STANDARD LESSON COMMENTARY

King James Version

2000–2001

International Sunday School Lessons

Edited by
Douglas Redford and Jonathan Underwood

Published by
STANDARD PUBLISHING

Eugene H. Wigginton, *President*
Mark A. Taylor, *Publisher*
Richard C. McKinley, *Director of Curriculum Development*
Carla Crane, *Assistant Director of Curriculum Development*
Jonathan Underwood, *Senior Editor of Adult Curriculum*
Cheryl Frey, *Office Editor*

Forty-eighth Annual Volume

©2000
STANDARD PUBLISHING
a division of STANDEX INTERNATIONAL Corporation
8121 Hamilton Avenue, Cincinnati, Ohio 45231

Printed in U. S. A.

In This Volume

Artists

TITLE PAGES: James E. Seward

Cover design by DesignTeam

Index of Printed Texts, 2000-2001

The printed texts for 2000-2001 are arranged here in the order in which they appear in the Bible. Opposite each reference is the number of the page on which it appears in this volume.

Cumulative Index

A cumulative index for the Scripture passages used in the STANDARD LESSON COMMENTARY
for the years September, 1998—August, 2001, is provided below.

V

How to Say It

Listed below are some of the names and other hard-to-pronounce words that you will encounter in the lessons covered in this book. (Because of space limitations, not every word that appears in the "How to Say It" boxes in each lesson has been included, but these will be the ones most often needed for general Bible study.) Notice that the page is perforated so that you can tear it out and keep it for later use in teaching or personal Bible study.

ABSALOM. *Ab*-suh-lum.
ADONIJAH. Ad-o-*nye*-juh.
AGABUS. *Ag*-uh-bus.
AHAB. *Ay*-hab.
AHAZ. *Ay*-haz.
AHAZIAH. Ay-huh-*zye*-uh.
AHIJAH. Uh-*high*-juh.
AMALEK. *Am*-uh-lek.
AMAZIAH. Am-uh-*zye*-uh.
AMMI. *Am*-my.
AMMONITES. *Am*-un-ites.
AMON. *Ay*-mun.
AMORITES. *Am*-uh-rites.
AMOZ. *Ay*-mahz.
ANANIAS. An-uh-*nye*-us.
ANTIOCH. *An*-tee-ock.
ANTIPAS. *An*-tih-pus.
APOLLOS. Uh-*pahl*-us.
AQUILA. *Ack*-wih-luh.
ARAMAIC. Air-uh-*may*-ick.
ARIMATHEA. *Air*-uh-muh-*thee*-uh (*th* as in *thin;* strong accent on *thee*).
ASHERAH. Uh-*she*-ruh.
ASHTAROTH. *Ash*-tuh-rawth.
ASSYRIA. Uh-*sear*-ee-uh.
AZARIAH. Az-uh-*rye*-uh.
AZOTUS. Uh-*zo*-tus.

BAALIM. Bay-uh-*leem*.
BALAAM. *Bay*-lum.
BALAK. *Bay*-lack.
BARAK. *Bair*-uk.
BEERSHEBA. Beer-*she*-buh.
BEN-HADAD. Ben-*hay*-dad.
BITHYNIA. Bih-*thin*-ee-uh.

CAESAREA. Sess-uh-*ree*-uh.
CANDACE. *Can*-duh-see.
CAPERNAUM. Kuh-*per*-nay-um.
CHEMOSH. *Kee*-mosh.
CHERITH. *Key*-rith.
CYPRUS. *Sigh*-prus.
CYRENE. Sigh-*ree*-nee.
CYRENIUS. Sigh-*ree*-nee-us.

DAGON. *Day*-gon.
DIAKONEO (Greek). dih-*ah*-ko-*neh*-o (strong accent on *neh*).

DIAKONOS (Greek). dih-*ah*-ko-nawss.
DIBLAIM. Dib-*lay*-im.

EDOMITES. *Ee*-dum-ites.
EHUD. *Ee*-hud.
ELIAB. Ee-*lye*-ab.
ELYMAS. *El*-ih-mass.
EMMAUS. Em-*may*-us.
EPHOD. ee-fod.
EPHRAIM. *Ee*-fray-im.
EUNUCH. *you*-nick.
EUPHRATES. You-*fray*-teez.

GAMALIEL. Guh-*may*-lih-ul.
GAZA. *Gay*-zuh.
GERIZIM. Guh-*rye*-zim or *Gair*-ih-zeem.
GETHSEMANE. Geth-*sem*-uh-nee.
GIBEAH. *Gib*-ee-uh.
GILBOA. Gil-*bo*-uh.
GILEAD. *Gil*-ee-ud.
GOLGOTHA. *Gahl*-guh-thuh.
GOMER. *Go*-mer.
GOMORRAH. Guh-*more*-uh.

HADES. *Hay*-deez.
HANNAH. *Han*-uh.
HAZOR. *Hay*-zor.
HEBRON. *Hee*-brun or *Heb*-run.
HERMON. *Her*-mun.
HEZEKIAH. Hez-ih-*kye*-uh.
HILLEL. *Hill*-el.
HIRAM. *High*-rum.
HITTITE. *Hit*-ite.
HOSEA. Ho-*zay*-uh.
HOSHEA. Ho-*shay*-uh.

ICONIUM. Eye-*co*-nee-um.
IMMANUEL. Ih-*man*-you-el.
ISH-BOSHETH. Ish-*bo*-sheth.
ISHMAEL. *Ish*-may-el.

JABBOK. *Jab*-ok.
JABESH GILEAD. *Jay*-besh *Gil*-ee-ud.
JABIN. *Jay*-bin.
JAEL. *Jay*-ul.
JAIRUS. *Jye*-rus or *Jay*-ih-rus.
JEBUSITES. *Jeb*-yuh-sites.
JEHOASH. Jeh-*hoe*-ash.

JEHORAM. Jeh-*ho*-rum.
JEHOSHAPHAT. Jeh-*hosh*-uh-fat.
JEHU. *Jay*-hew.
JEROBOAM. Jair-uh-*boe*-um.
JERUBBAAL. Jair-ub-*bay*-ul.
JEZREEL. *Jez*-ree-el or *Jez*-reel.
JOASH. *Jo*-ash.
JOPPA. *Jop*-uh.
JOSES. *Jo*-sez.
JOTHAM. *Jo*-tham.

KEDESH-NAPHTALI. Kee-desh-*naf*-tuh-lye.
KERITH. *Key*-rith.
KISHON. *Kye*-shon.
KRANION (Greek). kruh-*nee*-on.

LAZARUS. *Laz*-uh-rus.
LYSTRA. *Liss*-truh.

MACEDONIA. Mass-eh-*doe*-nee-uh.
MAGDALENE. *Mag*-duh-leen or Mag-duh-*lee*-nee.
MANAEN. *Man*-uh-en.
MANASSEH. Muh-*nass*-uh.
MATTHIAS. Muh-*thigh*-us.
MICAIAH. My-*kay*-uh.
MIDIAN. *Mid*-ee-un.
MILETUS. My-*lee*-tus.
MIZPEH. *Miz*-peh.
MOABITES. *Mo*-ub-ites.
MOLECH. *Mo*-lek.
MORESHETH. *Mo*-resh-eth.
MYSIA. *Mish*-ee-uh.

NAAMAN. *Nay*-uh-mun.
NABAL. *Nay*-bull.
NAPHTALI. *Naf*-tuh-lye.
NEBUCHADNEZZAR. *Neb*-yuh-kud-*nez*-er
     (strong accent on *nez*).
NICANOR. Nye-*cay*-nor.
NICOLAS. *Nick*-uh-lus.
NIGER. *Nye*-jer.
NINEVEH. *Nin*-uh-vuh.

OBADIAH. O-buh-*dye*-uh.
OMRI. *Ahm*-rye.

PAMPHYLIA. Pam-*fill*-ee-uh.
PAPHOS. *Pay*-fahss.
PARMENAS. *Par*-meh-nas.
PEKAH. *Peek*-uh.
PENTATEUCH. *Pen*-tuh-teuk.
PEREA. Peh-*ree*-uh.
PERGA. *Per*-guh.
PHILIPPI. Fih-*lip*-pie or *Fill*-ih-pie.
PHILISTIA. Fuh-*liss*-tee-uh.
PHILISTINES. Fuh-*liss*-teens or *Fill*-us-teens.
PHOENICIA. Fuh-*nish*-uh.
PISIDIA. Pih-*sid*-ee-uh.

PRISCILLA. Prih-*sil*-uh.
PROCHORUS. *Prock*-uh-rus.
PROSELYTE. *prahss*-uh-light.

QUIRINIUS. Kwy-*rin*-ee-us.

RABBAH. *Rab*-buh.
RAMAH. *Ray*-muh.
RAMOTH-GILEAD. *Ray*-muth-*gil*-ee-ud
     (strong accent on *gil*).
REHOBOAM. Ree-huh-*boe*-um.
REMALIAH. Rem-uh-*lye*-uh.
REZIN. *Ree*-zin.
RUHAMAH. Roo-*hah*-muh.

SAMARIA. Suh-*mare*-ee-uh.
SAMARITANS. Suh-*mare*-uh-tunz.
SANHEDRIN. San-*heed*-run or *San*-huh-drin.
SAPPHIRA. Suh-*fye*-ruh.
SELEUCIA. Sih-*lew*-shuh.
SEPTUAGINT. Sep-*too*-ih-jent.
SEPULCHRE. *sep*-ul-kur.
SERAPHIM. *sair*-uh-fim.
SERGIUS PAULUS. *Ser*-jih-us *Paul*-us.
SHEAR-JASHUB. *She*-are-*jah*-shub
     (strong accent on *jah*).
SHECHEM. *Shek*-em or *Shee*-kem.
SHILOH. *Shy*-lo.
SHITTIM. Shih-*teem*.
SICHEM. *Sigh*-kem.
SISERA. *Sis*-er-uh.

TABEAL. *Tay*-be-ul.
TABITHA. *Tab*-ih-thuh.
TEKOA. Tih-*ko*-uh.
TETRARCH. *teh*-trark or *tee*-trark.
THEOPHILUS. Thee-*ahf*-ih-luss.
THESSALONICA. *Thess*-uh-low-*nye*-kuh
     (strong accent on *nye*).
THEUDAS. *Thoo*-dus.
THYATIRA. *Thy*-uh-*tie*-ruh (strong accent on *tie*).
TIGLATH-PILESER. *Tig*-lath-pih-*lee*-zer
     (strong accent on *lee*).
TIMON. *Ty*-mon.
TISHBITE. *Tish*-bite.
TROAS. *Tro*-az.

URIAH. You-*rye*-uh.
URIM AND THUMMIM. *You*-rim and *Thum*-im.
UZZIAH. Uh-*zye*-uh.

ZAREPHATH. *Zair*-uh-fath.
ZEBULUN. *Zeb*-you-lun.
ZECHARIAH. Zek-uh-*rye*-uh.
ZEDEKIAH. Zed-uh-*kye*-uh.
ZELOTES. Zeh-*low*-teez.
ZIDONIANS. Zye-*doe*-nee-uns.
ZIKLAG. *Zik*-lag.

Fall Quarter, 2000

Rulers of Israel

(Judges, 1 and 2 Samuel, 1 Kings)

Special Features

Lessons

Unit 1: Judges of Israel

Unit 2: Saul and David

Unit 3: David and Solomon

About These Lessons

The lessons in this quarter survey the history of Israel from the period of the judges to the end of the united kingdom. They do so with a look at each of several great leaders of the nation during that time. From their successes and from their failures we can learn valuable lessons of faith.

Sep 3

Sep 10

Sep 17

Sep 24

Oct 1

Oct 8

Oct 15

Oct 22

Oct 29

Nov 5

Nov 12

Nov 19

Nov 26

Have You Heard the News?

TO HEAR THIS QUESTION automatically raises others. What kind of news? Is it good or bad? Does it involve me—or someone close to me?

The lessons for the coming year include both good and bad news. They show us that man's most pressing problems cannot be solved through economic, political, or military means. They are spiritual in nature. We are a broken people—broken by sin—and only by returning to our Creator can we be restored to wholeness.

The lessons for the fall and summer quarters are taken from the Old Testament. The fall quarter ("Rulers of Israel") covers the history of Israel from the judges through the reign of Solomon. The summer lessons proceed from that point and trace the tragic demise of God's people, climaxed by their captivity to pagans.

The lessons for winter and spring are drawn from the New Testament. Luke's Gospel (good news) enlightens our winter study, and in the spring we examine the book of Acts, which tells how the early church spread the good news of Jesus in Jerusalem, Judea, Samaria, and beyond!

Let this year's studies reinforce the truth that whatever the twenty-first century brings, the most important news of the century will be what it has been for the previous twenty: man has been ruined by sin, but God's redeeming love in Christ can make him all that God created him to be.

Now that's news worth hearing!

International Sunday School Lesson Cycle
September, 1998—August, 2004

YEAR	FALL QUARTER (Sept., Oct., Nov.)	WINTER QUARTER (Dec., Jan., Feb.)	SPRING QUARTER (Mar., Apr., May)	SUMMER QUARTER (June, July, Aug.)
1998-1999	God Calls a People to Faithful Living (Old Testament Survey)	God Calls Anew in Jesus Christ (New Testament Survey)	That You May Believe (John)	Genesis: Beginnings (Genesis)
1999-2000	From Slavery to Conquest (Exodus, Leviticus, Numbers, Deuteronomy, Joshua)	Immanuel: God With Us (Matthew)	Helping a Church Confront Crisis (1 and 2 Corinthians)	New Life in Christ (Ephesians, Philippians, Colossians, Philemon)
2000-2001	Rulers of Israel (Judges, 1 and 2 Samuel, 1 Kings 1-11)	Good News of Jesus (Luke)	Continuing Jesus' Work (Acts)	Division and Decline (1 Kings 12-22, 2 Kings 1-17, Isaiah 1-39, Hosea, Amos, Micah)
2001-2002	Jesus' Ministry (Parables, Miracles, Sermon on the Mount)	Light for All People (Isaiah 9:1-7; 11:1-9; 40-66; Ruth, Jonah, Nahum)	The Power of the Gospel (Romans, Galatians)	Worship and Wisdom for Living (Psalms, Proverbs)
2002-2003	Judgment and Exile (2 Kings 18-25, Jeremiah, Lamentations, Ezekiel, Habakkuk, Zephaniah)	Portraits of Faith (Personalities in the New Testament)	Jesus: God's Power in Action (Mark)	God Restores a Remnant (Ezra, Nehemiah, Daniel, Joel, Obadiah, Haggai, Zechariah, Malachi)
2003-2004	Faith Faces the World (James, 1 and 2 Peter, 1, 2, 3 John, Jude)	A Child Is Given (Samuel, John the Baptist, Jesus) Lessons From Life (Esther, Job, Ecclesiastes, Song of Solomon)	Jesus Fulfills His Mission (Death, Burial, and Resurrection Texts) Living Expectantly (1, 2 Thessalonians, Revelation)	Hold Fast to the Faith (Hebrews) Guidelines for the Church's Ministry (1, 2 Timothy, Titus)

Triumph and Trouble

by Orrin Root

DO YOU REMEMBER what we were doing in Sunday school a year ago? We were leaving Egypt with the children of Israel to travel to their promised land. For three months we followed them over the journey that took them forty years. At the end of November last year we saw them cross the Jordan into the promised land. There they followed God's leading, and He led them in triumphant conquest.

Now we are to take up the story of Israel at that point. During the upcoming thirteen lessons we shall consider what those people did for approximately the next four and a half centuries. It is a tale of both triumph and trouble.

Unit 1: September
Judges of Israel

Living in peace and prosperity year after year, the people of Israel began to think more about pleasure and comfort and less about God and His law. Carelessly they drifted into wrongdoing, and even joined in pagan religious rites.

Then came trouble. The Lord withdrew His protection. Armed raiders would sweep in from a neighboring country to drive away or destroy livestock and steal new harvests, killing anyone who got in their way. Peace and prosperity were replaced by helplessness and hunger.

In their misery the people remembered how God had helped them in former times. When they appealed to Him and went back to obeying His law, God provided a leader who rallied the people to resist and defeat the invaders. Peace and prosperity returned. But when all was well, the people again drifted away from God and His law.

That same pattern was repeated over and over through approximately three hundred years. (See the summary in Judges 2:11-19.) The leaders who rallied God's people are called *judges*. Twelve of them are named in the Biblical record, and four will be considered during our September lessons.

Lesson 1: Deborah. God chose this lady to be His prophetess, and men of Israel went to her to have their disputes settled according to God's law. Deborah instructed Barak to gather an army to defeat the Canaanites. So he and ten thousand men prepared to meet the fearsome Canaanite army, which was equipped with nine hundred iron chariots and countless horsemen and foot soldiers. Then the Lord took a hand in the battle. A terrific rainstorm and flood made the chariots and horses useless, and the Canaanites were soundly defeated.

Lesson 2: Gideon. God called Gideon to raise an army and drive out the Midianites and the Amalekites, who were robbing Israel at will. Gideon recruited thirty-two thousand men to help him, but the Lord said they were too many. The number was reduced to ten thousand, but that was still too many! When the number was reduced to three hundred, God used the tiny force to defeat countless thousands of the enemy.

Lesson 3: Samson. This hero raised no army—and needed none! Single-handedly he engaged the Philistines in conflict and won. On one occasion he was able to kill a thousand of them in a day; but he was not able to resist the charms of their women, especially the infamous Delilah.

Lesson 4: Samuel. Born to a godly mother who dedicated him to the Lord's service, the child Samuel was brought up by Eli the priest. From his youth he became recognized as God's prophet. That helped him to turn God's people back to the Lord and to end the long oppression of the Philistines. Prophetic insight also helped Samuel administer justice, and he became a loved and trusted judge of Israel.

Unit 2: October
Saul and David

Samuel's one notable failure was neglecting to bring up his sons to be like him. When he appointed them to be judges, they turned out to be mercenary scoundrels. Facing the prospect of being judged by such crooks, the elders of Israel asked Samuel to appoint a king for the nation.

That was not the best way to solve Israel's problem. Israel was designed to acknowledge God as their primary King, and He saw their request to Samuel as a rejection of Him (1 Samuel 8:7). The Lord warned that a monarchy would become expensive and oppressive. Still, the elders persisted in their request. The Lord consented without approving, and Israel became a monarchy. The lessons for October and November will tell of the first three kings.

Lesson 5: Saul Becomes King. God chose Saul to be Israel's first king. He was tall and handsome. Well pleased with the choice, the people voiced their approval with excitement.

Lesson 6: Saul Rejected and David Anointed. Saul began his reign with a glorious victory, but success seemed to go to his head. Soon he began to ignore God's leading and go his own way. His reign was then doomed to end in failure. The

Lord sent Samuel to anoint David to be the next king; but that was not made known to the public, for it was not yet time for Saul's rule to end.

Lesson 7: David Mourns Saul and Jonathan. By exhibiting valor in battle, David became a national hero. Saul became insanely jealous and ordered David killed. David fled to the desert and remained an exile until the Philistines defeated Israel and killed Saul and his son Jonathan. That opened the way for David to become king; but instead of rejoicing, David mourned sincerely for Saul and his son.

Lesson 8: David Becomes King of All Israel. When Saul was dead, the tribe of Judah promptly chose David to be its king. But Abner, general of Saul's army, named Saul's son Ish-bosheth as king. For seven years Israel was divided, and there was "long war" between the rival sides. Then both Abner and Ish-bosheth died, and David became king of the entire nation.

Lesson 9: God's Covenant With David. When David made Jerusalem his capital city, he soon brought the ark of the covenant there. He kept it in a tent, but proposed to build a house for it—a temple of stone and wood. That was a good thought, but it came before its time. The house for the Lord was to be built by David's son Solomon, who would be the next king. However, God promised to build an enduring house for David: a dynasty that would rule forever. Kings of David's family did rule in Jerusalem for centuries; but here we see a clear prophecy of Jesus, the King eternal. On the human side He is a son of David, and on the divine side He is the Son of God. He is ruling now, and His kingdom is forever.

Unit 3: November
David and Solomon

Young King David did the Lord's will, and the Lord blessed him with success and made little Israel into a mighty empire. But during what should have been David's mature years, he committed the sins of adultery and murder; and the latter years of his reign were plagued with trouble and sorrow. With difficulty he held the empire together and passed it on to his son Solomon.

Young King Solomon began his reign by serving God with a devotion like that of young King David. But at the end of November we shall see that old King Solomon drifted into sins more shameful than the sins of old King David.

What a warning is here for all of us! A good beginning is not enough. God's people must serve Him faithfully to the end.

Lesson 10: David and Bathsheba. When only skirmishes remained of his wars with the pagans, David stayed in Jerusalem. He left Joab in command of the army on the field.

Walking on the roof of his palace, David caught sight of a woman bathing on a neighboring roof or in a courtyard. Struck by her beauty, he brought her to his palace and to his bed. Then he plotted the death of her husband. Nathan the prophet pronounced God's sentence: "Now therefore the sword shall never depart from thine house" (2 Samuel 12:10). David's latter days were plagued by rebellions—led chiefly by his own sons.

Lesson 11: Solomon Succeeds David. In spite of these rebellions, David held his empire intact and handed it over to Solomon. He advised his son to obey God's law continually. Given a unique opportunity by God, Solomon requested and received a special gift of wisdom. His reign seemed to be bright with promise.

Lesson 12: Solomon Builds the Temple. Solomon amassed a fabulous income from taxes, from the tribute of pagan nations, and from his own business ventures. He built palaces and forts on a grand scale. Most significant of all his buildings was the exquisite temple of the Lord.

Lesson 13: Solomon's Mistakes. To maintain the stability of his empire, Solomon made treaties with foreign kings, taking daughters of those kings as his wives. But he allowed his pagan wives to bring their gods with them to Jerusalem. If that were not bad enough, Solomon then built shrines for those false gods. Finally, he actually joined in the pagan worship. So Solomon's efforts to strengthen his empire actually brought it to the brink of ruin.

Can you believe that the wisest ruler in the world blundered so foolishly? The warning to us should be clear: no good purpose is well served by disobeying God.

Answers to Quarterly Quiz
on page 8

Lesson 1—1. Sisera. 2. Barak. 3. Jael. **Lesson 2**—1. the angel of the Lord. 2. 10,000 men; 300 men. 3. "The sword of the Lord, and of Gideon." **Lesson 3**—1. Sorek. 2. Nazarite. **Lesson 4**—1. Eli. 2. "Speak, Lord; for thy servant heareth." 3. Ebenezer. **Lesson 5**—1. Benjamin. 2. the Lord. **Lesson 6**—1. Jesse. 2. false. 3. watching the sheep. **Lesson 7**—1. lovely and pleasant. 2. eagles, lions. **Lesson 8**—1. Hebron. 2. Jabesh-gilead. 3. forty. **Lesson 9**—1. Nathan. 2. established. **Lesson 10**—1. Uriah, Hittite. 2. Joab. 3. Nathan. **Lesson 11**—1. a thousand. 2. understanding, judge. **Lesson 12**—1. seven years. 2. David. **Lesson 13**—1. heart. 2. Chemosh. 3. one.

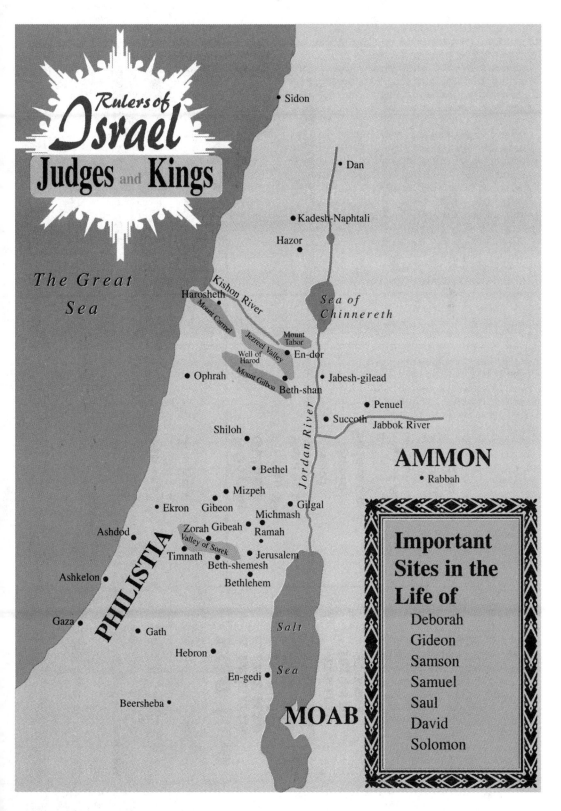

Rulers of
Israel
Judges and **Kings**

Sidon

Dan

Kadesh-Naphtali

Hazor

*The Great
Sea*

Harosheth
Kishon River

Mount Carmel

*Sea of
Chinnereth*

Mount
Tabor
Jezreel Valley

En-dor

Well of
Harod

Mount Gilboa

Ophrah

Beth-shan

Jabesh-gilead

Penuel

Succoth

Jabbok River

Shiloh

Jordan River

Bethel

AMMON

Rabbah

Mizpeh

Ekron   Gibeon

Gilgal

Michmash

Zorah Gibeah

Ramah

Ashdod

Valley of Sorek

Timnath

Jerusalem

PHILISTIA

Beth-shemesh

Ashkelon

Bethlehem

Gaza

Gath

Salt

Hebron

Sea

En-gedi

Beersheba

MOAB

**Important
Sites in the
Life of**
Deborah
Gideon
Samson
Samuel
Saul
David
Solomon

From Slavery to Slavery

Era	Leaders	Dates(B.C.)
Exodus and Wandering	Moses	1446-1406
Conquest and Settlement	Joshua	1406-1380
Judges	Deborah Gideon Samson Samuel	c. 1380-1050 c. 1250-1210 c. 1212-1172 c. 1110-1082 c. 1075-1020
United Kingdom	Saul David Solomon	1050-931 1050-1010 1010-970 970-931
Divided Kingdom	19 Kings of Israel 12 Kings of Judah 1 Queen of Judah	931-722
Judah Alone	7 Kings	722-587
Captivity		604-538

Leading With Success

by David Grubbs

SUCCESSFUL LEADERSHIP IS NOT FOUND in perfecting the process of leading, but in developing the heart of the leader. The key is not style but spiritual substance. This quarter's study of "Rulers of Israel" provides an opportunity to examine successful (and not-so-successful) leadership during the times of the judges and the reigns of the first three kings of Israel.

Some find the period of the judges confusing. Who were these people and how did they lead? The word *judges* makes one think that they were jurists sitting over courts of law. In a sense Deborah "held court" (Judges 4:4, 5), but she was also a prophetess. Jephthah was a warrior. Gideon was threshing wheat when God called him.

The judges may be best described as *deliverers*. God raised them up to deliver the Israelites "out of the hand of those that spoiled them" (Judges 2:16). They also called the people to repentance, challenging them to serve and worship God alone. Sadly, their influence was not lasting: "When the judge was dead, . . . they returned, and corrupted themselves more than their fathers, in following other gods to serve them" (Judges 2:19).

Israel's kings fit a leadership model that is more familiar to us and was certainly more familiar to Israel. Thus the people's reason for wanting a king: "that we also may be like all the nations" (1 Samuel 8:20). Had we been faced with the problems of Samuel's advanced age and the corrupt leadership of his sons, we too may have demanded a king "like all the nations."

The period of Israel's history covered in this quarter has much to tell us about good and bad leadership. What can we learn from it?

Fatal Errors in Leadership

1. Substituting secular government for personal responsibility. Israel functioned for centuries without a formal, secular government. God's law was sufficient. The chaos that resulted from forsaking that law is described in Judges 17:6: "In those days there was no king in Israel, but every man did that which was right in his own eyes." Making more rules, passing more laws, or increasing the size and scope of government is no substitute for keeping God's law.

2. Instituting another leadership model because it is contemporary and popular. The elders of Israel demanded a king, not because it was a proven model, but because it was a popular model. "All the [other] nations" had kings.

The most popular models of leadership today are not drawn from the political or military realms, but from the corporate world. Church "boards" (a corporate model) are being replaced by ministry teams (another corporate model). While not necessarily good or bad, the source of these models should be recognized.

3. Walking beyond the edge. There are rules and conventions beyond which a leader must not take his people. Leaders are change agents; their task is to lead people beyond the status quo. But not all change is good. Both Samson and Solomon exhibited an interest in foreign women—a practice that eventually drew both men away from God. Saul sought advice from a spirit medium (1 Samuel 28:3-19)—clearly a violation of God's law (1 Chronicles 10:13, 14).

While one may probe cultural and social conventions, Biblical doctrine must be carefully observed in the process. It must not be sacrificed merely for the sake of change.

4. Being jealous of the success of others. "Saul hath slain his thousands, and David his ten thousands" (1 Samuel 18:7). There was no more bitter sound in the ears of Saul than the success of David. Leadership in God's kingdom is not competitive; it is complementary. The crowning jewel is to be servant of all, as Jesus both taught and exemplified (Matthew 20:25-28).

Formula for Success

Successful leadership in the kingdom of God has a simple formula: be a person "after God's own heart." In telling Saul that he would lose his position of leadership, Samuel said, "The Lord hath sought him a man after his own heart, and the Lord hath commanded him to be captain over his people" (1 Samuel 13:14).

The life of King David (who succeeded Saul) was by no means perfect. However, his devotion to God was the hallmark of his reign as Israel's king. In a life filled with great accomplishments, one of his most cherished gifts to future generations is the Psalms. In addition, he is the most famous ancestor of Jesus, who is not called the Son of Jacob or the Son of Abraham, but the Son of David.

Successful leaders are spiritual leaders. They command respect because of the fruit of the Spirit in their lives. One can follow them with confidence, knowing that ultimately they follow Jesus—the greatest Leader of all.

Quarterly Quiz

The questions on this page may be used in several ways: as a pretest at the beginning of the quarter; as a review at the end of the quarter; or as a review after each lesson. The questions are based on the Scripture text of each lesson (King James Version). **The answers are on page 4.**

Lesson 1
1. Who was the leader of the Canaanite army? *Judges 4:2*
2. Whom did Deborah summon to lead Israel into battle against the Canaanites? *Judges 4:6*
3. Name the woman who struck and killed Sisera. *Judges 4:21, 22*

Lesson 2
1. Who told Gideon, "The Lord is with thee, thou mighty man of valor"? *Judges 6:12*
2. How many men were in Gideon's army just before they were tested at the water? How many were left after the test? *Judges 7:3-7*
3. What did Gideon's men cry as they went into battle? *Judges 7:20*

Lesson 3
1. Delilah lived in the valley of _____. (Jezreel, Sorek, or Elah?) *Judges 16:4*
2. Samson had been a _____ from birth, and that was the reason for his great strength. *Judges 16:17*

Lesson 4
1. At first, whom did Samuel think was calling him? *1 Samuel 3:5*
2. What did Eli tell Samuel to say to the Lord? *1 Samuel 3:9*
3. What was the name of the stone that Samuel set up to commemorate Israel's victory over the Philistines? *1 Samuel 7:12*

Lesson 5
1. From which tribe of Israel was Saul? *1 Samuel 9:1*
2. Who told the people that Saul had "hid himself among the stuff"? *1 Samuel 10:22*

Lesson 6
1. From among whose sons did the Lord say He would provide Israel a king? *1 Samuel 16:1*
2. Six of Jesse's sons passed before Samuel before David was summoned. T/F *1 Samuel 16:10*
3. What was David doing when he was summoned to appear before Samuel? *1 Samuel 16:11*

Lesson 7
1. With what two words did David describe Saul and Jonathan in his lament over their deaths? (wise and brave, lovely and pleasant, or true and faithful?) *2 Samuel 1:23*
2. Saul and Jonathan were also described as swifter than _____ and stronger than _____. *2 Samuel 1:23*

Lesson 8
1. To which city of Judah did David go to be made king of Judah? *2 Samuel 2:3, 4*
2. Men of a certain town were responsible for burying Saul. What was it? *2 Samuel 2:4*
3. David reigned as king a total of _____ years. *2 Samuel 5:4*

Lesson 9
1. Who told David, "Go, do all that is in thine heart; for the Lord is with thee"? *2 Samuel 7:3*
2. God promised that David's house, kingdom, and throne would be _____ forever. *2 Samuel 7:16*

Lesson 10
1. Bathsheba was the wife of _____ the _____. *2 Samuel 11:3*
2. To whom did David say, "Set ye Uriah in the forefront of the hottest battle"? *2 Samuel 11:14, 15*
3. To whom did David say, "I have sinned against the Lord"? *2 Samuel 12:13*

Lesson 11
1. How many burnt offerings did Solomon offer at Gibeon? *1 Kings 3:4*
2. Solomon asked God for "an _____ heart to _____ thy people." *1 Kings 3:9*

Lesson 12
1. How long did it take for Solomon to build the house of the Lord? *1 Kings 6:38*
2. God told Solomon to walk before Him as did _____. (Abraham, Moses, or David?) *1 Kings 9:4*

Lesson 13
1. Solomon's many wives "turned away his _____" from the Lord. *1 Kings 11:3*
2. Solomon built a high place for _____, the "abomination of Moab." *1 Kings 11:7*
3. How many tribes of Israel did God say He would give to Solomon's son? *1 Kings 11:13*

Deborah

September 3
Lesson 1

DEVOTIONAL READING: Psalm 68:1-6.

BACKGROUND SCRIPTURE: Judges 4, 5.

PRINTED TEXT: Judges 4:1-9, 14, 15, 17a, 21, 22a.

Judges 4:1-9, 14, 15, 17a, 21, 22a

1 And the children of Israel again did evil in the sight of the LORD, when Ehud was dead.

2 And the LORD sold them into the hand of Jabin king of Canaan, that reigned in Hazor; the captain of whose host was Sisera, which dwelt in Harosheth of the Gentiles.

3 And the children of Israel cried unto the LORD: for he had nine hundred chariots of iron; and twenty years he mightily oppressed the children of Israel.

4 And Deborah, a prophetess, the wife of Lapidoth, she judged Israel at that time.

5 And she dwelt under the palm tree of Deborah, between Ramah and Bethel in mount Ephraim: and the children of Israel came up to her for judgment.

6 And she sent and called Barak the son of Abinoam out of Kedesh-naphtali, and said unto him, Hath not the LORD God of Israel commanded, saying, Go and draw toward mount Tabor, and take with thee ten thousand men of the children of Naphtali and of the children of Zebulun?

7 And I will draw unto thee, to the river Kishon, Sisera the captain of Jabin's army, with his chariots and his multitude; and I will deliver him into thine hand.

8 And Barak said unto her, If thou wilt go with me, then I will go: but if thou wilt not go with me, then I will not go.

9 And she said, I will surely go with thee: notwithstanding the journey that thou takest shall not be for thine honor; for the LORD shall sell Sisera into the hand of a woman. And Deborah arose, and went with Barak to Kedesh.

.   .   .   .

14 And Deborah said unto Barak, Up; for this is the day in which the LORD hath delivered Sisera into thine hand: is not the LORD gone out before thee? So Barak went down from mount Tabor, and ten thousand men after him.

15 And the LORD discomfited Sisera, and all his chariots, and all his host, with the edge of the sword before Barak; so that Sisera lighted down off his chariot, and fled away on his feet.

.   .   .   .

17a Howbeit Sisera fled away on his feet to the tent of Jael the wife of Heber the Kenite.

.   .   .   .

21 Then Jael Heber's wife took a nail of the tent, and took a hammer in her hand, and went softly unto him, and smote the nail into his temples, and fastened it into the ground: for he was fast asleep and weary. So he died.

22a And, behold, as Barak pursued Sisera, Jael came out to meet him, and said unto him, Come, and I will show thee the man whom thou seekest. And when he came into her tent, behold, Sisera lay dead.

GOLDEN TEXT: Deborah said unto Barak, Up; for this is the day in which the LORD hath delivered Sisera into thine hand: is not the LORD gone out before thee?—Judges 4:14.

Lesson Aims

After participating in this lesson, each student will be able to:

1. Tell how God used Deborah to deliver His people from Canaanite oppression.

2. Explain from Deborah's example how behind-the-scenes leadership can be effective.

3. Seek a specific opportunity to serve the Lord and to give Him all the praise rather than to seek praise for oneself.

Lesson Outline

INTRODUCTION
    A. No Lapse in God's Vigilance
    B. Lesson Background
I. ISRAEL IN TROUBLE (Judges 4:1-3)
    A. Sin (v. 1)
    B. Punishment (v. 2)
    C. Distress (v. 3)
    Losing Streaks
II. LADY TO THE RESCUE (Judges 4:4-9)
    A. The Prophetess (vv. 4, 5)
    B. The Army (vv. 6, 7)
    C. The Leadership Team (vv. 8, 9)
III. VICTORY (Judges 4:14, 15, 17a, 21, 22a)
    A. Israel's Attack (v. 14)
    B. Enemy's Defeat (v. 15)
    C. A General's Death (vv. 17a, 21, 22a)
    Misplaced Trust
CONCLUSION
    A. Our Own Country
    B. What Can We Do?
    C. Prayer
    D. Thought to Remember

Introduction

"Johnny!" Mother's voice was sharp as the family gathered around the table. "Why do you keep coming to supper without washing your hands? You know I always send you back to do it."

Said Johnny, "Once you forgot!"

A. No Lapse in God's Vigilance

All through the book of Judges we read that the people of Israel always began to do wrong when they were safe and prosperous, and that God always punished them by allowing other peoples to ravage their land and terminate their prosperity. Not once did God forget. There was no lapse in His vigilance that would give the Israelites reason to hope there would be another. They often stopped thinking about God and His law, but God never stopped disciplining them and reminding them of the high cost of their disobedience.

B. Lesson Background

One year ago we began a series of thirteen lessons that traced the progress of Israel from slavery in Egypt to wandering in the wilderness and, finally, to conquering the land that God had promised to give them. With rare exceptions the people were faithful to God through those years of conquest, and He gave them victory over the pagan peoples who had lived there.

With undisputed possession of all the land they needed, God's people settled down to peaceful and prosperous living. This happy state continued as long as Joshua lived to lead them, and then for a few years more. As the faithful old leaders died, a new generation arose—a generation that did not remember the mighty miracles God had done to give them their good land. In their pursuit of profit and pleasure they forgot God and His law. So God allowed pagan tribes to invade Israel, stealing livestock and harvests and leaving the people in poverty and misery.

In their poverty and misery God's people remembered Him. They turned to Him and pleaded for His help. In response, God provided a leader who rallied the people to drive out the invaders and repossess their country. Peace and prosperity returned. Sadly, this same cycle of events was repeated over and over for approximately three hundred years.

Judges is the name given to those leaders whom God raised up to lead His people back to Him. This week our lesson concerns one of them. This judge was a lady. With the direction of God and the help of a man, she brought Israel from sin and misery to faithfulness and prosperity.

I. Israel in Trouble
(Judges 4:1-3)

A. Sin (v. 1)

1. And the children of Israel again did evil in the sight of the LORD, when Ehud was dead.

Ehud was a judge of Israel before the time of Deborah. His efforts on behalf of God's people are told in Judges 3:12-30. As indicated in Judges 2:18, 19, Ehud's influence kept the nation faithful to God as long as he lived. But *when Ehud was dead*, there was no one of like faithfulness and influence to take his place. In time *the children of Israel again did evil in the sight of the Lord.*

B. Punishment (v. 2)

2. And the LORD sold them into the hand of Jabin king of Canaan, that reigned in Hazor; the captain of whose host was Sisera, which dwelt in Harosheth of the Gentiles.

The Lord sold them into the hand of Jabin. This does not mean that Jabin paid anything to the Lord in return for his control of Israel; it means merely that God delivered Israel, or handed the people over, as if they had been sold. Back in the days when Joshua was leading and God was helping Israel, Joshua had promised two of the tribes a victory over the Canaanites in spite of their intimidating iron chariots (Joshua 17:17, 18). But now there was no godly leader like Joshua, and God was giving victory to Israel's enemies rather than to Israel.

King Jabin's capital was located at *Hazor*, far north in Israel's land (approximately nine miles north of the Sea of Galilee) in the territory belonging to the tribe of Naphtali. This means that we should understand *Canaan* in this verse to include, not the entire promised land (sometimes referred to as the land of Canaan), but the northern region of Canaan where the Canaanites were particularly strong. Apparently a large part of Jabin's army was stationed in *Harosheth*, located farther south in the plain of Jezreel. The troops there were commanded by *Sisera*.

C. Distress (v. 3)

3. And the children of Israel cried unto the LORD: for he had nine hundred chariots of iron; and twenty years he mightily oppressed the children of Israel.

With his impressive array of *chariots of iron*, Sisera easily terrorized the farmers of the valley and took whatever share of their harvests and livestock he chose to demand. This went on for *twenty years* because the people of Israel did not have the capability to oppose those chariots. So *the children of Israel cried unto the Lord.* [See question #1, page 16.]

LOSING STREAKS

Prairie View A & M (a small Texas college fifty miles northwest of Houston) once had a nearly invincible football team. They won five NCAA divisional titles in the 1950s and 1960s. But in 1989 the team began an eighty-game losing streak that broke the previous NCAA consecutive loss record by thirty games! The worst loss in the streak was by a score of 92-0! The nightmare finally came to an end on September 26, 1998, with a 14-12 victory over Langston University, nearly nine years after their last win.

Many factors contributed to the losing streak: unethical coaches, powerful opponents, lack of scholarships to attract good players, and perhaps even a losing mentality that developed as the streak went on.

In our text today, we see Israel in the throes of a twenty-year period of decline. After the death of the God-fearing judge Ehud, Israel had no strong leader. Her enemies—the Canaanites—were superior militarily. However, the most important factor in Israel's twenty-year "losing streak" was the attitude of the people: they had forgotten God. Only when they returned to Him in repentance and obedience did their dismal "streak" end.   —C. R. B.

II. Lady to the Rescue
(Judges 4:4-9)

A. The Prophetess (vv. 4, 5)

4. And Deborah, a prophetess, the wife of Lapidoth, she judged Israel at that time.

Like the other judges, *Deborah* was not elected by the people or appointed by anyone. God raised her up to help His people, and thus *she judged Israel at that time*. Here she is also described as a *prophetess*. Thus Deborah was not only the only judge who was a woman, but also the only one who is described as having the gift of prophecy. She needed no written law before her; her judgments came by direct inspiration from the almighty author of the law Himself.

5. And she dwelt under the palm tree of Deborah, between Ramah and Bethel in mount Ephraim: and the children of Israel came up to her for judgment.

The term *mount Ephraim* does not describe a single mountain, but all the hill country belonging to the tribe of Ephraim. No map can pinpoint the exact location of Deborah's *palm tree*, but it would have been somewhere in the hilly country near the middle of Israel's territory and within the land belonging to the tribe of Benjamin. The word *dwelt* may indicate either that she lived here or that this was the place at which she regularly dispensed justice to those who *came up to her for judgment.* Apparently this location became so familiar that it was known as *the palm tree of Deborah.*

VISUALS FOR THESE LESSONS

The visual pictured in each lesson (e. g., page 12) is a small reproduction of a large, full-color poster included in the *Adult Visuals* packet for the Fall Quarter. The packet is available from your supplier. Order No. 192.

B. The Army (vv. 6, 7)

6. And she sent and called Barak the son of Abinoam out of Kedesh-naphtali, and said unto him, Hath not the LORD God of Israel commanded, saying, Go and draw toward mount Tabor, and take with thee ten thousand men of the children of Naphtali and of the children of Zebulun?

Barak lived approximately eighty miles to the north of where Deborah held court, but it appears that he came promptly when Deborah *called* him. When he came, Deborah first made it clear that she was giving him the message of *the Lord God of Israel*, not her own. God wanted Barak to assemble an army of *ten thousand men* from the tribe of *Naphtali* (Barak's own tribe) and the neighboring tribe of *Zebulun*. He was to lead that army to *Mount Tabor*, a mountain (1,843 feet high) overlooking the valley of Jezreel. The Kishon River, mentioned in the next verse, flowed through that valley.

7. And I will draw unto thee, to the river Kishon, Sisera the captain of Jabin's army, with his chariots and his multitude; and I will deliver him into thine hand.

As mentioned in verse 2, *Jabin's army* was stationed at Harosheth, several miles to the west of Mount Tabor where the valley of Jezreel widened into a plain. The Lord promised to *draw* his army from that location and down the river to a point near Barak's position on Mount Tabor. *Sisera*, commander of that army, would bring his aforementioned nine hundred *chariots* of iron (v. 3). Probably *his multitude* included a large force of infantry that would accompany the chariots. The Lord planned to *deliver* those men *into* Barak's *hand*: that is, He promised victory to Barak and his army. [See question #2, page 16.]

C. The Leadership Team (vv. 8, 9)

8. And Barak said unto her, If thou wilt go with me, then I will go: but if thou wilt not go with me, then I will not go.

It is to Barak's credit that he trusted the Lord and recognized that Deborah was his "link with headquarters." He did not intend to be caught on Mount Tabor with ten thousand men and without God's guidance as to what to do next. If God's prophetess would *not go* with him on this mission, then he would *not go*.

Still, it seems to indicate some limitation in Barak's faith that he would set conditions on which he would obey what "the Lord God of Israel commanded" him to do (v. 6). As in the case of Gideon and his fleece (Judges 6:36-40), it seems the Lord responded on the basis of the faith that was expressed in spite of the clear need to grow in that faith.

9. And she said, I will surely go with thee: notwithstanding the journey that thou takest shall not be for thine honor; for the LORD shall sell Sisera into the hand of a woman. And Deborah arose, and went with Barak to Kedesh.

Thus the leadership team was formed. God would be the commander; Deborah would convey His orders to Barak; Barak would command the army. However, Deborah warned Barak that he would not receive the primary credit for Israel's victory. That would be given to *a woman*. At this point in the story, we might expect Deborah to be that woman, but she would not be.

Quickly Barak enlisted ten thousand men and led them to Mount Tabor, "and Deborah went up with him" (v. 10). Such a mobilization could not be kept secret, and Sisera soon learned about it (v. 12). To him it must have had all the appearances of an armed revolt among the Israelites. Sisera readied his chariots and infantry and set out from Harosheth to put the impudent rebels in their place. From their position on Mount Tabor, Barak and his men could see them coming. [See question #3, page 16.]

III. Victory
(Judges 4:14, 15, 17a, 21, 22a)

A. Israel's Attack (v. 14)

14. And Deborah said unto Barak, Up; for this is the day in which the LORD hath delivered Sisera into thine hand: is not the LORD gone out before thee? So Barak went down from mount Tabor, and ten thousand men after him.

The prophetess gave the command, and with it the promise of victory and the assurance that *the Lord* Himself was advancing to battle ahead of the *ten thousand men*. Encouraged by that promise, Barak led his troops down the slope of Tabor and across the valley floor to meet the chariots and infantry by the river.

It should be noted that this strategy seemed to favor Sisera, for it allowed him to fight where his

Visual for lesson 1
(See page 11 for ordering information.)

The visual for today's lesson will help your students place the events of the quarter's lessons in chronological order.

iron chariots could be used to their greatest advantage—in the level valley rather than on the slopes of the mountain. Perhaps Sisera anticipated an easy victory at little cost to himself or his men. The Lord, of course, had other plans.

B. Enemy's Defeat (v. 15)

15. And the LORD discomfited Sisera, and all his chariots, and all his host, with the edge of the sword before Barak; so that Sisera lighted down off his chariot, and fled away on his feet.

The Lord discomfited Sisera. For more about the Lord's action in this conflict, we turn to the song of victory in the next chapter of Judges. There we read that the Lord caused a spectacular cloudburst to come from the south (Judges 5:4, 5). Without being told all the details, we know that such a rain would have produced a flash flood on the Kishon. Quickly the river came forth from its banks. The soft ground turned to mud; the chariots bogged down to their axles. The rising flood overwhelmed both horses and men, drowned them, and swept their dead bodies away (5:21).

Those men who managed to make their way to dry ground above the flood were met with *the edge of the sword*—ten thousand vengeful swords in the hands of men smarting from twenty years of severe oppression. The Canaanites who did not die immediately raced back by the way they had come, but the men of Israel chased them all the way to Harosheth and killed every one of them (Judges 4:16).

C. A General's Death (vv. 17a, 21, 22a)

17a. Howbeit Sisera fled away on his feet to the tent of Jael the wife of Heber the Kenite.

Heber is described as a *Kenite,* meaning that he belonged to the tribe of "Hobab the father-in-law of Moses" (Judges 4:11). Originally the Kenites had become affiliated with the tribe of Judah to the south (Judges 1:16), but Heber and his wife *Jael* had chosen a more solitary life in the north. Apparently they were nomadic shepherds. On this occasion Jael was alone in the tent; perhaps Heber was away with the sheep.

The Kenites were not included among the oppressed Israelites; they were at peace with the Canaanites, as the latter part of this verse notes. Still, it seems that Jael's heart was with Israel. She recognized Sisera when he appeared, wearied by his long flight from the battlefield. Cordially she welcomed him into the tent and agreed to hide him there. After a drink of milk, he fell soundly asleep (vv. 18-20).

21. Then Jael Heber's wife took a nail of the tent, and took a hammer in her hand, and went softly unto him, and smote the nail into his

temples, and fastened it into the ground: for he was fast asleep and weary. So he died.

The *nail of the tent* was a tent peg. A heavy *hammer* was at hand for driving such pegs. Apparently Sisera was sleeping with his head flat on the ground. Jael came to him stealthily. With a few quick blows, she drove the stake through his head and into the ground. It was hardly necessary to add: *So he died.* [See question #4, page 16.]

22a. And, behold, as Barak pursued Sisera, Jael came out to meet him, and said unto him, Come, and I will show thee the man whom thou seekest. And when he came into her tent, behold, Sisera lay dead.

The record seems to indicate that some men of Israel saw Sisera leave his panic-stricken troops and race away alone to the north. But they proceeded to exterminate the army, and then returned to pursue the general. It was not hard to guess that he would hurry to his king at Hazor (v. 2), so they traveled in that direction. Perhaps they reached Jael's tent a day or two behind Sisera, but she had left Sisera's body undisturbed. Now, perhaps with some pride, she showed Barak what she had done. Thus, as Deborah had foretold (v. 9), the outstanding champion of the campaign was not Barak, but a woman—Jael.

At this point the war was not over, but a major blow had been struck against Israel's oppressors. Barak and his men pressed on until the Canaanites were subdued and their king was destroyed (Judges 4:23, 24). The oppression was ended, "and the land had rest forty years" (Judges 5:31).

MISPLACED TRUST

Ferdinand Marcos, who ruled as president of the Philippines from 1966 to 1986, once wrote in his diary: "I am president. I am the most powerful man in the Philippines. All that I have dreamt of I have. . . . . But I feel a discontent."

Marcos's discontent was appropriate. His delight and trust in the things that represented his worldly power became his undoing. Eventually, he was toppled from power, disgraced by charges that he had embezzled several billion dollars from the national treasury. The Swiss government returned to the Philippines more than $500 million that Marcos had hidden in private Swiss bank accounts. He died in exile—a broken, lonely man.

Sisera was a powerful general whose troops greatly outnumbered the ragtag army of Israelites and whose weaponry was vastly superior to theirs. His first mistake was to place his trust in military might, since the forces of nature's God made his armaments of no value. His second mistake was to place his trust in Jael, a woman unknown to him, whose hospitality would prove fatal.

Where do we place our trust? In the possessions that delight us, in the power we have at our disposal, or in the God whose wisdom can give us the proper perspective on life?   —C. R. B.

Conclusion

A. Our Own Country

These lessons are used in English-speaking countries more than anywhere else. Not for centuries has one of them been overthrown and oppressed by a foreign power. Does that mean we are as godly as we ought to be?

We doubt it. This dying century has seen such a surge of paganism in Europe and America that students of our time are calling it "the post-Christian era." Hardly any thoughtful observer will deny that our country is moving away from obedience to God rather than toward it.

B. What Can We Do?

We cannot recruit an army of ten thousand and "discomfit" all the sinners with the edge of the sword. What can we do for the salvation of our friends, our neighbors, our enemies, our country, our era?

We can bring people to Christ one by one. That was what Christians did when the church was beginning. They "went every where preaching the word" (Acts 8:4). Whom do you know who is not a Christian? Are you really trying to reach him? [See question #5, page 16.]

You don't know how? Then whom do you know who does know how? Perhaps you can go with him a few times, or many times, and see how he does it. Perhaps some more people in your church would like to know how. You can gather a class of six or ten or twenty and ask your minister or some other accomplished evangelist to teach you how to approach people and win them. Then you can form teams of two, divide the nearby homes among the teams, and cover your town with the gospel.

Of course, when someone is won to Christ that is only the beginning of what we can do. The next step is to make that person truly one of us. We can help him find his place in the work of the Lord. It may be mowing the lawn or singing in the choir. It may be trimming the shrubbery or teaching a Sunday school class. It may be repairing the roof or going out with another Christian to win his non-Christian friends.

Our problem is not that there is nothing we can do. Our problem is that we are not doing what we can. And that is a problem we can solve.

C. Prayer

Thank You, Father, for setting our tasks before us. Give us true hearts and willing minds and energetic bodies, we pray, that we may "do with our might what our hands find to do." Through Christ, our Lord, we pray, amen.

D. Thought to Remember

"There's a place for every worker
In the vineyard of the Lord."
—Noel A. McAulay

How to Say It

ABINOAM. Uh-*bin*-o-am.
BARAK. *Bair*-uk.
BETHEL. *Beth*-el.
CANAAN. *Kay*-nun.
CANAANITES. *Kay*-nun-ites.
EHUD. *Ee*-hud.
EPHRAIM. *Ee*-fray-im.
HAROSHETH. Huh-*roe*-sheth.
HAZOR. *Hay*-zor.
HEBER. *Hee*-ber.
HOBAB. *Ho*-bab.
JABIN. *Jay*-bin.
JAEL. *Jay*-ul.
JEZREEL. *Jez*-ree-el or *Jez*-reel.
KEDESH-NAPHTALI. *Kee*-desh-*naf*-tuh-lye (strong accent on *naf*).
KENITE. *Ken*-ite.
KISHON. *Kye*-shon.
LAPIDOTH. *Lap*-ih-doth.
NAPHTALI. *Naf*-tuh-lye.
RAMAH. *Ray*-muh.
SISERA. *Sis*-er-uh.
ZEBULUN. *Zeb*-you-lun.

Learning by Doing

This page contains an alternate lesson plan emphasizing learning activities.
Classes desiring such student involvement will find these suggestions helpful.

Learning Goals

After this lesson each student will be able to:

1. Tell how God used Deborah to deliver His people from Canaanite oppression.

2. Explain how Deborah's example shows that supportive, behind-the-scenes leadership can be effective.

3. Seek a specific opportunity to serve the Lord and to give Him all the praise rather than to seek praise for oneself.

Into the Lesson

Prior to class prepare a graffiti poster with the phrase, "An encourager is one who. . . ." Place this poster near the door to the classroom and attach a couple of markers. Ask each person coming into the classroom to complete the sentence by writing potential endings on the poster. *(Possible answers include: supports what you are doing; stands beside you in times of crisis; provides words of encouragement; believes in you; trusts in your ability to lead; stands behind you.)* When everyone has arrived, bring the poster to the front of the room and read the endings. State: "Now that we've listed some ways people encourage others, let's examine our text. Turn to the book of Judges, and let's learn from Deborah's example how we can be encouragers."

Into the Word

Divide the class into three groups and give each group one of these assignments. After ten minutes have each group report to the class.

Group 1: Read Judges 2:6-19 for the lesson background. Answer the following questions:

1. What happened after Joshua died? *(The next generation did evil, forsaking the Lord, vv. 11, 13.)*

2. Why did they forsake the Lord? *(They did not know Him or His works for Israel, v. 10.)*

3. How did the Lord respond to their sin? *(He delivered them to their enemies, v. 14.)*

4. How did God deliver the Israelites from their enemies? *(He raised up judges, vv. 16, 18.)*

5. What happened when the judge died? *(They sinned and forsook the Lord again, v. 19.)*

Group 2: Read Judges 4:1-9 and prepare to give a brief, one-minute summary of Ehud (from Judges 3:12-30). Then answer these questions:

1. Why did Israel cry out to the Lord? *(Sisera had nine hundred iron chariots and cruelly oppressed Israel for twenty years, v. 3)*

2. What evidence from the text suggests how the Israelites regarded Deborah? *(Prophetess, v. 4; Israelites came to her for judgment, v. 5; Barak came eighty miles in response to her request, v. 6; Barak accepted God's message through her, v. 8.)*

3. Why did Barak want Deborah to go with him to the battle? *(He believed she spoke God's message and wanted assurance that God was behind this operation.)*

Group 3: Read Judges 4:14, 15, 17a, 21, 22a; and 5:4, 5, 21. Answer the following questions:

1. How was Israel able to overcome the nine hundred chariots? *(Soldiers fought; the Lord discomfited Sisera and all his chariots, 4:15; severe rainstorm and flood, 5:4, 5, 21.)*

2. Explain the meaning of v. 9, "for the Lord shall sell Sisera into the hand of a woman." *(Reference to Jael, who drove a tent peg through Sisera's head so that he died, 5:21.)*

Into Life

Prepare a chart called "Principles to Apply," with three columns headed "Deborah," "Barak," and "Jael" on a large poster, an overhead transparency, or the chalkboard. Divide the class into three small groups and ask them to draw from this account at least one principle from each Biblical character. After a couple of minutes, ask each group to state the principles that the group discovered. Write those principles on the chart. Several principles could be suggested for each column, but make certain that the following principles are suggested and written on the chart. *(Deborah: gave supportive, behind-the-scenes leadership; Barak: did not seek his own glory, v. 9; Jael: took advantage of an unexpected opportunity.)*

Circle the Deborah principle stated above and compare it with the encourager list from "Into the Lesson." State: "Deborah was an encourager: she supported Barak in a dangerous situation; she got involved in community concerns; she shared God's word and stood beside Barak."

State: "I want each of you to select one person whom you can encourage. Tell the person sitting next to you how you will do that." Ask the class to pray in twos or threes for each other's commitment to encourage someone. Then lead the class in a prayer that God will help them take advantage of every opportunity to encourage someone and to give all the glory to God.

Let's Talk It Over

The questions on this page are designed to encourage review of the lesson Scriptures and to promote discussion of the lesson by the class. The answers provided are only discussion starters. Let your class talk it over from there.

1. Even though the Israelites cried out to the Lord for relief from the Canaanite oppression, He did not answer for twenty years. Why do you suppose God waited so long?

Actually, the text does not say that the Israelites cried to God for twenty years; it says that Jabin oppressed them for twenty years and that they cried unto the Lord. We do not know how many of those twenty years the Israelites spent in denial, refusing to address the Lord with their complaint, and then how many more they spent in unrepentant complaining. Finally, the Israelites began to develop the godly sorrow that is the key to genuine repentance (see 2 Corinthians 7:10). Only when they cried out in true repentance could God act to deliver them.

2. The narrative in Judges 4 places a great deal of emphasis on Sisera's nine hundred iron chariots. The Israelites apparently had none, but still they were willing to do battle. How do we today face seemingly unbeatable forces with confidence? What are some of the "iron chariots" that we face?

Perhaps Deborah reminded Barak and his army of what God did to Pharaoh's chariots during the crossing of the Red Sea (see Exodus 14:23-28). She could have recalled Joshua's victory over an earlier Jabin, when he disabled their horses and burned their chariots (Joshua 11:1-9). For the people of Deborah's time and for us there is a wealth of evidence that those who trust in God can win tremendous victories in the face of overwhelming odds.

Perhaps the presence of pornography or drugs in your town seems unbeatable. The secularization of society is also a formidable foe, crowding prayer, God's Word, and any mention of Jesus out of virtually every public arena. If we try to defeat these opponents on the chariots of power and politics, we will surely fail. We must fight with the weapons of spiritual warfare. "Some trust in chariots, and some in horses: but we will remember the name of the Lord our God" (Psalm 20:7).

3. Knowing that he would not receive the major credit for the triumph, Barak led his army into battle. How many Christians today do you think would undertake a significant ministry or project if they knew someone else would get the credit for any success achieved? How much should getting credit matter? Why?

Of course, we should be willing to serve simply for the honor of Christ. However, Christians are not immune to the hunger for praise and a moment in the spotlight. As often as possible we should thank one another for service and acknowledge the efforts of those who sacrifice time and energy to make the church better. But we should all dedicate ourselves to doing our best whether or not we are thanked, whether or not we are treated to public praise. See Matthew 6:1.

4. We can compare Jael's act with that of David in slaying Goliath (1 Samuel 17). In each case the victim was an enemy of God and His people. In one instance God used a woman with a tent peg and hammer to defeat that enemy, and in the other He used a boy with a sling and a stone. On both occasions God was given praise for the enemy's destruction (Judges 5:2-5; 1 Samuel 17:45-47). We are in the habit of viewing young David as a hero, but some have regarded Jael as a murderer. Why do you think that is so, and why should we regard Jael as heroic?

Jael's method was more deceptive, seeming to welcome Sisera in and then killing him in his sleep. David, of course, confronted the enemy face to face. Jael, however, lived among a tribe at peace with the Canaanites. Like Rahab of Jericho, she was forced to use stealth to assist the people of God. But if God had judged Sisera worthy of death, the means by which that death came about is secondary. Jael took a stand for God by killing Sisera and announcing the fact to Barak.

5. The lesson writer says winning people to Christ is the best solution to resolving our society's serious moral problems. Some critics may scoff that such a statement is too simplistic. After all, many professing Christians have made the news because of their involvement in adultery, pornography, political corruption, and other moral evils. How would you answer?

In spite of our failings, we Christians are involved in the most powerful venture on earth. Many believers can attest to the great change the gospel has brought to their lives. "If any man be in Christ, he is a new creature" (2 Corinthians 5:17).

Gideon

DEVOTIONAL READING: Joshua 1:1-9.

BACKGROUND SCRIPURE: Judges 6–8.

PRINTED TEXT: Judges 6:11-14; 7:1-7, 20, 21.

Judges 6:11-14

11 And there came an angel of the LORD, and sat under an oak which was in Ophrah, that pertained unto Joash the Abiezrite: and his son Gideon threshed wheat by the winepress, to hide it from the Midianites.

12 And the angel of the LORD appeared unto him, and said unto him, The LORD is with thee, thou mighty man of valor.

13 And Gideon said unto him, O my Lord, if the LORD be with us, why then is all this befallen us? and where be all his miracles which our fathers told us of, saying, Did not the LORD bring us up from Egypt? but now the LORD hath forsaken us, and delivered us into the hands of the Midianites.

14 And the LORD looked upon him, and said, Go in this thy might, and thou shalt save Israel from the hand of the Midianites: have not I sent thee?

Judges 7:1-7, 20, 21

1 Then Jerubbaal, who is Gideon, and all the people that were with him, rose up early, and pitched beside the well of Harod: so that the host of the Midianites were on the north side of them, by the hill of Moreh, in the valley.

2 And the LORD said unto Gideon, The people that are with thee are too many for me to give the Midianites into their hands, lest Israel vaunt themselves against me, saying, Mine own hand hath saved me.

3 Now therefore go to, proclaim in the ears of the people, saying, Whosoever is fearful and afraid, let him return and depart early from mount Gilead. And there returned of the people twenty and two thousand; and there remained ten thousand.

4 And the LORD said unto Gideon, The people are yet too many; bring them down unto the water, and I will try them for thee there: and it shall be, that of whom I say unto thee, This shall go with thee, the same shall go with thee; and of whomsoever I say unto thee, This shall not go with thee, the same shall not go.

5 So he brought down the people unto the water: and the LORD said unto Gideon, Every one that lappeth of the water with his tongue, as a dog lappeth, him shalt thou set by himself; likewise every one that boweth down upon his knees to drink.

6 And the number of them that lapped, putting their hand to their mouth, were three hundred men: but all the rest of the people bowed down upon their knees to drink water.

7 And the LORD said unto Gideon, By the three hundred men that lapped will I save you, and deliver the Midianites into thine hand: and let all the other people go every man unto his place.

. . . .

20 And the three companies blew the trumpets, and brake the pitchers, and held the lamps in their left hands, and the trumpets in their right hands to blow withal: and they cried, The sword of the LORD, and of Gideon.

21 And they stood every man in his place round about the camp: and all the host ran, and cried, and fled.

GOLDEN TEXT: Go in this thy might, and thou shalt save Israel from the hand of the Midianites: have not I sent thee?—Judges 6:14.

Rulers of Israel
Unit 1: Judges of Israel
(Lessons 1-4)

Lesson Aims

After studying this lesson, each student will be able to:

1. Recount the story of the unusual way in which God used Gideon to rescue Israel from the Midianites.

2. Explain why one's reluctance to serve the Lord should not be allowed to keep him or her from such service.

3. Seek an opportunity to encourage an individual who has been rather timid in serving the Lord to use his or her talents in His service.

Lesson Outline

INTRODUCTION
    A. Reluctant Leaders
    B. Lesson Background
  I. FINDING A LEADER (Judges 6:11-14)
    A. An Angel Visits (vv. 11, 12)
    B. Gideon Objects (v. 13)
    C. The Lord Sends (v. 14)
      "Look What I've Done!"
  II. REDUCING AN ARMY (Judges 7:1-7)
    A. From 32,000 to 10,000 (vv. 1-3)
    B. From 10,000 to 300 (vv. 4-7)
  III. DEFEATING AN ENEMY (Judges 7:20, 21)
    A. Lights and Noise (v. 20)
    B. Panic (v. 21)
    Too Much Light
CONCLUSION
    A. Examples
    B. The Process
    C. Prayer
    D. Thought to Remember

Introduction

A. Reluctant Leaders

Have you ever had difficulty getting someone to accept some task in the church? Reluctant leaders are not a new phenomenon in the work of the Lord. Isaiah volunteered, "Here am I; send me" (Isaiah 6:8); but some other outstanding leaders had to be "drafted." Do you remember how Moses protested when God appointed him to lead His people out of slavery (Exodus 3:11, 13; 4:1, 10, 13)? In this lesson we meet another reluctant leader.

B. Lesson Background

Last week we read that God used Deborah, Barak, and a powerful rainstorm to defeat the Canaanites and end their twenty-year oppression of Israel. Then "the land had rest forty years" (Judges 5:31). By that time most of the Israelites under sixty years old had no memory of the terrible oppression that had come because Israel had disobeyed God. They had not been involved in the momentous battle against the Canaanites. So this new generation began their own path of disobedience. For that reason, "the Lord delivered them into the hand of Midian seven years" (Judges 6:1).

The Midianites were nomads from the deserts east and south of Israel. They crossed the Jordan in great numbers, bringing countless thousands of sheep and cattle to pasture on the young barley and wheat in Israel. Thus deprived of their harvests, the Israelites found it hard to survive. Desperately they "cried unto the Lord" (Judges 6:6).

I. Finding a Leader (Judges 6:11-14)

Naturally the invaders from Midian were most interested in securing control of the plains, with their wide stretches of fertile farmland. As a result many Israelites fled to the hill country, where they found hiding places (Judges 6:2).

A. An Angel Visits (vv. 11, 12)

11. And there came an angel of the LORD, and sat under an oak which was in Ophrah, that pertained unto Joash the Abiezrite: and his son Gideon threshed wheat by the winepress, to hide it from the Midianites.

An *Abiezrite* was a member of one of the families of the tribe of Manasseh. *Ophrah* probably was located in the hills southeast of the plain of Jezreel, where Barak and the Israelites had routed the Canaanites. It seems that *Joash* and *his son Gideon* somehow had been able to grow and harvest a little wheat. Gideon was secretly threshing some of it in order to provide food.

A *winepress* usually consisted of a pit cut into the limestone rock that was common throughout Israel. There grapes were trodden to crush the juice out of them for wine—only now the pit also served as a hiding place. The phrase *by the winepress* is more accurately translated *in the winepress*. No doubt that is where Gideon was—down in the pit of the winepress and out of sight as much as possible since the Midianites would steal his wheat if they saw it. As Gideon worked, *there came an angel of the Lord, and sat under an oak* nearby.

12. And the angel of the LORD appeared unto him, and said unto him, The LORD is with thee, thou mighty man of valor.

For Gideon to hear himself described as a *mighty man of valor* must have sounded like cruel sarcasm. Some valor—hiding in a winepress to thresh a bit of wheat! [See question #1, page 24.] *The Lord is with thee* must have sounded unbelievable, too. Gideon had an immediate response to that claim.

B. Gideon Objects (v. 13)

13. And Gideon said unto him, O my Lord, if the LORD be with us, why then is all this befallen us? and where be all his miracles which our fathers told us of, saying, Did not the LORD bring us up from Egypt? but now the LORD hath forsaken us, and delivered us into the hands of the Midianites.

The Lord had indeed brought the people of Israel *up from Egypt* by means of *his miracles*. Gideon, however, had seen no wonders in his own time. He was quite right in saying, *The Lord hath . . . delivered us into the hands of the Midianites.* Judges 6:1 tells us exactly the same thing. But Gideon was wrong in saying, *The Lord hath forsaken us.* The Lord had delivered His people to the Midianites to turn them away from idolatry and other sins, and to bring them back to worshiping and obeying Him alone.

C. The Lord Sends (v. 14)

14. And the LORD looked upon him, and said, Go in this thy might, and thou shalt save Israel from the hand of the Midianites: have not I sent thee?

Here, as in several places in the Old Testament, there appears to be no clear distinction between the angel of the Lord and the Lord Himself. Someone has suggested that the angel was God "in one particular phase of His self-revelation." That seems to explain a concept that is difficult to understand fully.

Hiding in the winepress, Gideon must have wondered how he could have possessed any *might* of his own. How could someone like him *save Israel*? His family was a poor one in its tribe, and he was the least in his family (v. 15). But the Lord had a ready answer for him: "Surely I will be with thee" (v. 16).

After some further convincing, and at God's command, Gideon began to display his might. He destroyed an altar used in the worship of the imaginary god Baal (vv. 25-27). Men of the city wanted to kill Gideon for destroying Baal's altar, but his father dissuaded them (vv. 28-32).

Events moved swiftly after that. The Midianites assembled in a huge camp in the valley of Jezreel (v. 33). Gideon called for volunteers, and men from his tribe and three others responded (vv. 34, 35).

"LOOK WHAT I'VE DONE!"

For many years, the tallest building in the world was New York City's Empire State Building. In 1966 New York's World Trade Center claimed the title at 1,377 feet. Chicago's Sears Tower took the honor in 1973 (1,454 feet). In 1996 the crown passed to Kuala Lampur, Malaysia, where the Petronas Towers reached 1,483 feet.

A few years ago, top architects around the world claimed in a survey that the reason for such buildings is primarily "self-advertising" and "ego." We could have guessed that, couldn't we? How interesting, then, that God often looks elsewhere when He has a significant task to be done. When He looked for someone to lead His people against the Midianites, Gideon was working in a winepress, desperately hoping *not* to be noticed! Such people are more likely to credit God for their successes, but God often has to prod them into action.

Where do we fit in this picture? Are we willing to serve but wanting the credit, or humble but reluctant to serve? The story of Gideon teaches us a lesson about the kind of people whom God can use.   —C. R. B.

II. Reducing an Army
(Judges 7:1-7)

An army of thirty-two thousand assembled in answer to Gideon's call. Gideon may have thought that this number was much too small to fight the multitude of Midianites that filled a wide camp in the valley. But the Lord told Gideon that the army was too big!

A. From 32,000 to 10,000 (vv. 1-3)

1. Then Jerubbaal, who is Gideon, and all the people that were with him, rose up early, and pitched beside the well of Harod: so that the host of the Midianites were on the north side of them, by the hill of Moreh, in the valley.

Jerubbaal means "let Baal plead," a nickname Gideon picked up when he destroyed Baal's altar. When the people of the city came for Gideon, his father said, "Will ye plead for Baal? will ye save him? . . . If he be a god, let him plead for himself" (Judges 6:31). So from that day Gideon was known as Jerubbaal, "let Baal plead" (v. 32). The name appears fourteen times in Judges and 1 Samuel.

Gideon and his men made their camp on an elevated area where *the well of Harod* (a bountiful spring) provided an ample water supply. Since this spring was located at the northern foot of Mount Gilboa, this is most likely where Gideon and his men were camped. From this position they could look down on the enemy camp *in the valley* that was *north* of them.

2. And the LORD said unto Gideon, The people that are with thee are too many for me to give the Midianites into their hands, lest Israel vaunt themselves against me, saying, Mine own hand hath saved me.

The Lord explained why the army must be reduced in size. The battle must be won by a force so small that everyone would know without question that God had given the victory. [See question #2, page 24.]

3. Now therefore go to, proclaim in the ears of the people, saying, Whosoever is fearful and afraid, let him return and depart early from mount Gilead. And there returned of the people twenty and two thousand; and there remained ten thousand.

The proclamation went out through the camp of Israel: anyone who is *afraid* may be excused. More than two-thirds of the men happily departed *from mount Gilead* (most likely another name for Mount Gilboa).

B. From 10,000 to 300 (vv. 4-7)

4. And the LORD said unto Gideon, The people are yet too many; bring them down unto the water, and I will try them for thee there: and it shall be, that of whom I say unto thee, This shall go with thee, the same shall go with thee; and of whomsoever I say unto thee, This shall not go with thee, the same shall not go.

The army was still too big to serve the Lord's purpose. It had to be reduced again. A small stream flowed from the bigger spring near the camp. The men were to go down there for a drink, and God would reveal which ones should be selected for the coming battle.

5. So he brought down the people unto the water: and the LORD said unto Gideon, Every one that lappeth of the water with his tongue, as

Visual for lesson 2

The visual that corresponds to this lesson illustrates God's ability to do much with little. Discuss contemporary illustrations of the same concept.

a dog lappeth, him shalt thou set by himself; likewise every one that boweth down upon his knees to drink.

There are different ways of drinking from a running stream. One man would lap *with his tongue, as a dog lappeth*. This action is further explained in verse 6. He would cup the palm of his hand to dip a little water from the stream, then lap it from his hand with his tongue. Another man would kneel on both knees and bend forward, bringing his lips to the surface of the stream.

These ways of drinking seemed to show something about the attitudes of the men. They were camped in sight of the enemy, an enemy that greatly outnumbered them. At any time that enemy might decide to attack rather than wait to be attacked. A man who lifted a little water with his hand showed himself to be more alert and watchful, and more concerned about the possibility of sudden attack.

In contrast, one who put his face down to the water showed himself to be overconfident or careless, unaware of the potential danger. While he drank, the enemy could approach without his being aware of it. And he would drink more than the one who cupped a little in his hand. If he rose from his knees and discovered the enemy charging up the hill, his full stomach might keep him from doing his best in battle.

6. And the number of them that lapped, putting their hand to their mouth, were three hundred men: but all the rest of the people bowed down upon their knees to drink water.

By far the greater number of men relaxed and drank freely. It was obvious that they were more interested in satisfying their thirst than in staying ready for the possibility of conflict. [See question #3, page 24.]

7. And the LORD said unto Gideon, By the three hundred men that lapped will I save you, and deliver the Midianites into thine hand: and let all the other people go every man unto his place.

At this point, let's try to imagine what the Midianites were thinking in their camp in the valley. They had seen thirty-two thousand men of Israel gather on the hill above them. Then they had seen most of those Israelites go away. They must have wondered where all those men were going, and why. Were they planning to meet with other Israelites—thousands of them? Were they preparing to surround the camp of Midian with an overpowering army? When the number of men on the hillside shrank to *three hundred*, the thousands of Midianites likely felt more uneasy rather than more secure.

That was confirmed when later, under cover of darkness, Gideon and an aide sneaked near the enemy camp and heard the men of Midian talking. They learned that the Midianites indeed were apprehensive, fearing a devastating attack by Gideon and his men (Judges 7:9-14).

Encouraged by this information, Gideon went back to his own camp to prepare to carry out God's plan. The Midianites were to be routed by clever strategy rather than by force of arms. Gideon divided his three hundred men into three groups. Each man lighted a lamp (the Hebrew word could also describe a torch), but hid its flame in a clay pitcher or jar. Each man also took a trumpet. The three groups crept away silently in the darkness to their assigned places. [See question #4, page 24.]

III. Defeating an Enemy (Judges 7:20, 21)

The twelve hours of "night" (from 6:00 P.M. to 6:00 A.M.) were divided into three "watches" of four hours each. Near the end of the first watch Gideon and his men moved into position. At the beginning of the "middle watch," about 10:00 P.M. (v. 19), while sentries just roused from sleep were nervous amid the darkness around Midian's camp, Gideon blew his trumpet. The response was spectacular.

A. Lights and Noise (v. 20)

20. And the three companies blew the trumpets, and brake the pitchers, and held the lamps in their left hands, and the trumpets in their right hands to blow withal: and they cried, The sword of the LORD, and of Gideon.

Three hundred *lamps* gleamed in the darkness. Three hundred breaking *pitchers* shattered the silence. Three hundred *trumpets* blared, and three hundred voices shouted the battle cry to let the Midianites know what was upon them: *The sword of the Lord, and of Gideon!*

B. Panic (v. 21)

21. And they stood every man in his place round about the camp: and all the host ran, and cried, and fled.

The men of Israel did not need to draw their swords and charge. *They stood every man in his place.* They waved their lamps; they blew their trumpets; they shouted their battle cry—as they had been instructed to do.

In the dark camp of Midian, uneasy sleepers woke to the sound of three hundred trumpets and looked out at three hundred lamps like a line of fire around them. The startled Midianites must have thought that countless thousands of angry Israelites were upon them. Panic-stricken, they *ran, and cried, and fled.* No one paused to

light a lamp; no one took time to pack his belongings. Some did pick up their swords.

Charging out of their tents, the Midianites saw dark figures coming swiftly toward them. Swinging their swords in blind horror, they cut down their own comrades. In darkness and terror they ran screaming until they were out of breath and only faintly could hear the sound of the three hundred trumpeters, each of whom remained steadfast in his place. With scarcely a pause for rest, the Midianites pushed on toward the Jordan River and their homeland to the east of it (v. 22).

The rout of Midian was under way. Probably those men who had left the camp of Israel earlier now returned to chase the fleeing enemies, and other men of Israel joined in the pursuit (v. 23). Men from the tribe of Ephraim were alerted to intercept the fugitives (vv. 24, 25). Gideon then led his troops across the Jordan and defeated the Midianite army that remained there (Judges 8:10-12).

TOO MUCH LIGHT

Most people enjoy the added brightness that Christmas lights bring to December evenings. Many Christians see in the myriad of lights a symbol, not only of the season, but of Jesus, the "light of the world."

Some, however, don't quite see it that way. In Little Rock, Arkansas, Jennings Osborne's Christmas lights reached three million bulbs a few

---

How to Say It

ABIEZRITE. *A*-by-*ez*-rite (strong accent on *ez*).
BAAL. *Bay*-ul.
BARAK. *Bair*-uk.
CANAANITES. *Kay*-nun-ites.
DEBORAH. *Deb*-uh-ruh.
EPHRAIM. *Ee*-fray-im.
GIDEON. *Gid*-ee-un.
GILBOA. Gil-*bo*-uh.
GILEAD. *Gil*-ee-ud.
HAROD. *Hay*-rod.
ISAIAH. Eye-*zay*-uh.
JERUBBAAL. *Jair*-ub-*bay*-ul (strong accent on *bay*).
JEZREEL. *Jez*-ree-el or *Jez*-reel.
JOASH. *Jo*-ash.
MANASSEH. Muh-*nass*-uh.
MIDIAN. *Mid*-ee-un.
MIDIANITES. *Mid*-ee-un-ites.
MOREH. *Mo*-reh.
OPHRAH. *Ahf*-ruh.

years ago. It was then that his neighbors claimed, "That's too much light!" They filed a lawsuit to make him turn off some of his lights. Osborne fought the suit all the way to the Arkansas State Supreme Court. Alas, he lost, and the December nights became a bit darker in his part of Little Rock.

When Gideon's three hundred men had surrounded the Midianites in the dark of night, they blew their trumpets and lit their lamps. This sudden "light show" caused the Midianites to panic, and they fled in fear of a vastly greater army than was really there. Three hundred lamps may not provide a lot of light (at least by our standards), but they were too much for the enemies of God's people. On the other hand, those who are on God's side of the battle against evil never have to fear the light!   —C. R. B.

Conclusion

We're very blessed, aren't we? Nomads never bring their sheep and cattle across the river to devour our growing crops. What, then, does this lesson mean to us? Let's think about some things that do happen here.

A. Examples

Cora had never been in the room where the men's class met, but through the open door she saw the torn shade at the window. It looked disgraceful. A month later the door was open again, and the shade still looked disgraceful.

After church Cora stood on a chair and lifted the shade with its roller off the brackets. On Monday she took it to the hardware store and got a new one just like it. On Wednesday she went early to midweek Bible study and put the new shade in its place.

Home Daily Bible Readings

Monday, Sept. 4—The Midianite Oppression (Judges 6:1-10)

Tuesday, Sept. 5—The Call of Gideon (Judges 6:11-24)

Wednesday, Sept. 6—Sign of the Fleece (Judges 6:36-40)

Thursday, Sept. 7—Preparation for Battle (Judges 7:1-15)

Friday, Sept. 8—Defeat of the Midianites (Judges 7:16-25)

Saturday, Sept. 9—Pursuit of the Midianites (Judges 8:4-21)

Sunday, Sept. 10—Gideon's Latter Days (Judges 8:22-32)

On Sunday the men were delighted. Happily they commented, "They finally did something about that shade."

Dave was unhappy because his daughter didn't like Sunday school. The high school kids met with the adults, and they were bored. So Dave took it up with the teacher, who was also the preacher.

"Sam, how about starting a separate class for the high school kids?"

"Great idea," said Sam. "But a class needs two things: a teacher and a room."

"Couldn't we meet in the auditorium and let them have our room?"

"Maybe. How about a teacher?"

"There's Bill. He's both a teacher and a football coach. The kids think he's great."

Sam nodded. "OK. You get Bill to teach the kids, and I'll get our class to move."

Bill frowned at first, but on second thought he began to smile. "I'd really like to teach some Bible to those kids. In Sunday school I'd be free to shoot down some of the nonsense we read in the textbooks."

Not all the older folks like the auditorium, but they don't complain much because the high school class is growing every week.

B. The Process

You see the process, don't you? It goes something like this:

See the Problem. That isn't much, but it's a start.

Do Something. That's what Cora did about the window blind. There are other things that can be done single-handedly.

Get Help. Dave couldn't teach a high school class, but he knew who could.

Solve Problems. Moving the older adults' class may have been difficult, but it could be done once the benefits were clearly seen.

So what need do you see in your church? What can you do about it? Who can help? What problems will arise? How can they be solved? [See question #5, page 24.]

C. Prayer

Father in Heaven, the work before us is too great for our strength and too complicated for our understanding, but we know that nothing is beyond Your understanding or Your power. Trusting in You to supply what is lacking in us, we promise our best efforts to do Your will. In Jesus' name, amen.

D. Thought to Remember

Our trust in God is better than all our might.

Learning by Doing

This page contains an alternate lesson plan emphasizing learning activities.
Classes desiring such student involvement will find these suggestions helpful.

Learning Goals

After this lesson each student will be able to:

1. Recount the story of the unusual way in which God used Gideon to rescue Israel from the Midianites.

2. Explain why one's reluctance to serve the Lord should not be allowed to keep him or her from such service.

3. Seek an opportunity to encourage an individual who has been rather timid in serving the Lord to use his or her talents in His service.

Into the Lesson

Write on the chalkboard the word *reluctant* without the vowels: R _ L _ C T _ N T. Ask the class to fill in the blanks to discern a key word for today's lesson. Once the class identifies the word, ask, "Why are people sometimes reluctant to serve God?" *(They are uncertain of their talents or anxious about failure; they feel inadequate; they think they are too busy, that they don't have time.)*

State: "Our text today describes one who was reluctant to serve God. He gave some of the same reasons reluctant people today give for their unwillingness to be used by God. Let's turn to Judges 6 and find the reasons he gave and how he overcame them to become obedient to God."

Into the Word

Ask the students to read Judges 6:11-16 to see what excuses Gideon gave for his reluctance to do the Lord's work. Have each student discuss these reasons with one person sitting next to him or her. Allow about three minutes; then restate the question and write the suggested answers from the class on the chalkboard under the heading, "Excuses." *(He questioned whether the Lord was really with the Israelites, v. 13; he cited the absence of God's miracles, v. 13; he said the Lord had forsaken Israel, v. 13; his clan was the weakest in Manasseh, v. 15; he was the least in his family, v. 15).*

Summarize: "Basically, Gideon's excuses could be condensed to two: he doubted God's presence and he doubted his own ability." Write these two excuses on the chalkboard.

Ask the class to notice how God responded to Gideon's excuses. The Lord reassured Gideon that he should go and save Israel from the Midianites (cite verses 14 and 16). But Gideon wanted some signs. Divide the class into four groups,

asking each to read one of the following passages and to prepare a summary: 1. Judges 6:17-24; 2. Judges 6:25-32; 3. Judges 6:36-40; 4. Judges 7:9-14. After three to five minutes, ask the first three groups to summarize the signs the Lord gave to Gideon.

Read Judges 7:1-7 aloud. Ask, "Why did the Lord reduce Gideon's army from 32,000 to 300 men?" *(So Israel would not boast that they had saved themselves.)* To reassure Gideon once he had only 300 men, the Lord gave the sign of a dream. Ask the fourth group above to summarize this reassurance for the class. Conclude this Bible study with a brief summary of Israel's defeat of the Midianites (cite Judges 7:20, 21).

Into Life

State: "Gideon was reluctant because he doubted God's presence and doubted his own ability. What type of reassurance can we give someone today who is reluctant to get involved and serve the Lord?" *(Affirm that God is present and has not abandoned us; share God's Word— e.g., Philippians 4:13; affirm the person's giftedness and abilities; encourage the person to try.)*

State: "Churches are often ravaged and robbed of potential growth today by the lack of programs or workers. What lack of programs or personnel robs our church's growth today?" Write "Programs Needed" and "Personnel Needed" on the chalkboard, and write suggested answers of needed programs or personnel under the proper headings. *(Nursery or youth programs and workers; prayer ministry and workers; music leaders or choir members; ministry teams and workers.)*

Divide the class into the number of groups equal to the number of needed programs. Assign each group one program. Ask the groups to identify some individuals who have the gifts and abilities to serve in that particular program. Give the class five to seven minutes for this discussion. Finally, ask each group member to select one individual from their list to encourage, and to share with the members of their group the selected ways to reassure him or her. Ask each group to pray together for the opportunity to encourage the selected individuals.

(Be sure to coordinate your efforts with those who are responsible for recruiting various workers. Check with them before approaching any potential workers.)

Let's Talk It Over

The questions on this page are designed to encourage review of the lesson Scriptures and to promote discussion of the lesson by the class. The answers provided are only discussion starters. Let your class talk it over from there.

1. The angel of the Lord greeted Gideon as a "mighty man of valor." At the time Gideon seemed a man of cowardice more than valor. What is the value of speaking of others' potential more than what they have actually demonstrated?

The angel's words were an initial step in preparing Gideon for his impending role of military leadership. While reluctant at first, he eventually became a mighty man of valor. We can encourage one another in the church to become better leaders and workers and witnesses in similar fashion. When we focus on what God can do in a person's life more than on what the person has actually done with his or her own life, we encourage that one to press on and to do more and greater things in the power of God's strength.

2. The Lord is not dependent on the bigness of human organizations to accomplish great works. What is the significance of that fact for the church today? How should we apply that truth to our ministries?

The account of God's reducing Gideon's army is just one example of God's working with small numbers to accomplish tremendous results. Samson (Judges 15:14, 15) and Jonathan (1 Samuel 14:13, 14) played significant roles in two more. And of course we remember the powerful effect a small band of apostles exerted in spreading the gospel throughout the Roman Empire. This fact should inspire small congregations to plan prayerfully for mighty achievements, knowing that God delights in demonstrating His power through less impressive human enterprises. And this fact should serve as a reminder to large congregations that the bigness of their faith and commitment to God, rather than their abundant numbers, is the key to accomplishing great things for God.

3. The three hundred men who comprised Gideon's army were the ones who demonstrated their readiness for battle. Why is it important that we be alert and ready for battle today?

Are we too relaxed and complacent, while a crucial battle is being fought all around us? Hostile critics are undermining confidence in the Bible. Certain segments of the entertainment industry seem bent on making Jesus Christ an object of ridicule. Our moral system, once based on Biblical principles, is being set aside. And worst of all, the devil is blinding men and women to their need of salvation. We need to give fresh attention to the struggle Paul described in Ephesians 6:10-18, and we must be diligent in fitting ourselves with the armor described there. Timid, hesitant, complacent Christians must become warriors for Christ!

4. God's strategy for defeating the Midianites called for the use of empty jars, torches, and trumpets. God still uses ordinary things to accomplish His purposes today. What are some common human attributes that Christians can employ in God's service?

Some Christians possess a keen sense of humor. Often it is true that a lighthearted comment can be the "word fitly spoken" (Proverbs 25:11) to defuse a tense situation or to set a troubled individual at ease. Other Christians are gifted with listening ears. They are capable of sitting quietly and caringly while a person in distress unloads his or her burden. Of course there are many believers who can minister with their hands. They accomplish unspectacular but valuable service by typing, cooking, sewing, cleaning, doing mechanical work, etc. And others perform important service with their feet: visiting the sick and shut-ins, doing shopping for such persons, running other errands, etc.

5. Every church member should find something to do, and do it willingly, promptly, and efficiently. But how can we encourage such an attitude in our congregation?

Frequently we hear church members speaking in the third person regarding the congregation to which they belong: "*They* need to make some changes over there!" "What will it take to get *them* growing?" It is important that all church members see the congregation in terms of "we" and "us." Then they will view themselves as the possible suppliers of a need or the potential solution to a problem. Also, leaders of the church should not hesitate to make needs and problems known. Sometimes leaders "talk a problem to death" in their meetings, and then fail to bring it before the congregation. And while they are doing this, the man or woman with the solution may be sitting in a pew, awaiting the challenge to utilize his or her skills in Christ's service.

Samson

DEVOTIONAL READING: Psalm 145:14-21.

BACKGROUND SCRIPTURE: Judges 13–16.

PRINTED TEXT: Judges 16:4, 5, 16, 17, 19-22, 28-30.

Judges 16:4, 5, 16, 17, 19-22, 28-30

4 And it came to pass afterward, that he loved a woman in the valley of Sorek, whose name was Delilah.

5 And the lords of the Philistines came up unto her, and said unto her, Entice him, and see wherein his great strength lieth, and by what means we may prevail against him, that we may bind him to afflict him: and we will give thee every one of us eleven hundred pieces of silver.

. . . .

16 And it came to pass, when she pressed him daily with her words, and urged him, so that his soul was vexed unto death;

17 That he told her all his heart, and said unto her, There hath not come a razor upon mine head; for I have been a Nazarite unto God from my mother's womb: if I be shaven, then my strength will go from me, and I shall become weak, and be like any other man.

. . . .

19 And she made him sleep upon her knees; and she called for a man, and she caused him to shave off the seven locks of his head; and she began to afflict him, and his strength went from him.

20 And she said, The Philistines be upon thee, Samson. And he awoke out of his sleep, and said, I will go out as at other times before, and shake myself. And he wist not that the LORD was departed from him.

21 But the Philistines took him, and put out his eyes, and brought him down to Gaza, and bound him with fetters of brass; and he did grind in the prison house.

22 Howbeit the hair of his head began to grow again after he was shaven.

. . . .

28 And Samson called unto the LORD, and said, O Lord GOD, remember me, I pray thee, and strengthen me, I pray thee, only this once, O God, that I may be at once avenged of the Philistines for my two eyes.

29 And Samson took hold of the two middle pillars upon which the house stood, and on which it was borne up, of the one with his right hand, and of the other with his left.

30 And Samson said, Let me die with the Philistines. And he bowed himself with all his might; and the house fell upon the lords, and upon all the people that were therein. So the dead which he slew at his death were more than they which he slew in his life.

GOLDEN TEXT: O Lord GOD, remember me, I pray thee, and strengthen me,
I pray thee, only this once.—Judges 16:28.

Rulers of Israel
Unit 1: Judges of Israel
(Lessons 1-4)

Lesson Aims

After this lesson each student will be able to:

1. Give the details of Samson's demise and how God used it for good.

2. Tell why using God's gifts to promote His agenda rather than ours is the path to genuine fulfillment.

3. Tell how his or her own talents can be better used for God.

Lesson Outline

INTRODUCTION

  A. A Town Transformed

  B. Lesson Background

 I. SAMSON TRAPPED (Judges 16:4, 5, 16, 17)

  A. Evil Plot (vv. 4, 5)

  B. Endless Nagging (v. 16)

  C. Earnest Admission (v. 17)

    Giving In to Pressure

 II. SAMSON SUBDUED (Judges 16:19-22)

  A. Lost Strength (v. 19)

  B. Helpless Captive (vv. 20, 21)

    The Price of a Haircut

  C. New Hope (v. 22)

III. SAMSON AVENGED (Judges 16:28-30)

  A. Prayer for Strength (v. 28)

  B. Victory in Death (vv. 29, 30)

CONCLUSION

  A. Other Ancient Talents

  B. Today's Talents

  C. Prayer

  D. Thought to Remember

Introduction

Carson was an ordinary town. It had an ordinary high school and an ordinary church that most people ignored. Then Weber came to town.

A. A Town Transformed

Weber became janitor at the high school. He was an ordinary man who could do extraordinary things. When a student couldn't get his car started after school, Weber fixed it. Rejecting pay, he said, "Helping is more fun when you don't get paid. That's the way Jesus did it." The student wanted to know more about Jesus, and Weber took him to Sunday school. Because the student was a popular boy, friends started going with him.

Weber turned down overtime pay with the same kind of response when he worked all night to replace a broken pipe so that school could open in the morning. Impressed with Weber's dedication, the principal started going to church. Many of the teachers followed his example and took their families with them.

In his own neighborhood, Weber was everyone's helper. He led in making his block the neatest one in town. Happy neighbors responded by going to church with him, and they brought others. Soon the church had to build a bigger house.

That, in brief, is the story of a town that was changed because an ordinary man had an extraordinary talent for helping people and making friends. This week's lesson brings us a different story: the story of an extraordinary man who had an extraordinary talent for making enemies. But his enemies were God's enemies, and thus his story has a place in God's Word.

B. Lesson Background

Today's lesson background describes a time when Israel forgot God and fell into idolatry and other sins. Where have we heard that before? In the two lessons prior to this one, of course, and at many other places in the Old Testament. It was a pattern of behavior that was common during the period of the judges.

On this occasion the Lord delivered His sinful people to the Philistines, who lived in the southern coastal plain by the Mediterranean Sea. These oppressors harassed Israel, stealing the people's livestock and harvests for forty years (Judges 13:1).

Once more God set in motion a plan to rescue His people from their enemies. This plan, however, was quite different from what He had done in previous instances. He sent His angel to tell a childless couple that they would have a son who would be a Nazarite all his life. This meant that he would remain dedicated to the service of God. The sign of his dedication would be that his hair must never be cut. (Read more about the Nazarite vow in Numbers 6:1-21.) When the promised baby was born, he was named Samson (Judges 13:2-25).

As he grew to manhood, Samson began to demonstrate incredible strength. On one occasion, when a lion was about to attack him, Samson tore the beast apart with his bare hands (Judges 14:5, 6). In spite of Samson's failure to demonstrate a wisdom to match his strength, God repeatedly used his recklessness to punish the Philistines. During a conflict that followed

Samson's marriage to a Philistine girl, he twice put to death some of the Philistines and set fire to their ripened grain fields (Judges 14:10—15:8). When the Philistines came in great numbers to capture Samson, he picked up the jawbone of a donkey and killed a thousand of them (Judges 15:9-20).

Today's lesson text brings us to the final chapter of the story of Samson—perhaps the most noteworthy of the judges.

I. Samson Trapped
(Judges 16:4, 5, 16, 17)

It seems that Philistine women held a "fatal attraction" for Samson, but in the providence of God this proved fatal to his enemies. As noted above, when Samson married a Philistine girl, the resulting conflict brought death to Philistines, not Samson. When he visited another Philistine girl in Gaza, the Philistines shut and locked the gates of the city, planning to trap and kill him. But Samson simply pulled up the gates with the gateposts and carried them away (Judges 16:1-3).

Now we come to Samson's pivotal encounter with the infamous Delilah.

A. Evil Plot (vv. 4, 5)

4. And it came to pass afterward, that he loved a woman in the valley of Sorek, whose name was Delilah.

The valley of Sorek extended from near Jerusalem to the Mediterranean Sea, about eight and a half miles south of Joppa. From the little that is told of *Delilah*, we suppose that she was a Philistine woman of charming personality and pagan moral standards. Some students think that Samson married her. Whether he did or not, it seems clear that he often came to spend time with her, but was away long enough to let the Philistines plot with her in his absence.

5. And the lords of the Philistines came up unto her, and said unto her, Entice him, and see wherein his great strength lieth, and by what means we may prevail against him, that we may bind him to afflict him: and we will give thee every one of us eleven hundred pieces of silver.

The phrase *lords of the Philistines* describes the five men (Judges 3:3) who ruled the key cities situated in different parts of the Philistines' territory. They wanted to find out two things: what gave Samson his *great strength*, and how that strength could be overcome.

Vengeful as they were, these angry men did not want to kill Samson. They wanted to *bind him to afflict him*: they wanted to see him suffer in retaliation for all the suffering that he had brought upon the Philistines. The bribe they offered Delilah totaled fifty-five hundred *pieces of silver* (probably the *pieces* were shekels). The fact that during the time of the judges someone could be hired at a salary of ten shekels a year (Judges 17:10) indicates the enormous sum that was being offered to Delilah. That the Philistine rulers were willing to pay it shows their determination to rid themselves of Samson.

It appears that Samson, despite his unruly behavior, was something of a joker and a maker of riddles (see Judges 14:10-14). Here he teased Delilah three times, pretending to reveal to her the secret of his strength. Delilah tried each way and found it would not work (Judges 16:6-15). Urged on by thoughts of a lucrative reward, she kept on trying.

B. Endless Nagging (v. 16)

16. And it came to pass, when she pressed him daily with her words, and urged him, so that his soul was vexed unto death.

Delilah had reproached Samson for lying to her (vv. 10, 13) and had complained that he did not love her (v. 15). Now she resorted to ceaseless nagging until Samson could stand it no more.

C. Earnest Admission (v. 17)

17. That he told her all his heart, and said unto her, There hath not come a razor upon mine head; for I have been a Nazarite unto God from my mother's womb: if I be shaven, then my strength will go from me, and I shall become weak, and be like any other man.

Finally Samson gave in. He told Delilah the simple truth: if his hair was cut, his tremendous *strength* would be gone. Three times this woman had revealed her purpose to turn Samson over to the enemy (vv. 6-14), and now he was letting her know how it could be done. How could he be so blind to her intentions?

Apparently Samson had become accustomed to irresistible power. It seems that he really could not imagine himself weak and powerless, even when he divulged how he could be reduced to that state. At the moment, he could think only of putting an end to Delilah's continual nagging. That was the part of Samson's character that constantly led him into trouble: his desire to live for the moment and satisfy "the lust of the flesh" (Galatians 5:16). [See question #1, page 32.]

GIVING IN TO PRESSURE

An old story tells about Jim, a soldier who was sent off to battle. He left behind a wife whose talent seemed to be advising him about what he ought to do, how he ought to do it, and berating him if he didn't do it (or do it in the way she had suggested). It was what some call "nagging." Secretly Jim felt good about getting away from her barrage of counsel.

While Jim was at the battlefront, he received letter after letter from his wife advising him, "Try to get assigned away from the front lines," "Be sure you don't get captured," "Watch out so that you don't get shot," and so on. Finally, when Jim had become fed up with all of this advice from someone who had no idea what life in combat was like, he wrote his wife a letter. It contained two sentences: "Please stop sending me these nagging letters. Just let me enjoy this war in peace."

Samson's relationship with Delilah may have resembled the story of Jim. However, during a time of war with the Philistines, Delilah's nagging was not to assure Samson's safety, but to find a way to destroy him. When he finally gave in to her, the results were disastrous.

Like Samson, we face pressure from evil forces on a daily basis. And, like Samson, when we give in to the pressure to do wrong, the consequences can be devastating.   —C. R. B.

II. Samson Subdued
(Judges 16:19-22)

At last Delilah had the truth! Once more she sent word to the Philistine conspirators, confident that she could now deliver Samson into their hands (v. 18).

A. Lost Strength (v. 19)

19. And she made him sleep upon her knees; and she called for a man, and she caused him to shave off the seven locks of his head; and she began to afflict him, and his strength went from him.

Now the woman displayed nothing but tender affection for her man. She stroked and soothed him until he fell asleep *upon her knees*. There he lay undisturbed, oblivious to what proceeded to take place. Long and flowing, Samson's hair had been tied or braided in *seven locks*. A man removed them all. Thus Delilah *began to afflict him*, for *his strength*, which had kept him from being afflicted, *went from him*.

B. Helpless Captive (vv. 20, 21)

20. And she said, The Philistines be upon thee, Samson. And he awoke out of his sleep, and said, I will go out as at other times before, and shake myself. And he wist not that the LORD was departed from him.

Samson expected to overcome his attackers as he had always done before, for *he wist not* (that

is, he did not know) *that the Lord was departed from him*. Samson's strength was not really from his hair; it was from the Lord (Judges 14:6, 19; 15:14, 15). Samson had been devoted to the Lord by his parents' vow before he was born. His uncut hair was the sign of that vow (Judges 13:3-5). When Samson recklessly let the sign be removed, the Lord departed. Samson was now "like any other man" (v. 17). [See question #2, page 32.]

THE PRICE OF A HAIRCUT

Back in the 1940s, a man could get a haircut for a dollar or less. Of course, it didn't take much time for a barber to run a pair of electric clippers over a fellow's head. The "G.I." haircut went by various names: crewcut, buzz, butch, etc. And because American fighting men were heroes in those days, their hairstyle was very popular even among civilians.

How things have changed since then! Hair styles and lengths differ widely today. And so do the prices. Today a haircut may cost five or ten dollars at a small-town barber or upwards of fifty dollars at a salon in a bigger city. One barber reportedly charged Bill Clinton $200 to give the President a haircut aboard *Air Force One*. But the most expensive haircut of all time was the one into which Delilah lured Samson. That haircut cost Samson his dignity and strength as well as his locks. Ultimately it cost him his life.

It may be argued that our society makes too much out of how a man cuts his hair. But it's hard to overstate the cost to Samson of his haircut. Hairstyle (as well as most other issues of style) may be irrelevant, except when—as in

---

How to Say It

ANTIOCH. *An*-tee-ock.
APOLLOS. Uh-*pahl*-us.
AQUILA. *Ack*-wih-luh.
BARNABAS. *Bar*-nuh-bus.
DAGON. *Day*-gon.
DELILAH. Dih-*lye*-luh.
DORCAS. *Dor*-cus.
GAZA. *Gay*-zuh.
JOPPA. *Jop*-uh.
JOSES. *Jo*-sez.
MEDITERRANEAN. *Med*-uh-tuh-*ray*-nee-un (strong accent on *ray*).
NAZARITE. *Naz*-uh-rite.
PHILISTINES. Fuh-*liss*-teens or *Fill*-us-teens.
PRISCILLA. Prih-*sil*-uh.
SOREK. *So*-rek.
TABITHA. *Tab*-ih-thuh.

Samson's case—it reflects a change in our relationship with God.   —C. R. B.

21. But the Philistines took him, and put out his eyes, and brought him down to Gaza, and bound him with fetters of brass; and he did grind in the prison house.

Imagine the delight of the Philistines. Samson was in their power, and they lost no time in adding to his misery. First, they *put out his eyes.* Then they *brought him down to Gaza,* one of their principal cities, and *bound him with fetters of brass.* His superhuman power was gone; his human power was put to work turning a heavy millstone in order to *grind* wheat for his captors' food. That was a task sometimes given to an ox or a donkey.

C. New Hope (v. 22)

22. Howbeit the hair of his head began to grow again after he was shaven.

The sign of the vow was returning. Would Samson renew the vow itself? Would the Lord come back to him? Would Samson be strong again?

III. Samson Avenged (Judges 16:28-30)

The capture of Samson called for a celebration. The Philistines gathered for rejoicing and for giving thanks to Dagon, their supposed god. When the hearts of the revelers were merry, Samson was brought from the prison to make sport for them (vv. 23-25). We can only speculate as to what cruelties were involved in this "sport."

It is hard for us to imagine the shape of the building in which the celebration was held. Verse 27 simply calls it a "house." It may have been a temple dedicated to the worship of Dagon, in whose honor the Philistines had assembled. Verse 27 also tells us that about three thousand people were gathered on the roof of the structure to watch Samson.

At some point during the festivities, Samson asked to be led to the pillars "whereupon the house standeth" so that he could lean on them (v. 26). The stage was set for the final scene.

A. Prayer for Strength (v. 28)

28. And Samson called unto the LORD, and said, O Lord GOD, remember me, I pray thee, and strengthen me, I pray thee, only this once, O God, that I may be at once avenged of the Philistines for my two eyes.

Blinded by his enemies and abused to amuse them, Samson thirsted for vengeance as he once had thirsted for water: *strengthen me, . . . that I may be at once avenged of the Philistines for my*

O Lord God, remember me, . . . and strengthen me, . . . only this once.
Judges 16:28

Visual for lesson 3

The visual for today's lesson pictures Samson's final act by which he avenged himself and became God's instrument of judgment on the pagan Philistines.

two eyes. However, though Samson was making a request for himself, the vengeance that answered his prayer gave Israel freedom from Philistine oppression for some time. [See question #3, page 32.]

B. Victory in Death (vv. 29, 30)

29. And Samson took hold of the two middle pillars upon which the house stood, and on which it was borne up, of the one with his right hand, and of the other with his left.

As noted earlier, the design of this building is not made clear to us. What is clear is that Samson had been guided to *the two middle pillars upon which the house stood.* The stability of the entire structure depended on those two. In some way Samson *took hold* of those pillars, most likely bracing himself against them.

30. And Samson said, Let me die with the Philistines. And he bowed himself with all his might; and the house fell upon the lords, and upon all the people that were therein. So the dead which he slew at his death were more than they which he slew in his life.

Blinded, imprisoned, and tormented, Samson no longer cared to live. He wanted only for the Philistines to *die,* too. In answer to Samson's prayer, God gave him the strength he needed. With one great final effort he pushed (or pulled) the two main pillars out of place, and the building came tumbling down. *So the dead which he slew at his death were more than they which he slew in his life.* The five *lords* of the Philistines died in that catastrophe, and probably their subordinates as well. Eventually, however, the Philistines regained strength and again became a force capable of threatening Israel, which they did during the reigns of Saul and David.

The Bible adds a touching postlude in verse 31. Members of Samson's family came to dig his body from the rubble and take it home for an honored burial. More important, the inspired writer gives Samson an honored place in God's Book. With all his faults and follies, this man is worthy of honor. Among the heroes of Israel he stands alone. In the New Testament, the writer of Hebrews cites Samson as an example of faith in action (Hebrews 11:32). [See question #4, page 32.]

Conclusion

Samson might be called a two-talent man. He was gifted with enormous physical strength and with courage to use it against overwhelming odds. Beyond these, we see nothing to distinguish him. He did not have the moral purity we expect in a man of God. We see no wisdom in Samson's dealings with Philistine women, but God used even Samson's folly in this area to accomplish His purpose.

A. Other Ancient Talents

Apollos was a talented preacher, but his understanding of God's plan was incomplete. After receiving further instruction from Aquila and Priscilla, he continued using his talents and "helped them much which had believed through grace" (Acts 18:24-28).

Joses had such a talent for encouraging others that the apostles named him *Barnabas*, which means "son of encouragement." Note how he encouraged the poor brethren at Jerusalem (Acts 4:36, 37), Saul (Acts 9:26-28), the brethren in Antioch (Acts 11:19-26), and faltering John Mark (Acts 15:36-39).

Tabitha, also known as Dorcas, had a talent for needlework, and widows in Joppa treasured the coats and garments that she made for them (Acts 9:36-39).

Wonderful things happen when God's people use their talents to enrich one another and to hold forth the Word of life to all the world.

Home Daily Bible Readings

Monday, Sept. 11—Manoah Seeks Guidance (Judges 13:1-14)
Tuesday, Sept. 12—Manoah Offers a Sacrifice (Judges 13:15-25)
Wednesday, Sept. 13—Wedding Feast and Riddle (Judges 14:5-20)
Thursday, Sept. 14—Samson Defeats the Philistines (Judges 15:9—16:3)
Friday, Sept. 15—Samson and Delilah (Judges 16:4-17)
Saturday, Sept. 16—Samson's Capture (Judges 16:18-22)
Sunday, Sept. 17—Samson's Death (Judges 16:23-31)

B. Today's Talents

Tom was a "natural" at salesmanship. Back in 1936, when people were still feeling the effects of the Great Depression, his income averaged five hundred dollars a week. But Tom would have no part in evangelistic calling for the church. "That's not my responsibility," he said.

Mark is one of the most popular and most effective teachers in the local high school, while the little high-school class at church struggles along with a series of untalented and ineffective teachers. Mark turns a deaf ear to pleas that he teach that class. "I live with those kids five days a week," he explains. "Don't you think I deserve the weekend off?"

Marilyn has a big home and provides expert day care for babies, but she never works in the church nursery. Stewart is a landscape architect, but he can't find time to landscape the church lot. Mel is a building contractor. His new roof for the church was expertly done, but the price was high. The Merry Minstrels are so busy with weddings and parties that they turn down every invitation to bring special music at the church.

But the picture has a brighter side. Many talents are hard at work for the Lord. Laura works five days a week at Marilyn's day care center, but her chief joy is Sunday morning in the nursery at church. Annie teaches music and directs several singing groups in the high school, but she finds time to work with both the choir and the youth choir at church. Don's business is heating and air conditioning. He keeps the church's equipment in top condition, but laughs off every suggestion of payment. Mack's little truck farm produces mostly vegetables for the dinner table, but his little flower garden by the church door is a thing of beauty and a joy forever. And how the church is filled with food and gladness when the ladies combine their talents to produce a fellowship dinner!

What is your talent, your ability, your special gift from God? Is the Great Giver receiving any return? [See question #5, page 32.]

C. Prayer

How richly You have blessed our minds and our hands, our Father! What myriad ways You have set before us to make a living and to make our living happy! As we manage those gifts You have given, may we remember always that they come from You. In Jesus' name. Amen.

D. Thought to Remember

My talent is not really mine; it's God's.

Learning by Doing

This page contains an alternate lesson plan emphasizing learning activities.
Classes desiring such student involvement will find these suggestions helpful.

Learning Goals

After participating in this lesson, students will be able to:

1. Give the details of Samson's demise and how God used it for good.

2. Tell why using God's gifts to promote His agenda rather than ours is the path to genuine fulfillment.

3. Tell how their own talents can be better used for God.

Into the Lesson

Write on the chalkboard the following list of places: Zorah, Timnath, Lehi, Gaza, and valley of Sorek. Ask whether any in the class can guess which judge of Israel is the subject of today's study, based on these place names.

It would take a very well-versed student to identify Samson from this list, so be generous in your praise if anyone comes up with that answer. If not, give the following list and let them try again: jawbone of a donkey, unusual birth, gates of the city, Delilah, foxes and firebrands. This time nearly everyone should recognize that Samson is the subject.

If there is time, have the students try to match the items on the second list with the places in the first. Afterward, or instead, quickly summarize the information to provide some background. Samson's birth was to a couple from Zorah (Judges 13:2). At Timnath Samson tied firebrands to the tails of three hundred foxes and destroyed Philistine grain (14:1—15:5). It was at Lehi that Samson slew a thousand Philistines with the jawbone of a donkey (15:9-15). Samson carried the gates of Gaza off when the Philistines tried to trap him in that city (16:1-3). And Delilah lived in the valley of Sorek (16:4). She is a key player in today's lesson text.

Into the Word

Assign the members of your class the following roles: Samson, Delilah, Narrator, Lords of the Philistines (there were five but use at least two people for this role), Philistine People (Judges 16:24, 25).

1. *Samson Trapped, Judges 16:4-17.* Using the assigned roles, ask the class members to read this section of the text. Ask the class to answer the following questions. How did the rulers persuade Delilah to find out the secret of Samson's strength? (See verse 5.) What three unsuccessful methods did Delilah try to subdue Samson? (See verses 7-9, 11 and 12, 13 and 14.) Why did Samson finally reveal the truth about his strength? (See verses 15, 16.) What was the significance of Samson's uncut hair? (See Judges 13:3-5.)

2. *Samson Subdued, Judges 16:18-21.* Ask the class members to read their assigned words of the text. Then ask: What was the real source of Samson's great strength? *(The Lord's presence, v. 20.)* What did the Philistines do to Samson after capturing him? (See v. 21.)

3. *Samson Avenged, Judges 16:22-30.* Once again have the class members read their assigned words. Ask: What led to Samson's renewed strength? *(Hair began to grow; he prayed to the Lord for strength one more time.)* State: "So Samson died using God's gift of strength to deliver Israel from the hand of the Philistines."

Into Life

Samson broke his vow of devotion to the Lord, and the Lord departed from him. As a result of his failure, he was physically abused, disabled, and humiliated. If Samson had died in the prison, how would he have viewed his life before God? *(Unfulfilled; did not live up to God's purpose for his life.)*

What principles for living do we find in the life of Samson? *(Personal failure did not cause him to give up on God. He did not allow physical hardship, disability, or humiliation to keep him from serving God. He took advantage of the opportunity he had to use his gift from God. He asked the Lord for strength to use his talent. He was true to God's calling and purpose for his life.)*

Tell the class members to evaluate how closely each principle is followed in their own lives. Prepare a poster or transparency sheet with each of the above principles followed by a horizontal line. On the right side of the line write "Regularly Followed" and on the left side write "Seldom Followed." Ask each person to read each principle and evaluate himself or herself on how closely it is followed, mentally placing an "x" on the line. Next, ask the students to think about the gifts and abilities God has given them. Ask them to move into groups of three and to tell how their own talents can be better used for God. Lead the class in a prayer of commitment to use God's gifts for Him.

Let's Talk It Over

The questions on this page are designed to encourage review of the lesson Scriptures and to promote discussion of the lesson by the class. The answers provided are only discussion starters. Let your class talk it over from there.

1. Samson illustrates the wisdom of Paul's warning, "Let him that thinketh he standeth take heed lest he fall" (1 Corinthians 10:12). When we read of Samson's dealings with Delilah, we are amazed at his foolish overconfidence. Apparently he fancied that he was powerful enough that, even with his hair cut, he was more than a match for the Philistines. Sadly, he learned otherwise. How do people in our own time demonstrate a similar arrogance?

Many overestimate their physical prowess or intellectual superiority or personal charisma. In their arrogance they overextend themselves. They imagine that they can get away with bending the rules or deceiving their fellowmen or talking their way out of a jam. And, like Samson, they end up losing friends, power, and position.

2. Poor Samson! He had no idea that the Lord was no longer with him! How might a leader today get himself in a position where he is not following the Lord, but does not even know it? What can be done to help such a person return to the Lord?

It usually happens gradually, even as it did with Samson. While he kept lying to Delilah about the source of his strength, he kept getting closer and closer to the truth. Another key is pride, which was surely Samson's downfall. He couldn't have believed Delilah would not cut his hair after she had put to the test every other story he had told her. He must have thought he was invincible. Another problem Samson had was a failure to have anyone hold him accountable. Leaders today who are accountable to no one are in jeopardy of going the way of Samson.

Unfortunately, such a person will not usually listen to reason—until he has fallen. But he can be restored if he is offered love and forgiveness when that happens.

3. Samson prayed for strength so that he could gain revenge on his enemies. That may seem to us a selfish prayer. What, if anything, can we learn from Samson's prayer?

In spite of the outwardly selfish nature of this prayer, it accomplished something of benefit to the nation—a period of relief from Philistine oppression. Thus it is typical of Samson's life. So often he acted out of selfishness or in pursuit of his own lusts, and God used that to deliver His people. How much more could God have used a Samson whose heart was given completely to the Lord!

What about our own prayers? Do we keep God's honor and reputation uppermost in mind? Are we careful to give priority to prayer for friends, fellow members of the church, and other people we know? Are our hearts given wholly to the Lord, so that our prayers reflect that devotion?

4. Samson is one of the Old Testament heroes of the faith cited in Hebrews 11. Does that surprise you? What of Samson's life do you think earned him a place in the "roll call of the faithful"? What can we learn from his example?

In spite of Samson's many weaknesses, he did have faith. No doubt his earlier exploits were done with a recognition that his strength was from God. At some point he began to trust in his own might, but in the end he was forced to acknowledge God once again. Then he acted on his final prayer—believing God would answer.

Since we all are flawed in some way, it is encouraging to know that God uses flawed people to work His will. Of course, we should strive to overcome our flaws, but it is a relief to know that we do not have to be perfect and flawless in order for God to use us.

5. Some church members have unique talents that they utilize in their work, but seldom if ever employ in the betterment of the church. How can we challenge them to offer those talents freely in the cause of Christ?

Whatever the talent may be, it is God-given. We tend to view the ability to speak or sing or write or draw in that way, but other skills are also gifts of God. The lesson writer mentions several, and we could add still more: painting, plumbing, electrical work, typing, computer skills, accounting skills, and many more. Christians earn money by employing these skills, but since they come from the Creator, shouldn't they be made available to the church without cost? Of course, there are times when the church may need extensive use of these skills, and those occasions may require more time than the members can give on a voluntary basis. In such situations it is quite legitimate for the members to receive reasonable pay for their labors.

Samuel

DEVOTIONAL READING: Galatians 6:7-10.

BACKGROUND SCRIPTURE: 1 Samuel 3:1—4:1; 7:3-17.

PRINTED TEXT: 1 Samuel 3:2-10, 19-21; 7:3-5, 12.

1 Samuel 3:2-10, 19-21

2 And it came to pass at that time, when Eli was laid down in his place, and his eyes began to wax dim, that he could not see;

3 And ere the lamp of God went out in the temple of the LORD, where the ark of God was, and Samuel was laid down to sleep;

4 That the LORD called Samuel: and he answered, Here am I.

5 And he ran unto Eli, and said, Here am I; for thou calledst me. And he said, I called not; lie down again. And he went and lay down.

6 And the LORD called yet again, Samuel. And Samuel arose and went to Eli, and said, Here am I; for thou didst call me. And he answered, I called not, my son; lie down again.

7 Now Samuel did not yet know the LORD, neither was the word of the LORD yet revealed unto him.

8 And the LORD called Samuel again the third time. And he arose and went to Eli, and said, Here am I; for thou didst call me. And Eli perceived that the LORD had called the child.

9 Therefore Eli said unto Samuel, Go, lie down: and it shall be, if he call thee, that thou shalt say, Speak, LORD; for thy servant heareth. So Samuel went and lay down in his place.

10 And the LORD came, and stood, and called as at other times, Samuel, Samuel. Then Samuel answered, Speak; for thy servant heareth.

. . . .

19 And Samuel grew, and the LORD was with him, and did let none of his words fall to the ground.

20 And all Israel from Dan even to Beersheba knew that Samuel was established to be a prophet of the LORD.

21 And the LORD appeared again in Shiloh: for the LORD revealed himself to Samuel in Shiloh by the word of the LORD.

1 Samuel 7:3-5, 12

3 And Samuel spake unto all the house of Israel, saying, If ye do return unto the LORD with all your hearts, then put away the strange gods and Ashtaroth from among you, and prepare your hearts unto the LORD, and serve him only: and he will deliver you out of the hand of the Philistines.

4 Then the children of Israel did put away Baalim and Ashtaroth, and served the LORD only.

5 And Samuel said, Gather all Israel to Mizpeh, and I will pray for you unto the LORD.

. . . .

12 Then Samuel took a stone, and set it between Mizpeh and Shen, and called the name of it Ebenezer, saying, Hitherto hath the Lord helped us.

GOLDEN TEXT: Speak; for thy servant heareth.—1 Samuel 3:10.

Rulers of Israel
Unit 1: Judges of Israel
(Lessons 1-4)

Lesson Aims

After participating in this lesson, each student will be able to:

1. Relate the account of how God called Samuel, then used him to deliver Israel from the Philistines.

2. Explain the role of the Bible in providing us with a means of "hearing God's voice."

3. Develop or maintain a pattern of regular Bible study in order to stay sensitive to God's will.

Lesson Outline

INTRODUCTION

    A. Who Is Number One?

    B. Lesson Background

  I. GOD'S UNEXPECTED CALL (1 Samuel 3:2-10)

    A. Asleep in the Temple (vv. 2, 3)

    B. A Voice in the Night (vv. 4-7)

    C. The Right Answer (vv. 8-10)

  II. GOD'S ESTABLISHED PROPHET (1 Samuel 3:19-21)

    A. God Blesses Samuel (v. 19)

    B. Samuel's Reputation Grows (v. 20)

      Prophets, True and False

    C. God's Revelation Continues (v. 21)

  III. ISRAEL'S RETURN TO GOD (1 Samuel 7:3-5, 12)

    A. Appeal and Response (vv. 3, 4)

      Cleaning Out the Garbage

    B. Prayer and Victory (v. 5)

    C. Monument in Memory (v. 12)

CONCLUSION

    A. God's Ancient Speaking

    B. God's Speaking Today

    C. Prayer

    D. Thought to Remember

Introduction

The agnostic and the preacher were having a friendly argument:

Agnostic: If God wants me to believe in Him, He's got to let me know He's there.

Preacher: Look at the sun. Did you put it in place?

Agnostic: Maybe it's always been in place. Maybe it's eternal, as you say God is.

Preacher: Then take a look at yourself, or a mouse, or a bug. Surely, you're not going to say

that living things have been on earth forever, are you?

Agnostic: No. Scientifically speaking, the earth once was too hot to support life.

Preacher: And, scientifically speaking, every living thing comes from something that was living before. The living God put life on earth.

Agnostic: But you're assuming God exists. No one knows how life originated. One theory is as good as another. I'm not going to believe in God until I see some evidence I can accept.

Preacher: In other words, you will believe in God if He takes orders from you.

Agnostic: How's that again?

Preacher: You will believe in God if He obeys you, if He gives the kind of evidence *you* demand. Who do you think you are—some kind of "supergod"?

A. Who Is Number One?

How many human beings want to be "number one"! Like the agnostic portrayed above, some of them will believe in God if He provides the kind of evidence they demand.

Samuel had a better idea. Instead of trying to shape God according to his own wishes, he said, "Speak; for thy servant heareth."

B. Lesson Background

Hannah had no children. In the time and place in which she lived, this was thought to be a terrible hardship. More than that, some believed that it was a disgrace, a reproach, even a punishment or curse from God. To make matters worse for Hannah, her husband's other wife did have children, and she taunted Hannah unmercifully (1 Samuel 1:1-8).

Desperately Hannah prayed for a son; fervently she promised that she would give him to the Lord and signify his dedication by leaving his hair uncut (1 Samuel 1:9-11).

Finally Hannah did have a son, whom she named Samuel (1 Samuel 1:20). Unlike some who make promises to the Lord while in difficult circumstances, Hannah took her vow seriously. When the child was weaned (probably around the age of three), she left him with Eli the priest to be brought up in the service of God (1 Samuel 1:25-28; 2:11).

I. God's Unexpected Call
(1 Samuel 3:2-10)

As the years passed, this special child "grew on, and was in favor both with the Lord, and also with men" (1 Samuel 2:26). Our text takes up the story while Samuel was still a child (1 Samuel 3:1), but we are not told how old he was. Josephus, a noted Jewish historian who lived during the first century, says that he was twelve.

A. Asleep in the Temple (vv. 2, 3)

2. And it came to pass at that time, when Eli was laid down in his place, and his eyes began to wax dim, that he could not see.

Eli was "very old" (1 Samuel 2:22), and his eyesight was failing so *that he could not see* clearly. Perhaps that is mentioned at this point to explain why the boy Samuel was constantly at his call, night or day. Now it was night, and Eli had gone to bed.

3. And ere the lamp of God went out in the temple of the LORD, where the ark of God was, and Samuel was laid down to sleep.

The tabernacle had been set up at Shiloh soon after Israel had conquered the promised land and had divided it among the twelve tribes (Joshua 18:1). But in this verse we read of the *temple* rather than the tabernacle, and verse 15 mentions "the house of the Lord." We should not allow these differences in terminology to confuse us. In our own time a historic building is sometimes enclosed within a larger structure to protect it from the weather. Perhaps something similar had been done for the tabernacle.

Inside the tabernacle itself was *the lamp of God*, the seven-branched golden lampstand that gave light to the Holy Place (Exodus 25:31-40). In the Holy of Holies rested *the ark of God*, often called the ark of the covenant. Of course, Eli and Samuel did not sleep in the Holy of Holies or even in the Holy Place, where the lampstand was. They must have had bedrooms elsewhere in the larger (perhaps enclosed) structure that is here called *the temple of the Lord.*

The golden lampstand was replenished with oil every morning, for it was against the regulations of the law of Moses to allow the light to go out (Exodus 27:20, 21; 30:7, 8). That the incident recorded in our text is said to have occurred before *the lamp of God went out* indicates that it took place in the early morning hours, before all the oil was consumed.

B. A Voice in the Night (vv. 4-7)

4. That the LORD called Samuel: and he answered, Here am I.

In the darkness *Samuel* heard his name *called.* The voice probably awakened him from his sleep. Promptly he responded so that whoever had spoken would know that his words had been heard.

5. And he ran unto Eli, and said, Here am I; for thou calledst me. And he said, I called not; lie down again. And he went and lay down.

Naturally the boy thought the person speaking was Eli. What else could he think? But Eli had not *called,* nor had he heard anyone speak. Probably supposing that Samuel had been dreaming, Eli sent him back to bed.

6. And the LORD called yet again, Samuel. And Samuel arose and went to Eli, and said, Here am I; for thou didst call me. And he answered, I called not, my son; lie down again.

Again came the *call,* too plain to be unheeded. Samuel could only respond as he had done before, and Eli could only send him back to bed *again.*

7. Now Samuel did not yet know the LORD, neither was the word of the LORD yet revealed unto him.

Of course, Samuel had been taught about *the Lord.* He must have known that his mother had dedicated him to the Lord's service; he must have known that Eli was training him for that service. But he was not yet personally acquainted with the Lord; that is, the Lord had never spoken to him before. He must have been puzzled by the repeated sound of his name, but he had no reason to think that the Lord was speaking.

C. The Right Answer (vv. 8-10)

8. And the LORD called Samuel again the third time. And he arose and went to Eli, and said, Here am I; for thou didst call me. And Eli perceived that the LORD had called the child.

At last Eli *perceived* the truth. It was not that his young helper was dreaming; it was that *the Lord had called the child.*

9. Therefore Eli said unto Samuel, Go, lie down: and it shall be, if he call thee, that thou shalt say, Speak, LORD; for thy servant heareth. So Samuel went and lay down in his place.

Throughout this text, the word *Lord* is used to translate God's personal name, the name that is often rendered in English as "Jehovah." That name in later centuries was considered so sacred that Jews refused to speak it at all, lest they use

Visual for lesson 4

Today's visual reminds us that the Lord still speaks if we will but listen. He speaks to young and old alike through His Word.

that holy name in vain. Whenever they read the Scriptures and came to that name, they read "adonai," *the Lord,* instead. Many English translations use the name they read instead of the name that was written; but they print LORD in small capitals to let us know that it represents the more personal name.

10. And the LORD came, and stood, and called as at other times, Samuel, Samuel. Then Samuel answered, Speak; for thy servant heareth.

This time Samuel answered according to Eli's instructions—almost. Eli had told him to say, "Speak, Lord [Jehovah]; for thy servant heareth." Perhaps the boy was afraid to utter the sacred name. He answered, *Speak; for thy servant heareth.* [See question #1, page 40.]

The Lord then told Samuel that He would carry out His judgment against Eli and his family because Eli had failed to restrain the reckless wickedness of his sons (vv. 11-14). Eli had heard that before from another prophet (1 Samuel 2:27-36). Hearing it again from Samuel confirmed that the Lord had indeed spoken to him. The old man accepted his punishment with resignation (1 Samuel 3:15-18).

II. God's Established Prophet (1 Samuel 3:19-21)

A. God Blesses Samuel (v. 19)

19. And Samuel grew, and the LORD was with him, and did let none of his words fall to the ground.

Samuel grew, continuing in the service of God to which his mother had dedicated him (1 Samuel 1:11). *The Lord was with him,* so guiding his speech that *none of his words* could *fall to the ground;* that is, nothing he said was false or mistaken. What he said about the past or present

---

Home Daily Bible Readings

Monday, Sept. 18—Samuel Listens for God's Call (1 Samuel 3:1-9)
Tuesday, Sept. 19—Samuel Hears God's Message (1 Samuel 3:10-14)
Wednesday, Sept. 20—Samuel Becomes God's Prophet (1 Samuel 3:15—4:1)
Thursday, Sept. 21—Samuel Gathers Israel (1 Samuel 7:3-6)
Friday, Sept. 22—Defeat of the Philistines (1 Samuel 7:7-11)
Saturday, Sept. 23—Samuel Judges Victorious Israel (1 Samuel 7:12-17)
Sunday, Sept. 24—Always Be Watchful (Luke 12:35-40)

---

was true; what he said about the future came true in the proper time.

B. Samuel's Reputation Grows (v. 20)

20. And all Israel from Dan even to Beersheba knew that Samuel was established to be a prophet of the LORD.

Samuel's reputation spread *from Dan* in the far northern part of Israel *even to Beersheba* in the far south. The truth of his teaching and the accuracy of his predictions convinced *all Israel* that he was *a prophet of the Lord.* [See question #2, page 40.]

PROPHETS, TRUE AND FALSE

In March of 1997, thirty-nine members of the "Heaven's Gate" cult committed mass suicide. Their leader had told them that by this means they were preparing themselves to be transported to a spaceship that would fly them to Heaven on the tail of a comet.

William Proctor claims that these people were mistaken. The truth—according to Proctor—is that in 2001, thirty-three spaceships will land on top of one another on the San Diego property owned by Proctor's cult, the Unarius Academy of Science. Each of these ships will carry one thousand "space brothers" who will come to teach us how to live peaceably on earth. Unarius stands for Universal Articulate Interdimensional Understanding of Science, which claims to have five thousand members and asserts that nearly half a million people have read their books and seen their videos.

There is no end to the parade of misguided souls who seek enlightenment from mistaken and (often) unscrupulous people who claim to have secret knowledge. Time will prove William Proctor wrong soon enough, as it has every other prophet with fanciful ideas.

On the other hand, Samuel spoke the truth: his words were the words of the Lord. "All Israel" recognized that Samuel was a true prophet. As false prophets vie for our attention today, those who are wise will listen only for the words that come from God.   —C. R. B.

C. God's Revelation Continues (v. 21)

21. And the LORD appeared again in Shiloh: for the LORD revealed himself to Samuel in Shiloh by the word of the LORD.

The Lord appeared again, not just once, but many times *to Samuel in Shiloh.* The Hebrew text makes this clear, for it reads, "The Lord continued to appear in Shiloh." The last part of the verse explains that the Lord did not appear in a visible form to be seen by Samuel or anyone else; he *revealed himself to Samuel* through His *word.* Such a word was desperately needed in all Israel, for the nation was sinking into sin and idolatry.

III. Israel's Return to God (1 Samuel 7:3-5, 12)

Here we see an occasion where Israel's trouble came once more from the Philistines. As we saw in last week's lesson, Samson had won a significant victory over the Philistines; but they had recovered their power and now began once more to oppress Israel. Read about this in 1 Samuel 4. Israel was then under the dominance of the Philistines for twenty years, "and all the house of Israel lamented after the Lord"; that is, in their suffering and misery they turned to Him for help (1 Samuel 7:2).

A. Appeal and Response (vv. 3, 4)

3. And Samuel spake unto all the house of Israel, saying, If ye do return unto the LORD with all your hearts, then put away the strange gods and Ashtaroth from among you, and prepare your hearts unto the LORD, and serve him only: and he will deliver you out of the hand of the Philistines.

The law required the men of Israel to gather three times a year for the great national festivals of Passover, Pentecost, and Tabernacles (Exodus 23:14-17). Perhaps such a gathering provided an opportunity for Samuel to speak to *all the house of Israel.* Mourning over their oppression and appealing to God for help (v. 2) was good, but it was only a first step. The people needed to do more. If they were sincere in their appeal to God, they needed to get rid of the idols that offended Him.

Strange gods were foreign gods, imaginary gods of the pagans. The term *Ashtaroth* describes imaginary goddesses supposed to be associated with the imaginary gods (usually as their lovers). The presence of such supposed gods in Israel showed how far the people had drifted from worship of the one true God. The first of His Ten Commandments was, "Thou shalt have no other gods before me" (Exodus 20:3). If the people would obey that command, said Samuel, the true God would *deliver* them *out of the hand of the Philistines.* [See question #3, page 40.]

4. Then the children of Israel did put away Baalim and Ashtaroth, and served the LORD only.

Samuel's recommendation made sense, and the people followed it. *Baalim* (the plural of *Baal*) was a general name for all the false gods, even as the term *Ashtaroth* included all the false goddesses.

CLEANING OUT THE GARBAGE

The man who had lived in apartment 21 for eleven years drove a shiny new BMW sedan and wore nice clothes. He never spoke to neighbors, and no one knew what his living quarters looked like. Then one day he drove away with just a few boxes in his car. That's when the building manager discovered a literal garbage dump. Countertops were piled high with beer bottles, empty microwave dinner boxes, and assorted junk. The bathtub was covered with black mold except for where the tenant stood to take a shower. The bedroom was piled high with clothes except for the spot on the bed where he had slept. Perhaps the man figured it was easier to move and leave everything behind than to clean up the mess on a regular basis, as most folks do.

On a spiritual level, Israel had a similar problem. They had brought the gods of the pagans into their spiritual "house," polluting the land in which they lived and making it a spiritual garbage dump. However, since this was the land God had given them, they couldn't just move away and leave it all behind. Samuel called on them to do a thorough housecleaning, and they followed his command.

Housecleaning, whether physical or spiritual, is always hard work, but it pays the dividend of a more satisfying life. How many of us have learned the lesson the Israelites learned?

—C. R. B.

B. Prayer and Victory (v. 5)

5. And Samuel said, Gather all Israel to Mizpeh, and I will pray for you unto the LORD.

If Samuel's recommendation was given at one of the major national festivals, the people needed to return home in order to obey his words and get rid of their idols. Perhaps some time later, when Samuel was convinced that the idols were gone, he sent messengers throughout the villages

---

How to Say It

ADONAI (Hebrew). ad-o-*nye.*
ASHTAROTH. *Ash*-tuh-rawth.
BAAL. *Bay*-ul.
BAALIM. Bay-uh-*leem.*
BEERSHEBA. Beer-*she*-buh.
EBENEZER. Eb-en-*ee*-zer.
ELI. *Ee*-lye.
HANNAH. *Han*-uh.
JOSEPHUS. Jo-*see*-fus.
MIZPEH. *Miz*-peh.
PHILISTINES. Fuh-*liss*-teens or *Fill*-us-teens.
SHILOH. *Shy*-lo.

inviting the people to *gather* at *Mizpeh* for prayer. Mizpeh was a town in Benjamin, about seven and a half miles north of Jerusalem. Its central location made it an appropriate place at which to hold a national gathering. The people gathered as Samuel asked, and, with penitent fasting, they confessed their sins (v. 6).

The Philistines soon became aware of the gathering. Since this was not taking place at the time or the location of one of the national festivals, it must have appeared as if the Israelites were plotting a rebellion. The Philistines gathered their troops and determined to put a stop to that (v. 7). They arrived just as Samuel was offering a sacrifice and praying for Israel. The Lord answered his prayer with a terrific thunderstorm that "discomfited" the Philistines (vv. 8-10). (Recall a similar strategy that we saw God use in a previous lesson, in Judges 4:15; 5:4, 5, 21.) The Philistines took to their heels, and the men of Israel chased them back home (v. 11).

C. Monument in Memory (v. 12)

12. Then Samuel took a stone, and set it between Mizpeh and Shen, and called the name of it Ebenezer, saying, Hitherto hath the LORD helped us.

To commemorate Israel's triumph, *Samuel took a stone* and placed it as a monument to mark the occasion. The location of *Shen* is not certain; the word means "tooth" and may designate a sharp or pointed rock near the battle site. *The Lord* had *helped* His people at that spot. Samuel called the stone *Ebenezer,* which means "stone of help." [See question #4, page 40.]

Conclusion

A. God's Ancient Speaking

Over many centuries God spoke to His people through the prophets (Hebrews 1:1). Samuel is an example, but God spoke to His people through all the other prophets whose words are recorded in the Old Testament.

Then came the time when God spoke through His Son. Some editions of the New Testament have the words of Jesus printed in red, as if to set them apart and give them supreme importance. But much as we treasure those words, they are not all that God has said through His Son. Since the Holy Spirit inspired the writers of the New Testament (John 14:15-17, 26; 16:12-15), the teaching of those writers is the teaching of Jesus as truly as are the words printed in red.

B. God's Speaking Today

Today we do not expect to hear our names called in the night by the audible voice of God.

However, through the pages of the New Testament, God *is* speaking to us. Listen . . . .

At Home. "Wives, submit yourselves unto your own husbands, as unto the Lord. . . . Husbands, love your wives, even as Christ also loved the church, and gave himself for it; . . . Children, obey your parents in the Lord: for this is right. . . . Fathers, provoke not your children to wrath: but bring them up in the nurture and admonition of the Lord" (Ephesians 5:22—6:4).

At Work. "Servants, be obedient to them that are your masters according to the flesh, with fear and trembling, in singleness of your heart, as unto Christ. . . . Masters, do the same things unto them, forbearing threatening: knowing that your Master also is in heaven; neither is there respect of persons with him" (Ephesians 6:5-9).

In the Community. "Let every soul be subject unto the higher powers. For there is no power but of God: the powers that be are ordained of God" (Romans 13:1).

In the Church. "The elders which are among you I exhort. . . . Feed the flock of God which is among you. . . . Likewise, ye younger, submit yourselves unto the elder. Yea, all of you be subject one to another, and be clothed with humility" (1 Peter 5:1-5).

Why should we listen to God? Let's note a few good reasons:

1. God knows more than we do. Unless we acknowledge this in our actions as well as our words, we will be in trouble.

2. God loves us and wants us to do what is best for us. Unless we accept His direction, we will have to settle for less than the best.

3. No other advice is as good as God's advice. Unless we believe this, how can we say we believe in God at all?

So what are we waiting for? Let's be listening to God today.

When we say, "Speak, Lord; for thy servant heareth," we need to sit down with the Bible and listen—listen intently, listen for a long time, listen not only for what happened long ago, but especially for what God is saying to us today. [See question #5, page 40.]

C. Prayer

Great God in Heaven, we know that Your ways are above our ways and Your thoughts are above our thoughts, as far as Heaven is above the earth. Thank You for talking to us through Your holy Word. May we listen with alert minds and eager hearts. May we be quick not only to hear, but also to obey. In Jesus' name. Amen.

D. Thought to Remember
Listen to the Lord.

Learning by Doing

This page contains an alternate lesson plan emphasizing learning activities.
Classes desiring such student involvement will find these suggestions helpful.

Learning Goals

After this lesson each student will be able to:

1. Relate the account of how God called Samuel, then used him to deliver Israel from the Philistines.

2. Explain the role of the Bible in providing us with a means of "hearing God's voice."

3. Develop or maintain a pattern of regular Bible study to stay sensitive to God's will.

Into the Lesson

Write on the chalkboard the phrase, "Hearing God's Voice." When the students arrive they will read the phrase and begin to focus their thoughts on the lesson theme. Begin the class by asking, "What are the ways that people today claim to hear God's voice?" As answers are suggested, write them on the chalkboard.

State, "As you can see, people *claim* to hear God's voice in a variety of ways. But in the Bible, who actually heard God's voice? *(Examples include Adam, Abraham, Moses, Noah, Samuel, Elijah, Elisha, Peter, James, and John.)* Our text today centers on Samuel and his experience of hearing God's voice. God used Samuel to deliver Israel from the Philistines. Turn to 1 Samuel 3, and let's see how God called Samuel."

Into the Word

Read 1 Samuel 3:2-10, and give a brief lecture describing God's call of Samuel. Use the information in the lesson commentary. Make certain that you explain the following terms: *lamp of God, ark of God, temple of the Lord,* and LORD *(i.e., Jehovah).* Then ask, "Why did Samuel not immediately recognize the Lord's voice?" *(Word of the Lord was precious or rare in those days, v. 1; Samuel did not yet know the Lord, and the word of the Lord was not yet revealed to him, v. 7.)*

Ask someone in the class to read 1 Samuel 3:19-21, and then ask the following questions: "What is meant by the phrase, 'let none of his words fall to the ground' in verse 19?" *(Samuel did not speak anything false or misleading; all his predictions came true.)* What led to Israel's conclusion that Samuel was a prophet? *(The Lord revealed Himself to Samuel; his words were truthful and reliable; even his personal integrity was a contrast to Eli's sons.)* How did the Lord reveal Himself to Samuel in Shiloh? *(By the word of the Lord, v. 21.)*

Read 1 Samuel 7:3-5, 12, and then ask the following questions: "What were the Israelites supposed to do to be delivered from the Philistines?" *(Put away the strange gods and Ashtaroth; prepare their hearts for the Lord; serve Him only.)* Next, give a summary lecture over the events in 1 Samuel 7:6-11 that led to the setting up of the stone monument mentioned in verse 12. State: "So the Lord delivered Israel from the Philistines. But note the order. First the Lord revealed Himself to Samuel by the word of the Lord, 3:21. Then the word of the Lord through Samuel went to all Israel, 4:1. Next, Israel obeyed the word of the Lord, 7:4. Finally, the Philistines were subdued, 7:13. Hearing and obeying the word of the Lord were the key."

Into Life

Say, "Today we hear God's voice through the Bible. Our ability to hear God's voice and to stay sensitive to God's will increases the more we read, hear, and understand the Word of God." Divide the class into three equal parts and assign one of the following verses to each group: Psalm 1:1; 2 Timothy 2:15; Luke 11:28. For each verse ask: "What does this verse suggest we should do to hear God's voice and stay sensitive to God's will?" *(Daily reading and meditation; regular, ongoing study of the Word; hearing and obeying the Word.)* "What has been especially helpful for someone who wants to develop or maintain a pattern of regular Bible study?" (Write suggested answers on the chalkboard: *Set a definite time; a definite place; a specific process; a specific study topic; a specific person to study with; etc.*)

Prepare a handout called, "Tuning in God's Voice." Make two columns, the left one called "Helpful Suggestion" and the right one, "My Personal Plan." List the suggested answers (above) in the left column, and leave about five additional lines blank. Give each person a handout and ask the students to add any suggestions that may have come from the earlier discussion. Then ask the class to consider each suggestion and decide how it could be integrated into their lives. Ask them to write in the right column what they will do to tune in God's voice through His Word. After several minutes, ask them to share their plan with one other person. Lead the class in prayer to develop and maintain a pattern of regular Bible study.

Let's Talk It Over

The questions on this page are designed to encourage review of the lesson Scriptures and to promote discussion of the lesson by the class. The answers provided are only discussion starters. Let your class talk it over from there.

1. Eli told Samuel to say, "Speak, Lord; for thy servant heareth." Some people today say we should pray the same prayer. Others say such a prayer was for Samuel and other recognized prophets only. (See vv. 19, 20.) What relevance do you see for us today in Samuel's prayer?

Certainly we do not expect to receive revelation in the same manner as the inspired prophets. Otherwise, our "revelations" would be as authoritative as the Bible (2 Timothy 3:16; 2 Peter 1:20, 21). Still, God does speak to us through the Word. To read the Bible with Samuel's prayer on our lips can help us to avoid a merely mechanical Bible reading, simply trying to make it through so many verses or chapters each day rather than seeking to understand and apply them.

2. "All Israel from Dan even to Beersheba knew that Samuel was established to be a prophet of the Lord." What do all your neighbors know about you and your relationship with the Lord? What can or should you do to have a greater testimony in your community?

Western culture is not as open as it used to be. Neighborhoods used to be communities of friends; now they are often mazes of privacy fences. It is harder to be known in our communities than it once was. Even so, your neighbors ought to know you to be courteous and polite. Even more, they ought to know you to be compassionate. When someone in the neighborhood is in need, do they know you will be there to help? Have you reached out to get to know some of your neighbors so that you can minister to their needs and introduce them to Jesus? Have you invited any of them to worship with you?

3. Samuel showed the Israelites that deliverance would come when they obeyed the word of the Lord. What are some examples of how deliverance comes to people today when they obey God's Word?

People are delivered from sexual temptation when they consistently heed Jesus' warning in Matthew 5:28 about the peril of the lustful look. People gain deliverance from associations with worldly people and practices when they obey the command in 1 John 2:15: "Love not the world, neither the things that are in the world." Those who have made themselves slaves to the quest for material wealth can gain freedom by taking seriously Jesus' words in Luke 12:15: "Beware of covetousness: for a man's life consisteth not in the abundance of the things which he possesseth."

4. The stone called Ebenezer would remind the Israelites of how the Lord had helped them. Why is it important that we frequently remind ourselves of how the Lord has helped us? What are some appropriate occasions for engaging in this exercise of reminding ourselves?

We are prone to forgetfulness regarding God's help in times past, and that hinders us in facing present crises. In our forgetfulness we may give in to doubt and despair, and the quality of our service and our witness will be affected. One excellent occasion for reminding ourselves of God's past help is in the Communion service. We can review the previous week and gratefully enumerate those instances in which we have received divine help. Another occasion is our daily prayer time. Before we rush into our list of current needs, it is wise to praise and thank God for specific occurrences of His help in days or years past.

5. How can we best use the Bible to allow God to speak to us?

A regular reading from the Bible is an important part of the family's devotional life. Bible story books and devotional books are beneficial, but they should not replace the reading of the Word of God. Parents should emphasize at such times that it is God speaking, and every family member should listen carefully and reverently.

The public reading of Scripture in our worship services should be regarded as an important element in itself, and not merely the prelude to the minister's sermon. That reading should be done clearly and forcefully, and members should be urged to be attentive and reverent. It is a common practice for some readers to encourage hearers to follow along in their own Bibles. Besides the minister's reading of his sermon text, other Scripture readings are important in letting God speak to us and instruct us regarding our worship. We should frequently read those passages that describe the origin and purpose of the Lord's Supper, the appropriate attitude and practice regarding the offering, and the kind of praise we should express in our singing.

Saul Becomes King

DEVOTIONAL READING: Psalm 119:1-8.

BACKGROUND SCRIPTURE: 1 Samuel 9, 10.

PRINTED TEXT: 1 Samuel 9:1, 2a; 10:17-26.

1 Samuel 9:1, 2a

1 Now there was a man of Benjamin, whose name was Kish, the son of Abiel, the son of Zeror, the son of Bechorath, the son of Aphiah, a Benjamite, a mighty man of power.

2a And he had a son, whose name was Saul, a choice young man, and a goodly: and there was not among the children of Israel a goodlier person than he.

1 Samuel 10:17-26

17 And Samuel called the people together unto the LORD to Mizpeh;

18 And said unto the children of Israel, Thus saith the LORD God of Israel, I brought up Israel out of Egypt, and delivered you out of the hand of the Egyptians, and out of the hand of all kingdoms, and of them that oppressed you:

19 And ye have this day rejected your God, who himself saved you out of all your adversities and your tribulations; and ye have said unto him, Nay, but set a king over us. Now therefore present yourselves before the LORD by your tribes, and by your thousands.

20 And when Samuel had caused all the tribes of Israel to come near, the tribe of Benjamin was taken.

21 When he had caused the tribe of Benjamin to come near by their families, the family of Matri was taken, and Saul the son of Kish was taken: and when they sought him, he could not be found.

22 Therefore they inquired of the LORD further, if the man should yet come thither. And the LORD answered, Behold, he hath hid himself among the stuff.

23 And they ran and fetched him thence: and when he stood among the people, he was higher than any of the people from his shoulders and upward.

24 And Samuel said to all the people, See ye him whom the LORD hath chosen, that there is none like him among all the people? And all the people shouted, and said, God save the king.

25 Then Samuel told the people the manner of the kingdom, and wrote it in a book, and laid it up before the LORD. And Samuel sent all the people away, every man to his house.

26 And Saul also went home to Gibeah; and there went with him a band of men, whose hearts God had touched.

GOLDEN TEXT: Samuel said to all the people, See ye him whom the LORD hath chosen, that there is none like him among all the people?—1 Samuel 10:24.

Lesson Aims

After this lesson each student will be able to:

1. Summarize what today's text says about Saul and about the Israelites' acceptance of him as their first king.

2. Describe some of the ways in which God's rule over our lives today is threatened.

3. Pinpoint an area where God's authority as King needs to be allowed to have a greater impact.

Lesson Outline

INTRODUCTION
    A. Like Father, Unlike Son
    B. Lesson Background
  I. INTRODUCING SAUL (1 Samuel 9:1, 2a)
    A. Saul's Family (v. 1)
    B. Saul Himself (v. 2a)
 II. DEMAND FOR A KING (1 Samuel 10:17-19)
    A. God's Faithfulness (vv. 17, 18)
    B. Israel's Unfaithfulness (v. 19)
    Dreams of Perfection
III. KING AND KINGDOM (1 Samuel 10:20-26)
    A. The Choice (vv. 20, 21a)
    B. The Bashful King (vv. 21b, 22)
    Reluctant Heroes
    C. The King Is Accepted (vv. 23, 24)
    D. The Kingdom Is Described (vv. 25, 26)
CONCLUSION
    A. Every Man a King
    B. Prayer
    C. Thought to Remember

Introduction

From his infancy, Dave spent Sunday mornings in the church house: first in the nursery, then in the toddlers' room, and on through each grade of the Sunday school. In the high school class, he was a leader among the church youth and a second baseman on the softball team. No one was better known to church members young and old.

Then Dave went to college far from home. He stayed until his name was adorned with several degrees, then he became a professor and stayed on in that capacity. Only seldom did he visit his old home.

When Dave's son Joel graduated from high school, he too went to college far from home. From time to time, he took part of his weekend to stop by and visit Grandpa. When Grandpa and Joel stepped into the older adults' Sunday school class, the members greeted Joel with joy; but they called him Dave. Anyone could see that he was the "spitting image" of his father.

From such similarity comes the old saying, "Like father, like son." It comes from more important similarities too—similarities of character, purpose, and action. We expect the son of a good man to be a good man, and the son of a rascal to be a rascal. But it is not always so.

A. Like Father, Unlike Son

In real life, "Like father, *unlike* son" seems to be the principle at work sometimes. Last week we read of Eli, who brought up young Samuel as a wise and godly man. But Eli's own sons were scoundrels (1 Samuel 2:12-17).

The same tragedy was repeated in the next generation. Samuel became judge of all Israel. He was a prophet of God as well, and his judgments were always just and right. However, like Eli's sons, Samuel's sons were scoundrels. Samuel appointed them judges in Beersheba, but they "took bribes, and perverted judgment" (1 Samuel 8:1-3). The situation was so bad that it became a national scandal.

B. Lesson Background

The elders of Israel were concerned about this turn of events, as they should have been. Samuel was old; he could not judge Israel much longer. If his evil sons succeeded him, there would likely be little or no justice in the nation. Something had to be done, and the elders proposed what they thought was the best solution. They asked Samuel to appoint a king over Israel (1 Samuel 8:4, 5).

Samuel did not like that suggestion, and neither did God. Samuel even warned the people of all the negative consequences that would accompany having a king. But the people insisted, and God told Samuel to let them have their way. They would have to learn from their own mistake (1 Samuel 8:6-22). [See question #1, page 48.]

I. Introducing Saul
(1 Samuel 9:1, 2a)

After God instructed Samuel to let the people have a king, Samuel told the assembled people to return home (1 Samuel 8:22). They did not need to have a king named immediately. The Biblical writer then introduces Saul, the man who became Israel's first king.

A. Saul's Family (v. 1)

1. Now there was a man of Benjamin, whose name was Kish, the son of Abiel, the son of Zeror, the son of Bechorath, the son of Aphiah, a Benjamite, a mighty man of power.

First to be introduced is Saul's father, *Kish*. He was a member of the tribe of *Benjamin*. Several generations of his ancestors are named, but we know nothing more about any of them. Then Kish is described as *a mighty man of power*. Other versions read "valor" or "wealth" instead of *power*. Apparently Kish was a very prominent citizen, respected by his peers.

B. Saul Himself (v. 2a)

2a. And he had a son, whose name was Saul, a choice young man, and a goodly: and there was not among the children of Israel a goodlier person than he.

The words *choice* and *goodly* seem to describe a strikingly handsome fellow, a fine figure of a man. The *New International Version* says that Saul was "an impressive young man without equal among the Israelites."

The rest of chapter 9 and the first part of chapter 10 record a meeting of Samuel and Saul. At God's direction, Samuel anointed Saul to be king, but he did this privately. No one else knew about it.

II. Demand for a King
(1 Samuel 10:17-19)

At an earlier time, the elders of Israel had come to Samuel to demand a king, as we have noted in the introduction to this lesson. Now Samuel knew whom God had chosen to be that king. He therefore called a meeting of the people to let them know who would be their king and that God had chosen him. Samuel began by recalling the demand for a king that the people had expressed to him.

A. God's Faithfulness (vv. 17, 18)

17. And Samuel called the people together unto the LORD to Mizpeh.

The meeting at *Mizpeh* would have reminded the people that God had blessed them with a decisive victory over the Philistines at that place a few years earlier (1 Samuel 7:5-14).

18. And said unto the children of Israel, Thus saith the LORD God of Israel, I brought up Israel out of Egypt, and delivered you out of the hand of the Egyptians, and out of the hand of all kingdoms, and of them that oppressed you.

In these few words spoken by Samuel, God reminded the people of all the blessings and help He had given them in the past. He had rescued

them from their bitter bondage under *the hand of the Egyptians*. He had *delivered* them from *all kingdoms* that had opposed their march toward the promised land (Numbers 21:21-35). Once the people had taken possession of the promised land, the Lord had rescued them from all who had *oppressed* them.

B. Israel's Unfaithfulness (v. 19)

19. And ye have this day rejected your God, who himself saved you out of all your adversities and your tribulations; and ye have said unto him, Nay, but set a king over us. Now therefore present yourselves before the LORD by your tribes, and by your thousands.

Yes, God had been faithful to His people, rescuing them from every difficulty. But they had not been faithful to Him. In demanding a king, they were forgetting that God Himself was their real King. He had given them their law—a law that provided no central government to enforce it. Each person was responsible for his own obedience; each parent was responsible for teaching his children to obey.

Now, however, the people were asking for a king to enforce the law. In so doing, they were bypassing their own personal responsibility to obey and teach that law. They also wanted the king to be responsible for the national defense, to go out before them and fight their battles (1 Samuel 8:19, 20). What they failed to discern was that, if they had fulfilled their own responsibility by obeying the law, no battles would have been needed! The Lord would have given them victory over every foe.

The people had made their choice. Disregarding the warnings of God and Samuel, they had persisted in demanding a king. Therefore, said Samuel, they should prepare to *present* themselves before the Lord so He could designate the one from among them who should be their king. They should present themselves first by *tribes*, and then by smaller groups. The Hebrew word translated *thousands* can also mean "clans," and that is probably the meaning in this context. The tribes of Israel and the clans of families within those tribes were to present themselves. [See question #2, page 48.]

DREAMS OF PERFECTION

Most people have dreams of what life would be like if some part of it were "perfect" (whatever that means). For Gordon and Mary Aughinbaugh, the dream was a house with a spectacular ocean view in a very upscale community southwest of Los Angeles. It was to be a "perfect" $1.5 million, French-style manor that would "stand 900 years" (so the owners envisioned it).

But fifteen years after construction began, the house was still unfinished and the dream had turned into a nightmare. The couple became involved in lawsuits with three different contractors. The local homeowners' association sued to have the house torn down because it had been an eyesore for more than a decade. In fact, Mr. Aughinbaugh died before the house was finished, and it was sold to someone else, who completed the project.

Like many others since who have seen what their neighbors possessed and have dreamed of possessing it as their own, the Israelites saw that the nations about them had kings. They assumed that a king would be the "perfect touch" that would complete their struggle toward nationhood. And so, turning aside from the God who had been their flawless leader, they determined to be led by men who were flawed in sometimes serious ways.

Any "perfection" we seek in this world—without God and His help—is sure to disappoint us.
—C. R. B.

III. King and Kingdom (1 Samuel 10:20-26)

Though the people had rejected God in their demand for a king, Samuel wanted their first king to be God's choice; and He wanted the people to understand that God was making this choice.

A. The Choice (vv. 20, 21a)

20. And when Samuel had caused all the tribes of Israel to come near, the tribe of Benjamin was taken.

We need not suppose that entire tribes paraded before Samuel and the Lord. Perhaps one man was called forward to represent each tribe. We are not told exactly how *the tribe of Benjamin was taken* from the rest. Possibly the Urim and Thummim, which the high priest was to use

Visual for lesson 5

in making important decisions (Exodus 28:30; Numbers 27:21), were used to help make this choice (though we do not know exactly what the Urim and Thummim were or what using them involved).

Another suggestion is that a "casting of lots" of some kind was used and that God was asked to guide the result. For example, a white pebble might be placed in a jar with eleven dark ones. A man of each tribe would reach into the jar without looking and take a pebble. The tribe whose representative drew out the white pebble would be taken as the chosen tribe. Or, each tribe might mark a small stone with the name or symbol of that tribe. The stones would be put in a jar. Samuel, as God's prophet, would select one without looking, and the tribe indicated by that stone would be the chosen tribe. Whatever the procedure, Benjamin was revealed to be the chosen tribe.

21a. When he had caused the tribe of Benjamin to come near by their families, the family of Matri was taken, and Saul the son of Kish was taken.

Perhaps by the same procedure previously used, *the family of Matri was taken* from all the families of the tribe of Benjamin. By a final step, *Saul the son of Kish was taken*, chosen from all the men of Matri's family.

B. The Bashful King (vv. 21b, 22)

21b. And when they sought him, he could not be found.

Saul's absence here tells us that a man could be included among the candidates without even being present. Perhaps an elder of Matri's family wrote the names of the men of that family on separate stones, and Samuel or someone else randomly selected the stone with Saul's name on it. Whatever the process was, it is clear that all Israel was convinced, and rightly so, that God was making this choice.

When Saul's name was announced, of course everyone began looking for him. But *he could not be found.*

22. Therefore they inquired of the LORD further, if the man should yet come thither. And the LORD answered, Behold, he hath hid himself among the stuff.

Saul was not in the crowd. Was it possible that he had not arrived at Mizpeh yet? That question was put to the Lord, and He answered it plainly: Saul was hiding *among the stuff.* The Hebrew word rendered *stuff* seems to describe supplies of some kind (the *New International Version* uses "baggage"). People who walked two or three days to get to Mizpeh would have brought a lot of such items, including clothing, blankets, food,

The visual for today's lesson will help your students locate where the events of this lesson, and the other lessons of this quarter, took place.

and cooking utensils. Perhaps a particular area (possibly a large tent had been designated as what we might call a "baggage depot." There Saul *hid himself.*

The question of Saul's whereabouts was not so easily answered by a procedure such as "casting lots." That is one reason for putting a "perhaps" with the above suggestions of the procedure used to select who would be Israel's first king. We do not really know how the selection was made, and likewise we do not know how the Lord responded to this question. The most likely suggestion for the latter is that He inspired His prophet Samuel with the answer. At any rate, by some clear and unmistakable means, God revealed the truth to Samuel and the Israelites.

We need to remember that Saul knew in advance that he would be chosen as Israel's king. (See 1 Samuel 9:1—10:16.) Why, then, was he hiding? Was he bashful, afraid to face the stares of the crowd? Was he modest, shrinking from the praise that would be heaped upon him? Was he frightened by the responsibility he was being given? Keep in mind that this was something new for both him and the nation: Saul had never been a king, and Israel had never had a king. [See question #3, page 48.]

RELUCTANT HEROES

Some people intentionally become heroes: in warfare, in scientific endeavors (such as becoming astronauts), and in the field of sports. Marty Hornick, a U.S. Forest Service trails ranger, is one such intentional hero. He is a self-acclaimed "peak bagger" who has climbed Mt. Whitney hundreds of times.

But one day in 1991, Hornick proceeded on what became a record-setting climb. In just two hours, eight and a half minutes, he covered six miles of trail and gained 6,200 feet in elevation. And then, just three hours and twenty-three minutes after he started his climb, he was back at the Whitney Portals trailhead. His feat is significant because it was the fastest Whitney ascent ever— a notable achievement, given the fact that the mountain (at 14,494 feet) is the highest in the contiguous United States.

Saul apparently did not want to "set a record" as the first king of Israel. He hid "among the stuff," even though he already knew that God had chosen him to lead Israel as her king. Perhaps he was being genuinely humble, or perhaps he was stricken with a sense of the monumental task that lay before him.

Whatever Saul's motives for hiding himself, he was like many of us—reluctant to act when challenged to perform some significant task for the Lord. We never know how that challenge may be

Home Daily Bible Readings

Monday, Sept. 25—Saul Searches for the Man of God (1 Samuel 9:1-10)

Tuesday, Sept. 26—Samuel Recognizes Saul (1 Samuel 9:11-16)

Wednesday, Sept. 27—Saul Meets Samuel (1 Samuel 9:17-21)

Thursday, Sept. 28—Saul Anointed King (1 Samuel 9:22—10:1)

Friday, Sept. 29—Samuel Directs Saul (1 Samuel 10:2-8)

Saturday, Sept. 30—Saul Prophesies (1 Samuel 10:9-16)

Sunday, Oct. 1—Saul Proclaimed King (1 Samuel 10:17-26)

presented or how heroic our task may be. But God helps even reluctant heroes to find the strength to do what He asks of them.   —C. R. B.

C. The King Is Accepted (vv. 23, 24)

23. And they ran and fetched him thence: and when he stood among the people, he was higher than any of the people from his shoulders and upward.

Eager men *ran* to where the "stuff" was and escorted the reluctant king to the throng of his waiting people. Instantly everyone noticed that he was a head taller than any of them! He looked like a king!

24. And Samuel said to all the people, See ye him whom the LORD hath chosen, that there is none like him among all the people? And all the people shouted, and said, God save the king.

Samuel made two observations. First, *the Lord had chosen* this man to be their king. *All the people* had seen that no man or group of men had made the choice. If it was made by casting lots, they had asked God to determine the outcome; and they believed that He had done so.

Second, Saul's appearance seemed to verify the choice. Like a royal figure, he towered above the common people. Saul's fellow Israelites responded to Samuel's words with a roar of approval. Literally their words are *May the king live!* The *King James Version* substituted the shout of approval that was popular in the country and the era when it was first prepared: *God save the king!* [See question #4, page 48.]

D. The Kingdom Is Described (vv. 25, 26)

25. Then Samuel told the people the manner of the kingdom, and wrote it in a book, and laid it up before the LORD. And Samuel sent all the people away, every man to his house.

Having a king brought a new kind of government to Israel. Thus Samuel's next step was to tell the people what *the kingdom* should be like. No portion of this lecture has been preserved for us, but we can easily imagine some of its main points. First, God's law was still the law of the land. Second, each person still was responsible for his own obedience to the law. Third, the king also was to be bound by the law. He must not become an arbitrary tyrant. Emphasizing this would make it clear that kingship in Israel was to be significantly different from kingship in surrounding nations (even though one reason the people had demanded a king was a desire to be "like all the nations," 1 Samuel 8:5).

After giving this instruction to the assembled people, Samuel sent them home. He also *wrote* his words concerning the kingdom *in a book* (probably at a later time) and *laid it up* in the tabernacle *before the Lord*. There it would be available for future reference as needed.

26. And Saul also went home to Gibeah; and there went with him a band of men, whose hearts God had touched.

What does a new king do in a country that never had a king before? This one simply *went* back *home* to the farm, as other people did. (*Gibeah* was located about four miles southeast of Mizpeh.) Still, his life was not quite the same, for *there went with him a band of men, whose hearts God had touched*. Perhaps He touched their hearts with sincere concern for the king and the kingdom. As a result they volunteered to assist the new king in any way they could. [See question #5, page 48.]

The record adds that Saul wisely ignored the dissidents who sneered at him (v. 27); and when a national emergency arose, this new king knew what a king must do. In fact, he did it so well that the people enthusiastically reaffirmed their allegiance to him (1 Samuel 11).

Conclusion

A. Every Man a King

In recent centuries, kings have lost some of the sense of "enchantment" that at one time surrounded them. Some monarchies have become democracies; in others, kings are nothing more than figureheads. This change seems to be approved by nearly everyone (except the deposed kings).

Although a democracy can provide many freedoms and opportunities not available under a monarchy, many people today ignore the laws of democracies. Worse still, many renounce the rule of God. This seems to be the prevailing trend in our society, where a man will accept no

---

How to Say It

ABIEL. *Ay*-be-el.
APHIAH. Uh-*fye*-uh.
BECHORATH. Be-*ko*-rath.
BENJAMITE. *Ben*-juh-mite.
GIBEAH. *Gib*-ee-uh.
MATRI. *May*-try.
MIZPEH. *Miz*-peh.
THUMMIM. *Thum*-im.
URIM. *You*-rim.
ZEROR. *Zee*-roar.

---

king but himself. Proudly he announces that *he* will decide what is right for him.

God's Word teaches us to be obedient to the government we have, because it is ordained of God (Romans 13:1, 2). How many ordinary citizens ignore laws they consider trivial—traffic regulations, for example? How many of us are proud of our cleverness in avoiding the taxes that God's Word teaches us to pay (Romans 13:6, 7)? God's law said, "Thou shalt not steal" (Exodus 20:15). Still many citizens prefer their own rule: "I'm going to take care of myself." Our neighborhood supermarkets lose surprising sums to shoplifters, and some of them lose as much to pilfering employees.

God's law said, "Thou shalt not kill" (Exodus 20:13), and Jesus' apostle teaches us not even to hate (1 John 3:15). Still our morning paper reports a murder in our town, and probably your paper reports another in your town.

God's law said, "Thou shalt not commit adultery" (Exodus 20:14). Yet adultery is shown once or twice during a thirty-minute TV show that is supposed to portray real life. How often does it occur in life that is truly real?

How much better it would be if no man would think himself a king and no man would think any other man a king, but every man would bow in humble obedience to the King of kings and Lord of lords!

B. Prayer

Forgive us, Father, when we have turned aside from Your commands to follow our own inclination. Forgive us when we have ignored Your leading to follow human leaders. As we read Your Word, may our minds be keen to see Your will; may our hearts be strong to cherish it; may our bodies be quick to obey it. In Jesus' name, amen.

C. Thought to Remember

Christ is King!

Learning by Doing

This page contains an alternate lesson plan emphasizing learning activities. Classes desiring such student involvement will find these suggestions helpful.

Learning Goals

After this lesson each student will be able to:

1. Summarize what today's text says about Saul and about the Israelites' acceptance of him as their first king.

2. Describe some of the ways in which God's rule over our lives today is threatened.

3. Pinpoint an area where God's authority needs to be allowed to have a greater influence.

Into the Lesson

Prepare on the chalkboard or overhead transparency the following puzzle entitled, "Possible 'Gods' People Worship Today." Ask the class to read the four clues and call out the words that will fill in the blanks. Write the words on the puzzle as they are correctly identified.

1. __ __ __ __ __ __ __ __ __ __ __
2. __ __ __ __ __
3. __ __ __ __ __ __ __ __ __
4. __ __ __ __

1. Things that you own *(possessions)*
2. That which you spend *(money)*
3. Moses refused to "enjoy the _____ of sin" (Hebrews 11:25) *(pleasures)*
4. Seeking _____ and fortune *(fame)*

State: "People today worship possessions, money, pleasures, and fame. In reality, *self* sits on the throne as one's king, and people worship self instead of God. (Highlight the word *self* vertically on the puzzle grid, starting with the first *s* in *possessions* and reading down.) In the same way, the children of Israel rejected God as their true King and demanded an earthly king. Let's turn to 1 Samuel 9 and 10 for our lesson today."

Into the Word

The Israelites wanted to be like all the other peoples of the world with a king. They failed to realize that as God's people, they were to be different! First Samuel 9 introduces the man God chose to be king. Read 1 Samuel 9:1, 2 and ask the following questions: (1) What is meant by the description of Kish as a "mighty man of power"? *(Not physical strength but financial success; wealthy.)* (2) Describe the physical stature of Saul. *(A head taller than other Israelites; handsome.)*

Note that 1 Samuel 9:3—10:16 tells how Saul providentially was led to meet Samuel and was anointed king in a private ceremony. The remainder of our text tells of Saul's public coronation.

Ask a volunteer to read 1 Samuel 10:17-26 and then ask the following questions:

1. Why was the Israelites' demand for a king a rejection of their God? *(God was their King who had brought them out of Egypt and delivered them from all the kingdoms that oppressed them. This was just one more way they had forsaken God to serve themselves, 1 Samuel 8:8.)*

2. Saul knew in advance that he would be chosen. Why do you think he "hid himself among the stuff," 1 Samuel 10:22? *(Perhaps he was frightened by the responsibility, uncertain as to how the people would accept him, or maybe just bashful!)*

3. What was the people's response to God's selection of Saul as king? *(People readily accepted Saul as king.)*

4. Why did Samuel take the time to give all the instructions about the kingdom to the people and write them in a book? *(Israel had never had an earthly king, and instructions were needed now.)*

State: "Just as the people of Israel rejected God's rule over their lives, people today reject God's rule over their own lives. When we confess Jesus as Lord, we are saying that Christ is King of our lives."

Into Life

Ask the class to brainstorm some possible answers to this question: What are some ways that God's rule over our lives today is threatened? Write the suggested answers on the chalkboard or overhead transparency. After you have compiled a good-sized list, ask, "What are some areas where God's authority as King needs to have a greater impact in Christian lives today?" Write the suggested answers on the board. State: "In the final analysis, we either worship self by allowing personal desires, things, or people to control us, or we worship God. Take this commitment sheet and fill in the area where you want God to have more impact in your life." (Prepare a "commitment sheet" with the following information on it and distribute that sheet to the students.)

Father, I no longer want Your rule over my life to be threatened. I want You to be King over every area of my life. I want Your authority to have a greater influence in the following area of my life:

I surrender my will to You and ask You to strengthen me by Your Spirit. In Jesus' name I pray, amen.

Let's Talk It Over

The questions on this page are designed to encourage review of the lesson Scriptures and to promote discussion of the lesson by the class. The answers provided are only discussion starters. Let your class talk it over from there.

1. It was a lack of faith in God that led the Israelites to ask for a king. What are some errors human beings today make because of a similar lack of faith? How can we help one another to avoid or overcome such errors?

The Israelites' error was one of choosing sight over faith. A human king was someone they could see and, to some extent, control. We make the same mistake when we choose to act by what we can see and control instead of trusting the invisible God to accomplish His purpose. This is the error of those who fail to take the Bible seriously or fail to pray and expect God to answer. Sometimes we *claim* to believe the Bible and to believe in answered prayer, but we *act* as if we do not!

We need to examine ourselves regularly to see if we are walking by faith or by sight. When have we recently stepped out in faith to do something for the Lord? Perhaps meeting with another believer for regular prayer, Bible study, and mutual accountability could help us to be objective about whether or not we are acting by faith.

2. Samuel charged, "Ye have this day rejected your God . . . and ye have said unto him, Nay, but set a king over us." Then he proceeded, at God's direction, to give the Israelites a king. Why do you think God gave them what they wanted when what they wanted was wrong? In fact, God knew that future kings would often lead His people into idolatry and other sins. Why do you think He did that? What warnings do you see in this event for us?

When Jesus was questioned about divorce, He said, "Moses because of the hardness of your hearts suffered you to put away your wives: but from the beginning it was not so" (Matthew 19:8). It was similar hardness of heart that God acknowledged in allowing Israel to have a king. The people were determined to have a king, so God allowed it—and the harsh lessons the people would soon learn from having a king.

Some today take so much stock in the apparent success of their ideas that they assume God has blessed their efforts. Perhaps they should consider whether God is truly blessing or simply allowing their efforts!

3. Saul hid himself while he was being selected as king. It is generally believed that this was an indication of modesty or humility on his part. In his later years, however, Saul was proud, arrogant, and jealous. How can a person elevated to a place of leadership and influence maintain his initial humility?

We remember Paul's questioning of the proud church members at Corinth: "What do you have that you did not receive? And if you did receive it, why do you boast as though you did not?" (1 Corinthians 4:7, *New International Version*). He was addressing their attitude toward different teachers, but it applies well to our present topic. Both the ability and the opportunity to lead come from God, and we should never forget it. It is also helpful if we place a continual emphasis on ourselves as "servants" (2 Corinthians 4:5).

4. Some have suggested that the people of Israel let their emotions get away from them when they saw how impressive Saul's appearance was. What do you think? What can we learn from this event?

Of course, one's appearance cannot qualify a person for leadership. Samuel himself made this mistake later, when he went to Bethlehem to anoint Saul's successor. (See 1 Samuel 16:1-13.) But this was, indeed, a time of celebration. The Lord had chosen Saul to be their king, and they rejoiced in "the Lord's anointed."

We need to be careful not to select leaders (either politically or in the church) for merely emotional reasons. We do not have a Samuel to show us God's choice, so we must be careful and prayerful about our choices. But once the choice is made, let us rally behind the leader and encourage him to lead as God directs.

5. How can you tell when God has touched a person's heart today?

We do not know exactly what the writer meant by his use of this expression (v. 26), but we notice that these men stayed with the king. When God has touched people's hearts, they will be where the Lord's servant is. They will be eager to serve. They will stand up for the Lord and for His will. They will align themselves with God's choices.

When God has touched a person's heart today, others will see the result: faith, obedience, and commitment to God's Word—the word of truth.

Saul Rejected and David Anointed

DEVOTIONAL READING: Isaiah 55:6-11.

BACKGROUND SCRIPTURE: 1 Samuel 15:10—16:13.

PRINTED TEXT: 1 Samuel 16:1-13.

Oct 8

1 Samuel 16:1-13

1 And the LORD said unto Samuel, How long wilt thou mourn for Saul, seeing I have rejected him from reigning over Israel? fill thine horn with oil, and go, I will send thee to Jesse the Bethlehemite: for I have provided me a king among his sons.

2 And Samuel said, How can I go? if Saul hear it, he will kill me. And the LORD said, Take a heifer with thee, and say, I am come to sacrifice to the LORD.

3 And call Jesse to the sacrifice, and I will show thee what thou shalt do: and thou shalt anoint unto me him whom I name unto thee.

4 And Samuel did that which the LORD spake, and came to Bethlehem. And the elders of the town trembled at his coming, and said, Comest thou peaceably?

5 And he said, Peaceably: I am come to sacrifice unto the LORD: sanctify yourselves, and come with me to the sacrifice. And he sanctified Jesse and his sons, and called them to the sacrifice.

6 And it came to pass, when they were come, that he looked on Eliab, and said, Surely the LORD's anointed is before him.

7 But the LORD said unto Samuel, Look not on his countenance, or on the height of his stature; because I have refused him: for the LORD seeth not as man seeth; for man looketh on the outward appearance, but the LORD looketh on the heart.

8 Then Jesse called Abinadab, and made him pass before Samuel. And he said, Neither hath the LORD chosen this.

9 Then Jesse made Shammah to pass by. And he said, Neither hath the LORD chosen this.

10 Again, Jesse made seven of his sons to pass before Samuel. And Samuel said unto Jesse, The LORD hath not chosen these.

11 And Samuel said unto Jesse, Are here all thy children? And he said, There remaineth yet the youngest, and, behold, he keepeth the sheep. And Samuel said unto Jesse, Send and fetch him: for we will not sit down till he come hither.

12 And he sent, and brought him in. Now he was ruddy, and withal of a beautiful countenance, and goodly to look to. And the LORD said, Arise, anoint him: for this is he.

13 Then Samuel took the horn of oil, and anointed him in the midst of his brethren: and the Spirit of the LORD came upon David from that day forward. So Samuel rose up, and went to Ramah.

GOLDEN TEXT: The LORD seeth not as man seeth; for man looketh on the outward appearance, but the LORD looketh on the heart.—1 Samuel 16:7.

Rulers of Israel
Unit 2: Saul and David
(Lessons 5-9)

Lesson Aims

After this lesson each student will be able to:

1. Describe the process by which Samuel was led to anoint David as Israel's king.

2. Explain the importance of having one's heart wholly committed to the Lord.

3. List some actions or attitudes he or she can cultivate in seeking to serve the Lord wholeheartedly.

Lesson Outline

INTRODUCTION
   A. Use and Abuse of Power
   B. Lesson Background
I. SEARCH FOR A KING (1 Samuel 16:1-5)
   A. God's Prophet Sent (v. 1)
   B. Safety Promised (vv. 2, 3)
   C. Sacrifice Arranged (vv. 4, 5)
II. REJECTED CANDIDATES (1 Samuel 16:6-10)
   A. The Lord's Insight (vv. 6, 7)
   B. Parade of Possibilities (vv. 8-10)
     Faulty Expectations
III. THE ONE CHOSEN (1 Samuel 16:11-13)
   A. Youngest Son (v. 11)
   B. Anointed King (vv. 12, 13)
     The "Kid Brother" Syndrome
CONCLUSION
   A. Hunting Hidden Hearts
   B. Helpless Hasty Hearts
   C. Wholehearted or Halfhearted?
   D. Prayer
   E. Thought to Remember

Introduction

A. Use and Abuse of Power

"Power tends to corrupt, and absolute power corrupts absolutely." So wrote a British historian in 1887. History furnishes many examples, from corrupt King Ahab in the ninth century B.C. to corrupt Communist dictators in the twentieth century A.D.

Some men of power, however, are incorruptible. History tells us of Cincinnatus, a Roman general and statesman of the fifth century before Christ. Having led his people to a significant victory, he then resigned his office and went back to his farm. Americans honor George Washington.

After he had led an infant nation in war and peace and then served two terms as president, he declined a third term and went back to his plantation. Citizens lauded him as "the first, the last, the best; the Cincinnatus of the West."

B. Lesson Background

Last week we read of Saul, a modest man who hid from public acclaim on the day he was declared king of Israel. He then went back to the family farm; but when a national emergency came, he was ready. Boldly he raised an army and rescued a city of Israel that was being threatened by foreigners (1 Samuel 11). The new king went on to subdue other enemies of Israel (1 Samuel 14:47, 48), and Israel became an international power. At that point, having a king seemed to be yielding all the positive results for which Israel had hoped.

Tragically, Saul's humble and unpretentious spirit did not last. Success seemed to go to his head, and he began to revel in his power. Once, Saul took priestly prerogative and offered sacrifices rather than wait for Samuel. The prophet warned the king, "Thy kingdom shall not continue" (1 Samuel 13:13) because of his rash act. Later the Lord sent Saul to exterminate the nation of Amalek. Because of the wickedness of that nation, it was to be wiped out—men, women, children, even animals. But Saul thought he had a better plan. He spared the life of the Amalekite king and the best of the Amalekites' livestock.

This act marked the beginning of the end for Saul. The Lord rejected the disobedient king, and sent Samuel to tell him so—confirming the Lord's earlier warning. Saul's rule must end; the Lord had found a better man to take his place (1 Samuel 15:28).

I. Search for a King
(1 Samuel 16:1-5)

Saul had rejected the Lord, and the Lord had rejected Saul. God's prophet Samuel came no more to counsel the king; "nevertheless Samuel mourned for Saul" (1 Samuel 15:35). What a sad turn of events! Saul had begun his reign so nobly, wisely, heroically, and successfully. But now the disobedient king was doomed, and Samuel grieved for him.

A. God's Prophet Sent (v. 1)

1. And the LORD said unto Samuel, How long wilt thou mourn for Saul, seeing I have rejected him from reigning over Israel? fill thine horn with oil, and go, I will send thee to Jesse the Bethlehemite: for I have provided me a king among his sons.

The time to *mourn for Saul* was over. The Lord's prophet must be about the Lord's business, and that was the anointing of a man to replace Saul as *king*. This did not mean that the new king would take office soon. Saul himself had been anointed in private, when no one but he and Samuel knew about it (1 Samuel 9:27; 10:1). This new king's anointing would be known to only a few; Saul would remain king for several years to come. Samuel did not yet know whom he was to anoint, but it would be one of the *sons* of *Jesse*, a citizen of Bethlehem. [See question #1, page 56.]

B. Safety Promised (vv. 2, 3)

2. And Samuel said, How can I go? if Saul hear it, he will kill me. And the LORD said, Take a heifer with thee, and say, I am come to sacrifice to the LORD.

Modest Saul had been tolerant of those who had opposed his kingship (1 Samuel 10:27; 11:12, 13). But Saul was no longer modest and no longer tolerant. He had shown himself arrogant enough to go his own way in defiance of God's order. Now God was telling Samuel to anoint another man to replace Saul. If Saul heard about that, he would call it treason. It is likely that Samuel would be punished by death.

But the Lord had a ready answer for Samuel's dilemma. Saul need not know about the anointing. Samuel could take a *heifer* (young cow) to Bethlehem and offer a *sacrifice* there. Saul need not know about the other purpose of the trip.

3. And call Jesse to the sacrifice, and I will show thee what thou shalt do: and thou shalt anoint unto me him whom I name unto thee.

Samuel was to invite *Jesse to the sacrifice.* Later verses indicate that he was to invite Jesse's sons as well. In many sacrifices, only a small part of the sacrificed animal was actually burned on the altar. In this case, probably a part of the meat of the sacrificed heifer would provide a feast for the guests.

By this time, Samuel had been known as a judge of Israel for many years. It was not likely that any of the Israelites would have declined an invitation from him to attend a sacrifice. Once those invited were assembled, God would give Samuel further instructions as they were needed. Most important, He would tell him whom to *anoint.*

C. Sacrifice Arranged (vv. 4, 5)

4. And Samuel did that which the LORD spake, and came to Bethlehem. And the elders of the town trembled at his coming, and said, Comest thou peaceably?

The elders of the town trembled. Perhaps they had heard of Samuel's recent execution of the king of the Amalekites (1 Samuel 15:33). Had he come to *Bethlehem* to accuse the elders or the people of some terrible wrong? Or had he come *peaceably*? The elders were frightened.

5. And he said, Peaceably: I am come to sacrifice unto the LORD: sanctify yourselves, and come with me to the sacrifice. And he sanctified Jesse and his sons, and called them to the sacrifice.

Samuel reassured the elders: he had come *peaceably*. His purpose was *to sacrifice unto the Lord.* The text seems to indicate that he invited the elders to be present as well as Jesse and his sons, but in the following verses only Jesse and his sons are mentioned. Possibly the events recorded from verse 6 on involved a private meeting of only Samuel and Jesse and his sons, at some time during the proceedings.

A few generations ago in rural America, it was customary for farmers to take a bath on Saturday night. Then on Sunday morning they put on clean clothes to go to church. In a somewhat similar manner, the ancient Israelites *sanctified* themselves before meeting the Lord in a special way. Exodus 19:10-14 tells of an occasion when such ceremonial cleansing included putting on clean clothes. Note the special treatment that *Jesse and his sons* received, as they were prepared by Samuel himself. [See question #2, page 56.]

II. Rejected Candidates
(1 Samuel 16:6-10)

We are not told exactly when the sacrifice occurred following Samuel's arrival in Bethlehem. Our text proceeds to the primary reason for which the Lord had sent Samuel to Bethlehem.

A. The Lord's Insight (vv. 6, 7)

6. And it came to pass, when they were come, that he looked on Eliab, and said, Surely the LORD's anointed is before him.

Jesse and his sons met with Samuel at the place of sacrifice. Samuel first *looked on Eliab,* probably because he was the oldest of Jesse's sons (1 Samuel 17:28); and Samuel liked what he saw. *Surely* this fine-looking young man was to be Israel's next king!

7. But the LORD said unto Samuel, Look not on his countenance, or on the height of his stature; because I have refused him: for the LORD seeth not as man seeth; for man looketh on the outward appearance, but the LORD looketh on the heart.

People like to have a king or leader who looks the part—one who is tall and handsome and stands out from his peers. But other qualifications are more important. Samuel thought that no one could be a more capable king than Eliab, but the Lord knew better. He was looking for a man after His own *heart* (1 Samuel 13:14). [See question #3, page 56.]

B. Parade of Possibilities (vv. 8-10)

8. Then Jesse called Abinadab, and made him pass before Samuel. And he said, Neither hath the LORD chosen this.

Apparently Samuel had made known to Jesse his purpose to appoint a king as well as to offer a sacrifice. Jesse was presenting his sons one by one, probably in order of their ages. The Lord rejected the second as He had rejected the first.

9. Then Jesse made Shammah to pass by. And he said, Neither hath the LORD chosen this.

The third son likewise was rejected. It seems that the Lord, without words, made His will known to Samuel's mind, and Samuel conveyed that message to Jesse. From Samuel's youth he had thus been revealing the will of God, so that "all Israel from Dan even to Beersheba knew that Samuel was established to be a prophet of the Lord" (1 Samuel 3:20).

10. Again, Jesse made seven of his sons to pass before Samuel. And Samuel said unto Jesse, The LORD hath not chosen these.

No longer naming the *sons* one by one, the record adds that four more of them were presented before *Samuel.* Most likely they were presented one by one, and one by one *the Lord* rejected them.

FAULTY EXPECTATIONS

At 2:25 A.M. on February 25, 1942, the "Great Los Angeles Air Raid" began. Sirens sounded the alarm, searchlights swept across the sky to find invading Japanese warplanes, and anti-aircraft shells were fired into the darkness.

Later that morning, the *Los Angeles Times* gave a detailed account of the attack, but also mentioned (strangely) that "no bombs were reported dropped." Nevertheless, there were casualties.

How to Say It

ABINADAB. Uh-*bin*-uh-dab.
AHAB. *Ay*-hab.
AMALEK. *Am*-uh-lek.
AMALEKITES. *Am*-uh-leh-kites or Uh-*mal*-ih-kites.
BETHLEHEMITE. *Beth*-lih-hem-ite.
CINCINNATUS. Sin-sih-*nat*-us.
ELIAB. Ee-*lye*-ab.
RAMAH. *Ray*-muh.
SHAMMAH. *Sham*-uh.

Two people died of heart attacks during the excitement, and three died in traffic accidents during the blackout that occurred. The following day, however, the Secretary of the Navy admitted that the entire raid had been a mistake: there had been no enemy attack. Because of the tension surrounding World War II, people had been so certain that Japan would attack California that someone mistook weather balloons released that night for enemy aircraft!

Samuel discovered that faulty expectations can be misleading. None of the stalwart, older sons of Jesse was God's choice for the next king of Israel. Like Samuel, we tend to judge people by outward appearances, which often tell us nothing about their moral fiber. Our political (and even some religious) leaders have demonstrated this time and again. By now we should have learned our lesson.   —C. R. B.

III. The One Chosen (1 Samuel 16:11-13)

By this time, Samuel must have been puzzled. God had sent him to anoint one of Jesse's sons (v. 1). Now God had rejected seven of those sons, and no more were in sight. What could that mean?

A. Youngest Son (v. 11)

11. And Samuel said unto Jesse, Are here all thy children? And he said, There remaineth yet the youngest, and, behold, he keepeth the sheep. And Samuel said unto Jesse, Send and fetch him: for we will not sit down till he come hither.

Did *Jesse* have any other sons? That was Samuel's first question. Yes, said Jesse, but only one—*the youngest.* It had not seemed necessary to have him present. Surely *he* would not be chosen to rule his older brothers and the entire nation of Israel. Someone was needed to take care of the *sheep,* and naturally that duty had fallen to the "kid brother." But now all the other brothers had been rejected. There was nothing to do but send for the one who remained.

Note that the sacrifice that Samuel had come to offer has not been mentioned since verse 5. Perhaps at that point (when Jesse and his seven sons "were come") the sacrifice was offered. The meat for the family feast would then have been cooking while Samuel was searching for the chosen king. Perhaps Samuel now said, *We will not sit down* (to the feast) *till he come hither.* Or, possibly *we will not sit down* merely means that we will not rest—we will not end the search for God's chosen king—until the youngest son has been included.

B. Anointed King (vv. 12, 13)

12. And he sent, and brought him in. Now he was ruddy, and withal of a beautiful countenance, and goodly to look to. And the LORD said, Arise, anoint him: for this is he.

We can only guess how far away the young man was with the sheep, or how long it took for him to join the family. But when he came, he looked good—perhaps as good as the oldest son who had impressed Samuel at the beginning of his search (v. 6). Some students take *ruddy* to mean that the young man had a healthy outdoor complexion; others take it to indicate that he had red hair. The Hebrew phrase rendered *beautiful countenance* literally reads "beautiful eyes." His entire appearance made him *goodly to look to*. The Lord saw the young man's heart as well, and He gave Samuel a quick and clear message: *Arise, anoint him: for this is he.* [See question #4, page 56.]

THE "KID BROTHER" SYNDROME

The youngest child in a family often gets viewed with a certain amount of disdain. While older children in the family often think that the youngest child gets "babied" and catered to, psychologists tell us that the oldest child frequently enjoys advantages of parental attention that diminish as other children are born into the family. In some cases youngest children sometimes find that they are never quite recognized as having grown up, even when they reach adulthood.

However that might be, history has shown that oldest children are disproportionately represented among the kings and leaders of societies around the world. Thus it is not too shocking that Samuel was doubly surprised in his search for Israel's new king: first, that Eliab, Jesse's oldest son, was not the choice; and second, that David, the "kid brother" in a family of eight boys, was the choice.

David would prove that birth order has no bearing on God's call to service. Far more important than where we fit in our own families is where we fit in God's family. This is determined by our faithful response to God's will—and by nothing else. —C. R. B.

13. Then Samuel took the horn of oil, and anointed him in the midst of his brethren: and the Spirit of the LORD came upon David from that day forward. So Samuel rose up, and went to Ramah.

On an earlier occasion, Samuel had anointed Saul in private (1 Samuel 9:27; 10:1). Only Samuel and Saul knew about this until the time came to reveal the choice and let all Israel know that God had made it (1 Samuel 10:17-24). In the

Visual for lessons 6 & 8

The visual for today's lesson contrasts David's appearance in the eyes of his family with the potential God saw in him, and which he realized.

same way, the anointing of this new king was known only to his family (unless the elders of Bethlehem were also there). Undoubtedly any who were present were warned not to tell what had happened. If arrogant King Saul heard about it, surely he would want to kill both Samuel and the son of Jesse who was anointed (and probably any others who were witnesses).

The Spirit of the Lord came upon David. Now at last we are given the name of this youngest son of Jesse, who was anointed to be king. He was *David*. After becoming king, he would subdue enemy nations and build Israel into an empire. He would also become known as "the sweet psalmist of Israel" (2 Samuel 23:1), writing many of the songs we treasure in the book of Psalms.

Samuel rose up, and went to Ramah, which was his home (1 Samuel 7:17). For a long time the anointing of David seemed to make no difference. In fact, David did not become king until Saul was dead. In the meantime he served King Saul in several ways. His music subdued an evil spirit that troubled Saul (1 Samuel 16:14-23). He killed the giant Goliath, and the invading Philistines fled (1 Samuel 17:49-51). He led Saul's troops in battle so successfully that the king became jealous of his popularity (1 Samuel 18:5-9). When Saul determined to murder him, David fled instead of fighting (1 Samuel 19:8-18). Not until Saul was dead did David become king of Judah (2 Samuel 2:1-4), and then seven and a half more years passed before he became king of all Israel (2 Samuel 5:4, 5).

Israel is far away; Samuel, Saul, and David were long ago. What have they to do with the choices that we must make today and tomorrow? Let's see if we can glean some hints.

Conclusion

A. Hunting Hidden Hearts

Kings generally inherit their positions, but those who live in democratic societies have a voice in choosing the people who make their laws and enforce them. Like Samuel, we tend to look on the outward appearance; but the man with the handsome face and glib tongue is not necessarily the best. How can we know what is in his heart?

Alas, we often fail to do our homework. To take time to examine a candidate's positions would be a long and arduous task, and we have other things to do. So we vote blindly for our party's candidate. Then who is to blame if we are not well represented on a local, state, or national level?

B. Helpless Hasty Hearts

The prettiest girl in town may not become the best wife. The popular college football star, when he gets married, may forget all he ever learned about teamwork. Too many people choose their mates by outward appearance because that is all they can see. Worse yet, they choose when their own hearts are helpless—blinded by infatuation and incapable of sober thought. How can a boy or girl in love know anything about the heart of the beloved?

It takes time. It takes attention. But there are signals to look for. If a girl takes delight in teaching little ones in Sunday school, if she turns down a date with her boyfriend to go with them on an outing, if she happily washes dishes after a fellowship dinner at church, if she is considerate of her parents and careful not to worry them, if she is courteous and helpful to other adults—all of these provide glimpses of her heart. If a boy teases little children unmercifully and upsets a smaller child on a bicycle, if he scorns work day at church and cleanup day in the community, if he takes delight in disobeying his parents and makes fun of people feeble with age—watch out!

Home Daily Bible Readings

Monday, Oct. 2—Attack Against the Amalekites (1 Samuel 15:1-9)

Tuesday, Oct. 3—A New Word (1 Samuel 15:10-16)

Wednesday, Oct. 4—The Confrontation (1 Samuel 15:17-23)

Thursday, Oct. 5—God Rejects Saul as King (1 Samuel 15:24-29)

Friday, Oct. 6—Saul's Confession and Samuel's Departure (1 Samuel 15:30-35)

Saturday, Oct. 7—Samuel Is Sent to Bethlehem (1 Samuel 16:1-5)

Sunday, Oct. 8—David Is Anointed as King (1 Samuel 16:6-13)

Whatever actions a boy or girl consistently demonstrates are an indicator of the contents of his or her heart.

C. Wholehearted or Halfhearted?

Some of us don't even know our own hearts. In choosing a career, it is important to get acquainted with your heart and find a work you can put that heart into. Consider two examples.

At the age of five, Eddie announced his intention: "I'm going to be a preacher just like Ralph." Ralph was a young man who recently had become a preacher. Church members were proud of him. No one could remember when that church had sent out a preacher before. Happy Christians praised Ralph with enthusiasm. They expected great things from him.

Eddie never faltered in his determination. On "Youth Sunday" at his church, he always delivered better sermons than anyone else because he worked harder in preparation. He went to Bible college, graduated with honors, and became the minister of a large and growing church. He is happy, his family is happy, and his church is happy because Eddie's heart is in his work.

Meanwhile Ralph was failing in the ministry. He tried to put his heart into it, but his heart rebelled. He had a daily battle with himself, and it broke him down. He just didn't have the heart of a "people person." Finally he gave up the battle. He found an editorial job, working with words instead of people. He loved it with all his heart and did it with joy until he retired at eighty.

How do you feel about your job? Are you doing it with all your heart? Or are your heart and your work a bad match? If they are, maybe you can change your work. If that is impractical, maybe you can change your heart. Give it some thought. You don't want to be unhappy all your life. Can't you learn to love your work because it provides your daily bread, or because it provides a needed product for many people, or because it does some good in the world? [See question #5, page 56.]

D. Prayer

Father, we know that You have given us every talent, every ability, every usefulness we have. Help us to understand what we are and what we ought to be. For every work we do with joy we give You thanks. If we must do what we do not like, help us to do it with all our heart, remembering that we are doing it for You and not just for an employer. In Jesus' name. Amen.

E. Thought to Remember

"Whatsoever ye do, do it heartily, as to the Lord, and not unto men" (Colossians 3:23).

Learning by Doing

This page contains an alternate lesson plan emphasizing learning activities.
Classes desiring such student involvement will find these suggestions helpful.

Learning Goals

After this lesson students will be able to:

1. Describe the process by which Samuel was led to anoint David as Israel's king.

2. Explain the importance of having one's heart wholly committed to the Lord.

3. List actions and attitudes they can cultivate in seeking to serve the Lord wholeheartedly.

Into the Lesson

Bring to class a bag of balloons of different colors and shapes. Inflate one balloon with air, another with water, and, if possible, a third with helium. Ask each student to take a balloon from the bag for use later in the class. Begin the class by asking for various ways to use these balloons when filled with air, water, or helium. As ideas are mentioned, write them on the chalkboard or overhead transparency *(decorations, playing games, water bombs, to carry a message to someone)*. State, "By filling these balloons with air, water, or helium we can use them in different ways. Helium-filled balloons wouldn't work very well as water bombs! So what matters is what's inside! In the same way, God tells us in 1 Samuel 16 that it's what's inside that counts!"

Into the Word

Begin the background Bible study by dividing the class into three groups, asking each group to complete one of the following assignments.

Group 1: Read 1 Samuel 15:1-9; tell why Saul was rejected as king. *(He did not obey God and destroy all the Amalekites and their animals.)*

Group 2: Read 1 Samuel 15:11, 19-23; tell how Saul's failure was described by God and by Samuel. *(God: He "is turned back from following me, and hath not performed my commandments." Samuel: He did not obey the voice of the Lord; he did evil in the sight of the Lord; he rejected the word of the Lord.)*

Group 3: Read 1 Samuel 15:13, 20, 21, 24, 30; describe Saul's difficulty in accepting personal responsibility for his sin. *(First, he claimed to have "performed the commandment of the Lord," v. 13. Second, he blamed the people for taking the spoil, vv. 20, 21. Third, he admitted that he had sinned but blamed the people for his sin, v. 24. Finally, he confessed that he had sinned, v. 30.)*

After five minutes have each group report to the class.

Have a volunteer read 1 Samuel 16:1-13 aloud. Ask the following questions: (1) Why did the Lord send Samuel to Bethlehem? *(The Lord wanted Samuel to anoint the next king.)* (2) Why did the Lord instruct Samuel to take a heifer to Bethlehem? *(Samuel was fearful of Saul's finding out; the heifer was to be offered as a sacrifice to the Lord.)* (3) By what process did Samuel select the next king to anoint? *(Samuel invited Jesse and his sons to the sacrifice. As the sons passed by, the Lord would tell him which one to anoint.)* (4) Why was Samuel's initial choice of Eliab wrong? *(He looked at his outward physical stature and countenance, but the Lord looked on his heart and refused him.)* (5) Why was David selected to be the next king? *(Because his heart was wholly committed to the Lord, Acts 13:22.)*

Into Life

State: "David was selected because he was a man after God's own heart. He was wholly committed to the Lord. Why is it important to have one's heart wholly committed to the Lord?" As answers are suggested, write them on the chalkboard or an overhead transparency sheet so all can see. Then read aloud 1 Chronicles 28:9, David's instruction to Solomon.

Write "Attitudes" and "Actions" on the chalkboard. Divide the class into two sections for a "neighbor-nudge" activity. Assign one section to focus on "Attitudes" and the other section, "Actions." Ask each student to talk with someone sitting next to him or her to come up with suggested "Attitudes" and "Actions" that Christians need to cultivate to serve the Lord wholeheartedly. After several minutes, call for suggested answers, writing them under the respective heading.

When you have two good lists, observe that each of us has some growing to do to serve the Lord wholeheartedly. Ask each student to select from the lists one attitude and one action that he or she most needs to cultivate. Have the students inflate the balloons they took at the start of the class. They should write on their balloons the attitudes and actions they selected and then let the air out of the balloons. Encourage them to carry their balloons in a pocket or purse to remind them each day that it's what's inside that counts.

Close the session with a prayer of commitment. Or form a prayer circle and encourage each one who is willing to offer such a prayer.

Let's Talk It Over

The questions on this page are designed to encourage review of the lesson Scriptures and to promote discussion of the lesson by the class. The answers provided are only discussion starters. Let your class talk it over from there.

1. Samuel had been mourning over Saul's failure as king, but God told him it was time to take action. We also may be mourning over certain circumstances when God wants us to take action. Can you think of some examples?

Are we mourning over our church's failure to grow? Perhaps it is time to inaugurate a new means of outreach into the community. Are we mourning over the fact that young people in our town are getting into serious trouble with drugs, alcohol, and sex? Perhaps we can develop some kind of service or recreational program that will provide those young people with positive direction. Are we mourning over the immoral content of television programs today? When did we last write to a television network or station, or to an advertiser, and urge others to do the same?

2. The lesson writer compares the practice of sanctifying those who would attend the sacrifice with the old-fashioned custom of taking special care to clean up for attending worship services. Some would suggest our lack of such customs today shows we treat worship too casually. Others say such rituals were empty and without meaning. What do you think? In what ways—if any—do we "sanctify" ourselves for worship?

Certainly there was much in the Old Testament that was ritualistic. The writer of Hebrews calls it a "shadow" of the New Covenant reality (10:1). As for the old-fashioned Saturday night bath, hygiene at that time was not what it is today!

Still, there is a reason people chose to take their weekly baths on Saturday night instead of some other day, and that reason speaks to their devotion. And the writer of Hebrews exhorts Christians to draw near to God with their "hearts sprinkled from an evil conscience" (10:22). Surely we ought to approach an opportunity for worship (public or private) as an audience with the King of kings. We should do so "with reverence and godly fear" (Hebrews 12:28).

3. What are some of the mistakes we make when we focus too much on other people's outward appearance?

The handsome, immaculately groomed man and the attractive, well-dressed woman may be as good as they look, or they may be morally corrupt. We must keep in mind Jesus' warning about wolves "in sheep's clothing" (Matthew 7:15). We must look beyond the surface and focus on their fruits (Matthew 7:16-20). On the other hand, it may be tempting to discount another person simply because he or she is plain-looking, homely, or poorly dressed. James warns of such conduct in James 2:1-13.

4. If God "looketh on the heart," why does the Bible tell us of David's "beautiful countenance" and that he was "goodly to look to"?

Perhaps the description of David is here to prevent our going to the extreme of thinking that beauty is a thing to be shunned. That would be as wrong as choosing a leader simply because he is attractive. Or perhaps it gives us a contrast with Saul, who was also attractive and became vain. David was attractive but kept his humility.

Sometimes a person's character is reflected in his or her appearance. David's faith and courage, which enabled him to stand up against a lion and a bear (1 Samuel 17:34-37) and Goliath (1 Samuel 17:41-50), may well have been evident in his physical bearing. For us today a humble faith in God can keep us from the sneering countenance and haughty bearing that mars the appearance of a proud unbeliever. And our God-inspired love and compassion for others can keep us from the ugliness of a selfish, cold-hearted personality.

5. How can we find the kind of work for the Lord that we can do wholeheartedly? Why is this important?

The church is often hindered in its work by those who serve halfheartedly. Their lack of zeal results in work undone or poorly done. But the average congregation features all kinds of service opportunities, and any member can discover therein an area of work he or she can do with wholehearted devotion. Many churches make use of a talent-and-interest sheet. Every member is requested to fill out one of these and indicate what he or she would genuinely be interested in doing. It is important that members be honest in detailing their interests. It may seem more spiritual to take a place on an evangelism or missions committee. But if they are actually more interested in work on the building or grounds or assisting with secretarial work, that is the best choice to make.

David Mourns Saul and Jonathan

DEVOTIONAL READING: Psalm 77:1-9.

BACKGROUND SCRIPTURE: 1 Samuel 31:1—
2 Samuel 1:27; 1 Chronicles 10.

PRINTED TEXT: 2 Samuel 1:17-27.

2 Samuel 1:17-27

17 And David lamented with this lamentation over Saul and over Jonathan his son:

18 (Also he bade them teach the children of Judah the use of the bow: behold, it is written in the book of Jasher:)

19 The beauty of Israel is slain upon thy high places: how are the mighty fallen!

20 Tell it not in Gath, publish it not in the streets of Askelon; lest the daughters of the Philistines rejoice, lest the daughters of the uncircumcised triumph.

21 Ye mountains of Gilboa, let there be no dew, neither let there be rain, upon you, nor fields of offerings: for there the shield of the mighty is vilely cast away, the shield of Saul, as though he had not been anointed with oil.

22 From the blood of the slain, from the fat of the mighty, the bow of Jonathan turned not back, and the sword of Saul returned not empty.

23 Saul and Jonathan were lovely and pleasant in their lives, and in their death they were not divided: they were swifter than eagles, they were stronger than lions.

24 Ye daughters of Israel, weep over Saul, who clothed you in scarlet, with other delights; who put on ornaments of gold upon your apparel.

25 How are the mighty fallen in the midst of the battle! O Jonathan, thou wast slain in thine high places.

26 I am distressed for thee, my brother Jonathan: very pleasant hast thou been unto me: thy love to me was wonderful, passing the love of women.

27 How are the mighty fallen, and the weapons of war perished!

GOLDEN TEXT: The beauty of Israel is slain upon thy high places:
how are the mighty fallen!—2 Samuel 1:19.

Lesson Aims

After participating in this lesson, each student will be able to:

1. Summarize David's lament for Saul and Jonathan.

2. Tell how the expression of grief helps one to cope with a great loss.

3. Express his or her hope in Christ and how it helps in times of grief.

Lesson Outline

INTRODUCTION
  A. Waiting—and Waiting
  B. Lesson Background
 I. LAMENT FOR SAUL (2 Samuel 1:17-21)
  A. Prelude (vv. 17, 18)
  B. Israel Mourns (v. 19)
  C. Enemies Rejoice (v. 20)
  D. Mountains Are Barren (v. 21)
    Grieving for a Fallen Leader
 II. PRAISE FOR SAUL AND JONATHAN (2 Samuel 1:22-24)
  A. Their Courage (v. 22)
  B. Their Character (v. 23)
  C. Saul as Provider (v. 24)
III. LAMENT FOR JONATHAN (2 Samuel 1:25-27)
  A. Jonathan's Death (v. 25)
  B. David's Grief (v. 26)
    A Man's Tears
  C. Closing Words of Sorrow (v. 27)
CONCLUSION
  A. Love Your Enemies
  B. Sorrow and Hope
  C. Prayer
  D. Thought to Remember

Introduction

Marty and Mary were made for each other. Anyone could see that. They suspected it themselves the first time their eyes met. Enrolling as college freshmen when they were nearing thirty years of age, they felt worlds apart from their younger classmates but blissful with each other. In weeks they were thinking of marriage; in months they were talking about it.

But there was a problem—money, or the lack of it. Both of them were working their way through school, supplementing their earnings with student loans. Reluctantly they agreed that marriage must wait until one of them was earning a living wage. Work and studies left little time for dating, so four years dragged by with long waits between happy dates.

Then came graduation. Mary took a job in town; Marty took one a thousand miles away. For nearly two years they endured separation, but they paid off their loans. Then Marty made a down payment on a car, drove a thousand miles, was married, and took his bride home in celebration. Like characters in a storybook romance, Marty and Mary lived happily ever after.

A. Waiting—and Waiting

Haven't we all been dismayed by delay? Haven't you yourself had to wait and wait for an opportunity, a job, a promotion, a home, or something else that you desired and felt you deserved? Imagine how David felt when he knew that the Lord had chosen him to be king of Israel, yet year after year the throne remained in the control of a king whom the Lord had abandoned.

David had one great advantage. The Spirit of the Lord was with him (1 Samuel 16:13). Thus guided, he provides an admirable example for all of us who have to learn the difficult art of waiting. David became a loyal servant of the reigning king and learned to wait patiently for God's timing. He steadfastly refused to take any action against the king who was so eager to kill him (1 Samuel 24:2-7; 26:6-12).

B. Lesson Background

A band of Amalekites had invaded the southern part of Israel, burning a city and taking its people as captives. David and his men pursued the invaders, defeated them, and brought back the captives and the spoil (1 Samuel 30:1-20). Meanwhile the Philistines invaded farther to the north. Saul and his troops met them in a fierce battle in which Israel was soundly defeated. During the fighting, Saul was killed, along with Jonathan and two other sons of Saul (1 Samuel 31:1-7).

When David heard of this, did he rejoice in the death of the king who had been trying to kill him? No, he mourned; and we find a very touching expression of his grief in today's text.

I. Lament for Saul (2 Samuel 1:17-21)

Poets sometimes puzzle us with their figurative language. Sometimes they abandon the ordinary practices of grammar for the sake of meter and rhyme. For the same reason, they sometimes find and use words we never heard of before; or they use them in ways with which we are unfamiliar. We have to guess at the meaning or use a dictionary. In other cases they include a word that has more than one meaning, and again we have to guess at which meaning the poet is using.

The Hebrew poetry found in the Old Testament exhibits these same qualities. In addition, the poets sometimes abbreviate, and a translator has to add certain words to make sense in English. However, not all translators add the same words. Thus, if we read David's lament in two or more versions, we may find some puzzling differences. But regardless of the version used, the message of this text is unmistakably clear: David is expressing heartfelt grief at the deaths of Saul and Jonathan.

A. Prelude (vv. 17, 18)

17. And David lamented with this lamentation over Saul and over Jonathan his son.

We can understand why David felt grief for *Jonathan*, the dear friend who had turned against his own father and had risked his own life to save David from death (1 Samuel 20:30-34). More surprising is David's grief over *Saul*, the vindictive king who had pursued David relentlessly in order to kill him. But David's grief for Saul was real, too. Saul was God's anointed ruler, and for a time he had served God's people well. David loved and respected him for that. [See question #1, page 64.]

18. (Also he bade them teach the children of Judah the use of the bow: behold, it is written in the book of Jasher:)

Now our difficulty begins. Translating the Hebrew words as literally as possible, we read, "And he said to teach the children of Judah bow." Translators of the *King James Version* took that to mean that David instructed some unnamed persons to *teach* the men of the tribe of *Judah* how to use the *bow* (perhaps to prepare for the next battle against the Philistines who had defeated Saul).

The *New International Version* reads, "[David] ordered that the men of Judah be taught this lament of the bow." This seems to indicate that the lament that follows was known as simply "lament of the bow" (which perhaps eventually became its title), because it praises the bow of Jonathan (v. 22). Apparently David wanted his own tribe (the tribe of Judah) to learn the lament and thus commemorate the loss of Saul (even though Saul was of the tribe of Benjamin, not Judah).

The *New American Standard Bible* reads "the song of the bow" instead of "the lament of the bow." This may have the same meaning, but

some students believe it means that the following lament is to be sung to the tune of another song called "the Song of the Bow."

Whatever meaning we give to the first part of verse 18, the latter part tells us that the following lament, or else another song sung to the same tune, *is written in the book of Jasher*. The Hebrew word *Jasher* means straight, upright, or righteous. The book is also mentioned in Joshua 10:13, where it is said to contain the account of how the sun stood still to allow the Israelites to complete a great military victory during the time of Joshua. Apparently the book was a record of some of the significant people and events in the history of Israel. At some point it was lost or destroyed.

B. Israel Mourns (v. 19)

19. The beauty of Israel is slain upon thy high places: how are the mighty fallen!

What does the phrase *beauty of Israel* describe? It may refer to King Saul or to both Saul and Jonathan, who are the primary subjects of the lament. Or, it may refer to all the men of Israel slain in the battle with the Philistines—praising them as the finest men in Israel's army. Possibly a combination of both concepts is meant. The term *high places* apparently describes Mount Gilboa and the highlands around it (1 Samuel 31:1). [See question #2, page 64.]

C. Enemies Rejoice (v. 20)

20. Tell it not in Gath, publish it not in the streets of Askelon; lest the daughters of the Philistines rejoice, lest the daughters of the uncircumcised triumph.

Gath and *Askelon* were two of the Philistines' chief cities. David was wishing that the news of Saul's death could never be told there. His wish was in vain, of course. First Samuel 31:9, 10 tells how the news was heralded in every Philistine town.

D. Mountains Are Barren (v. 21)

21. Ye mountains of Gilboa, let there be no dew, neither let there be rain, upon you, nor fields of offerings: for there the shield of the mighty is vilely cast away, the shield of Saul, as though he had not been anointed with oil.

Mountains of Gilboa describes the highlands running southeast and south of the valley of Jezreel. These were verdant in spring. The steeper slopes were usually covered with woodlands, while on the level places one could produce fields of grain, some of which would be used as *offerings* to the Lord. In David's grief he longed for all that region to be desolate—a waterless desert—because of the tragedy that had taken place there; *for there the shield of the mighty* King *Saul* was *vilely cast away*. Other versions have *defiled*. The king's honored shield was disgraced by defeat, soiled by blood and by the dirt of the ground, and abandoned on the battlefield of defeat.

The final part of the verse presents another puzzle to the translator. Rendered word for word, it says, *the shield of Saul, not anointed with oil*. The *King James Version* takes that to mean that Saul's shield had been dishonored as if it were the property of some common soldier, not the anointed king of Israel. The *New International Version* says, "the shield of Saul—no longer rubbed with oil." Many students think that a warrior's shield was rubbed with oil to make it bright and shining. Others believe that the oil was meant to serve as a kind of lubricant, making arrows and spears glance off the shield more readily. But after the tragic battle on Mount Gilboa, Saul's shield was neither bright nor lubricated; it was defiled with blood and dirt—and David mourned.

GRIEVING FOR A FALLEN LEADER

"The president has been shot!" Most of us who were teens or adults in the United States on November 22, 1963, can remember where we were when we heard those fateful words about President John F. Kennedy. A man who was then a seminary student recalls that he was approaching the classroom building where two other students were discussing what had taken place. Just then a professor known for his partisan politics came out the door and asked what had happened. On hearing the news, his unthinking response was to utter words he would later regret: "Someone should have done it a long time ago!" As you might expect, news of his crass remark spread across the campus like wildfire. The following day he was forced to make a public apology.

One of the blessings of living in a democratic society is that we can have a part in choosing our

The beauty of Israel is slain upon thy high places: how are the mighty fallen!
2 Samuel 1:19

Visual for
lesson 7

Today's visual shows Mount Gilboa, where Saul and his sons died. Locate the site on a map. (See the visual for lesson 5.)

political leaders and can criticize them without fear of reprisal when they do not conduct themselves or the affairs of state as we think they should. Sometimes we find it difficult to honor the office while criticizing the person who holds it. But David's grief at the death of Saul provides a helpful model for us. Even though Saul had tried to kill David, David made his personal concerns subservient to the greater importance of his nation's well-being. Whenever our political leaders disappoint us, David's example is worth remembering. —C. R. B.

II. Praise for Saul and Jonathan (2 Samuel 1:22-24)

From a wail of grief, David's song now turns to a eulogy for the dead. Three of Saul's sons had been killed in the horrible battle (v. 2), but Jonathan had been David's special friend. The eulogy centers on Saul and Jonathan.

A. Their Courage (v. 22)

22. From the blood of the slain, from the fat of the mighty, the bow of Jonathan turned not back, and the sword of Saul returned not empty.

Jonathan and *Saul* had been both valiant and victorious in battle. *The bow of Jonathan* refers to Jonathan's distinguished activity in warfare. He had never turned back, retreated, or been frightened by the prospects of combat. The references to *blood* and *fat* call to mind the language of animal sacrifices, which is sometimes used in describing battles (cf. Isaiah 34:6, 7; Jeremiah 46:10). *The sword of Saul* likewise highlights Saul's activity in battle. It had *returned not empty*; that is, it had been successful and had accomplished its purpose.

These declarations of courage and success were no empty tributes. Remember how Saul had left the family farm to raise an army and win a dramatic victory (1 Samuel 11:1-11). Remember how Jonathan, with only one companion, had attacked a Philistine garrison and put it to flight (1 Samuel 14:1-23). Saul and Jonathan truly had been successful before that battle in which they died, and even in that fatal fight their courage had not weakened.

B. Their Character (v. 23)

23. Saul and Jonathan were lovely and pleasant in their lives, and in their death they were not divided: they were swifter than eagles, they were stronger than lions.

Perhaps when we think of Saul we remember the insane jealousy that moved him to try to kill David, who had done him nothing but good.

How to Say It

AGAPE (Greek). uh-*gah*-pay.
AMALEKITES. *Am*-uh-leh-kites or
    Uh-*mal*-ih-kites.
ASKELON. *As*-keh-lon.
GILBOA. Gil-*bo*-uh.
JASHER. *Jay*-sher.
JEZREEL. *Jez*-ree-el or *Jez*-reel.
PHILISTINES. Fuh-*liss*-teens or *Fill*-us-teens.

David, however, remembered how *lovely and pleasant* Saul had been before that. Saul had received a shepherd boy into the royal court and had promoted him to a place of command over many older men. [See question #3, page 64.]

Meanwhile, David and Jonathan had become the best of friends (1 Samuel 18:1-5). Jonathan disagreed vocally with his father's treatment of David (1 Samuel 20:32) and even helped David escape Saul's wrath (vv. 35-42). Yet he continued to serve faithfully in Israel's army under the command of his father. Together they died bravely on the field of battle.

C. Saul as Provider (v. 24)

24. Ye daughters of Israel, weep over Saul, who clothed you in scarlet, with other delights; who put on ornaments of gold upon your apparel.

Here David called the women of *Israel* to join him in mourning for Saul. Israel's first king had done much for them. They were able to wear fine clothing and golden jewelry because the nation had prospered during his administration. Some of these costly clothes and jewels were likely among the spoils of Saul's successful wars (1 Samuel 14:47, 48).

III. Lament for Jonathan
(2 Samuel 1:25-27)

The last stanza of David's lament expresses his grief over the loss of Jonathan, his dearest friend (1 Samuel 18:1).

A. Jonathan's Death (v. 25)

25. How are the mighty fallen in the midst of the battle! O Jonathan, thou wast slain in thine high places.

How are the mighty fallen! This cry of grief introduced the lament for Saul (v. 19); now it introduces the lament for Jonathan. But the Hebrew word for *mighty* is plural. The mourning is for both Saul and Jonathan, yes, and perhaps includes the warriors of Israel who died in the

battle with the Philistines. However, the latter line of the verse centers attention on *Jonathan*. Along with the other heroes of Israel, he was slain in that fierce battle on the *high places* of his homeland—the elevated terrain on and around Mount Gilboa.

B. David's Grief (v. 26)

26. I am distressed for thee, my brother Jonathan: very pleasant hast thou been unto me: thy love to me was wonderful, passing the love of women.

I am distressed for thee. The line may also be translated "distress is mine" or "grief is mine." The basic Hebrew verb means to be narrow or confining. David felt pressed and burdened by an overwhelming sense of grief over the death of his dearest friend. Many of us know that feeling, for we too have lost loved ones. Added to the crushing weight of sorrow is the feeling of utter helplessness. The dear one is dead. Nothing can be done about that. David's dear one was so close that he was more than a friend. David calls him *my brother Jonathan.*

There is no suggestion of a homosexual relationship in the closing line of this verse. David is simply stating that the strength of the bond between him and Jonathan was not one commonly found among men. First Samuel 18:1 describes this bond as follows: "The soul of Jonathan was knit with the soul of David, and Jonathan loved him as his own soul." [See question #4, page 64.]

A MAN'S TEARS

The Persian Gulf War of 1991 was carried off with such finesse that it seemed to be the product of cold, calculated military planning devoid of any humane considerations. However, President George Bush later revealed that it was not so. With uncharacteristic lack of guile for a politician, Bush said that he had broken into tears while praying the night before giving the command to go to war.

In speaking of the event, tears again came to his eyes. Later, when asked by reporters about the matter, he told of how he had been torn by the decision that had the potential to bring death in battle to thousands of enemies and allies alike. And once again, his eyes grew moist.

For many generations in Western culture, masculine tears have been thought of as a sign of weakness. Tears aren't part of the image of a "real man." But David was not ashamed to grieve publicly over the death of his beloved friend, Jonathan. Stern resolve in the face of danger may be a sign of manliness, but so are tears for the untimely end of a good person's life.   —C. R. B.

C. Closing Words of Sorrow (v. 27)

27. How are the mighty fallen, and the weapons of war perished!

How are the mighty fallen! This cry was the introduction of the lament for Saul (v. 19) and the lament for Jonathan (v. 25). Now it becomes the sorrowful conclusion of the entire elegy. How great and how sad is the contrast between *mighty* and *fallen!*

Obviously *the weapons of war* could not perish as the warriors themselves did, but the Hebrew word for *perished* can sometimes mean *lost.* (It is thus translated in 1 Samuel 9:3 and Ezekiel 34:16, for examples.) Perhaps the weapons left on the battlefield were gathered up by the Philistines who came back to steal the clothing of the dead (1 Samuel 31:8). Thus the dead warriors and their weapons were both lost to Israel.

Conclusion

A. Love Your Enemies

Jesus said, "Love your enemies" (Matthew 5:44). Long before He said it, David was demonstrating what it means. The word *love* is used so loosely today that we hardly know what it means when we hear it, for there are many kinds of love.

Jesus was talking about the most unselfish kind of love—the kind called *agape.* It is a love that is seen in the life as well as felt in the heart. Jesus explained it thus: "Love your enemies, bless them that curse you, do good to them that hate you, and pray for them which despitefully use you, and persecute you" (Matthew 5:44).

How do you feel toward those who mistreat you, slander you, insult you, abuse you? If you examine your heart and find no love for them, then fill your life with loving deeds. Do good to them at every opportunity you see, and make

some opportunities that you do not yet see. If you do this earnestly and conscientiously, you will be surprised by the love that begins growing in your heart.

B. Sorrow and Hope

"How are the mighty fallen!" That refrain in our text sets the tone of the entire lament. We are hearing a wail of sorrow untouched by hope. Saul and Jonathan were lovely and pleasant in their lives, but now they are dead. They were swifter than eagles and stronger than lions, but now they are dead. They were benefactors of Israel, but now they are dead.

In other Scriptures, however, we see indications that David expressed a clear hope of life after death. Mourning for his own young son, he said, "I shall go to him" (2 Samuel 12:23). Was he not hoping for a living reunion with his dead son? Then there is the triumphant conclusion of the best-loved of all David's songs: "I will dwell in the house of the Lord for ever" (Psalm 23:6). Surely David did not think that *forever* would end with his death, did he?

Today, because of Jesus' resurrection, Christian teaching is bright with the hope, not only that the dead bodies will rise at the last day (1 Thessalonians 4:16, 17), but also that death brings the Christian into the presence of Jesus. Contemplating the possibility of his own death, Paul longed "to depart, and to be with Christ; which is far better" (Philippians 1:23). He knew that to be absent from the body is to be present with the Lord (2 Corinthians 5:6-8).

When we lay our Christian loved ones in the grave, we grieve as David grieved for Saul and Jonathan; but we do not sorrow as others who have no hope (1 Thessalonians 4:13). Our grief is lightened because we know those loved ones are living now with Jesus, and we know that one day those bodies we lay in the graves will be raised alive, changed, and glorified to live forever with their spirits and with the Lord. [See question #5, page 64.]

C. Prayer

Heavenly Father, there is no sorrow too deep or dark to extinguish the hope You have given us. Thank You for the Savior who died for us. Thank You for the Scriptures that tell us of Him and His mercy. Thank You for Your people who walk with us and give us strength and comfort. Thank You for hope. In Jesus' name. Amen.

D. Thought to Remember

"Jesus Christ . . . hath abolished death, and hath brought life and immortality to light through the gospel" (2 Timothy 1:10).

Home Daily Bible Readings

Monday, Oct. 9—The Battle of Mount Gilboa (1 Samuel 31:1-7)

Tuesday, Oct. 10—The Rescue of Saul's Body (1 Samuel 31:8-13)

Wednesday, Oct. 11—The Amalekite Messenger (2 Samuel 1:1-16)

Thursday, Oct. 12—David's Lament (2 Samuel 1:17-27)

Friday, Oct. 13—Comfort in Times of Distress (Psalm 77:1-9)

Saturday, Oct. 14—Death of Saul and His Sons (1 Chronicles 10:1-7)

Sunday, Oct. 15—Burials and a Judgment Against Saul (1 Chronicles 10:8-14)

Learning by Doing

This page contains an alternate lesson plan emphasizing learning activities.
Classes desiring such student involvement will find these suggestions helpful.

Learning Goals

After this lesson each student will be able to:

1. Summarize David's lament for Saul and Jonathan.

2. Tell how the expression of grief helps one to cope with a great loss.

3. Express his or her hope in Christ and how that hope helps in times of grief.

Into the Lesson

Write the following on a poster: "When loved ones die unexpectedly, people react with. . . ." Place the poster on the wall with a couple of markers nearby. Encourage each person to write on the poster a completion to the partial statement. When class starts, call attention to the statement as completed by the students. *(Possible answers include shock, anger, weeping, grieving, blaming God, feelings of hopelessness or helplessness.)* State: "Our hearts respond with many emotions when we face the loss of loved ones. Some of these David experienced, as we see in our lesson today. But he also responded in ways that we have not mentioned. Let's see how he reacted to the loss of two friends, Saul and Jonathan."

Into the Word

Background. Begin the Bible study section of the lesson with a brief three- to five-minute lecture from 2 Samuel 1:1-16. State: "What is very interesting in this account is the totally unexpected response from David to the news of Saul's death. There was no rejoicing or celebrating now that he could officially become the king. There was no vindictiveness in spite of all that Saul had done to try to kill him. How did David respond to the news of Saul's death?" *(Tore his clothes, mourned, wept, fasted, and wrote a lament about his loss; he grieved.)* Summarize by saying, "David carried no grudge, no bitterness, no revengeful spirit toward Saul."

Ask the class whether anyone recalls the two opportunities David had had earlier when he could have killed Saul himself. (Read 1 Samuel 24:1-15; 26:1-16.) Ask, "Why did David refuse to try to kill Saul?" *(Saul was the Lord's anointed; David trusted the Lord to give him the kingdom in His own time and in His own way.)*

Lament for Saul and Jonathan. Prior to class prepare a summary on the chalkboard or a poster of David's lament for Saul and Jonathan. Use the three-section lesson outline: "Lament for Saul, 1:17-21"; "Praise for Saul and Jonathan, 1:22-24"; and "Lament for Jonathan, 1:25-27." Call attention to the outline as you summarize David's lament.

Ask a volunteer to read aloud 2 Samuel 1:17-27. Using the lesson commentary, identify the following terms or phrases: "beauty of Israel," "high places," "book of Jasher."

What praises for Saul did David emphasize in his lament? *(Mighty, v. 19; successful warrior, v. 22; lovely and pleasant, swifter than eagles, stronger than lions, v. 23; increased the wealth of Israel, v. 24)* What praises for Jonathan did David emphasize in his lament? *(courageous, v. 22; swift and strong, v. 23; loving friend, v. 26)* State: "We've seen David's grief at the death of Saul. What we need to see is that his expression of grief in this lamentation helped him to cope with this loss."

Into Life

When people today suffer the loss of a loved one, what do they often remember and talk about in their grief? *(They remember the things the loved one said or did and the good times that were shared together.)* State: "By remembering and talking about what our loved ones did or said, we express our grief over the loss. Such expression of grief helps us to cope with loss."

Have a volunteer read 1 Thessalonians 4:13-18 aloud. Ask the following questions: "How should Christians respond to the loss of loved ones?" *(We have sorrow and grief, but not in the same way as those who have no hope.)* "How does this passage help Christian people in their times of grief?" *(See v. 17.)* "How does the apostle Paul say to use this teaching?" *(See v. 18.)* State: "Death comes, but Christ overcomes!"

Give a four-inch-by-six-inch card to each person. Say, "Suppose the apostle Paul has found out that you have suffered the loss of a loved one and are grieving. So he writes a memo to you encouraging you to express your grief and your hope in Christ to help you in your time of grief. Use this card to write his memo to you." Give about five minutes for this activity. Then ask for volunteers to read their memos to the class. After several have done so, encourage all to keep their memos in their Bibles for future times of grief. Close the class in prayer, thanking God for the hope that we have in Christ.

Let's Talk It Over

The questions on this page are designed to encourage review of the lesson Scriptures and to promote discussion of the lesson by the class. The answers provided are only discussion starters. Let your class talk it over from there.

1. David mourned over Saul's death, primarily because the king was God's anointed. What are some other possible reasons for David's mourning, and how might they apply to our mourning over the death of an enemy?

David was certainly troubled over the *manner* of Saul's death. The king had perished in battle with pagans, which added a further tragic note to his death. We may feel that justice has been served when an enemy of the Christian faith or a terrorist or a vicious criminal dies. But if that death comes in a violent and unlawful manner, then the injustice is actually multiplied. Perhaps David harbored a hope that Saul would change his ways and return to faithfulness in serving God. When his death destroyed that hope, that would have made David's mourning more severe. We also may hope that wicked people will come to repentance and faith in God, and it can stir us to mourning when death eliminates such hope.

2. David's lament seems to have been not only for Saul and Jonathan, but for all the Israelite warriors who had fallen in battle to the Philistines. What significance do you see in that?

For one thing, it demonstrates that everyone is important, not just those with rank and recognition. The unknown many who support the work of the Lord and who serve behind the scenes are as important as those on the ministry staff who are in the public eye. We must never forget that.

It also reminds us of the importance of recognizing those who have sacrificed so much for our sakes. Nations set aside special days to commemorate the victims of past wars, but many citizens view these days as mere holidays. It is wise for all of us to use these days as occasions for sober reflection on the terrible price that must be paid to ensure freedom from tyranny.

3. David seemed to have the ability to focus on the good things he had experienced with Saul. How can we learn to concentrate on the good in people who treat us badly?

We are talking here about one practical application of the Golden Rule (Matthew 7:12). We certainly want other people to overlook our faults and weaknesses and put major emphasis on our positive qualities. It makes sense that we would do the same with them. Another helpful approach

to this matter is to examine why we sometimes offend other people and to apply our findings to those people who offend us. Are we sometimes impatient with people because we are under a great deal of pressure at work? Is there a physical reason (headaches, stomach problems, etc.) for occasional grouchiness? Perhaps those who vex us suffer from similar difficulties. We should view them with patience and understanding.

4. Those who condone homosexuality use many faulty studies and spurious statistics to declare it normal, genetic, and irreversible. Of course, the main thing they want to do is to make it acceptable. Thus they declare that the love between David and Jonathan was a homosexual love. How would you answer such a charge?

The Bible consistently condemns homosexual relations, but the friendship between David and Jonathan is heralded as pure and heroic. Nor is the Bible timid about condemning even its heroes for their failings—such as David's adultery with Bathsheba. But there is no mention, either to praise or condemn, of homosexuality here. Rather, the two had an uncommon friendship. They loved each other as brothers in an extraordinarily close family. Christian men today would do well to aim for the kind of manly demonstrative love for one another that David and Jonathan shared. See what is said about this loving friendship in 1 Samuel 18:1-4; 19:1-3; 20:1-42.

5. What comparisons and contrasts can we draw between the grief a Christian feels when a loved one dies and the grief of an unbeliever in a similar situation?

Both the Christian and the non-Christian experience real sorrow over their separation from their loved ones. The unbeliever views that separation as permanent, but the believer rejoices that it is just for a while. Both the Christian and the non-Christian may wrestle with the circumstances of the loved one's death. Whether it resulted from a sudden tragic accident or came at the end of a long lingering illness, they may ask why it should have happened that way. Often an unbeliever will become so obsessed over such questions that he will endanger his own emotional and physical health. The believer knows that in eternity all such questions will be answered.

David Becomes King of All Israel

October 22
Lesson 8

DEVOTIONAL READING: Psalm 78:67-72.

BACKGROUND SCRIPTURE: 2 Samuel 2–5; 1 Chronicles 11:1-3.

PRINTED TEXT: 2 Samuel 2:1-7; 5:1-5.

2 Samuel 2:1-7

1 And it came to pass after this, that David inquired of the LORD, saying, Shall I go up into any of the cities of Judah? And the LORD said unto him, Go up. And David said, Whither shall I go up? And he said, Unto Hebron.

2 So David went up thither, and his two wives also, Ahinoam the Jezreelitess, and Abigail Nabal's wife the Carmelite.

3 And his men that were with him did David bring up, every man with his household: and they dwelt in the cities of Hebron.

4 And the men of Judah came, and there they anointed David king over the house of Judah. And they told David, saying, That the men of Jabesh-gilead were they that buried Saul.

5 And David sent messengers unto the men of Jabesh-gilead, and said unto them, Blessed be ye of the LORD, that ye have showed this kindness unto your lord, even unto Saul, and have buried him.

6 And now the LORD show kindness and truth unto you: and I also will requite you this kindness, because ye have done this thing.

7 Therefore now let your hands be strengthened, and be ye valiant: for your master Saul is dead, and also the house of Judah have anointed me king over them.

2 Samuel 5:1-5

1 Then came all the tribes of Israel to David unto Hebron, and spake, saying, Behold, we are thy bone and thy flesh.

2 Also in time past, when Saul was king over us, thou wast he that leddest out and broughtest in Israel: and the LORD said to thee, Thou shalt feed my people Israel, and thou shalt be a captain over Israel.

3 So all the elders of Israel came to the king to Hebron; and king David made a league with them in Hebron before the LORD: and they anointed David king over Israel.

4 David was thirty years old when he began to reign, and he reigned forty years.

5 In Hebron he reigned over Judah seven years and six months: and in Jerusalem he reigned thirty and three years over all Israel and Judah.

GOLDEN TEXT: The LORD said to thee, Thou shalt feed my people Israel, and thou shalt be a captain over Israel.—2 Samuel 5:2.

> **Rulers of Israel**
> Unit 2: Saul and David
> (Lessons 5-9)

Lesson Aims

After participating in this lesson, each student should be able to:

1. Tell how David became king of all Israel after Saul's death.

2. Explain how David's reliance on the Lord's leading was key to his becoming king.

3. Suggest a means by which to determine the Lord's leading in an area of his or her interest.

Lesson Outline

INTRODUCTION
  A. Power Struggles
  B. Lesson Background
 I. KING OF JUDAH (2 Samuel 2:1-4a)
  A. Consulting the Lord (v. 1)
  B. Settling at Hebron (vv. 2, 3)
  C. Anointed by Judah (v. 4a)
II. GRATITUDE EXPRESSED (2 Samuel 2:4b-7)
  A. Reason (v. 4b)
  B. Blessing and Prayer (vv. 5, 6)
  C. Challenge (v. 7)
    Death With Dignity
III. KING OF ALL ISRAEL (2 Samuel 5:1-5)
  A. Tribes Speak (vv. 1, 2)
  B. Elders Anoint (v. 3)
    Two Kingdoms or One?
  C. David Reigns (vv. 4, 5)
CONCLUSION
  A. Good Guidance
  B. Courage to Act
  C. Determination to Do Right
  D. Trust in God
  E. Prayer
  F. Thought to Remember

Introduction

A. Power Struggles

Every four years the United States engages in a presidential election with much sound and fury, but the issues are decided by ballots, not bullets. It has been nearly a century and a half since America has experienced a bloody civil conflict. Some nations have survived much longer without civil war, but others have not been so fortunate. Early in the twentieth century, the bloody Bolshevik revolution was in the news; and now the Soviet empire that resulted has been broken up, though not without bloodshed. Most everyone who watches TV or reads the papers is aware of how civil war has engulfed several African nations in recent times.

Ancient Israel had its share of civil strife. Not long ago one of our lessons dealt with the judge named Gideon. When he died, one of his sons seized control by murdering seventy of his brothers and half brothers (Judges 9:1-6). But that was not the end of civil strife. It continued until the murderous son himself was killed in battle (Judges 9:50-56). Another civil war erupted when Israelites undertook to punish the men of Gibeah for an evil deed. Thousands of men were slain (Judges 19, 20).

Israel became a monarchy by popular demand and without a battle; but when the first king died, it took a long war (at least two years, according to 2 Samuel 2:10) before the next one was securely on the throne.

B. Lesson Background

When Saul died in battle, along with three of his sons and numerous soldiers in his army, Israel suddenly found itself without a king. Apparently distressed over being without a leader, the rest of Saul's army fled. Civilians living near the battlefield also vacated their towns. Philistines moved in and took possession of that section of Israel (1 Samuel 31:1-7).

Meanwhile David and his men were warring with Israel's enemies in the south (1 Samuel 30:1-20). Returning in victory to Ziklag, they were greeted by the news of Saul's defeat and death. David's lament for Saul and Jonathan formed the text of our lesson last week (2 Samuel 1:17-27). In today's lesson we consider events that transpired following Saul's death.

I. King of Judah
(2 Samuel 2:1-4a)

David had been sincerely loyal to Saul even when the king had hated him and wanted to kill him. Now the king was dead; yet David still desired to determine God's will before he made any move to claim the throne.

A. Consulting the Lord (v. 1)

1. And it came to pass after this, that David inquired of the LORD, saying, Shall I go up into any of the cities of Judah? And the LORD said unto him, Go up. And David said, Whither shall I go up? And he said, Unto Hebron.

When we pray, we do not expect an instant answer in plain words. We wonder how David was able to get such a response. Our question is not answered in this text, but from other Scriptures we can suggest a possibility. On another occasion when David inquired of God, he asked the priest to bring the ephod (1 Samuel 30:7, 8). The ephod was a kind of jacket. The elaborate one worn by the high priest is described in Exodus 28:5-14. Attached to the ephod was the breastplate of judgment (Exodus 28:15-30), and in the breastplate were the Urim and the Thummim (Exodus 28:30). Israel's leaders were to receive answers from God by means of these (Numbers 27:21; Ezra 2:63; Nehemiah 7:65).

The words *Urim* and *Thummim* may be literally translated *lights* and *perfections*. We do not, however, know exactly what these objects were; and we do not know how they conveyed God's answer to a specific question. Still, it seems probable that David often inquired of the Lord with the aid of the priest and received the Lord's answer by means of the Urim and Thummim.

In any case, the main point of this verse is that David sought the Lord's will, accepted it, and followed it. Do we sometimes fail because we proceed in our own way without even looking for leading from the Lord? Even when we see His way, do we sometimes think we can improve on it? Or do we, like David, look for the Lord's will, find it, and follow it? [See question #1, page 72.]

David was living in the territory held by the Philistines, where he had gone to escape the fury of King Saul. He had made peace with the Philistine king of Gath and had been permitted to live in Ziklag (1 Samuel 27:1-7). Now the Lord told him to go back to Israel—to the city of *Hebron*, which belonged to the tribe of *Judah*.

B. Settling at Hebron (vv. 2, 3)

2. So David went up thither, and his two wives also, Ahinoam the Jezreelitess, and Abigail Nabal's wife the Carmelite.

Several years (perhaps as many as fifteen) had passed since David had been anointed to be king. His heart must have leaped with eagerness when the Lord told him to make his move and claim the kingship.

Also noted is the fact that when David moved to Hebron, he took his two wives, *Ahinoam* and *Abigail*, with him. Ahinoam is called a *Jezreelitess*, probably to distinguish her from the wife of Saul (1 Samuel 14:50). Abigail had become David's wife following the death of her wicked husband Nabal (1 Samuel 25:39-42).

Some may question how David's having two wives could square with the description of him as a man after God's own heart (1 Samuel 13:14). Although polygamy was not God's intention for man (Genesis 2:24), it was a common practice in the ancient Near East (other notable examples are Abraham and Jacob). It should be noted, however, that such polygamous situations in Scripture are always accompanied by strife and turmoil in the home.

3. And his men that were with him did David bring up, every man with his household: and they dwelt in the cities of Hebron.

When *David* was a fugitive, hiding in the desert to elude Saul, he was joined by other *men* who were discontent or dissatisfied for some reason (1 Samuel 22:1, 2). Eventually their number grew to about six hundred (1 Samuel 23:13). These men followed David during his flight from Saul, and now they and their families returned with him to Hebron. *The cities of Hebron* included the smaller towns around it.

C. Anointed by Judah (v. 4a)

4a. And the men of Judah came, and there they anointed David king over the house of Judah.

In the last part of our text we shall see reasons why all Israel later accepted David as king (2 Samuel 5:1, 2). Those reasons must have seemed even more compelling to the *men of Judah*, David's own tribe; and those men likely saw other reasons as well. As Saul had become more and more unjust and cruel, they must have taken pleasure and pride in the clever way David was able to avoid the vindictive king. The farmers of Judah must have been grateful, because David and his six hundred men protected their flocks and herds by destroying their enemies in the south (1 Samuel 27:8, 9; 30:1-20). So it was likely with enthusiastic support that the *men of Judah came, and . . . anointed David king over the house of Judah*. However, they could not speak for all the other tribes of Israel. [See question #2, page 72.]

II. Gratitude Expressed (2 Samuel 2:4b-7)

David's first act as king was not to fortify the city of Hebron or to increase the size of his army. It was to send a message of thanks to the brave men who had been devoted to Saul.

A. Reason (v. 4b)

4b. And they told David, saying, That the men of Jabesh-gilead were they that buried Saul.

Gilead included the land east of the Jordan River that became Israel's possession. *Jabesh* was a town in that territory. In his first major military endeavor as king of Israel, Saul had saved this town from savage treatment by hostile neighbors (1 Samuel 11:1-11). At Hebron David learned that heroic men of that town had taken Saul's

Home Daily Bible Readings

Monday, Oct. 16—The Rival Kings (2 Samuel 2:1-11)

Tuesday, Oct. 17—Abner Defects to David (2 Samuel 3:6-21)

Wednesday, Oct. 18—Joab Murders Abner (2 Samuel 3:22-27)

Thursday, Oct. 19—David Mourns Abner (2 Samuel 3:28-39)

Friday, Oct. 20—The Death of Ish-bosheth (2 Samuel 4:1-12)

Saturday, Oct. 21—David, King of Israel, Captures Jerusalem (2 Samuel 5:1-12)

Sunday, Oct. 22—David Rules Israel From Jerusalem (1 Chronicles 11:1-9)

mangled body from the vindictive Philistines and had given it an honorable burial. (See 1 Samuel 31:8-13.)

B. Blessing and Prayer (vv. 5, 6)

5. And David sent messengers unto the men of Jabesh-gilead, and said unto them, Blessed be ye of the LORD, that ye have showed this kindness unto your lord, even unto Saul, and have buried him.

In last week's lesson we studied David's lament for Saul. It showed that David loved and respected Saul for what he had been and what he had done for Israel. Now once more David showed his admiration for Saul by his sincere pronouncement of blessing on the brave men who had risked their lives to show *kindness* to the dead king.

6. And now the LORD show kindness and truth unto you: and I also will requite you this kindness, because ye have done this thing.

David then asked that the Lord would reward those brave men by showing them *kindness and truth*, or by dealing kindly and justly with them. David added that he too would *requite* (reward) those men, though he said nothing about how or when he would do so.

C. Challenge (v. 7)

7. Therefore now let your hands be strengthened, and be ye valiant: for your master Saul is dead, and also the house of Judah have anointed me king over them.

The king so respected among those in Jabesh was *dead*; David was now *king* of Judah. There seems to be here an implied plea for the people of Jabesh to support him in his kingship because he also respected Saul. Later, when David did become king of the entire nation, he would be in

a position to reward Jabesh as he was promising to do (v. 6). [See question #3, page 72.]

DEATH WITH DIGNITY

One of the results of the many twentieth century advances in medical science has been a dramatic increase in life expectancy. New vaccines, medications, vitamins, surgeries, and therapies have been developed to treat ailments and diseases ranging from arthritis to heart disease to cancer. Millions of people have benefited.

There has also been what many call a "downside" to these advances. We can now extend a person's life into a weakened old age that may last for years. We are able to keep a body "alive" on life support systems long past the point at which he or she otherwise would have died.

One of the reactions to this has been a so-called "death with dignity" movement. Many people now write "living wills" to instruct family and physicians how they wish to be treated in the case of a terminal illness. They want to "die with dignity."

In our text, David commended the people of Jabesh-gilead for giving the body of Saul a dignified burial. While Saul's actions had often threatened David, he recognized that dignifying King Saul in his burial also dignified the kingship that David eventually assumed.

There is also a lesson here about treating the past in the "dignified" way God wants us to treat it. To minimize or detract from the work of our predecessors in our jobs or ministries minimizes us as well. God's kingdom is better served by letting the past "die with dignity."   —C. R. B.

III. King of All Israel (2 Samuel 5:1-5)

During Saul's reign, his second in command was Abner, who served as general of the army. Following Judah's declaration of David as king, Abner proclaimed that Saul's son, Ish-bosheth, was king "over all Israel" (2 Samuel 2:8, 9). Abner's army soon clashed with David's army, led by Joab (2 Samuel 2:12-32). Thus began a "long war between the house of Saul and the house of David: but David waxed stronger and stronger, and the house of Saul waxed weaker and weaker" (2 Samuel 3:1).

Eventually Abner must have realized that he was on the losing side of this war; nevertheless, the conflict continued. Then a quarrel took place between Abner and Ish-bosheth. Abner decided to desert Ish-bosheth and turn his support over to David. He urged the elders of Israel to do the same, and he himself went to David to express his personal support and his desire to "gather all

Israel" to "make a league," or agreement, with David (2 Samuel 3:6-21).

Not long afterward, both Abner and Ish-bosheth were killed by assassins. The nation was now leaderless (except for Judah); however, Abner had already persuaded most of its elders that it was in their interest to endorse David. Thus the stage was set for the events recorded in the last part of our text.

A. Tribes Speak (vv. 1, 2)

1. Then came all the tribes of Israel to David unto Hebron, and spake, saying, Behold, we are thy bone and thy flesh.

All the tribes of Israel were David's kinsmen; all were one family; all were descended from Jacob, whose other name was Israel. Therefore it was fitting for *David* to be king over all of them.

2. Also in time past, when Saul was king over us, thou wast he that leddest out and broughtest in Israel: and the LORD said to thee, Thou shalt feed my people Israel, and thou shalt be a captain over Israel.

The people of Israel stated three reasons for making David king of the entire nation: he was "kin" to the people whom he would be ruling (v. 1); he had proved competent when he was a general in Saul's army; and, most important, *the Lord* had designated him to be king. [See question #4, page 72.]

B. Elders Anoint (v. 3)

3. So all the elders of Israel came to the king to Hebron; and king David made a league with them in Hebron before the LORD: and they anointed David king over Israel.

The reasons listed in verses 1 and 2 seemed compelling (of course, at this point there was no other candidate for the throne). Gladly *David made a league* (the Hebrew word is the word usually translated "covenant") with *all the elders of Israel*, thus ending the long war. The elders then *anointed David king over Israel*.

TWO KINGDOMS OR ONE?

On November 27, 1941, the State of Jefferson officially seceded from both Oregon and California. The secessionists blocked Highway 99 (the main north-south highway in California at the time) and announced that they would "secede each Thursday until further notice." Their agenda was to force the leadership in California into building some good roads in what was then a largely undeveloped part of the state. On December 4, 1941, a Crescent City judge was inaugurated as acting governor of the new "state." However, three days later the Japanese attacked Pearl Harbor; and California and the entire nation turned their attention to more important matters that affected a much larger number of people.

When David was made king of Judah, the nation of Israel became divided. Conflict between supporters of David and supporters of Saul escalated. Eventually the violent deaths of Abner and Ish-bosheth, two leaders who could have created a separate kingdom, caused all Israel to realize that David was indeed the Lord's choice to rule all His people. This allowed David to consolidate his power.

Sometimes, in both church and society, selfish concerns so grasp our attention that only a momentous or disastrous event can bring us to our senses. Then we may realize that a greater cause is more important than one that pleases only ourselves.
               —C. R. B.

C. David Reigns (vv. 4, 5)

4, 5. David was thirty years old when he began to reign, and he reigned forty years. In Hebron he reigned over Judah seven years and six months: and in Jerusalem he reigned thirty and three years over all Israel and Judah.

David was king of *Judah seven years and six months* before he became king of all Israel; but that does not mean that the war mentioned in 2 Samuel 3:1 was that long. Ish-bosheth was king only two years (2 Samuel 2:10). The time of actual fighting would have been at least that, and probably not much longer. Thus the seven years and six months would include time both before the fighting started and after it ended.

Conclusion

No one can doubt that David was a remarkable young man. It seems that his every effort was crowned with success. Whether it was to conquer a well-armed giant with a single stone or become king of all Israel, David did it. How could he be so successful all the time? Several factors can be cited.

Visual for
lessons 6 & 8

Today's lesson is illustrated by the same poster as was used for lesson 6. The shepherd boy, by the grace of God, has become king!

A. Good Guidance

There is a clue in the first verse of our printed text for today: "David inquired of the Lord." That same statement appears again and again in the record. When faced with some difficult enterprise, David asked for instructions, got them, and obeyed them. That may leave us feeling deprived. We have no high priest with Urim and Thummim to obtain God's instructions for us. We have no inspired prophet to tell us exactly what God says.

Yet how well do we follow the instructions we do have? Consider one example. Jesus said, "Love your enemies, bless them that curse you, do good to them that hate you, and pray for them which despitefully use you, and persecute you" (Matthew 5:44). That is as plain as the instructions given to David, but how many Christians ignore it completely!

B. Courage to Act

If a lion or a bear threatens my sheep, I may be brave enough to wave something and yell. I am sure I will not catch the animal by the beard and kill him! But David did (1 Samuel 17:34-36).

If our church house is too small, or if one of our members is unemployed and hungry, or if we are not winning people to Christ, or if we have no positive influence in community affairs, is it because we do not know what is needed? Or is it because we are not daring and vigorous enough to do what needs to be done? [See question #5, page 72.]

C. Determination to Do Right

It was right to protect a sheep from a lion and a bear. It was right to pursue a troop of raiders and rescue the captives they had taken (1 Samuel 30:1-20). It was not right to assassinate the man whom God had chosen as king, not even when he threatened David's life. On one occasion, King Saul led his troops out in the desert to catch David and kill him. In the darkness of a desert night, David and Abishai sneaked past the sentries and found Saul sleeping on the ground. "Let me thrust him just once with my spear," whispered Abishai. "I won't need to hit him a second time." But David said no. It would not be right (1 Samuel 26:1-12).

When you are threatened, cheated, mistreated, injured, or insulted, you may hear an "Abishai" whispering, "Get even!" The Lord says, "Vengeance is mine; I will repay" (Romans 12:19). What do you say?

D. Trust in God

We ought to trust in God, but a word of caution is needed. Trust in God does not mean that we ought to be foolish. It was the devil who urged Jesus to jump from a pinacle of the temple, trusting God to keep His promise that angels would bear Him up. Jesus answered with another word from God: "Thou shalt not tempt the Lord thy God" (Matthew 4:5-7). To tempt God is to put Him to the test, to make Him prove what He has said. It would be wrong for Jesus to make that wild leap just to prove that angels would bear Him up—or just to draw a crowd.

How do we know what God wants us to do? We have the written Word that God has given, and we have the minds that God has given. With these we must discover what God wants us to do—and we must take care not to equate our own selfish desires with God's will.

Do you remember the praise given to the Christians in Macedonia who gave all they could, and even more than they could (2 Corinthians 8:1-3)? Many of us can do more than we think we can.

E. Prayer

Almighty God, we know Your way is always right. Thank You for the Bible that reveals Your way to us; thank You for minds to understand it. Father, we do want to do Your will. Empower our minds to understand it rightly, we pray; and empower both minds and bodies to obey it faithfully. In Jesus' name. Amen.

F. Thought to Remember

"Be ye doers of the word, and not hearers only" (James 1:22).

How to Say It

ABISHAI. Uh-*bish*-ay-eye.
AHINOAM. Uh-*hin*-o-am.
CARMELITE. *Car*-mul-ite.
EPHOD. *ee*-fod.
GIBEAH. *Gib*-ee-uh.
GIDEON. *Gid*-ee-un.
HEBRON. *Hee*-brun or *Heb*-run.
ISH-BOSHETH. Ish-*bo*-sheth.
JABESH-GILEAD. *Jay*-besh-*gil*-ee-ud (strong accent on *gil*).
JEZREELITESS. *Jez*-ree-el-ite-ess (strong accent on *ite*).
JOAB. *Jo*-ab.
MACEDONIA. Mass-eh-*doe*-nee-uh.
NABAL. *Nay*-bull.
PHILISTINES. Fuh-*liss*-teens or *Fill*-us-teens.
THUMMIM. *Thum*-im.
URIM. *You*-rim.
ZIKLAG. *Zik*-lag.

Learning by Doing

This page contains an alternate lesson plan emphasizing learning activities. Classes desiring such student involvement will find these suggestions helpful.

Learning Goals

After participating in this lesson, each student will be able to:

1. Tell how David became king of all Israel after Saul's death.

2. Explain how David's reliance on the Lord's leading was key to his becoming king.

3. Suggest a means by which to determine the Lord's leading in an area of his or her interest.

Into the Lesson

Prior to class draw a shield on a sheet of paper with a magic marker. Divide the shield into four sections and make enough copies for each person in the class. Begin this week's lesson by passing out one copy of the shield and a colored marker to each person. State: "To introduce today's lesson, I would like you to sketch in three sections of the shield your answers to three questions. Your sketches will portray various occupations. Here are the three questions: In section 1, when you were a child, what did you want to be when you grew up? In section 2, when you were older, what did others want you to be when you grew up? In section 3, as an adult, what have you become? You have three minutes to sketch your answers." When time is up, ask for volunteers to show their sketches and explain them to the class.

State: "Some of you decided to enter an occupation because that is what you wanted to do. Others chose a job because that is what someone else wanted you to do. Today's lesson centers on David's decision to go to Hebron to become king of Judah. Turn to 2 Samuel 2 to find out what guided his decision making."

Into the Word

Ask a class member to read 2 Samuel 2:1-7 and 5:1-5 aloud. To help students work through this text and understand how David became king of all Israel, ask the following questions.

1. What did David do before he went to Judah? *(He inquired of the Lord whether he should go.)*

2. To what city was David told to go? *(Hebron.)*

3. Who was Abigail? *(David's wife. Formerly she was the wife of Nabal, a Calebite who was surly and mean. She was intelligent and beautiful, 1 Samuel 25:3.)*

4. What did the men of Judah do to David? *(They made him king of Judah.)*

5. What people responded in kindness and buried Saul? *(The men of Jabesh-gilead.)*

6. How did David respond to this news of kindness toward Saul? *(He sent messengers to them to convey his blessings.)*

7. Why did the elders of Israel go to David in Hebron? *(They anointed David king of all Israel.)*

8. How long did David reign? *(Forty years.)*

Into Life

Say, "David knew he was to be the next king. He had been anointed by Samuel years before (1 Samuel 16:13). After Saul died, he rightfully could have gone up immediately to claim his position as king. But he chose not to do so. He would not take matters into his own hands. Instead, David relied on the Lord to guide his life. How did David's reliance on the Lord's leading affect his becoming king of all Israel?" *(He waited for the Lord to direct his life, telling him when to go and where to go. He trusted God's timing, waiting for the elders of Israel to come to him.)*

Ask, "What are some ways to determine the Lord's leading in our lives today?" *(Search Scripture for principles to apply; seek counsel and advice from godly Christians; pray for the guidance of the Holy Spirit.)*

Write on the chalkboard the following: Spiritual Life; Emotional Life; Social Life; Moral Life; Family Life; Church Life; Witnessing; Work/job. State: "As we look at these general categories, take a few moments to reflect on how regularly you follow the Lord's leading in these areas of your life. On a scale of 1 (never) to 5 (daily), rank how you regularly follow the Lord."

After a few moments ask whether every answer were a "5." State: "All answers below '5' indicate a need for a greater sensitivity to following the Lord's leading. Now think of a specific example in one of these areas where you especially need the Lord's leading in your life. Take the shield you used at the beginning of the lesson. In section 4 sketch what you believe God wants you to become or do in that specific area where the Lord's leading is needed."

Allow a couple of minutes for reflection and for sketching. Then ask the class to form groups of three to share their sketches and to close the class in prayer for each other. Encourage them to pray for the Lord's leading and for their willingness to recognize and respond to His leading.

Let's Talk It Over

The questions on this page are designed to encourage review of the lesson Scriptures and to promote discussion of the lesson by the class. The answers provided are only discussion starters. Let your class talk it over from there.

1. The lesson writer observes, "David sought the Lord's will, accepted it, and followed it." We cannot use the Urim and Thummim to do that, but how can we follow David's example?

Certainly prayer is important to this process. Since the Lord's Prayer offers us a pattern for our prayers, then every prayer should include a request for God's will to be accomplished. Whether or not we are praying for something specific, our theme should be, "Thy will be done." If we pray habitually in that way, it will affect our Bible reading. We will be alert to God's revealing of His will for us through His Word, and we will have programmed ourselves to accept and follow that will. The same thing will be true in regard to our hearing the Word taught and preached.

2. David waited quite a long time after his anointing before he actually became king. How would you advise a person who expressed frustration over a long wait for God to answer a prayer or to fulfill a promise?

We must always remember that God does not view time in the same way we do. (See Psalm 90:4.) We are often anxious about God's fitting *His* plans into *our* timetables.

Also, we must be sure to be submissive. We seldom have so clear a promise as David did. Did God really promise that for which we wait? Are we waiting for *God's* answer to our prayer—or are we expecting God to endorse our own answer?

Finally, we must remember that, during his waiting period, David served God and his nation. Our waiting time must also be a working time. (See Isaiah 26:8.) Of course, the work we do must not represent an effort to get ahead of God's timing! David did not hasten his acquisition of the throne by killing Saul or leading a revolt against him. Neither should we endeavor to do for ourselves what God has promised to do.

3. A cynic might accuse David of merely trying to "butter up" the men of Jabesh-gilead in order to gain their support for his rule over all Israel. But the Biblical account indicates that David's message of thanks was a genuine reflection of his feelings. Why is it important to be sincere in our gestures of praise and gratitude?

Anything less than sincerity in our speech is just plain dishonest. In our time the use of flattery, false praise, and insincere words of gratitude are often devices used by political candidates to gain the support of influential people. Even non-politicians are tempted to use such devices to curry favor with others to advance some plan or purpose. We must resist such temptation and avoid any attempt to manipulate other people with words that are "smoother than butter" and "softer than oil" (Psalm 55:21). We must consistently aim to speak words that will build up one another.

4. One reason the people of Israel were willing to make David their king was the military leadership he displayed while serving under King Saul. How important is it, when selecting leaders for the church, to examine previous leadership experience?

Among the qualifications Paul lists in 1 Timothy 3:1-7 for the office of bishop or elder is a special emphasis on a candidate's leadership in the home—note verses 4 and 5. Whenever an individual expresses an interest in being a leader in the church, the members can look to his home life, his business experience, and his previous service in the church to determine if he possesses the skills for the office he currently seeks. Does he have the ability to organize his time and effort so as to handle the work efficiently? Is he a "people person," able to communicate and cooperate with the members who must look to his leadership? Can he respond to problems promptly and effectively? These are marks of leadership that will fit him for weightier responsibilities.

5. David's courage was one of his outstanding attributes. How can we develop courage?

David's courage was closely connected with his faith in God. David's battle with Goliath is a good example. Unimpressed by Goliath's size and strength, David knew he served a God who was infinitely bigger and stronger than any man. We also will exhibit greater courage as we focus on our great God rather than on the size of our problems. David's courage also grew out of his wholehearted commitment to God's cause. (Read 1 Samuel 17:45-47.) Our courage will likewise grow stronger as we throw ourselves without reservation into the cause of Christ.

God's Covenant With David

DEVOTIONAL READING: 1 Kings 8:15-21.

BACKGROUND SCRIPTURE: 2 Samuel 7; 1 Chronicles 17.

PRINTED TEXT: 2 Samuel 7:1-13, 16.

2 Samuel 7:1-13, 16

1 And it came to pass, when the king sat in his house, and the LORD had given him rest round about from all his enemies;

2 That the king said unto Nathan the prophet, See now, I dwell in a house of cedar, but the ark of God dwelleth within curtains.

3 And Nathan said to the king, Go, do all that is in thine heart; for the LORD is with thee.

4 And it came to pass that night, that the word of the LORD came unto Nathan, saying,

5 Go and tell my servant David, Thus saith the LORD, Shalt thou build me a house for me to dwell in?

6 Whereas I have not dwelt in any house since the time that I brought up the children of Israel out of Egypt, even to this day, but have walked in a tent and in a tabernacle.

7 In all the places wherein I have walked with all the children of Israel spake I a word with any of the tribes of Israel, whom I commanded to feed my people Israel, saying, Why build ye not me a house of cedar?

8 Now therefore so shalt thou say unto my servant David, Thus saith the LORD of hosts, I took thee from the sheepcote, from following the sheep, to be ruler over my people, over Israel:

9 And I was with thee whithersoever thou wentest, and have cut off all thine enemies out of thy sight, and have made thee a great name, like unto the name of the great men that are in the earth.

10 Moreover I will appoint a place for my people Israel, and will plant them, that they may dwell in a place of their own, and move no more; neither shall the children of wickedness afflict them any more, as beforetime,

11 And as since the time that I commanded judges to be over my people Israel, and have caused thee to rest from all thine enemies. Also the LORD telleth thee that he will make thee a house.

12 And when thy days be fulfilled, and thou shalt sleep with thy fathers, I will set up thy seed after thee, which shall proceed out of thy bowels, and I will establish his kingdom.

13 He shall build a house for my name, and I will stablish the throne of his kingdom for ever.

. . . .

16 And thine house and thy kingdom shall be established for ever before thee: thy throne shall be established for ever.

GOLDEN TEXT: Thine house and thy kingdom shall be established for ever before thee: thy throne shall be established for ever.—2 Samuel 7:16.

Rulers of Israel
Unit 2: Saul and David
(Lessons 5-9)

Lesson Aims

After participating in this lesson, students should be able to:

1. Recount the covenant that God made with David and the circumstances under which He made it.

2. State how this covenant is fulfilled in Jesus and in the covenant He has established.

3. Praise God for the blessings of grace given in the New Covenant.

Lesson Outline

INTRODUCTION
    A. What David Did
    B. Lesson Background
  I. PLANS FOR GOD'S HOUSE (2 Samuel 7:1-7)
    A. David's Thoughts (vv. 1-3)
    B. God's Thoughts (vv. 4-7)
 II. GOD'S BENEFITS (2 Samuel 7:8-11a)
    A. To David (vv. 8, 9)
      Commoners or Royalty?
    B. To Israel (vv. 10, 11a)
III. TWO HOUSES (2 Samuel 7:11b-13, 16)
    A. David's House (v. 11b)
    B. David's Son (v. 12)
    C. God's House (v. 13)
    D. David's Kingdom (v. 16)
      An Everlasting Empire
CONCLUSION
    A. God's Covenants
    B. God's New Covenant
    C. Prayer
    D. Thought to Remember

Introduction

The election season is quite a time for those of us who live in democratic societies. Candidates are seen everywhere—debating in town meetings, making promises on television, and flaunting their names on billboards. Nearly all of them want to improve public education, stop the flow of illegal drugs, and reduce taxes. And when we elect the people who have clamored for change, isn't it amazing to see how few changes occur?

What would you do if you became king? Imagine you were living back in the time when the king's word was law, when he had a powerful army to back him, and when there was no opposition party. What would you do first? Most likely you would do none of the things that David did.

A. What David Did

One of King David's first acts was to capture Jerusalem (or Zion, as it is also called) and make it his capital city. That city had been captured and burned long before by members of the tribe of Judah (Judges 1:8); however, Joshua 15:63 notes that they were unable to drive out the Jebusites who were inhabiting the city.

Jerusalem's location on a hill made defending the city much easier; in fact, the Jebusites living there when David captured Jerusalem had felt confident that he would never enter the city (2 Samuel 5:6, 7). In addition, Jerusalem was located near the border of Judah and Benjamin; thus David did not appear to be favoring either Judah (which had earlier made him its king) or the remainder of his kingdom to the north.

Another noteworthy achievement in the early stages of David's reign was not of his choosing; it was forced on him. The Philistines who had defeated King Saul gathered their forces in order to let the new king know that they were still the dominant people of the region. But David twice defeated them, and for a time they gave Israel no more trouble (2 Samuel 5:17-25).

B. Lesson Background

Once David had gained firm control of his kingdom, he began to think about the ark of the covenant. For many years it had been separated from its original home in the tabernacle. The Philistines had captured it and taken it away (1 Samuel 4:1-11). But the ark brought only trouble to them, so they returned it to Israel. There it was kept in a private home (1 Samuel 5:1—7:2).

After becoming king, David wanted to bring the ark to Jerusalem. The first attempt ended in disaster because it was not carried properly (2 Samuel 6:1-11), but a second attempt was successful. The ark was then placed inside a tent that David provided for it (2 Samuel 6:12-19).

There was great rejoicing when Israel brought the ark to Jerusalem. David himself "danced before the Lord with all his might" (2 Samuel 6:14, 15) on this occasion. But soon the king began to have second thoughts. A portable tabernacle had been an appropriate place for the ark when Israel was traveling in the desert. It had been God's tent in the midst of the tents of His people. But now His people were living in houses. David himself was residing comfortably in a new palace in Jerusalem (2 Samuel 5:11). Shouldn't God's house be superior to David's?

I. Plans for God's House
(2 Samuel 7:1-7)

A. David's Thoughts (vv. 1-3)

1. And it came to pass, when the king sat in his house, and the LORD had given him rest round about from all his enemies.

With God's help, David had become undisputed king of all Israel. He had defeated, not only the Philistines, but any other *enemies* that had threatened the nation. Eventually a point was reached where no immediate military action was required. David was able to relax *in his house*, or palace.

2. That the king said unto Nathan the prophet, See now, I dwell in a house of cedar, but the ark of God dwelleth within curtains.

David's house was probably of stone on the outside, but on the inside it was covered with *cedar* brought from faraway Lebanon with the help of King Hiram of Tyre (2 Samuel 5:11). No doubt David's house was among the finest in Jerusalem, yet God's house in the same city was only a tent enclosed by *curtains*!

3. And Nathan said to the king, Go, do all that is in thine heart; for the LORD is with thee.

Without any additional words from David, *Nathan* knew what was in the king's *heart*. David wanted to build a house for the Lord—a house finer than the king's to serve as a fitting place for the ark of God. That sounded reasonable, so Nathan said, "Go ahead." [See question #1, page 80.]

B. God's Thoughts (vv. 4-7)

4. And it came to pass that night, that the word of the LORD came unto Nathan, saying.

Without waiting to be asked, Nathan had given an uninspired opinion to David. Without waiting to be asked, *the Lord* now gave His own *word* to Nathan.

5. Go and tell my servant David, Thus saith the LORD, Shalt thou build me a house for me to dwell in?

The Lord spoke to Nathan, but the message was for *David*. The question sounds as if He were saying, "Not so fast! Let's think this over." [See question #2, page 80.]

6. Whereas I have not dwelt in any house since the time that I brought up the children of Israel out of Egypt, even to this day, but have walked in a tent and in a tabernacle.

Approximately four and a half centuries had passed since the Lord had *brought up the children of Israel out of Egypt*. Through most of those centuries the people had been living in houses rather than in tents, but the Lord had never had a house of His own; that is, the ark that was the

symbol of His presence had never been kept in a house built and dedicated for that purpose. Its home was *in a tent—the tabernacle, which had* been specially made for it.

Significantly, the Lord did not say that He *dwelt* in a tent, but that He *walked in* a tent (see His promise in Leviticus 26:12). The tabernacle was His traveling house *even to this day*. It was not yet time for Him to have a more permanent home on earth.

7. In all the places wherein I have walked with all the children of Israel spake I a word with any of the tribes of Israel, whom I commanded to feed my people Israel, saying, Why build ye not me a house of cedar?

In all the places of their travels, the Lord had never *commanded* anyone in *Israel* to *build* a *house* for Him. That was David's idea, not God's. That is not to say it was a bad idea. Later in this text we shall see that it was a good one, and acceptable; but its time had not yet come.

II. God's Benefits
(2 Samuel 7:8-11a)

As He often did when asking His people to obey Him, God now paused to remind them that they were indebted to Him for benefits many and great. In this case He spoke of benefits to David personally as well as those to the nation as a whole.

A. To David (vv. 8, 9)

8. Now therefore so shalt thou say unto my servant David, Thus saith the Lord of hosts, I took thee from the sheepcote, from following the sheep, to be ruler over my people, over Israel.

David's rise from shepherd to king was not his own accomplishment; it was God's doing. (The word *sheepcote* describes a building in which sheep were kept.)

9. And I was with thee whithersoever thou wentest, and have cut off all thine enemies out of thy sight, and have made thee a great name, like unto the name of the great men that are in the earth.

This adds some details to the general statement found in verse 8. The Lord had been *with* David every step of the way from following sheep to leading people; the Lord had given him victory over *all his enemies*; the Lord had made him as famous as any of *the great men that are in the earth*. [See question #3, page 80.]

COMMONERS OR ROYALTY?

In Scotland several years ago, a baby girl born to a poor family of tenant farmers was given the name "Princess." But five months after her birth, the Registrar General in Edinburgh told her parents that the British Crown possessed a sole right to use the name, and that the little girl's name would have to be changed.

The family appealed to Queen Elizabeth, who replied through an aide that she took no offense at the choice of name. However, the bureaucracy still denied the family the use of the name. Finally, when the girl was two and a half years old, the government relented and notified her grateful parents that Princess would be allowed to keep her name.

David also came from a humble background. God took this shepherd boy and called him to be "ruler over . . . Israel." In similar fashion, He took a nation of slaves and made them His "peculiar treasure" (Exodus 19:5). Today God can turn a person from the most humble of origins into a member of Heaven's royal family. He will do so for any who will turn to Him through Jesus, the royal Son of David. —C. R. B.

B. To Israel (vv. 10, 11a)

10. Moreover I will appoint a place for my people Israel, and will plant them, that they may dwell in a place of their own, and move no more; neither shall the children of wickedness afflict them any more, as beforetime.

This repeats the promise God had given long before, beginning with Abraham (Genesis 12:1; 17:8). He would give His *people* a land of their own; He would establish them securely in that land; He would protect them from their pagan neighbors. Of course, this abbreviated form of the promise did not cancel the conditions that were attached to it. The people of Israel were to have the promised land and its abundant blessings as long as they obeyed God. If they disobeyed, they would forfeit those blessings and would lose possession of the land. This is stated at length in Deuteronomy 28:15-68.

11a. And as since the time that I commanded judges to be over my people Israel, and have caused thee to rest from all thine enemies.

This is connected closely with the last part of verse 10. Perhaps the meaning can be stated thus: The *people* of *Israel* had been afflicted by pagan tribes both before and during the time when God had appointed *judges* in Israel, but now God had given David and his people *rest* from such affliction. This peaceful rest would continue if both the king and the people obeyed God's law.

III. Two Houses
(2 Samuel 7:11b-13, 16)

David was thinking about building for the Lord a house—a magnificent temple that would stand through centuries of time. The Lord was steering David away from that plan because He had a better plan. The Lord promised to build a house for David—not a building of stone and wood, but a household, a family, a dynasty that would rule forever!

A. David's House (v. 11b)

11b. Also the LORD telleth thee that he will make thee a house.

David should give up the idea of building a house for the Lord; instead, he should consider the very different kind of *house* that the Lord was going to build for him.

B. David's Son (v. 12)

12. And when thy days be fulfilled, and thou shalt sleep with thy fathers, I will set up thy seed after thee, which shall proceed out of thy bowels, and I will establish his kingdom.

When David's life on earth was over, his son would take his place as king, and God would *establish his kingdom* as He had David's. Thus David's house, or family, would continue to rule.

C. God's House (v. 13)

13. He shall build a house for my name, and I will stablish the throne of his kingdom for ever.

This verse makes it clear that God did not forbid the building of a temple, but He wanted it to be done by David's son. Another passage tells us the reason for this: David was a "man of war"—a warrior who had "shed blood" (1 Chronicles 28:2, 3). This is not to say that David's activity in those battles was wrong. God approved David's wars and gave him victory in them, but still He

---

Home Daily Bible Readings

Monday, Oct. 23—Nathan's Prophecy (2 Samuel 7:1-11)

Tuesday, Oct. 24—Nathan Reveals God's Word (1 Chronicles 17:1-10)

Wednesday, Oct. 25—God's Promise to David Through Nathan (2 Samuel 7:12-17)

Thursday, Oct. 26—God Responds to David Through Nathan (1 Chronicles 17:11-15)

Friday, Oct. 27—David's Prayer (2 Samuel 7:18-29)

Saturday, Oct. 28—David's Thanksgiving (1 Chronicles 17:16-27)

Sunday, Oct. 29—God's Promise to David Fulfilled (1 Kings 8:15-21)

preferred to have His temple built by Solomon, a man of peace. (The name Solomon means "peaceful.")

David himself was at peace when he considered building a temple: "The Lord had given him rest round about from all his enemies" (v. 1). David had subdued many nations around Israel (2 Samuel 8:1-14; 10:1-19; 12:26-31). Under his leadership, Israel reached great prominence as a nation, but not without a significant amount of fighting.

This helps us to see a practical reason for postponing the temple building until the reign of Solomon. Senior citizens in Europe and America can remember the troubled years of World War II. Hardly anything was built unless it was needed in the war effort. Most available material and manpower were directed to that cause. So it was during the years of David's wars, and for that reason the building of the temple was left for a man of peace to undertake during a time of peace. At that point, Israel's men could be released from any military duty, and Solomon could assemble an army of workers to help with the temple (1 Kings 5:13-16).

David accepted God's decision without complaint. Later he received plans for the temple from the Lord, and then passed them on to Solomon to use in carrying out the task (1 Chronicles 22:2-5; 28:11-19).

Then the Lord added, *I will stablish the throne of his kingdom for ever*, thus adding *for ever* to the promise of verse 12. Certainly Solomon would not last forever, but the throne of his kingdom would. Because of the sins of the people, there were times when that promise seemed uncertain. At one point the people of Israel were captives in Babylon, having no king of their own. Then they were ruled by the Persians and later by the Romans.

But "when the fulness of the time was come" (Galatians 4:4), Jesus was born. He was a son of David, but, more importantly, He was the Son of God. He rules a kingdom "not of this world" (John 18:36), "which shall never be destroyed: and . . . shall stand for ever" (Daniel 2:44). [See question #4, page 80.]

D. David's Kingdom (v. 16)

16. And thine house and thy kingdom shall be established for ever before thee: thy throne shall be established for ever.

David's little kingdom of Israel would one day culminate in the great eternal kingdom of Jesus Christ. David's descendants would rule over the land of Israel; David's descendant, Jesus, would rule forever over the eternal kingdom—the "Israel of God" (Galatians 6:16).

AN EVERLASTING EMPIRE

In 1968 Mohammed Reza Pahlavi (Mo-*ham*-id Rih-*zah Pah*-luh-vee), the Shah of Iran, proclaimed himself "King of Kings, Light of the Aryans." In 1971 he declared a celebration of the twenty-five hundredth anniversary of the Persian Empire. The festivities lasted four days and cost one hundred million dollars! The guest list included six hundred dignitaries from sixty-nine nations.

Only eight years later, the fabled empire and the reign of this "King of Kings" lay in ruins. Muslim fundamentalists overthrew the Shah in 1979 and installed their religious leader, Ayatollah Khomeini (Eye-uh-*toll*-uh Ko-*may*-nee), as the sole ruler of their nation. The Shah had fancied himself to be ruler of an empire that had begun with Cyrus the Great in the sixth century B.C. (although he would have been hard-pressed to prove that connection). At any rate, the "timeless empire" that he envisioned came crashing down, and the nation was thrown into chaos.

This has been the fate of most of the world's kingdoms. Regardless of the pretensions of their leaders, nations rise and then fall, and other governments supersede them. So the promise to David that his throne would be established *forever* was startling news indeed. The New Testament reveals to us that Jesus Christ was the Son of David who has established this everlasting empire—a spiritual kingdom that is not of this world. What a privilege is ours to be citizens of such a kingdom! —C. R. B.

Conclusion

This week we are thinking of "God's Covenant With David." In our time the word *covenant* is not used very much, except in religious contexts. It means an agreement, a contract. Usually a contract between two persons confers certain benefits on each and makes certain demands of each. The Bible records several contracts between God

And thine house and thy kingdom shall be established for ever before thee: thy throne shall be established for ever.

Today's visual illustrates verse 16 of the printed text. Discuss how Jesus is the ultimate fulfillment of this promise to David.

Visual for lesson 9

How to Say It

BABYLON. *Bab*-uh-lun.
CYRUS. *Sigh*-russ.
HIRAM. *High*-rum.
JEBUSITES. *Jeb*-yuh-sites.
PHILISTINES. Fuh-*liss*-teens or *Fill*-us-teens.
TYRE. Tire.

---

and man. God has a glorious record of keeping every contract; man has a dismal record of breaking every one. [See question #5, page 80.]

A. God's Covenants

God's covenant with Adam provided a beautiful garden home with abundant food. It required Adam to dress and keep the garden and to abstain from eating the fruit of one certain tree. Adam broke the covenant and lost his home in the garden.

God's covenant with Noah offered safety in a devastating flood and the assurance that there would never be such a flood again. Noah kept this covenant. He believed God, obeyed Him, and praised Him.

The covenant with Abraham required him to trust God, to leave home and family, and to journey to an unknown land. It promised a great nation of descendants who would have a permanent home in that unknown land. Abraham was one of the better human covenant keepers; however, his record was not flawless. (See Genesis 12:10-20; 16:1-12.)

The covenant with the people of Israel promised them a permanent home in that same land that had been promised to Abraham. It promised abundant harvests, healthy livestock, and prosperity. It promised divine protection from enemies. But it also required them to obey the law that God gave at Sinai. In past lessons we have seen how abysmally the people failed in keeping that law, and how terribly they suffered from the invasions of enemies when divine protection was withdrawn. We shall see still more of their covenant breaking in lessons to come.

Why did all of those ancient covenants fail to produce the desired results? God was not at fault: He has never failed to keep a covenant. Every one of those covenants was shattered by the sins of men. History verifies the words of Scripture: "All have sinned" (Romans 3:23). Our own experience verifies it as well.

What we need, then, is a covenant that can overcome sin—one by which sinners can be forgiven, come into God's kingdom, and enjoy the blessings He is longing to give. That is exactly what God promised through His prophet Jeremiah (Jeremiah 31:31-34). And that is exactly what God now offers through Jesus, the Son of David and the Son of God.

B. God's New Covenant

"The wages of sin is death" (Romans 6:23). Therefore all mankind was doomed to die, from Adam down to me. That doom was of man's own doing, but God was not content to have it so. "For God so loved the world, that he gave his only begotten Son, that whosoever believeth in him should not perish, but have everlasting life" (John 3:16).

To put it in simple terms, Jesus died in my place, in your place, and in the place of all the sinners of the world. So you and I and all the sinners of the world can escape the death we deserve and have everlasting life.

That does not mean that every sinner will automatically live forever. No one is saved from death against his will. Each person still can choose, and most people choose to die (Matthew 7:13, 14).

That seems absurd, doesn't it? Why would anyone choose to die? One reason is that the same covenant that offers everlasting life to us also makes some demands on us. If we want Jesus to be our Savior, we must also take Him as our Lord. In the everyday language of our time, we must make Him our boss, we must obey Him, we must do His will rather than our own. Some people balk at that.

What happens if we disobey God after we have accepted His covenant and promised to obey Him? That depends on our attitude. "If we confess our sins, he is faithful and just to forgive us our sins, and to cleanse us from all unrighteousness" (1 John 1:9). But if we arrogantly cling to our own way when we know it is contrary to God's way, "there remaineth no more sacrifice for sins, but a certain fearful looking for of judgment and fiery indignation, which shall devour the adversaries" (Hebrews 10:26, 27).

The choice is ours.

C. Prayer

Almighty God, we are grateful for Your grace. We were lost and helpless on the way of death until You found us, holding out Your New Covenant and offering to forgive our iniquities and to remember our sins no more. With full hearts we praise You, Father. With all our hearts we promise to walk in Your way, and with all our hearts we plead that You will forgive our failures. In Jesus' name, amen.

D. Thought to Remember

We can choose death—or life.

Learning by Doing

This page contains an alternate lesson plan emphasizing learning activities.
Classes desiring such student involvement will find these suggestions helpful.

Learning Goals

After this lesson students will be able to:

1. Recount the covenant that God made with David and the circumstances under which He made it.

2. State how this covenant is fulfilled in Jesus and in the covenant He has established.

3. Praise God for the blessings of grace given in the New Covenant.

Into the Lesson

Write on the chalkboard the word *contract*. State: "To begin this class session, I'd like to give you a minute and a half to brainstorm as many different types of *contracts* as you can." As suggested contracts are called out, write them down on the chalkboard to form a list. *(Purchase of house or car; loan at the bank; marriage; job contract; remodeling contract; selling of a bond; will.)* State: "We are all very familiar with contracts. Many of us have signed contracts before. Now I'd like for us to think about the various parts of a contract. As you think of the items that make up a contract, call them out and we'll list them on the board." *(Names; dates; time frames; signatures; promises or benefits; responsibilities or conditions; an agreement.)*

State: "A contract is a binding agreement between two or more parties. Normally it contains promises and responsibilities made and accepted by all the participants. One party promises to provide certain goods or services when the other party fulfills certain responsibilities. Our lesson today centers on a contract or covenant made by God as the party of the first part with David and Israel as the parties of the second part. Let's turn to 2 Samuel 7 to see what promises and responsibilities are included."

Into the Word

Ask a volunteer to read aloud 2 Samuel 7:1-13, 16. Ask the following questions.

1. What were the circumstances that led to God's covenant with David? *(It was a time of peace from David's enemies. David had built a palace for himself, but the ark of God was still in a tent. David wanted to build a house for the ark of God.)*

2. Why did Nathan initially encourage David to build a house for the Lord? *(God had been with David, delivering him from all his enemies.)*

3. Describe the transition that the Lord brought about in David's life. *(From following sheep to being the ruler of God's people, Israel.)*

State: "Now that we've understood a little of the background of God's covenant with David, let's focus on the promises that the Lord gave David in this covenant." For this next question, divide the class into groups of three. Give to each group a large sheet of blank newsprint from an easel pad, along with a marker. Ask, "What promises did the Lord give to David in this covenant?" Allow about seven minutes for the groups to locate the answer and to write it on the paper.

When each group is finished, ask a member of the group to stick the paper on the wall so all can see. *(Possible answers: provide a permanent dwelling for Israel free from wickedness and affliction, vv. 10, 11; establish David's house forever, vv. 11, 16; give David a son who would build the temple after David's death, vv. 12, 13; David's son's kingdom and throne would endure forever, v. 16.)* State: "David accepted these promises without complaint. They had an immediate, contemporary application through David's son Solomon. But they also spoke of an eternal kingdom, an eternal throne, a house that would last forever—a partial glimpse of the New Covenant that Jesus established."

Into Life

Read Luke 1:31-33 and ask, "How is God's covenant with David fulfilled in Jesus and the New Covenant?" *(Jesus is a Son of David; He inherits the throne of David; His kingdom is forever.)* Divide the class into three groups of equal size. Assign one of the following passages of Scripture to each group: Matthew 26:28; Romans 11:27; Hebrews 9:15. Ask each group to tell how its passage describes this New Covenant. Allow ten minutes for discussion; then ask for answers to be reported to the class. *(Jesus' blood sealed the New Covenant; He is its mediator; the key provision is the forgiveness of sins.)*

Read Hebrews 8:6-13 and ask this question: "What are the blessings of grace given in the New Covenant?" Write suggested answers on the chalkboard or on an overhead transparency sheet. *(Laws in their minds and on their hearts; all will know the Lord in this covenant; wickedness is forgiven; sins remembered no more.)*

Let's Talk It Over

The questions on this page are designed to encourage review of the lesson Scriptures and to promote discussion of the lesson by the class. The answers provided are only discussion starters. Let your class talk it over from there.

1. How is David's desire to build God a house a good example for us to follow—even though God rejected David's plan?

David was disturbed over the contrast between his own comfortable palace and the relatively meager shelter the ark enjoyed. According to 1 Kings 8:18, God was pleased with David's intention. He told David, "Thou didst well that it was in thine heart." It is clear that David did not view such a construction project as one that would enhance his own reputation. Instead, he truly desired to bring glory to God.

What about our intentions? Do we pursue God's glory with the same drive as we pursue financial security and other comforts of this life? How about the building in which we worship? Is it a monument to God's glory? How does its appearance compare with the houses of those who worship in it?

2. In giving David an affirmative answer, Nathan gave what he *assumed* would be God's answer to David's request. He was right that God was pleased with David's heart, but he was wrong about God's intention for the temple. What can we learn from Nathan's mistake?

We ought to learn to be careful about speaking for God. Some people today easily speak about what God wants and what God has told them, but anything outside a clear Biblical statement is colored by our own biases and understanding. We need to be careful about affirming God's sanction to our own plans.

We also learn that God can be pleased with us even when He closes doors to our plans. We must be careful about interpreting circumstances as God's sign of pleasure or displeasure. Remember, God was pleased with Job, too, but He allowed much calamity and hardship to befall him.

3. God reminded David of how far He had brought him, from the humble life of a shepherd to the throne of Israel. How worthwhile do you think it is to ponder occasionally how far God has brought us? Why?

God has brought some Christians from a life ravaged by alcoholism to one characterized by productive service to others. Some believers with musical talent once employed that talent in bars and nightclubs, but now they use it to lift fellow believers in worship to God. Other saints can testify that they were foul-mouthed and abusive, but they have learned to use their tongues to praise God and edify their fellow human beings. In these and countless other ways God has brought His people from wasted, selfish, purposeless lives into dynamic service for Him. How that should inspire us to praise each time we ponder His wise and powerful leading! How it should stir us to give back to God for His glory every mighty blessing He has laid on us!

4. God promised David an everlasting kingdom, and David was awed by the promise. (See vv. 18ff.) What promises similarly bring you to respond with awe of God's wonderful nature?

When we read through 2 Samuel 7:18-29, we are impressed with David's sense of amazement toward God's past blessings and the even more awesome blessings to come. Today we often speak rather glibly about eternal life and sometimes fail to ponder what a tremendous prospect that is. Of course, it is impossible for us to grasp fully the concept of eternity. Nevertheless, it is important that we frequently remind ourselves that earth's death-shadowed existence will give way to a glorious life of endless hopes and joys and wonders! Jesus Christ, the fulfillment of the promise to David, holds the key to our eternal hope as well!

5. Human beings falter in living up to their responsibilities according to God's covenants, but He has always been and always will be faithful. How does it help you to meditate on the fact of God's faithfulness?

"If we believe not, yet he abideth faithful: he cannot deny himself" (2 Timothy 2:13). We are painfully aware of our own fickleness and inconsistency. We try to remain faithful to God, but we must confess to occasions when our faith grows weak and our obedience is imperfect. But God never wavers in His faithfulness to His covenant promises; He "remains faithful forever" (Psalm 146:6, *New International Version*). It is tempting for us to assume, in our times of weakness, that God has somehow abandoned us, that His promises are no longer in effect. But by meditating on the many Biblical assurances of His faithfulness, we can prevail over such doubts.

David and Bathsheba

DEVOTIONAL READING: Numbers 15:30, 31.

BACKGROUND SCRIPTURE: 2 Samuel 11:1–12:25.

PRINTED TEXT: 2 Samuel 11:2-5, 14-18, 26, 27; 12:13-15.

2 Samuel 11:2-5, 14-18, 26, 27

2 And it came to pass in an eveningtide, that David arose from off his bed, and walked upon the roof of the king's house: and from the roof he saw a woman washing herself; and the woman was very beautiful to look upon.

3 And David sent and inquired after the woman. And one said, Is not this Bathsheba, the daughter of Eliam, the wife of Uriah the Hittite?

4 And David sent messengers, and took her; and she came in unto him, and he lay with her; for she was purified from her uncleanness: and she returned unto her house.

5 And the woman conceived, and sent and told David, and said, I am with child.

· · · · · · · · · · · ·

14 And it came to pass in the morning, that David wrote a letter to Joab, and sent it by the hand of Uriah.

15 And he wrote in the letter, saying, Set ye Uriah in the forefront of the hottest battle, and retire ye from him, that he may be smitten, and die.

16 And it came to pass, when Joab observed the city, that he assigned Uriah unto a place where he knew that valiant men were.

17 And the men of the city went out, and fought with Joab: and there fell some of the people of the servants of David; and Uriah the Hittite died also.

18 Then Joab sent and told David all the things concerning the war.

· · · · · · · · · · ·

26 And when the wife of Uriah heard that Uriah her husband was dead, she mourned for her husband.

27 And when the mourning was past, David sent and fetched her to his house, and she became his wife, and bare him a son. But the thing that David had done displeased the LORD.

2 Samuel 12:13-15

13 And David said unto Nathan, I have sinned against the LORD. And Nathan said unto David, The LORD also hath put away thy sin; thou shalt not die.

14 Howbeit, because by this deed thou hast given great occasion to the enemies of the LORD to blaspheme, the child also that is born unto thee shall surely die.

15 And Nathan departed unto his house. And the LORD struck the child that Uriah's wife bare unto David, and it was very sick.

Nov 5

GOLDEN TEXT: Wherefore hast thou despised the commandment of the LORD, to do evil in his sight?—2 Samuel 12:9.

Lesson Aims

After participating in this lesson, each student will be able to:

1. Give the details of David's adultery and cover-up, as well as the terrible consequences that followed.

2. Explain the lessons that this account teaches us about the nature of temptation and the consequences of sin.

3. Suggest a specific step that he or she can take to resist a particular temptation.

Lesson Outline

INTRODUCTION
   A. Learning the Hard Way
   B. Lesson Background
 I. ADULTERY (2 Samuel 11:2-5)
   A. Temptation (v. 2)
   B. Investigation (v. 3)
   C. Sin (v. 4)
      Lust and Power
   D. Consequence (v. 5)
 II. MURDER (2 Samuel 11:14-18, 26, 27)
   A. Planned (vv. 14, 15)
   B. Accomplished (vv. 16, 17)
   C. Reported (v. 18)
      Guilty or Not?
   D. Hidden (vv. 26, 27)
III. PARDON AND PUNISHMENT (2 Samuel 12:13-15)
   A. Confession and Pardon (v. 13)
   B. Punishment Promised (v. 14)
   C. Punishment Given (v. 15)
CONCLUSION
   A. Wrong Leads to Wrong
   B. Wrong Is Hard to Hide
   C. Wrong Has Long-term Results
   D. Prayer
   E. Thought to Remember

Introduction

A. Learning the Hard Way

Summer vacation was in full swing. Sammy, Joe, and Mike were fishing in a little creek under tall sycamore trees, but the fish showed no interest in their worms. The boys were bored and ready for some other way to pass the time.

Then the Smoot boys came down the road. They were men, really, but everyone called them boys. On horseback, they were driving a small herd of cattle to the north range. Suddenly the three fishermen thought of something more exciting to do. They knew where the Smoot watermelon patch was, screened from the road by a patch of tall corn. Quickly they brought a big melon to the shade of a tree by the road. Opening it with a pocket knife, they scooped out the insides with grimy fingers until they were "full up to the ears," as Sammy put it. Then they stretched out on the ground for a nap.

Suddenly they were roused by the sound of hooves. The Smoot boys were coming back. The kids started to hurry back to the creek, but the riders pricked their horses into a gallop. "Split up!" yelled Sammy. "They can't catch us all."

The three ran in three different directions, but two were quickly overtaken. Mounted behind an older rider, each was taken to his home, where his father found a big switch and used it. (This was many years ago, when a switch was the accepted way of teaching a boy not to steal.)

Meanwhile, Sammy had escaped and headed straight for home, but he was nervous. He had no appetite for supper. Mom put a hand on his forehead to see if he had a fever. All night Sammy was restless. In the morning he only picked at his breakfast. Mom talked about taking him to town to see the doctor. At that point, Sammy burst into tears and sobbed out the story of the stolen watermelon. Dad found a big switch. After a painful whipping, Sammy felt better. At noon he was ready for a hearty meal.

Did an act of secret wrongdoing ever make you miserable? Did you feel better after the wrong became known? David had such an experience. It was so memorable that he wrote an account of it in one of his songs (Psalm 51). Now, some three thousand years later, his sin and his song are before us still.

B. Lesson Background

After David became king of all Israel, the Philistines assembled their forces in order to challenge his rule. David soundly defeated them (2 Samuel 5:17-25). Later victories over enemy nations are recorded in 2 Samuel 8:1-14. Then the Ammonites (to the east of Israel) enlisted the help of Syrians from the north to fight against Israel, but David's forces routed both Ammonites and Syrians until the Syrians were afraid to help the Ammonites any more (2 Samuel 10).

The war with the Ammonites was put on hold through the winter months, but resumed in the spring. This time David stayed in Jerusalem, putting Joab in command of the army. Again

Joab defeated the Ammonites, who took refuge in their chief city, Rabbah, where Joab initiated a siege (2 Samuel 11:1).

I. Adultery
(2 Samuel 11:2-5)

During this time David lived at ease in his palace in Jerusalem. It is certainly worth observing that in the past David had gone to battle with his men, as noted in the previous section. Now he was relaxing in Jerusalem "at the time when kings go forth to battle" (2 Samuel 11:1). Had David been where he was supposed to be, and had he been doing what he was supposed to be doing, perhaps the following sorry incident never would have occurred.

A. Temptation (v. 2)

2. And it came to pass in an eveningtide, that David arose from off his bed, and walked upon the roof of the king's house: and from the roof he saw a woman washing herself; and the woman was very beautiful to look upon.

Probably in the language of today we would say *afternoon* rather than *eveningtide*. Perhaps King David had been enjoying a midday nap on the *roof* of his palace. In the crowded city of Jerusalem, every house had a flat roof that could be used as we use a porch or patio—as a pleasant place to relax in the open air. When David *arose* from his nap and *walked* across the roof, he caught sight of a *beautiful* neighbor taking her bath. She may have been in an enclosed courtyard of the house where she lived, with walls around her but no roof overhead. David found the sight very attractive. [See question #1, page 88.]

B. Investigation (v. 3)

3. And David sent and inquired after the woman. And one said, Is not this Bathsheba, the daughter of Eliam, the wife of Uriah the Hittite?

Who was that lovely lady next door? David sent someone to find out. The investigator came back with the lady's name, her father's name, and her husband's name. Perhaps he also brought the information that her husband was miles away east of the Jordan, serving in the army that was besieging Rabbah.

C. Sin (v. 4)

4. And David sent messengers, and took her; and she came in unto him, and he lay with her; for she was purified from her uncleanness: and she returned unto her house.

This time *David sent* more than one messenger. If the woman seemed reluctant to come, they could bring her anyway. The text gives no hints

about her willingness or reluctance. Some students suppose that she was a virtuous woman who objected vigorously, though she was too dignified to be dragged kicking and screaming to the king. Others believe that she staged her bath with the deliberate purpose of seducing the king. Either explanation is mere speculation, however. The text focuses on David, and as for him, the record is clear. While for most of his life he did what was right in God's eyes, what he did on this occasion was wrong. "The thing that David had done displeased the Lord" (v. 27).

We are told that before committing this act, Bathsheba *was purified from her uncleanness*. This indicates that she had just become ceremonially clean, according to the law of Moses, following the time of uncleanness associated with the menstrual cycle (Leviticus 15:19-30). This also makes it clear that she was not already pregnant by Uriah when David *lay with her*.

LUST AND POWER

Former U. S. Secretary of State Henry Kissinger was once asked how a man of his rather plain appearance could date so many beautiful women. He replied, "Power is the ultimate aphrodisiac." Power seems to make many men feel as if they are invulnerable, and, in keeping with Kissinger's observation, many women seem to be drawn to men of power like moths to a flame. When those two forces come together, sin is frequently the result.

So it was with David. He reigned as king of Israel during a time when rulers could command absolute obedience from their subjects. We should not be surprised that he was tempted to use his position of power to satisfy his own lusts or that Bathsheba—if she acted willingly—responded to his invitation.

More important to us is how *we* conduct ourselves when opportunity and desire coincide. God still expects us—whether king or commoner—to exercise control over both our position and our passion. —C. R. B.

How to Say It

ABSALOM. *Ab*-suh-lum.
AMMONITES. *Am*-un-ites.
BATHSHEBA. Bath-*she*-buh.
ELIAM. Ih-*lye*-am.
HITTITE. *Hit*-ite.
JOAB. *Jo*-ab.
PHILISTINES. Fuh-*liss*-teens or *Fill*-us-teens.
RABBAH. *Rab*-buh.
SYRIANS. *Sear*-ee-uns.
URIAH. You-*rye*-uh.

D. Consequence (v. 5)

5. And the woman conceived, and sent and told David, and said, I am with child.

Bad news! Bathsheba was pregnant. Her adultery could not be denied. According to the law of Moses, both she and David should be put to death for this act (Leviticus 20:10). She simply relayed the news to the king without further comment. Now the matter was his to deal with. What would he do?

II. Murder
(2 Samuel 11:14-18, 26, 27)

David's first thought was to make it appear that Bathsheba's baby belonged to her husband, Uriah. So he sent for Uriah and encouraged him to go home to his wife. If he spent a night with her, everyone would assume that he was the father of Bathsheba's child. [See question #2, page 88.]

But Uriah was a loyal soldier. He thought it was not right for him to enjoy a night with his wife while his comrades were risking their lives on the field of battle. He spent two nights with David's men in Jerusalem, then returned to the siege (2 Samuel 11:6-13). So David was still left with his dilemma.

A. Planned (vv. 14, 15)

14. And it came to pass in the morning, that David wrote a letter to Joab, and sent it by the hand of Uriah.

This was the *morning* after Uriah's second night with the king's men. He was now going back to take his place with the troops besieging Rabbah. David gave him *a letter* to carry to *Joab*, commander of those troops.

15. And he wrote in the letter, saying, Set ye Uriah in the forefront of the hottest battle, and retire ye from him, that he may be smitten, and die.

It was murder that David ordered—murder disguised to look like death in *battle*, but still murder. Both David and his commander Joab were battle-hardened veterans. The loss of a few soldiers seemed to them a small thing. It happened in every conflict; it was the price of victory. Now it was to be the price of hiding the king's adultery. *Uriah,* who had shown such devotion to the king, was to be assigned to a place of intense fighting and then abandoned during the fighting to increase the likelihood of his death.

B. Accomplished (vv. 16, 17)

16. And it came to pass, when Joab observed the city, that he assigned Uriah unto a place where he knew that valiant men were.

Joab had *observed the city* enough to know that *valiant men* were posted in a certain place, probably to guard an important gate leading into the city. Israel's troops were all around the city so that no one could go out or come in; but they were too far away to be reached by arrows from the wall. Now Joab sent *Uriah* and some other men nearer the wall at the point where those valiant men were on guard. We are not told what the mission of the little group was supposed to be. Possibly they were to draw defenders out from the city so that the other troops could swarm in and overpower them.

17. And the men of the city went out, and fought with Joab: and there fell some of the people of the servants of David; and Uriah the Hittite died also.

Those valiant men whom Joab knew about did venture out to fight with the small detachment of his troops that had approached the wall. During the fighting some men of Israel were killed, and *Uriah* was one of them. [See question #3, page 88.]

C. Reported (v. 18)

18. Then Joab sent and told David all the things concerning the war.

Joab promptly *sent* a report *concerning the war* to David. He thought the king would be angry when he learned that some men had been killed because they had recklessly ventured near the wall; but he knew what would soothe that anger. The messenger must report, "Thy servant Uriah the Hittite is dead also." That, after all, was the king's objective. So King David sent back to Joab a message of assurance, telling him not to feel badly about the loss (vv. 19-25).

GUILTY OR NOT?

Marilyn Sheppard was a thirty-one-year-old mother and four months pregnant when she was beaten to death in July of 1954. In one of the most infamous murder cases of the twentieth century, her husband, Sam, was convicted of the murder. During the trial, the prosecution used prejudicial publicity about an earlier, extramarital affair in which the young doctor had been involved.

Ten years later, Sheppard was released from prison when a Federal District Court reversed the verdict. The federal judge called the first trial a "carnival" where "bedlam reigned." Some forty years after his wife was murdered, DNA tests completely exonerated Sam Sheppard. The so-called "love triangle" of which he was part apparently had nothing to do with the murder, even though the prosecution and news media placed considerable emphasis on the matter.

In David's situation, his extramarital affair was directly involved in the death of Uriah. Although technically Uriah was not "murdered," an honest appraisal shows that the results were the same as if David had bludgeoned Uriah to death himself. David had no way to rationalize or excuse what he had done, nor did he need to "appeal." He was simply guilty.

Sometimes we suffer from vicious rumors and the false opinions of others. But more often than not our troubles come because, like David, we have violated God's standard of righteousness.

—C. R. B.

D. Hidden (vv. 26, 27)

26. And when the wife of Uriah heard that Uriah her husband was dead, she mourned for her husband.

Bathsheba's mourning could not have been very long (we may wonder how sincere it was), but she did go through the motions.

27. And when the mourning was past, David sent and fetched her to his house, and she became his wife, and bare him a son. But the thing that David had done displeased the LORD.

Thus David's scheme seemed to have succeeded for the time being: he had a beautiful *wife* to add to those he already had, and soon she *bare him a son.*

It seems that Bathsheba became David's favorite wife. In his old age he bequeathed his kingdom to one of her sons (not the one whose birth is recorded here). Did he favor her because she really was the true love of his life? Or did he feel obligated to favor her because he had killed her husband? We do not know.

But the thing that David had done displeased the Lord. Thus David's scheme yielded a greater harvest of grief than of joy. We shall see a bit of that before we finish this lesson. Besides that, David himself was displeased with what he had done. We shall see a bit of that as well.

III. Pardon and Punishment (2 Samuel 12:13-15)

The first part of chapter 12 tells us that the Lord sent Nathan the prophet to rebuke David's sin. The prophet came with a parable. He told of a rich man who had plenty of lambs in his flock, but stole the one pet lamb of a poor man to prepare for dinner. When David angrily declared that such a man ought to be put to death, Nathan turned that judgment back on the king himself: "Thou art the man!" David had wives enough of his own, yet he had stolen the one wife of poor Uriah. To make matters worse, he had murdered Uriah himself.

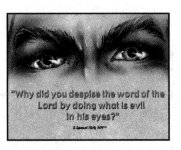

Visual for lesson 10

"Why did you despise the word of the Lord by doing what is evil in his eyes?"

Today's visual cites 2 Samuel 12:9. This verse reminds us that the Lord sees our sin, even as He saw David's, no matter how well we cover it up.

King though he was, David would not escape punishment. From his own family evil would rise against him, and his own wives would be stolen (2 Samuel 12:1-12). That startling condemnation brought forth David's confession that we see in the last section of our text.

A. Confession and Pardon (v. 13)

13. And David said unto Nathan, I have sinned against the LORD. And Nathan said unto David, The LORD also hath put away thy sin; thou shalt not die.

An evil king might have had Nathan beheaded, but David was a good king who had done an evil deed. When the fact of David's sin was plainly set before him, he humbly confessed it. Nathan then gave the welcome news: *The Lord also hath put away thy sin.* What that meant is explained in the next statement: *Thou shalt not die;* that is, David was not to be put to death immediately, as he himself had said he ought to be (v. 5). [See question #4, page 88.]

B. Punishment Promised (v. 14)

14. Howbeit, because by this deed thou hast given great occasion to the enemies of the LORD to blaspheme, the child also that is born unto thee shall surely die.

God's forgiveness does not remove all the evil consequences of an evil deed. David would not die immediately, but *the child* of his adultery would. The reason for this is given: *because by this deed thou hast given great occasion to the enemies of the Lord to blaspheme.* David had tried to hide his sin, but in time it would become known. The Lord's people would grieve (as we do upon reading of this incident) because the good king had done such a terrible deed. But the Lord's enemies would sneer. They would say, "What kind of a god is your God, that he blesses a king who does such a wicked thing?" However, when the child died, everyone would realize that the Lord was not blessing David's adultery. Thus the blasphemy of the enemies would be stopped.

C. Punishment Given (v. 15)

15. And Nathan departed unto his house. And the LORD struck the child that Uriah's wife bare unto David, and it was very sick.

So ends our printed text, but verse 18 adds that *the child* died after a week of sickness. Of course, that was not the end of David's punishment. The dire prediction of verses 11 and 12 remained to be fulfilled. [See question #5, page 88.]

Conclusion

The record of David's sin comes to us from centuries past, but it bristles with warnings for the present. Let's note some of them.

A. Wrong Leads to Wrong

David committed adultery, and then tried to hide his guilt by committing murder. That was some three thousand years ago, but only a few years ago a robber ran into the woods with a policeman in hot pursuit. The robber stopped behind a big tree until the pursuer came close, then shot him at point-blank range.

Very few of us have committed murder, but how many of us have done some trivial wrong and then lied about it? Whatever happened to the honest practice of admitting your wrong and taking the consequences?

B. Wrong Is Hard to Hide

Perhaps you have heard the saying, "Murder will out." It may not prove to be true in every case; however, on the day these lines were written, authorities in our area announced the solution of a murder committed eighteen years ago.

Home Daily Bible Readings

Monday, Oct. 30—David and Bathsheba's Affair (2 Samuel 11:1-5)
Tuesday, Oct. 31—David's Plot (2 Samuel 11:6-13)
Wednesday, Nov. 1—Uriah's Murder (2 Samuel 11:14-27)
Thursday, Nov. 2—The Prophet Nathan's Story (2 Samuel 12:1-6)
Friday, Nov. 3—The Judgment on David (2 Samuel 12:7-15)
Saturday, Nov. 4—Death of One Son, Birth of Another (2 Samuel 12:16-25)
Sunday, Nov. 5—Atonement for Sins (Numbers 15:27-31)

The messengers who took Bathsheba to David must at least have suspected his adultery. Joab knew about Uriah's murder, and perhaps some other soldiers did as well. Surely someone would talk, and the wrongs of the king would become so widely known that they would give the Lord's enemies an excuse to sneer both at David and at the Lord. Isn't it better to admit your wrongdoing than to have it exposed by others? Of course, it is better still not to do wrong.

"Be sure your sin will find you out." That is an oft-quoted saying from God's Word (Numbers 32:23). If we do manage to take some dark secrets with us to our graves, "we must all appear before the judgment seat of Christ" (2 Corinthians 5:10).

C. Wrong Has Long-term Results

When David was guilty of adultery, how could he be stern with a son who raped his half-sister (2 Samuel 13:1-19)? When he failed to punish that crime, how could he be stern with the girl's full brother when he killed the rapist (2 Samuel 13:20-29)? The killer did flee to a foreign land for a while (2 Samuel 13:37-39), but then was received back into the family (2 Samuel 14).

That killer was Absalom, a wild and willful young man who loved to be the center of royal attention (2 Samuel 15:1). He wanted to be king. It seems that he had a charming personality and no regard for truth or right. Secretly he won the hearts of many people and turned them against the king. When he thought he had followers enough, he led them in armed revolt, and David had to flee from Jerusalem (2 Samuel 15–17).

But David was still masterful in warfare. Though driven from his capital, he marshaled his loyal troops for a counterattack. The revolt was crushed. Twenty thousand men were killed, and Absalom was among them. Victory was complete, but the death of Absalom made David's triumph hollow (2 Samuel 18).

Thus Nathan's words in 2 Samuel 12:10-12 began to be fulfilled—and there was more to come. How many times David must have wished he had never seen that woman taking a bath!

D. Prayer

Thank You, Father, for the sobering lesson we have learned today. How often a wrong that seems trivial leads to another wrong, and thus wrong follows wrong until the throng of wrongs yields disaster! Thank You for the Holy Bible that shows us the right way. May we have clear eyes to see that way and stout hearts to follow it. In Jesus' name. Amen.

E. Thought to Remember

Do right.

Learning by Doing

This page contains an alternate lesson plan emphasizing learning activities.
Classes desiring such student involvement will find these suggestions helpful.

Learning Goals

After this lesson students should be able to:

1. Give the details of David's adultery and cover-up, as well as the terrible consequences that followed.

2. Explain the lessons that this account teaches us about the nature of temptation and the consequences of sin.

3. Suggest a specific step that he or she can take to resist a particular temptation.

Into the Lesson

Secure a video tape of the popular Disney film *Pinocchio*. Play a segment of the tape to begin your class session. Begin at the point where Pinocchio is sent to school. Show Pinocchio's meeting with the fox "Honest John" and his sidekick. See how they lure Pinocchio off the right path and into "show business." Stop the tape at the point where Jiminy Cricket sees Pinocchio perform and decides the puppet has done all right for himself.

Discuss how we are all tempted in similar ways. We intend to do right, but something or someone distracts us. We may even think we have done all right—for a while. Then turn the tape on again. Play it until Pinocchio is locked into a cage by his new owner. Point out that sin eventually shows itself to be a trap or prison.

Say, "In our lesson today we will consider the actions of one whom God considered exceptional but who gave in to temptation and committed a grievous sin. From this tragic chapter in David's life we will learn how we can seek righteousness and be careful in our actions and thoughts."

Into the Word

Ask a volunteer to read aloud 2 Samuel 11:2-5. Write the words *Sight, Search, Summons,* and *Surrender* on the chalkboard. Discuss how David fell into temptation and how there were deliberate steps taken. *Sight:* Do you think David just happened to be at that place at that time? Why or why not? *Search:* While "sight" may have been an accident, David did not stop the situation there. *Summons:* David found out the woman was someone's wife, but he sent for her anyway. *Surrender:* David surrendered to his basest instincts and committed adultery, resulting in Bathsheba's pregnancy. How might the story have been different had Bathsheba not conceived? Discuss, "At what point did 'temptation' become 'sin'?"

Summarize the events of 2 Samuel 11:6-13. Uriah, Bathsheba's husband, became an innocent victim in the next set of steps. Ask a volunteer to read aloud 2 Samuel 11:14-18, 26, 27; then give a brief lecture, noting the following three points. *Deception:* Discuss David's plan to set Uriah up to be killed. *Description:* Discuss Joab's report. Note the involvement of other innocent parties. *Displeasure of God:* God does not condone sin—even from favorite children. Note that not much is given along the way concerning God's displeasure—just a short statement. However, David's actions resulted in more grief than joy.

Finally David woke up. Summarize the events of 2 Samuel 12:1-12; then ask a third volunteer to read aloud 2 Samuel 12:13-15. Discuss the following steps in the conclusion of this situation. *Contrition:* Before confession was made, there had to be a realization that wrong had been done. With this realization David felt remorse. *Consequences:* Each sin has its consequence(s). In this case the son conceived would die. Discuss the severity of this consequence.

Into Life

Remind the students that David was a good person, but he was not perfect. Discuss how we may be like David or different from him.

Ask, "How does modern culture provide for the 'sight' step in various forms and various media?" When confronted with tempting sights or other tempting situations, we may react in different ways. Discuss how we exercise our will compared to the pull or influence of Satan.

Ask the students to list ideas that can help them to avoid temptation and sin. These might include the following:

1. Be more discerning in what we watch or read. Remember the little song that says, "Be careful little eyes what you see. . . ."

2. Be aware of seemingly innocent circumstances that lead to more serious consequences.

3. Pray for God's constant care.

4. Develop a habit of thinking through our actions to their conclusions.

5. Develop associations to help us avoid temptations.

In conclusion, urge the students to give careful thought to their actions, realizing that there are consequences to everything we do, and to resolve to apply God's guidance.

Let's Talk It Over

The questions on this page are designed to encourage review of the lesson Scriptures and to promote discussion of the lesson by the class. The answers provided are only discussion starters. Let your class talk it over from there.

1. The sight of Bathsheba either undressed or nearly so was the beginning of David's problems. Today nudity or scanty attire is common in our society. How can Christians avoid the potential temptations to lust and adultery?

Jesus spoke about casting away a lustful eye (Matthew 5:27-29), a vivid way of saying that we need to take drastic action against whatever could lead us into lust and adultery. Some Bible teachers believe that Christians should not watch television or attend movies. Other teachers believe these are permissible if they are used with care. Certainly there is much in those media that can excite to temptation. Similar observations could be made in regard to reading material and popular music. We are responsible for how we deal with the potential dangers in these and other areas. How drastic are we willing to be?

2. David hoped to make Bathsheba's pregnancy appear legitimate by calling Uriah home to spend a night or two with his wife. What are some devices people use today to cover up sin?

We could say that David tried to manipulate Uriah. That is certainly a tactic used often today. Politicians, businessmen, and ordinary people attempt to escape blame for wrongdoing by making other people appear responsible. Of course, outright lying is another tactic. It is frightening to see how even prominent, successful people do not hesitate to resort to lying, if it is to their advantage. Another popular tactic is to counterattack the person or group that has brought one's sins to light—questioning their honesty, their sanity, or their motives.

3. The record of David's wrongdoing illustrates how one sin leads to another. How can we guard against this problem in our own lives?

Perhaps David thought, "I have already sinned, so why should it make any difference if I sin again by arranging Uriah's death?" Whether or not David thought that way, such a statement does reflect the mind-set of many people today. But it is just that kind of thinking we must resist if we would keep our sin from escalating.

David did not suffer any immediate problems after his sin with Bathsheba, and that may have convinced him that he could also get away with murder. Again this is wrong thinking. The only way to keep sin from escalating is to stop. When we realize we have sinned, we must turn away, as did Peter when he "went out, and wept bitterly" (Matthew 26:75). When we realize that we have sinned, we must immediately confess our sin and claim the promise of 1 John 1:9.

4. David told Nathan, "I have sinned against the Lord." He made the same confession in the penitential prayer found in Psalm 51: "Against thee, thee only, have I sinned, and done this evil in thy sight" (v. 4). We may be inclined to object, "But he sinned against Bathsheba; he certainly sinned against Uriah; and as king he sinned against the people who entrusted that responsibility to him." Why is it important to see David's sin as "against the Lord"?

The Lord had commanded, "Thou shalt not covet thy neighbor's wife." But David coveted Uriah's wife. The Lord had commanded, "Thou shalt not commit adultery." But David committed adultery with Bathsheba. The Lord had commanded, "Thou shalt not kill [or murder]." But David murdered Uriah. Our sins frequently bring hurt to other human beings, but they are first of all violations of God's commands and sins against Him. Moreover, it is our sins against our holy God for which we will ultimately be held accountable, and it is for those sins that Jesus died!

5. God forgave David's sins, and yet the king would still suffer the consequences of those sins. What are some examples of the way this can happen today?

The person who abuses his body with alcohol and drugs can certainly obtain forgiveness for such a sin. But his physical health is likely to be impaired for a long time after he has broken the bad habit. The young woman who becomes pregnant out of wedlock can gain God's cleansing for the sin. But she may be faced with the difficult task of rearing her child alone. The habitual liar who forsakes his sin and receives God's forgiveness for it will probably still have to deal with distrust and suspicion on the part of people whom his lies have affected. The individual who destroys another person's property can seek and find both divine and human mercy, but he must nevertheless invest time and money in repairing the damage.

Solomon Succeeds David

DEVOTIONAL READING: Psalm 119:10-19.

BACKGROUND SCRIPTURE: 1 Kings 2:1-4; 3:1-15; 1 Chronicles 29:22-25; 2 Chronicles 1:1-13.

PRINTED TEXT: 1 Kings 2:1-4; 3:3-10.

1 Kings 2:1-4

1 Now the days of David drew nigh that he should die; and he charged Solomon his son, saying,

2 I go the way of all the earth: be thou strong therefore, and show thyself a man;

3 And keep the charge of the LORD thy God, to walk in his ways, to keep his statutes, and his commandments, and his judgments, and his testimonies, as it is written in the law of Moses, that thou mayest prosper in all that thou doest, and whithersoever thou turnest thyself:

4 That the LORD may continue his word which he spake concerning me, saying, If thy children take heed to their way, to walk before me in truth with all their heart and with all their soul, there shall not fail thee (said he) a man on the throne of Israel.

1 Kings 3:3-10

3 And Solomon loved the LORD, walking in the statutes of David his father: only he sacrificed and burnt incense in high places.

4 And the king went to Gibeon to sacrifice there; for that was the great high place: a thousand burnt offerings did Solomon offer upon that altar.

5 In Gibeon the LORD appeared to Solomon in a dream by night: and God said, Ask what I shall give thee.

6 And Solomon said, Thou hast showed unto thy servant David my father great mercy, according as he walked before thee in truth, and in righteousness, and in uprightness of heart with thee; and thou hast kept for him this great kindness, that thou hast given him a son to sit on his throne, as it is this day.

7 And now, O LORD my God, thou hast made thy servant king instead of David my father: and I am but a little child: I know not how to go out or come in.

8 And thy servant is in the midst of thy people which thou hast chosen, a great people, that cannot be numbered nor counted for multitude.

9 Give therefore thy servant an understanding heart to judge thy people, that I may discern between good and bad: for who is able to judge this thy so great a people?

10 And the speech pleased the Lord, that Solomon had asked this thing.

GOLDEN TEXT: Give therefore thy servant an understanding heart to judge thy people, that I may discern between good and bad.—1 Kings 3:9.

Rulers of Israel
Unit 3: David and Solomon
(Lessons 10-13)

Lesson Aims

After participating in this lesson, each student will be able to:

1. Tell about David's final counsel to Solomon and of Solomon's discerning request of the Lord.

2. Explain why God's wisdom is needed regardless of one's stage in life.

3. Make a commitment to pray daily for wisdom to live a life that honors the Lord.

Lesson Outline

INTRODUCTION
  A. Israel's New King
  B. Lesson Background
 I. ADVICE FOR A KING (1 Kings 2:1-4)
  A. Be Strong (vv. 1, 2)
  B. Obey God (v. 3)
  C. Think of the Future (v. 4)
      Good Advice
 II. SOLOMON'S DEVOTION (1 Kings 3:3, 4)
  A. Loving Obedience (v. 3)
  B. Generous Offerings (v. 4)
III. GOD'S GIFT TO SOLOMON (1 Kings 3:5-10)
  A. Unique Opportunity (v. 5)
  B. Past Gifts Acknowledged (v. 6)
  C. Solomon's Small Ability (v. 7)
  D. Solomon's Big Task (v. 8)
  E. Solomon's Request (v. 9)
      The Right Kind of Heart
  F. The Lord's Pleasure (v. 10)
CONCLUSION
  A. Unselfishness
  B. Obedience
  C. Keeping On
  D. Prayer
  E. Thought to Remember

Introduction

"The king is dead. Long live the king." When I first noticed that expression in my reading, it seemed silly. If the king was dead, he could not live at all. But Dad explained that this was an actual saying from history.

In a country that has a king, said Dad, almost everyone knows who the next king will be. Usually he is the oldest son of the present king. They call him the crown prince. Some time after a

king dies, a ceremony takes place during which the crown prince receives the crown; but in reality he is king as soon as his predecessor dies. When a herald goes out to announce the death of the king, he also shouts good wishes to the new king: "The [old] king is dead. Long live the [new] king."

A. Israel's New King

In the early years of Israel's experience with kings, the transition from king to king was not so smooth. The first king was Saul. After he died in battle, the general of his army attempted to make Saul's son Ish-bosheth the next king. But the tribe of Judah made David their king, and war ensued between Judah and the other tribes. Not until seven and a half years later, when Ish-bosheth and his general were dead, did David become king of all Israel (2 Samuel 5:5).

It appears that at some point during his reign, David's desire for his son Solomon to succeed him became known; however, not everyone was pleased with that choice. An older son, Absalom, gathered followers enough to stage a powerful revolt in an attempt to make himself king. But the revolt failed, and Absalom died during the conflict (2 Samuel 15—18).

Then a man named Sheba led another revolt, but he failed to gather enough followers to start a war. When Joab led his troops out to capture him, he took refuge in a walled city. Far from providing a refuge for him, the people of the city cut off his head and threw it over the wall to Joab (2 Samuel 20:1-22).

B. Lesson Background

When David was feeble with age, there was yet another attempt to take the throne by force. It was led by Adonijah, another son older than Solomon. He even enlisted the help of Joab, long-time general of David's army. They staged a celebration and announced that Adonijah was king. But David, though old, was not too feeble to respond to this challenge. Before Adonijah's celebration was over, David's supporters staged a similar celebration and announced that Solomon was king. Adonijah's supporters then deserted him. (Perhaps they remembered what had happened to Absalom's revolt!) So Adonijah's effort failed, and Solomon became king while David was still living (1 Kings 1:5-53).

I. Advice for a King
(1 Kings 2:1-4)

We are not told how old Solomon was when he became king. David called him "young and tender" (1 Chronicles 22:5). He called himself "a

unexpericed

little child" (1 Kings 3:7). Some Bible students suggest that he was not more than twenty, and may have been younger. But Solomon was not a "spoiled brat" like Adonijah, who had always been allowed to do as he pleased (1 Kings 1:5, 6). Solomon himself tells of how he had been taught to follow the path of wisdom by his father David (Proverbs 4:3-9). Our text begins with some of David's final instructions to Solomon.

A. Be Strong (vv. 1, 2)

1. Now the days of David drew nigh that he should die; and he charged Solomon his son, saying.

David's body was weakened by age (1 Kings 1:1), but his mind was alert, well informed, and capable of responding to a challenge, as Adonijah learned when he tried to take over the government (1 Kings 1:5-53). After officially making Solomon king, David realized that he would not live much longer. He therefore gave Solomon some final words of advice.

2. I go the way of all the earth: be thou strong therefore, and show thyself a man.

Older opponents of young Solomon might look on him as a mere boy; but he must *be strong* and *show* himself *a man*, taking the responsibility of government and ruling well. David had foiled Adonijah's attempt to seize the throne, but Solomon would have to deal with his continued plotting (1 Kings 2:13-25).

Solomon would also have to deal with Joab. This man, who was David's nephew, had long been a loyal and capable general of Israel's army; but he had killed Absalom in open defiance of David's order (2 Samuel 18:5, 9-15). He had murdered two capable military men who were his rivals for the position of commander (2 Samuel 3:22-27; 20:4-10). He had supported Adonijah, thus giving Solomon reason to question his loyalty. It was time for him to pay for his crimes (1 Kings 2:5, 6, 28-34). [See question #1, page 96.]

B. Obey God (v. 3)

3. And keep the charge of the LORD thy God, to walk in his ways, to keep his statutes, and his commandments, and his judgments, and his testimonies, as it is written in the law of Moses, that thou mayest prosper in all that thou doest, and whithersoever thou turnest thyself.

The first responsibility of a strong king must be to obey the Lord, who is far stronger and wiser. We need not pause to look for fine distinctions among the words *statutes, commandments, judgments,* and *testimonies.* All of these are *written in the law of Moses,* and all of that law must be obeyed. Only by obeying it faithfully could the king hope to *prosper* in everything he did.

C. Think of the Future (v. 4)

4. That the Lord may continue his word which he spake concerning me, saying, If thy children take heed to their way, to walk before me in truth with all their heart and with all their soul, there shall not fail thee (said he) a man on the throne of Israel.

The Lord had promised David that his descendants would rule in Israel forever (2 Samuel 7:8-16). David understood that to mean that they would continue to rule *if they* obeyed God, not if they disobeyed. Fresh in his memory were the disasters that had followed his own disobedience, and he warned Solomon to avoid such disasters by faithful obedience.

GOOD ADVICE

Robert Fulghum has been called America's most popular philosopher. He is perhaps best known for his book, *All I Really Need to Know I Learned in Kindergarten.* A book reviewer called Fulghum's advice "as universal as air." *All I Really Need to Know. . .* has been followed by several bestsellers, including one with the catchy title, *It Was on Fire When I Lay Down on It.*

Fulghum's fame apparently started with a simple list of advice from his kindergarten days. "Share everything. Play fair. Don't hit people. Put things back where you found them. Clean up your own mess. Don't take things that aren't yours. Say you're sorry when you hurt somebody," etc. The list was widely reproduced; a kindergarten teacher sent it home with her students, and the mother of one of them sent it to a New York literary agent. The agent asked Fulghum for more and sent all of the material to Random House. Within a decade, Fulghum had become a literary success on the basis of his homespun (and very practical) advice.

Home Daily Bible Readings

Monday, Nov. 6—David's Instructions to Solomon (1 Kings 2:1-9)
Tuesday, Nov. 7—Solomon's Prayer for Wisdom (1 Kings 3:1-9)
Wednesday, Nov. 8—God's Reply to Solomon's Prayer (1 Kings 3:10-15)
Thursday, Nov. 9—David's Prayer for Solomon (1 Chronicles 29:10-19)
Friday, Nov. 10—The Crowning of Solomon (1 Chronicles 29:21-25)
Saturday, Nov. 11—Solomon Sacrifices at Gibeon (2 Chronicles 1:1-6)
Sunday, Nov. 12—Solomon's Dream and Request for Wisdom (2 Chronicles 1:7-13)

David's advice to Solomon was more profound than any we may get from the pop philosophers of our time. His counsel came, not from kindergarten, but from a lifetime of walking with God (and sometimes *not* doing so!). He had learned that godliness is the only sure way to succeed in the areas of life that really count.   —C. R. B.

II. Solomon's Devotion
(1 Kings 3:3, 4)

The rest of chapter 2 records the death of David and the vigorous way in which Solomon secured his kingship, executing the treasonous Adonijah and Joab. Now we consider Solomon's attitude as he began his reign.

A. Loving Obedience (v. 3)

3. And Solomon loved the LORD, walking in the statutes of David his father: only he sacrificed and burnt incense in high places.

Solomon loved the Lord. At this point his heart was committed to obeying and serving God. He showed his love by living according to the *statutes* given him by *David his father.*

Only he sacrificed and burnt incense in high places. God's law was given before Israel reached the promised land, but it prescribed that any sacrifices and incense offered in the promised land should be offered in the place that God would "choose . . . to put his name there" (Deuteronomy 12:5-7). The *high places* were places of worship scattered throughout the country. This one exception to Solomon's devotion is a foreshadowing of the more grievous errors that would mar his later reign.

At this time the ark of the covenant (the special symbol of God's presence) was in Jerusalem, while the tabernacle, with the altar on which God had prescribed that all sacrifices be made, was located at Gibeon. It is unclear to us now which of those sites was the proper location for sacrifices. The lack of a central place of worship seems also to have left some question in the minds of the Israelites about the proper place for offering sacrifices (1 Kings 3:2). Even Samuel offered sacrifices at a high place (1 Samuel 9:11-14, 19, 25). It appears that the use of these high places was tolerated by God as long as such locations had no ties to pagan worship.

Later Solomon would build a temple in Jerusalem, and God would clearly designate it as the central place of worship. That will appear in our lesson next week. Once the temple was completed, worship at the high places was no longer tolerable. Even so, the practice persisted. Several of the later kings of Judah are noted as faithful except that the high places were not removed

---

How to Say It

ABSALOM. *Ab*-suh-lum.
ADONIJAH. Ad-o-*nye*-juh.
AMAZIAH. Am-uh-*zye*-uh.
AZARIAH. Az-uh-*rye*-uh.
GIBEON. *Gib*-ee-un.
ISH-BOSHETH. Ish-*bo*-sheth.
JEHOASH. Jeh-*hoe*-ash.
JOAB. *Jo*-ab.
JOTHAM. *Jo*-tham.
SHEBA. *She*-buh.

(e.g., Jehoash, 2 Kings 12:2, 3; Amaziah, 2 Kings 14:1-4; Azariah, 2 Kings 15:1-4; and Jotham, 2 Kings 15:32-35).

B. Generous Offerings (v. 4)

4. And the king went to Gibeon to sacrifice there; for that was the great high place: a thousand burnt offerings did Solomon offer upon that altar.

Probably the *high place* at *Gibeon* was considered *great* because the tabernacle was there. The proper procedure for making *burnt offerings* is described in Leviticus 1. Such an offering might be a bull, a sheep, or a goat. Presenting *a thousand* of them was generous—even for a *king.*

III. God's Gift to Solomon
(1 Kings 3:5-10)

The value of Solomon's gift to God was great, but the value of what God was about to give to Solomon was beyond any counting or measuring. As is often said, "You can't outgive God."

A. Unique Opportunity (v. 5)

5. In Gibeon the LORD appeared to Solomon in a dream by night: and God said, Ask what I shall give thee.

Fiction abounds in stories of a fairy, genie, or other imaginary creature who offers to grant one wish to a fortunate mortal. But we are reading factual history, and it records that *the Lord appeared to Solomon in a dream* and told him to make one request.

B. Past Gifts Acknowledged (v. 6)

6. And Solomon said, Thou hast showed unto thy servant David my father great mercy, according as he walked before thee in truth, and in righteousness, and in uprightness of heart with thee; and thou hast kept for him this great kindness, that thou hast given him a son to sit on his throne, as it is this day.

Before voicing any request, Solomon expressed his appreciation for what God had done for *David* his *father.* With rare exceptions, David had behaved *in truth, and in righteousness, and in uprightness of heart.* God had showed to him *great mercy,* or *great kindness.* In this verse the words translated *mercy* and *kindness* actually reflect the same Hebrew word. At other places in the *King James Version* this word is translated *loving-kindness, merciful kindness, goodness,* and *favor.* The word carries a depth of rich meaning, and any of these translations is an apt description of what God had shown toward David.

God's own summary of what He had done for David is found in 2 Samuel 7:8, 9: God had raised David from a shepherd to a king; God had been with him continually; God had given him victory over his enemies; and God had made him famous. Furthermore, God had promised that David's descendants would rule after him and that David's house and his kingdom would be established forever (2 Samuel 7:12, 16). Here Solomon acknowledged that God was beginning to keep that promise by giving the *throne* to him, David's *son.* [See question #2, page 96.]

C. Solomon's Small Ability (v. 7)

7. And now, O LORD my God, thou hast made thy servant king instead of David my father: and I am but a little child: I know not how to go out or come in.

The phrase *a little child* reflects Solomon's awareness of his inadequacy to rule Israel. At the same time, he came to the throne well prepared: undoubtedly his natural talent was great, and the teaching David had given him was no small thing. It included general instruction about doing right (Proverbs 4:3-9), and it provided practical advice for dealing with specific cases (1 Kings 2:1-9). Still, Solomon was right in recognizing that his ability was not enough to carry out the formidable challenge before him. [See question #3, page 96.]

Visual for
lesson 11

Today's visual illustrates Solomon's opportunity while it challenges students to consider their own priorities and opportunities.

D. Solomon's Big Task (v. 8)

8. And thy servant is in the midst of thy people which thou hast chosen, a great people, that cannot be numbered nor counted for multitude.

Some students estimate that there were more than six million people in Israel at this time. How could a new king know the needs of all of them, much less their wants? There were twelve tribes, every one of them motivated to some degree by tribal pride and jealousy. How could a king mold them into one nation under God? Solomon was wise enough to know that he was facing a fearsome task.

E. Solomon's Request (v. 9)

9. Give therefore thy servant an understanding heart to judge thy people, that I may discern between good and bad: for who is able to judge this thy so great a people?

An understanding heart! Living in the royal palace, Solomon needed heartfelt sympathy to appreciate the concerns of the millions of Israelites who lived in ordinary houses and toiled at ordinary tasks. He needed wisdom enough to understand the many regulations written in the law. He needed the practical good sense to apply those regulations fairly in all circumstances. [See question #4, page 96.]

Who is able to judge this thy so great a people? No one is able to do that; it is too much for any human being. Desperately the king needed wisdom from above, and it was to his credit that he realized what he needed.

THE RIGHT KIND OF HEART

A relatively few people with severe heart disease are fortunate enough to receive a heart transplant—one of the most remarkable achievements of modern medicine. But Greg Hamilton is one of very few people around the world who have had *two* heart transplants. It was not by design—several hours into the first operation it was discovered that Hamilton's blood type had been misidentified. Thus he was receiving a heart of the wrong blood type, which created a strong likelihood of his body's rejecting the new heart. So the surgeons finished the job, and Hamilton was placed at the top of the list to receive another new heart. A week later he got it, and less than two weeks after the second surgery he walked out of the hospital on the road to recovery.

When Solomon became king of Israel as a young man, he had much going for him. Not the least of his blessings was God's gift of the right kind of heart. While we know that "an understanding [or discerning] heart" does not refer to the literal heart that beat within Solomon's chest, it is a phrase that is pregnant with meaning. An attitude that reacts to every situation by first turning to God for wisdom is a blessing that all of us should seek.

No matter how low or high our station in life, such a "heart" should be among our deepest desires. This is all the more true if we are placed in positions of leadership in society or in the church.   —C. R. B.

F. The Lord's Pleasure (v. 10)

10. And the speech pleased the Lord, that Solomon had asked this thing.

A selfish man in Solomon's position might have asked for long life for himself and sudden death for his enemies, or for riches that would astound the world. But Solomon was not selfish. His request was not for himself; it was for the multitude of Israelites who depended on him for good and just government. Gladly the Lord gave Solomon what he *asked*: Solomon's wisdom became the wonder of the world and of the ages. There had never been, and never would be, anyone like him. [See question #5, page 96.]

And the Lord gave to Solomon what he had not requested: riches and honor unmatched among the kings of the world. Long life? That depended on Solomon. He could have it if he would continue to obey God and His law (vv. 11-14).

Conclusion

We have been reading of Solomon the young king. We have seen how he pleased God with a choice he made. But what about us? Can we apply this lesson to ourselves? Can we please God as Solomon did?

A. Unselfishness

God was pleased with Solomon's unselfish request. True, he asked for wisdom for himself, but he did so for the benefit of his people. He wanted to be wise enough to govern them well.

Unselfishness is one of the cardinal principles of Christian living. "Let no man seek his own, but every man another's wealth" (1 Corinthians 10:24). That does not mean that anyone should seek to take another's wealth for himself. It means that everyone should try to increase the other's wealth as well as his own. Some versions translate *good* instead of *wealth*, and this is quite proper. Each of us should seek all kinds of good for others, but material wealth is just one kind of good. If I work for wages, I am concerned about getting enough pay to live on; but I am no less concerned about giving my employer the full value of every dollar he pays me. If I am in a business of buying and selling, I am eager to make a profit; but I am no less eager to see that the buyer

also profits by his purchase. This is also true if I am engaged in manufacturing. Every good business transaction is profitable both to seller and to buyer. With such business God is pleased.

B. Obedience

Solomon understood that God had given David great mercy and kindness because David had made obeying God a priority (1 Kings 3:6). Likewise Jesus urges us not to be overly anxious about such items as food, clothing, and shelter. These will be provided for us if we give first priority to seeking God's kingdom and His righteousness—that is, making Him our King, being obedient subjects, and doing His will (Matthew 6:25-33).

Our obedience will not earn our place in Heaven, but it will please God and bring us a reward. Obeying Jesus is like building a house on the rock. Such a house will stand through all the storms that may come (Matthew 7:24, 25).

C. Keeping On

Looking at the paragraph in the Bible following our printed text, we see God's warning to Solomon. The king could have a long life if he kept on obeying God (1 Kings 3:14). But God's great kindness is withdrawn from one who turns away and stops obeying Him. In just two weeks we shall see how horribly Solomon failed to "keep on keeping on."

This emphasis on faithfulness is just as clear in the New Testament. Jesus said that one who fails to keep on in the Christian way is not fit for the kingdom of God (Luke 9:62). James said, "Blessed is the man that endureth temptation: for when he is tried, he shall receive the crown of life" (James 1:12). The writer of the letter to the Hebrews urged us to "hold fast the profession of our faith without wavering," and to "run with patience the race that is set before us" (Hebrews 10:23; 12:1). The apostle Paul wrote, "Be ye steadfast, unmovable, always abounding in the work of the Lord" (1 Corinthians 15:58).

"And let us not be weary in well doing: for in due season we shall reap, if we faint not" (Galatians 6:9).

D. Prayer

Our Father and our God, we are humbled by the responsibilities You have given to us as Your people. We ask of You the wisdom we need to do our task well, and we pledge our best efforts to follow Your leading now and always. In Jesus' name. Amen.

E. Thought to Remember

Keep on keeping on.

Learning by Doing

This page contains an alternate lesson plan emphasizing learning activities. Classes desiring such student involvement will find these suggestions helpful.

Learning Goals

After participating in this lesson, each student will be able to:

1. Tell about David's final counsel to Solomon and of Solomon's discerning request of the Lord.

2. Explain why God's wisdom is needed regardless of one's stage in life.

3. Make a commitment to pray daily for wisdom to live a life that honors the Lord.

Into the Lesson

Write the words *Wise* and *Foolish* on the chalkboard. Ask the students, "What are some of the wisest and the most foolish things you have ever done?" Make lists on the board from their responses. Next, ask the students to describe situations that seemed innocent at first but developed into problems.

Encourage students to share as much as they are willing to, but do not pressure anyone. (Note that there may be more willingness to share the wise but less interest in sharing the unwise!)

In studying this lesson, we should learn that we do make wise decisions and that the greatest of these is to devote our lives in unselfish obedience to God.

Into the Word

Briefly describe the lesson background; then read the printed text. Divide the class into three reporting groups and provide each group with its assignment. Have each group select a spokesperson who will report back to the whole class. (Answers are provided below for teacher's assistance.)

Group 1: Advice Given (1 Kings 2:1-3)

1. Who is giving advice? *(David.)*

2. What are the relative ages of the one giving advice and the recipient? *(David is very old, and Solomon is very young.)*

3. Why was the advice being given? *(To encourage obedience.)*

4. What advice was given? *(Be strong; obey God; think of the future.)*

Group 2: Advice Followed (1 Kings 3:3, 4)

1. To whom did Solomon show respect? *(David, God.)*

2. Did Solomon follow precisely the advice that was given him? *(No; he sacrificed and burned incense on the high places. Discuss how Solomon may have been trying to show love to God but was falling short.)*

3. How generous were Solomon's offerings? *(A thousand was very generous, even for a king.)*

4. This occasion happened before Solomon received a special measure of wisdom from God. How would you evaluate the wisdom he showed here? *(Solomon displayed a mature wisdom in listening to David and seeking to honor the Lord.)*

Group 3: God's Gift (1 Kings 3:5-10)

1. What was the gift? *(Wisdom.)*

2. Even before God granted his wish, Solomon showed wisdom. How? *(a. followed David's advice, b. expressed appreciation to God for blessings to David, his father, c. humbly asked God for the greatest gift possible.)*

3. Was the request selfishly motivated? Why or why not? *(There is no hint that it was. God would not likely have honored a selfish request.)*

Allow about ten minutes for the groups to work; then have each group share its responses. Discuss the answers given and be sure adequate information is reported on each.

Into Life

Ask Group 1 to defend the proposition, "Young people need God's wisdom to get along in life more than any other age group." Group 2 is to suggest reasons to support the idea that "Adults in the twenty to fifty-year-old age range need God's wisdom to get along in life more than any other age group." And Group 3 is to support the notion, "Older adults need God's wisdom to get along in life more than any other age group."

Give the groups three or four minutes to come up with a few arguments to support their positions. Summarize by saying, "Obviously we need God's wisdom no matter what age we are. Each phase of life offers its own challenges, but God gives us the wisdom to handle each one."

Ask, "How do we get such wisdom?" Let the students suggest some answers; then read James 1:5, 6. Ask, "How often do you think we ought to pray for this wisdom?" After a bit of discussion, your class should determine that we need God's wisdom on a daily basis. Distribute index cards and ask each student to write, "I will pray daily for wisdom to live a life that honors the Lord. I will do this. . . ." Students should write a time of day (specific—i.e., at 8:00 A.M.—or general, "when I get up"). Ask the students to keep these cards where they can serve to remind the students to pray each day for God's wisdom.

Let's Talk It Over

The questions on this page are designed to encourage review of the lesson Scriptures and to promote discussion of the lesson by the class. The answers provided are only discussion starters. Let your class talk it over from there.

1. David exhorted Solomon, "Be thou strong." Why do Christians need to take this exhortation to heart?

It is an exhortation that Paul frequently directed to his readers. (See 1 Corinthians 16:13; Ephesians 6:10; 2 Timothy 2:1.) In one of these cases the exhortation was, "Be strong in the Lord," and in another it was, "Be strong in the grace that is in Christ Jesus." We need to be strong to resist temptation. We need the Lord's strength to stand up to opposition. Encourage your students to suggest specific challenges for which divine strength is needed, and discuss ways to encourage and build up one another in the face of such challenges.

2. Solomon observed that God had shown kindness to his father David. What are some lessons in wisdom that he could have learned from David's example—both good and bad?

Of course, Solomon had not yet been born when David committed adultery with Bathsheba. But he certainly learned about it later, and he could see within the royal family the terrible consequences of the sin. He could and should also have learned that when David followed the Lord wholeheartedly, he was blessed by God. But when he failed to do so, terrible consequences ensued. (See 2 Samuel 24.) Discuss the value of imitating the lives of the faithful who have gone before us, perhaps even noting specific individuals in your church who can serve as examples. (See 1 Corinthians 11:1; Hebrews 13:7.) If you have mature adults in your class, you should challenge them to consider the impact of their own example on younger believers.

3. Solomon referred to himself as "a little child." The prophet Jeremiah later referred to himself as "a child" (Jeremiah 1:6). But while the Lord was pleased with Solomon's prayer, He was displeased with Jeremiah's. Why do you think God did not respond in the same way to these two incidents, and what lessons can we learn from the two of them?

Solomon was not trying to escape from his responsibility, as Jeremiah was. The king's description of himself as a little child was merely the prelude to his requesting divine help in order to rule effectively. The prophet's protesting that he was just a child came after the Lord announced that He had prepared Jeremiah from birth to be a prophet. So Jeremiah was voicing doubts about the Lord's wisdom in choosing him and equipping him. In this instance we should aim to be a Solomon rather than a Jeremiah. If the Lord has called us to a particular place of service, we should avoid focusing on our weaknesses and limitations, and look beyond them to what an all-wise and all-powerful God can do through us.

4. Solomon asked for an understanding heart. We, especially if we are in positions of leadership, should offer a similar prayer. What can we do to prepare ourselves for God's answer?

It would be foolish to ask for wisdom and understanding and at the same time neglect the wealth of wisdom to be found in God's Word. Every Christian—and especially each leader—should be a dedicated student of the Scriptures. And each time he opens his Bible, he should ask faithfully and unwaveringly for wisdom (see James 1:5, 6). It would likewise be foolish to ask for an understanding heart in ministering to human beings and at the same time live apart and aloof from people in need. We need to spend much time and effort becoming acquainted with the people around us. We will become wiser as we learn their hopes and dreams, their problems and needs.

5. One of the most striking aspects of Solomon's prayer at Gibeon is its unselfishness. He asked for help in serving his people, not for personal advantages. How can we gain the wisdom to lead a totally unselfish life?

One of the titles that has been given to Jesus is, "the Man for others." He lived His life in total unselfishness. He refused to employ His miraculous powers to benefit Himself but ministered with them to the blind, the lame, the lepers, and others in need. As John 17 demonstrates, He gave priority to praying for others. Each of us should aim to be "a man for others" or "a woman for others." To live up to such a title we must look for ways in which we can minister to our fellow human beings. Our prayers will be one way of testing our unselfishness. Do we focus on our own needs and wants, or do we labor in prayer on behalf of other people in need?

(handwritten annotations) 1K 6 temple 60 cubits long 20 wide 30 long / 13 yrs palace 7 yrs building temple / Palace long 100 cubits 50 wide 30 high 45 beams 15 in a row / Temple Furnishing I Kings 7-13

Solomon Builds the Temple

EVOTIONAL READING: Psalm 84:1-4.

ACKGROUND SCRIPTURE: 1 Kings 5:1-12; 6:1-38; 8:1—9:5.

RINTED TEXT: 1 Kings 6:37, 38; 8:22, 23, 27-30; 9:1-5.

1 Kings 6:37, 38

37 In the fourth year was the foundation of e house of the LORD laid, in the month Zif:

38 And in the eleventh year, in the month ul, which is the eighth month, was the ouse finished throughout all the parts ereof, and according to all the fashion of it. o was he seven years in building it.

1 Kings 8:22, 23, 27-30

22 And Solomon stood before the altar of e LORD in the presence of all the congrega- on of Israel, and spread forth his hands ward heaven:

23 And he said, LORD God of Israel, there no God like thee, in heaven above, or on rth beneath, who keepest covenant and ercy with thy servants that walk before ee with all their heart.

. . . .

27 But will God indeed dwell on the rth? behold, the heaven and heaven of eavens cannot contain thee; how much less is house that I have builded?

28 Yet have thou respect unto the prayer of y servant, and to his supplication, O LORD y God, to hearken unto the cry and to the rayer, which thy servant prayeth before thee day:

29 That thine eyes may be open toward is house night and day, even toward the place of which thou hast said, My name shall be there: that thou mayest hearken unto the prayer which thy servant shall make toward this place.

30 And hearken thou to the supplication of thy servant, and of thy people Israel, when they shall pray toward this place: and hear thou in heaven thy dwelling place: and when thou hearest, forgive.

1 Kings 9:1-5

1 And it came to pass, when Solomon had finished the building of the house of the LORD, and the king's house, and all Solomon's desire which he was pleased to do,

2 That the LORD appeared to Solomon the second time, as he had appeared unto him at Gibeon.

3 And the LORD said unto him, I have heard thy prayer and thy supplication, that thou hast made before me: I have hallowed this house, which thou hast built, to put my name there for ever; and mine eyes and mine heart shall be there perpetually.

4 And if thou wilt walk before me, as David thy father walked, in integrity of heart, and in uprightness, to do according to all that I have commanded thee, and wilt keep my statutes and my judgments;

5 Then I will establish the throne of thy kingdom upon Israel for ever, as I promised to David thy father, saying, There shall not fail thee a man upon the throne of Israel.

Nov 19

GOLDEN TEXT: Will God indeed dwell on the earth? behold, the heaven and heaven of heavens cannot contain thee; how much less this house that I have builded?—1 Kings 8:27.

Rulers of Israel
Unit 3: David and Solomon
(Lessons 10-13)

Lesson Aims

After participating in this lesson a student should be able to:

1. Recall key points from Solomon's prayer of dedication for the temple and from the Lord's response.

2. Tell why obedience to God's commands was important in Solomon's day and why it remains important today.

3. Suggest one act of obedience he or she can perform in the next seven days.

Lesson Outline

INTRODUCTION
  A. A Palace for King David
  B. A Tent for the Lord?
  C. Lesson Background
I. BUILDING THE TEMPLE (1 Kings 6:37, 38)
  A. Its Beginning (v. 37)
  B. Its Completion (v. 38)
II. SOLOMON'S PRAYER (1 Kings 8:22, 23, 27-30)
  A. Praise to the Lord (vv. 22, 23, 27)
  B. Plea for Mercy (vv. 28-30)
    Where Can You Find God?
III. THE LORD'S ANSWER (1 Kings 9:1-5)
  A. The Lord's Appearance (vv. 1, 2)
  B. The Lord's Acceptance (v. 3)
    True Significance
  C. Solomon's Responsibility (v. 4)
  D. The Lord's Promise (v. 5)
CONCLUSION
  A. The Fact of Sin
  B. Dealing With Sin
  C. Prayer
  D. Thought to Remember

Introduction

A. A Palace for King David

No visit to London is complete without a stop at Buckingham Palace, the residence of the royal family. Anyone who visits there gazes with respect at the magnificent edifice. When it was built, the king of England was James I, the same monarch to whom the famous *King James Version* of the Bible was dedicated. That version was published in 1611, just four years after the first British colony was established in North America.

In contrast to this, the United States seems like only a "beginner" nation. The first part of its president's home was not completed until 1800, but from the very start that house has been a national landmark. It seems that a king or a president cannot be allowed to live in an ordinary house. That would reflect badly on the entire nation.

After David became king of Israel, he conquered Jerusalem and made it his capital city (2 Samuel 5:6-9). He was then blessed with expert help in building a royal palace. King Hiram of Tyre not only supplied cedar from the northern mountains for timber; he also sent skilled builders to make for David what was likely the finest house in Israel (2 Samuel 5:11).

B. A Tent for the Lord?

David also wanted the new capital city to be the home of the ark of the covenant, the visible earthly symbol of God's presence. At one point the Philistines had captured the ark, but had soon returned it to Israel (1 Samuel 5:1—6:16). For years it had then been kept in a private house. Now David brought it to Jerusalem with fanfare and rejoicing, and set it in a tent that he had prepared for it (2 Samuel 6).

So the king of Israel had a palace, but the King of Heaven and earth had only a tent. That didn't look right to David. He wanted to build for the Lord a temple finer than his own palace.

However, the Lord's plan was not quite the same. He did not forbid building the temple, but He postponed it. David was a man of war. That in itself was not wrong. God approved his wars, but it was more appropriate for the Lord's temple to be built by a man of peace. David, said the Lord, should leave it for his son Solomon to do (1 Chronicles 22:6-10).

David humbly accepted God's will. Then, to help prepare Solomon for the work that he himself was not allowed to do, he began gathering various materials to be used in the project (1 Chronicles 22:2-5). In fact, 1 Chronicles 22:5 notes that David "prepared abundantly before his death." He did all he could to make sure this task would go smoothly for his son.

C. Lesson Background

The temple that Solomon built is described in chapter 6 of 1 Kings. God Himself was its architect. He revealed His plans to David, and David passed them on to Solomon (1 Chronicles 28:11, 12). The heart of the temple had the same sacred rooms as the tabernacle: the Holy Place and the Most Holy Place. The latter, which housed the ark of the covenant, was a cube—thirty feet long and wide and high. The Holy Place next to it was the same in width but was twice as long.

The height of the structure was notable—forty-five feet, rising like a tower above the court around it. Thus there must have been a large space under the roof of the temple and above the ceiling of the Most Holy Place. Across the front of the temple was a porch fifteen feet wide. Inside the temple the stone walls were covered with cedar, which was intricately carved and then overlaid with gold. Against the outside of the walls, three stories of side chambers were built. Above these side chambers, the temple walls had narrow windows that allowed some light to enter.

I. Building the Temple
(1 Kings 6:37, 38)

Our printed text begins with a brief description of the time it took to build the temple.

A. Its Beginning (v. 37)

37. In the fourth year was the foundation of the house of the LORD laid, in the month Zif.

Solomon began to build the temple *in the fourth year* of his reign. *The month Zif* was the second month of the Hebrew year. It was a springtime month, corresponding to the latter part of April and the first part of May on our calendar. The name *Zif* means splendor or beauty—most likely a reference to the growing and blooming that occurred during the month. In later years (following the return from captivity in Babylon) the same month was called *Iyar*, which has the same meaning.

B. Its Completion (v. 38)

38. And in the eleventh year, in the month Bul, which is the eighth month, was the house finished throughout all the parts thereof, and according to all the fashion of it. So was he seven years in building it.

Counting only complete years, it took *seven years* to finish the temple. Being a little more accurate, it took seven and a half years; for the work began in the second month of the fourth year of Solomon's reign and ended in the *eighth month* of the *eleventh year*. That month corresponds to the last part of October and the first part of November

on our calendar. It brought the beginning of the rainy season, and so it was named *Bul*, meaning rainy. [See question #1, page 104.]

II. Solomon's Prayer
(1 Kings 8:22, 23, 27-30)

First Kings 7:1-12 describes other buildings in the vicinity of the temple. Solomon's "own house" took thirteen years to build. It must have been a royal palace far grander than David's.

The structure known as "the house of the forest of Lebanon" probably had that name because its many pillars were made of cedar wood from Lebanon. No doubt they stood as majestically as the trunks of a forest. The purpose of this house is not stated. Perhaps it served as a guest house and reception area, for Solomon was visited by some of the great men and women of his time (1 Kings 10:24). The queen of Sheba is perhaps the most famous example (1 Kings 10:1-13). *half not told*

First Kings 7:13-22 records that Solomon commissioned an expert metal worker from Tyre to make two massive pillars of brass for the porch of the temple. The rest of that chapter describes the furnishings of the temple.

Chapter 8 of 1 Kings begins by telling how Solomon brought the ark of the covenant into the completed temple. A cloud of divine glory then filled that house—clear evidence that the Lord accepted it as His dwelling place among His people (1 Kings 8:10, 11). The rest of chapter 8 describes the dedication of the temple.

At this point our printed text includes some excerpts from Solomon's prayer.

A. Praise to the Lord (vv. 22, 23, 27)

22. And Solomon stood before the altar of the LORD in the presence of all the congregation of Israel, and spread forth his hands toward heaven.

Solomon had been speaking to the *congregation* (vv. 14-21). Now his upraised arms made it plain that he was speaking in prayer to God.

23. And he said, LORD God of Israel, there is no God like thee, in heaven above, or on earth beneath, who keepest covenant and mercy with thy servants that walk before thee with all their heart.

The *Lord*, Jehovah, stands alone as the one and only God. In all creation there is none to be compared with Him. One evidence of that is seen in the way He kept His *covenant*. He had made that covenant at Sinai when His people left Egypt. He had promised to bless them with prosperity and happiness if they would walk before Him *with all their heart*—that is, if they would obey His law sincerely and gladly. God's promise had been kept faultlessly for nearly five hundred

---

How to Say It

BABYLON. *Bab*-uh-lun.
BUL. Bool.
IYAR. *Ee*-yar.
SHEBA. *She*-buh.
ZIF. Zif.

years (1 Kings 6:1). The same covenant had promised disaster to the people if they did not obey, and that promise had also been kept.

Solomon then prayed that God would keep His recent promise that David's descendants would continue to rule (vv. 24-26); but our text omits that and goes on to the climax of Solomon's praise in verse 27.

27. But will God indeed dwell on the earth? behold, the heaven and heaven of heavens cannot contain thee; how much less this house that I have builded?

God is great beyond our comprehension. All of outer space is too small to contain Him. How absurd it would be to think that He could be found only in that tiny temple that Solomon had just completed! [See question #2, page 104.]

B. Plea for Mercy (vv. 28-30)

28. Yet have thou respect unto the prayer of thy servant, and to his supplication, O LORD my God, to hearken unto the cry and to the prayer, which thy servant prayeth before thee today.

Understanding that God was not confined to the temple, Solomon nevertheless pleaded that God would give attention to the *prayer* that he was about to speak as that temple was being dedicated. The next verse tells specifically what prayer he wanted to make.

29. That thine eyes may be open toward this house night and day, even toward the place of which thou hast said, My name shall be there: that thou mayest hearken unto the prayer which thy servant shall make toward this place.

Though God lived in the distant Heaven, Solomon prayed that He would give special attention to the temple *night and day*. Before Israel reached the promised land, God had promised that He would put His name at a specific place in

Home Daily Bible Readings

Monday, Nov. 13—Preparations for Building the Temple (1 Kings 5:1-12)
Tuesday, Nov. 14—Solomon Builds the Temple (1 Kings 6:1-13)
Wednesday, Nov. 15—The Interior of the Temple (1 Kings 6:14-22)
Thursday, Nov. 16—Dedication of the Temple (1 Kings 8:1-13)
Friday, Nov. 17—Solomon's Prayer of Dedication (1 Kings 8:22-30)
Saturday, Nov. 18—Rejoicing in the Sanctuary (Psalm 84)
Sunday, Nov. 19—God Again Appears to Solomon (1 Kings 9:1-9)

that land. That place was to be a special place of contact with God: people of Israel were to present their offerings there (Deuteronomy 12:10, 11). Then God had promised David that Solomon would build a place for God's name (2 Samuel 7:13). Now Solomon had completed the temple and placed in it the ark of the covenant, the visible symbol of God's presence. God had signaled His acceptance of the temple by filling it with His glory (1 Kings 8:10, 11). Surely this was the place of which God could say, *My name shall be there.*

True, God could not be confined to the temple; yet in a special sense He was there, as He had demonstrated by filling that place with His glory. Solomon asked for God's special attention, not only to the *prayer* he was making before the temple that day, but also to whatever prayer he later would *make toward this place.*

WHERE CAN YOU FIND GOD?

What would you say is the most awe-inspiring place on earth? Certainly one possibility would be Glacier Point in Yosemite National Park. There one can look straight down more than three thousand feet to the floor of Yosemite Valley, or north across the valley to Yosemite Falls (the highest falls in North America), or eastward toward the great monolith of Half Dome standing out against the backdrop of the snow-covered Sierra Nevada Mountains. Many people feel close to God in such a setting.

Another person might choose Victoria Falls in Africa as a place where they are reminded of the mighty power of God. Someone else might say, "Just let me sit in a peaceful garden. I can feel God's presence there." Still others have been known to claim that they can worship God better with a fishing pole in their hands than in any cathedral ever built. (We should be skeptical about this one!)

Obviously, as Solomon observed, no building—not even the heavens themselves—can contain the God we worship. However, He can and does inhabit both the world He made and the buildings we erect to aid us in worshiping Him. The issue is not so much *where* we find God, but *whether* we find Him. Private worship has its place, but God also commands us to join with others in seeking His presence. He promises to be there with us when we do so.   —C. R. B.

30. And hearken thou to the supplication of thy servant, and of thy people Israel, when they shall pray toward this place: and hear thou in heaven thy dwelling place: and when thou hearest, forgive.

Now Solomon pleaded that the Lord would hear not only his prayers, but the prayers that all

Israel would *pray toward* this special *place* of God's presence. *And when thou hearest, forgive.* Here we see that Solomon was thinking especially of sinful Israel's prayers for pardon. Read on in verses 31-40 to see this verified. Solomon was foreseeing the time when the people of Israel would fall into idolatry and other sins, as they had often done before. God would punish their sinning with national disaster, as He had often done before. In misery they would repent of their sins and plead for forgiveness, as they had often done before. Solomon prayed that God would be merciful and forgive them yet again. [See question #3, page 104.]

III. The Lord's Answer (1 Kings 9:1-5)

The latter part of chapter 8 records what happened after Solomon finished his lengthy prayer. Though he foresaw times when Israel would turn from God, the king urged the people to avoid such times by careful obedience to God. The completion of the temple was celebrated with a two-week festival; and then the people were dismissed to go home, still rejoicing in all the blessings the Lord had given them.

Now we turn to the Lord's answer to Solomon's prayer. Whether it was given during the two weeks of celebration or later, it is recorded in chapter 9 of 1 Kings.

A. The Lord's Appearance (vv. 1, 2)

1. And it came to pass, when Solomon had finished the building of the house of the LORD, and the king's house, and all Solomon's desire which he was pleased to do.

This makes it clear that we are now looking at a time not only after Solomon completed the temple, but also after he completed such buildings as the royal palace and the house of the forest of Lebanon (1 Kings 7:1, 2). In fact, *all* that Solomon had desired *to do* he had achieved. Some have suggested that this was a kind of crossroads in Solomon's reign and that God was appearing to him to remind him of his responsibility to be faithful as David his father had been.

2. That the LORD appeared to Solomon the second time, as he had appeared unto him at Gibeon.

At Gibeon the Lord had *appeared to Solomon* in a dream by night and had said, "Ask what I shall give thee" (1 Kings 3:5). Now He appeared again in a similar way.

B. The Lord's Acceptance (v. 3)

3. And the LORD said unto him, I have heard thy prayer and thy supplication, that thou hast

made before me: I have hallowed this house, which thou hast built, to put my name there for ever; and mine eyes and mine heart shall be there perpetually.

The Lord had *heard* Solomon's *prayer*, parts of which have been included in our printed text (1 Kings 8:22, 23, 27-30). In response He had *hallowed* the new temple: He had made it holy, set it apart, dedicated it as the place foretold in Deuteronomy 12:10, 11. It was to be the national worship center of Israel—the place where sacrifices and offerings would be made. God's *eyes* and *heart* would be there: He would be watching and cherishing that temple *perpetually.*

TRUE SIGNIFICANCE

Mickey's Dining Car has been located on Seventh Street in St. Paul, Minnesota, for some sixty years. For more than twenty of those years, city officials tried in vain to convince Eric Mattson, the owner of this old-fashioned eatery, that he ought to accept the inevitable and move his business elsewhere. Finally, the insurance firm that owned the surrounding property put up a seventeen-story, nearly one-half million square foot building that dwarfs the diner.

The dining car is officially known as an Art Deco Streamline Moderne-style car. That's important because this simple structure, originally one of thousands across America, is now one of only a few left. And because of its style and historic significance, Mickey's has been officially listed on the National Register of Historic Places. Neither the insurance company nor the city—which tried to move the diner so it could widen the street in front of it—can touch it.

The temple that Solomon built was never at the mercy of city bureaucrats or big business, since Solomon was both the king and the richest man around. However, the most important fact about the temple was that God had hallowed it with His presence—a fact far more significant than being listed on any "national register."

Use today's visual to encourage your students to share the awe expressed by Solomon at the greatness of our God, who cannot be confined or limited.

Visual for lesson 12

No matter how famous or important we may become, what matters most is whether our lives have been hallowed by the presence of God.

—C. R. B.

C. Solomon's Responsibility (v. 4)

4. And if thou wilt walk before me, as David thy father walked, in integrity of heart, and in uprightness, to do according to all that I have commanded thee, and wilt keep my statutes and my judgments.

With only a few exceptions, *David* had obeyed God with wholehearted devotion and upright living. If Solomon would do the same, he could be sure that God would keep the promise found in the next verse.

D. The Lord's Promise (v. 5)

5. Then I will establish the throne of thy kingdom upon Israel for ever, as I promised to David thy father, saying, There shall not fail thee a man upon the throne of Israel.

God had promised that David's *kingdom* would last *for ever*, and that one of David's descendants would always be king—but only if those descendants would obey Him sincerely (1 Kings 2:4). Now the Lord made the same promise to Solomon: his descendants would rule over Israel forever. Again the Lord stated the condition: the rule of Solomon's descendants would not be continuous unless their obedience to God was continuous (v. 4). [See question #4, page 104.]

This same warning is emphasized strongly in the verses that follow our printed text (6-9). If Israel turned to idolatry and wickedness, it would lose the promised land; and that magnificent temple would be destroyed. Sadly, this is eventually what happened (2 Kings 24:10-13; 25:8, 9, 13-17).

Conclusion

What is so attractive about doing wrong? All history proves that it is destructive; so why do most people still choose it (Matthew 7:13, 14)? Nothing could be plainer than the warning of 1 Kings 9:6-9. How could Solomon ever ignore it? He was gifted with more wisdom than any other man, yet even he played the fool. He disobeyed God, and brought his magnificent empire to the brink of disaster. We shall read about that in next week's lesson.

A. The Fact of Sin

This series of lessons has shown us how often and how dismally Israel failed to obey God, and thus forfeited His blessing. Wise King Solomon commented, "There is no man that sinneth not" (1 Kings 8:46). Thus he echoed the sad song of his father David: "They are all gone aside, they are all together become filthy: there is none that doeth good, no, not one" (Psalm 14:3). Centuries later Paul added this confirmation: "All have sinned, and come short of the glory of God" (Romans 3:23).

B. Dealing With Sin

"The wages of sin is death," wrote Paul in Romans 6:23, but that is not the entire story. He concludes on this most positive note: "but the gift of God is eternal life through Jesus Christ our Lord." All the sinners in the world were doomed to die, but Jesus died in their place.

Does that mean that all sinners are automatically saved from death? Certainly not. Each person can still choose, and many still choose the wide road that leads to destruction.

If I choose to live rather than to die, what can I do about it? Paul told the jailer in Philippi, "Believe on the Lord Jesus Christ, and thou shalt be saved" (Acts 16:31). To the Romans he wrote, "If thou shalt confess with thy mouth the Lord Jesus, and shalt believe in thine heart that God hath raised him from the dead, thou shalt be saved" (Romans 10:9). Sending other apostles to give doomed sinners His offer of life, Jesus said, "He that believeth and is baptized shall be saved; but he that believeth not shall be damned" (Mark 16:16). Giving instructions to convicted sinners, Peter said, "Repent, and be baptized every one of you in the name of Jesus Christ for the remission of sins, and ye shall receive the gift of the Holy Ghost" (Acts 2:38). Saul of Tarsus was agonizing in repentance when God's messenger told him, "Arise, and be baptized, and wash away thy sins, calling on the name of the Lord" (Acts 22:16).

Are all these quotations confusing? Are you wondering just what a person should do for his salvation? Then search the Scriptures. Search especially the New Testament, because it testifies most clearly about the New Covenant. Consider the teachings mentioned above; consider them in their context. Consider any other Scriptures that tell what one should do to be saved. Then do *everything* they say you should do. [See question #5, page 104.]

C. Prayer

Father in Heaven, how kind You are, and how limitless is Your love, reaching out to all the sinners in the world! Grateful for Your gracious forgiveness, grateful for the unfailing leading of Your Word, we pledge ourselves anew to seek Your way and to follow it. In our Master's name, amen.

D. Thought to Remember

Obey God.

Learning by Doing

This page contains an alternate lesson plan emphasizing learning activities.
Classes desiring such student involvement will find these suggestions helpful.

Learning Goals

After this lesson a student should be able to:

1. Recall key points from Solomon's prayer of dedication for the temple and from the Lord's response.

2. Tell why obedience to God's commands was important in Solomon's day and why it remains important today.

3. Suggest one act of obedience he or she can perform in the next seven days.

Into the Lesson

Ask the students to visualize a grand church building. Discuss what makes for a "grand" building (such as large doorways, wide hallways, stained glass, etc.). Note how the differing tastes of people will generate different responses.

Then ask, "What makes for a great church?" Responses here should focus on the people—showing love, acceptance, forgiveness, etc. Note the difference between a great *building* and a great *church*.

In today's lesson we shall see how important it was for Israel to have a temple, and Solomon's temple was truly grand. More importantly we shall see the need for faithful obedience to the Lord's commands.

Into the Word

Read 1 Kings 6:37, 38; 8:22, 23, 27-30; 9:1-5. Ask the students the following questions.

1. How long did it take to build the temple? *(Seven years; 6:38)*

2. In Solomon's prayer, how was God described? *(Unique in Heaven and on earth, Keeper of covenants; 8:22, 23)*

3. With whom did Solomon say the Lord keeps His covenants? *(God's "servants that walk before [Him] with all their heart"; 8:23)*

4. For what particular blessing on God's people did Solomon ask if they would pray toward the temple? *(forgiveness; 8:28-30)*

5. How did God affirm His pleasure at what Solomon had done? *(Appeared to Solomon the second time, as He had done at Gibeon [see lesson 11]; 9:1, 2)*

6. On what condition did God say He would establish Solomon's throne "upon Israel for ever"? *(If Solomon would walk as David did, in integrity of heart, in uprightness, and in obedience to God's commands; 9:4, 5)*

Ask the students to list and discuss significant elements of Solomon's prayer. Some of them follow:

1. Solomon recognized God's majesty and recounted God's consistent promises and blessings.

2. Solomon sought God's continued blessing for the people and acceptance of the temple as a place of special contact with Him.

3. The temple was important, but God's presence is even more important and is not limited to the temple.

4. Solomon sought God's grace for future generations, who were sure to err.

Ask the students to list and discuss the main points in God's answer.

1. God acknowledged Solomon's prayer and gave His blessing to the temple.

2. God confirmed His earlier promises with another, promising that David's kingdom would last forever if his descendants obeyed sincerely.

Into Life

Reflecting on Solomon's prayer, we can see many parallels to everyday life. Ask the class to comment on the following statements. How does today's lesson text instruct us about the issues raised in these statements?

1. Many associate their religious life with a specific place and/or time of worship.

2. Many associate worship with specific days or seasons.

3. We seek immediate results or gratification rather than exercise patience.

Comment on the following principles from God's response to Solomon.

1. God and His promises are everlasting.

2. Man will always be imperfect on his own. God has the perfect solution through His perfect Son.

3. The New Covenant with Christ continues God's promises.

4. Obedience to God and His commands is paramount among God's concerns for us.

If we would obey God, then we must know what He has commanded. Ask the class to suggest commands of God to which we need to give careful obedience. List these on the chalkboard. Then ask each student to choose one that he or she needs to be more diligent in obeying and to make a silent commitment to do so in the coming week.

Let's Talk It Over

The questions on this page are designed to encourage review of the lesson Scriptures and to promote discussion of the lesson by the class. The answers provided are only discussion starters. Let your class talk it over from there.

1. Solomon's temple was a magnificent structure. The length of time required for its construction speaks volumes about the splendor of it. Today many people feel that church buildings should be similarly ornate, while many others believe that spending money on aesthetics is wasteful. What do you think? Why?

The true temple of God today is the heart of the believer (1 Corinthians 6:19). The early church had no "church buildings" in which to meet. They met in the temple, in homes, and in other facilities. So there is no need to have a cathedral to worship God.

At the same time, a public building makes a statement to outsiders as well as to members. Certainly a congregation that builds a house of worship will want to make it fit the character of the neighborhood and not be an eyesore or a source of derision. Sacrificing to make a building especially lovely says something about the importance of what happens inside the building. The church building ought to be a tool that enhances the church's outreach. That will, no doubt, require a certain attention to aesthetics.

2. It was fitting that Solomon emphasized the fact that God was not confined to the temple, but greater than the expanse of the heavens. How can we overcome the tendency to confine our recognition of God to the church building?

Jesus pointed out to the Samaritan woman that "God is a Spirit: and they that worship him must worship him in spirit and in truth" (John 4:24). Worship can take place in our home, during lunch hour at our place of employment, in a quiet outdoor setting, and in many other places as well as in a church building. We must also recognize that God is watching us both while we are in the church building and outside of it. Some church attenders are notorious for donning a pious manner on Sunday and then laying it aside during the remainder of the week. God wants to be honored Monday through Saturday, as well as Sunday.

3. Suppose a Christian brother or sister said to you, "Solomon asked the Lord to give heed to the prayers for forgiveness of sin that were offered in connection with the temple. But we do not have a temple! How can I know that God

hears my prayers for forgiveness?" How would you answer?

We might turn to the book of Hebrews and see how the New Covenant is superior to the Old. Our "sanctuary" is not a temple but Heaven itself! (See Hebrews 9.) We might turn also to 1 John 1:9 for God's clear promise to hear and forgive His people when they confess sin. We can turn to Hebrews 4:16, which promises confident access to the "throne of grace." Perhaps we should remind our friend that the temple that Solomon built was ultimately destroyed, as was the temple that stood in Jesus' time, but the throne of grace can never be destroyed. We can always go there to "find grace to help in time of need."

4. God's promises to Solomon were clearly conditional ones: "*If* thou wilt . . . *then* I will" (1 Kings 9:4, 5). What are some conditional promises that God has made to human beings in the New Covenant age?

"If thou shalt confess with thy mouth the Lord Jesus, and shalt believe in thine heart that God hath raised him from the dead, thou shalt be saved" (Romans 10:9). Our salvation is conditional on our believing in Jesus Christ and confessing Him as Lord. "For we are made partakers of Christ, if we hold the beginning of our confidence steadfast unto the end" (Hebrews 3:14). Our continuing fellowship with Christ is conditional on our steadfastness in trusting and obeying Him. "If we confess our sins, he is faithful and just to forgive us our sins, and to cleanse us from all unrighteousness" (1 John 1:9). Our continuing cleansing from sin is conditional on our practicing personal confession of sin.

5. Some have claimed that the passages quoted in the conclusion to today's lesson are contradictory. How would you reply to such a charge?

It is true that the various passages cited give different information, but they do not give contradictory information. That is, none of them affirms what another denies. None prohibits what another commands. Different Scripture passages often give additional information to what is given elsewhere. The wise student takes all the passages he or she can and puts them together to get the complete picture.

Solomon's Mistakes

DEVOTIONAL READING: **Nahum 1:2-8.**

BACKGROUND SCRIPTURE: **1 Kings 11.**

PRINTED TEXT: **1 Kings 11:1-13a.**

1 Kings 11:1-13a

1 But king Solomon loved many strange women, together with the daughter of Pharaoh, women of the Moabites, Ammonites, Edomites, Zidonians, and Hittites;

2 Of the nations concerning which the LORD said unto the children of Israel, Ye shall not go in to them, neither shall they come in unto you: for surely they will turn away your heart after their gods: Solomon clave unto these in love.

3 And he had seven hundred wives, princesses, and three hundred concubines: and his wives turned away his heart.

4 For it came to pass, when Solomon was old, that his wives turned away his heart after other gods: and his heart was not perfect with the LORD his God, as was the heart of David his father.

5 For Solomon went after Ashtoreth the goddess of the Zidonians, and after Milcom the abomination of the Ammonites.

6 And Solomon did evil in the sight of the LORD, and went not fully after the LORD, as did David his father.

7 Then did Solomon build a high place for Chemosh, the abomination of Moab, in the hill that is before Jerusalem, and for Molech, the abomination of the children of Ammon.

8 And likewise did he for all his strange wives, which burnt incense and sacrificed unto their gods.

9 And the LORD was angry with Solomon, because his heart was turned from the LORD God of Israel, which had appeared unto him twice,

10 And had commanded him concerning this thing, that he should not go after other gods: but he kept not that which the LORD commanded.

11 Wherefore the LORD said unto Solomon, Forasmuch as this is done of thee, and thou hast not kept my covenant and my statutes, which I have commanded thee, I will surely rend the kingdom from thee, and will give it to thy servant.

12 Notwithstanding, in thy days I will not do it for David thy father's sake: but I will rend it out of the hand of thy son.

13a Howbeit I will not rend away all the kingdom; but will give one tribe to thy son.

GOLDEN TEXT: The LORD was angry with Solomon, because his heart was turned from the LORD God of Israel.—1 Kings 11:9.

Lesson Aims

After this lesson a student should be able to:

1. Tell what contributed to Solomon's demise and how God disciplined him.

2. Compare Solomon's sin with that of those who try to compromise faith in Christ.

3. Make a statement of uncompromising faith in Jesus Christ as the only Son of the one true and living God.

Lesson Outline

INTRODUCTION

  A. Israel Knew Better

  B. Lesson Background

  I. SOLOMON'S WOMEN (1 Kings 11:1-3)

    A. Foreign Women (v. 1)

    B. Forbidden Women (v. 2)

    C. A Thousand Women (v. 3)

      Simple Pleasures

  II. SOLOMON'S IDOLATRY (1 Kings 11:4-8)

    A. His Wandering Heart (v. 4)

    B. His False Gods (vv. 5-8)

      The Influence of "Outsiders"

  III. SOLOMON'S PUNISHMENT (1 Kings 11:9-13a)

    A. The Lord's Anger (vv. 9, 10)

    B. Punishment Promised (v. 11)

    C. Punishment Postponed (v. 12)

    D. Punishment Modified (v. 13a)

CONCLUSION

  A. The King Eternal

  B. The King's People

  C. Prayer

  D. Thought to Remember

Introduction

A. Israel Knew Better

Over the last three months our lessons have reminded us again and again of the misdeeds of Israel's people and of the punishment that followed. Their sin was the more shameful because the people knew better. At the beginning of their life as a nation, God had given them His law. He had assigned parents the duty of teaching it to their children—teaching it earnestly and constantly (Deuteronomy 6:6, 7). Priests had the duty of teaching the parents (Leviticus 10:8-11). When both parents and priests neglected their duty, God sent prophets to point out the misdeeds of the people.

In all of this, however, the people could not see the sorrowing face of their Father in Heaven. They saw the face and heard the voice of His prophet, so they tried to silence the prophet instead of correcting their way of living. Nothing but punishment could bring them to their senses. Oppressed by the various invaders whom God sent, they finally realized that their misery was the result of their sin. Prepared again to obey God, they pleaded with Him for mercy; and He rescued them from their misery.

B. Lesson Background

Our lesson title is "Solomon's Mistakes." That is a charitable way to put it. We might fittingly say, "Solomon's Sins," for surely Solomon knew better. We do not know how much he was schooled by faithful priests or tutored by Nathan the prophet; but we know that he recalled the teaching of his father David, a man after God's own heart (Proverbs 4:3, 4). In addition, he possessed a special gift of wisdom from God (1 Kings 3:11, 12). He himself became a noted teacher. "All the earth sought to Solomon, to hear his wisdom, which God had put in his heart" (1 Kings 10:24). "He spake three thousand proverbs" (1 Kings 4:32), many more than we see in the book of Proverbs.

Looking at the proverbs written in that book, we soon read, "The fear of the Lord is the beginning of knowledge" (Proverbs 1:7). Looking at the conclusion of one of Solomon's other books, we read, "Fear God, and keep his commandments: for this is the whole duty of man" (Ecclesiastes 12:13). Surely, we would think, so wise a man should never let himself be ensnared in wrongdoing. But he did—even though without doubt he knew better.

I. Solomon's Women
(1 Kings 11:1-3)

God's law did not forbid polygamy, but it did command that Israelites marry only other Israelites (Deuteronomy 7:1-4). Early in his reign, however, Solomon ignored that law, primarily for political reasons. He made an alliance with Pharaoh, king of Egypt, and strengthened the bond by taking that ruler's daughter as his wife (1 Kings 3:1). But that was only the beginning.

A. Foreign Women (v. 1)

1. But king Solomon loved many strange women, together with the daughter of Pharaoh, women of the Moabites, Ammonites, Edomites, Zidonians, and Hittites.

Here the word *strange* means foreign, or not of the nation of Israel. The *Moabites* lived east of the Dead Sea. The *Ammonites* lived east of Israel and north of Moab. The *Edomites* lived south of the Dead Sea. The *Zidonians* took their name from Zidon or Sidon, a city of Phoenicia north of Israel on the Mediterranean coast. The *Hittites* were prominent in Syria and Palestine for centuries. At this time they probably were strongest in the territory east of Phoenicia.

David had subdued these smaller nations and made them part of his empire, which was now ruled by Solomon. Each nation managed its own affairs but paid tribute to Israel. Since Solomon was respected and admired throughout the known world, there was a certain prestige in being associated with him. A foreign ruler might consider it a privilege to be a father-in-law to such a man. Also, if one of the subject kings ever thought of rebelling and refusing to pay tribute to Israel, he might be restrained by remembering that his daughter was in Jerusalem. She easily could be made a prisoner or a slave instead of a wife. [See question #1, page 112.]

B. Forbidden Women (v. 2)

2. Of the nations concerning which the LORD said unto the children of Israel, Ye shall not go in to them, neither shall they come in unto you: for surely they will turn away your heart after their gods: Solomon clave unto these in love.

God had told *the children of Israel* to destroy the pagan *nations* that inhabited the promised land. His people were not to associate with them; specifically, they were not to marry pagans (Deuteronomy 7:1-5). The reason was very simple: *they will turn away your heart after their gods.*

Solomon, however, became engrossed in preserving the stability of his empire. For political expediency he ignored God's law. He spoke affectionately to pagan kings; he took their daughters into his harem.

C. A Thousand Women (v. 3)

3. And he had seven hundred wives, princesses, and three hundred concubines: and his wives turned away his heart.

Israel had no king but God when the law was given, but the law included some specific regulations for the king who was to come later. One regulation forbade the king to "multiply wives to himself" (Deuteronomy 17:17). Solomon violated that one extravagantly!

It seems hard to believe that Solomon accumulated seven hundred princesses from the five small nations mentioned in verse 1. We know he made an alliance with Egypt and cemented it by marrying that king's daughter (1 Kings 3:1). It

may be that he did the same with countries west and south of Egypt, with the little kingdoms of Arabia, with whatever kingdoms there were in Asia Minor north of the Mediterranean, and even with some kingdoms in Mesopotamia. Even so, it appears that a smaller country must have had several of its princesses in Solomon's harem. Solomon was the greatest and most feared king on earth. It was an honor to be allied with him—and it was politically prudent as well.

Concubines have been described as "second-class wives." They had no royal fathers; they were not chosen for political purposes, and so their status was inferior. We wonder, then, why they were chosen. When Solomon saw an extremely beautiful woman, did he simply take her home to keep for his own? We wonder if these *three hundred* were the prettiest, the most vivacious, the most interesting, and the best loved of the thousand. We have no way to be certain. The record simply notes that the king had three hundred concubines.

Ominously the record adds that the warning of Deuteronomy 17:17 proved to be well founded: *his wives turned away his heart.* [See question #2, page 112.]

SIMPLE PLEASURES

Some teenage boys from the Los Angeles area were looking for some "innocent fun." They began playing with bulldozers at a construction site during the evenings after the work crews had

---

How to Say It

AMMON. *Am*-mun.
ARABIA. Uh-*ray*-be-uh.
ASHTORETH. *Ash*-toe-reth.
CHEMOSH. *Kee*-mosh.
EDOMITES. *Ee*-dum-ites.
HITTITES. *Hit*-ites.
JEROBOAM. Jair-uh-*boe*-um.
MEDITERRANEAN. *Med*-uh-tuh-*ray*-nee-un
    (strong accent on *ray*).
MESOPOTAMIA. *Mes*-uh-puh-*tay*-me-uh
    (strong accent on *tay*).
MILCOM. *Mill*-com.
MOAB. *Mo*-ab.
MOABITES. *Mo*-ub-ites.
MOLECH. *Mo*-lek.
PHARAOH. *Fair*-o or *Fay*-ro.
PHOENICIA. Fuh-*nish*-uh.
REHOBOAM. Ree-huh-*boe*-um.
SIDON. *Sye*-dun.
SYRIA. *Sear*-ee-uh.
ZIDON. *Zye*-dun.
ZIDONIANS. Zye-*doe*-nee-uns.

gone home. Apparently some of the boys knew how to "hot wire" the big diesel engines to start them without ignition keys.

One evening, one of the boys lost control of the bulldozer he was driving. The huge machine left the construction site and destroyed a major portion of a nearby church building before being stopped. Fortunately, this happened on one of the few nights when the building was not being used; so no one was injured or killed. One church member saw a positive side to the incident: with the publicity the church got, the whole community now knows about the church!

Solomon's dalliance with evil probably began innocently enough—at least in his opinion. He discovered that it was politically astute to marry the daughters of kings whose kingdoms were subject to Israel. No doubt Solomon also found the practice quite enjoyable as well. What harm could there be in such "simple pleasures"?

Through Solomon's "pleasure," however, he learned a hard lesson. What was formerly unthinkable became a fact of life: his foreign, idol-worshiping wives turned his heart to other gods. What the world calls expedient often leads to grievous sin.   —C. R. B.

II. Solomon's Idolatry
(1 Kings 11:4-8)

In the first of His Ten Commandments God said, "Thou shalt have no other gods before me" (Exodus 20:3). Perhaps Solomon had no intention of breaking that law when he let his Egyptian wife bring her religion with her to the palace in Jerusalem. But Solomon's tolerance of false religion led to support, and his support eventually resulted in actual worship.

A. His Wandering Heart (v. 4)

4. For it came to pass, when Solomon was old, that his wives turned away his heart after other gods: and his heart was not perfect with the LORD his God, as was the heart of David his father.

Who would have thought that the wisest man on earth would play the fool? Perhaps during the early years of his reign, when the words of *David his father* were still fresh in his mind, Solomon made an effort to distance himself from the pagan idols and practices of his many wives. But as he grew *old*, his will to resist seems to have weakened. In time, *his wives turned away his heart after other gods*.

B. His False Gods (vv. 5-8)

5. For Solomon went after Ashtoreth the goddess of the Zidonians, and after Milcom the abomination of the Ammonites.

Ashtoreth was a goddess worshiped by many pagans along the Mediterranean coast. She was portrayed in somewhat different ways in different towns and territories. Solomon followed the Zidonian version, probably because a wife from Zidon (Sidon) brought this goddess to Jerusalem.

As noted earlier, the *Ammonites* lived east of Israel. Different groups of them worshiped different versions of their so-called god, *Milcom*, who was also known as *Molech* (v. 7). Both names are derived from a word that means *king*. This deity was especially abominable because some of his worshipers burned their children in sacrifice to him, which Israelites were forbidden to do (Leviticus 18:21). Solomon did not go that far, but one of his descendants (approximately two centuries later) did (2 Kings 16:1-3).

6. And Solomon did evil in the sight of the LORD, and went not fully after the LORD, as did David his father.

Any involvement with false gods was *evil*. Solomon knew that, but for the sake of his wives he drifted into idolatry of various kinds. *David* in his later years was guilty of adultery and murder, but never of idolatry.

7. Then did Solomon build a high place for Chemosh, the abomination of Moab, in the hill that is before Jerusalem, and for Molech, the abomination of the children of Ammon.

A high place describes a place of worship. They were called high places because many of them were located on hilltops; but the name came to be given even to shrines that were set up in the valleys. The sites mentioned here most likely were situated on the Mount of Olives, which is a *hill that is before Jerusalem*.

As stated earlier, Moab was located east of the Dead Sea. Its people were neighbors of the Ammonites, and it seems that their god *Chemosh* was similar to *Molech*. Second Kings 3:26, 27 records that the king of Moab offered his son as a burnt offering, and a Moabite record (known as the Moabite Stone) adds that he made the offering to Chemosh.

Solomon's support of the high places helps us understand why God's plan was for Israel to worship Him at the one place that He would choose (Deuteronomy 12:10, 11). While worship at the high places was tolerated (1 Samuel 9:25), God knew that it also had the potential to open the door to the actual worship of false gods. This is exactly what happened in the case of Solomon.

8. And likewise did he for all his strange wives, which burnt incense and sacrificed unto their gods.

This does not mean that Solomon made seven hundred worship places for his seven hundred wives. Perhaps dozens of wives worshiped at

6 0 yrs old

each place he built. Still, there must have been a bewildering number of shrines in and near Jerusalem. Probably none of them was as big as the temple of the Lord, and none was as richly adorned with gold and silver; but a visitor in the area would not conclude that the Lord was the one and only God worshiped in Jerusalem. [See question #3, page 112.]

THE INFLUENCE OF "OUTSIDERS"

North America has always been a land of immigrants. In prehistoric times, they were apparently Asians who came across a "land bridge" between what is now Siberia and Alaska. At the beginning of the modern era of history, the immigrants were Europeans and Africans, the latter brought against their will. As the end of the twentieth century approached, the newcomers were primarily from Asia and Latin America.

As each wave of immigrants arrived, previous residents resisted yielding a measure of control over the land, the culture, and the social and governmental structures. This has been true whether the immigrants to an area were of a different race or nationality, or whether they were simply "outsiders" who didn't understand the customs of the places where they moved. "City folks" moving to small towns, "Yankees" moving to the South, or Southerners moving to New England have all found difficulty fitting in with their new environments.

Israel's problem in Solomon's time was that the immigrants (Solomon's wives) and their pagan culture (especially their worship) were readily accepted. Where Solomon should have resisted change, he gave in all too easily to his wives' pagan practices.

God's people are called to influence their surroundings, not to be influenced by them. Our contacts with "outsiders" should be designed to improve them, not to impair us.   —C. R. B.

III. Solomon's Punishment (1 Kings 11:9-13a)

Solomon had been doing just as he pleased for some time, and thus far his reign had been successful. That was true because he pleased to please God by worshiping Him and obeying Him. But now the voices of his wives seemed nearer, louder, and more insistent than the voice of God. So Solomon pleased to please his wives, and God was displeased.

A. The Lord's Anger (vv. 9, 10)

9. And the LORD was angry with Solomon, because his heart was turned from the LORD God of Israel, which had appeared unto him twice.

What Will Turn Your Heart?

The Lord was angry with Solomon, because his heart was turned from the Lord God of Israel.
1 Kings 11:9

Visual for lesson 13

The visual for today's lesson challenges us to learn from Solomon's tragic error. Discuss what turns people's hearts today and how the church can encourage faithfulness.

The Lord is rightly *angry* with wrongdoing, and Solomon's conduct was clearly wrong. With his great wisdom, he should have managed his own *heart* better; he should have kept it faithful to the Lord. His turning away was the more inexcusable because the Lord *had appeared unto him twice.* The first time He had granted Solomon's request for wisdom, and had added a bonus of riches and honor (1 Kings 3:5-14). The second time He had promised continued success to Solomon if Solomon remained faithful to Him, and disaster if Solomon did not (1 Kings 9:4-9). With that promise as plain as words could make it, how could Solomon turn from God? But he did. See the next verse.

10. And had commanded him concerning this thing, that he should not go after other gods: but he kept not that which the LORD commanded.

The law forbade idolatry (as clearly stated in the first two of the Ten Commandments). The Lord had appeared to Solomon and *commanded him concerning this thing* (1 Kings 9:6, 7). But Solomon had disobeyed.

B. Punishment Promised (v. 11)

11. Wherefore the LORD said unto Solomon, Forasmuch as this is done of thee, and thou hast not kept my covenant and my statutes, which I have commanded thee, I will surely rend the kingdom from thee, and will give it to thy servant.

With all his wisdom Solomon must have known that Israel had turned away from God time after time and that disaster had followed every instance of turning away. How could Solomon think that he could turn to idols without escaping punishment? Most likely he simply stopped thinking about pleasing God and thought only of pleasing his wives. [See question #4, page 112.]

The punishment prescribed by God must have hurt Solomon deeply. The *kingdom* that David his father had left him to rule and had prepared him to rule, and that represented Israel at the height of its glory, was to be taken from Solomon and given to a common *servant*.

C. Punishment Postponed (v. 12)

12. Notwithstanding, in thy days I will not do it for David thy father's sake: but I will rend it out of the hand of thy son.

Solomon certainly deserved punishment, but it was postponed—not for Solomon's sake, but for David's. *David* had served God heroically many years. God would not let his great empire collapse in ruin so quickly. The collapse would come after Solomon's *son* came to power. At that time, the *servant* mentioned in verse 11 (Jeroboam) became king of the northern portion of the kingdom after it divided (1 Kings 11:26-31; 12:20).

Did this mean that Solomon himself would escape punishment? No. God had promised long life to Solomon if he would be obedient to Him (1 Kings 3:14). But disobedient Solomon died rather young, probably no more than sixty years of age.

D. Punishment Modified (v. 13a)

13a. Howbeit I will not rend away all the kingdom; but will give one tribe to thy son.

In addition to declaring that Solomon's punishment would be postponed, God also modified the punishment by stating that Solomon's *son*, Rehoboam, would not lose *all the kingdom*. He would continue to rule the *one tribe* of Judah (1 Kings 12:17, 20), though some from the tribe of Benjamin also chose to support Rehoboam (1 Kings 12:21).

In the remainder of this verse, God repeated that He would allow Solomon's son to keep one tribe for David's sake and, in addition, "for Jerusalem's

sake which I have chosen." God had a great plan for David's kingdom, and His plan would not be frustrated by Solomon's sin. [See question #5, page 112.]

Conclusion

Since this is the final lesson of this series, let's leap over the centuries when David's descendants ruled in Jerusalem. Let's look briefly at the kingdom that "shall never be destroyed" (Daniel 2:44).

A. The King Eternal

There came a time when God's promise seemed to have failed: no man of David's family ruled in Jerusalem. But God's promise did not fail. During that time there was born a son of David who is also the Son of God. He is the King eternal.

This King "went about doing good" (Acts 10:38). The power of God was in His voice and in His fingertips. He gave hearing to the deaf, sight to the blind, health to the sick, and life to the dead. He shed no blood but His own, and by His death He conquered death. He rose triumphantly from the tomb; He soared beyond the skies to sit down at the right hand of God; He rules forevermore.

B. The King's People

If we are citizens of the kingdom eternal, our duty is basically the same as the duty of David and Solomon: *we ought to obey God*. This does not mean that we are under the law God gave at Sinai. With us God has made a New Covenant (Jeremiah 31:31-34). His supreme spokesman is not Moses but Jesus (Hebrews 1:1-4). What Jesus said is the supreme guide for our living. When Jesus went away, He sent the Holy Spirit to guide His apostles into all truth and to teach them the word and will of Christ (John 16:12-15). Therefore the inspired writings of those apostles are the teachings of Christ just as much as the words He spoke with His own mouth.

Through the open pages of the New Testament, God's Son speaks to us day by day. Let's listen. Let's allow nothing to keep us from time with God's Word, lest we become like Solomon—with a heart "turned from the Lord."

C. Prayer

We plead for mercy, Father, for we have disobeyed You. Please forgive us, and help us to bring under Your control all that we do, all that we say, all that we think, and all that we feel. In our Master's name. Amen.

D. Thought to Remember

Christ is King; obey Him.

Learning by Doing

This page contains an alternate lesson plan emphasizing learning activities.
Classes desiring such student involvement will find these suggestions helpful.

Learning Goals

After this lesson a student should be able to:

1. Tell what contributed to Solomon's demise and how God disciplined him.

2. Compare Solomon's sin with that of those who try to compromise faith in Christ.

3. Make a statement of uncompromising faith in Jesus Christ as the only Son of the one true and living God.

Into the Lesson

Write the following scrambled word on the chalkboard or on a large poster: MORPOSCIME. As the students arrive, ask them to try to unscramble the word. When it is time for the session to begin, see how many determined that the word is *compromise.* You might award a small token prize to all those who correctly unscrambled the word.

Ask, "Is compromise good or bad, and why do you think so?" In your discussion you should note that there are times when compromise is good. When issues like personal tastes and preferences are all that are at stake, compromise can be a means of making peace. But when the issue is a matter of right and wrong, compromise is a prescription for disaster. Solomon illustrates that sad fact in our lesson today.

Into the Word

Review the lesson background; then ask a volunteer to read the printed text, 1 Kings 11:1-13. Provide the students with copies of the following questions (they are in the student book) and ask them to write an answer for each one.

1. Who were some of Solomon's wives? *(The daughter of Pharaoh, Moabites, Ammonites, Edomites, Zidonians, and Hittites, v. 1.)*

2. What had God said about marrying foreign women? *("Ye shall not go in to them, . . . for surely they will turn away your heart after their gods," v. 2.)*

3. What happened when Solomon was old? *(His heart was turned away after other gods, v. 4.)*

4. How did Solomon show that his heart was turned to false gods? *(He "went after" Ashtoreth and Milcom, and he built high places for Chemosh and Molech—or Milcom—as well as the other gods worshiped by his wives, vv. 5, 7, 8.)*

5. What was God's reaction to Solomon's sin? *(He was angry, v. 9.)*

6. What would God do because of Solomon's sin? *(He would take the kingdom from Solomon's family and give it to his servant, v. 11.)*

7. When was God going to do this? *(When Solomon's son was king, v. 12.)*

8. How much was he going to take away? *(All but one tribe, v. 13.)*

Allow about five minutes for the class to work; then compare answers. Note information from the commentary pages that will enhance the students' understanding of these verses. Discuss how compromise led to Solomon's downfall.

Into Life

Present the class with the following case studies. (If time is short, assign one study to half the class and the second to the other half.)

First Case: The Altered Time Sheets

Randy is a service technician. His job is to repair small appliances brought to him by customers. The customers leave the appliances and come back at a later date to pick them up, at which time they pay for parts and labor.

Randy is new at the job, so he has no close friends. His boss has come to him and said, "No one knows how much time you really spend on a job. If you pad your time sheet a little, we'll take in more money and reach our sales goal. Then we all get bonuses from corporate headquarters. We're all counting on you, Randy. Don't let us down."

What would you advise Randy to do?

Second Case: The Generous Lover

Brenda's husband died three years ago, leaving her a minimal insurance benefit and three children, a fifteen-year-old daughter and two boys, nine and twelve. At first Brenda remained active with the church, but more and more she finds she has no time for extra activities and even misses Sunday mornings occasionally.

For the past six months she has been dating a very kind and generous man, and he has helped her pay some of her bills. They plan to get married, but they have not set a date. Recently, however, he has been insisting that he be allowed to spend the night with her. He says it's only right after all he's done to help her—and, besides, they are going to get married.

What would you advise Brenda to do?

Let's Talk It Over

The questions on this page are designed to encourage review of the lesson Scriptures and to promote discussion of the lesson by the class. The answers provided are only discussion starters. Let your class talk it over from there.

1. Solomon entered into marriage for wrong reasons. What are some unwise reasons people have for marrying today? How can we guide Christian singles into marrying for right reasons?

Far too often people are focused more on what they can *get* out of marriage than on what they can *give*. Such an approach is certain to lead to disappointment. Many appear to be looking for financial security when they marry. But can they remain committed to their spouses if loss of income or some other financial crisis hits? It is important that we emphasize Christian marriage as a commitment to mutual service for the glory of God. We need to teach and model that concept, and recognize it for the blessing that it is.

2. Solomon must have known what God's law said. Still, he took foreign wives. He must have thought, "They won't turn *my* heart away." Why do we so often think, "It won't happen to me" and refuse clear warnings of Scripture or helpful friends? How can we prevent such errors?

Clearly it is pride that makes us think this way, but we often do not recognize it. We really believe that our love for God will keep us faithful in spite of the things we add to our lives that will eventually pull us away from Him. So a young Christian girl begins to date a non-Christian boy. At first she remains faithful, but then she drifts away. A businessman tunes into adult entertainment while on business trips—and then one day he wonders what happened to his marriage. What other examples can your class name?

Of course, the solution is prevention. We need to take God's Word seriously and not put ourselves in situations where we will be tempted to compromise. We must not think of ourselves more highly than we ought! (See Romans 12:3; 1 Corinthians 10:12; Galatians 6:3.)

3. The lesson writer says, "A visitor in the area would not conclude that the Lord was the one and only God worshiped in Jerusalem." How long do you think it would take for a visitor to the average church member's home to conclude that person was a Christian? What kinds of evidence ought he to find? Why?

Our home testifies to the authenticity of our commitment to Christ. Are there magazines, books, videocassettes, and such items that would

suggest more than a passing interest in worldly pursuits? Is the music that is playing the kind that celebrates immorality? On the other hand, is there a Bible situated where it indicates frequent usage? Are paintings and plaques on display that honor Christ and the Word of God? Can the sounds of Christian music be heard? We can choose what kind of witness our home presents.

4. Solomon seems to have become more interested in pleasing his wives than in pleasing God. How can a Christian balance faithfulness to God with pleasing his or her spouse?

It is easy to say one must please God and not worry about what others think, but it is not so easy in practice. The Bible tells us to "live peaceably with all men" as much as possible (Romans 12:18), and that certainly includes with one's spouse. That illustrates the importance of marrying a Christian. If both partners agree that God must come first, then coming to a conclusion that encourages faithfulness is much easier. If the spouse is an unbeliever, then the Christian must make his or her priorities clear from the beginning. When God says something, the believer must obey, even if the spouse disapproves. This is difficult, and it requires one to be careful to discern between God's commands and one's own opinions. But it must be done.

5. God's purposes were not frustrated by Solomon's sin. How have you seen God work to accomplish His will in spite of errors made by humans? What kind of encouragement does this truth give you?

While God allows us to make our own choices, He is still in control. He even uses our mistakes to accomplish His purposes. Thus, the person who spends his youth in selfish and immoral pursuits can find, by the grace of God, that he can have a meaningful Christian witness later in life. The parent who worries that he or she did not do all that should have been done in child-rearing often finds that God has supplied the lack, and the child becomes a faithful servant of the Lord. Of course, we want to do all we can to follow the Lord, and disobedience will always have consequences. But God is greater than our faults and will cause "all things [to] work together for good to them that love God" (Romans 8:28).

Winter Quarter, 2000-2001

Good News of Jesus
(Luke)

Special Features

Lessons

Unit 1: A Savior Is Born

Unit 2: Mission and Ministry

Unit 3: Cross and Resurrection

About These Lessons

These lessons comprise the first section of a two-part study of the writings of Luke, the beloved physician. Taken from the Gospel of Luke, the lessons will remind us once again of the good news of Jesus—His miraculous birth, His powerful life, His challenging teachings, and His victorious death, burial, and resurrection. Do you know someone who needs some "good news"? Invite that one to study with you this quarter!

Dec 3

Dec 10

Dec 17

Dec 24

Dec 31

Jan 7

Jan 14

Jan 21

Jan 28

Feb 4

Feb 11

Feb 18

Feb 25

Quarterly Quiz

The questions on this page may be used in several ways: as a pretest at the beginning of the quarter; as a review at the end of the quarter; or as a review after each lesson. The questions are based on the Scripture text of each lesson (King James Version). **The answers are on page 116.**

Lesson 1

1. John the Baptist called those who came to be baptized a generation of _____. *Luke 3:7*
2. To what group did John say, "Exact no more than that which is appointed you"? *Luke 3:12, 13*
3. To what group did John say, "Be content with your wages"? *Luke 3:14*

Lesson 2

1. Who told Mary, "Hail, thou that art highly favored, the Lord is with thee"? *Luke 1:26-28*
2. Gabriel told Mary about someone else besides her who was going to have a child. Who was it? *Luke 1:36*

Lesson 3

1. Zechariah and Elisabeth's home was in the hill country of Judah. T/F *Luke 1:39, 40*
2. Mary said, "My _____ doth _____ the Lord, and my _____ hath _____ in God my Saviour." *Luke 1:46, 47*

Lesson 4

1. The "city of David" was called _____. (Nazareth, Bethlehem, or Jerusalem?) *Luke 2:4*
2. When the angel spoke to the shepherds, what were his first two words? *Luke 2:10*

Lesson 5

1. Simeon was said to have been waiting for the _____ of Israel. *Luke 2:25*
2. Simeon was told that he would not see death before a special event had happened. What was it? *Luke 2:26*
3. From which tribe of Israel was Anna? *Luke 2:36*

Lesson 6

1. In the synagogue at Nazareth Jesus read from one of the prophets. Which one? *Luke 4:17*
2. Those who heard Jesus in Nazareth wondered at the _____ _____ that proceeded out of his mouth. *Luke 4:22*
3. What two prophets did Jesus mention while speaking in the synagogue? *Luke 4:25, 26*

Lesson 7

1. A would-be disciple told Jesus that he first wanted to go and _____ his father. (comfort, bury, or help?) *Luke 9:59*

2. Jesus used an illustration about a man who built a _____ and did not count the cost. (house, wall, or tower?) *Luke 14:28*

Lesson 8

1. What two groups murmured against Jesus' eating with sinners? *Luke 15:2*
2. The prodigal son planned to ask his father to make him as one of the _____ _____. *Luke 15:19*

Lesson 9

1. The unjust steward in Jesus' parable thought that begging was a possible way out of his dilemma. T/F *Luke 16:3*
2. Jesus said, "Make to yourselves friends of the _____ of _____." *Luke 16:9*
3. Complete this statement of Jesus: "Ye cannot serve. . . ." *Luke 16:13*

Lesson 10

1. In what city did Zaccheus live? *Luke 19:1, 2*
2. What part of his goods did Zaccheus pledge to give to the poor? *Luke 19:8*
3. Quote Luke 19:10.

Lesson 11

1. Jesus said that the cup He gave to the disciples was the _____ _____ in His blood. *Luke 22:20*
2. During their meal together, an argument arose among the disciples. What was it about? *Luke 22:24*

Lesson 12

1. Name the three languages in which the title above Jesus' cross was written. *Luke 23:38*
2. What request did the thief on the cross ask of Jesus? *Luke 23:42*
3. On the day Jesus was crucified there was darkness from the _____ hour to the _____ hour. *Luke 23:44*

Lesson 13

1. What words of greeting did Jesus speak when He appeared to His disciples after His resurrection? *Luke 24:36*
2. Jesus said that all things written in the law of _____, in the _____, and in the _____ must be fulfilled concerning Him. *Luke 24:44*

Timeless Truths

by Johnny Pressley

WHY DO WE HAVE FOUR Gospel accounts of the life of Jesus? Isn't this just the same story being repeated? It is true that there is much overlap in material within the books of Matthew, Mark, Luke, and John, but it would be a mistake to think that the Gospel writers simply repeat each other. Each author uses a distinctive style and emphasizes certain themes for his readers. Thus our understanding of the life of Jesus has a richness that no single account could provide.

Matthew, for example, wrote primarily to Jewish readers. His Gospel cites a significant number of Old Testament messianic prophecies in order to show how Jesus fulfilled the promises that God's people had relied on for ages. Mark, on the other hand, seems to address a Gentile culture. By focusing on the miracles of Jesus, he demonstrates the powerful manner in which Jesus carried out His ministry. John adopts a more reflective manner and challenges philosophical minds with a portrait of Jesus as the true source of divine knowledge and wisdom.

Luke makes his distinctive contribution to our knowledge of Jesus by operating from a historian's perspective. It is Luke's intent to establish the historical reality of the life of Christ and to present the relevant historical facts. Thus he explains to his reader: "Therefore, since I myself have carefully investigated everything from the beginning, it seemed good also to me to write an orderly account for you, most excellent Theophilus, so that you may know the certainty of the things you have been taught" (Luke 1:3, 4, *New International Version*).

The lessons for this quarter are all drawn from the Gospel of Luke. Taken as a whole, they will serve to summarize the life of Jesus from His birth in Bethlehem, to His teaching ministry, and then to the climax of His suffering on the cross and resurrection from the grave. It is a familiar story, but it is one that deserves to be reviewed again and again. Each time we do, we discover a new perspective that deepens our understanding of, and our appreciation for, our Lord and Savior.

A Gift to Mankind

The first unit of five lessons is entitled, "A Savior is Born." Here we shall see the very first "Christmas gift," presented as God gives His beloved Son to mankind. A spirit of celebration and gratitude should spring from our study of the opening chapters of Luke as we are reminded of the angel's words to the shepherds: "Behold, I bring you good tidings of great joy, which shall be to all people. For unto you is born this day in the city of David a Saviour, which is Christ the Lord" (Luke 2:10, 11).

Lesson 1, "Preparing the Way," will highlight the ministry of John the Baptist as he made ready for the arrival of the promised Messiah. John's task was to create a climate of expectation in which Jesus could teach and minister effectively. His theme was repentance, something that is still required of any who wish to know Jesus as Lord and Savior.

Lesson 2, "Responding to God," will focus on the humility and trust of Mary as she welcomed the opportunity to fulfill God's role for her in bringing forth the long-awaited Messiah. This lesson will remind us of the kind of spirit that should characterize each of us, as seen in Mary's words: "Behold the handmaid of the Lord; be it unto me according to thy word" (Luke 1:38).

Lesson 3, "Praising God," will illustrate the nature of worship as we hear praise flow from the heart of the mother of Jesus. One of the most beloved prayers in Scripture is that spoken by Mary as she anticipates the birth of the Savior. *The Magnificat*, as Mary's praise is commonly called today, has been a source of inspiration for many and will move us to consider appropriate ways by which to exalt the name of the Lord and to express our gratitude for the "great things" He has done (Luke 1:49).

Lesson 4, "A Savior Is Born," will review what may be the most familiar chapter in the entire Bible—the Christmas story of Luke 2. We never tire of hearing about the baby Jesus' being born in humble surroundings and placed in a manger, or of the angel's announcing good news to the shepherds as they watched their flock by night. A devotional spirit will be most appropriate for the classroom, for this year the nativity story will be taught on a Christmas Eve Sunday.

Lesson 5, "Presented in the Temple," will focus on one of the lesser known events surrounding the birth of Jesus. As Mary and Joseph took their holy child into the temple shortly after His birth, they were confronted by an old man (Simeon) and an aged prophetess (Anna). Each acknowledged the significance of the child and expressed praise to God. This lesson will provide a final occasion to celebrate the birth of Christ as the holiday season draws to a close.

A Call to Service

The second unit of study, "Mission and Ministry," presents four lessons drawn from the teaching ministry of Jesus. In the texts selected for study, we shall see how Jesus revealed the nature of His ministry while urging His disciples to follow His example. Our goal will be to learn more about how we can be faithful servants of Christ in our world today.

Lesson 6, "Jesus in Nazareth," will give an example of the kind of opposition Jesus often confronted during His ministry. The occasion was Jesus' initial announcement to His hometown that He was, in fact, the fulfillment of the messianic prophecies. What should have been a cause for celebration turned into the first of many attempts on Jesus' life. Jesus' example shows us the kind of perseverance and determination needed when difficulties threaten to undermine our Christian service.

Lesson 7, "The Cost of Discipleship," will be one of the more challenging lessons in this quarter. It will remind us that Jesus' teaching on discipleship emphasizes a very demanding and rigorous commitment, comparable to what He Himself gave in His service to God. This lesson should call forth reflection and self-evaluation as we consider whether or not we are living up to the calling we profess.

Lesson 8, "Lost and Found," will highlight one of the best-known parables of Jesus—the parable of the "prodigal son." How well we remember the story of the foolish young man who left the comfort of his father's home and then squandered his inheritance! In this lesson we shall celebrate the grace of our Father, who continues to love us even when we have disappointed Him. But we shall also be challenged to develop the kind of repentance and humility that teaches us to appreciate God's grace.

Lesson 9, "Threat of Riches," will make a specific application of the discipleship theme to the way we manage our money and possessions. Worldly wealth can easily distract us from godly concerns, so much so that Scripture repeatedly cautions us to be wary of its appeal. In fact, our attitude toward worldly things is a good test of how much we are truly disciples of Christ.

The Way to Glory

The final unit of lessons, "Cross and Resurrection," focuses on the climax of the life of Christ—His death at Calvary and His resurrection from the dead. Of the four Gospels, Luke in particular develops the theme of Jesus' focus on the cross (Luke 9:51) and how an ever-present anticipation of His suffering and death carried Him to the completion of His ministry.

Lesson 10, "Going to Jerusalem," will provide an example of the clear perception Jesus had of the suffering that lay ahead of Him. It will also take us back to the favorite childhood story of Zaccheus, the little man in the sycamore tree. Here we shall explore again the Biblical themes of forgiveness and acceptance by God.

Lesson 11, "One Who Serves," will survey some of the events on the night when Jesus observed the Passover with His apostles and instituted the Lord's Supper. The truths regarding discipleship and service that were emphasized in our second unit of lessons were exemplified by the One who told His followers, "I am among you as he that serveth" (Luke 22:27).

Lesson 12, "Dying on a Cross," will focus on Luke's account of the greatest act of love in history. The lesson will give us another opportunity to reflect on Jesus' suffering at Calvary for the sins of the world.

Lesson 13, "Witnesses to the Resurrection," will serve as a fitting conclusion to our study of the life of Christ. Jesus' resurrection confirms that a complete atonement for sins was accomplished on the cross. It is His resurrection that gives us hope of our own resurrection to eternal life with Him.

The life, death, and resurrection of Jesus Christ do not belong in the realm of myth or legend; these are events that are firmly established in history. They are timeless truths to be cherished with all our hearts and to be proclaimed unashamedly to a lost world.

Answers to Quarterly Quiz on page 114

Lesson 1—1. vipers. 2. publicans. 3. soldiers. **Lesson 2**—1. Gabriel. 2. Elisabeth. **Lesson 3**—1. true. 2. soul, magnify, spirit, rejoiced. **Lesson 4**—1. Bethlehem. 2. "Fear not." **Lesson 5**—1. consolation. 2. before he had seen the Lord's Christ. 3. Asher. **Lesson 6**—1. Isaiah. 2. gracious words. 3. Elijah and Elisha. **Lesson 7**—1. bury. 2. tower. **Lesson 8**—1. the Pharisees and scribes. 2. hired servants. **Lesson 9**—1. false. 2. mammon, unrighteousness. 3. God and mammon. **Lesson 10**—1. Jericho. 2. half. 3. "For the Son of man is come to seek and to save that which was lost." **Lesson 11**—1. new testament. 2. which of them was the greatest. **Lesson 12**—1. Greek, Latin, and Hebrew. 2. "Lord, remember me when thou comest into thy kingdom." 3. sixth, ninth. **Lesson 13**—1. "Peace be unto you." 2. Moses, prophets, psalms.

117

Locating
the Lessons

Numerals indicate lesson numbers

GALILEE

SEA OF GALILEE

Nazareth
2 • 6

SAMARIA

Jordan River

PEREA

7 8 9

MEDITERRANEAN SEA

3
Hill
Country?
Jerusalem
•5 11 12 13

Jericho
10•

Wilderness of
1 Judea?

Bethlehem
4

DEAD
SEA

JUDEA

Good News for All

Matthew, Mark, and John all make some references to the impact of the gospel on all peoples. Consider Matthew's and Mark's record of Jesus' command to His disciples to go to "all nations" (Matthew 28:19) and "every creature" (Mark 16:15). Recall John's familiar words that "God so loved the world" (John 3:16).

Luke, however, demonstrates a particularly keen interest in God's concern for those considered outside the nation of Israel. This may have been of special significance to Luke since he himself, most likely, was a Gentile.

Consider the following references that are unique to Luke's writings:

Volume I: The Gospel of Luke

Reference	Incident	Significance
Luke 2:10	Shepherds in the field	"good tidings . . . to all people"
Luke 2:29-32	Simeon in the temple	Jesus is described as a "light to lighten the Gentiles"
Luke 3:6	John the Baptist's preaching	"all flesh" shall see God's salvation (all four Gospel writers quote from Isaiah; only Luke includes the reference to "all flesh")
Luke 4:25-27	Jesus in the Nazareth synagogue	God's special care for a Gentile widow and for Naaman (a Syrian)
Luke 10:25-37	Parable of the Good Samaritan	A Samaritan is commended for his kindness
Luke 14:15-24	Parable of the Great Supper	Those in the "highways and hedges" represent the Gentiles
Luke 17:11-19	Healing of the ten lepers	The only healed leper who thanks Jesus is a Samaritan

Volume II: The Book of Acts

Reference	Incident	Significance
Acts 1:8	Jesus' Great Commission	The apostles are told to go to the "uttermost part of the earth"
Acts 9:15; 22:21; 26:16-18	Commission to Paul	Paul is sent to the Gentiles
Acts 10:45; 11:18	Preaching to Cornelius	Gentiles accept the gospel
Acts 14:27	End of first missionary journey	God opens the "door of faith unto the Gentiles"
Acts 15:12-19	Jerusalem Conference	Gentiles' reception of the gospel is encouraged
Acts 20:21	Paul addresses Ephesian elders	Paul stresses his ministry to both Jews and Greeks
Acts 28:23-28	Paul in Rome	Gentiles' faith is highlighted

His Stories—and Ours

Using Stories to Teach the Story of Jesus

by Ronald G. Davis

As SOON AS THE TWO DISCIPLES of Jesus realized what had happened to them on the road to Emmaus, they had to find those who would want to know "what things were done in the way" (Luke 24:35). History is simply the "things done in the way" of daily life. Every person is a part of history. Every person has a history, for everyone experiences "things done in the way."

Luke wanted to tell the story of Jesus, even as it was "delivered . . . unto us" by those who "from the beginning were eyewitnesses, and ministers of the word" (Luke 1:2). Luke wanted to tell the stories of and about Jesus—stories that he rightly considered to be the most important personal history ever lived. And his Gospel reflects his high esteem for stories, or narratives, as the way to communicate the truth (the real Truth!) of history.

Any quick skimming of Luke's Gospel in a Bible version that uses paragraph headings is a journey through an index of one narrative after another. Luke's Gospel has more "stories"—that is, distinct narrative segments—than any of the others. In fact, about three-fourths of Luke's Gospel is narrative. And much of the material that is not narrative appears in the context of a narrative, such as when Jesus discussed future events on the occasion of walking by the temple area with His disciples (Luke 21:5-36). From Luke 9:51 through 18:14 Luke relates twenty-one stories that the other Gospels do not include.

Such a concern with narrative helped Luke achieve his purpose for writing his Gospel: to establish "the certainty of those things, wherein [Theophilus had] been instructed" (Luke 1:4). This concern for truth is seen in the Old Testament as well—from the events in Eden to the conflicts of Ezra and Nehemiah's time. The "things done in the way" reveal who God is and what His will is. History is truly "His story."

Stories and Wise Teachers

Now let us consider how much teachers of adults can learn from others who have attempted to communicate the truth of God's Word in story form.

While reading stories to adults may seem childish or out of place, this is a teaching method that can foster a wide range of learning opportunities for adults.

Few learners of any age can resist listening to a story (especially if it is short enough and age-appropriate in relevancy, content, and language). Reading aloud to adult students probably should seldom exceed four to five hundred words, and it should not last any longer than four to five minutes. While our major source of stories for reading (or telling) is the Bible itself, we must not overlook the wealth of significant stories to be gleaned from non-Biblical sources.

"Read Me a Bible Story, Teacher"

All the stories of the Bible have been told and retold in print. Some of these endeavors have followed Biblical texts closely, while others have used a well-informed imagination. (And some, of course, have used uninformed imaginations!) The "bare bones" nature of the Biblical accounts is by the Holy Spirit's design, so that (as John observed) we do not have to deal with an unmanageable collection of books (John 21:25).

Even stories published for children can provide ready instructional material for adults. Excellent compare-and-contrast activities and discussions can ensue. However, one must be cautious of any retellings that ignore or deny the inspirational, revelational nature of the contents of the Bible. At the same time, such retellings may offer useful insights into the thinking of those who consider Biblical stories to be in the same category as myth and legend (and they will offer your students a strong reminder that there are those who hold such views and who seek to influence children through their writings).

This quarter's studies from Luke's Gospel include some of the most familiar portions of Jesus' life and ministry: the beautiful birth narratives, the parable of the "prodigal son," Zaccheus's unique encounter with Christ, and the dramatic events surrounding Jesus' death at Calvary and His resurrection from the dead. As was the case in Luke's day, many have "taken in hand," as Luke himself did (Luke 1:1), the pen of narration and applied it to these and other stories.

Every religious publisher that prepares materials for children will have a selection of usable titles. (Most churches have such books lying around in their children's classrooms.) And most public libraries, in the religious section for children, shelve many relevant titles. Although the diligent searcher will find other good choices, a few worthy titles for this quarter's study from Luke follow.

Award-winning Christian writer Madeleine L'Engle prepared a series of stories on the life of Christ in *The Glorious Impossible* (Simon and Schuster, Inc., New York, 1990). This includes a telling of "The Annunciation," which would relate well to lessons 2 and 3 in this quarter.

The beautifully and authentically illustrated *The Blessing of the Lord* by Gary D. Schmidt (William B. Eerdmans Publishing Company, Grand Rapids, 1997), with artwork by Dennis Nolan, includes stories on "The Centurion at Calvary," related to lesson 12, and "Anna, Simeon, and the Blessing Fulfilled," which goes with lesson 5. Though these retellings are long, a teacher could use only selected portions for reading to the class.

One very popular series for children has been the Arch book collection from Concordia Publishing House. These versified retellings range from fair to excellent, but can be read quickly and with easy articulation and emphasis. Stories from the life and the parables of Jesus offer ready possibilities for use during this series from Luke's Gospel. (And adults might also enjoy the illustrations, which are easy to show as the text is being read!)

Holiday House, Inc., a leading New York publisher for children, has published a variety of religious titles, such as, *He Is Risen: The Easter Story* by Elizabeth Winthrop (1985), with illustrations by the noted children's artist Charles Mikolaycak. And popular children's writer/illustrator Tomie dePaola has done some significant work for Holiday House, including *The Miracles of Jesus* and *The Parables of Jesus*.

It is always interesting to compare and contrast what human writers do with a Biblical account with what the inspired writer has recorded. Sadly, several items are omitted even while non-Biblical events are added. Even worse, some factual information is distorted and denied. Most adults, however, will gain much from discussing the differences and the possible reasons for them. When a writer violates cultural, historical, or geographical facts, one is right to question his motives—or at least his understanding. This, of course, demands that the teacher and the members of the class have a solid background in the cultural, historical, and geographical setting of the Biblical narratives.

"Read Me More Stories, Teacher"

Many other stories worthy of use in instructing adults can be drawn from non-Biblical sources, both from the realms of fiction and non-fiction (especially biography). Tales from literature may help one illustrate the importance of standards of right and wrong, or, conversely, may highlight the contrasting worldview based on humanistic thinking. Even the well-known fables of Aesop can illustrate both, for not only is diligent effort touted as the secret to personal success (as in "The Ant and the Grasshopper"), but the "get-even" mentality is represented in "The Fox and the Stork," with the usual concluding moral stated: "One bad turn deserves another." (That's quite the opposite of the behavior taught by Jesus in the "Golden Rule.") And other fables from anonymous sources, such as "The Goose That Laid the Golden Egg," illustrate quite effectively the consequences of greed, which is one of the key issues of Jesus' parable studied in lesson 9, "Threat of Riches."

Of course, there is a wealth of biographical material that is worthy of use by the teacher, especially incidents from the "lives of the saints." These include vivid accounts from the classic *Foxe's Book of Martyrs* (originally compiled by John Foxe) to more contemporary examples of godly lives, such as those of Corrie Ten Boom and Aleksandr Solzhenitsyn. Lesson 7 in the coming series ("The Cost of Discipleship") can certainly be brought to life using some of the incidents recorded in Foxe's collection or some of Solzhenitsyn's stories of life in a Siberian gulag. Lesson 11, entitled "One Who Serves," gives the teacher an excellent opportunity to use illustrations from Ten Boom's account of the months she spent in a prisoner-of-war camp.

Finally, the teacher of adults must not overlook the compelling stories that appear in the daily news. These accounts show how man's behavior has changed little from the first century to the twenty-first. Prodigal son (and prodigal daughter) stories abound, for sin still abounds. Reading such items to the class (keep them fairly short) and asking for the way(s) in which a story parallels Biblical incidents will elicit both thought and insight—and this is exactly what the teacher of adults is after.

The Teacher's "Library"

Every wise teacher of adults should constantly be "collecting" stories that may prove to be useful in instruction. Keeping an eye on coming lessons and coming lesson series will enable one to spot just the right stories. Those read to children and grandchildren, those found in devotional and leisure reading, those heard or seen in daily news reports—all have the potential to become effective instructional material.

Who can resist a good story? Almost no one. Jesus knew that, and so did His Father. What about you?

Preparing the Way

DEVOTIONAL READING: Isaiah 40:1-5.

BACKGROUND SCRIPTURE: Luke 1:5-25; 3:1-22.

PRINTED TEXT: Luke 3:2b-18.

Luke 3:2b-18

2b The word of God came unto John the son of Zechariah in the wilderness.

3 And he came into all the country about Jordan, preaching the baptism of repentance for the remission of sins;

4 As it is written in the book of the words of Isaiah the prophet, saying, The voice of one crying in the wilderness, Prepare ye the way of the Lord, make his paths straight.

5 Every valley shall be filled, and every mountain and hill shall be brought low; and the crooked shall be made straight, and the rough ways shall be made smooth;

6 And all flesh shall see the salvation of God.

7 Then said he to the multitude that came forth to be baptized of him, O generation of vipers, who hath warned you to flee from the wrath to come?

8 Bring forth therefore fruits worthy of repentance, and begin not to say within yourselves, We have Abraham to our father: for I say unto you, That God is able of these stones to raise up children unto Abraham.

9 And now also the axe is laid unto the root of the trees: every tree therefore which bringeth not forth good fruit is hewn down, and cast into the fire.

10 And the people asked him, saying, What shall we do then?

11 He answereth and saith unto them, He that hath two coats, let him impart to him that hath none; and he that hath meat, let him do likewise.

12 Then came also publicans to be baptized, and said unto him, Master, what shall we do?

13 And he said unto them, Exact no more than that which is appointed you.

14 And the soldiers likewise demanded of him, saying, And what shall we do? And he said unto them, Do violence to no man, neither accuse any falsely; and be content with your wages.

15 And as the people were in expectation, and all men mused in their hearts of John, whether he were the Christ, or not;

16 John answered, saying unto them all, I indeed baptize you with water; but one mightier than I cometh, the latchet of whose shoes I am not worthy to unloose: he shall baptize you with the Holy Ghost and with fire:

17 Whose fan is in his hand, and he will thoroughly purge his floor, and will gather the wheat into his garner; but the chaff he will burn with fire unquenchable.

18 And many other things in his exhortation preached he unto the people.

GOLDEN TEXT: The voice of one crying in the wilderness, Prepare ye the way of the Lord, make his paths straight.—Luke 3:4.

> *Good News of Jesus*
> Unit 1: A Savior Is Born
> (Lessons 1-5)

Lesson Aims

After participating in this lesson, each student will be able to:

1. Summarize what Luke says about the message of John the Baptist.

2. Tell why some of the specific applications in John's message are important to a demonstration of repentance.

3. State one action he or she will take this week as a demonstration of repentance from past sins and commitment to the Lord.

Lesson Outline

INTRODUCTION
  A. "Allow Me to Introduce . . ."
  B. Lesson Background
I. JOHN AND HIS MINISTRY (Luke 3:2b-6)
  A. His Baptism (vv. 2b, 3)
  B. His Mission (vv. 4-6)
II. JOHN AND HIS MESSAGE (Luke 3:7-14)
  A. Stern Warnings (vv. 7-9)
  B. Practical Applications (vv. 10-14)
    Wearing and Sharing
    Preacher Pierce
III. JOHN AND THE MESSIAH (Luke 3:15-18)
  A. John's Notoriety (v. 15)
  B. John's Humility (vv. 16-18)
CONCLUSION
  A. Be Prepared
  B. Prayer
  C. Thought to Remember

Introduction

A. "Allow Me to Introduce . . ."

Public speaking is a great challenge under any circumstance, but many speakers will tell you that one of the greatest challenges is to introduce someone else. How do you prepare an audience for what the speaker is going to say? How much do you tell the people about the speaker? How much do you say about the subject?

John the Baptist was given a similar assignment: he was to introduce the Messiah. How was he to prepare the people for such an individual? How much should he tell them about Him? How much of the attention should he draw to himself? Judging from the Messiah's own words,

John did a superlative job in preparing the way for Jesus. Jesus once said, "Among them that are born of women there hath not risen a greater than John the Baptist" (Matthew 11:11).

John kept the primary focus of his ministry as "preparer" in mind, even when some of his own disciples expressed concern that Jesus was starting to gain a greater following than his. John was not jealous or upset to hear this; his response left no doubt that he was content to be what God had called him to be. "He must increase," said John of the Messiah, "but I must decrease" (John 3:30).

John the Baptist was willing to take second place—to tell others, "Allow me to introduce you to Jesus"—and then to slip into the background. That's not a bad description of our responsibility as disciples of Jesus today.

B. Lesson Background

Even though John the Baptist was content to take a back seat to Jesus, his ministry had a significant impact. At one point in Jesus' ministry Herod Antipas speculated that He might be John the Baptist returning from the dead (Matthew 14:2). During Jesus' final week of ministry the Jewish leaders did not want to appear critical of John lest they offend the crowds in Jerusalem (Matthew 21:23-27). Some of the men who became part of Jesus' twelve disciples were originally disciples of John the Baptist (John 1:35-42). John was also a man of godly courage, who was not afraid to tell a king the truth even though it cost him his life (Matthew 14:3-11).

Today's lesson serves not only as the introductory lesson to our studies from Luke's Gospel but also as the first in a unit of lessons that will take us through the Christmas season. This unit will focus on some of the unique contributions that Luke makes to our understanding of the birth of Christ and the events surrounding it. Some might question why we should pay attention to John the Baptist during the season when we celebrate the birth of Jesus. Just as John prepared people for the arrival of the Messiah on the stage of history, he can prepare us to celebrate the true meaning of the Christmas season.

I. John and His Ministry (Luke 3:2b-6)

A. His Baptism (vv. 2b, 3)

2b. The word of God came unto John the son of Zechariah in the wilderness.

John the Baptist was a prophet (Luke 7:26), cast in the same mold as the prophets of the Old Testament. When the text says *the word of God came unto John*, it is using words that remind us of the kind of call that summoned those men who proclaimed God's message fearlessly to His people Israel. Prophets did not invent their own messages; they were ministers of the oracles of God.

John is described as *the son of Zechariah*. Zechariah, whose name means "God remembers," was a priest. Luke is the only Gospel writer to mention him. Earlier Luke tells of how, when Zechariah was taking his turn of service in the temple, an angel (Gabriel) appeared to him and announced that he and his wife Elisabeth would have a son in their old age (Luke 1:5-23).

We may wonder why John conducted his ministry *in the wilderness*. Perhaps he was distancing himself from the religious establishment that resided in the cities. Some have speculated that John may have been a member of the Essenes, a sect of the Jews known for its simplicity and strictness of lifestyle. But there is no Biblical evidence to support such a notion.

3. And he came into all the country about Jordan, preaching the baptism of repentance for the remission of sins.

John's ministry took him *into all the country about Jordan*. Matthew says John preached "in the wilderness of Judea" (Matthew 3:1). Most likely Luke's words describe John's preaching in the desert areas on both sides of the Jordan River.

The reason John became known as "John the Baptist" (or "Baptizer") was his distinctive message and practice. He came *preaching the baptism of repentance for the remission of sins*. This explains why John remained close to the Jordan River: he wanted to remain close to a body of water in which to perform baptisms.

Christian baptism would later build on the concepts of repentance and remission of sins, adding a connection with the death, burial, and resurrection of Jesus and with the gift of the Holy Spirit (Acts 2:38). Thus John's baptism looked forward to the time when remission of sins could be offered as a result of Jesus' death and resurrection, just as the Old Testament sacrifices looked forward to Jesus' perfect sacrifice.

Was the idea of baptism totally contrary to Jewish thinking and experience? First-century Judaism did include a "proselyte baptism" to bring Gentile converts into the Jewish faith, but there is no clear evidence that this preceded John's baptism. John's baptism was unique in its form and, more significantly, in its purpose.

B. His Mission (vv. 4-6)

4. As it is written in the book of the words of Isaiah the prophet, saying, The voice of one crying in the wilderness, Prepare ye the way of the Lord, make his paths straight.

Here Luke quotes from *Isaiah 40:3*. The prophet's language describes what happened whenever a king prepared for a journey. Workers and soldiers would proceed in advance to make sure that the road on which the king would travel was smooth and safe. John saw himself as engaged in a similar task on behalf of the Messiah.

How were John's listeners to *prepare . . . the way of the Lord* and *make his paths straight*? By turning the people's attention to spiritual concerns, John was seeking to heighten their receptiveness to the Messiah's message of a spiritual kingdom. John had no desire to further his own agenda; "he was not that Light, but was sent to bear witness of that Light" (John 1:8). [See question #1, page 128.]

5. Every valley shall be filled, and every mountain and hill shall be brought low; and the crooked shall be made straight, and the rough ways shall be made smooth.

The figure of speech continues with a description of the process involved in preparing the Messiah's way, making it both smoother and straighter. John's preaching was aimed at encouraging his hearers to clear away any obstacles in their thinking and living that could cause them to miss "the salvation of God" (v. 6).

6. And all flesh shall see the salvation of God.

When the Messiah arrives, *all flesh* will *see* His *salvation*. While all four Gospel writers refer to Isaiah's prophecy (Matthew 3:3; Mark 1:3; John 1:23), only Luke includes this emphasis that Jesus came for all mankind, not just for the Jewish nation. This is one of Luke's major themes in both Luke and Acts (cf. Luke 2:10, 29-32; 13:29; 17:11-19; 24:47; Acts 1:8; 11:18; 13:41-48; 15:12-19). It was probably of special significance to him, since he himself, most likely, was a Gentile.

II. John and His Message
(Luke 3:7-14)

A. Stern Warnings (vv. 7-9)

7. Then said he to the multitude that came forth to be baptized of him, O generation of vipers, who hath warned you to flee from the wrath to come?

The use of the word *multitude* indicates a diverse group of people. Luke's emphasis is more

---

VISUALS FOR THESE LESSONS

The visual pictured in each lesson (e.g., page 124) is a small reproduction of a large, full-color poster included in the *Adult Visuals* packet for the Winter Quarter. The packet is available from your supplier. Order No. 292.

Visual for
lesson 1
(See page 123
for ordering
information.)

PREPARE YE THE WAY OF THE LORD, MAKE HIS PATHS STRAIGHT.

Today's visual gives a modern face to John's metaphor of preparing the way. Have the class suggest modern ways to reach the lost for Christ.

inclusive than that of Matthew, who calls attention to the Pharisees and Sadducees who came to John's baptism (Matthew 3:7). John's message would have been particularly irritating for the Jewish leaders to hear, but it was intended for everyone in his audience.

John's message was uncompromising, and his rhetoric was strong. He described the crowd as a *generation of vipers*. Later Jesus would use the same figure of speech to portray the Pharisees (Matthew 12:34). John's question, *Who hath warned you to flee from the wrath to come?* may have been tinged with sarcasm (particularly toward the Pharisees and Sadducees), indicating that they had heard numerous warnings concerning God's *wrath*. They simply refused to listen.

8. Bring forth therefore fruits worthy of repentance, and begin not to say within yourselves, We have Abraham to our father: for I say unto you, That God is able of these stones to raise up children unto Abraham.

John urged his hearers to *bring forth . . . fruits worthy of repentance*. It is important for every Christian to bear fruit. No one can see another person's heart. The only way to tell whether genuine repentance has occurred is by examining the deeds, or fruit, of someone's life. It has been said that while works do not justify us, they do identify us. [See question #2, page 128.]

John also urged his audience not to depend on their ancestry to save them. There was no security in saying, *We have Abraham to our* genealogical *father*. John declared that God could make *children* of Abraham out of *stones* if He so desired. Clearly the One who created man from the dust of the earth could also make people from stones; John's audience would have admitted that. That these new creations could be children of Abraham foreshadowed the Christian message that all people can by faith be children of Abraham (Romans 4:11, 12).

9. And now also the axe is laid unto the root of the trees: every tree therefore which bringeth

not forth good fruit is hewn down, and cast into the fire.

Here John used a figure of speech to illustrate impending judgment. He pictured a farmer cutting down a lifeless, fruitless *tree* and casting it into the *fire* to be burned. Why is it burned? Because it is useless. Recall words similar to these in John 15:6. [See question #3, page 128.]

B. Practical Applications (vv. 10-14)

10. And the people asked him, saying, What shall we do then?

The crowd responded to John's appeal in a way strikingly similar to the response to Peter's sermon in Luke's sequel, the book of Acts (2:37). They asked, *What shall we do then?*

11. He answereth and saith unto them, He that hath two coats, let him impart to him that hath none; and he that hath meat, let him do likewise.

To the crowd in general, John suggested a very practical application of his message: he urged compassion on the needy. In John's day, most people had no need of *two coats*, so John recommended sharing with anyone who had none. (The *coat* was a tunic worn by both men and women under one's outer garment or robe.)

John urged the sharing of *meat*, or food, with those who have none. If this spirit of kindness characterized disciples of John, how much more should it be the trademark of followers of Jesus!

WEARING AND SHARING

When the Communists controlled Eastern Europe, Christians in those countries came from time to time to Vienna, Austria, to a mission called Haus Edelweiss (House *Ay*-del-vice). In addition to offering Bible classes, the mission kept a used clothing room. Each guest was given an opportunity to spend a couple of hours there and take anything that he or his family could use. During one conference the weather turned rather cool, so my wife suggested some might want to make a second visit to the clothing room to get a sweater. Later a man from Estonia came to her with a sweater and said, "I would like to donate this to the clothing room. I already have a sweater."

This man's attitude toward his possessions reminded us of John the Baptist's challenge: "He that hath two coats, let him impart to him that hath none." We live in a world where many are poorly clothed. The need is so enormous that we cannot clothe them all. But if we can clothe one, we should. Likewise, we live in a world where millions are hungry. We cannot personally feed them all. But if we can feed one, we should.

We need to take John's teaching out of the realm of theory and put it into action. How many times do we look into our closets and say, "I don't have a thing to wear!" Wouldn't it be more accurate to say that we do not have anything we *want* to wear, or that we cannot decide what to wear?

Let's keep our eyes open to the blessings we have and to the needs of those around us. Many would dearly love to have what we often consider "nothing" to wear or "nothing" to eat. —R. C. S.

12. Then came also publicans to be baptized, and said unto him, Master, what shall we do?

Luke notes that even *publicans,* that is, tax collectors, came *to be baptized.* Tax collectors have never been popular, but in Jesus' day they were especially despised as thieves and traitors. They were viewed as traitors because of their cooperation with the Romans. They were regarded as thieves because many of them were! The Roman system of collection encouraged them to use strong-arm tactics and take more than was required, allowing them to pocket the surplus. Recall that Jesus made a great impact on two tax collectors in particular—Matthew and Zaccheus.

The use of the word *Master* by the publicans does not mean that they considered John the Messiah. The Greek term is more accurately rendered, "Teacher." It was simply a term of respect.

13. And he said unto them, Exact no more than that which is appointed you.

John commanded the publicans to take *no more than* what was required by law. Note that Zaccheus, following his encounter with Jesus, was so concerned about his own practices that he gave half of his wealth to the poor and offered to those whom he had wronged four times the amount they had been cheated (Luke 19:8).

14. And the soldiers likewise demanded of him, saying, And what shall we do? And he said unto them, Do violence to no man, neither accuse any falsely; and be content with your wages.

Home Daily Bible Readings

Monday, Nov. 27—The Prophecy of John's Birth (Luke 1:5-17)
Tuesday, Nov. 28—Too Good to Be True (Luke 1:18-25)
Wednesday, Nov. 29—John the Baptist's Birth (Luke 1:57-66)
Thursday, Nov. 30—Prophetic Words of Hope (Isaiah 40:1-5)
Friday, Dec. 1—John's Proclamation (Luke 3:1-6)
Saturday, Dec. 2—Baptism, Repentance, and Change (Luke 3:7-14)
Sunday, Dec. 3—The Truth Hurts (Luke 3:15-20)

Even *soldiers* were attracted to John's message. We do not know what kind of soldiers these were. Limited numbers of them were available to guard the king, to monitor the temple, and to escort tax collectors. Soldiers also served as a kind of police force. John urged these men to be ethical in their dealings with people. They were not to extort money or lie in making accusations.

John did not recommend that either tax collectors or soldiers resign from their positions. He told them to demonstrate integrity in everything they did, thus showing "fruits worthy of repentance" (v. 8). [See question #4, page 128.]

PREACHER PIERCE

He was a bi-vocational minister whom everyone called "Preacher Pierce." His full-time job was running a collection station for cream brought in by the local farmers. He owned the small building and all the equipment, and he had a contract with a company to collect and store the cream for a percentage of the money paid to the farmer. On one occasion, at the end of the month he kept the check that he received from the company and did not cash it. When the representative of the firm came by, Preacher Pierce told him, "This check is wrong, and I won't accept it."

The representative said, "That is the amount we agreed to pay you, and we will not pay you one penny more."

"You misunderstand," Pierce replied. "It's not that the check is too small. It's too big. I don't think I earned this much, and I won't accept it!"

It is interesting to consider this man's attitude in light of John the Baptist's challenge to "be content with your wages." Most people are discontent, not because they are paid too much, but because they believe they are paid too little! A great deal of envy, bitterness, anxiety, and frustration could be avoided if people took to heart the words of "Preacher John."

As for "Preacher Pierce"—what became of him? By refusing to accept what he thought he had not earned, he earned the respect of the entire community; and his ministry had an impact that it probably would not have had otherwise.

—R. C. S.

III. John and the Messiah
(Luke 3:15-18)

A. John's Notoriety (v. 15)

15. And as the people were in expectation, and all men mused in their hearts of John, whether he were the Christ, or not.

Some among the crowds *mused,* or wondered, if *John* himself *were the Christ.* It is clear, especially from the apostle John's account, that John the Baptist was not the Messiah and never claimed to be (John 1:8, 19-27; 3:28). He was true to his role as forerunner, calling attention only to his Successor, never to himself.

B. John's Humility (vv. 16-18)

16. John answered, saying unto them all, I indeed baptize you with water; but one mightier than I cometh, the latchet of whose shoes I am not worthy to unloose: he shall baptize you with the Holy Ghost and with fire.

To illustrate the superiority of the Messiah, John referred to his own baptism and compared it with the baptism that Jesus would institute. (Since John was known primarily for his baptism, this served as an especially effective comparison.) John said, *I indeed baptize you with water.* He then noted that the Messiah would administer a superior baptism: *he shall baptize you with the Holy Ghost and with fire,*

Some believe that the baptism with the Spirit refers to what happened on the Day of Pentecost when the Holy Spirit came upon the apostles (Acts 2:1-4). Others maintain that this baptism with the Spirit is identical with what is called the gift of the Holy Spirit—that is, the promise that the Holy Spirit will dwell in all Christians (Acts 2:38; 5:32; 1 Corinthians 12:13). Luke himself seems to indicate the former when he quotes the resurrected Christ telling the apostles to "wait for the promise of the Father" and adding, "For John truly baptized with water; but ye shall be baptized with the Holy Ghost not many days hence" (Acts 1:4, 5). The baptism *with fire* most likely describes God's judgment, given the reference to *fire* in verse 17.

Once again, John's humility is demonstrated in his acknowledgment that he was not *worthy to unloose* the *shoes* (sandals) of the Messiah. John refused to receive any acclaim that should go to the One whose way he was preparing.

17. Whose fan is in his hand, and he will thoroughly purge his floor, and will gather the wheat into his garner; but the chaff he will burn with fire unquenchable.

In continuing his description of judgment, John announced that the Messiah will come with a *fan.* This word describes the winnowing fork—a farm implement that was used on the threshing *floor* after wheat was cut during the harvest. First, the grain was separated from the straw, often by having oxen trample it. Then, in order to separate the kernel of *wheat* from the lighter shell or *chaff,* the grain was scooped up with a wide fork (the fan) and tossed into the air. The wind separated the light chaff from the heavier grain, which was then stored in a *garner,* or barn. In a similar way, the Messiah will separate the

truly repentant from the wicked, gathering the former to be with Him and destroying the latter (Matthew 13:41-43).

18. And many other things in his exhortation preached he unto the people.

We can only speculate about the content of these *other things* that John *preached.* About the purpose of this *exhortation* there need be no speculation. John's words were meant to point away from himself and toward Jesus. [See question #5, page 128.]

Conclusion

A. Be Prepared

John the Baptist's message speaks powerfully to Christians today. He taught that the process of preparing the way for the Messiah was to prepare one's heart through repentance and visible evidence of a reformed life.

How much more is this an appropriate way to prepare for Jesus' second coming! The world often associates repentance with an "old-fashioned" religion that has no relevance whatever to modern times. It will be more likely to understand the concept if it can see "fruits worthy of repentance" in the lives of God's people.

Most are acquainted with the Boy Scout motto: *Be prepared.* That's the substance of what John told people in his day; it describes the attitude of Christians as we consider the promised return of Jesus. And, like those in John's audience, we should look at our lives, take stock of our level of preparation, and ask ourselves the question, *What shall we do?*

B. Prayer

Father, I come to You for mercy, and I present to You my desire for a changed life. May it be evident to all that I am serving You. Strengthen me for the crucial task of being fruitful in a rotting world. In Jesus' name and for His sake, amen.

C. Thought to Remember

Repentance and reformation bring restoration.

How to Say It

ANTIPAS. *An*-tih-pus.
ESSENES. *Eh*-seenz.
GABRIEL. *Gay*-bree-ul.
ISAIAH. Eye-*zay*-uh.
PHARISEES. *Fair*-ih-seez.
SADDUCEES. *Sad*-you-seez.
ZACCHEUS. Zack-*kee*-us.
ZECHARIAH. Zek-uh-*rye*-uh.

Learning by Doing

This page contains an alternate lesson plan emphasizing learning activities.
Classes desiring such student involvement will find these suggestions helpful.

Learning Goals

After this lesson each student will be able to:

1. Summarize what Luke says about the message of John the Baptist.

2. Tell why some of the specific applications in John's message are important to a demonstration of repentance.

3. State one action he or she will take this week as a demonstration of repentance from past sins and commitment to the Lord.

Into the Lesson

Ask class members to imagine that the president of the United States (substitute the appropriate title and country if you live outside the U.S.) is coming to your town in one month. Discuss what would be done (and by whom) to prepare for this event. Encourage the class members to be as detailed as possible.

Tell the students, "When someone important is expected to arrive on the scene, there is always considerable preparation. Let's look at how the way was prepared for Jesus' ministry."

Into the Word

Examine the character of John the Baptist in parallel texts—Matthew 3:1-6; Mark 1:1-8; John 1:19-27. Assign each text to one third of the class for reading and thinking. Instruct the students to look for characteristics of John because they will be telling you what to list on the chalkboard. They may suggest *humble, obedient, simple, bold, rugged,* or *Biblically literate.* Read the list and comment on his obedience, sense of duty, and responsibility.

With this background understanding of John, ask a volunteer to read Luke 3:2b-18. Form groups of four or five, and ask the students to summarize the significance of each of the sections of text—vv. 2b-6, 7-9, 10-14, and 15-18. Discuss the responses as a class. Emphasize the following areas of significance:

Verses 2b-6: John's heritage (son of Zechariah, a Levite), his prophetic role (a word of God came to him; fulfills the prophecy of Isaiah 40:3-5).

Verses 7-9: the view of repentance as action.

Verses 10-14: specific applications.

Verses 15-18: preparation for the incarnation of God: Jesus.

Class members may ask some of the following questions or you may raise them.

"Why would the people wonder if John were the Christ?" *(The religious establishment was seeking a Messiah. The incorporation of Israel into the Roman Empire caused some to expect the coming of the Messiah.)*

"What is the difference between the baptism of John and Christian baptism as we know it today?" *(The baptism of John was in accordance with repentance and forgiveness of sins; Christian baptism builds on this—cf. Acts 19:4, 5. In addition, Christian baptism is intimately bound with the death, burial, and resurrection of Jesus Christ, which had not yet taken place.)*

Observe, "Many types of people were asking the *same* question of John that day: 'What shall we do?'" Discuss what the various responses that John gave have in common. Ask the students to suggest how we can act in the same spirit even if our specific actions may differ.

Into Life

Instruct the students to write the word *repent* vertically on a sheet of paper. Then ask them to use each letter of the word to begin a word or phrase that describes a specific action one might take today in demonstration of true repentance. Ask, "If we could bring John the Baptist back to life and have him visit our class, what might he say to us? If we asked, 'What shall *we* do?' how might he answer us?" Use the acronym to suggest some answers. As appropriate, have class members tell how they completed the acronym.

Observe, "We know Jesus is coming, and we often speak of being 'ready' for His return. How is preparation for Jesus' return similar to and different from the preparations for His first coming?" *(In each case the exact time of His coming was/is unknown. In both cases repentance was/is appropriate. In preparing for His first coming, John was preparing the people to hear and believe the message that was yet to be delivered. In our preparation, we want people to accept the truth already available. John prepared for Jesus to **begin** His work; we prepare for Jesus to **complete** His work.)*

Point out that John the Baptist fulfilled his responsibility in preparing the way for the coming of Jesus. Discuss, "What is our responsibility in preparing for the return of Jesus? What shall we do?" Close the lesson with a prayer for each class member to repent.

Let's Talk It Over

The questions on this page are designed to encourage review of the lesson Scriptures and to promote discussion of the lesson by the class. The answers provided are only discussion starters. Let your class talk it over from there.

1. What did it mean, in practical terms, for people to "prepare . . . the way of the Lord"? In what sense can we today "prepare . . . the way of the Lord"?

John used the vivid image of preparing the roadway for the safe and unobstructed arrival of a king. It is sin and competing loyalties that make the heart of any person a "wilderness" unfit for the arrival of the Lord. The lives of most of us could be represented by a roadbed obstructed by potholes left from eroding moral conviction and the debris of broken standards. John's call to "prepare . . . the way" focused on personal repentance, including a sincere effort at reform. People today need a similar preparation to allow Christ into their hearts and lives. We can prepare the way by helping people to focus on spiritual issues and to see their need for a Savior. Get as specific as the class is willing to be on ways to do this.

2. If some who came to John for baptism were insincere, what was motivating them? Why would anyone today pretend to follow Christ?

As more and more people responded to John's message, the nature of the response may have changed from a true revival to a social movement. It seems that some were motivated by the desire to be respected by the crowds who were flocking to John. From John's words it seems that some were seeking baptism as a spiritual merit badge rather than from genuine repentance. The motives of those who would pretend devotion to Christ today may be the same. It may be a way of avoiding arguments with a spouse or parent. It may bring entry into desired social circles. It could even be a misguided attempt to placate God by practicing certain religious rites and routines. Surface faith and pretended devotion do not go far with God (Isaiah 29:13; James 2:14-17).

3. What kind of "good fruit" demonstrates sincere repentance?

As godly sorrow leads to repentance, it seems reasonable to expect that some sorrow for past sin and faithlessness will accompany genuine repentance. Repentance is more than sorrow, however. It is a turning around, a change of course. One who truly repents will not frequent the places he once did. One who repents will not use the same kind of language she once did. The

truly repentant will not seek entertainment from the same sources they used to. Rather, they will replace all these with positive alternatives—friends who edify them, speech that is kind and gracious, entertainment that is wholesome.

4. What if your occupation were represented in the crowd? If someone with the same job as you asked John, "What shall we do?" what do you think John would have said?

Essentially John pleaded for honesty in his replies to the tax collectors and the soldiers. Surely that would be a major issue for anyone. But every occupation has its own particular temptations—tampering with time sheets, false reporting of inventory, taking excessively long breaks, embezzling funds, and many others. In addition to work-related behaviors, discuss personal honesty and integrity. What would John say about filing improper tax returns, claiming greater than actual losses on insurance claims, or withholding information about damage or mechanical problems when selling a used car? Again, get as specific as the class is willing to be.

5. John's task is our task—to point people toward Jesus. How are we tempted to draw attention to ourselves? How can we more effectively point people to Jesus?

While it is fitting and proper to recognize and honor those who do notable deeds, all our efforts pale in comparison with what Jesus has done. Keeping His life and ministry—especially His death, burial, and resurrection—in mind should help us keep the focus on Him. But when another is recognized for a service rendered and we are not, we easily fall into the trap of trying to make our contribution seem larger by minimizing that of the other person. Others, craving the attention given to those who contribute, throw themselves into some task or ministry. While service is commendable, seeking the praise of men is not. The value of our service is depreciated in God's eyes when it is done for men's applause.

We need a constant and consistent reminder that the Great Commission (Matthew 28:19, 20) is our mission in a nutshell. Everything we do needs to be measured by how or whether it helps to accomplish this great task—or whether it simply gives us an opportunity to be noticed!

Responding to God

DEVOTIONAL READING: Matthew 1:18-25.

BACKGROUND SCRIPTURE: Luke 1:26-38.

PRINTED TEXT: Luke 1:26-38.

Luke 1:26-38

26 And in the sixth month the angel Gabriel was sent from God unto a city of Galilee, named Nazareth,

27 To a virgin espoused to a man whose name was Joseph, of the house of David; and the virgin's name was Mary.

28 And the angel came in unto her, and said, Hail, thou that art highly favored, the Lord is with thee: blessed art thou among women.

29 And when she saw him, she was troubled at his saying, and cast in her mind what manner of salutation this should be.

30 And the angel said unto her, Fear not, Mary: for thou hast found favor with God.

31 And, behold, thou shalt conceive in thy womb, and bring forth a son, and shalt call his name JESUS.

32 He shall be great, and shall be called the Son of the Highest; and the Lord God shall give unto him the throne of his father David:

33 And he shall reign over the house of Jacob for ever; and of his kingdom there shall be no end.

34 Then said Mary unto the angel, How shall this be, seeing I know not a man?

35 And the angel answered and said unto her, The Holy Ghost shall come upon thee, and the power of the Highest shall overshadow thee: therefore also that holy thing which shall be born of thee shall be called the Son of God.

36 And, behold, thy cousin Elisabeth, she hath also conceived a son in her old age; and this is the sixth month with her, who was called barren.

37 For with God nothing shall be impossible.

38 And Mary said, Behold the handmaid of the Lord; be it unto me according to thy word. And the angel departed from her.

GOLDEN TEXT: And Mary said, Behold the handmaid of the Lord; be it unto me according to thy word.—Luke 1:38.

> ## Good News of Jesus
> Unit 1: A Savior Is Born
> (Lessons 1-5)

Lesson Aims

After participating in this lesson, each student will be able to:

1. Give the important details of Gabriel's message to Mary and her response to it.

2. Tell why Mary's response to God's will is an appropriate model for Christians.

3. Think of a difficult decision or issue he or she is facing, and commit that matter to God in simple faith.

Lesson Outline

INTRODUCTION
    A. The Importance of Motherhood
    B. Babies Change Everything
    C. Lesson Background
I. THE ANGEL'S MESSAGE (Luke 1:26-33)
    A. The Mother God Chooses (vv. 26-28)
    B. The Comfort God Brings (vv. 29, 30)
    C. The Child God Sends (vv. 31-33)
        Common Name, Uncommon Child
II. MARY'S RESPONSE (Luke 1:34-38)
    A. Her Question (vv. 34, 35)
    B. Her Sign (vv. 36, 37)
        Specializing in the Impossible
    C. Her Submission (v. 38)
CONCLUSION
    A. "Whatever"
    B. Something Special
    C. One Grand Package
    D. Prayer
    E. Thought to Remember

Introduction

A. The Importance of Motherhood

While both parents of a child are important, there has always been a special emphasis placed on motherhood. This is true even in our day, though some have tried to downplay the significance of motherhood. But no one can discount what it means when a woman bears in her own body the life of a growing baby. Her body sustains the very life of that child. Nor can anyone discount the pain involved in childbirth.

Clearly great sacrifices are made by a woman in order to bring a child into the world. Because of this and many other reasons, there is a unique bond between mother and child. This was particularly true in the ancient world, where the mother was the first and usually only teacher and caregiver for a child. What a humbling responsibility it was, then, for Mary to carry within her body the Messiah! Such a holy privilege had to be given to someone who could bear both the blessings and the burdens that accompanied the honor. Surely God found that kind of person in Mary of Nazareth.

B. Babies Change Everything

Every family has discovered that the addition of a baby changes everything—immediately! Everyone's schedule must be altered to accommodate the baby's needs. Not only will there be the new experience of midnight feedings, but regular meal times will never be the same. It is no longer as easy for a couple to take spontaneous trips, for provision must be made for the baby.

Certainly the addition of a baby changed everything for Mary and Joseph. They had to endure the changes to which all parents must adjust, but they faced the additional burdens that came from raising such an extraordinary child in such extraordinary circumstances.

Of course, there is another higher sense in which Mary and Joseph's baby has changed everything—for all people. Our world has never been the same since Jesus came. He has changed more than just our calendar; He has changed the way we look at God, ourselves, and the world. He continues to change individuals who come to Him in faith and obedience.

Let's look at how all this began, and let's consider it from Mary's perspective.

C. Lesson Background

Today's lesson forms an interesting kind of "package" with last week's and next week's. Last week we considered the impact of the ministry of John the Baptist. Next week we shall look at Mary's visit to Elisabeth, who was the mother of John the Baptist. This week we examine the announcement to Mary (described as a "cousin" of Elisabeth in Luke 1:36) that she would give birth to the Messiah.

Luke provides some significant details surrounding the birth of Jesus that are not found in the other Gospels. His account of what happened on the night of Jesus' birth is the fullest account of what we call the "Christmas story." Luke supplies information about the conception and birth of John the Baptist that no other writer does. We are also given a personal glimpse into the thoughts of Mary as she first became aware of her special role in God's plan.

In some ways, the account of the announcement to Mary resembles the account of the announcement to Zechariah concerning John the Baptist. Indeed, the same angel (Gabriel) appears to the individuals involved to tell them the startling news.

I. The Angel's Message
(Luke 1:26-33)

A. The Mother God Chooses (vv. 26-28)

26. And in the sixth month the angel Gabriel was sent from God unto a city of Galilee, named Nazareth.

Our text describes events that took place *in the sixth month*. This does not refer to the sixth month of the year, but to the sixth month of Elisabeth's pregnancy with John the Baptist. This is clear from the description of how Elisabeth "hid herself five months" in Luke 1:24 and from the angel's words concerning Elisabeth in verse 36: "this is the sixth month with her." The mention of Elisabeth's pregnancy indicates that Jesus was about six months younger than John the Baptist.

God's message to Mary was sent by way of *the angel Gabriel*. The name Gabriel can mean "mighty man of God" or "God is my hero." He *was sent* to the town of *Nazareth*, a small town in *Galilee* that covered approximately seven acres in New Testament times.

The designation Galilee means "the circle," indicating that the name must have referred originally to a group of towns that formed a rough circle in northern Palestine. By living this far north, the Jews in Galilee came into more frequent contact with Gentiles than did the Jews in Judea to the south. No doubt the distance to Jerusalem prevented many Galileans from attending some of the annual feasts in Jerusalem. These factors and others caused the Jews in Judea to consider Galileans inferior to themselves. Nazareth itself was held in such contempt that Nathanael, on hearing that Jesus was from Nazareth, wondered if any good could come from there (John 1:45, 46). [See question #1, page 136.]

27. To a virgin espoused to a man whose name was Joseph, of the house of David; and the virgin's name was Mary.

Even before we learn the name of the person to whom Gabriel was sent, we learn something more significant about her: she was a *virgin*. Matthew notes that the virgin birth fulfilled a prophecy spoken by Isaiah (Isaiah 7:14; Matthew 1:22, 23).

The virgin birth of Christ has troubled some people, for the very idea goes against the normal manner by which children are born. But this is to be expected in someone who was not a "normal" human being. If Jesus is the unique Son of God and Messiah, and One whose life was characterized by the miraculous, should it be any great surprise that He would come to the earth in a miraculous manner?

At this time, *Mary* was *espoused*, or betrothed, to *Joseph*. Jewish betrothal involved a step that was short of actual marriage but much stronger than our idea of engagement. If a girl's betrothed died, she was considered a widow. A betrothal could be abolished only by an act of divorce. And, while betrothal was considered a legal contract for a future marriage, sexual relations between the couple were not permitted until after the marriage ceremony. Still, sexual relations with someone other than the betrothed was considered adultery. This explains why, according to Matthew's Gospel, Joseph at first planned to divorce Mary upon learning of her pregnancy (Matthew 1:19).

Joseph was *of the house* or family *of David*. In Luke 2 we are told that this was the reason he went to Bethlehem, in obedience to the emperor's decree (Luke 2:1-4). Chapter 3 of Luke's Gospel includes a genealogy of Jesus (vv. 23-38), which is generally considered to trace His ancestry on Mary's side. Since this mentions David (v. 31), it appears that she also was a descendant of David.

28. And the angel came in unto her, and said, Hail, thou that art highly favored, the Lord is with thee: blessed art thou among women.

The *angel* Gabriel began his message with *Hail*, or "Greetings," followed by the declaration that Mary was considered *highly favored* by God. Gabriel's words indicate that Mary was a person of unique piety. We could expect no less for the mother of Jesus.

Mary was also informed that *the Lord is with thee*. She would need that comfort, not only on

---

Home Daily Bible Readings

Monday, Dec. 4—The Birth of Jesus Foretold (Luke 1:26-33)

Tuesday, Dec. 5—Mary Says Yes to God (Luke 1:34-38)

Wednesday, Dec. 6—The Joy of God's Presence (Psalm 16)

Thursday, Dec. 7—The Lord Helps Me (Psalm 121)

Friday, Dec. 8—The Miraculous Conception (Matthew 1:18-25)

Saturday, Dec. 9—The Genealogy of Jesus the Messiah (Matthew 1:1-17)

Sunday, Dec. 10—The Mercies of God (Lamentations 3:22-26)

this day, but in the difficult days that lay ahead. Such comfort was frequently offered to God's servants when they faced a particularly daunting task (Moses in Exodus 3:12; Joshua in Joshua 1:5; Gideon in Judges 6:12; Jeremiah in Jeremiah 1:8).

B. The Comfort God Brings (vv. 29, 30)

29. And when she saw him, she was troubled at his saying, and cast in her mind what manner of salutation this should be.

As we might expect, Mary at first was fearful of this messenger. Any angelic visitation usually produced great anxiety (Judges 6:22; Mark 16:5, 6; Luke 1:11, 12). In Mary's case, it was not just the appearance of the angel that caused concern; she also wondered about the meaning of the words that the angel had spoken. Humble people are always uneasy with high praise, and what higher praise could have been accorded Mary than this? No wonder *she was troubled*!

30. And the angel said unto her, Fear not, Mary: for thou hast found favor with God.

The angel's next words, *Fear not* are the same words the shepherds would hear outside of Bethlehem (Luke 2:10). As noted above, fear is a normal response to seeing an angel.

Not only did Mary have nothing to fear; she had much for which to be grateful. Once again she was told that she had *found favor with God*. What a compliment! This angelic visit was not to pronounce judgment; it was to announce God's choice of Mary for a special purpose. [See question #2, page 136.]

C. The Child God Sends (vv. 31-33)

31. And, behold, thou shalt conceive in thy womb, and bring forth a son, and shalt call his name JESUS.

Even though Jesus' birth was miraculous in that He was conceived in the *womb* of a virgin, it was in every other respect a normal human pregnancy and birth. The Son of God did not spring from the head of a god or grow from a flower or appear from the water. The accounts in the four Gospels exhibit none of the markings of ancient myths. Jesus entered the world as all human beings have—by birth. His coming to our world was characterized by a wonderful combination of the supernatural and the natural.

The name chosen for the child was *Jesus*, which is the Greek form of the Old Testament name *Joshua*. While this was a very common name, it was particularly appropriate for the Messiah, since it means, "The Lord is salvation." Just as Joshua led the children of Israel into the freedom of the promised land, so this new Joshua will lead His people from the slavery of sin into the freedom of eternal life.

COMMON NAME, UNCOMMON CHILD

Two boys, Joe and Max, were talking at the local playground one day. Max, who came from a well-to-do family and whose father was a prominent businessman, was bragging about all the nice things his family owned. Repeatedly he belittled Joe and his family in the process. Finally Joe said, "I've got something you don't have and probably never will have." "Like what?" asked Max. "The name Joe," replied Joe. Then he walked off, leaving Max standing speechless.

Jesus was a common name in the first century. Thus the designation "Jesus of Nazareth" was used to distinguish Mary's son from others of the same name. There is even another Jesus mentioned in the New Testament (Colossians 4:11).

Such a common name reflects the purpose for which Jesus came to earth. He was like us in so many ways: He was born; He grew from infancy to adulthood; He was hungry (Matthew 4:2) and tired (John 4:6); He was "tempted like as we are" (Hebrews 4:15).

And yet He was *un*common—*un*like us in so many ways. The most important of these was that, though tempted like us, He was "yet without sin" (Hebrews 4:15). This fact leads us to the heart of the gospel: the uncommon, sinless Son of God died in the place of common sinners.

Jesus was known by a common name, but He lived up to the meaning of that name—Savior—in a way that no one else could.   —R. C. S.

32. He shall be great, and shall be called the Son of the Highest; and the Lord God shall give unto him the throne of his father David.

While Jesus was a descendant of *David* and even though His reign was described as occurring on David's *throne*, He was not to be a king exactly like David. Jesus' kingdom was not political or earthly at all; it was a spiritual and heavenly kingdom, "not of this world" (John 18:36). The nature of Jesus' messiahship was a frequent source of contention among Jews in trying to evaluate Him. No one doubted that the Messiah would be a king, but they often assumed that He would rule according to the world's definition of "king," not God's.

How to Say It

GABRIEL. *Gay*-bree-ul.
GIDEON. *Gid*-ee-un.
ISAIAH. Eye-*zay*-uh.
JEREMIAH. Jair-uh-*my*-uh.
NAZARETH. *Naz*-uh-reth.
ZECHARIAH. Zek-uh-*rye*-uh.

Gabriel also referred to Jesus as *the Son of the Highest*, indicating His deity. (This is also emphasized in verse 35.) Later Zechariah spoke of John the Baptist as a "prophet of the Highest" (Luke 1:76). John was a spokesman for God; Jesus was the Son of God.

33. And he shall reign over the house of Jacob for ever; and of his kingdom there shall be no end.

Crowns and thrones of this earth will perish. How different is the *kingdom* of Jesus, of which *there shall be no end*! These words call to mind the promise that God gave to David, found in 2 Samuel 7:16: "And thine house and thy kingdom shall be established for ever before thee: thy throne shall be established for ever." (See also Daniel 2:44; 7:14.)

II. Mary's Response
(vv. 34-38)

A. Her Question (vv. 34, 35)

34. Then said Mary unto the angel, How shall this be, seeing I know not a man?

Mary's initial reaction was to question how the promised birth could occur, outside of normal sexual relations with a *man*. Such a birth seemed to defy all logic. While many today find the virgin birth a difficult truth to accept, we must keep in mind that this was no less true for Mary. Her response to Gabriel's message was different from Zechariah's unbelief (Luke 1:18-20). Her question indicated acceptance, but she was perplexed with a natural bewilderment. [See question #3, page 136.]

35. And the angel answered and said unto her, The Holy Ghost shall come upon thee, and the power of the Highest shall overshadow thee: therefore also that holy thing which shall be born of thee shall be called the Son of God.

In answer to Mary's inquiry, Gabriel declared that the *Holy Ghost* (Holy Spirit) would be responsible for the conception of the promised child. A veil of privacy continues to hide the mechanics of the act of conception and how God accomplished it. This is as it should be. Even a normal conception is filled with mystery and wonder and is most difficult to describe. Gabriel's words simply state that the entire process would be miraculous and that the child would not be the offspring of any earthly father. He *shall be called the Son of God.*

B. Her Sign (vv. 36, 37)

36. And, behold, thy cousin Elisabeth, she hath also conceived a son in her old age; and this is the sixth month with her, who was called barren.

Mary did not ask Gabriel for any kind of confirming sign, yet one was offered: the pregnancy of her relative *Elisabeth* (not necessarily an actual *cousin* as we use the term, but some kind of relative). [See question #4, page 136.] Elisabeth's conception, despite the fact that she had been childless and that both she and Zechariah were "well stricken in years" (Luke 1:7), was a sign that God could do whatever He wished.

This calls to mind women such as Sarah (Genesis 18:9-15), the mother of Samson (Judges 13:2, 3), and Hannah (1 Samuel 1:11), all of whom were considered barren. Yet God overruled their condition and gave them the privilege of becoming mothers (in Sarah's case, her age also appeared to prevent her from having children).

We can understand why Mary would later want to travel "with haste" to visit Elisabeth (vv. 39, 40). God had done something "impossible" for both of them!

37. For with God nothing shall be impossible.

This statement (or one similar in meaning to it) is made in more than one place in Scripture (Genesis 18:14; Jeremiah 32:17; Matthew 19:26), but here it is especially appropriate. The virgin birth is unique. To believe it, one must affirm that God is not limited by the so-called "laws of nature." Since He is the One who put those laws into effect, He can set them aside or override them at any time to accomplish His purposes. Thus *with God nothing shall be impossible.* [See question #5, page 136.]

SPECIALIZING IN THE IMPOSSIBLE

The songs and choruses that are sung in Christian youth camps change over the years—just as the songs we sing in worship services change over the years. One that was popular years ago, but is seldom heard today, is a chorus with these words: "God specializes in things thought impossible. He does the things others cannot do."* It's a lovely little song, and it speaks a great truth.

Certainly this was true in the case of Mary's pregnancy. No one could have accomplished this apart from the "laws of nature," except the One who established those laws!

We are not informed as to how the Holy Spirit accomplished the conception of Jesus within Mary's womb. If Gabriel's explanation had been phrased according to our modern understanding of genetics, it would have baffled men in the succeeding centuries and would have produced confusion instead of a sense of wonder. It was not considered necessary for Mary (or for us) to understand completely the ways of God.

*"Got Any Rivers," by Oscar C. Eliason. Copyright 1945, Benson Music Group. Used by permission.

Mary's task was, and ours is, simply this: to "walk by faith"—faith in a God who "specializes in things thought impossible" and "does the things others cannot do."   —R. C. S.

C. Her Submission (v. 38)

38. And Mary said, Behold the handmaid of the Lord; be it unto me according to thy word. And the angel departed from her.

Mary's submission to the Lord's will is a model for all Christians. She agreed to be God's *handmaid* (servant), to do whatever He asked. This responsibility was not a burden, but a blessing.

At this point Mary could not have been aware of all that she would have to face in fulfilling this extraordinary role. She would endure the gossips in Nazareth (speculating as to the *real* father of her child), the long trip to Bethlehem, the birth of her child in less than ideal conditions, the threat from jealous King Herod, and another long trip to Egypt and then back to Nazareth. She would watch as Jesus left the family circle to minister to people all over Galilee and Judea. Ultimately— and worst of all—she would watch as her son was crucified.

While Mary could not have anticipated most of this, the Biblical record indicates that she fulfilled all that was asked of her. This is not to say that her understanding of Jesus and His ministry was flawless. There were times when she did not grasp the full significance of who He was or what He had come to do (Luke 2:48-50; John 2:1-4). Still, when one considers the awesome responsibility given her, her faithfulness is exemplary.

Conclusion

A. "Whatever"

It has become a common practice whenever one wants to dismiss a comment or an opinion simply to shrug one's shoulders and say, "Whatever. . . ." In that context, the word is not an expression of commitment but of apathy.

Visual for lesson 2

Today's lesson visual reminds us that we, too, can serve God as Mary did. Adopting her attitude is the key to faithful service.

There is, however, a much better way to use this word. When we submit ourselves to Christ we say, "Whatever . . ." with an entirely different tone of voice and a different meaning. In using that word, we express our acceptance of *whatever* the Lord would have us do—not only whatever, but wherever, whenever, and however.

When someone surrenders himself to God, he commits himself to a life of both responsibility and privilege. It may be said that there can be no privilege without responsibility. The real joys of Christian living come to those who are willing to do "whatever"—great or small, public or private—to the glory of the One we love.

B. Something Special

There is something special about Christmas because there is something special about the first Christmas. Jesus was born into a special heritage, born to special parents, born in a special way, and born to fulfill a special purpose. The special heritage was the lineage of David. The special parents were Joseph, a man of righteousness and compassion, and Mary, a woman of singular virtue and commitment. Jesus was born in a special way through the virgin birth: a spiritual and biological miracle. Most of all, He was born to fulfill a special purpose—to save His people from their sins (Matthew 1:21) and to establish "a kingdom, which shall never be destroyed" (Daniel 2:44).

C. One Grand Package

During December it is appropriate to emphasize Jesus' birth. But in so doing, we should not overlook the impact of all of Jesus' life, including His teachings, miracles, death, resurrection, and promised return. One can imagine how odd it would seem to observe the birthday of any famous individual by focusing only on his birth and childhood and ignoring all the achievements of his adult life. The same is true of Jesus. At Christmas we should recognize that God has given us one grand package—one matchless life. This gift is ours to open and to treasure—not only at Christmas, but throughout the year.

D. Prayer

Father, help me, like Mary, to accept whatever task You give me. My task will certainly not be as great as hers, but that is all right. It is a privilege to serve You. Whether my task be great or small, may I say with a willing heart, "Yes, Lord." In Jesus' name, amen.

E. Thought to Remember

What is the best way to respond to God? As Mary did—with simple, trusting faith.

Learning by Doing

This page contains an alternate lesson plan emphasizing learning activities.
Classes desiring such student involvement will find these suggestions helpful.

Learning Goals

After this lesson each student will be able to:

1. Give the important details of Gabriel's message to Mary and her response to it.

2. Tell why Mary's response to God's will is an appropriate model for Christians.

3. Think of a difficult decision or issue he or she is facing, and commit that matter to God in simple faith.

Into the Lesson

Prepare a handout with the headings "Message" and "Response" at the top. In the Message column list the following: "Mommy, there's a monster in my closet!" "There's been an accident; you need to come to the hospital with me." "Schools are closed today because of the inclement weather." "If you'll invest just $5,000 in my new invention, you can double your money in a month!" "Mom, Dad, I'm getting married!" "If you will accept a transfer, we can offer you a position at the home office at twenty percent more than your current salary." "The world will end at midnight on December 31!"

As students arrive, give each one a handout. Ask the students to write how they would respond to each of the messages. (If any message on the list might prove difficult for your class because of recent events, feel free to omit it. For example, if your church has just lost one of its young people in a tragic accident, you might want to leave out the second message.)

After a few minutes, ask for responses. Discuss why some messages get an action response and other messages are dismissed. Observe that we respond to messages we believe. Then discuss what makes some messages believable and others not. Make the transition to the lesson by noting that Mary received a seemingly incredible message, but she believed it and responded in faith.

Into the Word

Ask a volunteer to read Luke 1:26-38 aloud. Then form groups of three or four students each and instruct the groups to list the main points of Gabriel's message. Give the students handouts similar to the one used at the beginning of the class, but the Message column should be blank. Using these handouts, the students should outline the main points of the message in the left column and the stages of Mary's response in the

right. It might be said that Mary's response to this incredible news was to experience some turmoil (v. 29a), consider the situation (v. 29b), gather appropriate information (v. 34), proclaim her primary role (v. 38a), and submit to the will of God (v. 38b).

Let the class discuss the main points of the message and the stages of Mary's response. Ask, "What factors would make this task difficult for Mary?" *(Social stigma, youth, uncertainty about whether Joseph would believe her, the importance of the task, etc.)* Note that Mary had already demonstrated a sense of duty and responsibility by submitting to the pledge to be married. These character traits continue to show in her faithful response to God's message through Gabriel. While we will not have the same kind of task as Mary did, her faithful response to a difficult duty is worthy of our imitation.

Into Life

Tell students to recall four or five of the most difficult situations they have faced in their lives. Encourage them to recall events from different time periods in life.

When everyone seems to have a mental list, ask students to choose situations that they are willing to discuss with their small group. Encourage them to consider all that was involved in dealing with their situations and compare theirs with Mary's. Finally, they should list their typical stages of response to difficult situations.

Tell students to return to their small groups. Have the groups discuss some wise, helpful, and godly stages in a plan for responding to difficult situations.

Then ask students to think of some difficult decisions or duties that they are currently facing. Ask each to consider what has already been discussed and to write out a plan for addressing the issue he or she is facing (even if it is only a first step and not the entire process).

Remind the class of Mary's sense of duty and responsibility: "When a plan of response is prepared, a person of duty will follow that plan even when it is difficult. Like Mary, our life of responsible faith includes turmoil, thoughts, questions, and submission."

Close by asking the students to commit their situations to God in silent prayer while you play a recording of the song, "Mary, Did You Know?"

Let's Talk It Over

The questions on this page are designed to encourage review of the lesson Scriptures and to promote discussion of the lesson by the class. The answers provided are only discussion starters. Let your class talk it over from there.

1. What significance, if any, do you see in the fact that God chose a woman of Nazareth, an obscure little Galilean village, to be the mother of Jesus?

Nazareth was perhaps the last place anyone would expect to produce a leader of any kind. It was not a center of commerce, politics, education, or religion. But the obscurity of Nazareth is in keeping with the rest of the story. Mary was not a woman of any social status or personal accomplishment. The announcement from Gabriel was made only to Mary, with no public proclamation. Obscurity at this point was a strategy for survival and would give Jesus a chance to grow up in a fairly normal existence. In addition, those who would later choose to follow Jesus would not be drawn to Him because He grew up with the privileges of place or status or acclaim. His character and His ministry alone would draw them to Him.

2. The angel Gabriel told Mary that she was "highly favored" and that she had "found favor with God." What does it mean to find favor with God? How do we do that?

The word for *favor* is often translated *grace* or *gift*. We often assume that God chose Mary because of her outstanding piety and spirituality. What little we know of Mary is in keeping with that assumption, but we actually know very little about her. Consider also that the gospel story is about God's showing favor (grace) to those who do not deserve it. "While we were yet sinners, Christ died for us" (Romans 5:8).

Certainly it can be said of all of us that we are "highly favored" because of what God chose to do for us. We cannot earn God's grace—or favor—by good deeds, but we can claim it by faith (Ephesians 2:8, 9). And as we walk by faith, we can approach the throne of grace and receive "grace to help in time of need" (Hebrews 4:16). In humility we find that God "giveth more grace" (James 4:6) as our situation demands.

3. Mary was confused. So she asked, "How shall this be, seeing I know not a man?" How can we encourage young people and others to ask questions freely when they do not understand theological issues?

The lesson writer notes the contrast between Mary's question and that of Zechariah (Luke 1:18), which expressed doubt and asked for a sign. Sometimes we confuse questions of doubt with simple, honest requests for information or clarification. We need to be slow to assume that a question is one of doubt, and answer with grace and kindness. If questioners regularly receive such respect, they will not be put off from asking more questions, and others will be likewise encouraged. Of course, if a person shows himself to be contentious, he needs to be handled somewhat differently. His questions must not be allowed to stir up strife within the church. Still, "speaking the truth in love" (Ephesians 4:15) is always a proper way to answer questions—whatever motivates them.

4. How would the news that Elisabeth had conceived be an assurance to Mary that Gabriel's message to her was true? What particular act of God gives you reassurance that His promises to you are true?

Elisabeth had been barren, and now, in her old age, was going to give birth. Mary would recognize this as a miracle. Obviously God was at work. Some explicit prophecies pertaining to a Messiah had been made hundreds of years before Jesus was born. Many generations lived in the hope of those prophecies, but died before they were fulfilled. The birth of Jesus—and His life, death, and resurrection—demonstrated God's power and willingness to keep those promises. Those events make us confident that the remaining promises of God will be fulfilled in His time.

In addition to the Biblical promises, your students may be able to cite answers to prayer or dramatic changes of lifestyle in themselves or people they know. These testify that God is still at work.

5. Mary had to believe that "with God nothing shall be impossible." How has God accomplished some blessing in your life in a surprising or even "impossible" way? Can you trust Him to do the impossible again?

We can draw reassurance from the mighty acts of God recorded in Scripture, but His providence today and His dramatic answers to prayer, in our experience or the experience of someone we know, will add current confirmation that He is trustworthy. Testifying of God's goodness is an encouragement to all who hear it.

Praising God

**Dec
17**

DEVOTIONAL READING: Psalm 34:1-3.

BACKGROUND SCRIPTURE: Luke 1:39-56.

PRINTED TEXT: Luke 1:39-55.

Luke 1:39-55

39 And Mary arose in those days, and went into the hill country with haste, into a city of Judah;

40 And entered into the house of Zechariah, and saluted Elisabeth.

41 And it came to pass, that, when Elisabeth heard the salutation of Mary, the babe leaped in her womb; and Elisabeth was filled with the Holy Ghost:

42 And she spake out with a loud voice, and said, Blessed art thou among women, and blessed is the fruit of thy womb.

43 And whence is this to me, that the mother of my Lord should come to me?

44 For, lo, as soon as the voice of thy salutation sounded in mine ears, the babe leaped in my womb for joy.

45 And blessed is she that believed: for there shall be a performance of those things which were told her from the Lord.

46 And Mary said, My soul doth magnify the Lord,

47 And my spirit hath rejoiced in God my Saviour.

48 For he hath regarded the low estate of his handmaiden: for, behold, from henceforth all generations shall call me blessed.

49 For he that is mighty hath done to me great things; and holy is his name.

50 And his mercy is on them that fear him from generation to generation.

51 He hath showed strength with his arm; he hath scattered the proud in the imagination of their hearts.

52 He hath put down the mighty from their seats, and exalted them of low degree.

53 He hath filled the hungry with good things; and the rich he hath sent empty away.

54 He hath holpen his servant Israel, in remembrance of his mercy;

55 As he spake to our fathers, to Abraham, and to his seed for ever.

GOLDEN TEXT: My soul doth magnify the Lord, and my spirit hath rejoiced in God my Saviour. For he hath regarded the low estate of his handmaiden.—Luke 1:46-48.

Good News of Jesus
Unit 1: A Savior Is Born
(Lessons 1-5)

Lesson Aims

After participating in this lesson, students will be able to:

1. List the elements of praise cited in the songs of Elisabeth and Mary.

2. Explain how these songs highlight the unique way in which God works.

3. Express their personal praise to God for His work in their lives.

Lesson Outline

INTRODUCTION
   A. Who Understands?
   B. Lesson Background
 I. THE SONG OF ELISABETH (Luke 1:39-45)
   A. Mary's Arrival (vv. 39, 40)
   B. The Baby's Reaction (v. 41)
   C. Elisabeth's Response (vv. 42-45)
   Joy in Believing
 II. THE SONG OF MARY (Luke 1:46-55)
   A. God's Blessings (vv. 46-48)
   Magnificent Music
   B. God's Character (vv. 49, 50)
   C. God's Ways (vv. 51-53)
   D. God's Care for Israel (vv. 54, 55)
CONCLUSION
   A. Do We Deserve It?
   B. Prayer
   C. Thought to Remember

Introduction

A. Who Understands?

If you are having a problem in your profession, who can understand that problem better than another person in the same profession? Physicians understand the problems of other physicians, while teachers can appreciate the problems of other teachers. That is the reason, among others, that there is a peer association for nearly every major profession.

If you are going through a trial of some kind, whether it involves sickness or some other personal crisis, who can understand your situation better than someone who has already been through it? Only an alcoholic can truly understand the struggles of an alcoholic. Only the widowed understand the special heartaches of widowhood. Only parents understand both the joys and frustrations that can make parenthood a joy one minute and an absolute nightmare the next. That is why there are so many effective support groups to help people cope with various crises.

As Mary faced the pressures and responsibilities accompanying her special pregnancy, with whom could she discuss her concerns? No one had ever gone through (or would ever go through!) what she would experience. The person whose situation most resembled hers was Elisabeth. She, too, was in the midst of an unusual pregnancy with an unusual child. She, too, was deeply committed to the Lord (Luke 1:5, 6). Even though there were differences in their respective situations, only Elisabeth could really understand what Mary was facing. Elisabeth would also believe Mary's explanation of what had happened. After all, the same angel who had visited Mary had also appeared to Elisabeth's husband Zechariah.

Also worth noting is the age difference between Mary and Elisabeth. Mary was quite young, perhaps in her early teens; Elisabeth was quite old, well past childbearing years. No doubt it was a comfort to Mary to have an older woman in whom to confide and from whom to receive advice. In addition, as noted in last week's lesson, Mary and Elisabeth were relatives (Luke 1:36).

Given all of these factors, it is not difficult to see why Mary would be interested in visiting Elisabeth and talking with her about the extraordinary news that Gabriel had brought.

B. Lesson Background

Today's lesson text immediately follows last week's text (from Luke 1:26-38). It ushers us into the private meeting that took place between Mary and Elisabeth. Both of them break forth in praise to God for His wondrous working in their lives. While their words are not actually called *songs* in the Scriptures, they resemble the songs of praise found in the Psalms of the Old Testament. Mary's praise in particular exhibits the characteristics of a poem that could be (and has been) set to music.

In addition, Mary's tribute displays a keen knowledge of the Old Testament Scriptures, especially of Hannah's words of praise uttered in gratitude to God for her son Samuel (1 Samuel 2:1-10). Since from early childhood boys and girls were taught the Scriptures, it would have been natural for Mary to recall some phrases from Hannah's poem and to use them in expressing her own gratitude to God for the special son she would bear.

I. The Song of Elisabeth
(Luke 1:39-45)

A. Mary's Arrival (vv. 39, 40)

39. And Mary arose in those days, and went into the hill country with haste, into a city of Judah.

The angel Gabriel had told Mary of Elisabeth's miraculous pregnancy (Luke 1:36), perhaps to let her know that she was not alone in her extraordinary condition. Here was someone else with a seemingly impossible pregnancy. Mary's pregnancy was miraculous because she was a virgin; Elisabeth's, because she had always been infertile and was now beyond the age of childbearing.

It appears that as soon as she could do so, Mary traveled *with haste* to see Elisabeth. We are not given the name of the town in the *hill country . . . of Judah* where Elisabeth lived. Mary's journey likely covered from sixty to seventy miles—quite a distance for her to travel. But such was the importance of visiting and talking with Elisabeth that distance was of little concern to Mary. [See question #1, page 144.]

40. And entered into the house of Zechariah, and saluted Elisabeth.

Saluted simply means that Mary greeted *Elisabeth*. This was a common practice, but it was to be followed by an uncommon reaction.

B. The Baby's Reaction (v. 41)

41. And it came to pass, that, when Elisabeth heard the salutation of Mary, the babe leaped in her womb; and Elisabeth was filled with the Holy Ghost.

It is not unusual for babies in the *womb* to kick, but Elisabeth could tell that these movements of the child inside her were out of the ordinary. Luke (a physician) uses the word *leaped* to describe what took place. This leaping was done with joy (v. 44), apparently because of what Mary's presence as the mother of the Messiah signified. Elisabeth's response to Mary's greeting was prompted by her being *filled with the Holy Ghost*.

C. Elisabeth's Response (vv. 42-45)

42. And she spake out with a loud voice, and said, Blessed art thou among women, and blessed is the fruit of thy womb.

The sheer excitement of Elisabeth is seen in the fact that she cried *out with a loud voice*. Empowered by God's Spirit, she acknowledged Mary's unique status *among women* and the uniqueness of the child in her *womb*.

While not of major significance, it is interesting that the word *blessed* used here is not the same Greek word that is rendered *blessed* in the Sermon on the Mount. The word in the Sermon on the Mount has the connotation of happiness or satisfaction. The word used by Elisabeth combines the Greek words for "good" and "word," resulting in the term we transliterate as "eulogy." This is not only a "good word" spoken of the deceased at a funeral. It is often used in the sense of speaking praise or pronouncing a blessing.

43. And whence is this to me, that the mother of my Lord should come to me?

In describing Mary as *the mother of my Lord*, Elisabeth humbly recognized the superiority of the One for whom her son would prepare the way. In the same way, John one day would draw attention away from himself to his far more worthy successor. (See John 1:29-34; 3:26-30.) Even though Elisabeth was joyous about her own pregnancy, it did not prevent her from being excited and happy about Mary and about the nature of the child she would bear. While Elisabeth felt a sense of honor, she acknowledged that Mary had been given an even greater honor. Like John, she was content to serve the Lord in a secondary role. [See question #2, page 144.]

44. For, lo, as soon as the voice of thy salutation sounded in mine ears, the babe leaped in my womb for joy.

Elisabeth was filled with wonder at the *joy* represented by her child's reaction to Mary's *voice*. It is interesting to compare this verse with John's later words in describing his joy at fulfilling his God-given assignment: "He that hath the bride is the bridegroom: but the friend of the bridegroom, which standeth and heareth him, rejoiceth greatly because of the bridegroom's voice: this my joy therefore is fulfilled" (John 3:29).

JOY IN BELIEVING

There's a lot of wisdom to be found on the bumper stickers that people put on their cars. One declares that April 1 is National Atheists' Day. When you remember that April 1 is April Fool's Day, you understand the message: "The fool hath said in his heart, There is no God" (Psalm 14:1).

The wise individual recognizes that faith in God makes life fit together and gives it meaning. The great British writer G. K. Chesterton once said that when he was an atheist, there was a large hole in his thinking that he could not fill. He discovered that it was a God-shaped hole, and he became a devout believer and a staunch defender of the Christian faith.

Atheism is not only foolish; it is futile. Ultimately it leaves one utterly hopeless in the face of death. In contrast, the two women in today's lesson, Mary and Elisabeth, found great joy in their faith in God and their acknowledgment of His power and presence. The apostle Paul writes of "joy . . . in believing" (Romans 15:13). Jeremiah said, "Thy word was unto me the joy and rejoicing of mine heart" (Jeremiah 15:16). Peter tells Christians that believing in Jesus has caused us to "rejoice with joy unspeakable and full of glory" (1 Peter 1:8).

You can buy a bottle of dish soap called "Joy," but real joy does not come in a bottle. Real joy comes only by believing God and trusting His promises. Such faith brought joy to Mary and Elisabeth and will bring lasting joy into the life of every believer.

If April 1 is National Atheists' Day, then every day is Believers' Day. Every day the person of faith can say, "This is the day which the Lord hath made; we will rejoice and be glad in it" (Psalm 118:24).   —R. C. S.

45. And blessed is she that believed: for there shall be a performance of those things which were told her from the Lord.

Elisabeth pronounced an inspired blessing on Mary, who believed Gabriel's message to her in spite of its "impossible" promise (Luke 1:37). Elisabeth also expressed an assurance that everything that Gabriel spoke would come to pass. Certainly she was the right person to offer such assurance. After all, she too had experienced the faithfulness of God in honoring His promises concerning an unusual conception.

Here the Greek word translated *blessed* is the same word as that used in the Beatitudes. It describes a blessing that is applicable to all Christians, who can take comfort in the assurance that God will keep His "exceeding great and precious promises" (2 Peter 1:4).

II. The Song of Mary
(vv. 46-56)
A. God's Blessings (vv. 46-48)

46. And Mary said, My soul doth magnify the Lord.

We come now to what is considered the song of *Mary*. Note that similar expressions of praise are recorded in the early chapters of Luke's Gospel. These include the words of Zechariah (Luke 1:67-79), of the angels who announced Jesus' birth (Luke 2:13, 14), and of Simeon in the temple (Luke 2:28-32).

Mary's song is often called *The Magnificat*, a title derived from the first word in the Latin translation. It is filled with words and phrases from the Old Testament. One commentator has counted twelve separate Old Testament references in it. We have already noted its similarity to Hannah's song of praise, found in 1 Samuel 2:1-10.

Mary's praise might easily have been a song, as illustrated by today's visual. Ask the class, "If you were to write a song of praise for what God has done for you, what would you include?"

Visual for lesson 3

Mary's song begins with her desire to *magnify the Lord*. We often think of magnifying as enlarging (which is what happens to an image when we use a magnifying glass). Certainly we cannot make the Lord larger, but we can enlarge His "image." The actual print on the page remains the same size even when we use a magnifying glass, but it appears larger. Even so our praise acts as a magnifying glass to others—God is seen more clearly, though He Himself remains unchanged. From the depths of her *soul* Mary was giving to the Lord a greater measure of reverence in expressing her awe at who He is and what He had done. [See question #3, page 144.]

MAGNIFICENT MUSIC

Every writer wants his last book to be his best book. Every artist wants his last painting to be his best painting. Every composer wants his last piece of music to be his best. Thus, for his final composition, the great composer Heinrich Schütz chose to write music to the words of Mary found in today's text. Her song is often called *The Magnificat*. Many composers before and after Schütz have written music for it. It is quite remarkable to think that these words, first spoken by a peasant girl from Galilee in the isolated Judean hill country of the first century, have been set to music and heard by millions. Truly God has "exalted them of low degree" (Luke 1:52).

But the lovely words of these verses deserve music—and the finest music. They are poetry at its best. They are theology of the highest caliber, describing God's marvelous ways. Let us not discount the guidance of the Holy Spirit in all of this. If the Spirit could create the child in Mary's womb (Luke 1:35), the same Spirit could create the poetry in Mary's mind.

These words of Scripture are called *The Magnificat* because of the first line: "My soul doth magnify the Lord." They could also be called *The Magnificat* simply because they are magnificent words!   —R. C. S.

47. And my spirit hath rejoiced in God my Saviour.

Together, verses 46 and 47 provide a good illustration of what is called *parallelism* in Biblical poetry. Quite simply this means that the same idea in one verse or part of a verse is repeated in a slightly different form in the next verse or part of the verse. *My spirit hath rejoiced in God my Saviour* is saying essentially the same thing as *my soul doth magnify the Lord*. Both phrases refer to praise that is not shallow or thoughtless, but originates from deep within one's being.

The word *Saviour* draws attention to the purpose that Mary's child was coming to fulfill—a purpose that is reflected in His name. An angel told Joseph, "Thou shalt call his name Jesus: for he shall save his people from their sins" (Matthew 1:21). That God would be so committed to saving sinful, rebellious humanity that He would sacrifice His own Son is something that should prompt us to praise Him as well.

48. For he hath regarded the low estate of his handmaiden: for, behold, from henceforth all generations shall call me blessed.

Mary's *low estate* describes her humble position in the social order of that day. There is no doubt that she and Joseph were rather poor. Recall that the offering they made at the temple for Mary's purification consisted of a "pair of turtledoves" (Luke 2:24)—the approved substitute for the more costly lamb (Leviticus 12:6-8). Carpenters in Jesus' day were not well paid. No doubt, this was especially true in a small town such as Nazareth. Since families contracted marriages and usually tried to select spouses who came from the same social strata, then most likely Mary's family also was not wealthy. Nevertheless, God chose the Messiah's mother from the ranks of the poor and lowly.

Mary and Joseph thus illustrate the beauty and wonder of the incarnation—that Immanuel ("God with us") would come to dwell with lowly, impoverished (not only physically, but also spiritually) humanity. Such are the surprising ways of the Lord. He "hath chosen the weak things of the world to confound the things which are

---

How to Say It

GABRIEL. *Gay*-bree-ul.
IMMANUEL. Ih-*man*-you-el.
JEREMIAH. Jair-uh-*my*-uh.
MAGNIFICAT. Mag-*nif*-ih-cot.
NAZARETH. *Naz*-uh-reth.
SIMEON. *Sim*-ee-un.
ZECHARIAH. Zek-uh-*rye*-uh.

---

mighty; . . . that no flesh should glory in his presence" (1 Corinthians 1:27-29).

Mary's declaration that future *generations* would call her *blessed* was not an arrogant boast. She spoke out of a sense of genuine humility that God would use her in such a wonderful way.

B. God's Character (vv. 49, 50)

49. For he that is mighty hath done to me great things; and holy is his name.

The *mighty* God had done *great things* with a humble peasant girl from an obscure Galilean village. Mary understood that the privilege of being the mother of the Messiah was something truly *holy*. We are reminded of the words at the beginning of the Lord's Prayer: "Hallowed be thy name" (Matthew 6:9). In Biblical thought, the *name* of a person represented the person. Thus to hallow a name is to hallow or revere a person. When Mary says that God's name is holy, she is declaring God Himself as holy.

50. And his mercy is on them that fear him from generation to generation.

While God's *mercy* receives particular emphasis in the New Testament because of its expression through Jesus Christ, mercy has always been part of God's character. Mary's statement resembles several Old Testament declarations of God as merciful (Exodus 20:6; 34:6, 7; Psalm 103:17; Micah 7:18).

[See question #4, page 144.] To *fear* God is not to cringe before Him in cowering terror. It means to acknowledge His holiness and purity and to recognize how unworthy we are of the mercy that He shows (Isaiah 6:1-5).

C. God's Ways (vv. 51-53)

51. He hath showed strength with his arm; he hath scattered the proud in the imagination of their hearts.

God's *arm* is a symbol of His *strength*. (Some of the many passages that use this term include Exodus 15:16; Deuteronomy 4:34; 1 Kings 8:42; and Psalm 98:1.) His power is so far beyond human capabilities that for us to become *proud* in our thoughts, words, and actions should be out of the question. Pride blinds us to what God, whose ways are so different from man's, is doing. For example, few could have imagined that here in the seclusion of the hill country of Judah, God's redemptive plan was unfolding. Likewise, most of those crowded into Bethlehem on the night Jesus was born had no idea that the Messiah was in their midst.

52. He hath put down the mighty from their seats, and exalted them of low degree.

[See question #5, page 144.] This verse and the next highlight how God's ways amount to a complete reversal of the world's standards. God humbles those who think they are secure in their position (think of wicked King Herod), and He elevates those from lower stations in life (think of Mary). As Jesus later taught, "Whosoever shall exalt himself shall be abased; and he that shall humble himself shall be exalted" (Matthew 23:12).

53. He hath filled the hungry with good things; and the rich he hath sent empty away.

Certainly those who hungered for physical food were fed during Jesus' ministry (Luke 9:16, 17). And Jesus issued a solemn warning to those who are rich (Luke 6:24). However, it may be more appropriate to view this verse in spiritual terms. Those who "hunger and thirst after righteousness" will find themselves *filled* (Matthew 5:6), while those who consider themselves in good standing with God are often blind to their desperate need for Him (Luke 18:9-14). This verse calls to mind Jesus' story of the rich man and Lazarus (Luke 16:19-31) with its vivid illustration that this life does not reveal the complete truth about riches and poverty.

D. God's Care for Israel (vv. 54, 55)

54. He hath holpen his servant Israel, in remembrance of his mercy.

The word *holpen* is an Old English participle for the word *help*. We would say that God "has helped" *Israel*. This help had been exhibited in numerous ways: the exodus, the provision for Israel's needs through forty years of wandering in the desert, deliverance from oppression by means of the judges, the prosperity during the reigns of godly kings, and the restoration after the Babylonian captivity to name just a few. Israel did not always deserve God's favor, as the Old Testament record clearly shows, yet He continued to show *mercy* to His chosen people.

Here, Mary's words point to the fact that the ultimate help to Israel is coming in the form of God's chosen Person—the Messiah. He is the ultimate sign of God's mercy, not only to Israel but to all of sinful humanity.

55. As he spake to our fathers, to Abraham, and to his seed for ever.

The term *fathers* describes the patriarchs (such as *Abraham*) and other men of faith in the Old Testament. God had promised to bless the entire world through Abraham's *seed*, or descendants (Genesis 12:3). As Paul notes, that promise of a *seed* is fulfilled in Jesus Christ (Galatians 3:16). The child whom Mary was carrying thus fulfilled not only Gabriel's words to her (Luke 1:26-38), but a plan that God had "foreordained before the foundation of the world" (1 Peter 1:20).

Luke 1:56 tells us, "And Mary abode with [Elisabeth] about three months, and returned to her own house." Apparently Mary remained with Elisabeth until John's birth and then returned to Nazareth. Eventually she would travel southward once more, this time to Bethlehem with Joseph. There she would see the "performance of those things which were told her from the Lord" (Luke 1:45).

Conclusion

A. Do We Deserve It?

The humility demonstrated by both Elisabeth and Mary should stir all of us to ask the question, "Do we deserve God's mercy and grace?" The answer is a clear *no*. What is the difference between mercy and grace? Some have stated it this way: mercy is not getting the punishment you deserve, and grace is getting something good you don't deserve. Thus they may be viewed as two sides of the same coin. Mercy is for the guilty; grace is for the undeserving.

From time to time people say something like, "I wish I could get what I deserve." But would we *really* want what we deserve—in the spiritual realm? Elisabeth and Mary both saw themselves as undeserving of God's great blessings. Shouldn't we all?

B. Prayer

Dear Father, as both Elisabeth and Mary did, I lift my voice in praise because of Your many blessings to Your people. I want to thank You because You have been so gracious to me personally. I may not be able to compose a song to Your glory, but there is a song in my heart. In Jesus' name, amen.

C. Thought to Remember

You will never run out of reasons to praise God.

Home Daily Bible Readings

Monday, Dec. 11—Gratitude (Psalm 34:1-4)
Tuesday, Dec. 12—It Is Good to Give Thanks (Psalm 92:1-4)
Wednesday, Dec. 13—Mary Visits Elisabeth (Luke 1:39-45)
Thursday, Dec. 14—Mary's Song of Praise (Luke 1:46-56)
Friday, Dec. 15—Sing to the Lord (Psalm 96)
Saturday, Dec. 16—Bless the Lord (Psalm 103:1-5, 19-22)
Sunday, Dec. 17—Daniel's Prayer and Praise (Daniel 2:17-23)

Learning by Doing

This page contains an alternate lesson plan emphasizing learning activities.
Classes desiring such student involvement will find these suggestions helpful.

Learning Goals

After this lesson students will be able to:

1. List the elements of praise cited in the songs of Elisabeth and Mary.

2. Explain how these songs highlight the unique way in which God works.

3. Express their personal praise to God for His work in their lives.

Into the Lesson

Tell the class to imagine that they just received an incredible challenge. Ask, "With whom would you want to talk about this challenge, and why?" Allow a little time for the students to think, and then ask for volunteers to give answers. As they do, gently prod the students to examine their connection with the people they mention.

Comment appropriately about the students' answers. Then say, "When we are facing a challenge, we often want to talk to someone who has faced the same challenge. In our Bible study today, a young woman goes to a godly older woman who will understand her circumstances."

Into the Word

Read Luke 1:39-55. Using information from the commentary and your own study, present a lecture on the relationship between Elisabeth and Mary. Include Mary's willingness to travel sixty or seventy miles (three to four days) for this counsel. Describe Elisabeth's circumstances, pointing out that she had experienced the faithfulness of God in honoring His promises and was quietly carrying out her responsibility to bear a promised special son. Here she rejoiced with Mary, who had received a similar promise. Her praise is instructive to us, both for its content and for the attitude it suggests.

Note that Mary was also prepared. Even though she experienced some turmoil, she submitted to the will of God. (Refer to last week's lesson.) Today we see that she knew her Scriptures so well that she could incorporate up to twelve separate Old Testament references in her praise. Mary's praise is poetic in form.

Divide the class into two groups. Ask one group to study Elisabeth's praise (vv. 41-45) and the other to examine Mary's (vv. 46-55). Have each group make a list of the elements of praise found in each expression of praise. After a few minutes ask the groups to report. Write their suggestions

on the chalkboard, an overhead transparency, or a chart tablet. Students should discover the following elements, or similar ones.

Elisabeth: Praise for what God was doing in Mary's life (v. 42); praise for being associated with His work (vv. 43, 44); confidence in God's continued working (v. 45).

Mary: God's blessings to her (vv. 46-48); God's superlative character (vv. 49, 50); God's concern for the downtrodden (vv. 51-53); God's concern for Israel (vv. 54, 55).

Into Life

Observe that Ken Medema, a Christian vocalist and pianist, urges people to use the history of their church to write a congregational song of praise. Say, "First, let's identify God's work in the life of this congregation, and then we will praise Him. Think of prayers that have been answered, people who have been won to Christ, spiritual growth, people sent out into ministry, and the like." Encourage students to talk about one or two of the significant events. Ask, "What did you experience when these events happened?"

As students list significant events in the life of the congregation and identify ways that God has cared for them, write their contributions on the chalkboard so that it will be available for reference. Be ready to add ideas that you have learned from your own research.

If your students are comfortable with creative writing assignments, invite them as individuals or small groups to prepare one of the following.

• Use the congregation's history to write lyrics to the tune of a well-known song.

• Write a poem of praise.

• Pen a letter of praise.

If your class is not ready for such creative writing assignments, lead them in writing an original responsive reading. Prepare an overhead transparency (or handout) that allows space for students to dictate a statement about God followed by the statement, "His mercy is on them that fear him from generation to generation." Provide space for another statement about God, followed by the response, "His mercy is on them that fear him from generation to generation." Follow that pattern for several repetitions. (See the pattern found in Psalm 136.)

Read the responsive prayer together to close your class session.

Let's Talk It Over

The questions on this page are designed to encourage review of the lesson Scriptures and to promote discussion of the lesson by the class. The answers provided are only discussion starters. Let your class talk it over from there.

1. Why do you think Mary made the long trip to see Elisabeth? How do you choose someone to confide in? What do you gain from that kind of relationship?

Pregnancy is the kind of life-changing circumstance that a woman wants to tell someone. In Mary's case, whom could she tell who would not react with skepticism at her story? Who would believe and celebrate with her that she was bearing in her womb the very Son of God? Because her relative Elisabeth had also experienced a miraculous conception, announced by an angel, she would be able to identify with Mary and give her the emotional support she needed.

It is a great blessing to have a trusted friend who will give an empathetic ear to whatever we need to share. It helps us process emotions, and it bolsters our hope and our courage. Christians need to cultivate such relationships with other Christians more often. Having a confidant can help one stay true and resist temptation as well as provide an outlet for expressing fears, hopes, joys, and other emotions.

2. Have you noticed that some people—very unlike Elisabeth—do not share the joy of others? Instead, they often feel diminished by another's success, good fortune, or recognition. Why is that? How can we respond more like Elisabeth in those situations?

Elisabeth was "filled with the Holy Ghost." Thus, her words were not entirely her own, but an expression of divine approval on Jesus, the "fruit of [Mary's] womb" (v. 42). Still, it is clear that Elisabeth appreciated her own role in the drama being played out—just as John would appreciate his own role in later days.

We, too, need a sense of God's purpose in our lives. We need an appreciation for what God is doing through each of His servants. Seeing ourselves as part of a body is helpful in this regard. Note Paul's description of the body in 1 Corinthians 12, especially verses 18-26.

3. Mary was eager to "magnify the Lord." How do believers today magnify the Lord? How is that important?

In this instance Mary "magnified" the Lord by testifying of what He had done and, in faith, looking ahead to what He would do. We magnify the Lord whenever we give genuine praise, when we call attention to God by proclaiming Him and His great deeds.

Our worship is important to God. He deserves all praise and honor and glory. He seeks those who worship Him "in spirit and in truth" (John 4:24). Worship is important to us because it reminds us of how great and wonderful God is. It renews our faith and devotion to Him. Worship is important for the sake of unbelievers. By the very fact that we worship God, unbelievers are confronted with the issue of faith versus unbelief. The content of our worship testifies of the truth about God and plants the seed of faith (Romans 10:17; 1 Corinthians 14:24, 25).

4. What does it mean to *fear* God? What is likely to be true of those who fear God?

The fear of God is the natural response to recognizing the disparity between who God is and what we are. You may call it awe, wonder, respect, reverence, or "the shivers." True worship is impossible without such a sense of this disparity. It is not a terror or panic—a fear that God is suddenly going to strike us dead. At the same time, it recognizes that He could and would even be justified in doing so if He did!

Those who fear God are also likely to have an attitude of humility, surrender, and obedience. God's mercy is upon those with such an attitude (v. 50). "God resisteth the proud, but giveth grace unto the humble" (James 4:6).

5. What does God have against "the mighty"? Does this mean that we should shun all positions of power and influence? Why or why not?

A consistent theme through the Bible is God's disapproval of the proud, the arrogant, and the self-promoting. Jesus made it clear that the greatest in His kingdom would be the servant and not one who likes to lord his position over others (Matthew 20:25-28). The Lord spoke woe to those who liked the chief seats in the synagogue and the titles that went with them (Luke 11:43). He warned that "whosoever exalteth himself shall be abased; and he that humbleth himself shall be exalted" (Luke 14:11). It is not that positions of leadership or influence are evil, but arrogance, self-promotion, and abuse of power are contemptible to God.

A Savior Is Born

December 24
Lesson 4

Dec 24

DEVOTIONAL READING: Matthew 16:13-16.

BACKGROUND SCRIPTURE: Luke 2:1-20.

PRINTED TEXT: Luke 2:4-20.

Luke 2:4-20

4 And Joseph also went up from Galilee, out of the city of Nazareth, into Judea, unto the city of David, which is called Bethlehem, because he was of the house and lineage of David,)

5 To be taxed with Mary his espoused wife, being great with child.

6 And so it was, that, while they were there, the days were accomplished that she should be delivered.

7 And she brought forth her firstborn son, and wrapped him in swaddling clothes, and laid him in a manger; because there was no room for them in the inn.

8 And there were in the same country shepherds abiding in the field, keeping watch over their flock by night.

9 And, lo, the angel of the Lord came upon them, and the glory of the Lord shone round about them; and they were sore afraid.

10 And the angel said unto them, Fear not: for, behold, I bring you good tidings of great joy, which shall be to all people.

11 For unto you is born this day in the city of David a Saviour, which is Christ the Lord.

12 And this shall be a sign unto you; Ye shall find the babe wrapped in swaddling clothes, lying in a manger.

13 And suddenly there was with the angel a multitude of the heavenly host praising God, and saying,

14 Glory to God in the highest, and on earth peace, good will toward men.

15 And it came to pass, as the angels were gone away from them into heaven, the shepherds said one to another, Let us now go even unto Bethlehem, and see this thing which is come to pass, which the Lord hath made known unto us.

16 And they came with haste, and found Mary and Joseph, and the babe lying in a manger.

17 And when they had seen it, they made known abroad the saying which was told them concerning this child.

18 And all they that heard it wondered at those things which were told them by the shepherds.

19 But Mary kept all these things, and pondered them in her heart.

20 And the shepherds returned, glorifying and praising God for all the things that they had heard and seen, as it was told unto them.

GOLDEN TEXT: For unto you is born this day in the city of David a Saviour, which is Christ the Lord.—Luke 2:11.

Lesson Aims

After this lesson each student will be able to:

1. Retell Luke's account of the birth of Jesus.

2. Contrast the humble scene of the nativity with the commercialism of the current celebration of Christmas.

3. Express a commitment to celebrating Christ's birth with a "spiritual pilgrimage" to Bethlehem to worship the Savior.

Lesson Outline

INTRODUCTION
   A. Something to Sing About
   B. Lesson Background
  I. BIRTH OF THE CHRIST CHILD (Luke 2:4-7)
   A. The Town (vv. 4, 5)
   B. The Time (vv. 6, 7)
 II. ANNOUNCEMENT OF THE BIRTH (Luke 2:8-14)
   A. The Angel's Appearance (vv. 8, 9)
   B. The Angel's Message (vv. 10-12)
    "This Day"
   C. The Angels' Praise (vv. 13, 14)
    Choir Practice
III. RESPONSE OF THE SHEPHERDS (Luke 2:15-20)
   A. The Shepherds' Visit (vv. 15, 16)
   B. The Shepherds' Witness (vv. 17-20)
CONCLUSION
   A. Being There
   B. Prayer
   C. Thought to Remember

Introduction

A. Something to Sing About

There is a legend concerning a little brown bird that lived in the stable where Jesus was born. According to this legend, the bird had never sung before. That night, hearing the angels' song to the shepherds, he learned to sing. In fact, the music that came from the little bird was the most beautiful and heavenly music anyone had ever heard. From that day forward people have listened to and enjoyed the nightingale, never realizing that it was imitating the angels' song.

This is only a legend, of course, and yet there is some truth in it. Because of what happened that night in Bethlehem, we have a reason to sing. Before Christ came, we had nothing to sing about. Because of Christ, that has changed. Let this story put a song in your heart this season.

What is it about Christmas that gives most people a lift? What makes them kinder and gentler? There is an extraordinary power in the story of the birth of Jesus, even for those who don't believe all of it. We have all seen some of the most secular people manifest a bit of the attitude of Jesus at Christmas, if only for a short while. For those who believe in Him as Savior, there is an abundance of joy that does not come and go with the season because they have come to know personally the purpose for which the baby was born.

B. Lesson Background

Luke provides more details about Jesus' birth than Matthew, Mark, or John do. At the beginning of his Gospel, Luke tells us that many other accounts of Jesus' life had been written (Luke 1:1, 2). It is interesting to speculate what these other accounts were like or what happened to them. Of far greater significance is the fact that the four we have in the New Testament are those Spirit-inspired records that are meant to lead the reader to faith in Jesus as God's Son (John 20:30, 31). Each Gospel tells the same story, but each has its own unique features. One of Luke's distinctive features is his account of the events surrounding Jesus' birth, which is the source of many of the readings traditionally used during the Christmas season.

Today's lesson may suffer somewhat from "over-familiarity." To gain a genuine appreciation of this lesson requires the desire to approach these words with a willingness to see their power afresh. This willingness will allow the reader to capture a bit of the excitement and wonder experienced by the original participants.

I. Birth of the Christ Child
(Luke 2:4-7)
A. The Town (vv. 4, 5)

4. And Joseph also went up from Galilee, out of the city of Nazareth, into Judea, unto the city of David, which is called Bethlehem, (because he was of the house and lineage of David,)

The Greek word rendered *city* is used to describe towns and villages as well as major cities. *Nazareth* was a small town in *Galilee* that was held in little regard by the people of Jesus' day (John 1:46). Nonetheless, it was situated close to several main trade routes; so it was not completely removed from the outside world.

The town of *Bethlehem* was a small village located just a few miles south of Jerusalem. Bethlehem held a special place in the heart of every Jew, for it was the hometown of King *David* (1 Samuel 16:1, 13). The name itself means "house

Bethlehem *Hous of bread*

of bread." Joseph and Mary would have traveled approximately eighty miles to go there—no easy journey for anyone, especially a pregnant woman.

5. To be taxed with Mary his espoused wife, being great with child.

This particular taxation (which affected the entire empire, according to verse 1) does not appear in Roman records. But this is no reason to conclude that it never took place. It was a common practice for the Romans to conduct such a tax or census in occupied territory. In fact, Luke records a similar census, taken later than the one mentioned here, in Acts 5:37. Luke's writing consistently reflects a careful attention to historical detail, and we can trust that this is the case here.

Mary was *great with child*, implying that she was getting close to the time of giving birth. She is described as Joseph's *espoused*, or betrothed, *wife*. This seems to suggest that they embarked on the journey to Bethlehem before they had completed their marriage ceremony. But Matthew tells us that Joseph "took unto him his wife: and knew her not till she had brought forth her firstborn son" (Matthew 1:24, 25). It is more likely, then, that they had had their wedding ceremony and even lived together as husband and wife. Technically, however, they would not have become husband and wife until their union was consummated— after Jesus was born. Matthew addresses the legal issue while Luke is more technical.

B. The Time (vv. 6, 7)

6. And so it was, that, while they were there, the days were accomplished that she should be delivered.

We do not know exactly how far along Mary was in her pregnancy when she and Joseph reached Bethlehem, nor do we know how much time passed after their arrival before the delivery occurred. We are simply told that, at some point during their stay in Bethlehem, *the days were accomplished that she should be delivered.*

This "accomplishment" also meant that the "fulness of the time" had come for God to "send forth his Son" (Galatians 4:4). With Jesus' birth, two of the most notable of Old Testament prophecies reached their "fulness": that He would be born of a virgin (Isaiah 7:14) and that He would be born in Bethlehem (Micah 5:2).

7. And she brought forth her firstborn son, and wrapped him in swaddling clothes, and laid him in a manger; because there was no room for them in the inn.

It is commonly assumed that Jesus was born in a stable because of the word *manger*. That term simply describes a feeding place for the animals. In the time of Jesus, animals were sometimes kept near a house in a separate space. Thus Mary and Joseph may have been taken to an area that belonged to the inn, but was not the portion where guests usually stayed.

Others have proposed that the birth of Jesus happened in a cave, which is also a place where animals were often kept. Wherever Jesus was born, it is clear that the event took place in very humble circumstances. Perhaps being away from the noise and confusion that probably characterized the inn during the time of taxation was, in some respects, to Mary and Joseph's advantage; at least it offered some privacy. [See question #1, page 152.]

That Jesus is referred to as Mary's *firstborn* implies that she had other children later. We know that Jesus had brothers (or more accurately, half-brothers) named James, Joses, Simon, and Judas, and that He had sisters (Matthew 13:55, 56). There is no reason from the Scriptures to assume anything other than that these were children of Mary and Joseph.

This verse also mentions the *swaddling clothes* in which Mary *wrapped* Jesus. These were the ordinary clothes placed on a newborn. They were folded around a baby to make him or her feel more comfortable, warm, and secure. The way in which they were wrapped made the baby look almost like a small mummy.

II. Announcement of the Birth (Luke 2:8-14)

A. The Angel's Appearance (vv. 8, 9)

8. And there were in the same country shepherds abiding in the field, keeping watch over their flock by night.

Even though much has changed around Bethlehem since the first century, *shepherds* still *watch . . . their flock* in the vicinity as these did. What time of year might this have been? We celebrate Christmas on December 25, but there is nothing in our text to indicate any specific season. Some argue that since winter is the rainy season in Israel, and that shepherds would not have been in the fields during the rainy season, Jesus could not have been born in the winter.

How to Say It

GABRIEL. *Gay*-bree-ul.
ISAIAH. Eye-*zay*-uh.
JOSES. *Jo*-sez.
MICAH. *My*-kuh.
NAZARETH. *Naz*-uh-reth.
SIMEON. *Sim*-ee-un.
ZECHARIAH. Zek-uh-*rye*-uh.

Others propose, however, that the shepherds in Bethlehem may have provided lambs for the temple sacrifices in Jerusalem, which was only a few miles away. Thus these shepherds would have been *in the field* throughout the year. Though we cannot know with certainty exactly when Jesus was born, this should not be allowed to affect our understanding of why He was born. There is no doubt whatsoever about that!

Why did the announcement of Jesus' birth come to shepherds? Was it because they raised the animals used in temple sacrifices—making them an appropriate group to welcome the Lamb of God? Was it because Jesus was a descendant of David, who was a shepherd? Was it because Jesus would one day describe Himself as "the good shepherd," who "giveth his life for the sheep" (John 10:11)?

Most likely shepherds were given this honor because they were among the humblest and most scorned individuals in the society of that time. Luke demonstrates a special interest in outcasts and in Jesus' concern for them (Luke 5:12-14, 27-32; 7:36-50; 10:25-37; 14:12-14; 15:11-24; 19:1-10), so he was likely impressed with the fact that the news of Jesus' birth first came to lowly shepherds. [See question #2, page 152.]

9. And, lo, the angel of the Lord came upon them, and the glory of the Lord shone round about them; and they were sore afraid.

What an interruption to an otherwise ordinary evening! Nothing could have prepared these simple shepherds for what they would experience. The wording in the Greek text literally reads, "They feared a great fear." This emphasizes even more the terror that filled the shepherds at the sight of *the angel of the Lord*.

B. The Angel's Message (vv. 10-12)

10. And the angel said unto them, Fear not: for, behold, I bring you good tidings of great joy, which shall be to all people.

Since the immediate reaction of the shepherds was fear, it was appropriate for the *angel* to begin his message with the words, *Fear not*. The reason that fear was not necessary was that the angel had come to convey a message of *good tidings*, not of judgment. The Greek phrase rendered *good tidings* or "good news" is closely related to a word that gives us our word "evangelism." The gospel is God's good news to a fallen world. Its product is *great joy* and its scope is universal—*all people*. The apostle John tells us that Jesus died for "the sins of the whole world" (1 John 2:2).

The angel who uttered these words is not named in the text. Could it have been Gabriel, whose appearances to Zechariah and Mary are recorded earlier by Luke? We are not told.

11. For unto you is born this day in the city of David a Saviour, which is Christ the Lord.

Let us focus on the three words used to describe Jesus: *Saviour*, *Christ*, and *Lord*. Jesus is *Saviour* because He came to be the atoning sacrifice for our sins. He is Messiah *(Christ)* because He is the "anointed" or "chosen one" who fulfills Old Testament prophecy. The term *Lord* calls attention to His authority over all things "in heaven and in earth" (Matthew 28:18). The verse is a comprehensive statement of who Jesus is and what He came to do. [See question #3, page 152.]

"THIS DAY"

The angel announced, "Unto you is born this day in the city of David a Saviour" (Luke 2:11). Of course, we do not know exactly what day *this day* was. We are not certain that Jesus was born on December 25—or, for that matter, in the month of December. And that, of course, is not really important. We have set aside a day to honor Christ's birth. What is important is that we use the day to honor Him. *Conceived*

We call this particular day *Christmas*; however, British writer Dorothy Sayers once suggested that we should call it *Wishmas*. She claimed that in fact this had already occurred and that Wishmas had superseded the commemoration of Christmas. It was marked, she said, by "the exchange of cards, bearing wishes for the recipients' material prosperity and frequently adorned with ice, snow, holly, and other polar symbols." She also noted that the day was characterized by "factitious heartiness and family friction."

Is it really true that the holiday known as Christmas is more correctly described as Wishmas? Has it lost its spiritual and Christian significance? No doubt it has for many. One liquor company erected a huge billboard at Christmastime right across the street from a church. The billboard showed the picture of a bottle of whiskey and declared, "The Spirit of Christmas!"

Brighter than the light of the angelic messengers was the "Light of the world" whose birth they announced. Display this visual as you discuss verse 11.

Visual for lesson 4

If we cannot turn Wishmas back into Christmas nationally, or even locally, we can certainly do so in our own hearts and homes. We can make certain that, at least for us and our families, "this day"—indeed, every day—will always honor Christ.   —R. C. S.

12. And this shall be a sign unto you; Ye shall find the babe wrapped in swaddling clothes, lying in a manger.

As noted in the comments under verse 7, it would not have been unusual to see a baby *wrapped in swaddling clothes*. What was remarkable was that the baby would be found *lying in a manger*.

C. The Angels' Praise (vv. 13, 14)

13. And suddenly there was with the angel a multitude of the heavenly host praising God, and saying.

First there was just *one angel*, now *suddenly* there was a *multitude*. Again, as with the words of Elisabeth (Luke 1:41-45) and Mary (Luke 1:46-55), the words of these angels are often considered their song, although the text simply records that they were *saying* them.

14. Glory to God in the highest, and on earth peace, good will toward men.

This account from Luke illustrates the two ways in which *glory* is used in Scripture. There is the *glory of the Lord* (v. 9), which is the radiant light that shone from the angel; and there is the *glory to God*, which describes the praise spoken by the multitude of angels.

The final phrase in this verse has been translated in two different ways. Our text reads *on earth peace, good will toward men*. More recent translations understand *good will* to be a description of the kind of men who are to receive *peace*. Readings such as "peace to men on whom his favor rests" (*New International Version*) and "peace among men with whom He is pleased" (*New American Standard Bible*) are suggested. All of these translations express the idea that mankind cannot experience genuine peace apart from God's Messiah. [See question #4, page 152.]

CHOIR PRACTICE

We would assume that a choir of angels should never need rehearsals. But just for a moment, try to imagine that it does. You are a member of the choir, and you are on your way to choir practice. "Where are we going to sing? It must be an important place for us to be rehearsing like this."

Another angel responds, "Earth."

"What? That disgusting little planet? Then surely we must be preparing to visit an important city on earth!"

"No, actually it's a rather small town—a town called Bethlehem."

"Well, then it must be an important audience—possibly kings or queens!"

"No, we're going to sing for shepherds out in a field!"

Of course, this is all imaginary, but such a hypothetical conversation can help us appreciate the wonder of what did take place on the night Jesus was born. To put it in a modern setting, what if the Mormon Tabernacle Choir were sent to sing in a remote country town? What if the Metropolitan Opera put on a performance in a town so small that they had to sing in a pasture because there was no auditorium?

Note the dramatic contrast portrayed in Luke 2: singers sent from Heaven and shepherds out in the field. Why did God choose to make the announcement of His Son's birth in this manner? Surely it calls attention to the essence of the "good news" of which the angel spoke. The sinless Son of God came to this "disgusting" world to save sinners. The Son of the Highest came to rescue the lowest.

True, the shepherds were not worthy to be the first to hear the good news. That is just the point—no one is worthy to hear it.   —R. C. S.

III. Response of the Shepherds (Luke 2:15-20)

A. The Shepherds' Visit (vv. 15, 16)

15. And it came to pass, as the angels were gone away from them into heaven, the shepherds said one to another, Let us now go even unto Bethlehem, and see this thing which is come to pass, which the Lord hath made known unto us.

Immediately the *shepherds* determined to travel to *Bethlehem* and to *see* for themselves the scene just described for them by the angel. Theirs is the kind of enthusiasm that we associate with people who become aware for the first time of what Jesus has done for them.

16. And they came with haste, and found Mary and Joseph, and the babe lying in a manger.

The shepherds *came with haste*, signifying the urgency of responding to the angel's message. Recall how Mary "went . . . with haste" to see Elisabeth following Gabriel's message to her (Luke 1:39). Do we treat the Lord's work with a similar sense of urgency?

B. The Shepherds' Witness (vv. 17-20)

17. And when they had seen it, they made known abroad the saying which was told them concerning this child.

Instantly these shepherds became evangelists and witnesses as they *made known abroad* what they had *seen* and what they had been *told*. With Jerusalem being as close as it was to Bethlehem, it is possible that word of the *child* reached the people there. If not, the news would be spread by way of Simeon and Anna (whom we shall consider in next week's lesson).

18. And all they that heard it wondered at those things which were told them by the shepherds.

Should any of us be surprised that *all they that heard it wondered* about what the *shepherds* described to them? It must have seemed unbelievable. Angels do not appear every day—but then, neither does the Messiah.

19. But Mary kept all these things, and pondered them in her heart.

Mary remained quiet through all of this. She did not go around town bragging about the identity of her child. Most likely she displayed the normal pride that any mother would demonstrate regarding her newborn. Although the shepherds must have told her what they had experienced, even these wondrous *things* she also *kept* within herself and *pondered . . . in her heart*. There is a time when the good news must be told to others, but there must also be moments for private reflection on what the Lord has done in our lives.

20. And the shepherds returned, glorifying and praising God for all the things that they had heard and seen, as it was told unto them.

We have already noted that the shepherds were in a sense evangelists, telling the news of Jesus' birth to others. Our lesson ends, however, with the shepherds' returning to their fields, *glorifying and praising God for all the things that they had heard and seen*. Just as Mary felt humbled to bear the Messiah, the shepherds must have felt humbled to be the first recipients of the news concerning the Messiah's birth. Moreover, they had opportunity to verify the angel's words and to see the Christ for themselves. They knew that all they had been *told* was true. Their lives would never be the same.

What about us and our witness today? Some who follow Jesus answer the call to vocational service in His name. That is, their vocation—what they do to earn a living—is itself related to the spread of the gospel. Most of us, however, serve Christ in more "secular" settings. Just as the shepherds *returned* to their fields, so we return to our occupations each day. In so doing, however, we also return to our "fields," for the places where we work are often fields "white already to harvest," as Jesus described them (John 4:35). There is a great need in these places for the faithful, consistent testimony of a dedicated Christian. Wherever we work, whether it be an office, an assembly line, a restaurant, a department store, or a farm, let us be committed to making a difference for Christ.

Conclusion

A. Being There

During the Christmas season, many people desire to travel to Bethlehem. They want to visit the site that has been traditionally identified as the birthplace of Jesus. Certainly there is something special and unforgettable about such an experience. However, far more important than visiting Bethlehem in that way is to visit it through a "spiritual pilgrimage" and to understand personally the significance of what took place there.

Have you *really* been to Bethlehem in this sense? If you embark on such a pilgrimage, you will find, as so many others have found, that it will change, not only your celebration of Christmas, but your life—forever. [See question #5, page 152.]

B. Prayer

Father, help me to move beyond what the world tells me Christmas is all about, for the world is often too busy and loses sight of the true meaning of Christmas. Help me to appreciate its real significance: You sent Your Son to save us from our sins. Having grasped that message, may I, like the shepherds, want to tell everyone I meet. Help me to have the courage to do that, in Jesus' name. Amen.

C. Thought to Remember

Jesus' coming changed an ordinary night into something extraordinary. He can do the same with our lives.

Learning by Doing

This page contains an alternate lesson plan emphasizing learning activities.
Classes desiring such student involvement will find these suggestions helpful.

Learning Goals

After participating in this lesson, each student will be able to:

1. Retell Luke's account of the birth of Jesus.

2. Contrast the humble scene of the nativity with the commercialism of the current celebration of Christmas.

3. Express a commitment to celebrating Christ's birth with a "spiritual pilgrimage" to Bethlehem to worship the Savior.

Into the Lesson

Prepare a video tape of the sights and sounds of Christmas around your community. Record activity at the mall, a program rehearsal, people's comments, and anything else you can think of. (If you do not have access to a video camera, you can still discuss the issues in the next paragraph. A video like the one described here would generate interest and enhance your discussion, but it is not vital to your discussion of these issues. Simply modify some of the instructions as needed.)

Begin the session by playing the video and asking, "What are some of the common images or concepts of Christmas? Which impressions would you label as Christian? Biblically accurate?" Allow answers. Then ask, "So does that mean that the people in the video were not Christians?" Allow response. Note, "It is possible that some of these people are Christians who have allowed modern Christmas celebration practices to invade their personal celebration, so that they have lost sight of the Christ, whose birth they are supposed to celebrate."

Into the Word

Most adults are familiar with movie posters. A movie poster is designed to convey the essence of a movie in one design. Some posters are such classics that they become collectors' items. Creating such a poster about the birth of Jesus will allow your students to put together the facts and express their appreciation for the purpose of His birth.

Ask a volunteer to read aloud Luke 2:4-20. Then form groups of no more than four students, and give each group a poster board and colored markers. If you think your students will be hesitant to be artists, provide magazines, old Christmas cards, scissors, and glue sticks. Explain that each group is to make an imaginary movie poster

for the birth of Jesus. You could show them a movie poster ad out of a magazine to stimulate their thinking. Tell the students to base their posters on today's text. Perhaps you could give a prize for the poster that displays the most scenes from, or in some other way displays a truth based on, Luke 2.

When work is completed, display the posters. Ask a representative from each group to explain his or her group's poster. Be especially sure that each spokesperson points out the connection between the group's work and the details of Luke 2.

After the reports, ask the class, "As you have worked on your posters, you have been forced to rediscover the excitement of the birth of Jesus. What are you already planning to do, or could you do, this evening or tomorrow to inject that excitement into the Christmas celebration of which you will be a part?" If you have a large class, let students share their thoughts and plans in pairs. This allows everyone the opportunity to speak in a non-threatening atmosphere.

Conclude this section by reading the text once again and by using material in the commentary to contrast Jesus' humble birth with the commercialization that surrounds Christmas today.

Into Life

Observe that even Christian families can get caught up in the commercialization of Christmas. It often takes a deliberate decision and plan to change such practices. Form small groups of students who will work together to suggest how a Christian individual, couple, or family could focus this year's Christmas celebration more on the true meaning of Christmas. Students should consider personal experiences, things they have read, and ideas prompted by brainstorming in their groups. Some suggestions might include attending a Christmas Eve worship service, serving Christmas dinner in a homeless shelter, inviting a person who lives alone to join one's family on Christmas Day, or giving anonymous gifts to people with notes saying that the gifts are given because of Christ's love. Let pairs pray together for each other's plans.

Close the session by singing one or more Christmas carols that hold no major errors. Suggested are "God Rest Ye Merry, Gentlemen," "Joy to the World," "O Come, All Ye Faithful," "O Little Town of Bethlehem," or "What Child Is This?"

Let's Talk It Over

The questions on this page are designed to encourage review of the lesson Scriptures and to promote discussion of the lesson by the class. The answers provided are only discussion starters. Let your class talk it over from there.

1. Although she was pregnant with the Son of God, Mary was not spared difficulty, discomfort, or frustration. Do you find that encouraging, discouraging, or neither? What does it tell you about your own difficulties?

We might think that Mary had every right to expect God to provide royal accommodations for His Son. But if she expected such an advantage, she surely did not receive it. The circumstances of Jesus' birth were surely not what she might have dreamed. We can only guess that her emotions might range from disappointment to frustration.

Still, Mary was the Lord's handmaid (Luke 1:38). Her difficulties were not evidence that she was out of harmony with God's will or guilty of some gross sin. She persevered, and God's will was accomplished—the Savior was born! When we experience difficulty and frustration, let us not give up or assume that God is not pleased with us. "Let us not be weary in well doing: for in due season we shall reap, if we faint not" (Galatians 6:9).

2. Why do you think the appearance of angels announcing Jesus' birth was given to only a few shepherds and not to crowds of people or to more influential people?

No doubt there are many reasons. Sending angels to Herod's court to announce Jesus' birth would have endangered the infant Jesus. (Note what happened when Herod did learn that a king had been born—Matthew 2.) Sending the angels to the Pharisees and Sadducees probably would have been equally dangerous. They were more interested in their own position and power than in pleasing God. They would have wanted to control the Messiah. And if they could not control Him, they would have tried to get rid of Him—which is exactly what they did thirty-three years later!

Sending the angels to shepherds demonstrates that Jesus was to be a Savior for all: not just for priests, not just for the highly religious, and not just for the "movers and shakers" in society. The angels brought "good tidings of great joy, which shall be to all people."

3. The angels used the terms *Savior, Christ,* and *Lord.* Do you think these terms are understood by the average person today? Why or why not? If not, what can we do to help such a person understand?

The title *Christ* means "anointed one," the Messiah of Old Testament prophecy. To appreciate its significance, one needs to know what the Old Testament foretold, including the references to David's throne and the Servant passages of Isaiah. The term *Savior* is always dependent on what one believes he or she needs to be saved *from*. *Lord* was the most common reference among Jews for God. They feared to pronounce the name of God, so they substituted *Lord*.

Few today will understand the Jewish nuance in these titles, but they can be understood in connection with the One who wore them. The more clearly we represent Jesus to people, the more significant these terms will become to them. Then we can help them to grow in their appreciation of Jesus by learning more about His titles.

4. Suppose a co-worker challenged the angelic message. "Peace on earth?" he might say. "I don't see any peace on earth! If the Bible is true, how come there is so much violence and hatred in the world?" How would you answer?

We should note that there are different kinds of "peace." Jesus was born in a time called the *pax Romana,* "the peace of Rome." Virtually the entire known world had been dominated by Rome, whose army kept a tight reign on any who might create insurrection. There were isolated incidents of strife and rebellion, but they were quickly squelched. Jesus did not come to impose such a peace. He came to bring peace with God (Romans 5:1). In the midst of turmoil and strife, one who is at peace with God has a "peace . . . which passeth all understanding" (Philippians 4:7).

5. How does your observance of Christmas glorify and praise God? How could you make it an even more God-glorifying event?

Unfortunately, Christmas for many is the glorification of an out-of-control materialism, or it is a secularized holiday for promoting personal peace and goodwill. Individuals and families may glorify God during this season by engaging in worship, either privately or with other Christians—or some of both. We glorify God by proclaiming the good news through drama, nativity scenes, caroling, cards, letters, and other ways. We also glorify God as we reflect His spirit of giving and give gifts or otherwise meet the needs of others.

Presented in the Temple

DEVOTIONAL READING: Isaiah 52:7-10.

BACKGROUND SCRIPTURE: Luke 2:21-40.

PRINTED TEXT: Luke 2:25-38.

Luke 2:25-38

25 And, behold, there was a man in Jerusalem, whose name was Simeon; and the same man was just and devout, waiting for the consolation of Israel: and the Holy Ghost was upon him.

26 And it was revealed unto him by the Holy Ghost, that he should not see death, before he had seen the Lord's Christ.

27 And he came by the Spirit into the temple: and when the parents brought in the child Jesus, to do for him after the custom of the law,

28 Then took he him up in his arms, and blessed God, and said,

29 Lord, now lettest thou thy servant depart in peace, according to thy word:

30 For mine eyes have seen thy salvation,

31 Which thou hast prepared before the face of all people;

32 A light to lighten the Gentiles, and the glory of thy people Israel.

33 And Joseph and his mother marveled at those things which were spoken of him.

34 And Simeon blessed them, and said unto Mary his mother, Behold, this child is set for the fall and rising again of many in Israel; and for a sign which shall be spoken against;

35 (Yea, a sword shall pierce through thy own soul also;) that the thoughts of many hearts may be revealed.

36 And there was one Anna, a prophetess, the daughter of Phanuel, of the tribe of Asher: she was of a great age, and had lived with a husband seven years from her virginity;

37 And she was a widow of about fourscore and four years, which departed not from the temple, but served God with fastings and prayers night and day.

38 And she coming in that instant gave thanks likewise unto the Lord, and spake of him to all them that looked for redemption in Jerusalem.

GOLDEN TEXT: Mine eyes have seen thy salvation, which thou hast prepared before the face of all people; a light to lighten the Gentiles, and the glory of thy people Israel.—Luke 2:30-32.

Good News of Jesus

Unit 1: A Savior Is Born

(Lessons 1-5)

Lesson Aims

After participating in this lesson, each student will be able to:

1. Summarize the reactions of Simeon and Anna upon seeing the Christ child.

2. Tell how these reactions reflected a hope based on the faithfulness of God and His promises.

3. Identify one person who does not have hope in Christ, and suggest a specific way to share with that person the good news of Jesus.

Lesson Outline

INTRODUCTION
    A. The Dignity of Age
    B. Lesson Background
 I. SIMEON (Luke 2:25-35)
    A. His Character (v. 25)
    B. His Hope (v. 26)
        Living in Hope
    C. His Praise (vv. 27-33)
    D. His Prophecy (vv. 34, 35)
II. ANNA (Luke 2:36-38)
    A. Her Identity (v. 36)
    B. Her Character (v. 37)
    C. Her Testimony (v. 38)
        Rest Stop
CONCLUSION
    A. The Wait Is Over
    B. Prayer
    C. Thought to Remember

Introduction

A. The Dignity of Age

Today's lesson focuses on the faith of two elderly saints. The Bible holds elderly people in high regard and teaches that they should be treated with respect (Leviticus 19:32; 1 Timothy 5:1). It tells us that God's care for individuals never diminishes, regardless of their age (Psalm 71:9, 18-21; Isaiah 46:3, 4).

For decades now people have talked about the "generation gap." Admittedly there is often tension between the generations. While some of their interests and concerns may differ, when one places the young and the elderly together, he often discovers that they display respect for one another. Each has much to offer the other: the young have ~~energy and enthusiasm~~; the elderly have ~~experience and wisdom~~.

One of the ways in which a society can be judged is by how it treats its elderly. Are they considered a burden or a blessing? How foolish to discount years of experience and the resultant wisdom of those years!

Today we will consider two elderly saints who are certainly worthy of honor. They met a young couple and their infant child in the temple in Jerusalem. In the process both young and old benefited. The young couple received additional confirmation of their child's importance in the plan of God. The elderly saints were rewarded for their years of faithful service and patient waiting on the Lord by being granted the privilege of seeing the fulfillment of their hopes—the Lord's Messiah.

B. Lesson Background

The occasion that brought Jesus and His parents to the temple involved the fulfillment of responsibilities prescribed by the law of Moses. Three duties were expected of the parents of a firstborn son: circumcision of the child, dedication of the child, and purification of the mother. Luke 2:21 tells us that Jesus was circumcised on the eighth day (no doubt while the family was still in Bethlehem). Also on this occasion He was officially given the name *Jesus*, although an angel had already instructed both Mary and Joseph as to what His name would be (Luke 1:31; Matthew 1:21).

In the case of John the Baptist, family members and friends gathered to mark his circumcision and naming (Luke 1:57-59). In contrast, Joseph and Mary were virtually alone in Bethlehem. Given the circumstances surrounding Mary's pregnancy and the skepticism that must have accompanied it, we wonder how many relatives and friends would have gathered for the occasion if Mary and Joseph had been at home. As it was, they were far from their family and friends in Nazareth when Jesus was born, so even the more supportive of them had no opportunity to share in this occasion.

Another responsibility concerned the mother. According to Leviticus 12, a woman was considered ceremonially unclean for a specified period of time following childbirth. During this time, she was not to participate in public worship services or other activities outside the home. This period of uncleanness was not intended to be a negative reflection upon women or upon childbearing; it was essentially a time of recuperation for the mother.

In order for the new mother to be able to return to her normal activities, including worship, she had to go through a ceremony of purification

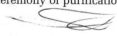

40 in case of mal

following the time specified in the law. This period of time was forty days in the case of a male child. Approximately one month later, the first-born was presented for dedication. While this was the general practice, it appears that Mary and Joseph combined the purification act with the dedication, making them part of one visit to the temple.

Luke 2:24 tells us that Joseph and Mary offered a sacrifice of two birds for Mary's purification. The law of Moses actually preferred a lamb and a bird, but allowed a couple to substitute a second bird if they could not afford a lamb (Leviticus 12:6-8). A couple with limited means could do as Joseph and Mary apparently did and let the bird offerings satisfy both the purification and dedication requirements.

It is interesting to consider where the incident studied today fits in relationship to the visit of the wise men and to the journey of Joseph, Mary, and Jesus into Egypt (Matthew 2:1-14). Probably these events followed this incident in the temple (though we cannot be sure how much time elapsed). It does not seem likely that Joseph and Mary's offering would have been a pair of birds if they had just received the treasures from the wise men. In addition, since Herod and "all Jerusalem" were "troubled" by the word of a new king (Matthew 2:3), the presentation of Jesus in the temple at that time would have been extremely risky. Some students are uncomfortable with this harmony because Luke says the couple and Jesus "returned into Galilee, to . . . Nazareth," after performing these things (2:39), not to Bethlehem (where the wise men would find them). But Luke chose not to include the visit of the wise men or the flight to Egypt at all, so it was proper for him simply to mention the return to Nazareth here.

We noted last week that Jesus' birth was witnessed by humble shepherds. Today we see how two humble and devout individuals—Simeon and Anna—rejoiced in His coming. Just as few realized what was happening in Bethlehem on the night Jesus was born, so did few probably notice what happened when a simple peasant couple entered the temple to fulfill the law.

I. Simeon
(Luke 2:25-35)

A. His Character (v. 25)

25. And, behold, there was a man in Jerusalem, whose name was Simeon; and the same man was just and devout, waiting for the consolation of Israel: and the Holy Ghost was upon him.

Simeon is not identified with any particular group, such as the Pharisees or Sadducees, but his reputation for integrity and righteousness is noted. [See question #1, page 160.] It has generally been assumed from the context that Simeon was an elderly man. There is, however, nothing in the text that explicitly mentions his age.

The phrase *consolation of Israel* refers to the messianic hope. To many, this hope carried political overtones. They believed that the Messiah would come and throw off the yoke of Roman rule, thus providing *consolation* to Israel and relief from the tyranny of pagans. Of course, Jesus' style of Messiah was quite different and was quite problematic for some.

Simeon is also described as someone *upon* whom was the *Holy Ghost*. This is important since, as the next verse states, the Holy Spirit was the source of a special revelation given to Simeon.

B. His Hope (v. 26)

26. And it was revealed unto him by the Holy Ghost, that he should not see death, before he had seen the Lord's Christ.

The Holy Ghost had assured Simeon that he would live to see *the Christ*. We can only wonder how long Simeon had waited and when he first received this promise. Perhaps day after day—for weeks and months and years—he had scanned the crowds that passed through the temple area and wondered if this would be the day he would see the Messiah. [See question #2, page 160.]

LIVING IN HOPE

Simeon is described as "waiting for the consolation of Israel" (Luke 2:25). He was sustained by hope—a hope that was finally realized when he saw the infant Jesus. We, too, are sustained by hope. The novel *Zorba the Greek* was written by Níkos Kazantzákis (*Nick*-oss Kah-zahn-*tsah*-kis). When Kazantzákis died in 1957, his philosophy of life was engraved on his tombstone: "I hope for nothing. I fear nothing. I am free." What a sad (and wrong) view of life! Lack of hope does not make us free. Hope makes us free. We cannot live without hope.

If you look up the word *hope* in Stevenson's *Home Book of Quotations,* you will read the entry "see also Optimism." But hope and optimism are not the same thing. Optimism is natural. Hope is spiritual. Optimism comes from a sunny disposition. Hope comes from faith. Optimism can fade with the passing years. Hope is eternal. We will not see our hope realized on earth as Simeon did. But our hope is no less real.

It was the blind songwriter Fanny Crosby who wrote the words, "And I shall see Him face to face, And tell the story—Saved by grace." Both Simeon and Fanny Crosby saw their hope fulfilled by seeing Jesus. Our hope assures us that we too "shall see him as he is" (1 John 3:2). —R. C. S.

C. His Praise (vv. 27-33)

27. And he came by the Spirit into the temple: and when the parents brought in the child Jesus, to do for him after the custom of the law.

Simeon was prompted *by the Spirit* to go to the *temple* on this day. There he would meet Mary, Joseph, and the infant *Jesus*.

The *custom of the law* mentioned here refers to the purification service for the mother and to the dedication service of the firstborn son. Though Luke's Gospel is characterized, as we have noted, by an emphasis on Jesus' concern for different groups of people, he notes that Jesus followed the important Jewish customs of His day (Luke 2:41; 4:16; 5:12-14; 17:11-14).

28. Then took he him up in his arms, and blessed God, and said.

What an amazing sight it must have been for Mary and Joseph to see aged Simeon lift up *in his arms* the infant Messiah! Just as God had impressed on Simeon that he would see the Messiah, so He impressed on him that Joseph and Mary's child was that special individual for whom he had been waiting so patiently.

29. Lord, now lettest thou thy servant depart in peace, according to thy word.

Simeon's words have come to be called the *Nunc Dimittis*, which is Latin for "you now dismiss." Having seen the promised Christ, Simeon knew that he could face death with *peace*. This is the reason it is assumed that Simeon was an old man. Now that the Lord's promise to him had been fulfilled, Simeon felt his life was complete. He did not mean that he longed for death, but that now he could die content with the knowledge that the Messiah had come!

The word translated *Lord* in this verse is not the word by which God is usually addressed. Instead, it is the word from which our word *despot* comes. It describes a sovereign master or owner. Simeon saw himself as a slave who was prepared to *depart*, or be released from, this life because his goal had been reached. He "had seen the Lord's Christ" (v. 26). Nothing else in the world held any attraction for him. He was satisfied.

30. For mine eyes have seen thy salvation.

Simeon's *eyes* had *seen [God's] salvation* in that he had looked upon the One who had come to bring salvation. Simeon probably did not grasp the full significance of his statement or just how that salvation would be provided (although later, in verse 35, he hinted at the suffering that Christ would undergo).

31. Which thou hast prepared before the face of all people.

Simeon gave thanks that the Messiah's salvation was being prepared with *all people* in mind. While many did not notice the humble birth of

Today's visual illustrates the vision of Simeon, who by the Spirit saw God's "salvation," which Jesus brought by the power of the same Spirit.

Jesus or this incident in the temple, the impact of His extraordinary birth and life was meant to be felt by succeeding generations of peoples around the world. In the early chapters of his Gospel, Luke's interest in all people is seen in the words of the angels to the shepherds (Luke 2:10) and in the preaching of John the Baptist (Luke 3:6), as well as here.

32. A light to lighten the Gentiles, and the glory of thy people Israel.

[See question #3, page 160.] Luke often records events in which *Gentiles* or other outcasts were included in or affected by the ministry of Jesus. (See "Good News for All" on page 118, as well as comments under Luke 2:8 on page 148, for examples.) Here Jesus is called *a light to . . . Gentiles* as well as to *Israel*. This emphasis, however, is not exclusively Luke's. Even Matthew, the most "Jewish" of the Gospels, includes indications that Jesus came to bless Gentiles (the visit of the wise men is a good example).

Luke's second book, the book of Acts, shows how the gospel message was first proclaimed among the Jews and eventually came to be preached among the Gentiles. Such an outreach did not come easily for the church. It is one thing to quote Jesus' Great Commission and quite another to practice it.

33. And Joseph and his mother marveled at those things which were spoken of him.

Both Joseph and Mary had already seen and heard more than enough concerning Jesus to cause them to marvel; yet Simeon's words on this occasion produced a similar effect.

D. His Prophecy (vv. 34, 35)

34. And Simeon blessed them, and said unto Mary his mother, Behold, this child is set for the fall and rising again of many in Israel; and for a sign which shall be spoken against.

Simeon's welcome was also filled with words of warning. That Jesus would cause *the fall and rising again of many in Israel* indicates how Jesus would become a kind of "watershed." Some would believe in Him and find eternal life; others "received him not" (John 1:11). Some experienced His "consolation" (v. 25); others rejected it.

Simeon further warned that Jesus would face stern opposition. While Jesus was extremely popular at times, certain individuals or groups, unhappy with Him or jealous of His success, spoke *against* Him and His teachings. [See question #4, page 160.]

Even today, the idea of rising or falling is an apt way to describe how there is no middle ground concerning Jesus. It is impossible to remain neutral about Him.

35. (Yea, a sword shall pierce through thy own soul also;) that the thoughts of many hearts may be revealed.

The previous verse noted that Simeon's warning was directed specifically to Mary. These are not exactly the kind of words that a young mother wants to hear. The opposition against Jesus would become so pronounced, said Simeon, that it would wound Mary, piercing her very *soul*. No doubt it was difficult for Mary when the religious and political leaders began their verbal attacks against Jesus. Most agonizing of all, of course, was the pain she endured in watching her son die the humiliating death of crucifixion. The fact that Jesus Himself would be pierced is clear from the word *also*. Thus, even at this early stage in the life of Christ, we see the foreshadowing of the cross.

How are *the thoughts of many hearts . . . revealed* through Jesus? They are revealed by the persons' response to Him. What Jesus said and what He did, particularly in His death and resurrection, challenge individuals to look at themselves and to confront the questions of eternal significance. Thus you can tell what a person is really like by his view of Jesus and His teachings.

Home Daily Bible Readings

Monday, Dec. 25—The Consecration of the Firstborn (Exodus 13:11-16)
Tuesday, Dec. 26—According to the Law (Luke 2:21-24)
Wednesday, Dec. 27—Our Love for God (Deuteronomy 6:1-9)
Thursday, Dec. 28—Adoration and Prophecy of Simeon (Luke 2:25-35)
Friday, Dec. 29—The Good News of Peace (Isaiah 52:3-10)
Saturday, Dec. 30—Adoration of Anna (Luke 2:36-38)
Sunday, Dec. 31—Honor Widows Who Hope in God (1 Timothy 5:3-8)

During His earthly ministry, Jesus possessed special insight into the thoughts of people (John 2:24, 25). Even now, whenever we read His teachings and consider His example, we see His unique insight into the human condition.

II. Anna
(Luke 2:36-38)
A. Her Identity (v. 36)

36. And there was one Anna, a prophetess, the daughter of Phanuel, of the tribe of Asher: she was of a great age, and had lived with a husband seven years from her virginity.

Simeon was not identified as a prophet, yet he, through God's Spirit, prophesied on this day. *Anna*, on the other hand, is described as a *prophetess*. Her name is essentially the same as the Old Testament character Hannah, and it means "grace."

Anna is described as *the daughter of Phanuel*. We know nothing else about this man, but he was probably well known at the time for his name to be mentioned here.

Anna is also described as a member *of the tribe of Asher*. When the promised land had been divided among the twelve tribes, Asher was assigned an area along the Mediterranean coast north of Mount Carmel. Although many of the people of this northern tribe had been carried away by the Assyrians (following the conquest of the northern kingdom by Assyria in 722 B.C.), the tribe had not completely lost its identity.

Luke also mentions that Anna was widowed *seven years* into her marriage and never remarried. Life could be very difficult for widows in the ancient world. They were often poverty stricken and the targets of unscrupulous practices, sometimes from supposedly religious individuals (Luke 20:45-47). Luke's unique references to widows (here; 4:25, 26; 7:12; 18:1-8) comprise another indication of his Gospel's concern for those considered outcasts by society.

B. Her Character (v. 37)

37. And she was a widow of about fourscore and four years, which departed not from the temple, but served God with fastings and prayers night and day.

Anna's devotion to God was such that she *departed not from the temple*. This may simply mean that she stayed there all day, not that she lived there. It is possible, however, that she lived in one of the rooms adjoining the temple and did volunteer service there. The depth of her spiritual commitment is clear from the statement that she *served God with fastings and prayers night and day*. [See question #5, page 160.]

There is some disagreement among Bible students regarding Anna's age. Some believe that the text is saying that Anna was currently a widow and currently *fourscore and four years* (eighty-four years) old. Others suggest that she had been widowed for eighty-four years, which, if true, would make Anna over a hundred years old. Such a scenario, though unusual, would not have been impossible.

C. Her Testimony (v. 38)

38. And she coming in that instant gave thanks likewise unto the Lord, and spake of him to all them that looked for redemption in Jerusalem.

Anna's testimony concerning the child was far more public than Simeon's was. Like the shepherds, she too was a kind of evangelist, telling people who *looked for redemption* that their looking was over; the Messiah had come! It appears that her proclamation concerning Jesus was not limited to the people in the temple. She conveyed the news wherever she could find an interested hearer.

REST STOP

The minister arrived early for the morning service, but one person was already seated in the sanctuary. She was sitting in the back, at the end of the pew, half asleep. The minister walked over and teased her about getting her nap finished before he began to preach. "This is the only place I can get any rest," she said. At first he thought that she had back trouble and that the contour of the padded pew gave her relief. But as they talked on, he realized she meant something else. She worked a full-time job outside the home and cared for all the household duties in the home. When she came to the church building, it was the only time she could get any rest.

Many have experienced rest in the church—not physical rest, but spiritual and emotional rest. Guilt-laden people say, "This is the only place I can get any rest." Sorrow-laden people say, "This is the only place I can get any rest." Worried people say, "This is the only place I can get any rest." Even people in physical pain can find relief in worship. As an old hymn says, "O Love that wilt not let me go, I rest my weary soul on Thee."

Both Simeon and Anna found peace and rest in the place that had been dedicated to the worship and service of God. Many today will testify that there is something about the atmosphere of a modern house of worship that brings a sense of contentment and rest to their bodies, their minds, and their souls.
—R. C. S.

Conclusion

A. The Wait Is Over

One of the toughest things to do in life is to wait. When we are children, we think that Christmas will never come or that the school year will never end. When we are waiting for news from a medical test, the minutes seem like days.

In the time in which Simeon and Anna lived, there was a general hope and expectation in Israel that God was about to do something. Along with these two, we know that Joseph of Arimathea also possessed such a hope (Luke 23:50, 51). People were praying for and watching for a Messiah. They took a new interest in the promises of the prophets. They held tightly to every hint in the Scriptures of the Messiah's coming. There must have been times when they thought this event would never happen, yet they continued to trust God's promises.

On the day that Joseph and Mary entered the temple with the infant Jesus, two faithful saints of God—Simeon and Anna—learned that the long wait was over. God was acting. God was coming in the form of a baby to meet human need. No wonder these devout believers lifted their voices in praise.

Today people are still in need of the light and salvation that Jesus came to bring. Like Anna, we must tell everyone we can about this good news.

B. Prayer

Dear Father, thank You for sending us light. Thank You for sending us salvation. We recognize that these have come to us through a person—Jesus. He gives us reason to raise our voices in praise, just as Simeon and Anna did. In His dear name we pray. Amen.

C. Thought to Remember

No matter what your age may be, God always gives you reason to hope and to look forward to tomorrow.

How to Say It

ARIMATHEA. *Air*-uh-muh-*thee*-uh (strong accent on *thee*).
ASSYRIA. Uh-*sear*-ee-uh.
MEDITERRANEAN. *Med*-uh-tuh-*ray*-nee-un (strong accent on *ray*).
NUNC DIMITTIS. Nunk Dih-*mit*-us.
PHANUEL. *Fan*-you-el.
PHARISEES. *Fair*-ih-seez.
SADDUCEES. *Sad*-you-seez.
SIMEON. *Sim*-ee-un.

Learning by Doing

This page contains an alternate lesson plan emphasizing learning activities.
Classes desiring such student involvement will find these suggestions helpful.

Learning Goals

After participating in this lesson, each student will be able to:

1. Summarize the reactions of Simeon and Anna upon seeing the Christ child.

2. Tell how these reactions reflected a hope based on the faithfulness of God and His promises.

3. Identify one person who does not have hope in Christ, and suggest a specific way to share with that person the good news of Jesus.

Into the Lesson

Before the class arrives write, "Promises! Promises!" on the chalkboard or on a large poster. Below that write, "How promises affect my behavior." As students enter the room, direct their attention to what you have written. Allow some time for the students to think, and then ask for responses. Ask for volunteers to tell about times they have said—or wanted to say—"Promises! Promises!" Why did they doubt? Were they right about the promises' not being kept, or were they surprised? How do we respond to promises that we believe?

Make the transition to Bible study by saying, "In our lesson today we will meet two people who believed God's promise to send a Messiah. Their faith led them to dramatic encounters with baby Jesus in the temple."

Into the Word

Ask a volunteer to read Luke 2:25-38. Then divide the class into two groups. Ask the first group to consider Simeon and the second to consider Anna. Each group should determine how belief in God's faithfulness had guided Simeon's or Anna's life until the important day recorded in our text. The groups should also tell how these two saints displayed their faith in God's keeping His word when they saw Jesus.

After ten minutes, ask a reporter from each group to stand and summarize the group's findings. Some suggested discoveries follow.

Simeon: His "waiting for the consolation of Israel" (v. 25) is evidence that Simeon trusted God to keep His word. Probably his presence at the temple was additional evidence. His prayer that he could depart in peace was a prayer of triumph and anticipation of God's putting into place His plan of salvation. His prophecy, while troubling, was a confident expression of hope that God would work out His plan even through distress.

Anna: Her continual presence at the temple was, no doubt, a demonstration of her faith and hope in God to provide a Redeemer. Her fastings and prayers also demonstrated her faithfulness. She gave thanks to God for the Christ child, and spoke of Him "to all them that looked for redemption" (v. 38). Comment on how our willingness to talk to others about Jesus shows our own faith.

Into Life

Comment on how Simeon and Anna demonstrated their hope in God's salvation even without knowing all the details. Jesus was but a baby, and was probably but a youth when these two saints died. But we know the rest of Jesus' life. We know the convincing proofs He gave to show that He was sent by God, that He is "the Christ, the Son of the living God" (Matthew 16:16). We know of His death, burial, and resurrection. How much more ought we to be confident of His identity and of His ability to provide salvation!

But many today do not know Him. Ask the class to think of five non-Christians whom they know. Have them write the names of the people they think of. Then ask them to think about which of these they can talk with this week about the Lord—as Anna told all those looking for redemption. Are there individuals on your students' lists who are seeking the Lord? Have some of them expressed interest in your students' faith or in the church? Have they visited the worship service? Have some of them had recent experiences that may serve to awaken spiritual interest or desire?

Ask the students also to think about the people with whom they have the most credibility. Are there co-workers with whom they have a closer relationship than with others? Are there people on their lists who seek them out for advice?

Have the students consider practical matters such as how often they see the people they listed. Are there some they know they will see every day this week, or at least once during the week?

Have the students evaluate all the information; then ask each one to choose one person from his list with whom he will share the good news of Jesus this week. Brainstorm some specific ways of doing that, and then ask each student to choose one of the methods discussed and make plans to share the gospel this week.

Let's Talk It Over

The questions on this page are designed to encourage review of the lesson Scriptures and to promote discussion of the lesson by the class. The answers provided are only discussion starters. Let your class talk it over from there.

1. Whom have you known personally whom you would describe as "just and devout"? How does his or her example influence you and others?

The description of Simeon as just and devout tells us much about his character. Since he was devout toward God, we may assume he was a student of the Scriptures and morally scrupulous. Synonyms for just are fair, upright, and impartial.

If you have been privileged to know someone like that, surely it has influenced you for good. The devout tend to inspire devotion in others, and the behavior of the just makes us ashamed of our pettiness and prejudice. "Just" and "devout" are terms we do not often hear today. Let us be sure that the qualities have not disappeared, but are being displayed in our own lives.

2. Simeon was promised that he would see the Messiah in his lifetime. How do you suppose that promise affected him? How would your life be different if you knew the Lord would return in your lifetime?

Every day when Simeon woke up he must have thought, "Perhaps this is the day I will see the Christ." That sense of expectation certainly would have affected his attitude. Simeon believed that no matter how difficult life became, he would live to see the promised Messiah. That kind of trust adds endurance in the face of hardship, courage in the face of threats, and faithful obedience in the face of weariness or temptation to sin.

The same things are true of a vivid hope in the return of Jesus. If we truly believe that He may return at any time, we are moved to greater faithfulness and courage. We do not need an assurance that Jesus will come in our own lifetimes, however, for we have the sure word that He will, indeed, return—and that we will be with Him forever. That is an even better promise than the one to which Simeon clung!

3. Simeon saw Jesus as a "light to lighten the Gentiles" as well as "the glory of . . . Israel." How does his statement speak to the mission of the church today?

The Jews in Simeon's day would have agreed that the Messiah would be the glory of Israel. Most of them had a very nationalistic view of the Messiah. They believed He would restore independence to Israel and reestablish the throne of David in Jerusalem. The Gentiles were not included, except as objects of judgment and wrath.

Simeon had a divine vision for the ministry of the Messiah as extending to all people. The church today must not forget that the good news of Jesus is for every nation and every culture. We must make every effort to reach the lost in foreign lands through sending and supporting missionaries. And we must reach out to those of different cultures and ethnic backgrounds in our own country. We must welcome them to our own church through deliberate planning and programming. And we must reach out to where they are to tell them the good news of Jesus.

4. "This child is set for the fall and rising again of many in Israel; and for a sign which shall be spoken against." How do these words continue to apply wherever Christ is proclaimed?

Once confronted with the life of Jesus, the teachings of Jesus, and the claims of and about Jesus, it is impossible to remain neutral. Jesus was and is a very controversial figure. Those who reacted to Him with self-righteous, defensive pride were brought low by His stinging rebuke. Those who responded in humble faith were elevated to a new status with God. It is still true that, concerning Jesus, people are polarized into two camps.

5. How is God served by the "fastings and prayers" of someone like Anna? Who carries on this "service" today?

We live in a culture that glorifies self-reliance and a "can do" approach to problem solving. People with those values tend to look on behaviors like fasting and prayer as doing next to nothing. They may wonder how fasting and prayer can qualify as "serving" God. The Bible, however, portrays fasting and prayer as of great importance, often resulting in God's direct intervention. Many believers today are recognizing the value of these disciplines and are arranging their schedules to make time for this "service" to God. Challenge your students to participate in a ministry of fasting and prayer, especially if your church is about to launch a new enterprise (a building project, sending out a mission team, etc.), is wrestling with a difficult decision, or is dealing with some crisis.

Jesus in Nazareth

DEVOTIONAL READING: Isaiah 61.

BACKGROUND SCRIPTURE: Luke 4:14-30.

PRINTED TEXT: Luke 4:16-30.

Luke 4:16-30

16 And he came to Nazareth, where he had been brought up: and, as his custom was, he went into the synagogue on the sabbath day, and stood up for to read.

17 And there was delivered unto him the book of the prophet Isaiah. And when he had opened the book, he found the place where it was written,

18 The Spirit of the Lord is upon me, because he hath anointed me to preach the gospel to the poor; he hath sent me to heal the brokenhearted, to preach deliverance to the captives, and recovering of sight to the blind, to set at liberty them that are bruised,

19 To preach the acceptable year of the Lord.

20 And he closed the book, and he gave it again to the minister, and sat down. And the eyes of all them that were in the synagogue were fastened on him.

21 And he began to say unto them, This day is this Scripture fulfilled in your ears.

22 And all bare him witness, and wondered at the gracious words which proceeded out of his mouth. And they said, Is not this Joseph's son?

23 And he said unto them, Ye will surely say unto me this proverb, Physician, heal thyself: whatsoever we have heard done in Capernaum, do also here in thy country.

24 And he said, Verily I say unto you, No prophet is accepted in his own country.

25 But I tell you of a truth, many widows were in Israel in the days of Elijah, when the heaven was shut up three years and six months, when great famine was throughout all the land;

26 But unto none of them was Elijah sent, save unto Zarephath, a city of Sidon, unto a woman that was a widow.

27 And many lepers were in Israel in the time of Elisha the prophet; and none of them was cleansed, saving Naaman the Syrian.

28 And all they in the synagogue, when they heard these things, were filled with wrath,

29 And rose up, and thrust him out of the city, and led him unto the brow of the hill whereon their city was built, that they might cast him down headlong.

30 But he, passing through the midst of them, went his way.

Jan 7

GOLDEN TEXT: The Spirit of the Lord is upon me, because he hath anointed me to preach the gospel to the poor; he hath sent me to heal the brokenhearted, to preach deliverance to the captives, and recovering of sight to the blind, to set at liberty them that are bruised, to preach the acceptable year of the Lord.—Luke 4:18, 19.

Good News of Jesus
Unit 2: Mission and Ministry
(Lessons 6-9)

Lesson Aims

After this lesson each student will be able to:

1. Tell what happened in Nazareth when Jesus identified Himself as the fulfillment of one of Isaiah's prophecies of the Messiah.

2. Compare the prophesied role of the Messiah with Jesus' ministry and with that of the church today.

3. Give a specific example of how the church can continue the messianic ministry Isaiah prophesied and Jesus fulfilled.

Lesson Outline

INTRODUCTION
 A. Going Home
 B. Lesson Background
I. A GOSPEL MISSION (Luke 4:16-21)
 A. Announced in the Synagogue (vv. 16, 17)
  The Worth of Worship
 B. Foretold in Prophecy (vv. 18, 19)
  The Year of the Lord
 C. Fulfilled by Jesus (vv. 20, 21)
II. A SKEPTICAL RESPONSE (Luke 4:22-27)
 A. The Crowd's Reaction (v. 22)
 B. Jesus' Defense (vv. 23-27)
III. A DETERMINED SPIRIT (Luke 4:28-30)
 A. Facing Hostility (vv. 28, 29)
 B. Pressing Forward (v. 30)
CONCLUSION
 A. Preconceptions
 B. Prayer
 C. Thought to Remember

Introduction

A. Going Home

Students of American literature are familiar with the works of Thomas Wolfe, a novelist who lived during the first half of the twentieth century. One of his most well-known novels is entitled *You Can't Go Home Again*. Certainly there is a measure of truth to that. Going home can be difficult if an individual left home amidst a flurry of high expectations but then fell flat on his face in failure.

On the other hand, going home can be one of the most thrilling, rewarding experiences of a person's life if the individual lived up to, or even

exceeded, the expectations surrounding him. And if he left home with few thinking that his chances for success were very great, going back home to headlines of "Local Boy [or Girl] Makes Good" would be especially satisfying.

In today's lesson we consider what happened when Jesus made His first visit back to His hometown of Nazareth after He had begun His messianic ministry. One would think, given the excitement over Jesus' ministry to this point, that the reception of the townspeople would have been most favorable. But such was not the case; in fact, the residents of Nazareth became not only unfriendly, but hostile.

B. Lesson Background

From the story of the presentation of Jesus in the temple (the subject of last week's lesson), our study of the Gospel of Luke moves forward to Jesus at age thirty (Luke 3:23). It was then that He initiated His ministry as Messiah by means of His baptism in the Jordan River (Luke 3:21, 22).

From the river to the wilderness, the Holy Spirit led Jesus to a confrontation with the devil. This time of temptation tested the resolve of the Messiah. Though physically weakened by forty days of fasting (Luke 4:1, 2), Jesus proved to be stronger than any scheme of the tempter. He was now ready to pursue His ministry in earnest.

After first spending some time in Jerusalem and the surrounding vicinity, Jesus led His disciples north to Galilee (Luke 4:14), where together they ministered for nearly two years. There He began to visit some of the synagogues in Galilee, where He was "glorified of all" (Luke 4:15). Eventually He came to His hometown of Nazareth.

I. A Gospel Mission
(Luke 4:16-21)

A. Announced in the Synagogue (vv. 16, 17)

16. And he came to Nazareth, where he had been brought up: and, as his custom was, he went into the synagogue on the sabbath day, and stood up for to read.

Though Jesus had been born in Bethlehem, not far from Jerusalem, He was *brought up* in the town of *Nazareth*. We have noted in previous lessons that in Jesus' day Nazareth was a small village of little notoriety. It was considered by many to be too remote and uncultured to produce anything good, let alone a Messiah (John 1:46). Yet Jesus was respectful enough of His hometown to give its residents the opportunity to hear the good news of His appointment by God as the Messiah.

It was Jesus' *custom* to attend worship services in a Jewish *synagogue* every *sabbath day* (i.e.,

Saturday). It is important to note that, while on the one hand Jesus did not consider Himself to be bound by man-made traditions such as not healing on the Sabbath (Luke 6:6-10), He was nevertheless fully committed to the letter and spirit of God's Word. The consistent picture throughout all four Gospels is that Jesus was faithful in observing the requirements of the Old Testament law. The seriousness with which He pursued the religious practices of His day serve to inspire us in our walk with the Lord today. [See question #1, page 168.]

THE WORTH OF WORSHIP

Some time ago a lady by the name of Mary Ellen Benson was fined five dollars for not attending meetings of Local 356 of the United Papermakers Union. The reason she did not attend was that the meetings were held on Sunday mornings during the time of her church's worship services. She refused to pay the fine, so the union took her to court. The court ordered her to pay and added court costs of $5.40. So skipping the union meetings cost Mrs. Benson $10.40. But the worth of worship is much, much more than that!

Jesus recognized the priority of worship. It was His "custom" to be present at the services held each Sabbath at the synagogue in Nazareth (Luke 4:16).

Many today object, "Look at all the problems in the church! It's full of hypocrites! I can live a life just as good and as pleasing to God without the church as I can with the church." But does today's church have any more problems than the synagogues did in Jesus' day? (Think of the "hypocrites" whom Jesus often confronted who were in regular attendance at the synagogues!)

If Jesus recognized the necessity of regular worship—if He saw the value of observing this "custom" faithfully—what about us? The writer of Hebrews says it well: "Not forsaking the assembling of ourselves together, as the manner of some is; but exhorting one another: and so much the more, as ye see the day approaching" (Hebrews 10:25). —R. C. S.

17. And there was delivered unto him the book of the prophet Isaiah. And when he had opened the book, he found the place where it was written.

It was a common synagogue practice in first-century Judaism to show respect to visiting teachers by inviting them to read Scripture aloud and then give their exposition of the passage read. This custom afforded Jesus a ready opportunity to proclaim His gospel message in every city and village that He visited on a Sabbath day. The apostle Paul later made it "his manner" (or

custom) to turn this tradition into an evangelistic opportunity as he traveled about (Acts 17:2).

The *book* that was handed to Jesus resembled a scroll of Scripture texts more than a modern book. We are not told whether Jesus requested this particular scroll or simply accepted whatever book of Scripture was currently being used in this synagogue's rotation of Bible reading. No doubt He knew, whether by His own request or by divine foreknowledge, what scroll He would be reading. The one that He was given was the Old Testament *prophet Isaiah.* Immediately Jesus sought out a well-known messianic text—Isaiah 61:1, 2. By careful design Jesus turned that day's reading into an extraordinary event. A familiar prophecy was read aloud by the One who had come to fulfill it!

B. Foretold in Prophecy (vv. 18, 19)

18. The Spirit of the Lord is upon me, because he hath anointed me to preach the gospel to the poor; he hath sent me to heal the brokenhearted, to preach deliverance to the captives, and recovering of sight to the blind, to set at liberty them that are bruised.

The prophecy that Jesus chose to read was clearly a reference to the Messiah, which means *anointed* one. The Messiah of Jewish expectation was not merely one who was anointed with oil, but anointed with the *Spirit of the Lord.*

Having identified the source of power for the Messiah, the prophet then set forth a summary of God's agenda for the Messiah. It was not exactly what the first-century Jews were hoping for. They wanted a deliverer to destroy the hated Romans—or at least to banish them from the Jewish homeland—and reestablish the political empire that David and Solomon ruled.

How to Say It

CAPERNAUM. Kuh-*per*-nay-um.
CHERITH. *Key*-rith.
ELIJAH. Ee-*lye*-juh.
ELISHA. Ee-*lye*-shuh.
ISAIAH. Eye-*zay*-uh.
MEDITERRANEAN. *Med*-uh-tuh-*ray*-nee-un (strong accent on *ray*).
MESSIANIC. mess-ee-*an*-ick.
NAAMAN. *Nay*-uh-mun.
NAZARETH. *Naz*-uh-reth.
SIDON. *Sye*-dun.
SYNAGOGUE. *sin*-uh-gog.
SYRIAN. *Sear*-ee-un.
TYRE. Tire.
ZAREPHATH. *Zair*-uh-fath.

Isaiah's picture was quite different. First, the Messiah was appointed to *preach the gospel,* or good news, of God's salvation. The Greek verb used in this text is one from which we get the term "evangelist." It literally refers to proclaiming aloud good news.

It is difficult to know whether we should interpret the next portion of Isaiah's prophecy in literal terms or in a way that applies the language to spiritual concerns. Certainly we can acknowledge the fact that Jesus' ministry did reach out to both the spiritual and physical needs of the people He met. His "good news" made a difference in peoples' lives in more than one way, and His work serves to remind us that we too need a view of ministry that is broad enough to respond to both spiritual and physical needs. [See question #2, page 168.]

19. To preach the acceptable year of the Lord.

Here the term *year* is not describing a calendar year. It refers instead to the era when all of the above actions would take place—in other words, the messianic age. Many Bible students have seen a reference in Jesus' words to the Old Testament Year of Jubilee (Leviticus 25:8-55). At that time, which was to occur once every fifty years, slaves were freed, debts were canceled, and ancestral property that had been sold during the previous fifty years (because of poverty) was returned to the family that originally owned it. Whereas Isaiah first uttered these words to promise Israel deliverance from captivity in Babylon and repossession of her "property" in the promised land, Jesus used it to announce deliverance from sin and its consequences.

THE YEAR OF THE LORD

Jesus told those who had gathered in the synagogue in Nazareth that He had come to proclaim "the acceptable year of the Lord" (Luke 4:19). It is interesting that the symbol A.D. (as in A.D. 2001) stands for the Latin phrase *anno Domini,* which means "in the year of the Lord." Some today who prefer an alternative dating system refer, not to years A.D., but to years C.E. (Christian Era or Common Era) and to years B.C.E. (Before the Christian/Common Era).

While Jesus was not referring to a calendar year when He spoke of "the year of the Lord," the phrase should merit special consideration as we embark on a new year of 2001. Will this be "the year of the Lord"—the year that we will become more firmly committed to living under the lordship of Jesus in our daily lives? Could this *really* be the year of the Lord, in that it will be the year of Christ's return?

Whatever the year is, it ought to be "the year of the Lord" in the sense that we increase our

Visual for lessons 5 & 6

Display the poster from last week's lesson. Note how Jesus' claim fulfilled not only Isaiah's prophecy, but the prophecy of Simeon as well.

faith in the Lord and yield our lives more completely to His service.   —R. C. S.

C. Fulfilled by Jesus (vv. 20, 21)

20. And he closed the book, and he gave it again to the minister, and sat down. And the eyes of all them that were in the synagogue were fastened on him.

Jesus followed the customary practice for speaking in a synagogue. Out of respect for the Word of God, a speaker would stand while reading aloud a Scripture text (v. 16), but then it was acceptable to sit down while speaking and teaching. On this occasion of Jesus' first sermon in His hometown, *the eyes of all . . . were fastened on him* as they listened intently to see what He would say regarding His ministry of preaching and healing that had caused such a stir throughout Galilee (v. 14).

21. And he began to say unto them, This day is this Scripture fulfilled in your ears.

This day is this Scripture fulfilled in your ears. This was a bold statement to make. Jesus was doing significantly more than simply claiming to be a new kind of prophet or rabbi. The Messiah held a one-of-a-kind position rooted in the hopes of the Jewish faith—hopes that were especially intense at this time. By identifying Himself with this prophecy, Jesus provided both an announcement of His ministry plans and a means for the people to measure whether or not He lived up to the divine standard for the Messiah.

II. A Skeptical Response (Luke 4:22-27)

A. The Crowd's Reaction (v. 22)

22. And all bare him witness, and wondered at the gracious words which proceeded out of his mouth. And they said, Is not this Joseph's son?

It is probable that the words recorded in verse 21 do not comprise all that Jesus said before the crowd responded. Matthew and Mark both note that Jesus taught at Nazareth (Matthew 13:54; Mark 6:1, 2), which most likely included additional words beyond those recorded by Luke. Whatever the content of Jesus' teaching, reaction to it was swift. Those in attendance began to *bare him witness*, expressing to one another their opinion of what Jesus had said and claimed.

Reaction from the crowd appears to have been mixed. On the one hand, they seemed to enjoy Jesus' style and delivery and to relish the messianic possibilities within His *gracious words*. On the other hand, the people found it hard even to imagine that one of their own—from their insignificant town—could actually turn out to be someone as profoundly important as the Messiah. *Is not this Joseph's son?* they asked. As they did so, they must have spoken with a certain measure of skepticism or even derision. After all, a lowly carpenter's son is not a likely candidate to become a royal, messianic figure. This latter view seems to have been more commonly held; both Matthew and Mark note that the audience was "offended" at Jesus (Matthew 13:57; Mark 6:3). [See question #3, page 168.]

B. Jesus' Defense (vv. 23-27)

23. And he said unto them, Ye will surely say unto me this proverb, Physician, heal thyself: whatsoever we have heard done in Capernaum, do also here in thy country.

Jesus perceived the crowd's growing skepticism. He knew that they were expecting Him to defend His messianic claim by producing supernatural manifestations before their eyes. After all, they had *heard* reports of Jesus' performing miracles *in Capernaum* prior to His arrival in Nazareth. The Gospels do not record any details from this preliminary work in Capernaum, but it must have been impressive enough that rumors had spread all the way out to Nazareth. Now the townspeople wanted to see some of these wonders for themselves.

24. And he said, Verily I say unto you, No prophet is accepted in his own country.

Throughout His preaching ministry, Jesus often noted the tragic irony that the very nation that claimed to be devoted to Jehovah God had a long history of killing His messengers (Luke 11:49-51). False prophets had always been welcomed because they preached what the people wanted to hear. But a genuine *prophet* with a challenging message from God was usually not *accepted in his own country*.

The phenomenon Jesus described has its parallel in our experiences today. It is often quite difficult for someone to be taken seriously by the people who have known him the longest and the best. Images from their past often shape their perception of the present, not allowing them to see individuals in a new and different light. Apparently the memories of Jesus growing up in Joseph's humble home kept the people of Nazareth from accepting Jesus as someone to listen to and heed. Today we sometimes quote the saying, "Familiarity breeds contempt." This is in essence the idea Jesus was expressing in His words, *No prophet is accepted in his own country.*

25. But I tell you of a truth, many widows were in Israel in the days of Elijah, when the heaven was shut up three years and six months, when great famine was throughout all the land.

The tone of Jesus' remarks in the synagogue had taken a decisive turn. Whereas He began with "gracious words" (v. 22) about the fulfillment of messianic prophecy, the predominantly skeptical reaction of His audience prompted Him to speak words of rebuke. Using illustrations from the lives of two great Old Testament prophets, Jesus told how a hostile reception to a messenger of God can result in blessings being taken away and given to others more receptive.

The prophet *Elijah* pronounced a drought upon *Israel* that lasted for *three years and six months* (1 Kings 17:1; James 5:17). This resulted in a severe *famine . . . throughout all the land*. But Elijah did not provide supernatural relief for the hungry of Israel, in large part because they were under God's discipline. They had failed to heed the preaching of Elijah and other prophets of God, and they were suffering the consequences.

26. But unto none of them was Elijah sent, save unto Zarephath, a city of Sidon, unto a woman that was a widow.

After Elijah hid himself for a while on the east side of the Jordan near the little brook of Cherith (1 Kings 17:3), God instructed him to relocate to the small town of *Zarephath*. This was located on the Mediterranean coast in the region of *Sidon*, approximately fourteen miles north of Tyre. There Elijah was to seek out the hospitality of a particular *widow*. Though her food supply was almost exhausted, she shared what little she had with this prophet of God, and was thereby blessed with sufficient food for the duration of the drought (1 Kings 17:8-16).

27. And many lepers were in Israel in the time of Elisha the prophet; and none of them was cleansed, saving Naaman the Syrian.

Like his predecessor Elijah, *Elisha* worked in an environment of hostility, experiencing rejection by both the king of *Israel* and the people. Thus his miracle-working power was allowed to bless someone outside of Israel—*Naaman*, whose account is told in 2 Kings 5:1-19.

Naaman was a captain in the army of the neighboring country of Syria, which was at odds with Israel during the ministry of Elisha. He had some form of leprous skin disease, which, though apparently not contagious (since he was still on "active duty"), was nevertheless serious enough that he desired relief. He was instructed by Elisha to dip seven times in the Jordan River, and upon his obedience to the word of God he was healed (2 Kings 5:14).

Jesus' point in calling attention to this story was to emphasize that there were *many lepers* in *Israel* that Elisha could have healed; however (as was shown in the preceding example from Elijah's ministry), blessings of God are often withheld from those who reject the preaching of God's servants. Nazareth was being warned in no uncertain terms that it was headed down a similar path of disaster. [See question #4, page 168.]

III. A Determined Spirit (Luke 4:28-30)

A. Facing Hostility (vv. 28, 29)

28. And all they in the synagogue, when they heard these things, were filled with wrath.

The majority of the people who heard Jesus speak reacted with anger at His rebuke. Their earlier anticipation at seeing one of their own return home was now replaced with a violent rage. [See question #5, page 168.]

29. And rose up, and thrust him out of the city, and led him unto the brow of the hill whereon their city was built, that they might cast him down headlong.

There is not enough information here to know exactly what the crowd intended to do with Jesus. Their plan to *cast him down headlong* from the *brow of the hill* could be read as an attempt to kill Him by throwing Him off a cliff. However, the topography of Nazareth resembles

a sloping hill more than a mountainous cliff. What Luke may be describing here is the preliminary steps to a stoning. It was common practice among the Jews to cast a person to be stoned down into an area below the crowd, where they could then throw stones from above.

B. Pressing Forward (v. 30)

30. But he, passing through the midst of them, went his way.

Luke does not explain how Jesus survived this threat. Perhaps He used His supernatural power to shield Himself from the crowd and then passed *through the midst of them* unharmed. Or it may be that He challenged their intimidation with a powerful presence and an unyielding resolve, thereby defusing the situation before it could get further out of hand.

Regardless of how Jesus escaped from this scene, He was not moved from the mission He had announced in the synagogue. Jesus *went his way* and immediately proceeded to carry out the gospel agenda prophesied in Isaiah 61, undaunted by this or any other opposition He would encounter.

Conclusion

A. Preconceptions

What a frustrating thing it is to attempt to get people to try something that we know will be good for them, only to have them say, "I'll try it, but I know I'm not going to like it." Sometimes they are pleasantly surprised, and our pleas and assurances are vindicated. But too often our good intentions are wasted as a biased attitude refuses to give the item a fair chance. "How can anyone be so closed-minded?" we wonder—that is, until we recall those occasions when our preconceived notions turned out to be just as mistaken.

The gospel of Jesus Christ deserves a fair hearing, with no bias or prejudice, lest a truly good thing be lost. At the same time, we who are followers of Jesus should determine that nothing we say or do will cause others to be biased against Him. We must, by our conduct, lead others closer to Jesus, not drive them farther away from Him.

B. Prayer

Father, thank You for sending Your Son Jesus Christ to be our Savior and Lord. May we always be receptive to His words. May we continue to carry out His mission of proclaiming "the acceptable year of the Lord." In Jesus' name. Amen.

C. Thought to Remember

Jesus came to fulfill the Scripture; the church is to proclaim that fulfillment.

Home Daily Bible Readings

Monday, Jan. 1—Tempted As We Are (Luke 4:1-13)
Tuesday, Jan. 2—A Mission to the People (Luke 4:14-21)
Wednesday, Jan. 3—The Good News of Deliverance (Isaiah 61)
Thursday, Jan. 4—His Own Received Him Not (Luke 4:22-30)
Friday, Jan. 5—The Healing of Naaman (2 Kings 5:1-14)
Saturday, Jan. 6—The Rejection of Jesus (Matthew 13:54-58)
Sunday, Jan. 7—Whoever Does the Will of God (Mark 3:31-35)

Learning by Doing

This page contains an alternate lesson plan emphasizing learning activities.
Classes desiring such student involvement will find these suggestions helpful.

Learning Goals

After this lesson each student will be able to:

1. Tell what happened in Nazareth when Jesus identified Himself as the fulfillment of one of Isaiah's prophecies of the Messiah.

2. Compare the prophesied role of the Messiah with Jesus' ministry and with that of the church today.

3. Give a specific example of how the church can continue the messianic ministry Isaiah prophesied and Jesus fulfilled.

Into the Lesson

People have many roles in their lives. Our roles often define who we are or what we will do. These roles are also used by others to determine their acceptance or rejection of us. Ask, "What are some of the roles you play in life?" In groups of four have the students share roles—e.g., parent, plant supervisor, Little League coach, deacon, etc.

Continue with this activity by asking the groups to discuss the following questions:

• "Which role provides you the most fun?"
• "Which role do you find the most rewarding?"
• "Which role provides the most challenge?"
• "Which role gives you the most frustration?"

As you make the transition to the Bible study, ask whether anyone has ever been rejected in any role. Ask volunteers to tell how they have experienced rejection and how they responded.

Say, "Today we will examine an episode in which Jesus revealed His identity and work in Nazareth. Within that revelation was a challenge of ministry to His followers. We will see how a similar challenge is given to us today."

Into the Word

Prepare a three- to five-minute lecture using material from the lesson commentary's Introduction section. Then have a student read Luke 4:16-30 aloud. After this person reads the text, appoint at least three groups of four students. If you have more students, give the assignments to more than one group. Each group should appoint a reporter to write answers on a poster you have mounted on the wall and to explain the group's answers to the class.

Group 1: Responses of People

1. What positive responses to Jesus are seen in this passage?

2. What negative responses to Jesus are seen in this passage?

3. What changes are recorded in this passage to bring forth these different responses?

Group 2: The Roles of the Messiah

1. List the six roles of the Messiah as presented by Jesus in this passage.

2. Give examples from Jesus' ministry that fulfilled these roles.

3. What do you think the people expected from Jesus after He read these words?

Group 3: Handling Rejection

1. What kind of rejection did Jesus face in this passage?

2. How did Jesus handle this rejection?

3. What does this passage teach us about handling rejection?

Into Life

Draw attention to the answers on Group 2's poster. Be sure to highlight the six points that Jesus made about His ministry: preach the gospel, heal the brokenhearted, proclaim freedom to prisoners, perform acts of mercy, pursue release for the oppressed, proclaim God's grace to sinners.

Discuss the following questions.

1. How do these six points compare with the role that the church is to play in the world today?

2. What response should we expect from the world if we are involved in such a task?

3. What would it cost the church to perform these roles in the community?

Discussion of these points should reveal that the church is to fulfill these tasks in the world today. Even as we do so, the same responses can be expected: praise, amazement, disbelief, anger, and rejection.

Bring enough bulletins or calendars from your church for each group. Using the six areas of mission delineated by Group 2, evaluate your church's schedule. Place each scheduled activity in an area of mission. Ask, "After checking our church's activities, in which area of mission do you believe we are the strongest? In which area are we the weakest? What activities should we consider to better fulfill the messianic ministry Jesus has given us?"

Close with prayer for greater wisdom in selecting activities that will help the church accomplish Jesus' ministry.

Let's Talk It Over

The questions on this page are designed to encourage review of the lesson Scriptures and to promote discussion of the lesson by the class. The answers provided are only discussion starters. Let your class talk it over from there.

1. It was Jesus' custom to go to the synagogue on the Sabbath. What excuses do some people today give for not attending worship services? How does Jesus' example answer those excuses?

Jesus could have given many of the excuses we hear so often if He had chosen not to attend synagogue worship. *"There are hypocrites in the church."* Not all those who attended synagogue had pure motives or a pure heart. *"I don't get anything out of it."* Jesus was certainly capable of contributing far more than He received at the synagogue. In fact, He was there obviously for what He could contribute, not what He could get. Why are *we* in worship? *"It's my only day to sleep in."* During the years when crowds of people were following Him, Jesus had difficulty finding time or place for rest. But He did not skip worship to catch up on His rest.

Gathering with God's people for corporate worship was a priority with Jesus. Should it not also be a priority among His followers?

2. How do those who minister in the name of Jesus continue to "heal the brokenhearted, to preach deliverance to the captives, and recovering of sight to the blind, to set at liberty them that are bruised"?

Christians believe that the gospel is "the power of God unto salvation" (Romans 1:16). The gospel we share is a message of life and hope that does bring healing to the brokenhearted. It is a message of forgiveness and restoration that brings deliverance to those who are captive to sin. It is the truth that reveals right and wrong, thus giving sight to those who are blind. It is a call to purpose and meaning that gives liberty to those who have been bruised by their own vain efforts.

3. The people in Nazareth were amazed at the "gracious words" that Jesus spoke. Do people consider your words "gracious"? Why or why not? How can we speak "gracious words"?

Luke does not go into detail, but Matthew and Mark tell us that Jesus taught the people in Nazareth and that the people were impressed with the wisdom that had been "given unto him" (Matthew 13:54; Mark 6:2). Apparently they saw Jesus' wisdom as a gift, or a grace, from God.

Our words can be gracious when they demonstrate the grace of God. Paul tells us our words are to be "always with grace, seasoned with salt" (Colossians 4:6). This, too, calls for wisdom from God (Colossians 4:5), which can be ours for the asking, if we will ask in faith (James 1:5, 6).

4. Jesus cited examples of blessings that went to those outside Israel because they had a simple trust in God. What blessings do you think you, your church, or your community may have missed because of skepticism and doubt?

Matthew notes that Jesus "did not many mighty works [in Nazareth] because of their unbelief" (Matthew 13:58). Who knows how many sick or disabled or demon-possessed continued to suffer there because of their lack of faith? Listen to the testimonies of the faithful today, at what God has done in their lives. These are the blessings that would be lacking if those saints had no faith.

Has your church had to put up with inferior or deteriorating facilities? Is there frequent turnover in the ministry positions because the salary is not sufficient to hold a minister there? Perhaps greater faith on the part of those who give would lead to upgraded facilities, more staff, and/or long-term ministries. Think about the expanded ministry and outreach your church could have—and the blessing that these would be to every member as well as to the community—if everyone grew in his or her faith.

5. The people of the Nazareth synagogue reacted to Jesus' message with rage. How do you normally respond to a convicting message or a rebuke? What determines whether a person responds with anger or with grace?

The natural response to criticism is to defend and to seek to justify oneself. Some will even attack the one with the message of rebuke—if not physically, then verbally. But the response that leads to growth, and the one the Christian ought to follow, is thoughtful self-assessment and repentance where needed. The truth delivered in love should be received in love. Reproof and rebuke are a part of the ministry of the Word of God (2 Timothy 4:2). Even if we believe that the person with the rebuke is wrong, we can respond graciously, examine the words and our own lives to see if there might be some basis for the criticism, and then do whatever we believe to be God's will—whether we make a change or not.

The Cost of Discipleship

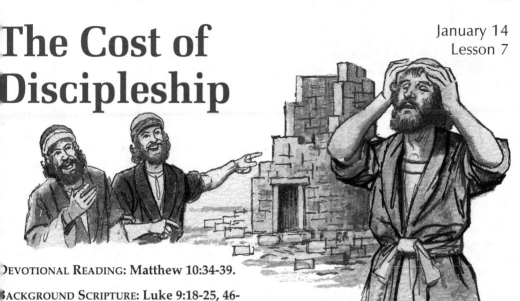

DEVOTIONAL READING: Matthew 10:34-39.

BACKGROUND SCRIPTURE: Luke 9:18-25, 46-62; 14:25-35.

PRINTED TEXT: Luke 9:57-62; 14:25-33.

Luke 9:57-62

57 And it came to pass, that, as they went in the way, a certain man said unto him, Lord, I will follow thee whithersoever thou goest.

58 And Jesus said unto him, Foxes have holes, and birds of the air have nests; but the Son of man hath not where to lay his head.

59 And he said unto another, Follow me. But he said, Lord, suffer me first to go and bury my father.

60 Jesus said unto him, Let the dead bury their dead: but go thou and preach the kingdom of God.

61 And another also said, Lord, I will follow thee; but let me first go bid them farewell, which are at home at my house.

62 And Jesus said unto him, No man, having put his hand to the plow, and looking back, is fit for the kingdom of God.

Luke 14:25-33

25 And there went great multitudes with him: and he turned, and said unto them,

26 If any man come to me, and hate not his father, and mother, and wife, and children, and brethren, and sisters, yea, and his own life also, he cannot be my disciple.

27 And whosoever doth not bear his cross, and come after me, cannot be my disciple.

28 For which of you, intending to build a tower, sitteth not down first, and counteth the cost, whether he have sufficient to finish it?

29 Lest haply, after he hath laid the foundation, and is not able to finish it, all that behold it begin to mock him,

30 Saying, This man began to build, and was not able to finish.

31 Or what king, going to make war against another king, sitteth not down first, and consulteth whether he be able with ten thousand to meet him that cometh against him with twenty thousand?

32 Or else, while the other is yet a great way off, he sendeth an ambassage, and desireth conditions of peace.

33 So likewise, whosoever he be of you that forsaketh not all that he hath, he cannot be my disciple.

GOLDEN TEXT: Whosoever doth not bear his cross, and come after me, cannot be my disciple.—Luke 14:27.

Lesson Aims

After this lesson the students will be able to:

1. Summarize Jesus' teaching about the demands of discipleship according to today's text.

2. Tell why encouraging people to "count the cost" should be an integral part of evangelism.

3. Pinpoint an excuse that they have been using to avoid a deeper commitment to Christ, and express a commitment to strengthen their discipleship.

Lesson Outline

INTRODUCTION
    A. "A Few Good Men"
    B. Lesson Background
  I. DECISIVE ACTION (Luke 9:57-62)
    A. No Hesitation (vv. 57, 58)
      Homeless
    B. No Conditions (vv. 59, 60)
    C. No Regrets (vv. 61, 62)
      No Time for Good-byes
 II. FULL DEVOTION (Luke 14:25-27)
    A. Setting Priorities (vv. 25, 26)
    B. Carrying the Cross (v. 27)
III. CAREFUL THOUGHT (Luke 14:28-33)
    A. Finish What You Start (vv. 28-30)
    B. Do Whatever Is Needed (vv. 31-33)
CONCLUSION
    A. Counting the Cost
    B. Prayer
    C. Thought to Remember

Introduction

A. "A Few Good Men"

The recruitment posters for the Marine Corps make a powerful statement. The Corps is not for everyone—only for the best among recruits. As their motto says, they want only "a few good men." Now, on the one hand, we like an open policy that allows anyone who wishes to participate in a program to do so. For some activities that may be the only way we will get in. On the other hand, we admire programs that operate with tough admission standards, that bring together the best and most talented people they can find, and then put out a "product" that is a cut above the rest. And while the latter approach may discourage some, for others it is the kind of challenge that draws them in.

Although the invitation to be a disciple of Christ is open to all, the standards set forth by the Master are rather demanding. Our Lord is not as interested in the numbers He recruits as He is in the quality of service we give. Only those who are ready to give Jesus their best need apply.

B. Lesson Background

Luke 9:51 is an important transitional statement in Luke's account of the life of Jesus. It may be considered a framework for viewing the remainder of his Gospel. It reads, "And it came to pass, when the time was come that he should be received up, he steadfastly set his face to go to Jerusalem." This shows Jesus' awareness that the time of His death, by which He would fulfill His Father's plan, was approaching. However, Luke does not say that this was Jesus' final journey to Jerusalem. It appears that this journey marked the beginning of a time of ministry in Judea, during which, according to John's record, the Feast of Tabernacles was observed (John 7:1-10). This ministry is recorded in Luke 9:51—13:21. It was during this trip toward Jerusalem that Jesus encountered the would-be disciples mentioned in the first part of today's printed text. This probably occurred about six months prior to the Lord's crucifixion.

The second portion of our text comes from Luke 14:25-33. By this time, Jesus' ministry had moved into Perea—the territory located across the Jordan River from Samaria and Judea. Here, where "great multitudes" were following Jesus (v. 25), He gave one of His most straightforward descriptions of what it really means for a person to follow Him. This incident must have taken place sometime following the observance of the Feast of Tabernacles (John 10:40 records Jesus' movement "beyond Jordan"). The cross was now only three to four months away.

I. Decisive Action
(Luke 9:57-62)

A. No Hesitation (vv. 57, 58)

57. And it came to pass, that, as they went in the way, a certain man said unto him, Lord, I will follow thee whithersoever thou goest.

Luke may have intended a special meaning in his expression *as they went in the way*. Earlier we called attention to Luke 9:51 as a framework for viewing the second half of Luke's Gospel. According to this verse, as Jesus entered the final months of His ministry, He "steadfastly set his face to go to Jerusalem." Whatever He said or did from this point on was keenly focused on His impending death. Thus it may be Luke's intent to say *as they went in the way* toward Jerusalem—as Jesus anticipated the cross that lay ahead—He spoke of the cost of being His disciple.

We can certainly commend the enthusiasm for service expressed in the words, *Lord, I will follow thee whithersoever thou goest.* Indeed, discipleship does require a "wherever you want me" attitude. But Jesus was well aware that words of commitment are more easily spoken than acted on. Too many times we say the right words without giving thought to the implications they have for our lives. Thus, in the next verse, Jesus responded with a challenge that may be summarized as, "Do you really understand what you are getting yourself into?"

58. And Jesus said unto him, Foxes have holes, and birds of the air have nests; but the Son of man hath not where to lay his head.

The path of service and ministry for God often requires some personal sacrifices of us, as demonstrated by the One who went before us on this same path. *The Son of man hath not where to lay his head.* Jesus' fulfillment of His messianic ministry did not allow Him to settle down with a house, a family, and a regular paying job. He was constantly on the move—living a modest lifestyle and depending on the generosity and hospitality of others. [See question #1, page 176.]

HOMELESS

In 1970 Jim Vernon founded a ministry in Atlanta, Georgia, known as "Jesus Place Inner City Mission." His primary purpose was to serve the homeless people who lived under the bridges and viaducts of the city. Initially the ministry was conducted out of a storefront; it now operates from a donated church building.

For a period of time in between those two locations, the ministry of "Jesus Place" actually operated out of Jim Vernon's van. The ministry had lost the lease to the storefront, and the church building had not become available. During these uncertain days, Jim drove down an Atlanta street and picked up a homeless man. Seeing the words "Jesus Place" on the side of the van, the man asked, "Where is this Jesus Place?"

"You're sitting in it," said Vernon.

"Oh, I guess that makes sense," said the man, "because Jesus was homeless, too."

We sometimes forget that homelessness was something to which Jesus was accustomed. He began His earthly life homeless in Bethlehem. As G. K. Chesterton wrote, Bethlehem was the place "where the Son of Man was homeless and where all men are at home."

Sometimes people identify Jesus with settled, secure middle-class homeowners. In fact, we should identify Him with the rootless, homeless people of society and of the world. It is not surprising that the church has often been the only agency that shows any real compassion for homeless people. The church helps them because their need is so great—but also helps in the name of the One who became homeless that we may one day live in His home!   —R. C. S.

B. No Conditions (vv. 59, 60)

59, 60. And he said unto another, Follow me. But he said, Lord, suffer me first to go and bury my father. Jesus said unto him, Let the dead bury their dead: but go thou and preach the kingdom of God.

On the surface it appears that this man was simply asking for time to provide a proper burial for his *father.* It is not readily evident how a few days' delay for a funeral would interfere with Jesus' ministry plans. After all, Scripture clearly teaches a responsibility for us to honor and care for our parents (Exodus 20:12; 1 Timothy 5:8). Perhaps what the man actually desired was to remain at home and care for his father until after he had died and was buried, whenever that might be. After all, in that time and place burials were virtually immediate after a death. If the man's father were already dead, he should have been at home making the arrangements for the burial even then.

We can see, then, why Jesus rejected his proposal. Caring for one's parents can last several years, but Jesus had only a few months (approximately six) remaining in His ministry on earth. He needed this man's help right then, not several years down the road. The immediate urgency of His mission called for disciples who were ready to serve immediately.

With this understanding in mind, it seems most likely that Jesus was making a play on words when He spoke of *the dead* in verse 60. He was suggesting to this man that he leave his father in the care of family members who were "spiritually dead" and had no interest in serving Jesus to the extent that this man did.

We can learn a lesson for our own situation from Jesus' wise counsel. It is still true today, for

---

How to Say It

AMBASSAGE. *am*-buh-sij.
ELIJAH. Ee-*lye*-juh.
ELISHA. Ee-*lye*-shuh.
MALACHI. *Mal*-uh-kye.
PEREA. Peh-*ree*-uh.
SAMARIA. Suh-*mare*-ee-uh.

some of us, that we could decide to put aside our earthly interests and actively pursue Christian service; and someone would be available to take over what duties we left behind. (This is true whether the people we would leave behind were Christians or "spiritually dead.") Most parents will not suffer if left in the immediate care of our siblings who do not share our interest in leaving home in order to serve the Lord. Community programs and activities will still continue even if we are no longer involved. Rarely would a business shut down because one employee decided to quit and go to Bible college.

When we realize that most people will not answer the call to vocational service for Christ, then those of us who are considering such service should determine whether or not our earthly concerns should be allowed to outweigh the opportunities that God has placed before us.

C. No Regrets (vv. 61, 62)

61. And another also said, Lord, I will follow thee; but let me first go bid them farewell, which are at home at my house.

This request to *bid . . . farewell* to one's family before setting out to follow Jesus sounds very similar to what Elisha asked of the prophet Elijah when he was summoned to leave home and become his disciple (1 Kings 19:19, 20). However, there is a difference. In the case of Elisha, when he went home to say good-bye to his father and mother, he went with a heart that was ready and willing to leave everything and follow the prophet. His attitude is evidenced in his sacrificing two oxen to celebrate his prophetic call and then immediately leaving to follow after Elijah (1 Kings 19:21).

But the attitude of the man who approached Jesus was apparently not as eager as Elisha's. Judging by Jesus' response, this man seems to have had some misgivings about leaving his home and family, and thus may have had an attachment that would interfere with his ability to give full attention to the service that Jesus would require of him.

62. And Jesus said unto him, No man, having put his hand to the plow, and looking back, is fit for the kingdom of God.

This imagery of plowing should speak clearly to each one of us, even if we have never personally used a horse or mule to drag a *plow* through a field. We know from other experiences what is the best strategy for making a straight line, whether we are putting down white chalk on a baseball field, dragging a stick on the ground to make a line in the dirt, or just trying to walk a straight path through an open field. If, as we walk, we have our head turned around watching the line

Crosses are never on sale;
Crosses are always full price.
Luke 14:27

The cross demanded all that Jesus had, and the Lord asks no less of His disciples. Use today's visual poster to remind your class of that fact.

Visual for lesson 7

behind us, the twist of the body will throw off our sense of balance and we will digress from the straight line we intended. To stay on course, we must set our sights ahead on a distant object and let it serve as a bearing that keeps us on a straight path.

The man in this story apparently did not yet have his sights fully set on Jesus. He was *looking back* on something that still held his attention—in this case, family and home life. His divided interests threatened any long-term commitment that he might make to the Lord's work.

For this reason, Jesus warned him (and warns us) that he must first determine if in fact he is ready to make service for Jesus his first priority before he even starts down that pathway. To begin with only a half-hearted interest is to run the later risk of frustration and disappointment. Both the disciple and the work of the *kingdom* are thereby harmed. [See question #2, page 176.]

NO TIME FOR GOOD-BYES

Does it ever seem to you that Jesus was the most unreasonable man who ever lived? What could be more natural than to want to go home and say good-bye to one's family? However, keep in mind that saying good-bye can take a long time. Some couples will recall a time, before they were married, when it took half an hour just to say good night! Farewells can take time.

Remember also that Jesus could read the heart of the man who made the request to return home, while we can read only his words. Perhaps Jesus knew that the young man's parents would try to persuade him not to go after Jesus if he went back home to see them.

The encounters described in Luke 9:57-62 reveal an urgency about the work of the kingdom that must not be missed. It is easy for us to forget that urgency. Not a moment of time should be wasted. The return of Christ may be nearer than we think. Our opportunities may be fewer than we think. The one we hope to win to Christ may not have many years, or even days, ahead of him or her. (We may not have many years, or even days, ahead of us!)

The novelist Rebecca West once observed that we cannot imagine Jesus hurrying—yet there was always an urgency about His efforts. While we should never be frantic about our work, we should certainly be urgent.   —R. C. S.

II. Full Devotion
(Luke 14:25-27)

A. Setting Priorities (vv. 25, 26)

25. And there went great multitudes with him: and he turned, and said unto them.

Throughout His ministry Jesus attracted *great multitudes* of people. Had He been interested in sheer numbers of followers, He could have achieved His goal very easily. However, the commitment found within these large crowds was always mixed. Many of them had no interest in Jesus beyond His ability to perform dramatic miracles. Now, with the cross just a few months away, Jesus wanted the multitudes to realize what being identified with Him was going to cost.

26. If any man come to me, and hate not his father, and mother, and wife, and children, and brethren, and sisters, yea, and his own life also, he cannot be my disciple.

Here is one of the most puzzling statements made by Jesus in the Gospels—we must *hate* those we love the most if we are to be disciples of Jesus. Given Jesus' frequent emphasis on love, it is hard to imagine that He would ever encourage hatred, especially toward our own families.

Jesus' meaning is better understood when we take into consideration that He was using a figurative expression from the ancient world. When contrasting one's feelings toward two different persons or objects, to say that you *love* one and *hate* the other simply means that you have a preference for the former over the latter. In this usage, the word *hate* really means "to love less than" something else. Thus the Mosaic law could speak of a man who loved two women enough to marry them both (Deuteronomy 21:15-17), but had a preference for one ("the beloved") over the other ("the hated"). Likewise, Jacob is said to have "loved" Rachel and to have "hated," or had lesser affection for, Leah (Genesis 29:30, 31). This language is even used of God's attitude toward Jacob and Esau (Malachi 1:2, 3).

Thus we can see that Jesus was emphasizing the superior love and devotion that He deserves over any other person or object. Jesus was not promoting feelings of hatred toward family and friends; He was setting forth the degree of commitment required of anyone who aspires to be

His disciple. This interpretation is confirmed by Jesus' words on another occasion: "He that loveth father or mother more than me is not worthy of me: and he that loveth son or daughter more than me is not worthy of me" (Matthew 10:37).

The standard of priority commitment to Jesus Christ lends itself to many applications. For example, as Christians we are to be respectful to all in authority over us, including *father and mother*. But if ever told to do something that is clearly a sin, our first priority is to honor the will of God (Acts 5:29). Furthermore, serving Christ will not necessarily require that we forego marriage or a family, or that we move away from our parents and siblings. But a committed disciple is willing to do so if that would best serve the kingdom.

A disciple must likewise be willing to give up personal comfort and worldly gain for the sake of serving the Lord. And, if called upon to make the ultimate sacrifice, a true disciple is willing even to die for the cause of Christ. [See question #3, page 176.]

B. Carrying the Cross (v. 27)

27. And whosoever doth not bear his cross, and come after me, cannot be my disciple.

At the time Jesus spoke these words, His audience did not yet understand the theological implications that we see in the word *cross*. For them, a cross would bring to mind a slow, torturous death—the most horrible way to die that they could imagine. It was this level of suffering that Jesus said His followers must be willing to endure if they were to be true disciples. If we say that we want to follow Jesus, then we should not "marvel" if our path leads us through opposition and hardship (1 John 3:13); for that is exactly the kind of path that our Master Himself had to walk.

III. Careful Thought
(Luke 14:28-33)

A. Finish What You Start (vv. 28-30)

28. For which of you, intending to build a tower, sitteth not down first, and counteth the cost, whether he have sufficient to finish it?

In Biblical times a landowner would often *build* a *tower* in order to keep an eye on his fields and, especially, his vineyards (Mark 12:1). A wise landowner would first take inventory of his time, laborers, and finances to determine whether or not he had *sufficient* resources to *finish* the project in a reasonable amount of time. [See question #4, page 176.]

29, 30. Lest haply, after he hath laid the foundation, and is not able to finish it, all that behold it begin to mock him, saying, This man began to build, and was not able to finish.

The gospel message that invites all to follow Christ carries with it a warning that a person must first "count the cost" before he responds. Thus our evangelistic efforts should not only show people the benefits and joys of becoming a Christian, but also the expectations and difficulties that accompany this decision. This is not to say that discipleship is optional. The one who "counts the cost" and determines that he cannot pay it does so to his own peril. Rather, he must count the cost and determine to pay it!

Furthermore, as each of us considers what types of service and ministry we will pursue in behalf of our Lord and Savior, we should carefully assess our abilities and opportunities and our strengths and weaknesses, lest we take on a task of service that we are not able to complete. Again, this does not suggest that ministry is optional. Rather, it is a challenge to consider the cost of ministry and make preparations to pay it. And once we have made a commitment to serve, we must resolve not to allow any discouragement or distraction to pressure us to quit before we have given our best effort to accomplish what we said we would do. [See question #5, page 176.]

B. Do Whatever Is Needed (vv. 31-33)

31. Or what king, going to make war against another king, sitteth not down first, and consulteth whether he be able with ten thousand to meet him that cometh against him with twenty thousand?

Whether the party involved be a nation or an individual, we do not regard lightly any offense or threat by our enemies. The impulse to fight and to defend our honor and our lives comes from a strong inner passion. These emotions can serve to sustain us through the duration of a conflict, but they can also cloud our judgment if we impulsively take on a battle for which we are not prepared. A wise leader holds his emotions in check while he assesses the prospects for victory.

32. Or else, while the other is yet a great way off, he sendeth an ambassage, and desireth conditions of peace.

A king who foresees unacceptable losses or certain defeat in battle would be wise to send an *ambassage*, or delegation, to attempt to negotiate a peaceful solution to the conflict. Though this will likely require giving away something to the enemy, that is preferable to a humiliating defeat.

The choice to follow Jesus should be based not on the emotions of the moment, but on careful reflection regarding the demands of discipleship. Only those who are prepared to do "whatever it takes" to serve Christ should sign on for duty.

33. So likewise, whosoever he be of you that forsaketh not all that he hath, he cannot be my disciple.

What an excellent summary of all that Jesus had taught regarding discipleship! Commitment to Christ requires nothing less than everything we can give Him. It is truly "all or nothing."

Conclusion

A. Counting the Cost

Are you familiar with the expression, "Don't bite off more than you can chew"? We can imagine a person stuffing his mouth with so much food that he cannot easily chew or swallow. As a result, it is impossible for him to gain any enjoyment or satisfaction from what he is eating. And, of course, we can understand the point that it is foolish to say "yes" to more responsibilities than we can realistically manage. We who are disciples of Jesus need to weigh carefully the many opportunities for service and to choose the one that best matches our gifts and abilities. Jesus deserves only our best and will settle for nothing less.

"Counting the cost" is also imperative for those who are not yet disciples. And as they weigh that choice, they must consider not only what it costs to follow, but what it means to reject Christ's call. Yes, it costs to follow Jesus—some even lose their lives in His service. But the cost of not following, of remaining lost for eternity, is far greater!

B. Prayer

Father, help us to be faithful in our service for Christ, always giving our all for the One who gave His all at the cross. In Jesus' name, amen.

C. Thought to Remember

"Whosoever he be of you that forsaketh not all that he hath, he cannot be my disciple" (Luke 14:33).

Home Daily Bible Readings

Monday, Jan. 8—On the Master's Mission (Luke 9:1-9)

Tuesday, Jan. 9—Hospitality Refused (Luke 9:51-56)

Wednesday, Jan. 10—The Christ and His Suffering (Luke 9:18-27)

Thursday, Jan. 11—The Would-be Followers of Jesus (Luke 9:57-62)

Friday, Jan. 12—Warnings and Encouragements (Luke 12:4-12)

Saturday, Jan. 13—Guilt by Association (Luke 22:54-62)

Sunday, Jan. 14—The Cost of Being a Disciple (Luke 14:25-33)

Learning by Doing

This page contains an alternate lesson plan emphasizing learning activities.
Classes desiring such student involvement will find these suggestions helpful.

Learning Goals

After this lesson the students will be able to:

1. Summarize Jesus' teaching about the demands of discipleship according to today's text.

2. Tell why encouraging people to "count the cost" should be an integral part of evangelism.

3. Pinpoint an excuse that they have been using to avoid a deeper commitment to Christ, and express a commitment to strengthen their discipleship.

Into the Lesson

Every day people use excuses to explain the lack of follow-through on projects, commitments, and relationships. Hang a large sheet of paper on the classroom wall or use an overhead projector transparency. Write the word *EXCUSES* vertically. Students are to think of words that they might use as excuses for lack of following through on something. Words could include: **E**ducation, e**X**tra work, **C**ost, not **U**nderstanding, **S**chedule, Entertainment, and lack of **S**kills.

Say, "Often we are excited about new opportunities that look too good to be true. What scheme has been attractive to you? Perhaps you sought a new car, an addition to your house, or a college education. Each of those comes with hidden price tags." Have the class brainstorm a list of some of the "hidden costs" to the above activities. *(Examples may include less money for other activities, loss of free time, dust and mess around the house, etc.)*

Perhaps you have had class members who remarked, "I thought becoming like Jesus and following Him would be simple. It seems that I have struggled from day one!" Discuss why that expectation is not warranted.

Then say, "Today we are going to explore the challenges put forth by Jesus concerning the cost of following Him. We will be asked to evaluate our willingness to pay the cost of discipleship."

Into the Word

Ask a volunteer to read Luke 9:57-62 and another to read Luke 14:25-33. Then provide copies of the following questions and allow students several minutes to answer them. Use these as a guide to discussion in studying the passage. (You will want to be familiar with the commentary material for difficult questions that may arise during the study.)

1. What is the most important thought in this passage?

2. What is the key verse in this passage?

3. Why did Jesus need to teach this lesson?

4. What is the most practical teaching in this passage for you?

5. If you had been in the crowd before Jesus, what would you have asked Him?

After discussing students' findings ask, "What do each of these teachings tell us about giving our lives to Jesus?" Students should see that there is a cost to following Jesus, a cost that is too seldom emphasized.

Into Life

Prepare a chart with the following headings: "Benefits" and "Costs." Say, "Suppose that you are asked to develop a brochure for our evangelism program here at church to help people understand the cost of following Jesus. Using this chart, what would you include?" Answers should include promises Jesus made concerning the new life, as well as the things that would need to be given up as the Christian becomes more like Jesus.

Discuss how such a tool would be helpful for a person making a decision for Christ. Would it help a person not to be too hasty, but also give a realistic picture of the cost of discipleship?

Most of us began following Jesus with the best of intentions. Just as the people in the text today, we would follow Jesus anywhere. However, we too can make excuses. Prepare three posters with the following headings: "Comfort," "Social Concerns," and "Family Concerns."

Have your students gather in three groups. Ask each group to write on one of the posters excuses that the group members have heard people use to keep from developing stronger discipleship. Some might include: "I really don't have time for devotions. I need to get a lot of sleep." "You don't understand; I am involved in so many community events." "My family wouldn't understand my being at Bible study on a weeknight."

Ask the students to tell what it has cost them to follow Christ. Then encourage students to confess excuses that they have used to avoid deeper commitment to Christ, and encourage them to commit to strengthening their discipleship. Have each group member pray for greater resolve on behalf of the member on his or her right.

Let's Talk It Over

The questions on this page are designed to encourage review of the lesson Scriptures and to promote discussion of the lesson by the class. The answers provided are only discussion starters. Let your class talk it over from there.

1. Jesus had very little in the way of material goods—not even a place "to lay his head" (Luke 9:58). As a disciple of Jesus, what do you expect in the way of material security?

It is very easy to look around at what others have and want to have the same things. In many cases we have lost sight of the eternal perspective in favor of the temporal. Jesus did not want people to follow Him with the expectation that they would be enriched materially. He objected when He perceived that the crowds were seeking Him because they wanted Him to feed them again (John 6:26, 27). His own lifestyle, dependent on the hospitality of others, is an indicator that material gain should not be a motive for discipleship.

We may or may not be blessed with wealth. All that we are promised is that the Father knows our needs and that we need not worry about them if we seek the kingdom of God (Matthew 6:31-33).

2. What difficult choices have you had to make to maintain following Jesus as the first priority in your life?

This can be a time of helpful affirmation of some who have struggled financially or socially but remained faithful to the Lord through their difficulties. Let their testimonies be an encouragement to all, but be careful that the discussion does not become a "Can-you-top-this?" exercise.

Use the discussion also to help the students see that, when confronted with a choice, loyalty to Jesus as Lord may be at stake. Caring for an aging parent is a good thing, but according to our text the call of discipleship requires something different. Are there *good* things your students are choosing that are consuming the time that could be given to serving Christ? Has any of them ever deliberately chosen to live below one's means in order to supply greater resources to Christ's work? Has anyone ever rearranged his or her "obligations" in order to respond to the call to service?

3. Can you give an example of an instance when loyalty to Christ must take precedence over family members or even your own life?

In a Christian family, it is not usually necessary to choose between the family and the Lord—the family as a whole chooses to follow the Lord. That may mean, however, that the family voluntarily does without some luxuries in order to give

more to the Lord's work. It may mean the family does not go to the beach for a week's vacation, but spends the week serving on a mission trip or in Christian service camp.

Whenever the expectations of non-Christian family members come into conflict with the teaching and example of Jesus, the choice can become more painful. The examples your students cite may be hypothetical or they may be actual, but encourage wide participation.

4. No one can predict what suffering or sacrifice may be required in order to follow Christ for the rest of one's life. Without that information, how can anyone commit to discipleship?

No matter what age we are when we accept Jesus as Lord and Savior, there is no way we can know how that commitment may be tested in the future. We cannot predict what rejections we may suffer because of our faith. We cannot predict how Christians will be regarded generally in the culture or by the powers of government, the media, or business. The trend of secularization, however, seems to be resulting in a drift in our lifetime from disregard to outright contempt for Christianity in society. If a commitment to Christ is to endure, it cannot be based upon the best possible circumstances. Although we cannot predict tomorrow, we may assume that faith will require some sacrifice and trial. If we assume the standard of Revelation 2:10—"faithful unto death"—then we will have the proper foundation on which to base our choices.

5. What "unfinished towers" stand as reminders of partial commitment or broken vows in your life? How can you better follow through on the commitment you have made to the Lord?

Do you have a rowing machine collecting dust in your basement? How about an exercise bike or a treadmill? These rusting relics remind some of us of commitments we once made but failed to follow through on. How about a book on Christian living that has hardly been read, or guides for daily devotions that have not been used beyond some past February? These speak of a different kind of commitment that may also have been dropped. Do not pressure the students to respond, but allow time for some introspection.

Lost and Found

January 21
Lesson 8

DEVOTIONAL READING: Ephesians 1:15–2:5.

BACKGROUND SCRIPTURE: Luke 15.

PRINTED TEXT: Luke 15:1, 2, 11-24.

Luke 15:1, 2, 11-24

1 Then drew near unto him all the publicans and sinners for to hear him.

2 And the Pharisees and scribes murmured, saying, This man receiveth sinners, and eateth with them.

. . . .

11 And he said, A certain man had two sons:

12 And the younger of them said to his father, Father, give me the portion of goods that falleth to me. And he divided unto them his living.

13 And not many days after the younger son gathered all together, and took his journey into a far country, and there wasted his substance with riotous living.

14 And when he had spent all, there arose a mighty famine in that land; and he began to be in want.

15 And he went and joined himself to a citizen of that country; and he sent him into his fields to feed swine.

16 And he would fain have filled his belly with the husks that the swine did eat: and no man gave unto him.

17 And when he came to himself, he said, How many hired servants of my father's have bread enough and to spare, and I perish with hunger!

18 I will arise and go to my father, and will say unto him, Father, I have sinned against heaven, and before thee,

19 And am no more worthy to be called thy son: make me as one of thy hired servants.

20 And he arose, and came to his father. But when he was yet a great way off, his father saw him, and had compassion, and ran, and fell on his neck, and kissed him.

21 And the son said unto him, Father, I have sinned against heaven, and in thy sight, and am no more worthy to be called thy son.

22 But the father said to his servants, Bring forth the best robe, and put it on him; and put a ring on his hand, and shoes on his feet:

23 And bring hither the fatted calf, and kill it; and let us eat, and be merry:

24 For this my son was dead, and is alive again; he was lost, and is found. And they began to be merry.

GOLDEN TEXT: This my son was dead, and is alive again;
he was lost, and is found.—Luke 15:24.

Good News of Jesus
Unit 2: Mission and Ministry
(Lessons 6-9)

Lesson Aims

After participating in this lesson, the students will be able to:

1. Tell how the prodigal son in Jesus' parable left his father's home and was later reconciled to his father.

2. Tell how this parable pictures our heavenly Father's compassion for repentant sinners.

3. Acknowledge that they are represented by the prodigal son, and give thanks for the Father's stubborn love for them.

Lesson Outline

Introduction

A. What a Waste!

"What a waste!" we often say or think when we hear a news story about an athlete who is suspended for drug use, a good student who drops out of school, or a teen who runs away from home and gets caught up in the dangers of life on the streets. And how easy it is for us to write off such people and assume that they will never amount to much of anything.

But the good news of Jesus Christ is that by God's grace there is always room for repentance, for forgiveness of the past, and for a new beginning. Lost lives—even those believed to be "too far gone"—can be reclaimed, if they can be led to

a humble repentance before God. Jesus' classic story of the prodigal son serves to remind us of this important Biblical truth.

B. Lesson Background

Today's text follows where last week's study left off (14:25-33). Luke 15 is well-known for its three parables about lost items—a lost sheep, a lost coin, and a lost son. However, the emphasis in these parables is not only on the word *lost*, but also on the *joy* that results from finding what was lost. And just as Heaven rejoices each time a person comes to know Jesus Christ as Lord and Savior (Luke 15:7, 10), so likewise we should be filled with excitement and appreciation whenever a lost person "comes home" to the Father.

I. Sinful Attitudes
(Luke 15:1, 2, 11-13)

A. Bitter Spirit (vv. 1, 2)

1. Then drew near unto him all the publicans and sinners for to hear him.

Throughout His ministry Jesus reached out to all people, particularly those commonly rejected as society's outcasts. Perhaps the most notable example of this was the *publicans*, or tax collectors. This group was viewed with special scorn, for reasons that went beyond the fact that people naturally resist paying taxes. Because the publicans acted as agents of the Roman Empire, they were judged as "traitors" for working in league with those considered oppressors of Israel. In addition, the power given to publicans easily lent itself to abuse, serving to increase the hatred of the general populace toward all publicans.

In addition to the publicans, other groups were looked down upon by many of the Jews. These disfranchised people included the blind, the lame, and the poor (as in Luke 14:21). Also included were those with disreputable lifestyles, such as prostitutes, thieves, and swindlers. All such people were commonly lumped together in the category of *sinners*.

While neither publicans nor other sinners were welcome in respectable gatherings of that day, they were always treated in a gracious manner by Jesus. Note that these people came *near* Jesus *to hear* Him. At the end of the previous chapter Jesus concluded His teaching on discipleship with the words, "He that hath ears to hear, let him hear" (Luke 14:35). While the religious leaders dismissed Jesus' teaching, the publicans and sinners gladly listened to and carefully considered His message. [See question #1, page 184.]

2. And the Pharisees and scribes murmured, saying, This man receiveth sinners, and eateth with them.

Often during His ministry Jesus faced a barrage of complaints and criticisms from *the Pharisees and scribes,* two of the ruling classes within the Jewish community. They considered it a violation of Mosaic law to have any association with people who did not live up to their high moral standards. They possessed no evangelistic vision of reaching out to the lost or of joyfully receiving *sinners* who chose to draw near to God. The gracious manner of Jesus stood in sharp contrast to their bitter spirit, which was later illustrated by the attitude of the prodigal's older brother (vv. 25-32). [See question #2, page 184.]

EATING WITH SINNERS

Lawrence of Arabia was one of the most adventurous personalities of World War I. During his travels through the Middle East, he found hospitality in the home of a desert sheik who was thought to be on the side of the enemy. After they had eaten together, the sheik told Lawrence that he would no longer be in any danger. According to the social customs of the Middle East, once two men had eaten together there was a bond between them. This custom is still observed. An Arab bus driver for a Holy Land tour bought bread and gave some to every tourist. "Now we are friends," he told them, "because we have eaten together."

Such a perspective helps us understand the Pharisees and scribes' evaluation of Jesus: "This man receiveth sinners, and eateth with them." Jesus is a friend of sinners! How appalling!

Of course, we realize that if Jesus had not eaten with sinners, He would always have eaten alone. There was no one else with whom He *could* eat! True, He was eating with sinners, but His critics were sinners, too—as are we all. In fact, Jesus came to our world not only to eat with sinners, but to *die for* them. He is a friend of sinners! How amazing!   —R. C. S.

B. Selfish Lifestyle (vv. 11-13)

11. And he said, A certain man had two sons.

Jesus did not give names to the characters in this parable, nor did He indicate whether or not it was taken from a real life situation. Nevertheless, the circumstances Jesus described would have seemed quite realistic to His audience.

12. And the younger of them said to his father, Father, give me the portion of goods that falleth to me. And he divided unto them his living.

The law of Moses established some basic guidelines regarding family inheritances. The oldest son was to receive a double portion of the father's estate (Deuteronomy 21:15-17). This was to be a majority share of money and property, at least two times as much as the other brothers

and sisters received. In the situation described by Jesus, the process of dividing the goods was fairly simple: two-thirds would go to the older son and one-third to the *younger.*

Though as a general rule inheritances were not distributed until after the death of a father, they could be disbursed at any time the father wished. For instance, a man growing old and feeble might choose to go ahead and invest his oldest son in his position as chief heir and then live under his care. Likewise, a father could give permission to any of his younger children to go ahead and try to establish themselves in the world with their smaller portion.

13. And not many days after the younger son gathered all together, and took his journey into a far country, and there wasted his substance with riotous living.

The description of the *younger son* gathering up all his money and taking off to *a far country* has a modern ring to it. It sounds like the son or daughter who can hardly wait to get as far away from parental oversight as possible. Didn't this father realize what his son would do with the money he received? Perhaps he did, but this is not indicated in the parable. Every parent, however, has wrestled with the decision to give a child freedom and responsibility when he or she is not certain how the child will handle it.

Sadly (and with a folly not uncommon when young people first step out on their own) the younger son *wasted his substance with riotous living.* We can imagine what this involved—perhaps an abundance of eating, drinking, and entertaining friends and female companions—the lure of "wine, women, and song." Note the older brother's complaint to his father that "this thy son" had "devoured thy living with harlots" (v. 30).

It is this young man's selfish and foolish spending spree that has earned him the title "the prodigal (wasteful) son." And in this behavior his true character was revealed. He exhibited no thought of acting with prudence and discretion, and showed no concern for honoring his father and his family. He was simply focused upon himself and his desire to enjoy all the worldly pleasures that money could buy.

II. Humble Repentance
(Luke 15:14-19)

A. Hitting Bottom (vv. 14-16)

14. And when he had spent all, there arose a mighty famine in that land; and he began to be in want.

Eventually an extravagant and wasteful lifestyle takes its toll on a young man's financial resources. Running out of money is a problem

---

How to Say It

BATHSHEBA. Bath-*she*-buh.
PHARISEES. *Fair*-ih-seez.

---

under any circumstances, but it is even more serious when *a mighty famine* has struck the *land*.

15. And he went and joined himself to a citizen of that country; and he sent him into his fields to feed swine.

The younger son *joined himself to* a *citizen*, meaning that he agreed to work for a man who offered him employment. His employer was a resident of the unnamed *country* to which the young man had traveled. Judging from the brief references to this land as well as the presence of *swine*, it seems that the young man was no longer among his fellow Jews but was now residing in Gentile territory. Working for a Gentile master would likely disturb the conscience of many a Jew, since the law of Moses discouraged any intimate association with Gentiles (Acts 10:28). However, during a famine one must seek wages wherever he can find someone willing to pay them.

How this young man's pride must have taken a beating throughout this disheartening turn of events! Not only did he have to deal with the loss of all his money (and thus the loss of all the companions whom his money had attracted), but now he was forced to accept the terms of a Gentile master. And that was not the end of the indignities he experienced. For in his fall from what he had once perceived as the good life, there would be no "modest setbacks," as we like to say. His life came crashing down all the way to "rock bottom." He was hired to *feed swine*.

Swine were among the animals that, according to the law of Moses, were to be considered "unclean" by the Jews (Leviticus 11:7; Deuteronomy 14:8). These ritualistic distinctions of "clean" and "unclean" formed much of the basis of the ethnic identity of the Jewish people. Yet in his abject desperation, with starvation looming before him, the young man forced himself to violate his conscience and his heritage, thus destroying whatever self-respect and dignity he may have had left. And even this was not the full extent of his downfall.

16. And he would fain have filled his belly with the husks that the swine did eat: and no man gave unto him.

In His masterful telling of this story, Jesus brought His Jewish audience to a point where their hearts would have ached for this young man. For no matter how foolish he had been, no Jew deserved this fate: *he would fain have filled his belly with the husks that the swine did eat.* Apparently he was so hungry that he longed to eat the food that he was putting out for the pigs. These *husks,* or "pods" as the Greek text indicates, were likely what are called carob pods. This crop was specifically grown for feeding livestock, but it was sometimes eaten by the poor during times of severe hardship. Such was the plight of the prodigal. For a Jewish man to be envious of pigs indicates what little self-respect remained in him.

To emphasize further the young man's sorry condition, Jesus then added, *And no man gave unto him.* No doubt the prodigal could not help but notice that there was no help forthcoming from the "friends" who had helped him spend his money. He was truly alone and helpless—quite a contrast from the cocky young man who had so rudely demanded his father's inheritance.

While it might have seemed that this situation was completely hopeless, such was not the case. God always holds before us a hope for recovery and renewal, even in our darkest moments. However, we cannot see it, nor can we pursue it, until first our pride has been broken and our spirit has been humbled. For it is in our times of failure that we finally see our foolish and sinful choices for what they truly are. It is in our deepest despair that we realize the need to approach our Father with the humility to admit that we were wrong and to seek His grace and mercy. [See question #3, page 184.]

B. Confessing Sin (vv. 17-19)

17. And when he came to himself, he said, How many hired servants of my father's have bread enough and to spare, and I perish with hunger!

Deep despair can either break a man down to the point of giving up on life, or it can challenge him to fight back and consider all his options, no matter how unpromising they might be. The latter was the case with our young man, as in the field with the swine *he came to himself.* This meant much more than regaining a level of mental composure that would enable him to assess his situation and form a plan of action. To "come to yourself" was an expression for repentance, which is a common theme linking all three of the parables in this chapter of Luke (15:7, 10). The young man was now beginning to see the reason for his troubles and was on the verge of accepting responsibility for his own foolish mistakes.

During this process, the young man began to reflect on the status of the *hired servants* in his father's household. They received a fair wage for their labor, along with sufficient food to eat.

Their condition, compared with his own sorry existence, led the young man to devise a plan where moments before all had seemed hopeless. [See question #4, page 184.]

18. I will arise and go to my father, and will say unto him, Father, I have sinned against heaven, and before thee.

The words of repentance are short and simple, yet so difficult to say: *I have sinned.* None of us likes to admit that we were wrong. But genuine repentance requires that we set aside any defense of our actions and honestly admit our sin.

This young man's sin was both *against heaven* and *before* his *father.* Certainly his conduct had shown disrespect to his father. But first and foremost, he had sinned against God. All of our wrongful actions against others are ultimately sins against God. After all, our misdeeds are a violation of the instructions God has clearly revealed to us in His Word; thus they are a resistance to the will of God over our lives. For example, David's adultery with Bathsheba was certainly a departure from the fidelity he owed to his family, and it was a despicable treatment of one of his most loyal officers and that man's wife. And yet, behind all of this was a blatant sin against God Himself. As David put it, "Against thee, thee only, have I sinned, and done this evil in thy sight" (Psalm 51:4).

19. And I am no more worthy to be called thy son: make me as one of thy hired servants.

I *am no more worthy to be called thy son,* the young man intended to say to his father. While he was still physically and legally the man's son, he did not feel that he deserved to be treated as a son after what he had done. Living as one of the *hired servants* under his own father's roof would be a fitting punishment, or so he thought. His public humiliation would serve to vindicate his father, to declare that he had been right all along.

The spirit of humility and repentance was now running so deep within the soul of the young man that he was willing to do anything he must in order to make things right again with his father and thereby save himself from complete ruin. Note how his attitude had changed from "give me" (v. 12) to *make me.*

III. Gracious Welcome
(Luke 15:20-24)

A. Loving Father (vv. 20, 21)

20. And he arose, and came to his father. But when he was yet a great way off, his father saw him, and had compassion, and ran, and fell on his neck, and kissed him.

The *father saw* his returning son *when he was yet a great way off.* Perhaps he just happened to

look out on the horizon at the time his son was approaching, or possibly he had been watching and hoping for his son's safe return. The latter is certainly appropriate when this story is applied to our Father in Heaven.

As for the traditional protocol of that era, the father tossed aside all formalities. He *ran* to greet his son, *fell on his neck* and hugged him, and *kissed him.* The reason for this dramatic reception: the father's heart was filled with *compassion* for his errant son. Perhaps, for the sake of emphasis, it would be better not to title this story "the Prodigal Son," but to call it instead "the Gracious Father."

HOLY LOVE

One evening Richard Wurmbrand, who ministered for many years in lands under the control of Communism, was talking with a man from Romania. The man did not know that Wurmbrand, a Christian, was also a former Jew. The man boasted of killing Jews during the Holocaust. Then Wurmbrand told him that he himself was a Jew and so was his wife. He said that his wife was sleeping in the next room. He then proposed an experiment. The two men would go in and tell Wurmbrand's wife the man's story and see what she would do.

So the men did this. Wurmbrand told his wife, "This man is the murderer of your sisters, your brother, and your parents. What do you have to say to him?" In response Wurmbrand's wife put her arms around that man's neck. Both wept. It was a scene of holy love. Wurmbrand then said to the man, "If my wife, who is only human, can do this—if she can love you like this, knowing what you have done, and can forgive you—then how much more will God, who is love!"

As instructive as it is for us to see ourselves in the prodigal son, it is also important that we see God in the forgiving father. The parable shows us a God who is not distant and far removed from us—even when we have treated Him with

Wanted: Alive!

Offense: Wasting an Inheritance

Reward: Love and Forgiveness

*Many people think sin makes us "unwanted" by God. The theme of today's text, illustrated by the lesson visual, is that even though we sin, God **wants** us!*

Visual for lesson 8

the utmost contempt. He is ever and always the compassionate Father, longing for us to come home.   —R. C. S.

21. And the son said unto him, Father, I have sinned against heaven, and in thy sight, and am no more worthy to be called thy son.

The son immediately began the repentance speech that he had rehearsed in the field with the swine. But before he could complete it, the father interrupted his words and chose to disregard any thought of humiliating his son. He had more noble plans in mind.

B. Joyous Reception (vv. 22-24)

22. But the father said to his servants, Bring forth the best robe, and put it on him; and put a ring on his hand, and shoes on his feet.

The father called for his *best robe* and bestowed on his son a treatment reserved for honored guests. He offered full admission back into his home by giving his son *a ring,* perhaps a signet ring that symbolized authority (cf. Genesis 41:42). He rejected the idea of his son's showing penance as a household servant. Instead, he had him fitted with *shoes* (more precisely, leather sandals)—a luxury not often enjoyed by mere *servants.* The reception of the son back into the home he had abandoned was complete and uninhibited, and it was founded entirely on the grace of the father.

23. And bring hither the fatted calf, and kill it; and let us eat, and be merry.

Fresh meat was not a regular part of meals in that day and culture. Grains and fruit were the norm. A *fatted calf* was used for special occasions, and today was such. The joy of the father at receiving back his lost son was similar to that portrayed in the other two parables in this chap-

ter—when a shepherd found his lost sheep (Luke 15:5, 6) and a woman found her lost coin (v. 9).

As it is in Heaven (Luke 15:7, 10), so should it be on earth among God's people. All of us should rejoice at seeing lost souls rescued and saved. The callous attitude of the Pharisees and scribes in this regard had initiated this series of parables (v. 2). May it not be our attitude as well. We should practice an evangelism that shares the gospel with every creature (Mark 16:15), offer a Christian hospitality that gladly welcomes all repentant sinners into our fellowship (James 2:1-9), and envision an assembly both on earth and in Heaven that encompasses "all nations, and kindreds, and people, and tongues" (Revelation 7:9). [See question #5, page 184.]

24. For this my son was dead, and is alive again; he was lost, and is found. And they began to be merry.

When the *son* chose to abandon his home, his family relationship was *dead.* But more to the point for us, he had been spiritually dead because of the sinful lifestyle he pursued. The message of Jesus' parable is that an enthusiastic "welcome home" is always available for each one of us through the grace and mercy of our loving heavenly Father.

Conclusion

A. "Was Blind, But Now I See"

"Amazing grace! how sweet the sound, That saved a wretch like me! I once was lost, but now am found, Was blind, but now I see." Perhaps no song is more cherished among Christians than this old hymn. Certainly no message is any dearer to our hearts than the story of our Father's amazing grace for sinners such as ourselves. The thought should fill us with a "joy unspeakable and full of glory" (1 Peter 1:8).

Moreover, what God has done for us should prompt us to show kindness and compassion to others, even as we have received it ourselves. Once we realize what it means to "come home" to the Father, we are to search for those still wandering, who need to know that they can stop running. The Father longs for them to come home.

B. Prayer

Father, we thank You for the grace You have shown to us in spite of our failings before You, and we thank You for Your Son Jesus, in whose name we pray. Amen.

C. Thought to Remember

"I say unto you, there is joy in the presence of the angels of God over one sinner that repenteth" (Luke 15:10).

Home Daily Bible Readings

Monday, Jan. 15—Lost Sheep and Lost Coin (Luke 15:1-10)

Tuesday, Jan. 16—Lost Son (Luke 15:11-16)

Wednesday, Jan. 17—Repentance, Return, and Rejoicing (Luke 15:17-24)

Thursday, Jan. 18—A Plea for Pardon (Psalm 51)

Friday, Jan. 19—No One Cares for Me (Psalm 142)

Saturday, Jan. 20—Your Sins Are Forgiven (Mark 2:1-12)

Sunday, Jan. 21—The Elder Brother (Luke 15:25-32)

Learning by Doing

This page contains an alternate lesson plan emphasizing learning activities.
Classes desiring such student involvement will find these suggestions helpful.

Learning Goals

After this lesson the students will be able to:

1. Tell how the prodigal son in Jesus' parable left his father's home and was later reconciled to his father.

2. Tell how this parable pictures our heavenly Father's compassion for repentant sinners.

3. Acknowledge that they are represented by the prodigal son, and give thanks for the Father's stubborn love for them.

Into the Lesson

Today's lesson focuses on grace and forgiveness. Begin the lesson by putting your students into groups of three. Prepare the following questions on paper for each student. Ask the students to choose to answer the question with which they are most comfortable.

1. If you could wave a magic wand over your life and make it perfect, how would it be different from the way it is now?

2. If you could rewind the "tape" of your life and live a year over again, which one would it be? Why?

3. What was your most embarrassing moment?

Allow ten minutes for this exercise, as people will have to think about their answers. This introduction will prepare them for identifying with the prodigal in today's lesson.

Say, "Each of us has issues in which he has not lived up to God's standard. Sometimes we have been willful about it, other times ignorant. In today's lesson we shall see just how far God's grace goes in reaching us when we need Him."

Into the Word

It is critical for your students to understand the context of today's lesson. Select someone early in the week to review the lesson commentary and other materials concerning Luke 15:1, 2. He or she will prepare a five-minute report on the crowd that was present when Jesus spoke. Be sure to contrast the ones who gathered around Jesus with the ones who murmured against Him.

Create three groups of up to to six students each, and give them the following assignments. (If you have more than eighteen students, create more groups and repeat assignments.)

Group 1. Use a concordance to find Old Testament verses with references to God as "Father"—especially from Psalms and Isaiah. List as many as you can, and be prepared to report on these verses to the class.

Group 2. Read Luke 15:11-24. Prepare a short drama on the events told here. You will present this drama to the class.

Group 3. Read Luke 15:11-24. Prepare a short drama putting the events in terms of a "sinner" and God rather than a son and a father. Decide what characters need to be present; then write the dialog. Present this drama during the session.

Be sure that materials needed are present: a concordance, Bibles or a printed text of the Scripture, and props or clothing to add realism to the dramas.

After fifteen minutes call the groups together. Have Group 2 present its drama. If any questions arise from the presentation, refer to the commentary for answers.

Ask Group 1 to present the results of its Scripture search. Ask the class, "In this parable, who is the father?" Then say, "By our Scripture search, it is reasonable to assume that the scribes and Pharisees understood Jesus' point. God is gracious toward those who stray from His way."

Into Life

Ask Group 3 to present its drama. After the presentation ask, "How do you think most people would have felt when they first saw the father again? How do you think most people would have reacted had they *been* the father? What does this passage tell us about repentance?" (See the commentary section, "Humble Repentance," pages 179-181.) "What does this passage tell us about God's grace?" (See "Gracious Welcome," pages 181, 182.)

As a result of this lesson, each student should recognize personal similarities to the prodigal. The following exercise will allow them to confess sin and give thanks to God for His forgiveness.

Ask each student to complete the following silently: "My struggle with sin involves _____." You can give categories such as family, finances, friends, faithfulness, business, emotions, self-discipline, sexual issues, etc. Remind believers of the promise of forgiveness in 1 John 1:9. If you have non-Christians in the class, invite any who wish to do so to remain after class to talk about the forgiveness available through Jesus' blood.

Close the class with a prayer of confession and of thanksgiving for God's forgiveness.

Let's Talk It Over

The questions on this page are designed to encourage review of the lesson Scriptures and to promote discussion of the lesson by the class. The answers provided are only discussion starters. Let your class talk it over from there.

1. Is our church attracting a large number of "sinners" who want to inquire about Christian teaching? Why or why not? How can our church become more appealing to "sinners"?

If unbelievers or lapsed believers feel comfortable meeting with your church, they probably do so because of your intentional effort to make them feel welcome. What signals are you sending out to those who are strangers to your fellowship and even strangers to Christianity? How would you grade your hospitality? Are the ministries of your church designed to meet the needs of the already initiated, or are you creatively and thoughtfully reaching out to those who are not yet disciples?

Jesus did not condone sin, but His care for people caused them to feel welcome in His presence. It should be the goal of His people to welcome sinners into His presence and help them to find His saving grace.

2. In what situations do you associate with unbelievers? How may Christians associate with unbelievers and not compromise our witness?

It is a good thing to invite unbelievers to church or to social functions with our church friends, but the most effective method of evangelism is sharing the gospel friend-to-friend. To have much of an influence on unbelievers, we may have to venture onto their turf, just as Jesus did when He visited the home of Levi the tax collector. Most of us already have some association with unbelievers because we work with them or they are our neighbors. We can demonstrate the love of Christ by taking initiative to show kindness to them. We can plan to share time with them and share experiences with them without compromising our moral standards. When values or standards come into conflict, it may become an opportunity to talk about our faith.

3. In circumstances of severe suffering, the prodigal repented of his ways. What are some of the circumstances that are likely to be turning points for people today?

If you have students who came to the Lord as adults, perhaps they can relate what situations became turning points for them. Many believers can tell of feeling empty in spite of financial success and other seemingly positive factors in their lives. Perhaps it was the consistent witness of a Christian co-worker that turned such a one to the Source of real success.

Others may have experienced negative circumstances—financial difficulty, health problems, a broken relationship, loss of a job, legal problems, or an accident or other brush with death. Any of these may serve to turn a person away from material pursuits to seek the Lord. In these situations as well, the testimony of a committed believer is usually what turns the unbeliever in the right direction.

4. The prodigal found courage to return home because his father had a reputation as kind and generous. How can we convince spiritual prodigals that the heavenly Father is kind and generous?

The Christian gospel is based on the love of God. "God so loved the world, that he gave his only begotten Son . . ." (John 3:16). As Christians we have the privilege of sharing the good news of God's grace and forgiveness extended to sinners. Not only can we share the story of Jesus and relate what He taught about the love of the Father, but we can testify about the Father's love shown to us personally. Also, we can emulate the Father's love and acceptance in the way we treat those who are seeking Him.

5. How can Christians add more celebration when modern prodigals turn to God?

In Jesus' story the father threw a huge party at the return of his son who had been "lost." If we had a banquet whenever someone made a public profession of faith or was baptized before the church, we would probably see people feigning faith just for the party. Still, it seems that celebration is warranted. The form of celebration will vary from place to place, and your students can probably suggest several specific ways.

Perhaps we need a greater sense of what it means for a person to be "lost." We don't use that word much anymore, speaking instead of the "unchurched" or some other sterile term. The father felt keenly the hopeless estate of his son— he had been dead, but now he was alive. If we appreciate the hopeless condition of the lost— spiritually dead and bound for Hell—we will surely celebrate when they are saved from that!

Threat of Riches

DEVOTIONAL READING: Luke 12:13-21.

BACKGROUND SCRIPTURE: Luke 16.

PRINTED TEXT: Luke 16:1-13.

Luke 16:1-13

1 And he said also unto his disciples, There was a certain rich man, which had a steward; and the same was accused unto him that he had wasted his goods.

2 And he called him, and said unto him, How is it that I hear this of thee? give an account of thy stewardship; for thou mayest be no longer steward.

3 Then the steward said within himself, What shall I do? for my lord taketh away from me the stewardship: I cannot dig; to beg I am ashamed.

4 I am resolved what to do, that, when I am put out of the stewardship, they may receive me into their houses.

5 So he called every one of his lord's debtors unto him, and said unto the first, How much owest thou unto my lord?

6 And he said, A hundred measures of oil. And he said unto him, Take thy bill, and sit down quickly, and write fifty.

7 Then said he to another, And how much owest thou? And he said, A hundred measures of wheat. And he said unto him, Take thy bill, and write fourscore.

8 And the lord commended the unjust steward, because he had done wisely: for the children of this world are in their generation wiser than the children of light.

9 And I say unto you, Make to yourselves friends of the mammon of unrighteousness; that, when ye fail, they may receive you into everlasting habitations.

10 He that is faithful in that which is least is faithful also in much: and he that is unjust in the least is unjust also in much.

11 If therefore ye have not been faithful in the unrighteous mammon, who will commit to your trust the true riches?

12 And if ye have not been faithful in that which is another man's, who shall give you that which is your own?

13 No servant can serve two masters: for either he will hate the one, and love the other; or else he will hold to the one, and despise the other. Ye cannot serve God and mammon.

Jan 28

GOLDEN TEXT: Ye cannot serve God and mammon.—Luke 16:13.

Lesson Aims

After this lesson each student will be able to:

1. Recount Jesus' parable of the dishonest steward.

2. Tell how a story about a person's unethical behavior can serve as an example to Christians.

3. Pinpoint an area where he or she has been trying to "serve two masters," and suggest ways to put God first.

Lesson Outline

INTRODUCTION
 A. No Regrets?
 B. Lesson Background
I. WASTED OPPORTUNITIES (Luke 16:1-3)
 A. Falling Short (vv. 1, 2)
 B. Filled With Despair (v. 3)
II. SWIFT RECOVERY (Luke 16:4-8)
 A. The Steward's Plan (vv. 4-7)
 B. The Owner's Praise (v. 8)
III. FAITHFUL SERVICE (Luke 16:9-13)
 A. Responsible in Everything (vv. 9-11)
  Friend or Foe?
 B. Devoted to the Master (vv. 12, 13)
CONCLUSION
 A. "Well Done"
 B. Prayer
 C. Thought to Remember

Introduction

A. No Regrets?

One of Frank Sinatra's most popular songs was entitled "My Way." In it he mentioned that he'd had a few regrets, but not enough of them to mention. Part of his statement is true. We do not care to mention our regrets about the past, though not because they are "too few." The truth is that all of us have made many, many mistakes of which we do not wish to be reminded. And the more we grow spiritually, the more sensitive we become regarding the sinful and foolish things we have done—and still do.

What a blessing it is that God allows "second chances"—not that we can undo the past, but we can put it behind us and move ahead. Through Christ we can be forgiven of the sins of yesterday and resolve to be better and to do better by the

power of His Spirit in us. Although we cannot look back and honestly say "no regrets," we must not allow ourselves to be burdened with guilt about the past; for we are strengthened and encouraged by the abundant grace of God.

B. Lesson Background

Jesus' parables, taken as a whole, reveal His extensive knowledge of the variety of life experiences within His age and culture. He could tell stories about children playing in the marketplace and about a housewife baking bread or searching a room for a missing coin. He could paint verbal pictures of a fisherman with his net, a farmer sowing seed or pruning his vineyards, and a shepherd seeking a lost lamb. He could draw imagery from a king preparing for battle or planning a royal wedding feast. And, as will be seen in today's text, Jesus could draw an important spiritual lesson from the management (or more accurately, mismanagement) of an estate by a steward. His teaching ministry demonstrates that much of life readily lends itself to spiritual parables and analogies well suited for our edification.

The chapter from which today's lesson is taken follows the one from which last week's study of the prodigal son was drawn. Jesus was still in Perea, east of the Jordan River from Samaria and Judea. Approximately three to four months remained until His crucifixion.

I. Wasted Opportunities (Luke 16:1-3)

A. Falling Short (vv. 1, 2)

1. And he said also unto his disciples, There was a certain rich man, which had a steward; and the same was accused unto him that he had wasted his goods.

Jesus often told parables that likened our Christian duty to that of a *steward*. A steward served as a manager of a wealthy man's estate. His responsibilities varied; for instance, he could serve as a household manager, supervising the various servants (cf. Matthew 24:45) and overseeing the household budget and all expenditures. Or, as in the case of the steward in this parable, he could be the equivalent of our modern business manager. With the estate of a landowner, that role would involve selling the goods produced from the land—seeking the best price and maximum profit for the owner. The steward would also need to purchase whatever supplies were needed for further production.

A household steward was typically a slave trained in management. A business steward could likewise be a slave, but it was not uncommon for this to be a hired position. The latter appears to be the case with the steward in our parable, who was facing accusations of mismanagement. Had he been a slave, he could have anticipated a severe beating, if not death. But the punishment that this man faced was the loss of his job (v. 2)—the appropriate penalty for a hired employee.

The accusation against this steward was that he had *wasted* the owner's *goods*; that is, he had mismanaged the business affairs entrusted to him. Perhaps he had made some careless transactions or failed to take advantage of some profitable opportunities. It may be that his weakness was in record keeping, and that inventory and receipts were not being fully accounted.

Whatever the problems, the steward was not accused of dishonesty or embezzlement (as some commentaries suggest). The same Greek word used for the prodigal son when he "wasted" his inheritance (Luke 15:13) is applied to this steward as well. Of course, it is little consolation to be spared a charge of criminal misconduct in favor of being branded incompetent. For a business steward, either charge could ruin a career.

2. And he called him, and said unto him, How is it that I hear this of thee? give an account of thy stewardship; for thou mayest be no longer steward.

In the process of having his employee *give an account of thy stewardship*, the owner would usually want to conduct what we call an "audit" of the ledger books. This accounting would serve to confirm whether or not the accusations of poor management were true. However, apparently enough was already known or assumed by the owner that the fate of the steward was already determined: he was to be dismissed from his employment.

Truly this story is a parable with applications to many of us as we reflect on the personal stewardship of our lives. It is with deep regret that we look back and acknowledge our careless mistakes, our halfhearted efforts, and our wasted opportunities. And there is one more thing we share in common with this steward—the mistakes of the past often catch up with us, threatening our present security and our future prospects. How much better we would be now if only we had made better choices in our past! [See question #1, page 192.]

B. Filled With Despair (v. 3)

3. Then the steward said within himself, What shall I do? for my lord taketh away from me the stewardship: I cannot dig; to beg I am ashamed.

Were the charges of mismanagement actually true? Apparently so. An audit of the ledgers could have exonerated an innocent man, but the steward had already accepted the inevitable. His initial reaction to the prospect of dismissal from his job was a deep sense of despair.

I cannot dig, the steward lamented. He seems afraid to face a type of employment for which he may have had no training or experience. Perhaps he wondered whether or not he possessed the stamina to keep up with a more physically demanding job. For many a modern "desk jockey," the prospects of an abrupt switch to manual labor could produce similar feelings of apprehension. Furthermore, this steward would probably need to adjust to the loss of a level of income to which he had grown accustomed.

If the steward was not willing to do any of the lesser jobs that were available, his only other option might be *to beg.* That, however, was unacceptable, for he was *ashamed* to stoop to such tactics. Indeed, begging for a handout by its very nature assaults one's self-esteem and dignity. This steward would have none of that. And yet, with either of the options before him, pride would take a beating. When someone in a professional career deliberately chooses to give up the "rat race" for a simpler lifestyle, we admire the person. But when someone is fired for incompetence and is forced to abandon his career and aspirations and settle for something less, we pity him.

Consider the depth of despair being experienced by the steward in this parable. Some of us have "been there," and we have felt our world come crashing in on us; we feared that life would never be the same again. Even if we have not felt such despair personally, we have seen it in others and have witnessed its demoralizing and debilitating effects. The situation Jesus portrayed is unfortunately all too real in our time.

II. Swift Recovery
(Luke 16:4-8)

A. The Steward's Plan (vv. 4-7)

4. I am resolved what to do, that, when I am put out of the stewardship, they may receive me into their houses.

Deep despair over a set of circumstances can often lead to inactivity and thus to further problems. Not so with this steward. He took control of his emotions, thought carefully about his situation, and *resolved* to initiate a plan of action. It is this determination and will power in the face of certain failure that will later serve as the steward's redeeming quality in the lesson to be learned from this parable.

The steward's scheme was designed to win the favor of the businessmen with whom he had been dealing on behalf of the landowner. He hoped that placing before them an exceptionally good financial opportunity would ingratiate himself with them, thereby setting himself up for future employment options.

5. So he called every one of his lord's debtors unto him, and said unto the first, How much owest thou unto my lord?

In his role as a business manager, the steward would have regularly set up buying and selling transactions, and would have been responsible for calling in debts on behalf of the landowner. To put it in contemporary terms, his "signature" would have been as good as the owner's. Thus the steward was taking advantage of his position of authority while it still remained intact in order to carry out his plan.

6. And he said, A hundred measures of oil. And he said unto him, Take thy bill, and sit down quickly, and write fifty.

The first businessman owed the landowner's estate *a hundred measures of oil*. The *New International Version* provides a modern equivalent by saying "eight hundred gallons." This would have been a large transaction in that day, likely to be paid off in increments over a period of time. Here was the steward's offer: he would discount the debt by half if the businessman would act *quickly* and pay in full right then. This would amount to such a tremendous savings that anyone with the resources to pay would leap at the opportunity.

It is not likely, as some assume, that this offer was based on the steward's cutting out his commission on the transaction. Fifty percent is much too large a figure for a commission. It is more likely that the steward was undercutting the real value of the original deal simply to buy the good favor of this businessman. In any event, one who had been filled with desperation over his plight

was now moving swiftly with a strategy to ensure his survival.

7. Then said he to another, And how much owest thou? And he said, A hundred measures of wheat. And he said unto him, Take thy bill, and write fourscore.

The second businessman received an offer comparable to that given to the first man. Once again the *New International Version* suggests a modern equivalent of the amount owed—in this case, "a thousand bushels." While not the fifty percent reduction the first debtor received, the twenty percent discount would represent a substantial savings and make for an attractive offer. The parable records only two transactions by the steward, but the implication is that there were as many others as he could arrange.

B. The Owner's Praise (v. 8)

8. And the lord commended the unjust steward, because he had done wisely: for the children of this world are in their generation wiser than the children of light.

With this verse we can see why most Bible students consider this parable to be a tricky passage to interpret. The actions of the steward in offering these "discounts" were clearly unethical. He is referred to as an *unjust steward*—or, as other translations put it, dishonest. He had not acted in the best interest of the landowner; his actions were focused purely on his own self-preservation.

It is not that the steward acted illegally, for as steward he had full authority to make any deal that he wanted to make. Certainly we would expect him to know better than to cross the line into criminal mischief, knowing that he was currently under close scrutiny. But in the business world, legal is not necessarily the same as ethical. Thus, while the original charge against him was that he had been wasteful and had poorly managed his duties (v. 1), here he had pushed the boundaries of ethical responsibility and was declared *unjust*.

So how can a dishonest character such as this steward serve as the main character in a parable intended to teach positive spiritual lessons? Actually, Jesus did this more than once in His teaching. Consider, for example, His parable of the "unjust judge" in Luke 18:1-8. Jesus described this judge as one who "feared not God, neither regarded man" (v. 2). He responded to a widow's plea for justice only because her persistent appeals wearied him. And yet this "unjust judge," as he is called, was used to teach us a lesson regarding prayer. Obviously Jesus was not saying that God is unjust or that He does not care about our needs and concerns. No, the lesson in

---

Home Daily Bible Readings

Monday, Jan. 22—The Dishonest Manager (Luke 16:1-8)

Tuesday, Jan. 23—Faithful Stewardship (Luke 16:10-13)

Wednesday, Jan. 24—Give to God (Deuteronomy 14:22-26)

Thursday, Jan. 25—The Law and God's Kingdom (Luke 16:14-18)

Friday, Jan. 26—Rich Man, Poor Man (Luke 16:19-26)

Saturday, Jan. 27—Warnings About Riches (Luke 16:27-31)

Sunday, Jan. 28—Respect the Great King (Psalm 24)

this parable is in the widow's persistence, not in the moral character of the judge (or of the widow, for that matter).

Even granting that Jesus could use a dishonest character in a parable, why did *the lord* commend this steward, and how can he serve as an example for us? First, he was not commended for his unethical conduct, but for his shrewdness. When Jesus notes that *he had done wisely,* He actually means that the steward had carried out his scheme with great craft and cunning. When his life was unraveling before him, he refused to be defeated. His actions themselves were not commendable, either to the landowner or to Jesus. And he is not to be respected by us for his motives of self-interest, for he showed little regard for the best interests of the man whose property he managed. But his ability to devise a prudent plan in the midst of professional and emotional turmoil was impressive even to the landowner who was firing him. [See question #2, page 192.]

It is the steward's refusal to be defeated and his dogged determination to succeed that are commended to Jesus' followers, that is, to *the children of light.* Of course, Jesus expects our actions to be more honorable than those of the steward; but our resolve to succeed should be no less intense than was his. Believers are encouraged to act as *wisely* with spiritual matters as unbelievers do with earthly ones. We are urged to make present investments in future, and eternal, "securities."

III. Faithful Service (Luke 16:9-13)

A. Responsible in Everything (vv. 9-11)

9. And I say unto you, Make to yourselves friends of the mammon of unrighteousness; that, when ye fail, they may receive you into everlasting habitations.

Mammon of unrighteousness refers to worldly wealth and material possessions. There is nothing inherently evil about such wealth, but there is nothing inherently righteous about it either— thus it is *un-*, or not, righteous. To *make to yourselves friends of* this *mammon* means to make friends by means of, or by using, such wealth.

But how and why are we to make friends through our worldly possessions? Perhaps Jesus is offering practical advice for our interaction with people on earth; that is, good deeds and acts of kindness in sharing worldly goods toward others will often "come back" to bless those who do them. This may have been what the steward had in mind when he reduced the indebtedness of his lord's debtors. Perhaps he hoped that, once he was out of work, they would repay his kindness by assisting him with food or housing.

How to Say It

PEREA. Peh-*ree*-uh.
SAMARIA. Suh-*mare*-ee-uh.

However, Jesus' statement that people will *receive you into everlasting habitations* suggests a loftier idea. It may be that He is challenging us to use our material wealth in ways that will win us "friends in Heaven"—that is, in ways that will encourage the spread of the gospel and will win people to Christ. In other words, Jesus is saying that our wealth should always be used in a manner that pleases God and advances His cause. We should be as shrewd in using wealth in this honorable manner as the steward was in promoting his self-serving agenda.

FRIEND OR FOE?

Several years ago a wealthy automobile dealer in Tampa, Florida, got into an argument with his wife. This was not an infrequent event for the couple, but on this occasion the wife shot and killed her husband. Later, when she was being interviewed by the press, she said, "It's all because of the money. I wish there had never been any money at all!" No doubt many others have expressed the same wish, after coming to realize that the money they had thought would bring them happiness brought nothing but misery.

Jesus encouraged us to "make to yourselves friends of the mammon of unrighteousness" (Luke 16:9). Many have found mammon to be a foe more than a friend, a hindrance more than a help, a curse more than a blessing. Some make a living stealing money, but money is itself a thief—robbing people of genuine peace and happiness and, in many cases, destroying their most important relationships.

Jesus counsels us to use money in a wise way, not to let money use us in a wasteful way.

—R. C. S.

10. He that is faithful in that which is least is faithful also in much: and he that is unjust in the least is unjust also in much.

This verse states a most valuable rule for daily life. How well we handle current tasks and decisions implies how well we would manage greater responsibilities, if given the opportunity to do so. Unfortunately, many people put forth a halfhearted effort in some of their current work, while maintaining that they would surely do better if they had better work to do. [See question #3, page 192.] Consider responses to each of the following hypothetical situations.

"If I were promoted to manager of this store, I would really put forth my best effort." *But then, why aren't you giving your best effort now?*

"If I were alone on a trip and approached by a prostitute, I would surely say no." *But then, how well are you resisting the lustful images that come your way each day?*

"If I were a millionaire, I would give away a lot of money to Christian work." *But then, how generous are you now in what you give from your current income?*

"If I were an overseas missionary, I would evangelize as many people as I could." *But then, to how many of your friends and neighbors did you witness today?*

"If I were facing a martyr's death, I would boldly testify to my faith." *But then, how boldly do you speak the name of Jesus even now among friends and colleagues?*

If we are not doing our best with what we have been given now, we are only kidding ourselves to imagine that we would do better if given greater opportunities.

11. If therefore ye have not been faithful in the unrighteous mammon, who will commit to your trust the true riches?

Here Jesus mentions once again the specific issue of the *unrighteous mammon* (worldly wealth). His words indicate that how we handle these riches determines whether God will commit to our care *true riches*. Consider a similar principle stated by Paul concerning leadership: "If a man know not how to rule his own house, how shall he take care of the church of God?" (1 Timothy 3:5). [See question #4, page 192.]

The right use of wealth is certainly not a condition of salvation, but a wrong use of it indicates that one's life is not under the lordship of Christ as much as it ought to be. As Jesus pointed out, "Where your treasure is, there will your heart be also" (Matthew 6:21). Much of the spiritual riches that could be ours (in areas such as faith and love) often go unclaimed because we are selfish with our material wealth.

B. Devoted to the Master (vv. 12, 13)

12. And if ye have not been faithful in that which is another man's, who shall give you that which is your own?

This verse is yet another way of stating the lesson in the previous verse. The true and eternal wealth (which is really our *own* and which the world cannot take away) will not be ours at all if we cling selfishly to worldly wealth (which was never ours to begin with but came from someone else—and ultimately from God).

13. No servant can serve two masters: for either he will hate the one, and love the other;

or else he will hold to the one, and despise the other. Ye cannot serve God and mammon.

Here is the crux of the matter: who is really in control of your life? A life dedicated to accumulating *mammon* will time and again run into conflicts with the demands of serving *God*. The more the pursuit of earthly things becomes a priority, requiring our time and energy, the more our devotion to Christ and His ministry will diminish. And what is said about mammon could be said just as well about anything in this life that we value: nothing should ever be permitted to stand in the way of our commitment to Jesus Christ. [See question #5, page 192.]

Conclusion

A. "Well Done"

How satisfying it is to be commended for our efforts by our peers—to receive awards and commendations, or a promotion and a raise. But none of this compares with the commendation that awaits us at the final judgment if we have been faithful in all things in the sight of Jesus. The world may scoff at our devotion to the cause of Christ and our disdain for the pleasures it counts dear. To hear these words from the Master will be worth whatever ridicule or opposition we have had to endure:

"Well done, good and faithful servant; thou hast been faithful over a few things, I will make thee ruler over many things: enter thou into the joy of thy lord" (Matthew 25:23).

B. Prayer

Father, strengthen us when we are weak. Help us to be faithful stewards for You in every situation. Help us not to fall prey to the temptation to "serve two masters." In Jesus' name. Amen.

C. Thought to Remember

"He that is faithful in that which is least is faithful also in much" (Luke 16:10).

Today's visual reminds us that we cannot go two ways at once. Discuss some of the choices that have to be made in order to serve God and not money.

Visual for lesson 9

Learning by Doing

This page contains an alternate lesson plan emphasizing learning activities.
Classes desiring such student involvement will find these suggestions helpful.

Learning Goals

After this lesson each student will be able to:

1. Recount the parable of the dishonest steward.

2. Tell how a story about a person's unethical behavior can serve as an example to Christians.

3. Pinpoint an area where he or she has been trying to "serve two masters," and suggest ways to put God first.

Into the Lesson

Search newspapers, newsmagazines, or business papers for articles concerning "good" and "bad" managers. Place the chairs of the room in circles of four with an article in each circle. Students will summarize the article, identifying the positive or negative nature of the person.

You may also introduce this lesson by asking, "If you could have any job in the world right now, what job would you like to have? Don't let issues related to changing jobs affect your answer—issues like changing your kids' schools, moving, and the like. Simply consider the job itself—what is your dream job? Why?" Allow the groups a few minutes for discussion.

Make the transition to today's Bible study by saying that we will be looking at a story about a man who was on the verge of losing his "dream" job and what he decided to do about it.

Into the Word

Begin with a brief lecture using the lesson commentary's introductory materials and the following statement: "Today's lesson encourages us to look beneath the surface a bit. We are challenged by Jesus' commendation of someone who was dishonest. Our study is designed to uncover this mystery. What we have here is a person who has made mistakes and needs a second chance."

Prepare a handout with the following questions. Ask students, in groups of four, to work quickly on the assigned task. (You may need to ask some groups to complete the same question or task as one or more other groups.)

1. Why does Jesus need to tell this story to His disciples? *(Perhaps He is indicating that planning and possessions can be important for the kingdom. The disciples could see wealth as evil, or they could become preoccupied with amassing wealth, as the Pharisees described in v. 14.)*

2. Recount the details of Jesus' parable (vv. 1-8). What surprises you most about this story?

3. Name one other parable where Jesus uses a dishonest character to teach a spiritual lesson. *(Luke 18:1-8.)* What is the lesson we should learn here? *(It is the refusal of the steward to be beaten down and his dogged determination to succeed.)*

4. What is the meaning of Jesus' words "faithful in the unrighteous mammon"? *(NIV-"trustworthy in handling worldly wealth")*

5. What does this passage teach about handling money?

6. What is the problem with trying to serve two masters?

Allow ten minutes for research, and then call for reports. Observe that some difficult questions are raised by this passage.

1. Jesus said, "They may receive you into everlasting habitations." But we cannot earn or buy our salvation. Explain this expression. *(Use notes in the commentary under verse 9.)*

2. Some say that in this passage Jesus condones greed and dishonesty. What is wrong with that view? *(See verses 10-13.)*

These difficult verses force us to determine whom we shall serve. Jesus leaves no "wiggle room" for His disciples. "Choose," He says.

Into Life

There are three areas that this parable challenges us to evaluate. The first is our trustworthy character. Use the lesson commentary material under verse 10 to challenge students to greater commitment in what they are presently doing.

Second, prepare a short checklist concerning the students' relationship with money. Ask each student to check the most appropriate statement.

__ God wants me to be trustworthy in my money management.

__ I must stop serving money and serve God.

__ I need to use my money to help others.

__ I need to make wise, honest business decisions.

Third, while money may have been a focus of this lesson, there are other "masters" that compete with our allegiance to God. Say, "On the back of the sheet used for the checklist, list some of the 'masters' you have served in the past. List some that tug for your allegiance now. Write one practical change you can make in your life so that you can serve God more completely."

Close with this prayer, "Lord, I cannot serve two masters. Help me to value what You value. Today, I choose You! Amen."

Let's Talk It Over

The questions on this page are designed to encourage review of the lesson Scriptures and to promote discussion of the lesson by the class. The answers provided are only discussion starters. Let your class talk it over from there.

1. The steward was called to "give an account" of his stewardship. How would you fare if called to "give an account" of your management of the resources God has made available? How does knowing that you will someday be asked for such an accounting affect the decisions and choices that you make each day?

Have you been a wise manager of money? Have your practices in the making, the spending, and the saving of money been selfish, or have they brought honor to God? Consider your use of time—have you redeemed good value out of every day God has given you? Do you claim uncommitted hours as "your time" to practice being a couch potato, or do you use those hours to improve yourself, to work on your relationship with God, or to bless others? How about your potential for influence? Have you capitalized on the opportunities to be an influence for good with your children, with your work associates, and with your neighbors? Do they know more about the will of God and the Christian life because of watching you?

Having the mindset of a manager will influence nearly every choice we make in life. Our personal welfare and desires are not our only reference point. We must consider God's desires and aim for the outcomes that deliver the greatest good.

2. The steward in Jesus' story is commended for his shrewd plan of action. What kind of actions characterize the wise Christian steward today?

It is wise to remember that an accounting must finally be given and that we should make choices thoughtfully, with regard to the will of God and the needs of those around us. It is also wise to use resources in a generous way toward others, since money does not last beyond this life, but relationships do. We are not to try to "buy friends," but our use of resources clearly demonstrates the kind of regard we have for other people. That kind of attitude is noticed and remembered, not only by those who benefit, but by our Lord as well.

3. What kind of behavior demonstrates a faithfulness that suggests that one can be trusted to be faithful with greater things?

Have you ever thought, "If I were rich, I would be generous to the church, to missionaries, and to those in need"? In this text Jesus calls our bluff! He claims that we would handle large amounts of wealth in the same way we have handled small amounts. If we have been careless, selfish, or stingy with what we have, there is no reason to think that we would suddenly be prudent and generous with more. If you are praying for greater material resources, greater opportunity, or greater responsibility, begin by demonstrating that you can be trusted with greater things by the wise use of what you already have.

4. What are the "true riches" to which Jesus refers (verse 11)? Why are they more valuable than "mammon"?

God has much more to bestow and distribute than material wealth. Jesus is probably referring to the truth of the gospel, the message of salvation, gifts of ministry, and opportunities for service and influence when He speaks of "true riches." These are of greater value than mammon because they pertain to that which is eternal. In the Sermon on the Mount Jesus warns, "Lay not up for yourselves treasures upon earth, where moth and rust doth corrupt, and where thieves break through and steal: but lay up for yourselves treasures in heaven . . . " (Matthew 6:19, 20).

5. What are some decisions or choices that you have made because you serve the Lord—and what different choices or decisions do you think you would have made if mammon were your god?

Students may name many choices, both major and minor. Some who have aptitude for lucrative careers may tell how they chose other paths that provided greater opportunities to serve God. No matter what career one chooses, he or she will face a variety of choices with regard to making, spending, giving, and saving money. If mammon is master, one may cast aside scruples of honesty and integrity in order to improve the bottom line. On the other hand, the one who serves God will sacrifice personal gain, when necessary, in order to follow the path of honesty. When mammon is god, then it is really self who rules, for one will make decisions based on what brings to him- or herself the greatest personal pleasure. The one who serves God will seek to advance His cause without regard to personal profit.

Going to Jerusalem

DEVOTIONAL READING: Matthew 10:32-39.

BACKGROUND SCRIPTURE: Luke 18:15—19:10.

PRINTED TEXT: Luke 18:31-34; 19:1-10.

Luke 18:31-34

31 Then he took unto him the twelve, and said unto them, Behold, we go up to Jerusalem, and all things that are written by the prophets concerning the Son of man shall be accomplished.

32 For he shall be delivered unto the Gentiles, and shall be mocked, and spitefully entreated, and spitted on:

33 And they shall scourge him, and put him to death; and the third day he shall rise again.

34 And they understood none of these things: and this saying was hid from them, neither knew they the things which were spoken.

Luke 19:1-10

1 And Jesus entered and passed through Jericho.

2 And, behold, there was a man named Zaccheus, which was the chief among the publicans, and he was rich.

3 And he sought to see Jesus who he was; and could not for the press, because he was little of stature.

4 And he ran before, and climbed up into a sycamore tree to see him; for he was to pass that way.

5 And when Jesus came to the place, he looked up, and saw him, and said unto him, Zaccheus, make haste, and come down; for today I must abide at thy house.

6 And he made haste, and came down, and received him joyfully.

7 And when they saw it, they all murmured, saying, That he was gone to be guest with a man that is a sinner.

8 And Zaccheus stood, and said unto the Lord; Behold, Lord, the half of my goods I give to the poor; and if I have taken any thing from any man by false accusation, I restore him fourfold.

9 And Jesus said unto him, This day is salvation come to this house, forasmuch as he also is a son of Abraham.

10 For the Son of man is come to seek and to save that which was lost.

Feb 4

GOLDEN TEXT: The Son of man is come to seek and to save that which was lost.—Luke 19:10.

Good News of Jesus
Unit 3: Cross and Resurrection
(Lessons 10-13)

Lesson Aims

After this lesson each student will be able to:

1. Tell how Jesus met and accepted Zaccheus.

2. Explain why Zaccheus is a good illustration of Jesus' mission "to seek and to save that which was lost."

3. Identify a "Zaccheus" among his or her own acquaintances and suggest one means of reaching this person with the gospel.

Lesson Outline

INTRODUCTION

  A. The Lazarus Man

  B. Lesson Background

I. THE MEANS ANNOUNCED (Luke 18:31-34)

  A. Delivered and Degraded (vv. 31, 32)

  B. Dead, Then Alive (v. 33)

  C. Deaf to Jesus' Words (v. 34)

II. THE METHOD APPLIED (Luke 19:1-7)

  A. Being Seen (vv. 1-4)

  B. Being Known (vv. 5, 6)

    Known by Name

  C. Being Judged (v. 7)

III. THE MISSION ACCOMPLISHED (Luke 19:8-10)

  A. Repentance (v. 8)

    The Execution of Restitution

  B. Redemption (v. 9)

  C. Reminder (v. 10)

CONCLUSION

  A. Keep Your Eye on the Ball

  B. Prayer

  C. Thought to Remember

Introduction

A. The Lazarus Man

In October of 1975 a man in our congregation proposed that we reach out to the less fortunate in our community in a very special way. He suggested that the families in our church sacrifice their usual Thanksgiving celebrations and prepare a Thanksgiving meal for people in a part of town that was far removed from our nice suburbs. The proposal was met with genuine enthusiasm, and we began making preparations.

When Thanksgiving came, we gathered in a storefront that we had rented for the occasion. We did all the cooking and set tables for seventy-five

people. We had distributed flyers for several days, and our efforts at publicity were very successful. Before long, we realized that we were going to have to buy more food and get more people to cook. Some stood as they ate their meals because there were not enough chairs.

After the meal, we conducted a Thanksgiving service with music and preaching. One man had come in to eat toward the end of the meal. He had not received as much to eat as some others, but he did not complain. It appeared that he had been drinking. His clothes were little more than rags. He clung tenaciously to his one valued possession—a heavy winter coat.

As we began our Thanksgiving service, the man wandered to a metal chair in the back row. As we began to sing one of the traditional Thanksgiving hymns, one of our men noticed that the man did not have a hymnal. He went over and sat down beside him. He moved his chair close to the man and wrapped his arm around the back of the man's chair so that they could share a hymnal. After the service the two men stood and talked for a long time. They were an odd sight—one was a pathetic alcoholic; the other was a highly respected educator.

Later I questioned my friend about his encounter with the man. When I asked about his name, my friend said that he thought he should be named, "Lazarus." I asked why, and he replied, "Because he stinketh." We laughed a little about that, but it was a laugh tinged with sadness. My friend had told the man how much Jesus loved him and wanted to free him from his bondage to sin. The man then began to cry and promised to think about the things he had been told. He also promised to read the Bible my friend had given him.

I wish I could report a happy ending to this story, but all I have is a question mark. We never heard from the man again. He had gladly received food for his body. Our prayer was that he also received food for his soul.

B. Lesson Background

Today's lesson begins our final unit of study from the Gospel of Luke. Appropriately it focuses on the death and resurrection of Jesus. Jesus had been trying to prepare His followers for the horrible ordeal that awaited Him in Jerusalem. (Luke records previous warnings in Luke 9:22, 44, 45; 12:50; 13:33; and 17:24, 25.) To this point, Jesus had met with little success in making them understand what was about to happen.

As Jesus embarks on this pivotal journey with the Twelve, He will try once again to prepare them for the events in Jerusalem. As the group passes through Jericho, He will also illustrate for

His followers, in an unforgettable manner, the true nature of His mission: "to seek and to save that which was lost" (Luke 19:10).

I. The Means Announced (Luke 18:31-34)

In the time of Jesus, Israel was waiting and longing for the Messiah to come. To many, the need for the Messiah had never been more urgent: the Romans had conquered much of the world, and Israel had not been spared their tyranny.

Jesus of Nazareth, while He appeared to do and to say much that seemed messianic, did not meet many of the popular expectations. He did not assemble an army or wield mighty weapons. He did not talk of overthrowing Rome or of delivering Israel. In fact, He later encouraged people to "render therefore unto Caesar the things which be Caesar's" (Luke 20:25). However, none of this was as astonishing as the fact that Jesus proposed to "deliver" His people and fulfill His Father's will by means of a cross.

A. Delivered and Degraded (vv. 31, 32)

31. Then he took unto him the twelve, and said unto them, Behold, we go up to Jerusalem, and all things that are written by the prophets concerning the Son of man shall be accomplished.

As previously noted, Jesus had made numerous attempts to warn His disciples of His impending death. Now, as Passover approached and they made their last trip to *Jerusalem*, He tried again to prepare them for the horrible events that lay ahead. Here He introduced a new element into His predictions of His death: it would accomplish what the *prophets* had *written . . . concerning the Son of man.* Thus, while Jesus' death would be tragic and shameful, it would be no accident. It would mark the fulfillment of a plan, revealed by God to His spokesmen of the past (1 Peter 1:10-12).

From our vantage point, many of these prophecies are obvious; they include Psalm 22:1-31; Isaiah 52:13—53:12; and Daniel 9:24-27. But as we shall see, the disciples did not yet grasp what Jesus was telling them. [See question #1, page 200.]

32. For he shall be delivered unto the Gentiles, and shall be mocked, and spitefully entreated, and spitted on.

Contrary to the popular opinion of the time, the Messiah was not going to be welcomed with open arms and treated as a V.I.P. He was going to be *delivered unto the Gentiles.* The people of His "own nation" (John 18:35) would hand Him over to the people whom they hated so deeply—the

Romans. That is how intense the religious leaders' hatred of Jesus had become.

We may become angry when we read about Jesus' unjust treatment at the hands of the Romans: *mocked, and spitefully entreated, and spitted on.* But let us never forget that our sin was the reason He endured that suffering. Such was the depth of His love for lost humanity. We must never take that love for granted.

B. Dead, Then Alive (v. 33)

33. And they shall scourge him, and put him to death; and the third day he shall rise again.

Now came the most unthinkable part of Jesus' description of His future treatment. He would be *put . . . to death.* Peter told his audience on the Day of Pentecost, "Jesus of Nazareth, . . . being delivered by the determinate counsel and foreknowledge of God, ye have taken, and by wicked hands have crucified and slain" (Acts 2:22, 23). Yes, wicked men had crucified Jesus; but it was according to God's plan. Jesus was a volunteer on a rescue mission. It is not entirely correct to say that men took the life of Jesus; He gave His life to save mankind (John 10:18).

Had Jesus spoken only of His death, His disciples would have been left without hope. But Jesus never leaves His followers without hope. He reminded His disciples that death would not triumph. Jesus would *rise again* on the *third day* after being crucified.

C. Deaf to Jesus' Words (v. 34)

34. And they understood none of these things: and this saying was hid from them, neither knew they the things which were spoken.

It is easy for us to look back on this scene and wonder how the disciples could have been so ignorant. However, let us remember that we have twenty centuries of hindsight that the disciples did not!

That the meaning of Jesus' words *was hid from them* does not imply that God was doing the hiding. The meaning was hidden from the disciples because of their own preconceived ideas and motives concerning the Messiah's mission. When Jesus first spoke plainly of being killed, Peter chastised Him for suggesting such foolishness (Matthew 16:21, 22). The disciples soon became

---

How to Say It

JERICHO. *Jair*-ih-co.
LAZARUS. *Laz*-uh-rus.
MESSIANIC. mess-ee-*an*-ick.
ZACCHEUS. Zack-*kee*-us.

preoccupied with planning their own places in the kingdom that they believed Jesus would rule (Matthew 18:1). Even on the night before He died, they argued about their position in Jesus' kingdom (Luke 22:24). Like many in their day, they rejected the idea of a Messiah who would suffer and die. That was not what they wanted to hear, so they simply refused to accept it. They apparently thought Jesus was using figurative language that they could not understand (cf. Mark 9:10).

We may look at the disciples' shortcomings with a critical eye, but are we not like them? Jesus spoke many difficult truths. Do we accept them all or just the ones we want to hear? Do we turn the other cheek? Do we pray for those who persecute us? Do we love our enemies? Do we love the lost? Do we invest in God's kingdom rather than in earthly wealth? We may think that the disciples were deaf to Jesus' words, but are we qualified to claim that we have been model followers of Jesus? [See question #2, page 200.]

II. The Method Applied
(Luke 19:1-7)

A. Being Seen (vv. 1-4)

1. And Jesus entered and passed through Jericho.

On their way to Jerusalem, *Jesus* and His disciples *passed through* the town of *Jericho*, approximately twelve miles northeast of Jerusalem. It was located on one of the lowest points in the Jordan valley, some eight hundred fifty feet below sea level. Jerusalem, by contrast, was situated in the Judean hills at about twenty-six hundred feet above sea level.

2. And, behold, there was a man named Zaccheus, which was the chief among the publicans, and he was rich.

Home Daily Bible Readings

Monday, Jan. 29—The Coming of the Kingdom (Luke 17:20-30)

Tuesday, Jan. 30—Keep On Praying (Luke 18:1-8)

Wednesday, Jan. 31—The Pharisee and the Publican (Luke 18:9-14)

Thursday, Feb. 1—Innocence and Humility (Luke 18:15-17)

Friday, Feb. 2—The Rich Ruler (Luke 18:18-30)

Saturday, Feb. 3—Join the Procession (Luke 18:31-43)

Sunday, Feb. 4—Jesus and Zaccheus (Luke 19:1-10)

Zaccheus collected taxes for the Romans. The Jews who performed that service for the Romans were hated for two reasons: first, they were considered traitors (since they were employed by the people who were considered Israel's oppressors); and second, they were usually wealthy because Rome cared little if they overcharged the people and kept some of the money for themselves. As *chief among the publicans*, Zaccheus was hardly the most popular man in Jericho; but being *rich* may have made up for not having a lot of friends. [See question #3, page 200.]

3. And he sought to see Jesus who he was; and could not for the press, because he was little of stature.

We do not know why Zaccheus was so interested in Jesus, but, like many others, he wanted *to see* Him. This was an important first step. Perhaps Zaccheus's riches had left him feeling spiritually empty. But a crowd had gathered, which posed a problem for Zaccheus. Because of his short *stature*, he could not see over the people.

4. And he ran before, and climbed up into a sycamore tree to see him; for he was to pass that way.

Zaccheus was not easily discouraged. He *ran* ahead to a spot where a *sycamore tree* stood beside the road, and he *climbed up into* the tree so that he could *see* Jesus as He passed by. When it comes to spiritual matters, how easily do you give up? If something takes time, effort, and sacrifice, do you bail out? Zaccheus is a great example of perseverance in the face of obstacles.

The tree that Zaccheus climbed (also called a sycamore-fig tree) was a wide, sturdy tree with low limbs that allowed even a short man like Zaccheus to climb into it. It was also well-known for the shade it provided from the heat. [See question #4, page 200.]

B. Being Known (vv. 5, 6)

5. And when Jesus came to the place, he looked up, and saw him, and said unto him, Zaccheus, make haste, and come down; for today I must abide at thy house.

Zaccheus caught Jesus' eye, and Jesus immediately responded to the obvious eagerness of this man in the tree. Jesus knew Zaccheus's name, but more important He knew what was in his heart. Jesus quickly and lovingly responded to the longing of Zaccheus by inviting Himself to Zaccheus's house.

It is God's desire to know us. He created us in order to have an intimate fellowship with us. Sin ruined that fellowship, but God wants it restored. That is the reason Jesus came. Is it not amazing to think that the Creator of the universe desires such intimacy with us?

KNOWN BY NAME

It has been said that nothing sounds sweeter to any man or woman than the sound of his or her own name. That is the reason motivational speakers urge their audiences to learn people's names. They even suggest certain techniques for remembering names, such as repeating a person's name while we are conversing with him or her. Perhaps we have heard a person say, "Your face is familiar, but I can't recall your name." Some people might be offended at hearing that.

A. B. "Happy" Chandler served as governor of Kentucky, as a United States senator, and also as the commissioner of baseball. It was said that, because of his phenomenal memory and a real effort he made to remember names, he never forgot the name of any person he met.

The fact that Jesus called Zaccheus by name tells us as much about Jesus' knowledge of and compassion for the individual. Jesus did not say, "Hey, you—you, up in the tree there—get down!" He called Zaccheus by name. Such are God's dealings with His creation. Recall His speaking by name to Abraham (Genesis 22:11), Moses (Exodus 3:4), and Samuel (1 Samuel 3:4-10).

It is not at all hard to believe that the very hairs of our head are numbered by such a God. He who created us in His image knows each one of us personally and individually, and He sent His Son to die for each one of us. We are never simply "John Doe" or "Jane Doe" to the Christ!

—R. C. S.

6. And he made haste, and came down, and received him joyfully.

Zaccheus must have been ecstatic to hear Jesus' words. Not only was he going to get to see Jesus, but he was going to have Him as a guest in his home! Such an enthusiastic response should cause us to ask ourselves just how welcome we have made Jesus feel in our own homes.

C. Being Judged (v. 7)

7. And when they saw it, they all murmured, saying, That he was gone to be guest with a man that is a sinner.

Everywhere Jesus went there was a critic, or so it seemed. Here in Jericho His intention to go home with Zaccheus confounded and disturbed the crowd that had gathered. Wasn't He aware of Zaccheus's position and reputation? How could He socialize with such a man? But Jesus was often criticized for making friends with the wrong people. Instead of cultivating the companionship of the pious, He associated with prostitutes, lepers, and tax collectors. Yes, the people were right about Zaccheus: he was indeed a *sinner*—but so was each of them.

In Jericho Jesus showed His disciples the nature of His mission. Despite the judgmental attitude of others, Jesus extended His love and grace to any who wanted to know Him. That invitation is still open: He still welcomes those who want to know Him and to learn about Him because He is so eager to know us and fellowship with us. Do we as Christ's people communicate that truth in our outreach? If not, why not?

III. The Mission Accomplished (Luke 19:8-10)

A. Repentance (v. 8)

8. And Zaccheus stood, and said unto the Lord; Behold, Lord, the half of my goods I give to the poor; and if I have taken any thing from any man by false accusation, I restore him fourfold.

We do not know what Jesus and Zaccheus discussed in Zaccheus's home. At some point, Zaccheus was apparently challenged to follow a new Master. He responded by making a radical pledge to *the Lord*: he would give *half* of all he had *to the poor* and offer a quadruple repayment to anyone he had cheated. This *fourfold* return went far beyond the requirements of the law of Moses, which stipulated that one restore twenty percent more (one-fifth) than he had wrongfully taken (Leviticus 6:1-5; Numbers 5:5-7).

It is easy to express repentance in words. To follow up with action is more difficult. True sorrow for sin manifests itself in a change of direction that is reflected in a desire to make amends for one's wrong actions wherever possible. Zaccheus went from being a taker to being a giver! Which category describes you? [See question #5, page 200.]

THE EXECUTION OF RESTITUTION

Wedding Nurseries is a well-known business in St. Petersburg, Florida. It has supplied ornamental plants to the city for a long time. As is the case with most plant nurseries, this one discovers from time to time that some of its plants have been stolen. In fact, one young man stole plants repeatedly and was never caught. But then he became a Christian. To demonstrate his repentance and his commitment to his new way of living, he brought back *three truckloads* of plants that he had stolen from the nursery. (He even brought back plants that he had raised from the plants he had stolen!) Clearly this man wanted to make restitution for what he had done in his past.

While we often talk about repentance, we seldom discuss restitution. Of course, in some situations restitution for past wrongdoing cannot be made. If we have ruined someone's reputation, we cannot easily make restitution. And there are cases where even an attempt at restitution would only make matters worse.

However, there are situations where it is possible to make restitution; and where that is possible, it needs to be done. A teenage girl told her minister that as a child she had stolen candy from a store. But that was in another city, and the store was no longer in business. The minister told her that her forgiveness did not depend on restitution, but that she might feel better if she did such an act. So he told her to buy some candy of equal value and give it to a poor child. She did this and felt immeasurably better.

Zaccheus did not buy his forgiveness, nor did this teenage girl. But an act of restitution can express how grateful we are to be forgiven and how much we love the One who has forgiven us.

—R. C. S.

B. Redemption (v. 9)

9. And Jesus said unto him, This day is salvation come to this house, forasmuch as he also is a son of Abraham.

Jesus knew the content of Zaccheus's heart and the genuineness of his repentance. He saw that Zaccheus's god of money had been dethroned. Faith in earthly riches had been replaced by faith in the living God. It is by faith that we come to God (Hebrews 11:6). It is by faith that we become children of Abraham (Romans 4:13-16; Galatians 3:29). Zaccheus, a descendant of Abraham in the flesh, was now also a *son of Abraham* by faith.

C. Reminder (v. 10)

10. For the Son of man is come to seek and to save that which was lost.

Son of man was Jesus' most commonly used title for Himself. (In the Gospels it is never used by anyone except Jesus.) Its messianic significance is clear from its use in Daniel 7:13, 14. Here the Son of man responded to the faith of Zaccheus by proclaiming that His mission was *to*

Visual for
lesson 10

The son of man is come to seek and to save that which was lost.
Luke 19:10

Today's lesson visual illustrates verse 10 of our Scripture text. Discuss how we today can participate in seeking and saving the lost.

seek and to save that which was lost—in other words, people just like Zaccheus.

We have seen in a previous lesson (lesson 8) how Jesus used parables to illustrate God's desire to reclaim that which was lost (Luke 15). Zaccheus provided a personal and dramatic illustration of this desire. As Jesus approached Jerusalem (and therefore Calvary), He wanted to impress on His disciples what His ministry was all about. He had come to change people's lives by bringing them from darkness to light, from slavery to freedom, from sin to salvation. In Zaccheus His followers could see a living example of "mission accomplished."

Conclusion

Jesus came from Heaven to earth on a rescue mission. He came to reunite sinners with a perfect, holy God by means of His atoning death. Jesus' love for sinners is illustrated by His compassion for Zaccheus. Man's greatest need is still the restoration of fellowship with God, but we can never accomplish that ourselves. God, in love and mercy, reached out and, in Christ, did for us what we could not do for ourselves.

A. Keep Your Eye on the Ball

Anyone who has played baseball knows that to be a successful batter, you must keep your eye on the ball. Sometimes in the church we get sidetracked. We take our eyes off the ball. The gospel is about salvation. That is its focus.

The church can put its time, energy, and financial resources into many good causes. We can work to help the poor. We can work to stop abortion. We can try to help young people stop the violence in their schools and neighborhoods. All of those are good things to do. But the church must never get so busy doing good things that it forgets the main thing—the purpose for which Jesus came and the mission He left to His followers: "to seek and to save that which was lost."

B. Prayer

Father, help us to see the lost through Your eyes. Remind us that we once were separated from You, and may this motivate us to reach out to the least and the last and the lost. We thank You for sending Jesus on His marvelous rescue mission. May His love be in our hearts and His truth be on our lips as we seek to be lights in a dark world. In Jesus' name. Amen.

C. Thought to Remember

God's love for the lost is beyond our ability to understand. But we know it is real because of Jesus.

Learning by Doing

This page contains an alternate lesson plan emphasizing learning activities.
Classes desiring such student involvement will find these suggestions helpful.

Learning Goals

After this lesson each student will be able to:

1. Tell how Jesus met and accepted Zaccheus.

2. Explain why Zaccheus is a good illustration of Jesus' mission "to seek and to save that which was lost."

3. Identify a "Zaccheus" among his or her own acquaintances and suggest one means of reaching this person with the gospel.

Into the Lesson

To begin the class, distribute copies of a handout containing the following information:

"In a rural midwestern community, a toddler has fallen down a newly dug well, twenty feet deep. The well is only two feet wide—too narrow for an adult to climb down. The child is wedged in head first, near the bottom of the well, too far down to reach by hand through the opening. Rescuers fear that pulling the child out with a rope will seriously hurt him. Widening the well could cause a mud slide that would bury him. How can they rescue him?"

Ask students to suggest ways to save the child, writing their advice on a chalkboard. When they finish making suggestions, tell them the child was actually rescued by digging a shaft beside the well, then tunneling beneath him. Then tell your class that this lesson will provide an opportunity to discuss strategies for saving the lost.

Into the Word

Choose three students to read aloud today's text: Luke 18:31-34; 19:1-10. One will be the narrator, reading most of the verses. Another will read the words of Jesus in 18:31-33; 19:5, 9, 10; a third will read Zaccheus's words in 19:8.

Next, divide your class into an equal number of groups composed of four to six students per group. Half of your groups will do Study A, below. The other half will do Study B. After they finish their studies, have each group report its findings to the class.

Study A: Compare Luke 18:31-34 with Luke 5:35; 9:22, 44, 45; 12:49, 50; 13:32, 33; 17:22-25. Then answer the questions below.

1. How many times did Jesus warn His disciples that He had to die?

2. How did the disciples react to His predictions? Why didn't the disciples understand Jesus' warnings?

3. Luke 18:34 says the meaning of Jesus' explanation was hidden from the disciples. What or who was responsible for hiding the truth?

4. In 1 Corinthians 15:3-8, Paul lists what he calls the matters of "first importance" for the Christian. Compare his listing with Luke 18:31-33. Why are these truths so important?

Study B: Provide copies of the chart below (without the material that appears in parentheses). Give the class the following instructions: "Read Luke 19:1-10 and complete this chart, indicating how Zaccheus and the crowd in the story reacted to Jesus. Answer the discussion questions that follow."

Verses	What Jesus Did	Zaccheus's Response	The Crowd's Response
1-4	(Came to Jericho)	(Eager to see Jesus)	(Flocked to see Jesus)
5-7	(Asked to stay with Zaccheus)	(Received Jesus joyfully)	(Murmured against Jesus)
8-10	(Taught and forgave him)	(Repented and made amends)	(No reaction)

1. Why was there such a difference between the crowd's reaction to Jesus and Zaccheus's reaction?

2. Summarize Jesus' techniques for evangelizing Zaccheus. Which of them can we use today?

Into Life

Discuss the following scenarios with your class. If time is short, divide the class into three groups and give one scenario to each group. The groups can summarize their findings for the class.

1. Steve has always been a follower. He is a kind-hearted person, but he has allowed bad friends to get him into trouble with drugs and alcohol. What can be done to lead him to Christ?

2. Jennifer has a drive to succeed in business. She has devoted her life to success. Everything else, including family, friends, and God, is secondary. What strategy would you develop to present the gospel to her?

3. Michael is an intellectual. His college studies in science and philosophy have convinced him that God doesn't exist. How would you penetrate his wall of unbelief?

To close the study, urge each student to pick some unsaved person—a Zaccheus—to reach with the gospel and to develop a strategy for leading that person to Christ.

Let's Talk It Over

The questions on this page are designed to encourage review of the lesson Scriptures and to promote discussion of the lesson by the class. The answers provided are only discussion starters. Let your class talk it over from there.

1. Jesus knew that going to Jerusalem would result in suffering and death for Him, but still He went there. The suffering that awaited Him was a necessary part of God's plan for our redemption. What about us? Should we walk into situations we know will result in confrontation? How do we know when to stand against opposition and when to walk away?

While no one else need ever face persecution or death for the same reason as Jesus did, we are called to "follow his steps" (1 Peter 2:21). Our suffering does not secure salvation, either for ourselves or for others, but it does demonstrate our faithfulness. Such faithfulness is required by our Lord, even "to the point of death" (Revelation 2:10, *New International Version*). Whenever that faithfulness is challenged, we must stand firm, in spite of the danger that may come to us. On the other hand, there are many occasions when facing danger and opposition will accomplish no real purpose, and avoiding the danger becomes the prudent course of action. The apostle Paul left Damascus in a basket to escape the Jews who were plotting against him (Acts 9:23-25), but he went to Jerusalem ready to face imprisonment and death when he believed that such a course of action was the Lord's will (Acts 21:10-14).

2. From our vantage point, it seems preposterous that the disciples could misunderstand what Jesus was telling them. But the disciples pictured Jesus reigning over a kingdom in which they would enjoy privileged positions of power. This concept was so firmly planted in their minds that they literally could not conceive of Jesus' being put to death in Jerusalem. What truths have some people today "misunderstood" because the truth is contrary to their preferred ideas?

There are so many such ideas that a brief list without much explanation is all there is room for here. Some people have dismissed the reality of the devil or of Hell because they cannot imagine such things as consistent with a "God of love." Humanism has so dominated western education that many people seem unable to believe in the Biblical account of creation. Jesus' demand to take up one's cross to follow Him is blurred by the "health and wealth" gospel preached by some so-called evangelists. How many more "misunderstandings" can your students suggest?

3. Zaccheus was rich, but his wealth did not bring him contentment. In what do people today wrongly seek to find contentment? How can we help them to find true joy in Jesus?

Money still has the same allure as it did in Jesus' day; many pursue it above all else. Others believe education or political power holds the promise of a better world. We know that only Jesus can bring lasting fulfillment to life. To communicate that truth, Christians must demonstrate by their behavior that they believe it. Too often, Christians are running after the same things that the world seeks. We must live our faith and build bridges of friendships to those who do not know the Lord. Then we will find opportunities to voice our faith in a context in which we can be heard.

4. How can we tell who is interested in the gospel today when nobody is climbing trees to see Jesus? How do we know how to target our message?

Of course, the gospel is for all, and we want to proclaim the gospel to everyone we can. If we have an opportunity to share our faith, we should do so—to anyone. There are times, however, when we must choose. Taking one course of action will, of necessity, eliminate other possible courses. As we plan our outreach, we must consider the needs of potential hearers and which needs we are equipped to meet. Try to get specific about the resources on hand at your church and the people available, and develop a plan that uses all of them to the best advantage.

5. Being in the company of Jesus had a profound effect upon Zaccheus. How could you increase the power of your example and your witness to the lost people you meet?

~~One cannot give away what he does not have.~~ If we want to attract people to the personal peace that comes from knowing Christ, we must be living examples of that peace. If we are just as riddled with guilt and just as anxious about life as unbelievers, what reason is there for them to seek our Lord? The more we become products of God's transforming grace, the more that we display the fruit of the Spirit (love, joy, peace, . . .), the more interest others will have in hearing about our faith. What kind of advertisement does your life provide for the value of Christianity?

One Who Serves

DEVOTIONAL READING: Mark 10:35-45.

BACKGROUND SCRIPTURE: Luke 22:1-30.

PRINTED TEXT: Luke 22:14-30.

Luke 22:14-30

14 And when the hour was come, he sat down, and the twelve apostles with him.

15 And he said unto them, With desire I have desired to eat this passover with you before I suffer:

16 For I say unto you, I will not any more eat thereof, until it be fulfilled in the kingdom of God.

17 And he took the cup, and gave thanks, and said, Take this, and divide it among yourselves:

18 For I say unto you, I will not drink of the fruit of the vine, until the kingdom of God shall come.

19 And he took bread, and gave thanks, and brake it, and gave unto them, saying, This is my body which is given for you: this do in remembrance of me.

20 Likewise also the cup after supper, saying, This cup is the new testament in my blood, which is shed for you.

21 But, behold, the hand of him that betrayeth me is with me on the table.

22 And truly the Son of man goeth, as it was determined: but woe unto that man by whom he is betrayed!

23 And they began to inquire among themselves, which of them it was that should do this thing.

24 And there was also a strife among them, which of them should be accounted the greatest.

25 And he said unto them, The kings of the Gentiles exercise lordship over them; and they that exercise authority upon them are called benefactors.

26 But ye shall not be so: but he that is greatest among you, let him be as the younger; and he that is chief, as he that doth serve.

27 For whether is greater, he that sitteth at meat, or he that serveth? is not he that sitteth at meat? but I am among you as he that serveth.

28 Ye are they which have continued with me in my temptations.

29 And I appoint unto you a kingdom, as my Father hath appointed unto me;

30 That ye may eat and drink at my table in my kingdom, and sit on thrones judging the twelve tribes of Israel.

**Feb
11**

GOLDEN TEXT: He that is greatest among you, let him be as the younger;
and he that is chief, as he that doth serve.—Luke 22:26.

Good News of Jesus
Unit 3: Cross and Resurrection
(Lessons 10-13)

Lesson Aims

After this lesson each student will be able to:

1. Give the details surrounding Jesus' institution of the Lord's Supper.

2. Contrast the attitude required for a proper observance of the Lord's Supper with the attitude that the disciples displayed on this occasion.

3. Write a Communion meditation that incorporates Jesus' call to humility in discipleship.

Lesson Outline

INTRODUCTION
    A. "I Am the Greatest"
    B. Lesson Background
  I. THE PASSOVER (Luke 22:14-20)
    A. Eagerness Expressed (vv. 14-16)
    The Loving Cup
    B. Old Meal Observed (vv. 17, 18)
    C. New Meal Instituted (vv. 19, 20)
 II. THE BETRAYER (Luke 22:21-23)
    A. Warning (v. 21)
    B. Woe (v. 22)
    C. Worry (v. 23)
III. THE DISPUTE (Luke 22:24-30)
    A. Confusion (v. 24)
    B. Comparison (v. 25)
    C. Challenge (vv. 26, 27)
    Here to Help
    D. Commendation (vv. 28-30)
CONCLUSION
    A. True Greatness
    B. Prayer
    C. Thought to Remember

Introduction

A. "I Am the Greatest"

The young boxer from Louisville, Kentucky, had lightning quick hands and feet. He was equally quick with a quote or a quip. When he entered the ranks of professional boxing and began to make his mark, he soon became associated with a slogan that is readily recalled nearly forty years later: "I am the greatest!" While few could argue with Cassius Clay (later Muhammad Ali) in his assessment of his boxing skills, many were offended by such brashness. In those days, humility was a quality that most people admired.

Today it is the lack of humility that seems to be more highly valued. Humility is equated with weakness or the lack of "self-esteem." Elevation of self to a place above others (at any cost) is considered part of getting ahead in the world. In the days when beepers were in frequent use, I remember being told by one man (seeking to impress me with his status) that he was not a person to be beeped. He was the one to do the beeping!

Jesus, the Creator of the universe, the King of kings and Lord of lords, never spoke a word of self-adulation. He refused to be governed by the world's standard of greatness. He knew that greatness in God's eyes comes through humble service. And He gave His disciples (and us) a powerful example to follow!

B. Lesson Background

Jesus and His disciples had come to Jerusalem for the Passover feast. His enemies had anticipated His arrival for this occasion. They had spent months scheming to kill Jesus and thought that the Passover might provide the opportunity they desired. They also knew, however, that Jesus was a very popular figure with vast numbers of people (Luke 22:2). He had been teaching in the temple, where many gathered to hear Him speak (Luke 21:37, 38). The religious leaders were fearful of the turmoil that could erupt if the populace became aware of their intentions concerning Jesus.

None of this caught Jesus by surprise. He knew what was being planned. He had come to Jerusalem to offer Himself as a sacrifice for the sins of the world. Recall the words of Luke 9:51, which tells us that "when the time was come that he should be received up, he steadfastly set his face to go to Jerusalem." He alone recognized the eternal significance of the events that were about to unfold in Jerusalem.

By the time of the events recorded in today's printed text, preparations already had been made for the Passover meal. A place had been secured. A lamb had been slain. All other necessary arrangements had been made. Despite the numerous warnings of Jesus, His disciples did not seem to appreciate the gravity of this observance of the Passover, as we shall see.

In studying the text of this week's lesson, the student should be aware that Luke's account of events differs somewhat from that of the other Gospel writers. He includes material that other writers omit and omits information that others include. (Similar variations can be seen when comparing the records of almost any incident in the life of Christ.) When all four Gospels are harmonized, the student of the Bible is presented with a complete picture of the events that transpired on this occasion. Whatever differences are present do not weaken or destroy the integrity of any of the Gospel accounts. The differences most difficult to harmonize concern the arrangement of the material. In these we are forced to conclude that not all the accounts are given in chronological order. While that may seem strange in our time-bound culture, topical or other arrangements of historical information were common in the first century.

I. The Passover
(Luke 22:14-20)

A. Eagerness Expressed (vv. 14-16)

14. And when the hour was come, he sat down, and the twelve apostles with him.

Jesus *sat down* with *the twelve apostles* to observe the Passover. Passover marked the remembrance of God's salvation of His people on that night when all the firstborn in Egypt were killed (Exodus 11:4—12:30). Even though this feast of remembrance had been celebrated for centuries, it still held great significance in teaching the young and refreshing the memory of the old. The Jews were not to forget what God had done in delivering their ancestors from cruel bondage in Egypt.

While this feast was usually observed in families, Jesus chose to observe it with the people closest to Him.

15. And he said unto them, With desire I have desired to eat this passover with you before I suffer.

In this verse we are given a glimpse into the heart of Jesus. The phrase *with desire I have desired* may be rendered, "I greatly, or eagerly, desire." Jesus was always eager to do what God had asked His people to do. But this night was special, and Jesus had been looking forward to it with anticipation. [See question #1, page 208.]

For Jesus, *this passover* was meaningful, not only as a means of looking back but also as a way of looking ahead. He was eating this meal *before* He would endure His suffering on behalf of those enslaved to sin, in order to "deliver them, who through fear of death were all their lifetime subject to bondage" (Hebrews 2:15).

Jesus was also eager to be *with* those whom He loved. Jesus had chosen these twelve men, had invested much of His life in them, and had come to love them in spite of their many weaknesses. As John notes, "Having loved his own which were in the world, he loved them unto the end" (John 13:1). The work of His kingdom would be placed in their hands. Even though they had failed Him at times and would desert Him this very night, we should not forget that He wanted to be with them at this Passover.

THE LOVING CUP

In medieval times, on the twelfth night after Christmas, people gathered to celebrate the conclusion of the Christmas season. During the meal, all who were present drank from a two-handled cup. Since this cup was intended to be shared, it came to be known as a "loving cup."

Today a "loving cup" refers to a trophy that one receives after winning a contest. But on the night *before* the cross, at the *beginning* of His anguish over the sins of the world, Jesus sat down to share a cup with His closest followers. It would be proper to refer to this as a "loving cup" because Jesus loved these men so deeply (John 13:1). He had looked forward "with desire" to the Passover that He celebrated with them (Luke 22:15).

Today the Communion cup is always a shared cup. This is true even if a church uses individual cups, which is the practice in most congregations. Though each of the people who partakes has a cup, each cup is shared with Christ. And each cup is a loving cup, pledging our love for Christ and for His people even as we celebrate His love for us. It is no wonder that John Brokhoff entitled his book about Communion, "A Table for Lovers." At the Lord's table, we renew our love for Jesus and for one another.   —R. C. S.

16. For I say unto you, I will not any more eat thereof, until it be fulfilled in the kingdom of God.

Jesus knew that this was the last Passover meal that would ever be necessary. There was one final Passover Lamb to be slain, and He was "the Lamb of God, which taketh away the sin of the world" (John 1:29; cf. 1 Corinthians 5:7). Once He had been slain, there would be no more need for animal sacrifices (Hebrews 9:11-15).

Throughout His ministry Jesus had spoken of the *kingdom of God*, or kingdom of Heaven (Matthew 4:17; Mark 1:14, 15). Most of His listeners did not understand what He meant by these terms. They expected the Messiah to sit on a physical throne and restore the political nation of Israel to its past glory. But Jesus knew the true nature of the kingdom of God: it is radically different from all earthly kingdoms. Jesus is its King, and His throne is within the hearts of those who acknowledge His kingship. The kingdom could not be inaugurated until after Jesus' death and resurrection.

Jesus' statement that He would *not any more eat thereof, until it be fulfilled in the kingdom* is taken by some to mean that He will not share in this feast again until the "marriage supper of the Lamb" in the heavenly kingdom (Revelation 19:9). Others believe that Jesus was referring to the spiritual union that Christians enjoy with Him whenever they celebrate the Lord's Supper.

If that is so, then this union was experienced just a few weeks later when the church began on the Day of Pentecost and began to observe the "breaking of bread" (Acts 2:42). Perhaps one should accept a combination of these views: the spiritual union here on earth will be consummated by the visible presence of Jesus in Heaven.

B. Old Meal Observed (vv. 17, 18)

17. And he took the cup, and gave thanks, and said, Take this, and divide it among yourselves.

The fact that Luke mentions another cup later in connection with the "new testament" (verse 20) indicates that the *cup* that Jesus *took* at this point was one of the cups included in the Passover observance. In a traditional Passover meal, there were four occasions when the participants would drink a cup of the fruit of the vine. Each cup had a distinctive theme, often accompanied by prescribed words, songs, and prayers. The first two cups were taken prior to the main meal, and the latter two cups were taken after the meal. The third cup was called the Cup of Redemption, which celebrated Israel's redemption from bondage in Egypt.

This third cup may have been the cup that Jesus now told His disciples to *divide* among themselves. He would then have used the fourth and final cup to institute a new kind of memorial to a new kind of redemption. However, others believe that the cup of this verse was the final cup and that the cup of verse 20 was a different cup to mark a new and different memorial.

18. For I say unto you, I will not drink of the fruit of the vine, until the kingdom of God shall come.

Jesus' promise that He would *not drink . . . until the kingdom of God shall come* is similar to His promise about eating, explained under verse 16.

C. New Meal Instituted (vv. 19, 20)

19. And he took bread, and gave thanks, and brake it, and gave unto them, saying, This is my body which is given for you: this do in remembrance of me.

The coming of the kingdom was contingent on the willingness of the King of kings to become the sacrificial Lamb of God. Jesus came to earth to take that responsibility upon Himself. He came to give Himself willingly as an atoning sacrifice for the sins of all humanity (1 John 2:2).

This sacrifice was what Jesus proceeded to call attention to by instituting a new kind of memorial feast. He *took bread* (the unleavened bread that remained from the Passover observance), once again *gave thanks*, broke it, and *gave* it to His disciples. He stated that the bread was His *body, given* for them. Previously Jesus' followers had heard Him

refer to Himself as the "bread of life" (John 6:48). They had heard Him tell a great crowd that they should eat His flesh (John 6:53-58). Although the disciples probably did not grasp the true significance of Jesus' words, they knew that He was speaking metaphorically and not advocating cannibalism. What they did not realize was how quickly that body would be taken from them and be torn and broken—at the cross.

Jesus has instructed His followers to remember Him by means of breaking bread and drinking of the fruit of the vine (cf. 1 Corinthians 11:23-25). This act is not magical or mystical. It simply uses common—yet significant—items to remind us of Jesus and His love. [See question #2, page 208.]

20. Likewise also the cup after supper, saying, This cup is the new testament in my blood, which is shed for you.

Jesus then gave a *cup* to His disciples, instructing them to use it to remember His *blood*, which He would *shed* for them. That cup and its contents represented a *new testament*, or covenant—a new stage in God's dealings with humanity. People would no longer anticipate the coming of the Messiah. They would look back on His coming as a historical event and celebrate His death. The blood of Jesus, having the power to cleanse from sin (1 John 1:7), must not be forgotten. The fruit of the vine forever serves as an apt reminder. [See question #3, page 208.]

II. The Betrayer
(Luke 22:21-23)

A. Warning (v. 21)

21. But, behold, the hand of him that betrayeth me is with me on the table.

Jesus knew of Judas's treachery. At this point He told the disciples that one of them would betray Him; but in the tension and confusion of the hour, the disciples did not discern the identity of the schemer. Imagine the sorrow in Jesus' heart as He spoke of how one who was eating with Him at that moment would soon betray Him!

Here is where it is apparent that Luke's account of the events in the upper room is not chronological. The other Gospels give the indication that Judas was not present at the institution of the Lord's Supper (in other words, that the act of identifying the betrayer occurred before the institution of the Supper). It seems that Luke's record is topical and that he placed the institution of the Supper at the beginning for emphasis.

B. Woe (v. 22)

22. And truly the Son of man goeth, as it was determined: but woe unto that man by whom he is betrayed!

Jesus knew that His death was part of a plan set in place by His Father and that this plan was coming to fruition. But He also made it clear that this did not excuse the actions of His betrayer. Betraying the *Son of man* was not an act to be taken lightly.

C. Worry (v. 23)

23. And they began to inquire among themselves, which of them it was that should do this thing.

Immediately the disciples expressed their dismay over Jesus' unexpected announcement. None of them believed himself capable of such a hideous act. Judas, of course, knew he was "that man" (v. 22), though none of the other disciples realized the significance of his sudden departure (John 13:21-30). [See question #4, page 208.]

III. The Dispute (Luke 22:24-30)

A. Confusion (v. 24)

24. And there was also a strife among them, which of them should be accounted the greatest.

Even now, with the cross just hours away, Jesus' disciples still had their heads in the clouds. They were still being influenced by the notion that He was going to overthrow the Romans, sit on a throne in Jerusalem, and rule the nation of Israel. They, His loyal followers, would have positions of power and prestige in His kingdom. Because they were confused about the nature of Jesus' kingdom, they were confused also about the path to greatness in that kingdom.

B. Comparison (v. 25)

25. And he said unto them, The kings of the Gentiles exercise lordship over them; and they that exercise authority upon them are called benefactors.

Jesus tried to show the disciples a different way to greatness by contrasting His way with the world's concept of greatness. The disciples knew how the *Gentiles* (or pagan peoples) became powerful: they exercised authority over their subjects by forcing them into submission. Sometimes they tried to compliment themselves for their treatment of their subjects by referring to themselves as *benefactors* of the poor and underprivileged. Such self-promoting leadership was the very type exhibited by the disciples as they bickered over who was the greatest.

C. Challenge (vv. 26, 27)

26. But ye shall not be so: but he that is greatest among you, let him be as the younger; and he that is chief, as he that doth serve.

Jesus rejected the worldly path to greatness and instructed the disciples in a better, godly way. In the Jewish home, the oldest son inherited a larger portion of the father's estate than any of the *younger* children. The disciples were all acting like oldest sons, each claiming that he should have the most prominent position in Jesus' kingdom. Jesus told them to begin thinking like youngest sons—those considered worthy of the least honor. If they truly wanted to sit in *chief* positions, they must be willing to *serve*. That is what greatness means in Jesus' kingdom! [See question #5, page 208.]

27. For whether is greater, he that sitteth at meat, or he that serveth? is not he that sitteth at meat? but I am among you as he that serveth.

Here Jesus used another illustration to make His point about greatness. Most people consider the master of the house more important than the one who serves him his meals. Such thinking is not the rule in Jesus' kingdom. There the virtue is in serving, not in being served. Jesus Himself lived by this principle: *I am among you as he that serveth*. John tells how Jesus, on this night, washed the feet of His disciples (John 13:1-15). And in just a few hours He would "give his life a ransom for many" (Matthew 20:28) in the ultimate act of service.

HERE TO HELP

Near the end of the nineteenth century a New York newspaperman named Jacob Riis (*Rees*) wrote a book entitled *How the Other Half Lives*. It described the deplorable conditions in the slums of New York City, including the vice and crime that occurred there. The book was read by future U.S. President Theodore Roosevelt, who went immediately to the newspaper office. When he found out that Riis was not in his office, Roosevelt

Home Daily Bible Readings

Monday, Feb. 5—The Plot to Kill Jesus (Luke 22:1-6)

Tuesday, Feb. 6—The Preparation of the Passover (Luke 22:7-13)

Wednesday, Feb. 7—The Feast of Unleavened Bread (Exodus 12:14-20)

Thursday, Feb. 8—The Institution of the Lord's Supper (Luke 22:14-23)

Friday, Feb. 9—Jesus Foretells His Betrayer (John 13:18-30)

Saturday, Feb. 10—The Dispute About Greatness (Luke 22:24-30)

Sunday, Feb. 11—The Request of James and John (Mark 10:35-45)

left a note: "I have read your book, and I have come to help."

It is easy to complain about conditions in society, in the world at large, or in our own city or community. And there are plenty of people who will agree with our pessimistic assessment. But finding the people who are willing to work personally for a better world or a better community is another matter. Only a few are willing to say, "I have come to help."

Jesus did not come to our world simply to point a finger and cite all the wrongs we had done. He came to help. He told His disciples, "I am among you as he that serveth." Although Luke does not mention it, by this time in the evening Jesus probably had washed His disciples' feet. It was an act of service that stunned the disciples, but it was only a precursor to His greatest act of service—His death on the cross.

Jesus did more than just lecture about service: He truly *served*. He practiced what He preached.

—R. C. S.

D. Commendation (vv. 28-30)

28. Ye are they which have continued with me in my temptations.

Jesus spoke of the disciples' devotion to Him during His *temptations*, or trials. He knew that they would soon disappoint Him by fleeing from the garden, but in this moment He spoke in gentle, affectionate terms of appreciation.

29. And I appoint unto you a kingdom, as my Father hath appointed unto me.

The disciples would not sit on earthly thrones, wear crowns, or hold scepters. Instead, they would have the wonderful privilege of being the first to proclaim the story of Jesus and His glorious *kingdom*. They would tell of the life, death, and resurrection of the King of kings. Yes, they would be great, but on Jesus' terms, not theirs.

30. That ye may eat and drink at my table in my kingdom, and sit on thrones judging the twelve tribes of Israel.

Visual for lesson 11

Borrowing an image from John 13, today's visual suggests one means by which Jesus might have ended the disciples' dispute about greatness.

Jesus' commendation of His disciples concluded with a stirring pronouncement. They would be privileged to *eat and drink* with Him in His *kingdom* as He had promised earlier (vv. 16, 18). In addition, they would rule *Israel* in a way they had never imagined. By the preaching of the gospel of Christ, these same men who had gathered with Jesus at this Passover celebration would set a standard by which all people—both Jews (those of Israel) and Gentiles—will be judged. They, through the proclamation of the gospel, would open the doors to the kingdom of Heaven (Matthew 16:18, 19). That took place for the first time on the Day of Pentecost, and it continues today through the preaching of the apostolic message by the church.

Conclusion

A. True Greatness

What makes a person great? In our culture we often equate greatness with being a celebrity. We idolize sports figures and entertainers. Even in the church we can fall into this trap. Everyone knows who the soloist was in the morning worship. How many people know who stayed in the nursery and changed diapers?

No one would deny that we live in a me-first, blow-your-own-horn, climb-over-others-to-get-to-the-top world. Humility is scoffed at; arrogance is admired. Heroic figures are those who tell us how great they are rather than prove it by their lives. Style is more important than substance. Public relations is the name of the game.

John tells us of another event that happened in the upper room. During the evening, Jesus took a towel and a basin of water and performed the most menial task of a household servant. He washed the feet of the disciples (John 13:4, 5). Think of it: the most powerful person ever to walk on earth was kneeling to wash the dirty feet that would soon carry away the men who would desert Him when He needed them most. Such is the nature of true greatness.

B. Prayer

Father, help us to reject the standards of the world and to seek to be great in Your eyes. Help us to remember Jesus' death when we observe the Lord's Supper, and help us to remember His life and example when we get too wrapped up in becoming great in the eyes of men. Humble us, and remind us how to attain greatness in Your kingdom. Thank You for loving us. We ask all things in the name of our King. Amen.

C. Thought to Remember

True greatness is attained by following Jesus.

Learning by Doing

This page contains an alternate lesson plan emphasizing learning activities.
Classes desiring such student involvement will find these suggestions helpful.

Learning Goals

After this lesson students should be able to:

1. Give the details surrounding Jesus' institution of the Lord's Supper.

2. Contrast the attitude required for a proper observance of the Lord's Supper with the attitude that the disciples displayed on this occasion.

3. Write a Communion meditation that incorporates Jesus' call to humility in discipleship.

Into the Lesson

Distribute copies of the following agree-disagree exercise, and ask your students to circle the response that best reflects their opinion for each statement.

1. The Lord's Supper is primarily a remembrance of Christ's death. Agree or disagree?

2. The Lord's Supper reminds us to be like Christ in our daily lives. Agree or disagree?

3. A servant's attitude is necessary to observe the Lord's Supper properly. Agree or disagree?

4. Few Christians exhibit a proper attitude when they observe the Lord's Supper. Agree or disagree?

5. It is impossible for a person to take the Lord's Supper properly if he is conceited or hates another person. Agree or disagree?

Discuss your students' answers briefly, noting their views on each statement. Then tell your class that today's lesson will deal with the attitude required to observe the Lord's Supper properly.

Into the Word

Hand out copies of the matching test below. Instruct your students to match each event with its corresponding Scripture reference by looking up the references in the Bible. Correct answers are indicated in parentheses.

___ 1. Peter and John prepare an upper room and the Passover meal. (c)

___ 2. Jesus and the Twelve observe Passover. (f)

___ 3. Jesus washes the disciples' feet. (b)

___ 4. The traitor is identified. (d)

___ 5. The disciples argue over greatness. (g)

___ 6. Jesus predicts Peter's denial. (e)

___ 7. Jesus institutes the Lord's Supper. (a)

a. Luke 22:17-20   e. Luke 22:31-34
b. John 13:1-20   f. Luke 22:14-16
c. Luke 22:7-13   g. Luke 22:24-30
d. Luke 22:21-23

When your students complete the test, review the correct answers. As you do, you will want to discuss the circumstances and chronology of the events (they are listed in chronological order) surrounding the inauguration of the Lord's Supper. Discuss the following questions.

1. Luke indicates that Jesus made extensive preparations for this special Passover meal. How should we prepare to take the Lord's Supper? *(Focus on preparing one's heart.)*

2. Paul calls Jesus "our Passover" (1 Corinthians 5:7). How was this true? What was the purpose of His suffering? *(Jesus delivered us from bondage to sin, as God delivered the Israelites from Egyptian bondage at the first Passover.)*

3. What lesson did Jesus teach by washing the disciples' feet? *(Humility.)* Who usually performed such a task? (See 1 Samuel 25:41.) *(The lowest servant.)* What does that tell us about the nature of leadership in God's kingdom? *(Leadership is best exercised through service.)*

4. How could the disciples argue over greatness after Jesus washed their feet and after He announced that one of them was a traitor? Contrast their attitudes with Jesus'.

5. What is the purpose of the Lord's Supper? *(Jesus said it was to be done in remembrance of Him, v. 19. It is an expression of love and gratitude to Him and an expression of unity with His body.)*

Into Life

Ask each student to write a brief Communion meditation, using Luke 22:14-30; John 13:1-20; 1 Corinthians 11:20-32; and Philippians 2:1-11 as source material, on the general subject of discipleship. Students may wish to focus on one of the following themes:

1. It is impossible for a person to take the Lord's Supper properly if he is conceited or hates another person (Luke 22:24-27; 1 Corinthians 11:22; Philippians 2:3).

2. A servant's attitude is necessary to observe the Lord's Supper properly (Luke 22:24-27; John 13:12-17; Philippians 2:1-8).

3. The Lord's Supper reminds us to be like Christ in our daily lives (Luke 22:24-27; John 13:14-16; Philippians 2:5).

When the students have finished, call for volunteers to share their meditations with the class. Collect the completed meditations for possible use in your congregation's worship services.

Let's Talk It Over

The questions on this page are designed to encourage review of the lesson Scriptures and to promote discussion of the lesson by the class. The answers provided are only discussion starters. Let your class talk it over from there.

1. The expression Jesus used to explain His "desire" to eat the Passover with His disciples (v. 15) is a very intense one, but John does not tell us *why* Jesus was so eager to do this. Why do you think it was so important to Jesus to share this "Last Supper" with His disciples? What significance is there for us in Jesus' desire?

There are probably many reasons Jesus wanted to share this meal with His disciples. The fellowship around a table is always special, and it was especially so in Jesus' day. Jesus probably drew strength for His upcoming ordeal by being with His closest friends. He also equipped them, to some extent, for what was ahead.

Of course, Jesus also knew He would institute the Lord's Supper on this occasion. This memorial is so significant that we are not surprised that Jesus was eager to do this. Christians ought to anticipate each observance of the Lord's Supper with a similar eagerness.

2. Jesus said, "This do in remembrance of me" (v. 19). What do you remember about Jesus when you partake of the Lord's Supper?

This question will allow your students to share how they make the meditation time during Communion significant. Of course, Jesus' sacrificial and atoning death is foremost among what we should remember. The love that His death expressed is also something worth noting (1 John 4:9, 10). Some will mention the awful suffering Jesus endured on our behalf. Some will note His humiliation and how that speaks against our own displays of pride. Perhaps some will note Jesus' faithfulness to the will of God and how that encourages them to be faithful.

3. The concept of a "new testament" (or covenant) between God and His people must have been a revolutionary concept for the disciples. In fact, it seems to have been so much so that they missed the point until after Jesus' resurrection. How well do you adapt to new and different ways of doing things? Why?

Struggles over following tradition and being contemporary seem to be a constant in the church. Whatever the issue, some people resist change ferociously. Others blindly accept change just because the new thing is "different." Either position can be harmful. Tradition gives stability

to a group; change produces stress. Sometimes that stress is good, as in "growing pains."

Of course, Jesus made the change of covenants by virtue of His authority as King of kings. We must not change anything He has ordained. At the same time, as we follow His command to make disciples of all the nations, we will find that change is often needed. Let us be mature enough to make the changes that can improve our obedience to the Lord, even while we resist changes that would oppose His will. When the change involves something between the two, let us be loving and mature enough to choose a course of action that pleases the Lord.

4. When Jesus said that one of the Twelve would betray Him, Matthew tells us they all began to ask, "Is it I?" (Matthew 26:22). None pointed a finger at another, but instead each looked at himself. We should similarly examine our own lives for evidence of betrayal. How can we do that?

The quiet time generally afforded us during the Lord's Supper is an ideal time to do so. Paul wrote, "Let a man examine himself, and so let him eat of that bread, and drink of that cup" (1 Corinthians 11:28). We can also take time daily for self-examination along with confession and repentance when necessary. Whenever we hear or read of the faith and faithfulness of others, we can ask, "Would I be as faithful in the same circumstance?" When we hear of a believer who is caught in an embarrassing sin, we can pray, "Lord, would I have done any better in that same situation?"

5. Jesus claimed that true greatness is measured in the number you serve, not in the number you command. How have you seen the truth of Jesus' words displayed in life?

The answer to this question may be quite generic. Think of the doctors and other medical professionals, psychologists and other counselors, ministers, missionaries, and social workers who are "great" based on the number they serve. Or your class may be specific. Perhaps there are outstanding examples among the students' personal acquaintances who demonstrate a servant's heart. Use each example as motivation to the class to think first of serving, not of being served.

Dying on the Cross

DEVOTIONAL READING: Luke 23:50-56.

BACKGROUND SCRIPTURE: Luke 23:13-56.

PRINTED TEXT: Luke 23:33-49.

Luke 23:33-49

33 And when they were come to the place, which is called Calvary, there they crucified him, and the malefactors, one on the right hand, and the other on the left.

34 Then said Jesus, Father, forgive them; for they know not what they do. And they parted his raiment, and cast lots.

35 And the people stood beholding. And the rulers also with them derided him, saying, He saved others; let him save himself, if he be Christ, the chosen of God.

36 And the soldiers also mocked him, coming to him, and offering him vinegar,

37 And saying, If thou be the King of the Jews, save thyself.

38 And a superscription also was written over him in letters of Greek, and Latin, and Hebrew, THIS IS THE KING OF THE JEWS.

39 And one of the malefactors which were hanged railed on him, saying, If thou be Christ, save thyself and us.

40 But the other answering rebuked him, saying, Dost not thou fear God, seeing thou art in the same condemnation?

41 And we indeed justly; for we receive the due reward of our deeds: but this man hath done nothing amiss.

42 And he said unto Jesus, Lord, remember me when thou comest into thy kingdom.

43 And Jesus said unto him, Verily I say unto thee, Today shalt thou be with me in paradise.

44 And it was about the sixth hour, and there was a darkness over all the earth until the ninth hour.

45 And the sun was darkened, and the veil of the temple was rent in the midst.

46 And when Jesus had cried with a loud voice, he said, Father, into thy hands I commend my spirit: and having said thus, he gave up the ghost.

47 Now when the centurion saw what was done, he glorified God, saying, Certainly this was a righteous man.

48 And all the people that came together to that sight, beholding the things which were done, smote their breasts, and returned.

49 And all his acquaintance, and the women that followed him from Galilee, stood afar off, beholding these things.

GOLDEN TEXT: And when Jesus had cried with a loud voice, he said, Father, into thy hands I commend my spirit: and having said thus, he gave up the ghost.—Luke 23:46.

Good News of Jesus
Unit 3: Cross and Resurrection
(Lessons 10-13)

Lesson Aims

After this lesson each student will be able to:
1. Relate the details of the crucifixion of Christ, according to Luke's account.
2. Explain the significance of the cross in the redemptive plan of God.
3. Praise God for Jesus' atoning death at Calvary.

Lesson Outline

INTRODUCTION
    A. The Man in the Water
    B. Lesson Background
  I. THE CHRIST (Luke 23:33-38)
    A. Crucified (v. 33)
      The Honor Guard
    B. Compassionate (v. 34)
    C. Cursed (vv. 35-37)
    D. Confirmed (v. 38)
 II. THE CRIMINALS (Luke 23:39-43)
    A. Rude (v. 39)
    B. Repentant (vv. 40-42)
    C. Rewarded (v. 43)
III. THE CLIMAX (Luke 23:44-49)
    A. Darkness (vv. 44, 45)
    B. Death (v. 46)
      Steering by the Cross
    C. Declaration (v. 47)
    D. Distress (vv. 48, 49)
CONCLUSION
    A. It Took a Death to Bring Us Together
    B. Prayer
    C. Thought to Remember

Introduction

A. The Man in the Water

In January of 1982 an Air Florida aircraft taking off from Washington, D.C., on a cold, snowy day crashed into a bridge and plunged into the Potomac River. As television reporters with their camera crews arrived and began to cover the tragedy, they broadcast an event on live television that few who witnessed will ever forget.

By the time rescue efforts could be organized, the plane had virtually disappeared beneath the surface of the Potomac. Most of the passengers either had been killed already or were trapped in the wreckage beneath the water. At the surface of the water, a handful of survivors were in immediate peril of freezing or drowning. It was clear that both the location of the crash and the bitter winter weather were going to make rescue efforts difficult.

Soon a helicopter flew above the survivors bobbing in the icy water. The helicopter crew dropped a flotation device on a tether. Those in the water were either too weak or confused to be lifted into the helicopter, so they were dragged to shore where they were met by medics and others involved in the rescue operation.

As millions watched on live television, a true hero emerged. Whenever the helicopter returned to the survivors and the flotation device was lowered, a man in the water would gather in the device, hand it to another survivor, and help him or her attach it properly. Finally, the only person left in the water was the man himself, who had been so willing to make sure that everyone else was rescued. But when the helicopter returned to get him, he had slipped beneath the surface of the water. This man had died saving the lives of several other people.

B. Lesson Background

Jesus' mission was coming to its climax. He had celebrated the Passover with His disciples. He had washed their feet to illustrate the path to greatness in God's kingdom. He had agonized in the garden of Gethsemane, pondering the awful weight of man's eternal destiny. He had suffered the humiliation of illegal trials throughout the night. He had been mocked and spit upon. A crown of thorns had been jammed onto His head. He had struggled beneath the weight of the cross until a man named Simon was pressed into service to carry it to the place of execution.

As these events unfolded, Jesus' enemies must have rejoiced. Finally, they thought, they would be rid of the man who had been a thorn in their sides for far too long. In contrast, those who had been followers of Jesus now followed at a distance, viewing the macabre scene and wondering if God would intervene. They did not realize that what was about to transpire just outside Jerusalem was, in fact, God's intervention: Jesus was fulfilling the plan of His Father by giving Himself to die for the sins of the world. The world has never seen another such compelling demonstration of love.

I. The Christ
(Luke 23:33-38)

Many kings in history have been willing to put their subjects to death in order to save themselves. King Jesus was willing to be put to death in order to save His subjects. Such is the depth of God's love for us!

A. Crucified (v. 33)

33. And when they were come to the place, which is called Calvary, there they crucified him, and the malefactors, one on the right hand, and the other on the left.

The Roman soldiers and the men who were to be *crucified* arrived at the *place* of execution, which was known as the "place of a skull" (Matthew 27:33; Mark 15:22; John 19:17). The word rendered *Calvary* here is *kranion,* the Greek word for "skull." *Calvary* derives from the Latin translation of *kranion.* Matthew, Mark, and John (in the references cited above) also note the Aramaic term for the place, which is "Golgotha." It is unclear whether the name derived from the appearance of the place (perhaps it looked something like a skull) or from the presence of skulls and other bones from the many executions. Both explanations have been suggested.

Crucifixion was a gruesome, torturous way to kill a person. The Romans had "perfected" it to make it especially so. They knew how to carry out a crucifixion so that death came slowly—usually by suffocation as the body sagged beneath its own weight and compressed the lungs. Shock, fatigue, and blood loss complicated the respiratory problem. Death would finally come only when a person could no longer lift himself by pushing on the nails in his feet to straighten his body and thus expand his lungs. To this agony the Son of God submitted Himself for you and me.

Jesus was not alone at Calvary. Two other men were also crucified that day. We do not know their names. We know only that they were *malefactors,* or criminals. Matthew and Mark call them thieves (Matthew 27:38; Mark 15:27). Thus the Romans added to Jesus' humiliation by crucifying Him between two lawbreakers. The only perfect person in history was treated as a common criminal. This calls attention to the purpose of Jesus' death: to die in the place of sinners. He became "sin for us, who knew no sin" (2 Corinthians 5:21).

THE HONOR GUARD

In Greece the Orthodox Church has an interesting custom that it observes on the Saturday before Easter Sunday. A picture of Christ is brought into the church building and used as a symbol of the tomb of Jesus. It is placed in a prominent part of the building and surrounded by flowers. Then four soldiers stand as an honor guard, each at a corner of the picture. Other soldiers take their places when their shift is completed. All day Saturday the honor guard stands at attention beside the picture. Then at midnight there is a great celebration, and early on Easter Sunday morning the same picture is carried through the streets in a great procession accompanied by joyful worshipers.

Jesus, of course, was assigned no "honor guard" when He died. Instead, He was crucified between two thieves. Yet it was actually a mark of honor for Jesus that He should be flanked by sinners in His death, for He came to the world to die for sinners.

While the presence of the thieves may have been intended to shame and degrade Jesus, it was something foreseen hundreds of years earlier: "He was numbered with the transgressors," said Isaiah (Isaiah 53:12). This was just one instance of how, at the cross, the enemies of Jesus engaged in actions and spoke words that were, unintentionally, most appropriate. It was fitting that Jesus should die *between* sinners, for He came to die *for* them.   —R. C. S.

B. Compassionate (v. 34)

34. Then said Jesus, Father, forgive them; for they know not what they do. And they parted his raiment, and cast lots.

We do not know the precise moment at which Jesus spoke these words. Many believe that *Father, forgive them; for they know not what they do* was the first of the seven sayings uttered by Jesus at the cross. It is often assumed that He said this after the cross had been raised. It is possible, however, that these words were spoken even as Jesus was being nailed to the cross.

Whatever the timing, there is perhaps no greater expression of compassion known to man than these words of Jesus. Jesus wanted the men responsible for His present agony to be forgiven—to have the opportunity to repent of their sin and experience His love. Concerning the Jewish leaders, Acts 6:7 records that "a great company of the priests were obedient to the faith." Some of the Pharisees became Christians (Acts

---

How to Say It

CALVARY. *Cal*-vuh-ree.
CENTURION. sen-*ture*-ee-un.
GETHSEMANE. Geth-*sem*-uh-nee.
GOLGOTHA. *Gahl*-guh-thuh.
HADES. *Hay*-deez.
ISHMAEL. *Ish*-may-el.
KRANION (Greek). kruh-*nee*-on.
MAGDALENE. *Mag*-duh-leen or
          Mag-duh-*lee*-nee.
MALEFACTORS. *mal*-ih-fac-terz.
PHARISEES. *Fair*-ih-seez.

15:5), the most notable example being Paul (Philippians 3:5).

The callousness of the Roman executioners is evident from their activity amidst the suffering going on around them. They were playing a game, casting *lots* for Jesus' *raiment*, or clothing, specifically for his seamless "coat" or tunic (John 19:23, 24). Crucifixion was "business as usual" for them; they hardly noticed the agony of their victims. Their actions, however, fulfilled an Old Testament prophecy (John 19:24; cf. Psalm 22:18). [See question #1, page 216.]

C. Cursed (vv. 35-37)

35. And the people stood beholding. And the rulers also with them derided him, saying, He saved others; let him save himself, if he be Christ, the chosen of God.

Some of the Jewish *rulers* journeyed to the site of the crucifixion. They were delighted to see that their strategy for getting rid of Jesus had worked. They *derided* Him with taunts, implying that if He were the true Messiah, surely He could *save himself* from this injustice (if it really was injustice). Surely if He were the *Christ, the chosen of God*, God would intervene and rescue Him. These men did not understand that the very act they were witnessing was what the chosen of God had come to do. *Others* would never be *saved* if Jesus decided to *save himself* from the cross.

36. And the soldiers also mocked him, coming to him, and offering him vinegar.

Once the crosses had been erected, the job of the *soldiers* was simply to watch the crowd and make sure that order was maintained. To pass the time, the soldiers engaged in activities like gambling for the victims' clothes (as we have seen). Sometimes they made sport of those who were dying by playing little jokes on them, and some students believe Luke's mention of offering Jesus wine *vinegar* at this point—soaking a rag or sponge with vinegar and raising it to His mouth on a spear or pole—indicates it was part of the soldiers' mocking. Other students believe that a consideration of all four Gospel accounts suggests that there may have been mixed motives involved in offering the vinegar to Jesus. The vinegar itself appears to have been the same cheap wine used by the soldiers for their own refreshment.

37. And saying, If thou be the King of the Jews, save thyself.

The soldiers did not concern themselves with Jesus' claim to be the Messiah. They were aware of the title He had been given—*King of the Jews*. They knew something of kings and royalty, and they could see that the man on the cross before them bore none of the usual marks of royalty. To the soldiers Jesus was just another rabble-rouser who ran into trouble with the authorities. That some considered Him a King only served as fodder for their mockery. [See question #2, page 216.]

D. Confirmed (v. 38)

38. And a superscription also was written over him in letters of Greek, and Latin, and Hebrew, THIS IS THE KING OF THE JEWS.

The charges against a crucified person were often written on a board and placed at the top of the victim's cross. No legal charge had been made against Jesus, so Pilate ordered that the charge presented by the Jews themselves be displayed. This also gave Pilate an opportunity to ridicule the Jews by proclaiming a tortured, dying man to be their king. What Pilate failed to comprehend was that by posting this sign, he was declaring a glorious truth. He had unwittingly confirmed the royal status of Jesus, who was not only the King of the Jews, but the "King of Kings, and Lord of Lords" (Revelation 19:16).

II. The Criminals (Luke 23:39-43)

A. Rude (v. 39)

39. And one of the malefactors which were hanged railed on him, saying, If thou be Christ, save thyself and us.

The selfish motives of this thief are evident. He had heard the claims that Jesus was the *Christ*. His concern, however, was not in acknowledging Jesus as the Anointed One of God; all he wanted was to be freed from the agony of the cross.

B. Repentant (vv. 40-42)

40. But the other answering rebuked him, saying, Dost not thou fear God, seeing thou art in the same condemnation?

The other thief did not share the cynicism of the first one. He *rebuked* the first thief for his words and attitude, asserting that he was hardly in a position to be condemning someone else.

41. And we indeed justly; for we receive the due reward of our deeds: but this man hath done nothing amiss.

What did this thief know about Jesus? Judging from his words in verse 42, it is clear that he knew something about Jesus' kingdom. Apparently he was aware also of Jesus' righteous character. He recognized that Jesus was being executed unjustly, whereas he and the other thief were receiving exactly what they deserved.

42. And he said unto Jesus, Lord, remember me when thou comest into thy kingdom.

There is an obvious tone of humility and repentance in the words of this thief. He acknowledged Jesus as *Lord* and asked that Jesus *remember* him when His *kingdom* was established. Again, we do not know what concept of the kingdom this man had, but he knew that he wanted to be where Jesus was. [See question #3, page 216.]

C. Rewarded (v. 43)

43. And Jesus said unto him, Verily I say unto thee, Today shalt thou be with me in paradise.

Many have tried to use this thief as an example of how a person today can be saved. All that an individual needs to do, so these students say, is to appeal to Jesus to save him. But we must keep in mind that at this point Jesus was still alive. Hebrews 9:15-17 is quite clear that the will or "new testament" established by Jesus did not go into effect until His death (as is true of any will or testament). While Jesus was living, He, as the "testator," had every right to declare someone saved since He could read the hearts of men (John 2:25). Thus Jesus could declare that the thief would be with Him in paradise. Today our situation is quite different; with Jesus' death, burial, and resurrection having occurred, it is our responsibility as Christians to declare the "terms of pardon" as recorded in the New Testament.

Paradise refers to the temporary abode of the righteous dead. It was a portion of Hades to which Jesus went during the time between His death and resurrection (1 Peter 3:18-20).

III. The Climax
(Luke 23:44-49)

A. Darkness (vv. 44, 45)

44. And it was about the sixth hour, and there was a darkness over all the earth until the ninth hour.

As noon (*the sixth hour* by Jewish reckoning) approached, *darkness* came *over all the earth*. It remained until three in the afternoon (*the ninth hour*). It was as if God drew a curtain of darkness to conceal His Son from the evil eyes of those who would torment His body and soul.

45. And the sun was darkened, and the veil of the temple was rent in the midst.

Another astonishing occurrence took place in the *temple*. The curtain separating the Most Holy Place from the Holy Place was suddenly *rent*, or torn—being divided in two. It tore from the top to the bottom, indicating that this was an act of God, not of man (Matthew 27:51). This act symbolized the new accessibility of God to man, for Jesus, by His death, was opening the way for all men to approach God (Hebrews 9:1-8; 10:19-22).

B. Death (v. 46)

46. And when Jesus had cried with a loud voice, he said, Father, into thy hands I commend my spirit: and having said thus, he gave up the ghost.

With one last burst of strength, Jesus *cried with a loud voice*, entrusting His *spirit* to the *Father*. The dramatic events of that pivotal day had come to a climax. Under a darkened sky, the Son of God had paid the penalty for mankind's sin. The world would never be the same! [See question #4, page 216.]

STEERING BY THE CROSS

The only constellation that appears on a national flag is a group of stars called the Southern Cross. (You can see it on the flags of Australia and New Zealand.) It is not there just because the constellation is so prominent in their skies, though absent from the skies in the northern hemisphere. It is also there because early explorers in the South Pacific navigated by those stars. They determined the direction that their ships should take by following the Southern Cross.

Like these explorers, we who are Christians navigate our lives by a cross—the cross of Christ. Some choose to steer their lives away from the cross. They find it offensive, irrelevant, or meaningless. But we steer our lives by the cross. We see in the sacrifice of the Lord Jesus a nobility that we try to emulate in our daily living. He died for others; we try to live for others. We steer by the cross, for we see it as God's "plus sign."

Just as the Southern Cross pointed explorers and sailors to a safe harbor, the cross of Christ guides our way to the only truly safe haven—Heaven. As long as we navigate by the cross, we are guaranteed to arrive home safely.   —R. C. S.

C. Declaration (v. 47)

47. Now when the centurion saw what was done, he glorified God, saying, Certainly this was a righteous man.

The *centurion* (a Roman) was probably the man in charge at the crucifixion. He *glorified God* and acknowledged that Jesus was *a righteous*

Today's visual reminds us that Jesus was in His Father's hands, even at the moment of His awful death.

Visual for lesson 12

man. At what point had the centurion become aware of this truth? We do not know. Perhaps the inexplicable darkness made a convincing impact on him. Perhaps the exchange of words between Jesus and the thief was persuasive. Or perhaps this centurion, who may have seen hundreds or even thousands of men die, took note of Jesus' words and actions and realized that this was no ordinary man.

D. Distress (vv. 48, 49)

48. And all the people that came together to that sight, beholding the things which were done, smote their breasts, and returned.

All crucifixions were gruesome. The crucifixion of Jesus had been accompanied by a series of highly unusual circumstances. Perhaps the sum total of events persuaded some who were present that a terrible injustice had been committed. They *smote their breasts*, or beat their chests, which was a sign of fear, anguish, and grief (Luke 18:13). They left the scene and *returned*— either to their daily activities or, perhaps, to their homes. One wonders how they could return to routine matters after such a spectacle. They knew that the events they had witnessed were unlike any they had ever seen before. [See question #5, page 216.]

49. And all his acquaintance, and the women that followed him from Galilee, stood afar off, beholding these things.

We know from John's Gospel that some of Jesus' closest followers and His mother stood near the cross as He was dying (John 19:25-27). Others, however, *stood afar off* at a distance. These included some of the *women . . . from Galilee*, one of whom was Mary Magdalene (Matthew 27:55, 56). They were probably among those mentioned in Luke 8:2 and 3, who supported Jesus' ministry.

Home Daily Bible Readings

Most of us have lost loved ones. We know how difficult this is. Try to imagine what it would be like to see a loved one unjustly accused, denied justice, subjected to whipping and mocking, and finally nailed to a cross and displayed before the public. We cannot begin to know the anguish in the hearts of those followers of Jesus who saw these events unfold. The One on the center cross was not just a casual acquaintance. He was their friend. They had seen Him gather little children into His lap. They had seen Him cry with friends at the death of a loved one. They had witnessed His concern over the hunger of large crowds of people. They knew Him as a compassionate, generous, kind, gentle man. Now He was dead, and for many, their hopes and dreams died with Him that day. However, as we know, this was only a temporary setback. Three days later the gloom of the cross would be erased by the glory of the empty tomb.

Conclusion

A. It Took a Death to Bring Us Together

The story of the Old Testament patriarch Abraham is familiar to many. Not as familiar, however, is an event that took place after Abraham's death. When Abraham died, a reunion took place. Genesis 25:9 tells us that Isaac and Ishmael buried their father. These men had been separated for approximately seventy-five years (cf. Genesis 17:17; 21:8-14; 25:7). It took their father's death to bring them back together!

God and man are separated by sin. Man is incapable of bridging this enormous gap by himself. But God, in His infinite mercy and grace, sent His own Son to do for us what we could never have accomplished for ourselves. It took a death to bring us together! What happened on Calvary two thousand years ago is still touching lives every day and for all of eternity. "God commendeth his love toward us, in that, while we were yet sinners, Christ died for us" (Romans 5:8).

B. Prayer

Heavenly Father, keep us mindful of the price of our salvation. May our every word, thought, and action express to You our gratitude for what Jesus has done for us. Rekindle our passion for lost souls. Energize us through the Holy Spirit so that we may be ambassadors for Christ, telling all we meet of the love, compassion, mercy, and grace of Him who willingly went to Calvary to die for our sins. In His glorious name we pray, amen.

C. Thought to Remember

It took Jesus' death to bring God and us together.

Learning by Doing

This page contains an alternate lesson plan emphasizing learning activities.
Classes desiring such student involvement will find these suggestions helpful.

Learning Goals

After this lesson each of your students will be able to:

1. Relate the details of the crucifixion of Christ, according to Luke's account.

2. Explain the significance of the cross in the redemptive plan of God.

3. Praise God for Jesus' atoning death at Calvary.

Into the Lesson

Distribute these open-ended statements on paper and instruct your students to complete them.

1. When I think of Jesus dying on the cross, I. . . .

2. If I had been present at Christ's crucifixion, I. . . .

3. If Jesus had not died on the cross, I. . . .

When they finish, ask volunteers to share their work. Tell your class that today's lesson will deal with the significance of Christ's death on the cross.

Into the Word

Give a brief lecture to provide some background, using information in the commentary section and other sources available to you. Note *why* crucifixion was used as a form of execution (to humiliate the victim and deter others from breaking the law) and *how* crucifixion was carried out (several types of crosses were used; the most common was probably the "T" shaped cross; the victim was tied or nailed to the cross). Observe also that victims could survive for days before suffocating or dying of exposure and shock. Emperor Constantine finally ended the practice in the fourth century because of its cruelty.

To explore today's text, divide the class into small groups. Each group is to examine how some of those present at the crucifixion of Jesus reacted to His execution. After reading Luke 23:33-49, each group should write a brief description of the crucifixion from the points of view of one of the following: Jesus, the Jewish people, the religious rulers, the Roman soldiers, Jesus' disciples, and the crucified thieves. After a few minutes have each group report its findings to the class.

Distribute the outline below (if you use the student quarterly, use the proper page in that book for this activity). Use the outline to discuss the reasons for Jesus' death. (Leave blanks in place of the underlined words.) Students should fill in the blanks during the discussion.

A. What Did Sin Do to Man?

1. It made him **guilty** of breaking God's law. So, man owed God **payment** in penalty for every sin (Ezekiel 18:20; Romans 2:5-11; 5:12-14; 6:23; James 2:10).

2. It placed a **barrier** between man and God, disrupting **fellowship** between the two (Isaiah 59:2).

3. It left man unable to save himself from the penalty for **sin**. Unless his sins are paid for by someone else, he is **doomed** (Romans 2:12-25; 3:19-26).

B. What Did Jesus' Death Accomplish?

1. His death was a *propitiation* or *substitutionary sacrifice.* He took the **punishment** man deserved because man's **guilt** was transferred to Him (Romans 3:25; 5:6-8; 2 Corinthians 5:21; 1 Timothy 2:6; Hebrews 2:9; 1 Peter 2:24; 3:18; 1 John 2:2).

2. His death *redeemed* man from **bondage** to sin and paid the penalty owed God (Matthew 20:28; Luke 24:21; Romans 3:24; 8:23; Galatians 3:13; 1 Timothy 2:6).

3. His death *reconciled* man to **God** by breaking down the sin barrier between the two (Romans 5:8-11; 2 Corinthians 5:18-21; Ephesians 2:16; Colossians 1:21, 22).

4. His death *justified* man, so God could declare him **"not guilty"** even though man deserved to die for his sins (Romans 3:26; 5:9, 19).

Into Life

How can we express our thanks for all Christ has done for us? For one thing, we can praise the Father and the Son for their gracious love. For this activity, distribute a hymnal to every student. Ask each group to write its own "Easter cantata," based on the outline above, by selecting a different hymn stanza to illustrate each point, then writing a brief narration to explain the stanza's significance. So, to illustrate Christ's sacrificial death, students might use the second stanza of "Beneath the Cross of Jesus." When the groups finish, ask each to share its work with the class (singing is optional).

Let's Talk It Over

*The questions on this page are designed to encourage review of the lesson
Scriptures and to promote discussion of the lesson by the class. The answers
provided are only discussion starters. Let your class talk it over from there.*

1. The Roman soldiers displayed a callous disregard for life when they gambled for the clothing of Jesus. What evidence of a similar callousness do you see in our own society? How can we appeal to such a culture with the love of Christ?

Your students may cite several examples, including the popularity of gruesome movies with gratuitous violence and gore, the acceptance of abortion on demand—including some forms of it that are brutally painful to the baby—and the ease with which some people divorce their mates in times of long-term illness. Each of these, along with any number of other examples, displays a selfishness that completely disregards the feelings and rights of another in the pursuit of personal convenience or pleasure.

2. Many people taunted Jesus while He hung on the cross, including curious onlookers, religious leaders, and soldiers. Which do you think hurt the most, and why? Whose rejection and/or taunts hurt you the most? What can you do about it?

Some might suggest that the taunting of the religious leaders was the "unkindest cut." These were men who should have known from the Scriptures who Jesus was—but they rejected Him. Perhaps, however, there were those in the crowd whom Jesus had helped. To see them now turn on Him must have cut as deeply as the thorns digging into His brow. The soldiers added their jeers to physical torture—was theirs the most hurtful? Or maybe the worst of all was not the taunts at all, but the silence of His supporters!

We all face a certain measure of ridicule and rejection. Some comes from people who should know better, and some comes from people who at one time seemed our friends. Whatever its source, Jesus' example helps us to bear it. See Hebrews 12:3, 4; 1 Peter 2:21-23.

3. From Matthew 27:44 we know that both thieves at first mocked Jesus. One of them, however, apparently had a sudden change of heart. What do you think changed His mind about Jesus? How can we help hardened unbelievers to make such a dramatic turn?

Probably there were several factors at work. The repentant thief obviously knew Jesus was a righteous person. Seeing the injustice played out, even though he at first joined in the taunts, must have preyed on his conscience. Perhaps it was the sudden darkness, which Luke mentions just two verses later, that made him listen to the inner voice of his conscience. Or perhaps it was something in the way Jesus conducted Himself—something that seemed powerful even in the midst of His execution—that convinced the thief that Jesus would indeed come into His kingdom.

It is that kind of demeanor on the part of Jesus' followers today that has the most power to affect unbelievers. If we display a faith that says our God can bring victory even in the midst of apparent tragedy and defeat, the world will notice and begin to listen to our message.

4. What is significant to you about the fact that Jesus was praying to the Father ("Into thy hands I commend my spirit") at the moment of His death? What does it say to you about God's presence in your own life during trying times?

Whatever Jesus meant by quoting Psalm 22:1 (see Matthew 27:46; Mark 15:34), He was not left alone by His Father. He prayed to God and expected to be heard. He was doing His Father's will, and the Father would see to it that the intended result was accomplished. Jesus would sit again at the right hand of God.

When we face trials, we may feel that God has abandoned us. Instead we should commit our ways to the Father. Even if a believer's trial should end in his or her death, God is still in control and will bring glory to Himself through the believer.

5. Some who witnessed the crucifixion "smote their breasts," presumably in fear or grief. For whom is Jesus' crucifixion a fearful thing? Why?

Perhaps some who witnessed Jesus' death realized the gravity of what they had done. If Jesus was in fact the Christ, what hope could there now be for a world that put Him to death? What kind of judgment might God bring on them? Today, those who have disregarded Jesus and have refused to acknowledge Him as Lord have reason to fear. If they have shown contempt for God's greatest gift of love and the only remedy for our sin and guilt, there is nothing left for them but condemnation.

Witnesses to the Resurrection

DEVOTIONAL READING: Matthew 28:16-20.

BACKGROUND SCRIPTURE: Luke 24:13-53.

PRINTED TEXT: Luke 24:33-49.

Luke 24:33-49

33 And they rose up the same hour, and returned to Jerusalem, and found the eleven gathered together, and them that were with them,

34 Saying, The Lord is risen indeed, and hath appeared to Simon.

35 And they told what things were done in the way, and how he was known of them in breaking of bread.

36 And as they thus spake, Jesus himself stood in the midst of them, and saith unto them, Peace be unto you.

37 But they were terrified and affrighted, and supposed that they had seen a spirit.

38 And he said unto them, Why are ye troubled? and why do thoughts arise in your hearts?

39 Behold my hands and my feet, that it is I myself: handle me, and see; for a spirit hath not flesh and bones, as ye see me have.

40 And when he had thus spoken, he showed them his hands and his feet.

41 And while they yet believed not for joy, and wondered, he said unto them, Have ye here any meat?

42 And they gave him a piece of a broiled fish, and of a honeycomb.

43 And he took it, and did eat before them.

44 And he said unto them, These are the words which I spake unto you, while I was yet with you, that all things must be fulfilled, which were written in the law of Moses, and in the prophets, and in the psalms, concerning me.

45 Then opened he their understanding, that they might understand the Scriptures,

46 And said unto them, Thus it is written, and thus it behooved Christ to suffer, and to rise from the dead the third day:

47 And that repentance and remission of sins should be preached in his name among all nations, beginning at Jerusalem.

48 And ye are witnesses of these things.

49 And, behold, I send the promise of my Father upon you: but tarry ye in the city of Jerusalem, until ye be endued with power from on high.

GOLDEN TEXT: And that repentance and remission of sins should be preached in his name among all nations, . . . And ye are witnesses of these things.—Luke 24:47, 48.

Lesson Aims

After this lesson the students will be able to:

1. Describe what happened when Jesus appeared to His disciples after His resurrection and how He proved to them that He was alive.

2. Explain why the resurrection of Jesus is crucial to our faith in Him as Lord and Savior.

3. Develop a plan (or involve themselves in a program) that will help them become better prepared to present a witness to the risen Christ.

Lesson Outline

INTRODUCTION
  A. The Nature of Christian Faith
  B. Lesson Background
 I. THE MEETING (Luke 24:33-35)
  A. Witnesses Gather (v. 33)
  B. Witnesses Testify (vv. 34, 35)
 II. THE MASTER (Luke 24:36-46)
  A. Declaration (vv. 36-38)
  B. Demonstration (vv. 39-43)
   Meeting for Eating
  C. Discourse (vv. 44-46)
   To Be Continued
III. THE MISSION (Luke 24:47-49)
  A. Message (v. 47)
  B. Messengers (v. 48)
  C. Might (v. 49)
CONCLUSION
  A. "I Serve a Risen Savior"
  B. Prayer
  C. Thought to Remember

Introduction

A. The Nature of Christian Faith

Why do you believe that Jesus of Nazareth is the promised Messiah, the Son of God? Why do you believe that He came forth from the tomb to live again? You may have a hereditary faith—"Grandma believed it, and so do I." You may have a "substitutionary confidence" faith—"the preacher believes it, and if it's good enough for him, it's good enough for me." You may have an uninformed faith—"I don't know why I believe; I just do."

We owe the world something better than such inferior brands of faith as these. The apostle Peter gave this charge to all believers: "Sanctify the Lord God in your hearts: and be ready always to give an answer to every man that asketh you a reason of the hope that is in you, with meekness and fear" (1 Peter 3:15). If we are going to persuade others of the truth of the gospel, our faith needs to be capably defended. We must know what we believe and *why* we believe it.

The resurrection of Jesus is the central event of the Scriptures. Thus our ability to defend that event is of paramount importance. Fortunately, God did not leave us in the dark. He gave us abundant evidence on which our trust can be built. Christian faith is not, as some have suggested, a leap in the dark. Faith is, by God's provision, a walk in the light!

B. Lesson Background

The reality of Jesus' death (our topic last week) had settled in on His followers. His body had been hastily laid in a tomb. The burial procedures were not completed because of the time of Jesus' death and the need to place His body in a tomb before the Sabbath began at sundown.

Early on the first day of the week, after the Sabbath had passed, some women went to the tomb to finish the burial procedures. When they arrived, the tomb was opened and empty, and Jesus was not there (Luke 24:1-3). Two angels told the women that He was alive (vv. 4-6). Later Jesus Himself appeared to Mary Magdalene (Mark 16:9-11; John 20:11-18) and then to the rest of the women (Matthew 28:9, 10). At some point He also appeared to Peter (Luke 24:34).

That same day two men walked from Jerusalem to the little village of Emmaus, located about seven miles northwest of Jerusalem. As they walked, Jesus joined them, but they did not recognize Him. They explained the events that had transpired in Jerusalem over the past few days (Luke 24:14). They told Jesus of the reports of the empty tomb (vv. 22-24). Jesus then explained to the men the Old Testament Scriptures about the suffering and resurrection of the Messiah (v. 27).

When the three men arrived at Emmaus, the two whom Jesus had joined extended their hospitality to Him and asked Him to join them for a meal. As He broke the bread that they shared, His true identity was revealed to them; then He "vanished out of their sight" (vv. 30, 31).

I. The Meeting
(Luke 24:33-35)

The events of that first day of the week were, without doubt, confusing and distressing for Jesus' disciples. Were the reports true? The tomb was indeed empty, but did that mean that Jesus was alive? Perhaps His body had simply been stolen. Perhaps all of this was a plot by the Jews to ferret out the true followers of Jesus, arrest them, and charge them with some crime. The disciples desperately needed some firm assurance that the reports they were hearing were true. As they gathered together in secret, they did so in fear (John 20:19).

A. Witnesses Gather (v. 33)

33. And they rose up the same hour, and returned to Jerusalem, and found the eleven gathered together, and them that were with them.

The two men from Emmaus were so excited about Jesus' appearance to them that they immediately hurried back to *Jerusalem*. On arriving, they *found* the place where Jesus' followers had *gathered*. [See question #1, page 224.]

The eleven is how the closest disciples of Jesus were known at this point, for Judas had hanged himself (Matthew 27:3-5). The remaining group of eleven is identified by that number, even though Thomas was not with them on this occasion (John 20:24). Jesus would appear to them all a week later and assure Thomas that the testimony of the other disciples was true (John 20:25, 26).

The men from Emmaus apparently knew the place where the disciples were meeting. We can imagine that they could hardly contain their excitement as they hurried to Jerusalem. They knew that rumors were circulating rapidly within the company of Jesus' followers. They could add another piece of evidence to the testimony of those who claimed Jesus was alive!

B. Witnesses Testify (vv. 34, 35)

34. Saying, The Lord is risen indeed, and hath appeared to Simon.

This verse is a bit confusing because it is not clear who is speaking. Did the two from Emmaus say this? That seems unlikely. How would they have known of the appearance to *Simon* Peter? Even if they had known, it would have been unnecessary to say this when Peter was standing in the room with them. It is more likely that the individuals reporting the resurrection and the appearance to Peter were those already in the room. What they had to say would have been news to the two men from Emmaus.

35. And they told what things were done in the way, and how he was known of them in breaking of bread.

Now it is the two from Emmaus who get to tell their exciting news. Yes, they know Jesus is alive, and not just because they have already heard a report of His resurrection. They themselves have seen Him! He has walked with them,

talked with them, and eaten with them! [See question #2, page 224.]

Imagine the scene as the disciples looked at each other in wide-eyed wonder. Here was further proof of what had seemed too good to be true. One might suspect the assertions of only one or two people who claimed that they had seen Jesus alive. Now, however, the testimony from credible witnesses was becoming more and more persuasive.

II. The Master
(Luke 24:36-46)

A. Declaration (vv. 36-38)

36. And as they thus spake, Jesus himself stood in the midst of them, and saith unto them, Peace be unto you.

With beautiful simplicity the Scripture states that *Jesus himself stood in the midst of them.* There is no explanation of exactly how this was done. Most important is the fact that Jesus was there! He addressed His disciples with the customary greeting of *peace.*

37. But they were terrified and affrighted, and supposed that they had seen a spirit.

To say that the men in that room were surprised would be a significant understatement! Jesus was dead; they had seen Him die. They had watched as He was carried to Joseph's tomb and placed in it. Despite reports that He was alive again, to witness His sudden appearance in the middle of a group of people and in a room where the doors were shut (John 20:19) was startling to say the least. Luke tells us the disciples *were terrified and affrighted*—so taken aback that they thought they were seeing a *spirit*, or ghost.

38. And he said unto them, Why are ye troubled? and why do thoughts arise in your hearts?

Jesus mildly rebuked the disciples for being *troubled* at His appearance. Had He not told them on previous occasions that He would not only be killed but would rise from the dead (Luke 9:22, 44; 18:31-33)? Jesus knew their *thoughts* and the questions and doubts that flooded their minds. He attempted to calm their fears even as He had done prior to His death when He told them, "Let not your heart be *troubled*" (John 14:1).

How to Say It

EMMAUS. Em-*may*-us.
ISAIAH. Eye-*zay*-uh.
MAGDALENE. *Mag*-duh-leen or Mag-duh-*lee*-nee.
PENTATEUCH. *Pen*-tuh-teuk.

B. Demonstration (vv. 39-43)

39. Behold my hands and my feet, that it is I myself: handle me, and see; for a spirit hath not flesh and bones, as ye see me have.

To allay the fears of His disciples, Jesus instructed them to examine Him closely. They had seen Him with their eyes and heard Him with their ears; now He told them to use another of their senses—touch. No, their eyes and ears were not playing tricks on them. This was not a *spirit* standing before them. A spirit might be seen or even heard, but everyone knew that a spirit had no *flesh and bones*.

40. And when he had thus spoken, he showed them his hands and his feet.

Jesus also offered the disciples the opportunity to examine *his hands and his feet*. There they would find the flesh wounds made by the nails that held Jesus to the cross. John notes that Jesus also permitted them to examine the wound that the spear had made in His side (John 20:20). He wanted the disciples to be completely convinced of His identity. The proclamation of the gospel was going to be entrusted to them. They must be absolutely certain of Jesus' bodily resurrection!

41. And while they yet believed not for joy, and wondered, he said unto them, Have ye here any meat?

In spite of the evidence before them, the disciples *believed not for joy*. We usually think of Thomas as the "doubting disciple," yet certainly the rest of the group required some convincing as well! Perhaps the disciples' joy was tempered by a fear that something might happen to "burst the bubble" and bring them back to reality. [See question #3, page 224.]

Then Jesus spoke again. He asked for something to eat. This provided further proof that He was not a spirit or an illusion. He was there with them in the body that they recognized, and He was hungry.

42. And they gave him a piece of a broiled fish, and of a honeycomb.

Despite the excitement of the day, the disciples were still in need of nourishment. Thus there was food present in this room. The men *gave* Jesus *a piece of a broiled fish* and part of *a honeycomb*.

43. And he took it, and did eat before them.

Jesus *took* the food that was offered and ate it in the disciples' presence. (Spirits could not do this!) What an encouragement to these men to see Jesus eating with them just as He had before! [See question #4, page 224.]

MEETING FOR EATING

If you ever visit a congregation when the people are having a church dinner, you will often hear someone say, somewhat apologetically, "One thing for sure about this church—we're good eaters." Someone even went so far as to poke fun at such events in a little poem written in fractured English:

> We met and we et.
> And if we hadn't have et,
> We wouldn't have met.

But no one should criticize meeting for eating. Consider how often we find the risen Christ sharing a meal with His disciples. He did it at Emmaus. He did it in Jerusalem in the incident found in today's text. He did it when He cooked breakfast by the Sea of Galilee for seven of His followers (John 21:9-13).

Certainly such incidents prove the reality of the resurrection, but they teach us much more than that. Whenever a congregation comes together to eat a meal, something happens that is not visible. There is a spiritual dimension to such gatherings that should never be overlooked. Compare the church family with the human family. Family mealtimes are important; and when families are too hurried to eat together, something important is lost. Opportunities for talking, laughing, sharing, and dreaming are wasted. One cannot imagine a family reunion without a time for eating together. One cannot imagine a holiday family gathering without a meal being shared. It is an expression of togetherness and solidarity.

So it is with the church family. When Jesus ate with His disciples, He underscored the spiritual blessings that come when Christians eat together. Is it any wonder that the most important time in our worship is when we observe the Lord's *Supper* in remembrance of Jesus and with others in God's family?   —R. C. S.

C. Discourse (vv. 44-46)

44. And he said unto them, These are the words which I spake unto you, while I was yet with you, that all things must be fulfilled, which were written in the law of Moses, and in the prophets, and in the psalms, concerning me.

Jesus was the Master Teacher, and He saw this occasion as a teachable moment. He reminded the disciples that He had talked to them about the *things* that would happen to Him. In addition He noted that none of this had happened by accident; all of it was prophesied in what we know as the Old Testament Scriptures. Here Jesus mentions the three main sections of the Scriptures as first-century Jews divided them—*the law of Moses* (the Pentateuch), *the prophets*, and *the psalms*. The disciples had the privilege of seeing events that *fulfilled* prophecies that had been *written* hundreds of years before.

45. Then opened he their understanding, that they might understand the Scriptures.

Jesus knew that there was far more to be done with the disciples than simply validating His resurrection. They needed to understand the Old Testament prophecies about Him in order to appreciate how the resurrection was God's supreme act of authenticating Jesus as the Messiah.

So Jesus continued to teach His disciples, helping them to *understand the Scriptures* and the plan of God recorded in them. At times it appears that these men did not pay adequate attention to Jesus while He walked the dusty roads of Palestine with them. Now, however, they must have been listening with "new ears." Just a few hours earlier, their Instructor had been lying in a tomb. Now He was with them, enjoying their food and fellowship. He had their undivided attention!

Understanding the Bible is vital to the life of every Christian. By it we learn of God's special interest in mankind. By it we learn about sin and our condemnation because of sin. By it we learn of Jesus and His death for our sins. By it we learn of God's promise of His Spirit to live in us. By it we learn of our eternal home—the place God Himself has prepared for His people. Never let your Bible gather dust on a shelf or a coffee table. It is God's love letter to you!

46. And said unto them, Thus it is written, and thus it behooved Christ to suffer, and to rise from the dead the third day.

It *behooved* (or, it was necessary for) *Christ to suffer*. That had been prophesied in Scriptures such as Psalm 22:1-21 and Isaiah 53. But so had the fact that He would *rise from the dead the third day*. That had been prophesied in passages including Psalm 16:9-11; Isaiah 53:10, 11; and Jonah 1:17 (cf. Matthew 12:40). Jesus had clearly fulfilled these prophecies.

TO BE CONTINUED

Many of us have become deeply involved in watching a television program, hardly aware of the passing of time. Just when it seems that we are reaching a pivotal moment in the action, the TV picture freezes, and at the bottom of the screen appear the words: *To Be Continued*. We realize, to our dismay, that we are going to have to wait another week to find out what happens.

As Jesus was dying on the cross, one of the statements He uttered was, "It is finished" (John 19:30). And certainly that was true in that He had paid the price "in full" for the sins of the world. But there was more to come. The resurrection of Jesus tells us that His death on the cross was not the conclusion of God's work. His plan was "to be continued"—and so it was three days later when Jesus arose.

We are reminded that it is only when we look back at the cross from the vantage point of the resurrection that the cross makes any sense at all. Few people doubt that Jesus died on the cross. Many doubt that He rose from the dead. It is amazing that those who doubt can see any value in Jesus, any helpful lessons from His life, or any relevance in His teachings. But when you include, as you must, the resurrection, then and only then does the story of Jesus become truly good news. Only then do we share in the victory that Jesus secured. We realize that death is not the end for those who trust Jesus; life is "to be continued"—with Him!　　　　　　—R. C. S.

III. The Mission
(Luke 24:47-49)

A. Message (v. 47)

47. And that repentance and remission of sins should be preached in his name among all nations, beginning at Jerusalem.

In addition to predicting events such as the life, death, and resurrection of the Messiah, the Scriptures also foretold that these redemptive acts of God were to be accomplished on behalf of *all nations*—not just the Jews. We can see indications of God's interest in all peoples as early as His promise to Abram: "In thee shall all families of the earth be blessed" (Genesis 12:3). The book of Isaiah is full of such prophecies (Isaiah 2:1-4; 19:16-24; 25:6-9; 42:1-4; 49:5-7; 51:4-6; 55:5; 60:1-3; 61:1-9).

B. Messengers (v. 48)

48. And ye are witnesses of these things.

Not everyone could know Jesus as those gathered in that room knew Him. They had heard His teachings. They had seen Him command the forces of nature. They had watched as He brought healing to lives ravaged by disease and affliction, causing the deaf to hear, the blind to see, the lame to walk, and the lepers to be made

Visual for lesson 13

Today's visual recalls some of the events in Jesus' life of which we are "witnesses." Discuss ways to give testimony of Jesus to your community.

whole. They had seen Jesus bring the dead back to life. Then they had seen Him die. Now they beheld Him alive again.

To all of these wonderful works—and more—these men were *witnesses*. They would bear the responsibility of telling the world what they had seen and heard. [See question #5, page 224.]

C. Might (v. 49)

49. And, behold, I send the promise of my Father upon you: but tarry ye in the city of Jerusalem, until ye be endued with power from on high.

Jesus knew that He would not be able to stay with His followers indefinitely. He would appear to them a few more times, but forty days after His resurrection He would leave them. He would ascend to His *Father*, as He said He would do (John 20:17), and would return at a time known only to the Father (Matthew 24:36; Acts 1:7, 11). He knew that the instructions He was giving His disciples at this point were crucial to their future success in taking His message to the world.

Jesus' departure was necessary in order for Him to *send the promise* of the Father *upon* the disciples. This promise referred to the prophecy of Joel regarding the coming of the Spirit upon God's people (Joel 2:28-32), which would be fulfilled seven weeks later on the Day of Pentecost (Acts 2:1-4). During the night before His death, Jesus had spoken to the disciples of the Spirit's coming (John 14:15-26; 16:7-15). Now He assured them again that, although He would be leaving them, they would never be alone. The Father would empower them through the Spirit to face the exciting, but challenging, days ahead.

Jesus also instructed His followers to *tarry* (stay) *in the city of Jerusalem* until the Spirit had *endued* them with *power*. Apparently this did

Home Daily Bible Readings

Monday, Feb. 19—The Sign of Jonah (Matthew 12:38-42)

Tuesday, Feb. 20—The Resurrection of Jesus (Mark 16:1-8)

Wednesday, Feb. 21—The Walk to Emmaus (Luke 24:13-27)

Thursday, Feb. 22—Recognizing Jesus and Testifying of Him (Luke 24:28-35)

Friday, Feb. 23—Jesus Appears to His Disciples (Luke 24:36-49)

Saturday, Feb. 24—Reassurance (John 20:19-23)

Sunday, Feb. 25—The Commissioning of the Disciples (Matthew 28:16-20)

not mean that they could never travel beyond Jerusalem at this point, because Jesus later met with some of His disciples in Galilee (Matthew 28:16-20; John 21:1-3). They were, however, back in Jerusalem by Pentecost.

Conclusion

The resurrection is God's "exclamation point" in verifying Jesus' identity. The resurrection is proof positive that Jesus is exactly who He said He was. Paul tells us that Jesus was "declared to be the Son of God with power, by the resurrection from the dead" (Romans 1:4).

In 1 Corinthians 15 Paul again addresses the importance of the resurrection. There he points out that the resurrection of Jesus is central to the Christian faith. Without it we have no assurance and no hope. If Christ is not alive, death retains its sting. The grave is still frightening. Life after death remains forever in the realm of the unknown. Christian faith becomes an exercise in futility.

A. "I Serve a Risen Savior"

These words are taken from a well-known hymn: "I serve a risen Savior, He's in the world today." Part of the words in the chorus of that hymn are as follows: "You ask me how I know He lives? He lives within my heart." While that is a wonderful thought, we need to remember that our faith is not founded on emotional experience. It is based firmly on facts. These facts are clear. Jesus of Nazareth claimed to be the Son of God and did many mighty works to substantiate that claim. He died on a cross. He rose from the dead. Eyewitnesses spoke and wrote of all these events.

We believe in a risen Savior because we have abundant eyewitness testimony on which to base our belief. We serve that Savior because the persuasive testimony of the eyewitnesses has convinced us of the truth of their message. Jesus lived, died, and by the power of God lives again. We, too, "are witnesses of these things."

B. Prayer

Father, may the testimony of those who saw the resurrected Christ stir us as we read it today. May we appreciate the reality of that miracle more than ever before. Use us to tell others of the joy of new life in Christ. Compel us to proclaim our faith boldly and to touch the lives of others. In Jesus' wonderful name we pray. Amen.

C. Thought to Remember

Faith is not a leap in the dark—it is a walk in the light!

Learning by Doing

This page contains an alternate lesson plan emphasizing learning activities.
Classes desiring such student involvement will find these suggestions helpful.

Learning Goals

After this lesson your students will be able to:

1. Describe what happened when Jesus appeared to His disciples after His resurrection and how He proved to them that He was alive.

2. Explain why the resurrection of Jesus is crucial to our faith in Him as Lord and Savior.

3. Develop a plan (or involve themselves in a program) that will help them become better prepared to present a witness to the risen Christ.

Into the Lesson

Frank Capra's classic movie *It's a Wonderful Life* concerns a well-intentioned but disillusioned character, George Bailey, who decides to end his life. To convince George not to commit suicide, an angel grants George's wish that he never had been born. Once George sees how many lives are changed for the worse because he was not there to help, he decides that life is worth living after all.

Ask your class to imagine what the world would be like—religiously, morally, politically, and socially—if Jesus had not risen from the dead. Give them paper to record their answers or refer them to the student book, where this exercise is printed.

When they finish, discuss their answers. Then tell your class that today's lesson will deal with the impact of Christ's resurrection on the world.

Into the Word

You will need to provide some background for today's lesson text. These details are rather familiar to most Christians, so perhaps a question-and-answer session will help you bring out the necessary details. Ask the following questions and see whether members of the class can answer. If not, provide the Scripture references and let the class search out the answers. Provide the Scripture references also when the questions are answered correctly so that those who did not know the answers can look up the Scriptures and read the information for themselves.

1. How do we know Jesus really died on the cross? *(A soldier pierced His side with a spear, John 19:33, 34; a centurion confirmed His death, Mark 15:44, 45.)*

2. What happened to Jesus' body after He died? *(It was buried in a tomb [Luke 23:50-53] with a stone rolled across the entrance [Matthew 27:60] and a detachment of soldiers guarding it [Matthew 27:62-66].)*

3. Who first saw Jesus after His resurrection? *(Mary Magdalene, Mark 16:9; John 20:11-18.)*

4. Who saw Him next? *(The other women who had come to the tomb, Matthew 28:9, 10.)*

5. Two unnamed disciples walked with Jesus to Emmaus, not recognizing Him at first. Describe this encounter. *(See Luke 24:13-32.)*

Point out that when we read, "They rose up . . . and returned to Jerusalem" in our text, the *they* are these two disciples from Emmaus. They arrived back in Jerusalem in time to be present for Jesus' first appearance to the apostles as a group (except for Thomas—see John 20:19-24). Then have a volunteer read Luke 24:33-49.

Ask, "From this text, what evidence do you find for the resurrection of Jesus?" Have students call out answers while you write them on the chalkboard. The following should be included: a reported appearance to Simon (i.e., Peter or Cephas, v. 34; see also 1 Corinthians 15:5); the witnesses saw and heard Jesus (v. 36); they were invited to see His wounds and touch Him to prove He was not a mere spirit or ghost (vv. 37-40); He ate physical food (vv. 41-43); He taught them insights from the Scriptures (vv. 44-47); He commissioned them as witnesses (vv. 48, 49).

Read 1 Corinthians 15:1-19; then ask someone to summarize what Paul says about the significance of Jesus' resurrection. *(It is the foundation of our faith and hope. Without it our faith is useless and we are still lost!)*

Into Life

Next, say, "Now that we've discussed the importance of the resurrection to the Christian faith, what are we to do to share this knowledge with the lost?" Write the following headings on the chalkboard, or make a handout for the class with these two headings at the top of the page: "What We Are Doing," and "What We Could Do."

Ask students to list in the first column what your congregation is doing to evangelize the lost. Then ask them to brainstorm other ways to evangelize. Write these suggestions in the second column. Allow students to choose what they think is the most promising method and make definite plans to carry it out. You may need further meetings to work out details. Close with a prayer for boldness in telling of Jesus.

Let's Talk It Over

The questions on this page are designed to encourage review of the lesson Scriptures and to promote discussion of the lesson by the class. The answers provided are only discussion starters. Let your class talk it over from there.

1. Following Jesus' death, the eleven and others of Jesus' followers were gathered together in Jerusalem. How does being with other Christians help us in times of grief?

The death of Jesus left His most devoted followers sharing the pain of grief. These disciples had left all to follow Jesus, and they had shared many of the same experiences during their weeks and months with Him. In the face of their loss, they still could cling to one another. All of them must have found comfort in knowing that the others understood their sorrow. The void created by Jesus' absence could be partially filled by reviewing together their treasured memories of Him. In our experience of grief today, Christian fellowship can be a similar blessing. It is a consolation to know that our Christian friends understand and care. It is healing just to talk about our memories of a departed loved one and to be reminded of the Christian hope that includes eternal life beyond the grave.

2. Read Luke 24:30, 31 to see how Jesus "was known of them in breaking of bread" (v. 35). Why do you think this act was significant in the disciples' recognition of Jesus? How can people "recognize" Jesus today?

For Mary Magdalene it was the special way Jesus called her name. For these disciples, who must have eaten with Jesus many times, it was the way He "took bread, and blessed it, and brake, and gave to them" (v. 30). Perhaps He looked them in the eye as He handed them the bread. Perhaps it was the special way that He addressed His Father in prayer. There was something special, something intimate, about that moment.

The disciples recognized One they had seen before in a familiar act. People today have never seen Jesus, but there are certain things they expect from Him. One is to be treated with love. When Jesus' disciples act in genuine love toward others, those others will see and recognize Jesus in them.

3. The disciples "believed not for joy" (v. 41). In other words, they thought Jesus' presence among them was just "too good to be true"! People may feel the same way about the claims of the gospel. Why? How can we convince them that the claims of the gospel—as great as they are—really are true?

Most people have the idea that "you get what you pay for." Salvation by grace, as a free gift (Ephesians 2:8-10), seems just "too good to be true." Some have fallen prey to con schemes that were, indeed, too good to be true; they have promised themselves they will not fall for such a thing again.

When sharing the gospel with such people, it is important that we demonstrate that we have nothing to gain personally from their acceptance of the gospel. This means that Christian family members and friends have more credibility with these folk than paid evangelists have. It is important that we maintain our credibility by respecting others and showing unselfish love toward them. Then perhaps they will accept the good news for what it is.

4. The resurrection was confirmed to the disciples a number of times and in a number of ways. For you, which is the most compelling reason to believe in the risen Lord?

This question has many possible answers. For some, the Biblical accounts of the risen Jesus' appearing to His disciples are the most convincing. The lack of refuting evidence from the enemies of Jesus and their inability to produce a body are significant. The power of this message and the movement created in Jerusalem such a short time after Jesus was crucified there is proof to some. The failure of any alternate explanations and the endurance and spread of the Christian faith through the centuries are persuasive. For many, however, the most compelling confirmation is the work of Christ in the lives of people today—especially in their own lives.

5. What obligation, if any, do believers today have for being witnesses to the resurrection, preaching "repentance and remission of sins . . . among all nations"?

We believe that it is God's will that repentance and remission of sins be preached among all nations, and that He has made no provision for that to happen except through believers' carrying the message. We are witnesses to the resurrection by virtue of our relationship with the risen Christ. We who are in Christ have a message to share, and the gift of the Holy Spirit empowers us to share it.

Spring Quarter, 2001

Continuing Jesus' Work
(The Book of Acts)

Special Features

Lessons

Unit 1: Beginning in Jerusalem

Unit 2: Witnessing in Judea and Samaria

Unit 3: Spreading the Gospel Into All the World

About These Lessons

The book of Acts, or "The Acts of the Apostles," is the focus of this quarter's lessons. It has also been called "The Acts of the Holy Spirit," for it is clearly the Spirit who is driving the action and not the apostles themselves. One teacher always added a "Chapter 29" to his syllabus. That was the chapter not yet written, for the Spirit is still driving the church to fulfill the mission given by Christ—and He is not finished with us yet.

Mar 4 · Mar 11 · Mar 18 · Mar 25 · Apr 1 · Apr 8 · Apr 15 · Apr 22 · Apr 29 · May 6 · May 13 · May 20 · May 27

Quarterly Quiz

The questions on this page may be used in several ways: as a pretest at the beginning of the quarter; as a review at the end of the quarter; or as a review after each lesson. The questions are based on the Scripture text of each lesson (King James Version). ***The answers are on page 228.***

Lesson 1

1. To whom did Luke address the book of Acts? *Acts 1:1*
2. For how many days did Jesus show Himself alive after His resurrection? *Acts 1:3*
3. What phrase is used to describe the distance between the Mount of Olives and Jerusalem? *Acts 1:12*

Lesson 2

1. On the Day of Pentecost, what did the "cloven tongues" that appeared look like? *Acts 2:3*
2. In what four activities did the early church continue "steadfastly"? *Acts 2:42*

Lesson 3

1. At what hour did Peter and John come to the temple to pray? *Acts 3:1*
2. John told the lame man, "Silver and gold have I none." T/F *Acts 3:6*
3. The Jewish leaders took note of the _____ of Peter and John. (appearance, miracles, or boldness?) *Acts 4:13*

Lesson 4

1. Name the Pharisee who addressed the Jewish council concerning the apostles. *Acts 5:34*
2. What two men did Gamaliel mention in his speech? *Acts 5:36, 37*

Lesson 5

1. The Grecian believers were murmuring against the Jewish believers because a certain group was being neglected. Which group? *Acts 6:1*
2. How many men were selected to take care of this matter? *Acts 6:3*
3. What were Stephen's last words before he died? *Acts 7:60*

Lesson 6

1. Who traveled to Samaria to preach Christ? *Acts 8:5*
2. Philip's ministry in Samaria included doing miracles. T/F *Acts 8:6, 7*
3. Whom did Philip ask, "Understandest thou what thou readest?" *Acts 8:27, 30*

Lesson 7

1. What question did the angel at Jesus' tomb ask the women? *Luke 24:5*

2. Following his conversion, Saul stayed in Damascus and preached Christ in which place? (synagogues, homes, or by the riverside?) *Acts 9:20*

Lesson 8

1. To what city did Cornelius send messengers to find Peter? *Acts 10:32*
2. In whose house was Peter staying? *Acts 10:32*
3. Peter told the house of Cornelius that God is no _____ of _____. *Acts 10:34*

Lesson 9

1. Who was sent from Jerusalem to assist the church in Antioch? *Acts 11:22*
2. Where did Barnabas go to find Saul? *Acts 11:25*
3. Name the prophet who predicted a time of "great dearth throughout all the world." *Acts 11:28*

Lesson 10

1. Who left Paul and Barnabas when they arrived at Perga? *Acts 13:13*
2. Paul and Barnabas shook the dust off their feet when they left Antioch of Pisidia. T/F *Acts 13:14, 51*

Lesson 11

1. Paul and Barnabas and others traveled to _____ to speak to the _____ and _____ about the issue of circumcising Gentiles. *Acts 15:2*
2. Who said, "Why tempt ye God, to put a yoke upon the neck of the disciples?" *Acts 15:7, 10*

Lesson 12

1. In a vision, Paul saw a man from _____. *Acts 16:9*
2. Who is described as a seller of purple from Thyatira? *Acts 16:14*
3. What question did the Philippian jailer ask Paul and Silas? *Acts 16:30*

Lesson 13

1. From what city did Paul send for the elders of the Ephesian church? *Acts 20:17*
2. Paul told the elders that he was going to _____. (Damascus, Jerusalem, or Antioch?) *Acts 20:22*
3. How long had Paul labored in Ephesus? *Acts 20:31*

Unfinished Business

by Edwin V. Hayden

BEFORE WE PROCEED with your new proposal, Brother Jones, we need to act on an item of business left over from our previous meeting. We have a motion before us—properly made, seconded, and discussed at some length—but neither accepted nor rejected by a determinate action of the body. We may approve, reject, or table the motion. But we must deal with it in some way before we go on."

The rules of order call for finishing what you have started before you start something else.

What Jesus Did

When God sent His Son into the world, He provided the way to finish what He started in creation—to bring into fellowship with Himself those whom He made in His own likeness and image. Jesus recognized an unchanging responsibility to pursue that purpose to its end: "My meat is to do the will of him that sent me," He said, "and to finish his work" (John 4:34). "I have glorified thee on the earth," He prayed within hours of His crucifixion. "I have finished the work which thou gavest me to do" (John 17:4).

Forty days after that work was completed, Jesus ascended into Heaven. From His exalted position as Lord and Christ, He sent the Holy Spirit to lead and empower His chosen apostles to convey His message, directly and indirectly, to the entire inhabited earth. The book of Acts describes the way in which Jesus' ministry became the ministry of the Spirit-empowered apostles. Our studies for this quarter provide highlights from that account of the Lord's ongoing ministry to all mankind.

Beginning in Jerusalem

Our four lessons in March develop the theme introduced by Jesus in a final conversation with the apostles and recorded in Luke 24:46, 47: "It behooved Christ to suffer, and to rise from the dead the third day: and that repentance and remission of sins should be preached in his name among all nations, *beginning at Jerusalem*."

Lesson 1, from Acts 1, deals with "The Promise of the Spirit's Power." This promise was very specific, given to the apostles who remained after the death of Judas. The promise was to be fulfilled "not many days" after it was spoken (Acts 1:5). We can accept, then, with the utmost confidence the record of the words and deeds of the apostles on and after the fulfillment of Jesus'

promise at Pentecost. Their teachings must remain the standard by which all other teachings and truth claims are measured.

Lesson 2, "The Holy Spirit Comes in Power," focuses on the opening and closing portions of Acts 2. These tell how the Holy Spirit came upon the apostles in dramatic fashion. They also show the Spirit's power in working through Peter's message (vv. 14-36) to convince and convict sinners. As a result, three thousand hearers were baptized.

Lesson 3, "The Holy Spirit Works With Power," deals with the Spirit's working through the apostles Peter and John, as seen in Acts 3 and 4. First, we read of a miracle of healing in the case of a lame man at the temple gate. Then noted is the response of the "unlearned and ignorant" apostles to an official order that they soft-pedal their insistence that the Lord Jesus was not only the source of the healing miracle, but also the only source of salvation for all mankind.

Lesson 4, "Obedient to the Spirit," from Acts 5, reveals an increasing level of opposition to Jesus from the Jewish leaders. Failing in their efforts to silence the apostles by threats and commands, the authorities added imprisonment and beatings. The apostles responded that they were committed to obeying God rather than men. They rejoiced in being counted worthy to suffer shame for the sake of their Lord.

Witnessing in Judea and Samaria

The four lessons in April follow the pattern of Jesus' directive in Acts 1:8: "Ye shall be witnesses unto me both in Jerusalem, and in all Judea, and in Samaria."

Lesson 5, "Empowered to Serve," is taken from portions of Acts 6 and 7. It calls attention to the church's care for the needy folk in its midst. As that need grew with the growing church, so did the apostles' need for helpers to relieve them of having to address material concerns. Seven carefully selected men were ordained for the work with the laying on of the apostles' hands. One of them, Stephen, was finally stoned to death following his bold rebuke of the Jews for their rejection and slaying of Jesus.

Lesson 6, "Witnessing Beyond Jerusalem" (from Acts 8), follows the preaching of Philip to the people of Samaria and to an Ethiopian on his way home from worshiping in Jerusalem. Philip heard the Ethiopian reading Isaiah's prophecy of

God's Suffering Servant. Philip explained the application to Jesus, and when the traveler pointed out available water, Philip baptized him.

Lesson 7, "Proclaiming the Risen Lord," provides a suitable study for our annual celebration of Jesus' resurrection. Part of the printed text comes from Luke 24, where angels at the empty tomb announced the historic event. The other part of the printed text is taken from Acts 9. It highlights the testimony that Saul of Tarsus bore concerning the risen Lord after encountering Him on the way to Damascus and being baptized by a disciple named Ananias. Saul astonished observers at Damascus by boldly preaching Jesus as the Christ.

Lesson 8, "Gentiles Receive the Spirit," draws from a part of Acts 10 to tell how the gospel was first proclaimed to Gentiles. As Peter presented the gospel in the house of Cornelius, the Holy Spirit came upon these Gentiles; and they spoke in languages that they had never studied or learned, just as the apostles had done on the Day of Pentecost. Thus assured that these Gentiles were acceptable with God, Peter commanded that they be baptized.

Spreading the Gospel Into All the World

Our lessons for the last week in April and the four weeks in May build on Jesus' promise that the Spirit-empowered apostles would become His witnesses to the "uttermost part of the earth" (Acts 1:8).

Lesson 9, "The Church in Antioch," draws from Acts 11 and 13 to tell of the church that was established in Antioch of Syria, where Christ's followers were first called Christians. The church received encouragement from Barnabas, who came from Jerusalem and later brought Saul from Tarsus to join in the work. Eventually, the Holy Spirit directed the church to send Barnabas and Saul to preach in areas not yet reached with the gospel.

Lesson 10, "Mission to Gentiles," draws from Acts 13 to tell of evangelizing done by Saul (now called Paul) and Barnabas in Cyprus and in Antioch of Pisidia. They preached first in synagogues to Jews and to proselytes to Judaism. When certain Jews resisted and opposed the gospel, Paul and Barnabas took their message to Gentiles in the city with such success that Jewish jealousy finally drove them to other communities. Believers were left rejoicing in the Spirit.

Lesson 11, "The Jerusalem Conference," is taken from Acts 15. There we read of a problem that arose from the missionaries' work among the Gentiles. Certain Jewish Christians insisted that Gentiles could not be saved without first having been circumcised according to the law of Moses.

Paul and Barnabas were asked to discuss the problem with the apostles and elders in Jerusalem, and they did so. After hearing testimonies of the Holy Spirit's work among the Gentiles through the gospel, the gathering concluded that circumcision should not be required of Gentile converts.

Lesson 12, "Responding to Need," draws from Acts 16 and tells of events in Philippi of Macedonia during Paul's second missionary journey. Notable was the conversion of a businesswoman, Lydia, and her household. Also recorded was the conversion of a jailer whom Paul and Silas taught and led to Christ following a dramatic midnight earthquake.

Lesson 13, "Serving With Humility," includes a text from Acts 20. There Paul summarizes his ministry among the Ephesians as he addresses the elders of that church at the close of his third missionary journey. Paul had endured many hardships (and he expected others even more severe), but he desired only to finish the ministry that Jesus had assigned to him. He urged the elders to exercise a similar faithfulness in the face of coming dangers and difficulties.

When Jesus departed this earth, He conveyed His ongoing ministry to the Spirit-led apostles. When the apostle Paul neared the conclusion of his third missionary journey, he conveyed the ongoing responsibility to the elders with whom he had labored. The fulfillment of Jesus' Great Commission—the unfinished business of worldwide evangelism—continues to be conveyed to generation after generation of committed, Spirit-filled Christians, including us.

Answers to Quarterly Quiz
on page 226

Lesson 1—1. Theophilus. 2. forty. 3. a sabbath day's journey. **Lesson 2**—1. fire. 2. the apostles' doctrine, fellowship, breaking of bread, and prayers. **Lesson 3**—1. the ninth. 2. false. 3. boldness. **Lesson 4**—1. Gamaliel. 2. Theudas and Judas of Galilee. **Lesson 5**—1. the Grecian widows. 2. seven. 3. "Lord, lay not this sin to their charge." **Lesson 6**—1. Philip. 2. true. 3. the Ethiopian eunuch. **Lesson 7**—1. "Why seek ye the living among the dead?" 2. synagogues. **Lesson 8**—1. Joppa. 2. Simon (a tanner). 3. respecter, persons. **Lesson 9**—1. Barnabas. 2. Tarsus. 3. Agabus. **Lesson 10**—1. John (Mark). 2. true. **Lesson 11**—1. Jerusalem, apostles, elders. 2. Peter. **Lesson 12**—1. Macedonia. 2. Lydia. 3. "Sirs, what must I do to be saved?" **Lesson 13**—1. Miletus. 2. Jerusalem. 3. three years.

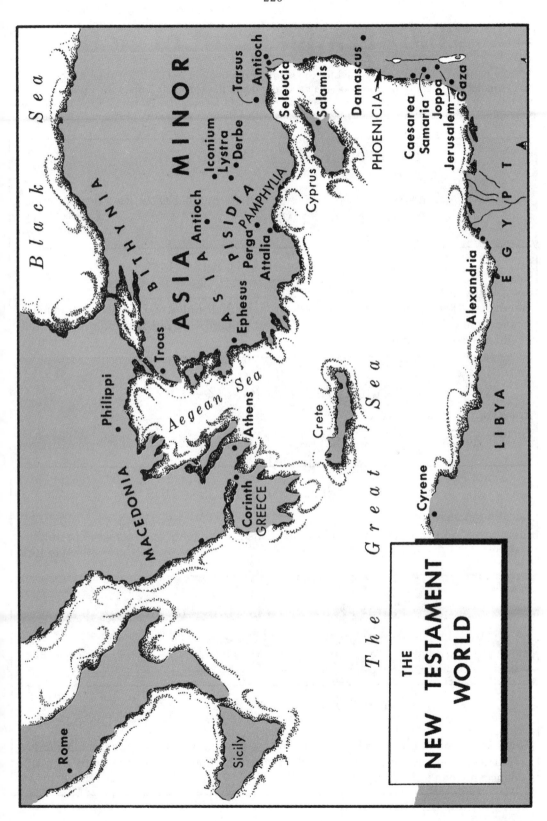

THE
NEW TESTAMENT
WORLD

The Arrangement of Acts

Many outlines have been suggested for the study of the book of Acts. C. H. Turner's suggestion of six chronological "panels" in the book may actually come the closest to Luke's own plan as he laid out the material. Each "panel" covers a particular time and focuses on (though not exclusively) one geographical area. In addition, each one concludes with a distinct summary statement in the text.

Panel One   Acts 1:1—6:7

Location: Jerusalem

Summary: "And the word of God increased; and the number of the disciples multiplied in Jerusalem greatly; and a great company of the priests were obedient to the faith."
—Acts 6:7

Panel Two   Acts 6:8—9:31

Location: Judea and Samaria (and Galilee)

Summary: "Then had the churches rest throughout all Judea and Galilee and Samaria, and were edified; and walking in the fear of the Lord, and in the comfort of the Holy Ghost, were multiplied."
—Acts 9:31

Panel Three   Acts 9:32—12:24

Location: Syria; Gentiles included

Summary: "But the word of God grew and multiplied."
—Acts 12:24

Panel Four   Acts 12:25—16:5

Location: Asia Minor

Summary: "And so were the churches established in the faith, and increased in number daily."
—Acts 16:5

Panel Five   Acts 16:6—19:20

Location: Gospel introduced in Europe; churches strengthened in Asia Minor

Summary: "So mightily grew the word of God and prevailed."
—Acts 19:20

Panel Six   Acts 19:21—28:31

Location: The church reaches Rome

Summary: "And Paul . . . received all that came in unto him, preaching the kingdom of God, and teaching those things which concern the Lord Jesus Christ, with all confidence, no man forbidding him."
—Acts 28:30, 31

The Acts of People

Making Bible People More "Personal"

by Ronald G. Davis

ALTHOUGH THE BOOK FROM WHICH this quarter's lessons are drawn is usually called "The Acts of the Apostles," Acts is a book about a wide range of *people*: men and women, slave and free, Greek and Barbarian, Jew and Gentile, noble and ignoble. Acts is a book about people who came face-to-face with the gospel of Jesus Christ. The issue in every such encounter was this: "Will the gospel be allowed to demonstrate its power, or will it be met and resisted by a 'force field' of personal will?"

The book of Acts revels in the many times when the answer to this question was, "Yes!" But it is painfully honest in recording that sometimes the answer was, "No, I won't let it!" Of course, the "No" reflects on the will of the person involved, not on the character of the gospel. We know that "the gospel . . . is the power of God unto salvation to every one that believeth" (Romans 1:16).

A study of Acts ought to fortify the Christian's confidence in the gospel's power to change lives. Students should walk away from such a series strongly committed to the proposition: "The gospel preached, taught, and modeled can work with any person—regardless of social status, religious background, or ethnic heritage."

The teacher of this series will want to personalize the studies—that is, to make the people of the first century alive and as real as family members and neighbors. Two approaches to making that happen follow. One we will call *Label Makers*; the other we will call *Dramatic Interviews*.

Label Makers

Consider some of the significant individuals in the lessons to be studied this quarter: Peter, Stephen, Philip, the Ethiopian eunuch, Saul/Paul, Barnabas, Cornelius, Lydia, the Philippian jailer, and the Ephesian elders. For each one there is a collection of labels that fits him or her to a tee. Developing such a list of labels—some obvious, some not so obvious—is a worthwhile activity for any class. The teacher has two sources for such a list: 1) make the list himself and introduce it to the students for their consideration and explanation, or 2) have the class itself develop the list.

Look at this list of characteristics for the Ethiopian eunuch of Acts 8:26-39 (lesson 6): *man, Ethiopian, eunuch, outsider, alien, African, steward, powerful, responsible, literate, treasurer,* *worshipful, committed, wealthy, humble, hospitable, listener, servant, curious, concerned, responsive, obedient, joyful, confused, open, rider, opportunist, mutilated.*

And consider this list for the Philippian jailer of chapter 16 (lesson 12): *callous, obedient, careful, thorough, diligent, wise, responsible, loyal, opportunistic, fatherly, kind, joyful, hospitable, Roman, scared, homeowner, believer.*

Can you explain all the labels suggested? Can your students? Can you add to the lists? Can your students?

As a teacher, if you have compiled your own list, you could show all the contents at once and ask your class to identify the reason each term would be appropriate; or you could read/write one word at a time, followed by the same call for student response. If you ask the class to devise the list, consider displaying a large cutout of a person on the wall and then asking class members to approach and write their labels on the cutout. (Label the cutout across the head with the name of the person under consideration.) Some will enjoy the graffiti nature of this activity, and having the cutout on the wall for a week or two may help the students remember the study and its applications to their lives.

Another approach to developing such a list is to give each student a three-by-five index card or a half-sheet of paper and ask each to write down three words that could be used to describe the person who is the subject of the study. Cornelius, the centurion, is the subject of lesson 8 of this quarter. Have students read the entire account of Cornelius in Acts 10; then give them this statement to complete by using three one-word responses: "Cornelius was (a). . . . " (The optional *a* gives the students the opportunity to complete the statement with either an adjective [devout, wise, etc.] or a noun [soldier, leader, etc.]).

After three or four minutes, ask students to read "the one word on your list that you doubt anyone else has" or, "the one word on your list that you think most people included." After a word is read, ask for a show of hands of others who included the same word. This will allow a comparison and contrast of lists and will provide a thorough description/characterization of Cornelius. Labels a teacher might expect to hear most often include *God-fearing, Roman, devout, centurion, generous, prayer* (all from the lesson text); labels that might appear on a few lists include: *expectant, kind, hospitable, baptized, listener, afraid, well-to-do.* For those words that no other class member included, you will want to ask the reader to explain his choice. For example, if someone had the word *visionary*, he might explain it on the basis of Acts 10:3 ("he saw in a vision"). If someone included *mistaken*, he might use Acts 10:25 and 26 in his explanation. In most such activities, some students will include words the teacher has never considered, and usually they will have interesting and even insightful explanations for the choices.

For some individuals and classes, preparing an acrostic using the key character's name is an enjoyable and profitable "label-making" activity. Such a longer name as *Cornelius* lends itself to acrostic-making. Consider: **C**ommander, **O**bedient, **R**espected, **N**otable, **E**xpectant, **L**oving, Ital**i**an, **U**nusual, **S**pirit-filled. Shorter names or titles may lend themselves to sentence acrostics. Consider the Ephesian elders of lesson 13 (Acts 20:17-32): **E**phesian **l**eaders **d**early **e**ncouraged (by) **r**eminding **s**ervant.

Dramatic Interviews

A dramatic or dramatized interview presents an up-close-and-personal look at a particular Biblical person. A "pretender" (actor/actress) is called on to answer questions about the person being represented—questions with factual responses based on history, geography, culture, and the Biblical record, and questions with only speculative responses (though even those responses should have some reasonableness to them). A few props or a bit of costuming can be used, but neither needs to be present for such an activity to be effective.

The teacher can play the role of the one interviewed, the interviewer, or neither. (He may wish to recruit someone from within the class or from outside the class to fill these roles.) Such interviews can be carefully "scripted" or almost spontaneous. Each approach offers some legitimate learning opportunities for the class. The interviews can be conducted in a one-on-one, "TV newsmagazine" setting or in a "press conference" arrangement. The latter offers more student involvement; the former may be "safer" and more controlled.

Stephen is the primary subject of lesson 5 this quarter and could serve as the ideal subject of a dramatic interview. If a teacher recruits another person to be Stephen, the actor can be interviewed across the table with such questions as these: (1) Stephen, could you describe the situation that led to your being selected to help with the ministry to the widows? (2) What are some of the "great wonders and miracles" you were able to do? (3) Why, do you suppose, did the Jews begin to argue with you? (4) How could your accusers say, "Stephen has spoken words of blasphemy against Moses and against God"? What had you been saying that led them to make such a charge? (5) When you were on trial before the Sanhedrin, how was your experience there similar to Jesus' experience? (6) Your summary of the Old Testament, moving from Abraham through the prophets, is a marvelously concise history. How did you learn that history so well? (7) Briefly describe your vision of the heavenly throne room. What sort of encouragement was that to you? (8) Stephen, give our class one final word of encouragement. What do you think we most need to hear? (Note that whoever participates in this interview will need to be familiar with the entire account of Stephen as recorded in Acts 6 and 7.)

If the teacher decides to let the class, or a representative group of four to six, do the interviewing, he can prepare and assign questions to each member of the group, he can recruit his panel early and ask them to develop their own questions, or the questions can be worded spontaneously by the members after a brief introduction by the teacher. If the individual playing the role of the Bible person wants to be more confident in responding during the interview, it will help to have the questions pre-arranged, with a copy given to the individual before the class session. But if that person is willing, spontaneous and unknown questions will probably elicit a more interesting response.

"Getting to Know You"

The words of an older popular song, "Getting to know you; getting to know all about you," state a worthy goal for a study of the book of Acts. Getting to know the people there, learning that they were real people struggling to stay faithful to Christ in an amoral or even immoral culture, and sensing their deep faith and commitment to the gospel—achieving these goals will make this quarter's study a valuable one for your adult students.

Probably every member of your adult class has experienced a period of doubt and discouragement. (Some may be experiencing such a time right now.) To study the book of Acts is to study those individuals who are now among "so great a cloud of witnesses" and whose example can encourage us to "run with patience the race that is set before us, looking unto Jesus" (Hebrews 12:1, 2). By getting to know them, we can run our race with greater confidence.

The Promise of the Spirit's Power

DEVOTIONAL READING: **John 16:7-14.**

BACKGROUND SCRIPTURE: **Acts 1.**

PRINTED TEXT: **Acts 1:1-14.**

Acts 1:1-14

1 The former treatise have I made, O Theophilus, of all that Jesus began both to do and teach,

2 Until the day in which he was taken up, after that he through the Holy Ghost had given commandments unto the apostles whom he had chosen:

3 To whom also he showed himself alive after his passion by many infallible proofs, being seen of them forty days, and speaking of the things pertaining to the kingdom of God:

4 And, being assembled together with them, commanded them that they should not depart from Jerusalem, but wait for the promise of the Father, which, saith he, ye have heard of me.

5 For John truly baptized with water; but ye shall be baptized with the Holy Ghost not many days hence.

6 When they therefore were come together, they asked of him, saying, Lord, wilt thou at this time restore again the kingdom to Israel?

7 And he said unto them, It is not for you to know the times or the seasons, which the Father hath put in his own power.

8 But ye shall receive power, after that the Holy Ghost is come upon you: and ye shall be witnesses unto me both in Jerusalem, and in all Judea, and in Samaria, and unto the uttermost part of the earth.

9 And when he had spoken these things, while they beheld, he was taken up; and a cloud received him out of their sight.

10 And while they looked steadfastly toward heaven as he went up, behold, two men stood by them in white apparel;

11 Which also said, Ye men of Galilee, why stand ye gazing up into heaven? this same Jesus, which is taken up from you into heaven, shall so come in like manner as ye have seen him go into heaven.

12 Then returned they unto Jerusalem from the mount called Olivet, which is from Jerusalem a sabbath day's journey.

13 And when they were come in, they went up into an upper room, where abode both Peter, and James, and John, and Andrew, Philip, and Thomas, Bartholomew, and Matthew, James the son of Alpheus, and Simon Zelotes, and Judas the brother of James.

14 These all continued with one accord in prayer and supplication, with the women, and Mary the mother of Jesus, and with his brethren.

GOLDEN TEXT: Ye shall receive power, after that the Holy Ghost is come upon you: and ye shall be witnesses unto me both in Jerusalem, and in all Judea, and in Samaria, and unto the uttermost part of the earth.—Acts 1:8.

Continuing Jesus' Work
Unit 1: Beginning in Jerusalem
(Lessons 1-4)

Lesson Aims

After this lesson students should be able to:

1. Describe how Jesus prepared His apostles to be His witnesses.

2. Tell how Acts 1:8 can serve as a model for evangelistic efforts today.

3. Suggest a specific way to act as a witness for Jesus in the coming week.

Lesson Outline

INTRODUCTION
   A. Evidence for the Defense
   B. Lesson Background
I. A PERIOD OF PROOFS (Acts 1:1-5)
   A. Introduction to the Book (vv. 1, 2)
   B. Evidence of the Christ (v. 3)
   C. Baptism of the Spirit (vv. 4, 5)
II. A PROMISE OF POWER (Acts 1:6-11)
   A. Time of the Kingdom (vv. 6, 7)
   B. Power of the Witnesses (v. 8)
     Sharing Good News
   C. Certainty of Jesus' Return (vv. 9-11)
     "Because It Is There"
III. A PRAYER OF PREPARATION (Acts 1:12-14)
   A. Returning to the City (v. 12)
   B. Gathering to Pray (vv. 13, 14)
CONCLUSION
   A. Wanted: Witnesses
   B. Prayer
   C. Thought to Remember

Introduction

A. Evidence for the Defense

Suppose a friend of yours told you that last year an alien spaceship flew over his house and landed in a nearby field. You are naturally skeptical and begin to ask him some important questions. "What specifically did you see? Who else saw it? Do all the witnesses' stories agree? What evidence do you have? *I've* never seen a flying saucer, so why should I believe you? And if this thing landed, where is it now?"

Tough questions . . . questions similar to those that Christians sometimes face when they share with others the good news of Jesus Christ. Quite often today, a skeptical world demands that believers have more to offer than just a nice story.

Can a person living in the twenty-first century really believe that Jesus of Nazareth is the Son of God who died for our sins and was raised from the dead to ascend to the right hand of Almighty God? The answer is, "Yes, you can believe—and you don't have to abandon your rational mind."

Jesus was well aware of how difficult it can be to lead people to faith, so He prepared a group of specially instructed and empowered men to be His official witnesses to their world and to ours. Today's lesson describes the last stage of that training before the apostles would embark on their worldwide task.

B. Lesson Background

Our printed text includes the opening verses of the book known as "The Acts of the Apostles." That title, however, is somewhat misleading. The "acts" and words of only two apostles dominate the book: Peter in the first twelve chapters and Paul in the last sixteen. However, the focus on their ministries gives us an accurate representation of the general witness and preaching of all the apostles.

The author of Acts is Luke, the beloved physician and a co-worker of Paul. Judging from the events recorded at the end of the book (Paul's journey to Rome and his imprisonment there), Luke probably wrote Acts around A.D. 62. Luke's Gospel and Acts form a two-volume presentation of the life of Christ and the first years of Christ's church. In fact, Acts forms a kind of "bridge" from the Gospels to the epistles. Without it, the letters of Paul, James, Peter, John, and Jude would be far more difficult to understand.

I. A Period of Proofs
(Acts 1:1-5)

Luke begins by connecting the book of Acts with his Gospel. He takes the last major event in his Gospel (the ascension of Jesus into Heaven, Luke 24:50-53) and expands on it in the opening verses of Acts.

A. Introduction to the Book (vv. 1, 2)

1, 2. The former treatise have I made, O Theophilus, of all that Jesus began both to do and teach, until the day in which he was taken up, after that he through the Holy Ghost had given commandments unto the apostles whom he had chosen.

The *former treatise*, or book, refers to Luke's Gospel. Both the Gospel and Acts are addressed to the same individual, *Theophilus*. Who was he? Since Luke describes him by the title "most excellent" in Luke 1:3, Theophilus was probably a Gentile who was a high official in the service of Rome.

He may have been Luke's "patron" in writing these books. Apparently he had received some instruction about Jesus, and Luke's carefully researched Gospel reinforced the reliability of all he had heard (Luke 1:1-4). Perhaps Theophilus was considering becoming a Christian or was a new believer whom Luke wanted to encourage in the faith.

Luke says that his Gospel told how Jesus' ministry *began* until He ascended into Heaven; Acts, in turn, tells how Jesus' ministry continued after His ascension through His *apostles* and His church. Notice that Luke emphasizes Jesus' actions by putting *to do* before *teach*. The apostles' preaching in Acts focused on Jesus' miracles, including His death for us and His resurrection, rather than His ethical teaching. The gospel that saves us centers on what Jesus did (1 Corinthians 15:1-4).

B. Evidence of the Christ (v. 3)

3. To whom also he showed himself alive after his passion by many infallible proofs, being seen of them forty days, and speaking of the things pertaining to the kingdom of God.

One matter about which the apostles had to be utterly convinced was that Jesus had overcome death. In fact, Jesus went out of His way to make sure that the apostles had all the *proofs* they needed. So He invited them to look at His nail marks and spear wound, to touch Him, to give Him food to eat, and even to thrust their hands into His wounds (Luke 24:37-43; John 20:27). With such a continual stream of evidence that Jesus was alive again, the apostle John could say that the apostles' message was based on what they had heard, seen, and handled concerning the "Word of life"—that is, Jesus (1 John 1:1-3). [See question #1, page 240.]

The subject of Jesus' post-resurrection teaching was the *kingdom of God*, just as that had been the subject of His public ministry before (Luke 4:43). As described in the Lord's prayer, God's kingdom is present when those who are His subjects do His will here on earth as it is done in Heaven (Matthew 6:10). With the establishment of Jesus' church on the Day of Pentecost, the *kingdom of God* describes both the church's present identity and its future goal.

C. Baptism of the Spirit (vv. 4, 5)

4. And, being assembled together with them, commanded them that they should not depart from Jerusalem, but wait for the promise of the Father, which, saith he, ye have heard of me.

On one occasion, Jesus was *assembled together with* His apostles. He warned them not to go their separate ways, as they may have done earlier during this forty-day period (John 21:1-14). Instead,

they were to stay together in *Jerusalem* and *wait for the promise of the Father*, which, as the next verse shows, referred to the coming of the Holy Spirit. The Spirit was not a new subject to the apostles; they had *heard* Jesus speak of Him on the night before His crucifixion (John 14:16, 17, 26; 15:26, 27). [See question #2, page 240.]

5. For John truly baptized with water; but ye shall be baptized with the Holy Ghost not many days hence.

This verse calls to mind *John* the Baptist's prophecy of how Jesus' ministry would supersede his own (Luke 3:16). People can administer water baptism—whether John, the apostles, or any Christian. But only Jesus can immerse (the meaning of the word "baptize") people *with* (or "in") the Holy Spirit.

Baptism in the Holy Spirit is mentioned only seven times in the Bible. The first four are the Gospel accounts of John the Baptist's prediction that the One coming after him would baptize with the Holy Spirit (Matthew 3:11; Mark 1:8; Luke 3:16; John 1:33). The next occurrence is our text in Acts 1:5. Jesus' comment here points directly to the Spirit's filling of the apostles at Pentecost (Acts 2:4). The sixth reference is found in Acts 11:16, where Peter connects the Lord's promise of the Spirit's filling with events at the household of Cornelius as well as with the filling of the apostles "at the beginning." Thus the baptism in the Spirit is historically connected with just two events—the filling of the apostles at Pentecost and the filling of Cornelius's household. These two events mark the first gospel presentations to the Jews and then to the Gentiles.

The seventh and final verse describing a Spirit baptism is found in 1 Corinthians 12:13. Here Paul notes that all Christians have been baptized "by one Spirit . . . into one body." (The Greek word

Home Daily Bible Readings

Monday, Feb. 26—The Promise of the Holy Spirit (Acts 1:1-5)

Tuesday, Feb. 27—The Ascension of Jesus (Acts 1:6-11)

Wednesday, Feb. 28—Jesus Appoints the Twelve (Mark 3:13-19)

Thursday, Mar. 1—The Acts of the Apostles Begin (Acts 1:12-20)

Friday, Mar. 2—The Voice of the Lord (Psalm 29)

Saturday, Mar. 3—The Suicide of Judas Iscariot (Matthew 27:3-10)

Sunday, Mar. 4—Matthias Chosen to Replace Judas Iscariot (Acts 1:21-26)

that is translated "by" is the same word that is used in the other six passages, where it is translated "with.") Here, however, Paul is not discussing the Spirit baptism that Jesus administered. Instead, he is talking about the unity of the church based on the fact that all Christians have been "baptized into one body." Given the fact that there is only "one baptism" (Ephesians 4:5), it seems best to understand 1 Corinthians 12:13 as a reference to the "gift of the Holy Spirit" that accompanies the baptism in water that all Christians are to experience (Acts 2:38). Biblically, then, the promise of Jesus' baptizing in the Spirit is applied to only two important occasions in the book of Acts.

The apostles had to wait ten days for the Spirit's coming. We know this because Jesus was with them after His resurrection for forty days (v. 3) and the Spirit came at Pentecost—a feast held fifty days after the Passover celebration during which Jesus died and rose again.

II. A Promise of Power
(Acts 1:6-11)

A. Time of the Kingdom (vv. 6, 7)

6. When they therefore were come together, they asked of him, saying, Lord, wilt thou at this time restore again the kingdom to Israel?

The apostles' question was not unreasonable. Jesus had been teaching them about the *kingdom of God* (v. 3) and He had promised the coming of the Holy Spirit, which Israel had always associated with the restoration of its greatness as an independent nation (Ezekiel 36:22-28). In the first century, many believed that this restoration would be accompanied by the overthrow of the Roman forces who occupied the country.

Throughout Jesus' ministry the apostles had been interested in becoming leaders in the restored kingdom of which He spoke (Matthew 20:20-28; Luke 22:24-30). Their interests, however, had been tainted by the popular thinking. Even now, with Jesus' death and resurrection

Visual for lesson 1

This map in the Adult Visuals *kit will give your students a visual representation of the spread of the gospel in the book of Acts.*

having taken place, the apostles' question revealed that they still held certain misunderstandings about what Jesus had taught them. [See question #3, page 240.]

7. And he said unto them, It is not for you to know the times or the seasons, which the Father hath put in his own power.

Jesus responded to the apostles' question by telling them that information about God's timetable was not meant for them. Such knowledge was not necessary for the apostles to have in order to complete their mission. In fact, such knowledge is reserved by God the *Father* for Himself (Mark 13:32). The focus of Jesus' teaching about the end times is not to provide us with a handy chart outlining when and how He will return to reign over all; His main concern is that we be active and faithful servants, ready for the Master to return at any moment (Mark 13:33-37).

B. Power of the Witnesses (v. 8)

8. But ye shall receive power, after that the Holy Ghost is come upon you: and ye shall be witnesses unto me both in Jerusalem, and in all Judea, and in Samaria, and unto the uttermost part of the earth.

Instead of giving the apostles a timetable, Jesus gave them a task: He told them that they were to be His *witnesses* to the entire world. He also assured the apostles that the Spirit's coming would give them the *power* that they would need to be effective witnesses.

What power did Jesus mean? At least three types are indicated in the Bible. One power that the Spirit gave the apostles was the ability to accurately recall and proclaim all that Jesus taught them during His three and a half years of public ministry. Furthermore, the Spirit would reveal to them any additional truths as they would need them (John 14:26; 15:26, 27; 16:13-15). A second witness power given to the apostles was the ability to perform attesting signs and wonders to confirm that their message came from God and was true (Acts 2:43; 5:12; 2 Corinthians 12:12).

The third power that accompanied the apostles' preaching was the working of the Holy Spirit on the hearts of the hearers of the gospel to convict them of their sin and of their need for a Savior (John 16:7-11). This power is still available whenever we share the gospel with others.

This verse may be considered a "key" that "unlocks" the development of the rest of the book of Acts. Jesus told His disciples to fulfill their task in three stages: in Jerusalem (as told in Acts 1-7), in Judea and Samaria (chapters 8-12), and throughout the known world (chapters 13-28). This pattern for evangelism is one that all of us can use; we can begin with reaching those close to us even as we keep the ends of the earth as our ultimate goal. [See question #4, page 240.]

SHARING GOOD NEWS

Where should a single, eighty-one-year-old man go in search of a wife? Apparently it depends on what his mother thinks! An Associated Press story datelined in Corbeil, Ontario, a few years ago offered an interesting perspective on how to find a suitable marriage partner.

At the time the story was printed, the gentleman in question had a 117-year-old mother who believed it was important for her son to have a good wife and some kind of social life. "Mom" lived in a home for senior citizens. She made sure that all the "younger" women in the home were aware of some good news: her son was a fine man who would make some woman an excellent husband!

You have to admire this woman's zeal. She had some good news, and she began spreading it to anyone who would listen. She started where she was and took the message to the ends of her limited universe!

Jesus directed His apostles to take much the same approach in spreading the gospel. They were to start where they were and not stop until they had spread the message to "the uttermost part of the earth." We Christians, both individually and collectively (as the church), have not really fulfilled the Great Commission until we have evangelized our own "Jerusalems" and have also found some means of helping to spread the gospel to the far corners of the earth.   —C. R. B.

C. Certainty of Jesus' Return (vv. 9-11)

9. And when he had spoken these things, while they beheld, he was taken up; and a cloud received him out of their sight.

As He had foretold, Jesus now left the earth to return to His Father (John 16:28). The *cloud* into which He ascended may have been simply an ordinary cloud that finally hid Him from the apostles' view. However, it is also possible that this was the cloud of glory associated with the presence of God in the Old Testament and with Jesus at His transfiguration (Exodus 40:34; Mark 9:7).

10. And while they looked steadfastly toward heaven as he went up, behold, two men stood by them in white apparel.

The *two men* who *stood by* the apostles are not specifically identified, but their sudden appearance and *white apparel* (cf. Matthew 28:3; John 20:12) leave little doubt that they were angels.

11. Which also said, Ye men of Galilee, why stand ye gazing up into heaven? this same Jesus, which is taken up from you into heaven, shall so come in like manner as ye have seen him go into heaven.

The gentle angelic rebuke seems to say, "Why are you staring at the sky? Unlike His transfiguration, Jesus will not rejoin you when the clouds roll back. But He will return. Until He does, remember: you have His orders to carry out!"

The promise to the apostles (and to us) is that *this same Jesus* will return in the same way He left: personally, visibly, bodily, unexpectedly, and gloriously. The early Christians lived with a joyous expectation of Jesus' imminent return. This promise encouraged them as they moved out to win as many as possible to His kingdom before He came again. Our expectation of Jesus' coming should do the same for us, for this is certain: every day we are closer to His return.

"BECAUSE IT IS THERE"

Many will recognize the words, "Because it is there," as the answer given by George Mallory, the famous English mountain climber, when he was asked why he wanted to climb Mount Everest. On his third attempt to scale the mountain, in 1924, Mallory was last seen moving toward his goal before a cloud enfolded him about eight hundred feet below the summit.

It is not known whether Mallory conquered Everest before Sir Edmund Hillary and Tenzing Norgay (who succeeded in 1953). The latter pair can prove their feat by documentary evidence, including the photographs they took while on the peak. Even when the remains of Mallory were found in 1999 approximately two thousand feet below the summit of Everest, the question remained unanswered. A broken rope about his waist and a fractured leg indicate that he died in a fall. His camera (which might have provided evidence of his having reached the summit) was never found.

Jesus has not been seen since He ascended into a cloud in the Judean sky nearly two thousand years ago. However, unlike George Mallory, the fact of Jesus' success in achieving His life's mission is attested to by a host of eyewitnesses whom He had instructed in the meaning of His life, death, and resurrection. Their testimonies,

---

How to Say It

ALPHEUS. Al-*fee*-us.
BARTHOLOMEW. Bar-*thah*-luh-mew.
CORNELIUS. Cor-*neel*-yus.
JOSES. *Jo*-sez.
MATTHIAS. Muh-*thigh*-us.
SAMARIA. Suh-*mare*-ee-uh.
THEOPHILUS. Thee-*ahf*-ih-luss.
ZELOTES. Zeh-*low*-teez.

recorded in Scripture, give us assurance of the trustworthiness of the Christian message. We can trust what those witnesses say "because they were there." —C. R. B.

III. A Prayer of Preparation (Acts 1:12-14)

A. Returning to the City (v. 12)

12. Then returned they unto Jerusalem from the mount called Olivet, which is from Jerusalem a sabbath day's journey.

Luke's Gospel records that the apostles had followed Jesus out of *Jerusalem* toward Bethany, which is just over the crest of the *mount called Olivet*—i.e., the Mount of Olives (Luke 24:50, 51). After Jesus ascended to Heaven, the disciples *returned* to the city with great joy and anticipation (Luke 24:52, 53). Their *journey* was no farther than Jews were allowed to travel on a *sabbath*—about three quarters of a mile.

B. Gathering to Pray (vv. 13, 14)

13. And when they were come in, they went up into an upper room, where abode both Peter, and James, and John, and Andrew, Philip, and Thomas, Bartholomew, and Matthew, James the son of Alpheus, and Simon Zelotes, and Judas the brother of James.

This "witness list" includes those who had once fled into the night when Jesus was arrested. Now they waited eagerly to proclaim publicly their Lord and Savior. Soon the name of Matthias will be added to this list to replace the betrayer, Judas (Acts 1:26).

14. These all continued with one accord in prayer and supplication, with the women, and Mary the mother of Jesus, and with his brethren.

Besides the apostles, *the women* who had followed Jesus during His ministry and Jesus' *brethren* are mentioned. This is the last New Testament reference to *Mary the mother of Jesus.* Just as she appeared at the beginning of Luke's Gospel (Luke 1:26, 27), she appears here at the beginning of the church. Jesus' *brethren* (more accurately, half-brothers) were James, Joses, Simon, and Judas (Matthew 13:55). They had not believed in their

brother before He was crucified (John 7:5). But apparently, when the resurrected Jesus appeared to one of them (James, 1 Corinthians 15:7) their doubts were transformed into faith. James became an important leader in the Jerusalem church (Acts 15:13; cf. Galatians 2:9).

As Luke leaves this group of believers waiting for the promise of the Spirit, he notes that they were *with one accord*; that is, they were united in a common purpose and mission. In addition they *continued . . . in prayer.* Their attitude does not appear to be one of agonizing and pleading for the Spirit to come. Instead, they appear certain that Jesus' promise would be fulfilled, leaving them filled with courage, expectancy, and joy. Christ's witnesses could hardly wait to begin the grand task of proclaiming the living Lord. [See question #5, page 240.]

Conclusion

A. Wanted: Witnesses

While none of us can be witnesses of the resurrection as the apostles could, each of us can give a testimony for Jesus in other ways. We can share with those who do not know Jesus the good news based on the apostles' witness. We can also share how Jesus has changed our lives and given us new hope and joy in His grace and forgiveness. We can show how Jesus can change a person's character to become like His own by demonstrating the fruit of the Spirit.

What all of this comes down to is this: we witness of Christ through the total commitment of our lives to serve Him and further His kingdom wherever we are. It is interesting that by the end of the New Testament, the word for "witness" had taken on an additional meaning: it described a person willing to give up his life for his faith in Jesus (Revelation 2:13). This has come into our language as the word "martyr"—one whose witness to Jesus is signed in blood.

Whether or not we are called to give testimony in this way, may we all be faithful witnesses of Jesus as we await His return.

B. Prayer

You call us, O Lord, to a faith in Jesus Christ founded on the bedrock testimony of faithful witnesses and confirmed miraculously by Your power and Your Spirit. May our testimony to Jesus be equally faithful so that the gospel may reach out to the ends of the earth to save the lost. In Jesus' name. Amen.

C. Thought to Remember

Christian witnesses confirm their testimony by the way they live and by the way they die.

VISUALS FOR THESE LESSONS

The small visual pictured in each lesson (e.g., page 236) is a small reproduction of a large, full-color poster included in the *Adult Visuals* packet for the Spring Quarter. The packet is available from your supplier. Order No. 392.

Learning by Doing

This page contains an alternate lesson plan emphasizing learning activities. Classes desiring such student involvement will find these suggestions helpful.

Learning Goals

After this lesson each student will be able to:

1. Describe how Jesus prepared His apostles to be His witnesses.

2. Tell how Acts 1:8 can serve as a model for evangelistic efforts today.

3. Suggest a specific way to act as a witness for Jesus in the coming week.

Into the Lesson

To introduce today's lesson, lead your students in writing a true-false quiz based on the content in today's lesson text. The purpose of a true-false quiz is to cause class members to open their Bibles and say, "It says right here. . . ." Or you may use the quiz below to shorten this portion of the lesson. (Two of these statements will require more information than can be gleaned from the Bible text alone—numbers 5 and 7. Use the commentary section to answer these, as they provide helpful background for the students.)

1. Jesus told His disciples not to leave Jerusalem until the Day of Pentecost. *(False, v. 4.)*

2. The Great Commission is given in Acts 1:8. *(True.)*

3. God selected Matthias to replace Judas as one of the twelve apostles. *(True, vv. 24-26.)*

4. Luke identifies himself as the author of Acts. *(True, v. 1.)*

5. Theophilus may have been the patron who sponsored the writing of Luke and Acts. *(True.)*

6. The names of the twelve apostles are given in Acts 1. *(True, v. 13—plus Matthias, v. 26.)*

7. "The Acts of the Apostles" is a good title for Luke's second book. *(False, see p. 234.)*

8. After the resurrection, the apostles finally understood the kingdom of God. *(False, v. 6.)*

9. There were three thousand disciples with the Twelve in Acts 1. *(False, v. 15.)*

10. Jesus appeared after His resurrection over a period of fifty days. *(False, v. 3.)*

Into the Word

Have your students work in small groups to outline the first fourteen verses of Acts. Encourage each group to read the text at least twice, list the main idea in each verse or paragraph, and then try to connect the ideas with an acrostic (the first letter of each point spells a word) or an alliteration (each title begins with the same letter). For example, steps 2 and 3 might produce:

1-3   Acts Introduced
4-6   Await the Holy Spirit
7, 8   All the World
9   Ascension
10, 11   Angelic Message
12-14   Apostles at Prayer

Into Life

Option 1: Letter Writing

Almost every church has members who are living away from home attending a college or university. A letter from a concerned Christian back home would be welcome mail.

Bring paper, envelopes, stamps, and addresses to class. (Your church secretary or the students' mothers can help with the addresses.) Ask each class member to write a letter to a college student explaining why the testimony of God's chosen witnesses is a better foundation for our faith than an individual believer's personal religious experience. You may want to provide copies of the lesson commentary for this project.

Option 2: Memorization

Encourage your class members to memorize Acts 1:8 during the class period. Select one of the following methods or use another of your own choosing.

1. Read the verse aloud several times. Then have all Bibles closed and ask each person to take a turn saying one word of the verse until the whole verse has been recited.

2. Use hand gestures. For example, when the class says the word *ye* or *you*, have them point to themselves or to one another. For *power*, flex your biceps in a classic body builder's pose. *The Holy Ghost* is symbolized by the flapping wings of a bird coming down on one's head. Emphasize the eyewitness testimony of the apostles by pointing to your eyes as you say *witnesses*. *Jerusalem* is indicated by pointing to the spot where you are standing. *All Judea* is indicated by tracing a circle around you, and *unto the uttermost part of the earth* is indicated by a larger circle covering all points of the compass.

3. Write the verse with the reference on a chalkboard or marker board. Have the class read the verse aloud together a couple of times; then erase one or two words. Continue erasing words one or two at a time until nothing remains and everyone is quoting the verse from memory.

Let's Talk It Over

The questions on this page are designed to encourage review of the lesson Scriptures and to promote discussion of the lesson by the class. The answers provided are only discussion starters. Let your class talk it over from there.

1. Of the "many infallible proofs" by which Jesus "showed himself alive" after His resurrection (Acts 1:3), which do you find most convincing? Why? How can you use this evidence to share the gospel with another person?

As your students comment on what evidence is most convincing for them, be sure to note the great variety of evidence. Jesus appeared on multiple occasions to multiple persons and was witnessed through a variety of senses: sight, hearing, and touch. He ate with the apostles (Luke 24:41-43 and probably John 21:9-15). The apostles were so convinced of Jesus' resurrection that they were transformed from timid and fearful sheep scattering when the Shepherd was struck (Matthew 26:31) to the bold and confident men who stood up to the Sanhedrin, as recorded in Acts 4 and 5.

2. Jesus reassured the apostles regarding "the promise of the Father" with the reminder that they had heard it from Him. Of what promises do you await fulfillment with the assurance that the promises came from Jesus?

One of the most powerful and reassuring promises from the lips of Jesus is this: "If I go and prepare a place for you, I will come again, and receive you unto myself; that where I am, there ye may be also" (John 14:3). This same promise is repeated in Revelation 22:12—"Behold, I come quickly; and my reward is with me." This might be a good time to have the class look up as many occasions as they can find in the New Testament where Jesus promises to return.

There are others as well. Jesus has promised that, in spite of the trouble we face in life, He will give us peace (John 16:33). He has promised to sustain us as we seek first His kingdom and righteousness (Matthew 6:33).

3. The lesson writer says the apostles' understanding of the kingdom "had been tainted by the popular thinking." In what ways are modern Christians' ideas "tainted by the popular thinking" of our day? How can we prevent such influence from corrupting our views?

This discussion may go in a variety of directions. One would be to debunk several supposed Scriptural quotations that are not in the Bible. Many believe that the adage, "God helps those who help themselves," is in the Bible. It isn't. In

truth, God helps those who realize they cannot help themselves (Romans 5:6). A salesman for a popular brand of vacuum cleaner quoted what he thought was Scripture when he said, "Cleanliness is next to godliness." But that's not in the Bible either. One of the most serious errors is the belief that if I work hard, don't drink or smoke, tell the truth, and love my spouse and my children, then I'll go to Heaven. Paul tells us it is "by grace [we are] saved through faith; and that not of yourselves: it is the gift of God: not of works" (Ephesians 2:8, 9)

4. Acts 1:8 is frequently used as a model for evangelism. Suggest some specific strategies for testifying of Christ in each of the four levels mentioned: local (Jerusalem), regional (Judea), national (Samaria), and global (uttermost part of the earth).

Here is a chance to get very practical with the lesson. What specific needs can your class address in your community to provide a means of sharing the good news with those closest to you? What about the larger region around you—can you support a new church nearby, perhaps in the inner city, or maybe in a fast-growing suburb? Can you work with other churches to sponsor evangelistic efforts to an unreached people group in this country or on foreign soil? How about a mission trip by your class or some members of your class and others in the church?

5. Early disciples were of "one accord." How can such unity be achieved today? What can you do to promote it?

To discern how unity can be achieved *today*, perhaps we need to discover the basis of the disciples' unity *then*. They never sat down and drew up a creed and pledged their loyalty to that. They did not hold unity meetings with the Jews and seek to find common ground between their faith and that of Judaism. They simply were loyal to Jesus Christ alone and preached His gospel. Those who accepted Christ accepted Him alone as "the way, the truth, and the life" (John 14:6). They shared the same mission—that of making disciples of all nations (Matthew 28:19, 20). If we would have unity today, then each of us must have a wholehearted devotion to Jesus as Lord and to obedience to His Great Commission.

The Holy Spirit Comes in Power

DEVOTIONAL READING: John 3:5-8.

BACKGROUND SCRIPTURE: Acts 2.

PRINTED TEXT: Acts 2:1-4, 37-47.

Acts 2:1-4, 37-47

1 And when the day of Pentecost was fully come, they were all with one accord in one place.

2 And suddenly there came a sound from heaven as of a rushing mighty wind, and it filled all the house where they were sitting.

3 And there appeared unto them cloven tongues like as of fire, and it sat upon each of them.

4 And they were all filled with the Holy Ghost, and began to speak with other tongues, as the Spirit gave them utterance.

· · · · · · · · · · ·

37 Now when they heard this, they were pricked in their heart, and said unto Peter and to the rest of the apostles, Men and brethren, what shall we do?

38 Then Peter said unto them, Repent, and be baptized every one of you in the name of Jesus Christ for the remission of sins, and ye shall receive the gift of the Holy Ghost.

39 For the promise is unto you, and to your children, and to all that are afar off, even as many as the Lord our God shall call.

40 And with many other words did he testify and exhort, saying, Save yourselves from this untoward generation.

41 Then they that gladly received his word were baptized: and the same day there were added unto them about three thousand souls.

42 And they continued steadfastly in the apostles' doctrine and fellowship, and in breaking of bread, and in prayers.

43 And fear came upon every soul: and many wonders and signs were done by the apostles.

44 And all that believed were together, and had all things common;

45 And sold their possessions and goods, and parted them to all men, as every man had need.

46 And they, continuing daily with one accord in the temple, and breaking bread from house to house, did eat their meat with gladness and singleness of heart,

47 Praising God, and having favor with all the people. And the Lord added to the church daily such as should be saved.

GOLDEN TEXT: Peter said unto them, Repent, and be baptized every one of you in the name of Jesus Christ for the remission of sins, and ye shall receive the gift of the Holy Ghost.
—Acts 2:38.

Continuing Jesus' Work
Unit 1: Beginning in Jerusalem
(Lessons 1-4)

Lesson Aims

After this lesson students should be able to:

1. Describe the events of Pentecost and the earliest days of the church.

2. Explain the importance of each element of worship cited in Acts 2:42.

3. Consider one of the elements cited in Acts 2:42 and suggest some specific steps he or she can take to grow in maturity in that area.

Lesson Outline

INTRODUCTION

  A. Finding the Power to Change

  B. Lesson Background

I. THE SPIRIT DESCENDS (Acts 2:1-4)

  A. Wondrous Wind (vv. 1, 2)

  B. Testifying Tongues (vv. 3, 4)

    An Unquenchable Fire

II. THE CROWD RESPONDS (Acts 2:37-41)

  A. Inspired Instructions (vv. 37, 38)

  B. Warning Words (vv. 39-41)

    Yes or No?

III. THE CHURCH GROWS (Acts 2:42-47)

  A. Primary Practices (v. 42)

  B. Startling Signs (v. 43)

  C. Common Concern (vv. 44-47)

CONCLUSION

  A. The Task Continues

  B. Prayer

  C. Thought to Remember

Introduction

A. Finding the Power to Change

Even the most attractive celebrity has some physical attributes that are less than perfect in someone's eyes. That is the reason plastic surgeons have waiting lists of hopeful people longing to change for the better. However, the most difficult task on the face of the earth has to be the permanent and positive transformation of the human soul. Thousands of self-help books, programs, and organizations have claimed to have the power to make lasting and beneficial changes in people. Yet whatever temporary improvements occur tend to be followed by long-term failures.

Jesus claimed that He had come to bring us life "more abundantly" (John 10:10). He insisted that real change comes only "from the inside out" (Mark 7:21-23). Such change requires a special kind of power.

On the Day of Pentecost, when the church began, Jesus sent the Holy Spirit to enter obedient believers and to begin building new lives. Those new lives made up the new body of Christ, His church. Today's lesson focuses on how God brought the church into being.

B. Lesson Background

According to Acts 1, following Jesus' ascension into Heaven the apostles were guided by God in selecting a replacement for Judas. This man, Matthias, most likely joined the other apostles during the time that they were "continually in the temple, praising and blessing God" (Luke 24:53). There must have been tremendous excitement among the apostles. They could hardly wait to share the good news of Christ's resurrection. Still, they followed Jesus' instructions and remained together until they were clothed "with power from on high" (Luke 24:49).

I. The Spirit Descends
(Acts 2:1-4)

A. Wondrous Wind (vv. 1, 2)

1. And when the day of Pentecost was fully come, they were all with one accord in one place.

The feast of Pentecost was one of the three great sacred assemblies of the Jewish religion. The word *Pentecost* means fifty because the observance of this feast fell fifty days after the Passover Sabbath. That means that Pentecost would have occurred on the first day of the week. The church was born on the day we call Sunday.

Although Luke does not mention it, Pentecost was a harvest feast that celebrated the end of the barley harvest. Out of all the days that God could have chosen to begin His church, He chose a harvest celebration to plant the seed of the gospel and reap His first crop of souls.

Luke states that *they* were all together as this pivotal time approached. But what group does the pronoun *they* indicate? Some students believe it refers to the one hundred twenty disciples mentioned in Acts 1:15. Others argue that it refers only to the twelve apostles.

The one hundred twenty has been suggested primarily because that group included both men and women. And, at the beginning of his address to the crowd, Peter linked the events of Pentecost with the prophecy of Joel, who predicted that the Spirit of God would be poured out on both men and women (Acts 2:16-21; cf. Joel 2:28-32). But this prophecy can also be understood to refer to all the work of the Holy Spirit from that first day (when the church began) until the day when Christ comes again—a period of time when many men and women would be filled with the Spirit.

It is better to understand the word *they* as a reference to the apostles. Consider the following:

• The immediate antecedent—the group named in the previous verse—is the apostles (1:26).

• The group consisted only of Galileans (2:7).

• The group consisted only of men (2:13).

• The group is specifically identified as Peter and the other eleven apostles—twice (2:14, 37).

Some have suggested that the *one place* where the apostles were gathered was the upper room mentioned in Acts 1:13. If so, they must have left that place as the crowd began to gather. Otherwise they could not have addressed so large a crowd that three thousand hearers could respond to their message. For that reason, many students believe that the *one place* was somewhere around the temple courts—perhaps near the Court of the Gentiles. Such a place would have been large enough to accommodate the thousands who would soon convene to hear the apostles' preaching. That the place is called a "house" in verse 2 is not a problem, since the temple—or even the tabernacle—is also called a house (Matthew 21:13; Mark 2:26; John 2:16, 17; Acts 7:47).

2. And suddenly there came a sound from heaven as of a rushing mighty wind, and it filled all the house where they were sitting.

The first of a cluster of four events described is a *sound*—a sudden noise that resembled the echoing roar of a *mighty wind*. Note that Luke does not say that an actual wind was present, only the sound that a wind would make. He seems to have been using a play on words, for the Greek word that is translated *wind* is also the word that is translated, on some occasions, as *spirit*. Like the wind, the Holy Spirit is unseen but not unnoticed: His movement is mysterious and powerful, and the effects of His working are undeniable (John 3:8).

B. Testifying Tongues (vv. 3, 4)

3. And there appeared unto them cloven tongues like as of fire, and it sat upon each of them.

Here Luke tries to describe the second event, which was something the apostles saw. The shape of what they saw resembled a group of *tongues*, apparently similar to human tongues. The brightness of the tongues was like flickering *fire*. The movement of the tongues was to divide from a central point (the word *cloven* actually means "separated" or "distributed") until one bright shape came to rest on *each* apostle.

That these flames were shaped like tongues may point to the Spirit-empowered preaching about to

take place. It may further suggest the effect that God's Word has on human hearts; it makes them "burn" (Luke 24:32; cf. Jeremiah 20:9).

AN UNQUENCHABLE FIRE

Those four "doughnuts" of black rubber on which our cars ride are infinitely better than the solid tires that were used on early automobiles. The smooth ride and precise handling that we enjoy in our cars are two of the numerous benefits of modern technology. However, there is a downside to these wonders: disposal. The state of California alone discards thirty million used tires every year, and that's a problem.

One summer day, near the town of Tracy, California, a pile of seven million used tires caught fire. The shape of tires makes such a fire very difficult to extinguish. Air is trapped and readily available to feed the fire even as water or other flame retardants are blocked from reaching it. Thus, months later, the "tire fire" was still burning out of control, sending a pall of black, pollutant-filled smoke over the countryside.

On the Day of Pentecost, a strange phenomenon occurred. The place where the apostles were gathered was filled with the roar of a "rushing mighty wind"—perhaps like the sound of a tornado. Then, what resembled a flame appeared upon each of the apostles.

This was the beginning of a "fire" that has been impossible to extinguish. It was a fire that burned, not on the heads, but in the hearts of those who became fervent followers of Jesus Christ. Two millennia later, the message of the gospel is still a consuming fire that has spread around the world, burning the pollution of sin out of the hearts of those who yield to the cleansing power of Jesus. —C. R. B.

4. And they were all filled with the Holy Ghost, and began to speak with other tongues, as the Spirit gave them utterance.

The last two events were another pair of miracles. The first miracle was that the Holy Spirit of God *filled* twelve ordinary human beings. The second miracle provided the apostles with the ability they needed to preach directly to the hearts of the crowd that was gathering. The *Spirit* enabled the Twelve to speak to each group in its native tongue or dialect. [See question #1, page 248.]

II. The Crowd Responds
(Acts 2:37-41)

Peter and the apostles used this unique opportunity to proclaim publicly for the first time that Jesus of Nazareth is the Lord of glory and the Messiah whom Israel had awaited for so long.

Central to his message was the fact that, though they had crucified Jesus, God had raised Him from the dead (v. 32). Peter's declaration that God had made Jesus "both Lord and Christ" (v. 36) struck a blow at the people's messianic hopes. They had rejected the very Messiah they had awaited for centuries—what hope was left for them?

A. Inspired Instructions (vv. 37, 38)

37. Now when they heard this, they were pricked in their heart, and said unto Peter and to the rest of the apostles, Men and brethren, what shall we do?

The sting of guilt *pricked* the hearts of many in the crowd like a sharp needle. When they realized what they had done in crucifying the Son of God, they pleaded to the apostles, *What shall we do?* Should they offer an abundance of animals as a sacrifice for their sins? Should they pray for God to forgive them? Should they promise to be better and try harder? Should they punish themselves for the terrible thing they had done? [See question #2, page 248.]

Similarly, many today realize that they have disobeyed God; and they too wonder what they should do about it. Listen to Peter's answer.

38. Then Peter said unto them, Repent, and be baptized every one of you in the name of Jesus Christ for the remission of sins, and ye shall receive the gift of the Holy Ghost.

Peter responded with two commands and two promises. The first command was that those who believe in Jesus as the Messiah must *repent*. To repent is to turn around, to turn from sin and self-centeredness to obedience to God. This change of attitude results in a change of life, as we begin to embrace new habits and new goals. Repentance does not mean that we suddenly become perfect, but rather that we start moving in a new direction, daily striving to become more like Christ.

The second command was that those who believed and repented should *be baptized . . . in the*

"Repent, and be baptized every one of you in the name of Jesus Christ for the remission of sins, and ye shall receive the gift of the Holy Ghost."

Acts 2:38

Display today's visual as you prepare to discuss today's Golden Text, Acts 2:38.

Visual for lesson 2

name of Jesus Christ. Water baptism was designed by God to be a common experience uniting all Christians (Ephesians 4:4-6). Sadly, baptism has often divided Christians instead of uniting them. Perhaps it would help to note that certain conditions must exist before an act can be called Christian baptism.

First, the person who is baptized must believe in Jesus Christ (Mark 16:15, 16). Baptism without personal faith is not Biblical baptism. Being baptized is an act of faith; it is not a work that we do to please God. In fact, we cannot baptize ourselves. Baptism is passive—it is something we allow another to do to us. Christian baptism is to be done *in the name of Jesus Christ*—that is, under His authority and by His terms. In baptism we reenact what Jesus did for us: we die (to sin, in repentance), we are buried (in the water), and we are resurrected, or brought forth from the water, into "newness of life" (Romans 6:1-4).

Second, baptism is a decision that each person must make for himself or herself. Just as *every one* of us must decide to repent, so also each of us must decide to be baptized.

Third, God expects each person who believes in Christ to be baptized into Him. The New Testament knows nothing of the idea of an unbaptized believer. As baptism assumes faith, faith also assumes baptism. Jesus expected that anyone who decided to be His disciple after His death, resurrection, and ascension should be baptized (Matthew 28:19, 20).

The two promises attached to faith in Jesus Christ, expressed in repentance and baptism, are the *remission* (forgiveness) of our *sins* and the reception of the Holy Spirit. We should not think that God forgives our sins as a "reward" for our faith, repentance, and baptism. We are saved by the grace of what Jesus did for us, not by any goodness of anything that we do for Him.

The second promise we receive is the *gift of the Holy Ghost*, who comes to dwell within us and renew us so that we may grow daily to become more like Christ. As forgiveness removes the condemnation of our sin, so the Holy Spirit breaks our slavery to sin.

B. Warning Words (vv. 39-41)

39. For the promise is unto you, and to your children, and to all that are afar off, even as many as the Lord our God shall call.

Peter told his audience that the *promise* of which he spoke was for three groups. The first was the crowd before him who had gathered to observe Pentecost. They represented all of that generation of Jews. The second group comprised the *children* of those gathered—in other words, the generation that was to come. This indicated that God's promise was not limited simply to the time of the apostles' ministry.

The third group included *all* others, no matter how *afar off* they were, which indicated that the promise of the gospel was not to be limited by any national or geographical boundaries. Peter himself later saw the church incorporate both Jews and Gentiles into one body, worshiping the same Lord. God delights in shattering all man-made barriers with the gospel of Jesus Christ. [See question #3, page 248.]

The phrase *as many as the Lord our God shall call* brings to mind the concluding words of Joel's prophecy (Joel 2:32). It should be noted that this verse also includes the words, "Whosoever shall call on the name of the Lord shall be delivered." Thus God's call does not diminish the need for human responsibility. We answer God's call by calling on His name (Acts 22:16).

40. And with many other words did he testify and exhort, saying, Save yourselves from this untoward generation.

This clearly indicates that, although many in the crowd were convicted, they were not yet saved. They were part of the *generation* whose lives were not directed toward God, but away from Him (this is the meaning of the word *untoward*). The most obvious sign that this generation was corrupt was the fact that they had rejected and crucified Jesus Christ.

41. Then they that gladly received his word were baptized: and the same day there were added unto them about three thousand souls.

With this verse, Luke announces the spiritual harvest that the Lord reaped at the harvest festival of Pentecost. Those in the crowd who believed what Peter preached about Jesus, who in turn were ready to put their faith in Jesus, and who were prepared to repent of their sins *were baptized*—most likely in some of the many pools in Jerusalem. [See question #4, page 248.]

To baptize this many people on *the same day* should not be considered impossible. The apostles would not have had to do all the baptizing. If those who had been baptized in turn baptized others, the entire group of three thousand could have been baptized in a few hours.

YES OR NO?

For decades Jack Smith was a popular columnist for the *Los Angeles Times*. One of his most memorable columns was entitled, "The Everlasting Yea—or Nay." In it he compared the way in which computer circuits respond only to 1 or 0 (on or off, yes or no) with the way the human brain functions. His conclusion was that even life's most complicated quandaries can be resolved by asking the right simple questions.

How to Say It

GALILEANS. Gal-uh-*lee*-unz.
MATTHIAS. Muh-*thigh*-us.
MESSIANIC. mess-ee-*an*-ick.

For example, do we get up? Go to work? Stay at home in bed? These simple questions can have a profound influence on our lives, and the answers to them are simply *yes* or *no*. Everything from our choice of dinner menu to our choice of a life's mate can be boiled down to a *yes* or a *no*.

Smith noted that even great, history-making questions (Should the American colonies declare independence? Should Imperial Japan attack Pearl Harbor? Should America drop the atomic bomb?) all were decided with a simple *yes*.

When the gospel was presented to the crowd that had gathered on that Pentecost, the key issue came down to a simple *yes* or *no*. It still does: those who gladly receive the apostolic message of the crucified and risen Christ say *yes* to what He has done and respond to Him in faith-filled obedience.   —C. R. B.

III. The Church Grows
(Acts 2:42-47)

A. Primary Practices (v. 42)

42. And they continued steadfastly in the apostles' doctrine and fellowship, and in breaking of bread, and in prayers.

The early Christians were a devoted people; they lived their faith *steadfastly* in regard to four essential elements of church life. First, all came under the instruction of the *apostles' doctrine*, or teaching, whether in large groups at the temple or in smaller groups in homes (v. 46).

Second, the Jerusalem church devoted itself to *fellowship*—a commonly shared life. They created a new and close community within the city as they supported and encouraged each other.

The third and fourth items to which these believers committed themselves relate to their worship. While *breaking of bread* may simply mean sharing a meal, here Luke probably means the Lord's Supper, or Communion. Finally, *prayers* were a vital part of the early church—a theme emphasized throughout Acts (4:24-31; 6:4, 6; 11:4, 5; 12:5; 13:3; 14:23; 16:25; 22:17; 28:8).

B. Startling Signs (v. 43)

43. And fear came upon every soul: and many wonders and signs were done by the apostles.

Miraculous *wonders and signs* supported the authority of the apostles' teaching, for such demonstrations of God's power indicated that they spoke on His behalf (Hebrews 2:3, 4). Luke gives several examples of such miracles in the rest of his account (Acts 3:1-10; 5:12-16; 8:13; 9:32-42; 14:8-10; 19:11, 12; 20:9-12; 28:7-9).

C. Common Concern (vv. 44-47)

44, 45. And all that believed were together, and had all things common; and sold their possessions and goods, and parted them to all men, as every man had need.

What Luke describes here is not the establishment of an early Christian commune; it is simply a description of how wealthier Christians helped their poorer brothers and sisters. Some *sold their possessions and goods* and gave to those who *had need*. This was an example of voluntary generosity, not a continuing pattern that was meant to be compulsory for all Christians for all time. (That certain families kept their private homes is clear from the next verse.) [See question #5, page 248.]

46. And they, continuing daily with one accord in the temple, and breaking bread from house to house, did eat their meat with gladness and singleness of heart.

At this early stage in the development of the church, Christians and Jews could still worship in the same areas without animosity. The *daily* meetings *in the temple* probably took place during the regular prayer times and may have included teaching sessions conducted by the apostles. In addition, these Christians met together in private homes to share their meals and their joy.

47. Praising God, and having favor with all the people. And the Lord added to the church daily such as should be saved.

Although the Christians would continue to be faithful in *praising God*, the *favor* of the public was something that the church could not expect

to enjoy forever. This "honeymoon period" would soon be replaced by opposition and persecution. But *the Lord* was able to use both good times and bad to keep adding *to the church* those who were being *saved* (as He still is). The Lord blesses human efforts in His behalf and brings growth to the church (1 Corinthians 3:7-9).

New Christians become a part of the church at the same moment that they are saved. They must not be left alone, for they have been born into a spiritual family who should care for them, nourish them, and encourage them. Each of us must work to ensure that our church does not produce "spiritual orphans" who feel abandoned the moment they get out of the baptistery.

Conclusion

A. The Task Continues

Luke's record indicates that every Christian has four joyful responsibilities that come with being a follower of Jesus Christ. First, we are responsible to worship and obey God. Second, we are responsible to learn the teaching of the apostles and submit to it. Third, we are responsible to encourage, share with, and worship with one another. And fourth, we are responsible to the people of the world, to share with them the good news of God's love found in Jesus Christ. God's Spirit will work through our words to convince them of the truth of the gospel. Then, when they accept Christ, we can continue the process by teaching them these four responsibilities so that they in turn may teach them to others.

As we pursue these tasks, let us remember that we are empowered by the same God who sent His Spirit to His church on the Day of Pentecost. We can preach the same gospel, call for the same kind of response, teach the same apostles' doctrine, share the same fellowship, and accept the same responsibilities as the early church. As we do, we will see that the Lord is faithful and that He can still add to our number daily those who are being saved.

B. Prayer

O God of Pentecost! You sent Your Son to save us and Your Word to guide us. You sent Your Spirit to empower us and Your people to encourage us. May we as Your church be faithful to the example and design You have given us in the Holy Bible, and may all that we do give You praise forever. Through Jesus Christ, amen.

C. Thought to Remember

God's church, which began on Pentecost, is the same church whose purpose and activities we seek to reproduce today around the world.

Home Daily Bible Readings

Monday, Mar. 5—The Festival of Weeks (Pentecost) (Leviticus 23:15-21)

Tuesday, Mar. 6—The Coming of the Holy Spirit (Acts 2:1-13)

Wednesday, Mar. 7—Joel's Prophecy (Acts 2:14-21)

Thursday, Mar. 8—Peter Preaches About Jesus, the Messiah (Acts 2:22-36)

Friday, Mar. 9—The First Converts (Acts 2:37-42)

Saturday, Mar. 10—Life Among the Believers (Acts 2:43-47)

Sunday, Mar. 11—The Believers Share Their Possessions (Acts 4:32-37)

Learning by Doing

This page contains an alternate lesson plan emphasizing learning activities.
Classes desiring such student involvement will find these suggestions helpful.

Learning Goals

After participating in this lesson, each student will be able to:

1. Describe the events of Pentecost and the earliest days of the church.

2. Explain the importance of each element of worship cited in Acts 2:42.

3. Consider one of the elements cited in Acts 2:42 and suggest some specific steps he or she can take to grow in maturity in that area.

Into the Lesson

Nothing parallels the excitement of starting a new congregation. The participants in planting a new church must grapple with the essential elements that make the church the unique institution that God has ordained. Tell your class members to pretend that they are the planning committee for a new church planting. Ask the learners to turn to the persons seated next to them and spend a minute or two describing the essential features of the church.

Make the transition to the Bible study by saying, "We have been wrestling with what constitutes the essential features of the church. Our text today spells out those qualities in the historical account of the establishment of the first church—the church formed on the Day of Pentecost in Acts 2."

Into the Word

Use one or more of the following activities to involve your students in a study of today's lesson text.

Newspaper Report

Ask your class members to pretend that they are newspaper reporters assigned by *The Jerusalem Herald* to cover the events on the Day of Pentecost described in Acts 2. Newspapers should present a balanced story that covers the five "W" questions—"Who?" "What?" "When?" "Where?" "Why?"—and "How?"

Warm up for writing by having your class members read the text at least twice. Then establish an outline of the events to be covered. Decide which participants should be interviewed and quoted in the article. Conclude by brainstorming for an eye-catching headline. (Directions for this activity are included in the student quarterly, *Adult Bible Class*.)

Diary or Journal Entry

The Day of Pentecost recorded in Acts 2 was a unique and memorable day in history. What impact did these events have on those who were present? We cannot really know in detail. But it is enlightening to try to imagine.

Ask your class members to write a diary or journal entry as if they were present for the events recorded in Acts 2. In preparation for writing, have your students read the text several times.

Into Life

Use one or more of the following activities to help your students make application of today's lesson text.

Evaluation

Every church has the four elements listed in Acts 2:42 as a part of their church experience. Ask your class to evaluate your church in each of these four areas: the apostles' teaching, fellowship, breaking of bread, and prayer. Then select the one that is weakest and develop a plan to improve your church in that area.

Chart

Make a large copy of the following chart to compare the characteristics of the church in Acts 2 with your church today. Characteristics of the Christians in Acts 2 are identified on the left side. Use the right column to note a similar practice or experience in your church. If your church does not have a corresponding practice or experience, suggest an appropriate activity that the class can plan to encourage growth in that area.

Text	Acts 2 Church	Our Church
2:37	people cut to the heart	
2:38	repentance, baptism	
2:39	promise is universal	
2:40	powerful preaching	
2:41	baptism	
2:42	apostles' teaching	
	fellowship	
	breaking of bread	
	prayer	
2:43	sense of awe	
2:44	togetherness	
2:45	shared with needy	
2:46	happily eating together	
2:47	praising God	

Let's Talk It Over

The questions on this page are designed to encourage review of the lesson Scriptures and to promote discussion of the lesson by the class. The answers provided are only discussion starters. Let your class talk it over from there.

1. The apostles' preaching in languages they had never studied or learned was a powerful demonstration that God was the author of their message. How can we convince people today that the gospel is true and of God?

Encourage your students to tell how they have been able to make headway with convincing unbelievers to accept the truth of the Bible. If discussion is slow, consider what makes this task so difficult. The rejection of the concept of absolute truth is certainly one factor. Ask the class to suggest ways to deal with this problem. For example, we can challenge the notion that there are no absolutes—or that anyone really believes that. If your neighbor who says there are no absolutes needs surgery, will just anyone do? Is it absolutely necessary to have a surgeon? If the appendix is the problem, does the patient think it absolutely imperative that the appendix—and only the appendix—be removed? If there are absolutes in medicine, then why not in spiritual matters?

2. The people who heard Peter's accusation that they had crucified the One who was "both Lord and Christ" were "pricked in their heart"— they felt guilty. How appropriate is it to use guilt as a motivating factor to lead people to Christ?

Conventional wisdom eschews the idea of guilt as a motivating factor. But when one has done wrong, then he or she is guilty—and guilt is the appropriate feeling to go with that reality. Manipulating a person into feeling guilt is certainly wrong, but telling the truth so that a person realizes he or she has done wrong is not manipulation. And if the person feels guilty about that, then it may well be the work of the Spirit—convicting the person of sin. We must avoid manipulation, but we ought not to feel bad if a guilty person feels honest guilt.

3. The gospel breaks down the barriers that divide and separate people. In what ways have you seen the gospel break down barriers? How can we be more effective in taking the gospel across barriers in our own community?

Certainly every student in your class who is a believer can tell how the gospel crossed the barrier of sin in his or her own life. Perhaps there are some who can tell how the gospel broke down walls of prejudice in their lives and helped them reach out to someone of another race or socio-economic level. Is your church reaching out to people different from yourselves? Perhaps a wealthy suburban church runs a soup kitchen in the inner city or provides assistance to homeless people. Another church may open its doors to sponsor an Alcoholics Anonymous group or to provide facilities for a crisis pregnancy center.

Again and again the New Testament repeats the refrain that the gospel is for both men and women, both Jews and Gentiles, both slave and free (Romans 10:12, 13; Galatians 3:28; Colossians 3:11). The gospel is for everyone; no one is excluded. Let us demonstrate our belief in that truth by our actions.

4. The early church won three thousand converts on its first day of operation. What can we learn from their strategy that can help us have that kind of success in our evangelistic efforts?

First, the apostles talked to the people in their own language (Acts 2:4-8). Sometimes people who do not regularly attend church services think we Christians have a language all our own. We must avoid "churchy" sounding language and speak plainly.

Second, Peter focused on the death and resurrection of Jesus (vv. 22-36). Jesus must be at the center of our witnessing if we are to have any influence on other people.

Third, Peter boldly called for repentance (v. 38). We can't expect people to take us seriously if we do not present the gospel's radical demands. Peter did not say, "Sign a card and join the church." He said, "Repent, and be baptized."

5. The success of the early church was due in part to the willingness of all to share what they had with those who were in need. How can we live out that principle in the church today?

While the church cannot provide for every need of every person in the community, the New Testament is clear in stating that the church should care for those in its own fellowship (Romans 12:13; Galatians 6:10; Hebrews 13:1). Ask students to suggest some specific ways your church can do that without becoming enablers of those who could provide for themselves but don't, and without becoming so suspicious of all who voice needs that we fail to help those the Bible says we should assist.

The Holy Spirit Works With Power

DEVOTIONAL READING: 1 Corinthians 1:26-31.

BACKGROUND SCRIPTURE: Acts 3:1—4:22.

PRINTED TEXT: Acts 3:1-10; 4:1-4, 13.

Acts 3:1-10

1 Now Peter and John went up together into the temple at the hour of prayer, being the ninth hour.

2 And a certain man lame from his mother's womb was carried, whom they laid daily at the gate of the temple which is called Beautiful, to ask alms of them that entered into the temple;

3 Who, seeing Peter and John about to go into the temple, asked an alms.

4 And Peter, fastening his eyes upon him with John, said, Look on us.

5 And he gave heed unto them, expecting to receive something of them.

6 Then Peter said, Silver and gold have I none; but such as I have give I thee: In the name of Jesus Christ of Nazareth rise up and walk.

7 And he took him by the right hand, and lifted him up: and immediately his feet and ankle bones received strength.

8 And he leaping up stood, and walked, and entered with them into the temple, walking, and leaping, and praising God.

9 And all the people saw him walking and praising God:

10 And they knew that it was he which sat for alms at the Beautiful gate of the temple: and they were filled with wonder and amazement at that which had happened unto him.

Acts 4:1-4, 13

1 And as they spake unto the people, the priests, and the captain of the temple, and the Sadducees, came upon them,

2 Being grieved that they taught the people, and preached through Jesus the resurrection from the dead.

3 And they laid hands on them, and put them in hold unto the next day: for it was now eventide.

4 Howbeit many of them which heard the word believed; and the number of the men was about five thousand.

. . . .

13 Now when they saw the boldness of Peter and John, and perceived that they were unlearned and ignorant men, they marveled; and they took knowledge of them, that they had been with Jesus.

GOLDEN TEXT: Now when they saw the boldness of Peter and John, and perceived that they were unlearned and ignorant men, they marveled; and they took knowledge of them, that they had been with Jesus.—Acts 4:13.

Continuing Jesus' Work
Unit 1: Beginning in Jerusalem
(Lessons 1-4)

Lesson Aims

After this lesson students should be able to:

1. Tell how the Spirit's power was seen in the healing of the lame man and in Peter and John's response before the Sanhedrin.

2. Explain how our treatment of society's "outcasts" demonstrates whether we have "been with Jesus."

3. Form a plan for ministering to someone in their neighborhood or community whose situation and needs are often ignored.

Lesson Outline

INTRODUCTION
    A. Majoring in "Minor People"
    B. Lesson Background
  I. APOSTOLIC MIRACLE (Acts 3:1-10)
    A. A Beggar's Request (vv. 1-5)
    B. Peter's Response (vv. 6-8)
      A Remarkable Cure
    C. The Crowd's Reaction (vv. 9, 10)
 II. APOSTOLIC MESSAGE (Acts 4:1-4, 13)
    A. Producing Opposition (vv. 1-3)
    B. Bearing Fruit (v. 4)
    C. Causing Wonder (v. 13)
      Unlikely Spokesmen
CONCLUSION
    A. Take the Risk
    B. Prayer
    C. Thought to Remember

Introduction

A. Majoring in "Minor People"

Often many of us find ourselves surrounded by what might be called "minor" characters—people who pass in and out of our days so quickly and quietly that we tend to ignore them. (Of course, we can also be minor characters in other people's lives.)

What changes someone from a minor character into a "real" person? That usually takes place when we choose to focus on such a one and to care about him or her as someone made in the image of God. We begin looking directly at that individual, speaking with and really listening to the person. We make a connection that goes beneath mere surface concerns.

Some people seem doomed to the continual role of a "minor character"—just a part of the scenery in other peoples' lives. They wait for someone to notice (*really* notice) them in their loneliness and isolation. Today's lesson focuses on an incident when Peter transformed a lame man's life by really seeing him, speaking to him, and taking his hand in Jesus' name. This action and the events that followed resulted in many coming to faith in Christ and in an opportunity for Peter and John to demonstrate the character of Christ.

And it all began with majoring in what seemed to be a "minor" person.

B. Lesson Background

Part of last week's lesson was taken from the closing verses of Acts 2, where Luke describes the life of the early church in Jerusalem. He notes that the Christians continued to worship in the temple, that the apostles were empowered to do miracles as a sign of God's blessing on their message, and that the church was growing daily. Moving from these general descriptions, Luke then focuses on one specific incident that illustrates how the Spirit empowered the apostles' ministry.

This particular incident is also pivotal in showing the beginning of opposition to the preaching of the gospel. As was the case with Jesus, the primary adversaries of the apostles were the Jewish religious leaders. A miracle of healing impressed the crowds and led many to be open to the preaching of Peter. This openness was not shared by the temple leaders, however, and they moved quickly to attempt to silence the apostles. The way in which Peter and John responded to being jailed and interrogated had a telling impact on the Sanhedrin (the Jewish ruling council). These leaders seemed to consider the boldness and wisdom of Peter and John to be as miraculous as the healing of a lame man. And this is a "miracle" that God can reproduce in us.

I. Apostolic Miracle
(Acts 3:1-10)
A. A Beggar's Request (vv. 1-5)

1. Now Peter and John went up together into the temple at the hour of prayer, being the ninth hour.

Peter and John are prominent both in the Gospels and in the early chapters of Acts. Here they *went up together into the temple.* (They literally *went up,* for the temple grounds were higher than the city, and the temple itself sat atop four ascending terraces.) The Jews paused for prayer three times each day: at the time of the morning sacrifice (9:00 A.M.), the time of the evening sacrifice (3:00 P.M.), and at sunset. *The ninth hour* was not 9:00 A.M., as we might suppose. The Jews counted the day as starting at 6:00 A.M. The ninth hour, then, would have been nine hours after that—3:00 P.M.—the second *hour of prayer* during the day.

2, 3. And a certain man lame from his mother's womb was carried, whom they laid daily at the gate of the temple which is called Beautiful, to ask alms of them that entered into the temple; who, seeing Peter and John about to go into the temple, asked an alms.

As the two apostles entered the *temple* grounds, they passed a *lame* man begging *alms* from the worshipers who passed by. Throughout this passage, Luke (the physician) seems to take a particularly medical interest in this man. First, he notes that the man's inability to walk was a congenital problem, making it especially unlikely that he could ever be helped (John 9:32). Second, the man was over forty years old (Acts 4:22). This was not a case of temporary paralysis; the man's condition was well-known to all. He always had to be *carried* to the temple, since he was unable to walk on his own. His primary means of support was begging for alms from passersby.

The lame man was *laid daily at the gate . . . which is called Beautiful*. This was most likely the great Eastern gate (or Nicanor Gate), which was the largest entrance into the temple area. When the man saw *Peter and John* approaching, he cried out to them for alms.

4, 5. And Peter, fastening his eyes upon him with John, said, Look on us. And he gave heed unto them, expecting to receive something of them.

Both of the apostles stopped and focused their attention on the lame beggar. They did not have to stop; like most in the crowds around them, Peter and John could have walked right by the man. But they acted as Jesus would. They gave time and attention to one who meant little or nothing in most people's eyes. In fact, many thought that such a congenital deformity as this man's was a sign of God's judgment on the sin of either the man or his parents (John 9:2). But Jesus had taught the apostles that this was not so (John 9:3). Today Christians also need to be on the lookout for the physically challenged and for others who are often treated as though they were invisible. [See question #1, page 256.]

B. Peter's Response (vv. 6-8)

6. Then Peter said, Silver and gold have I none; but such as I have give I thee: In the name of Jesus Christ of Nazareth rise up and walk.

Peter removed the beggar's false expectations so that he could replace them with far greater

ones. The apostle informed the poor man that he would get no money from Peter because he had *none*. Instead, what the beggar was about to receive was of far greater value than any amount of money. What Peter did have was the power given by the Holy Spirit to perform signs and wonders. Thus he gave the man a second command: *In the name of Jesus Christ of Nazareth rise up and walk*.

7. And he took him by the right hand, and lifted him up: and immediately his feet and ankle bones received strength.

With a firm grasp, Peter *took* the beggar *by the right hand, and lifted him up*. [See question #2, page 256.] As he did so, sudden changes took place in the lame man's body. The physician Luke carefully describes both the speed of the healing and its location. He uses very specific terms for the *feet and ankle bones*. When he says that these bones *received strength*, he uses a medical term that commonly described the mending of broken bones. Such healing usually involves a lengthy, tiring process, but in this instance it happened *immediately* by the power of God. The lame man felt this dramatic change in his long-standing condition and responded just as dramatically.

8. And he leaping up stood, and walked, and entered with them into the temple, walking, and leaping, and praising God.

Now the beggar completed the action that Peter's initiative began. For the first time in his forty-some years, he sprang to his feet! He *stood* for a moment, perhaps just experiencing what it felt like to stand upright and to look people in the eye. He began to walk, getting used to the sensation of carrying his own weight instead of being carried around by others.

Then the joy of this man's healing and his new freedom took hold of him. As he accompanied the apostles into the *temple* area, he began *leaping* up and down and shouting praise to the God who had set him free. Such worship might have seemed excessive and far too exuberant for those calmly strolling toward the temple to pray. But this man's life had been suddenly and radically

---

How to Say It

GALILEANS. Gal-uh-*lee*-unz.
KHRUSHCHEV. *Kroosh*-shef.
LEVITES. *Lee*-vites.
NAZARETH. *Naz*-uh-reth.
NICANOR. Nye-*cay*-nor.
SADDUCEES. *Sad*-you-seez.
SANHEDRIN. San-*heed*-run or *San*-huh-drin.

changed. Now he could go anywhere and do anything; he could live a normal life. No wonder he could not stop *walking, and leaping, and praising God!* The wonder is that many of us who have been set free by Christ have forgotten how to rejoice and praise God for the glorious things He has done for us. [See question #3, page 256.]

A REMARKABLE CURE

In 1999 Lance Armstrong became only the second American ever to win the classic Tour de France bicycle race. But when he won the grueling, 2,288-mile, three-week-long ride over the mountains and plains of France, it wasn't his nationality that made his victory such a spectacular achievement.

Three years earlier, Armstrong had been told that he had an aggressive cancer in his abdomen, lungs, and brain. There was a fifty percent chance that he would die and only a ten percent chance that he would ever ride a bicycle in competition again. When he conquered these seemingly insurmountable odds to win the Tour de France, one sportswriter called his victory "the greatest comeback in the history of all sports." Some even called it a "miracle."

The lame man in our lesson text today had even less of a chance at a normal life than Lance Armstrong did. Forget any idea of athletic competition: this man had *never* walked in his entire life! No "miracle cures" of modern medical science and no "grit" and determination such as Armstrong displayed in his recovery could overcome the fact that this man simply *could not walk.* But God's power immediately turned this man into a leaping, praising "athlete"!

Thanks be to Him who can accomplish what man's ability cannot.   —C. R. B.

C. The Crowd's Reaction (vv. 9, 10)

9, 10. And all the people saw him walking and praising God: and they knew that it was he which sat for alms at the Beautiful gate of the temple: and they were filled with wonder and amazement at that which had happened unto him.

The actions and shouts of the healed man soon caught the attention of those in the temple. For a moment they were likely annoyed by someone interrupting the solemn time of prayer. Then those who knew the man saw his face and realized that, to their astonishment, this was the lame man they had just passed and had passed so many times before at the temple gate. An excited murmur spread through the crowd. A miracle had happened! The worshipers were *filled with wonder and amazement.* As they gathered around the apostles and the formerly lame man,

the stage was set for Peter and John to explain this remarkable turn of events.

II. Apostolic Message
(Acts 4:1-4, 13)

In Acts 3:12-26 Luke records Peter's words to the throng gathered in the temple area. First, he made it clear that he and John did not heal the lame man by their own power. God had healed him in order to glorify Jesus Christ, the very One whom these crowds had disowned and killed, but whom God had raised to life. The lame man's healing demonstrated that the name of Jesus was as authoritative now as when He was on earth.

Peter then called for the people to repent of their sins, turn to God, and believe in Jesus Christ. He warned them that this same Jesus will one day return and restore the universe and will judge those who have not obeyed Him. The crowds listened intently, and many did respond to Peter's preaching (Acts 4:4). However, this sudden interruption in the worship schedule had not gone unnoticed by those charged with keeping peace in the temple.

A. Producing Opposition (vv. 1-3)

1. And as they spake unto the people, the priests, and the captain of the temple, and the Sadducees, came upon them.

While Peter and John were still preaching, they were suddenly surrounded by a group of angry men. The leader was *the captain of the temple,* who was the priest in charge of the temple police. He was second only to the high priest in authority, and he was charged with keeping order in all the courts of the temple.

The *Sadducees* were the dominant party among the priests and controlled the office of the high priest. They rejected any belief in angels or in the resurrection of the dead (Acts 23:8). Many were wealthy landowners, and, to remain financially secure, were willing to cooperate with the hated Romans when necessary. They knew that the Roman army could be called in to crush any civil disorder (such as the uproar caused by the preaching of the apostles after the healing of the lame man). Something had to be done.

2. Being grieved that they taught the people, and preached through Jesus the resurrection from the dead.

These Jewish leaders were deeply disturbed by the apostles' actions on two counts. First, they were upset that the apostles had *taught the people* who gathered for worship in the temple. As the officials saw it, the apostles were agitators stirring up unrest among the crowds. They were interrupting the established order of worship for the day and keeping the people from fulfilling their religious duties. Furthermore, the apostles were threatening the authority of the religious leaders by publicly teaching new doctrines that had not been cleared by the officially sanctioned teachers of the law. The right to teach the people was a privilege that was jealously guarded by the Jewish authorities for themselves alone.

Second, the religious leaders were disturbed because of the content of the apostles' teaching. Peter and John were proclaiming *through Jesus the resurrection from the dead.* This would have especially enraged the Sadducees, who had publicly argued for years that a resurrection from the dead was a myth. The apostles had to be stopped. After all, when they preached that Jesus was raised from the dead, they not only implicitly taught that the Sadducees were wrong to deny the resurrection, but they also charged the Jewish religious leaders with being responsible for the crucifixion of One whom God had glorified by bringing Him up from the grave. To protect their reputation and authority, the temple elite had to act immediately. [See question #4, page 256.]

3. And they laid hands on them, and put them in hold unto the next day: for it was now eventide.

The temple guards arrested the apostles under the authority of the captain of the temple and with the approval of the Sadducees. The arrest seems to have included the healed lame man, since later he is described as "standing with" the apostles before the Jewish leaders (Acts 4:14). The prisoners were then taken to some place of custody to be jailed overnight. This was probably a guarded room near the temple.

The apostles were held until *the next day* because it was too late for the people who would judge them to convene and hold a hearing. Apparently Peter's sermon was considerably longer than the excerpt Luke has recorded, since the healing occurred at around 3:00 P.M. (see verse 1), and it was now *eventide* (evening).

The apostles' hearing was to be held before the Jewish high council, or the Sanhedrin. It was composed of seventy priests, Levites, and elders, with the current high priest serving as the leader. Most of these men lived in Jerusalem, but many of them also had country estates outside of the city. This was why it would take time to notify all the members of the council and gather them together to deal with Peter and John.

B. Bearing Fruit (v. 4)

4. Howbeit many of them which heard the word believed; and the number of the men was about five thousand.

In spite of the fact that the two preachers had just been arrested, the response to their message was extremely positive: *many of them which heard the word believed.* Aside from Peter and John, there must have been many other Christians in the crowd going to the temple to pray that day. These unknown believers must have completed the work of the apostles by baptizing the new converts and helping them to get started in their new life with Christ. Here Luke notes that the total number of believing *men was about five thousand;* thus this figure does not include the women and children in the church at that time.

At this point, Luke goes on to describe what happened when the apostles and the lame man appeared before the Sanhedrin the next day. By the power of the Holy Spirit, Peter gave a simple yet courageous defense for the apostolic preaching in Jesus' name. His argument was based on the undeniable fact of two miracles: the healing of a lame man and the resurrection of Jesus Christ from the dead. His conclusion was that Jesus Christ is the one and only means of salvation (v. 12). Luke then comments on the reaction of the Sanhedrin to the apostles' words.

C. Causing Wonder (v. 13)

13. Now when they saw the boldness of Peter and John, and perceived that they were unlearned and ignorant men, they marveled; and they took knowledge of them, that they had been with Jesus.

This Jewish ruling council was composed of some of the most powerful and intelligent men in all Judea. These men were experts in interpreting the Old Testament law. Most of the common prisoners brought before such a court were too intimidated to present a powerful and coherent case in their defense. But the apostles were an exception. They were confident in Christ and empowered with *boldness* by the Holy Spirit.

The members of the council realized that the apostles *were unlearned and ignorant men;* that is, they had had no formal rabbinical training in interpreting the Old Testament Scriptures. They

Since we have "been with Jesus," we will "obey God rather than men."
Acts 4:13 & 5:29

Today's visual dramatizes the conflict between Jesus' disciples and the Sanhedrin. Display it as you discuss verse 13.

Visual for lessons 3, 4

were common people, not priests or experts in the law. They held no public office or titles; they were ordinary men. How were they to explain the remarkable courage and clarity of these two untrained Galileans? And how could they explain the man who was healed who stood beside the apostles? The minds of the Sanhedrin *marveled* at the seeming contradiction between the commonness and the power of Peter and John. Then the truth began to dawn on them.

Not long before, someone else had stood before the council. He too was a commoner from Galilee with no formal training. But He had also spoken with extraordinary power and performed wondrous miracles. He was the very One whom these apostles proclaimed as the Savior risen from the dead. It became obvious that Peter and John had to have *been with Jesus*—walking with Him, learning from Him, and growing more like Him. Jesus Christ was the only possible explanation for the transformed lives of these men. By the power of Jesus, lame men began to leap and cowards became courageous. Today it should also be obvious from our lives that we are living with Jesus and are being transformed into His likeness. [See question #5, page 256.]

UNLIKELY SPOKESMEN

During what came to be called the famous "kitchen debate" in Moscow, Russia, on July 24, 1959, Nikita Khrushchev told then-Vice President Richard Nixon, "In another seven years we will be on the same level as America. . . . We will bury you." By this he meant that capitalism would die and that Marxist Communism would be victorious in the battle for political primacy in the world.

So it was that an unlikely candidate for United States citizenship took his oath of citizenship on another July day, exactly forty years later. This person was none other than Khrushchev's son, Sergei. The younger Khrushchev and his wife had been living and working in America since 1991. They had come to enjoy the fruits of the capitalism that was supposed to have been "buried" long ago. They have now become the unlikely spokespersons of the American way of life. In fact, they own two cars and have a suburban house with central air conditioning, a Jacuzzi, and an entertainment center!

The Jewish Sanhedrin had had enough trouble with the "unlearned" rabbi from Nazareth who had won the hearts of the Jewish people with His criticism of the Jewish aristocracy. Now they were forced to deal with the powerful witness of some unlikely spokesmen—Jesus' equally "unlearned" followers. They did not realize that truth cannot be silenced, even though it is spoken by unsophisticated, "common" people.

—C. R. B.

Conclusion

A. Take the Risk

Peter and John risked becoming major people in a minor person's life. They cared enough to step out of the background and get involved. Because they were willing to serve one person in Jesus' name, they gained a greater opportunity to serve many people in Jesus' name. And when confronted by opposition, the apostles responded with Christlike courage and wisdom, so that even their enemies could see the character of Christ in their lives.

Every day each of us encounters people who could simply remain "minor characters" in our lives if we choose to ignore them and go our way. But what if we consciously notice them, speak to them, and actually get to know them? If we treat them as Jesus would, we might see how the Lord can heal their hearts through our words and our touch. And when they look into our eyes and see the compassion and respect there, they might tell us that now they know that we have been with Jesus because they see His love in us.

B. Prayer

Father, give us Your eyes to see those around us. Give us Your heart to care about them. Give us Your boldness to share Jesus with them so that His love may be seen in us. May our godly character give You glory through Jesus Christ, amen.

C. Thought to Remember

Many people believe that the way Christians treat them is the way that Jesus would treat them, and that should be true.

Learning by Doing

This page contains an alternate lesson plan emphasizing learning activities.
Classes desiring such student involvement will find these suggestions helpful.

Learning Goals

After this lesson students will be able to:

1. Tell how the Spirit's power was seen in the healing of the lame man and in Peter and John's response before the Sanhedrin.

2. Explain how our treatment of society's "outcasts" demonstrates whether we have "been with Jesus."

3. Form a plan for ministering to someone in their neighborhood or community whose situation and needs are often ignored.

Into the Lesson

Have your class brainstorm for the qualities and characteristics that identify a true Christian. List your class members' responses on a white board or overhead projector—or tape a large piece of paper to the wall and use a broad-tipped marker. Explain to your class that in brainstorming you do not stop to evaluate answers—just keep writing them as fast as possible and let students "feed on" other students' responses.

Make the transition to the Bible study by saying, "The last verse of our text today says that the Jewish leaders took note that the disciples 'had been with Jesus.' As we study today's lesson, watch for the qualities and characteristics we have listed to see how many of them show up in the disciples' lives."

Option

Invite a children's Bible school class to visit your class with a rendition of the children's song, "Peter and John Went to Pray." Older adults especially enjoy the vitality of singing children. The song will provide a natural entrance into the study of a familiar passage.

Into the Word

Divide you class into small groups—no more than four to a group. Have the members of each group select one or two of them to play characters mentioned in today's text. (Possible characters to portray include Peter and John, the former lame man, the leader of the Sanhedrin, the captain of the temple guard, a couple from the crowd, and one or two of the five thousand believers.) The other members of the group will interview these characters, asking them questions about the events recorded in Acts 3 and 4. Allow time for the group to prepare; then ask each group to record its interview on a cassette tape. If you have time, you can play some or all of these recordings like a radio broadcast.

While each group is recording its interview, help the remaining students make a second chart similar to the one created in the brainstorming activity above, this time listing characteristics and qualities demonstrated in the lives of the apostles in today's text. List the verse numbers and write the qualities that your class members identify from each verse. For example:

3:1—They were regular in prayer.

3:4—They noticed the poor and needy out of the crowds of people.

3:6—They carefully explained what they were going to do.

3:7—They personally touched the poor and needy man.

Into Life

Have each learner compare the list of qualities from the brainstorming activity and the characteristics identified in the apostles and make a revised list of the qualities that identify a true Christian. Then ask the learners to evaluate where they are in their personal development. Say, "On a scale from 0 to 5, where 0 means 'I haven't even started yet!' and 5 means 'I am mature in this characteristic,' put your numbers in the right margin in the character study."

Today's text shows that followers of Jesus are sensitive to the poor and needy of society. Have your class plan an activity that reaches out to meet the needs of those often overlooked or ignored in our society. A visit to a nursing home or resident home for adults with mental retardation are two possibilities. Preparing small favors for residents and sharing a favorite verse are two ways of helping visitors interact with residents.

Close your class with a time of prayer for the persecuted church. Have a leader pray for various missionaries and the problems they face. (Missionaries whom your church supports, or their forwarding agents, can provide you with information for specific prayer.) After the leader prays for each group, have the class respond in unison with a prayer based on Acts 4:13 like this one:

"Lord, give courage to these disciples, as You did to Peter and John. May their detractors be astonished, not by their education or abilities, but by the fact that they have been with Jesus."

Let's Talk It Over

The questions on this page are designed to encourage review of the lesson Scriptures and to promote discussion of the lesson by the class. The answers provided are only discussion starters. Let your class talk it over from there.

1. Peter and John focused their full attention on the lame man and his obvious need. Why do we sometimes have a hard time seeing the needs of the people around us? How can we do a better job of being sensitive to other people's needs?

We can become so caught up with the events and circumstances in our own lives that we don't take the time or expend the energy to focus on someone else's needs. That is one problem. Another problem is that the needs are so many and so severe that we have learned to tune them out. So we can look right at a person in need, smile benignly, and walk on without really seeing him or feeling his need.

Jesus saw each person as a person, not as a problem or an obstacle or a need. That is what we must do. We must feel the pain of the unemployed man, the single parent, the woman who is caring for a husband dying of cancer, and parents with a prodigal child. We need to see them as persons whom we can touch with the love of Christ.

2. Peter took the right hand of the lame man and helped him stand up. How can we give people in need a helping hand?

We are tempted to go to one of two extremes on this issue. One extreme is to say we can't help everyone, so we won't help anyone. Peter could not and did not help everyone in need, either. But he did help the one he saw.

The other temptation is to do too much for people in need. As a result, we stifle their own initiative and make them dependent on the help we and others provide. When our resources run out, the needy are in even worse condition than before.

We need to do what we can for people—and what they can't. What they can do, we need to encourage them to do and even assist them in doing. If a man loses his job, instead of giving a gift of money—except, perhaps, for some emergency help with immediate necessities—we can help him find a new job. This will mean involvement and commitment on our part, but it is something we can do to really make a difference.

3. When the lame man was healed, he began leaping and shouting, praising God for the miracle. No doubt many of those who saw him were annoyed by his emotional outburst, thinking it inappropriate for a place of worship. Why are

many of us reluctant to be emotional about the good things that God does in our lives?

Certainly we are different emotionally. When some people hear good news, they jump up and down and scream. Others respond with a quiet "That's great." But all people make some kind of emotional response. We just need to accept that the way others express their emotions is right and natural for them. The quiet one should accept the more vocal praiser. And the exuberant one should not question the spiritual fervor of the quiet one.

We can become overly concerned about what other people in the church will think of us if we do something "inappropriate." But that didn't stop the healed lame man. He was simply praising God!

4. The temple authorities wanted to stop Peter and John from talking about Jesus Christ. Why is there opposition to the preaching of the gospel? Why do some people always get angry when the name "Jesus" comes up?

Opposition to the gospel springs from a variety of sources. The craftsmen at Ephesus opposed the gospel because it was having a negative impact on their livelihood (Acts 19:23-27). Some people oppose the preaching of the gospel out of jealousy and envy (13:45; 17:5). Still others oppose the gospel for religious reasons: they do not agree with what is being said (14:1, 2).

We have to understand that the claims of Jesus—and thus of the gospel—are very exclusive. "I am the way," Jesus said. "There is none other name," echoed Peter. In today's inclusive, "tolerant" society, such exclusivism is not tolerated!

5. The members of the Sanhedrin recognized that Peter and John "had been with Jesus" (Acts 4:13). How can people tell that we have been with Jesus?

People will know if we live in the presence of Jesus. They will know by our values, our vocabulary, our interests, and our commitments. They will know by the way we treat other people—especially our spouses and our children. They will know by the way we spend our time and our money and our energies. They will know by the things we talk about—and the things we *don't* talk about.

Obedient to the Spirit

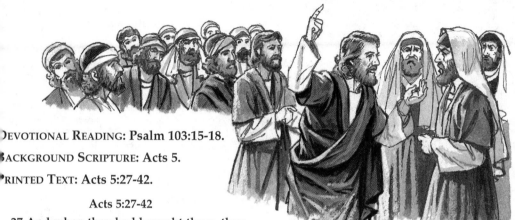

DEVOTIONAL READING: Psalm 103:15-18.

BACKGROUND SCRIPTURE: Acts 5.

PRINTED TEXT: Acts 5:27-42.

Acts 5:27-42

27 And when they had brought them, they set them before the council: and the high priest asked them,

28 Saying, Did not we straitly command you that ye should not teach in this name? And, behold, ye have filled Jerusalem with your doctrine, and intend to bring this man's blood upon us.

29 Then Peter and the other apostles answered and said, We ought to obey God rather than men.

30 The God of our fathers raised up Jesus, whom ye slew and hanged on a tree.

31 Him hath God exalted with his right hand to be a Prince and a Saviour, for to give repentance to Israel, and forgiveness of sins.

32 And we are his witnesses of these things; and so is also the Holy Ghost, whom God hath given to them that obey him.

33 When they heard that, they were cut to the heart, and took counsel to slay them.

34 Then stood there up one in the council, a Pharisee, named Gamaliel, a doctor of the law, had in reputation among all the people, and commanded to put the apostles forth a little space;

35 And said unto them, Ye men of Israel, take heed to yourselves what ye intend to do as touching these men.

36 For before these days rose up Theudas, boasting himself to be somebody; to whom a number of men, about four hundred, joined themselves: who was slain; and all, as many as obeyed him, were scattered, and brought to nought.

37 After this man rose up Judas of Galilee in the days of the taxing, and drew away much people after him: he also perished; and all, even as many as obeyed him, were dispersed.

38 And now I say unto you, Refrain from these men, and let them alone: for if this counsel or this work be of men, it will come to nought:

39 But if it be of God, ye cannot overthrow it; lest haply ye be found even to fight against God.

40 And to him they agreed: and when they had called the apostles, and beaten them, they commanded that they should not speak in the name of Jesus, and let them go.

41 And they departed from the presence of the council, rejoicing that they were counted worthy to suffer shame for his name.

42 And daily in the temple, and in every house, they ceased not to teach and preach Jesus Christ.

GOLDEN TEXT: Then Peter and the other apostles answered and said, We ought to obey God rather than men.—Acts 5:29.

Continuing Jesus' Work
Unit 1: Beginning in Jerusalem
(Lessons 1-4)

Lesson Aims

After this lesson students should be able to:

1. Summarize the viewpoints expressed at the apostles' trial before the Sanhedrin and the outcome of the trial.

2. Tell how joyful obedience in the face of opposition can testify to the power of the gospel.

3. Ask God for boldness in confronting a specific situation where a Christian's testimony is needed.

Lesson Outline

INTRODUCTION
    A. How Can I Be Bold?
    B. Lesson Background
  I. APOSTLES' TESTIMONY (Acts 5:27-32)
    A. Charge of Disobedience (vv. 27, 28)
    B. Defense of Obedience (vv. 29-32)
 II. GAMALIEL'S ADVICE (Acts 5:33-39)
    A. Learn From the Past (vv. 33-37)
    B. Leave These Men Alone (vv. 38, 39)
     Good Advice
III. TRIAL'S OUTCOME (Acts 5:40-42)
    A. Council's Decision (v. 40)
    B. Apostles' Response (vv. 41, 42)
     They Could Not Be Silenced
CONCLUSION
    A. Bold Believers
    B. Prayer
    C. Thought to Remember

Introduction

A. How Can I Be Bold?

Boldness is a willingness to take risks. It chooses to stand and state clearly what must be said, regardless of the cost. For a Christian, boldness involves using every available opportunity to act and speak in ways that honor God, even when others may disapprove and our hearts are pounding with fear. Boldness is courage in action. But boldness is difficult for many of us because we do not like to offend anyone or risk the pain of rejection or persecution.

In today's text, we see how the apostles boldly gave their witness before a hostile audience. Even though they faced a painful beating and the possibility of death, their faith in Jesus Christ en-abled them to proclaim Him without compromise and to experience joy as a consequence of their suffering. Their example encourages us to be bold in Christ.

B. Lesson Background

From last week's study of Acts 4, we learned how the Sanhedrin (the Jewish ruling council) tried to stop Peter and John from preaching about Jesus to the crowds at the temple. The apostles were released with a warning to stop evangelizing. Instead, they returned to the group of believers and organized a prayer meeting to ask God for greater boldness in preaching Jesus. God responded by empowering those present so that they "spake the word of God with boldness" (Acts 4:31).

At the beginning of Acts 5, we read of a Christian couple who tried to cover their greed with a show of generosity. Ananias and Sapphira dropped dead because of their sin, and, as a result, a respectful fear spread through the church (v. 11). Still, the church grew as the apostles preached and healed many people. Their successful evangelism soon aroused the jealous wrath of the Sanhedrin, who had all the apostles arrested and held overnight for trial.

Near dawn an angel came and released the apostles, telling them to go back to the temple area and resume their preaching. Thus, when the Sanhedrin sent to have the jailed prisoners brought before them, the officers sent found no one in the cells. They ran back to the council to announce that the twelve were missing. Then, in the middle of their report, another messenger announced that the apostles were back in the temple grounds—preaching again! This time the captain of the guard took some men to re-arrest the apostles (quietly) and to return them for trial before the Sanhedrin.

Amazingly, the council seemed uninterested in how the miraculous escape from jail had occurred. This group was far more concerned with the apostles' stubborn refusal to keep silent about Jesus.

I. Apostles' Testimony
(Acts 5:27-32)

A. Charge of Disobedience (vv. 27, 28)

27. And when they had brought them, they set them before the council: and the high priest asked them.

Previously only Peter and John had faced this group of educated, powerful men. The Sanhedrin (consisting of seventy such men) regarded with suspicion these disciples of Jesus who could heal the sick and escape from locked and guarded rooms. The *high priest* (most likely Annas, as noted in Acts 4:6) was the president of the *council* and thus began the hearing. The same group that tried Jesus was about to put His disciples on trial.

28. Saying, Did not we straitly command you that ye should not teach in this name? and, behold, ye have filled Jerusalem with your doctrine, and intend to bring this man's blood upon us.

The high priest brought three charges against the apostles. First, they had ignored the previous warning given to Peter and John not to preach in Jesus' name (Acts 4:18). Notice that the high priest refused even to say the word, "Jesus"; he simply stated that the apostles were teaching *in this name*. He then stated the second charge against the apostles: they had not only refused to be silent concerning Jesus, but they had also *filled* the entire city with their *doctrine*, or teaching. They had made Jesus "the talk of the town." The high priest, however, tried to diminish this accomplishment by claiming that the doctrine the apostles taught was theirs, originating from them and not from God.

The third accusation against the apostles was that they had blamed the Sanhedrin for Jesus' death. The high priest's reference to bringing Jesus' *blood* upon the Sanhedrin may reflect what transpired during His trial before Pilate. After the Roman governor had declared Jesus to be innocent and had publicly washed his hands, he stated that he was innocent of the blood of "this just person." Then the crowd (spurred by the religious leaders) shouted back at Pilate that they would accept the responsibility for Jesus' blood (Matthew 27:24, 25). Perhaps these men feared that their words were coming back to haunt them. [See question #1, page 264.]

B. Defense of Obedience (vv. 29-32)

29. Then Peter and the other apostles answered and said, We ought to obey God rather than men.

Peter's defense is quite similar to the one he made to the Sanhedrin the last time that he and John appeared before them (Acts 4:19): what *God* says is more important than what *men* say. [See question #2, page 264.]

30. The God of our fathers raised up Jesus, whom ye slew and hanged on a tree.

Peter then called attention to another contrast between the will of God and the will of the council. God *raised up Jesus* from the dead after the council had *hanged* Him *on a tree* (the cross).

The law of Moses declared that the body of anyone who was executed for a crime should be hung on a tree for public display and that such a person had God's curse upon him (Deuteronomy 21:22, 23). The members of the council had treated Jesus in this manner, intending to humiliate Him. They did not realize that in so doing, they were fulfilling the promises made by God to their fathers. The curse associated with Jesus' death was not for His own sins; He was "made a curse for us" (Galatians 3:13) by taking the punishment that we rightfully deserved for our sins.

31. Him hath God exalted with his right hand to be a Prince and a Saviour, for to give repentance to Israel, and forgiveness of sins.

For someone to be *exalted with* (or to) the *right hand* of a monarch meant that the ruler had given that individual both honor and authority. This is also clear from the titles of *Prince* and *Saviour* that are used to describe Jesus.

Peter then elaborated on how Jesus provides salvation. First, Jesus is said to *give repentance*. This does not mean that Jesus forces anyone to repent, but He provides what is necessary for us to carry out this crucial step of returning to God. Jesus has sent the Holy Spirit to convict us of our sins (John 16:7-11). He has shown us the love of God by giving His life to pay for our sins (1 John 4:9, 10). Because of this, it is now possible for us to turn from our sins and turn back to God.

Second, when we repent we receive *forgiveness of sins* through Christ's sacrifice for us. As Peter preached on the Day of Pentecost, repentance and forgiveness are closely linked (Acts 2:38). Only Jesus could provide these blessings, not only for *Israel* but for the entire world.

32. And we are his witnesses of these things; and so is also the Holy Ghost, whom God hath given to them that obey him.

Peter concluded his defense by stating the *witnesses* whose testimony supported his case. This was in keeping with the requirements of the law of Moses (Deuteronomy 17:6). Peter himself, along with the rest of the apostles, made up one group of witnesses to who Jesus is and what He has done. The second witness was the *Holy*

Since we have "been with Jesus," we will "obey God rather than men."

Acts 4:13 & 5:29

Use the same visual as you used last week to illustrate today's lesson. Refer to it as you discuss verse 29.

Visual for lessons 3, 4

Ghost, who supported the apostles' testimony by empowering them to do miraculous signs (Hebrews 2:3, 4).

Peter then reminded the Sanhedrin that God gives His Spirit only to those who *obey* Him (Acts 2:38). The apostles were obeying God by continuing to preach Jesus, even when this meant disobeying the council. (Peter's words implied that the Sanhedrin was disobeying God by hampering the apostles' ministry.)

II. Gamaliel's Advice
(Acts 5:33-39)

A. Learn From the Past (vv. 33-37)

33. When they heard that, they were cut to the heart, and took counsel to slay them.

The members of the Sanhedrin realized that only death could stop the apostles' testimony, and, at that moment, the council was so outraged that they actually might have executed the Twelve (as they later did Stephen). [See question #3, page 264.]

34. Then stood there up one in the council, a Pharisee, named Gamaliel, a doctor of the law, had in reputation among all the people, and commanded to put the apostles forth a little space.

At this pivotal moment, the Lord supplied a voice of calm and reason. *Gamaliel* was the greatest Jewish teacher of his day. The apostle Paul (when he was Saul) studied under Gamaliel before he became a Christian (Acts 22:3).

Gamaliel was the head of an important rabbinical school in Jerusalem, the school of Hillel (named for Gamaliel's grandfather). This school promoted a rather loose interpretation of the law of Moses while remaining true to the traditions of the Pharisees. (The other school in Jerusalem, named after a Rabbi Shammai, was much more strict.) Gamaliel demonstrated his broad-minded attitude in his suggestion on how to deal with the *apostles*. First, he had them removed so that he could speak freely about their case.

35, 36. And said unto them, Ye men of Israel, take heed to yourselves what ye intend to do as touching these men. For before these days rose up Theudas, boasting himself to be somebody; to whom a number of men, about four hundred, joined themselves: who was slain; and all, as many as obeyed him, were scattered, and brought to nought.

Gamaliel began by solemnly warning the Jewish leaders to be careful in their handling of these followers of Jesus. He separated himself from his companions' murderous intent by stating that it was they who needed to evaluate their thinking. In typical rabbinical style, Gamaliel appealed to recent well-known events to remind his hearers of the lessons of history.

Gamaliel's first illustration called attention to a man named *Theudas*. The only information we know about this person and his followers is what Gamaliel tells us. In 4 B.C. King Herod the Great died. In the power vacuum that followed, many insurrectionists rose up trying to seize control. The situation became so bad that the Roman army came in to put down all the uprisings. Theudas may well have been one of these insurgent leaders. His boast to be *somebody* was likely a claim to be a prophet of God or even the Messiah.

Theudas attracted a small following of *four hundred* men (many more than Jesus' twelve). However, as soon as Theudas was killed, his movement fell apart. Gamaliel was suggesting that perhaps Jesus' cause would also end up as a pointless attempt to gather a following.

37. After this man rose up Judas of Galilee in the days of the taxing, and drew away much people after him: he also perished; and all, even as many as obeyed him, were dispersed.

Thanks to the writings of a first-century historian named Josephus, we know more about *Judas of Galilee*. In A.D. 6 the Roman governor of Syria and Judea, Quirinius (called Cyrenius in Luke 2:2), took a census of the territories he controlled in order to determine how much he could raise in taxes from them. Judas of Galilee publicly opposed the census and its taxation, claiming that this action was just the first step to enslaving the Jews and causing them to serve another god.

To protect the liberty of his people and to uphold the holy name of the Lord, Judas called on all Jews to oppose this taxation—by force if necessary. He attracted a large following to his endeavor. However, once more the might of Rome crushed the uprising through a series of violent campaigns, and Judas died. Afterward, all the people whom Judas had persuaded to join his cause *dispersed* and returned to their normal lives, except for those injured or killed.

Although Judas of Galilee had been very popular for a time, at this point the only group who followed his anti-Roman philosophy was the group known as the Zealots. Gamaliel seemed to be saying that the Sanhedrin tolerated the Zealot movement, so why not be equally tolerant of these followers of Jesus?

B. Leave These Men Alone (vv. 38, 39)

38. And now I say unto you, Refrain from these men, and let them alone: for if this counsel or this work be of men, it will come to nought.

Gamaliel now stated his position: *refrain from these men, and let them alone*. Whatever the apostles' plans and activities may be, if their movement is merely the remains left over from the followers of some dead fanatical leader, it will disappear on its own without help from the Sanhedrin. The council should just be patient, and perhaps this latest "fad" will die out on its own or be destroyed as the others were. There was, however, another possibility to consider.

39. But if it be of God, ye cannot overthrow it; lest haply ye be found even to fight against God.

Gamaliel went on to say something like this: "What if these followers of Jesus are telling the truth and doing God's bidding? Do you really think we can successfully *fight against God*? We are supposed to be the religious leaders of our people; do we want to appear to be God's enemies? No! So again I say, leave these men alone!" [See question #4, page 264.]

Gamaliel's argument does make a certain amount of sense. And yet, while it is true that Christ's disciples will win in the end, that does not mean that, in the here and now, it will always appear that we are winning. Sometimes, for a certain period of time, it may seem as if the church is failing miserably or even dying. Such a momentary setback does not mean that we are not truly doing the will of God. Nor is it true that apparent success and growth of false teachers' ministries are evidence that these are being blessed by God.

Thus, despite what Gamaliel advised, momentary victories or defeats do not reveal what will ultimately be approved or disapproved before the Lord. God has shown us His will through Jesus and in the Bible; our job is to be faithful in following His will, whether we seem to be winning or losing at any particular time.

GOOD ADVICE

"Dear Abby" once advised a woman not to have the local newspaper correct the obituary of her recently deceased mother. The obituary had incorrectly added nine years to the mother's age. Abby's response was, "Let it alone."

Abby then quoted a series of small-town newspaper ads that continued to compound an error printed in the first ad. A man was selling a sewing machine. Buyers were instructed to call after 7 P.M. and "ask for Mrs. Kelly who lives with him cheap." The following day the editor published a correction: "ask for Mrs. Kelly who lives with him after 7 P.M." On the third day came another correction: "ask for Mrs. Kelly who loves with him."

Finally, the seller of the sewing machine placed an ad saying that he no longer had a sewing machine for sale. He had smashed it and disconnected his phone! He added, "I have not been carrying on with Mrs. Kelly. Until yesterday she was my housekeeper, but she quit."

The members of the Sanhedrin were somewhat like that poor editor. The more they tried to address their concerns about the apostles, the more their frustration grew. Gamaliel reminded them of some recent history and then gave some good advice: If God is not in this movement, don't worry about it; but be careful—lest you find yourselves fighting against God.   —C. R. B.

III. Trial's Outcome
(Acts 5:40-42)

A. Council's Decision (v. 40)

40. And to him they agreed: and when they had called the apostles, and beaten them, they commanded that they should not speak in the name of Jesus, and let them go.

The Sanhedrin *agreed* with Gamaliel that killing the apostles would not be wise. At the same time, these men had to be given some kind of punishment for disobeying the explicit instructions of the council. So each apostle was *beaten*, most likely with the standard thirty-nine lashes. The number was carefully counted so that the punishment did not exceed the forty lashes allowed by the law (Deuteronomy 25:3).

The Sanhedrin then solemnly repeated to the Twelve the commandment that they had already broken: do not ever preach *in the name of Jesus* again. Then the apostles were released. The members of the council no doubt hoped that the sting of the whip would silence these troublemakers. How wrong they were!

B. Apostles' Response (vv. 41, 42)

41. And they departed from the presence of the council, rejoicing that they were counted worthy to suffer shame for his name.

The apostles' will to serve Jesus was not broken by the beating they received; on the contrary,

---

How to Say It

ANANIAS. An-uh-*nye*-us.
ANNAS. *An*-nus.
CYRENIUS. Sye-*ree*-nee-us.
GAMALIEL. Guh-*may*-lih-ul.
HILLEL. *Hill*-el.
JOSEPHUS. Jo-*see*-fus.
PHARISEE. *Fair*-ih-see.
QUIRINIUS. Kwy-*rin*-ee-us.
SANHEDRIN. San-*heed*-run or *San*-huh-drin.
SAPPHIRA. Suh-*fye*-ruh.
SHAMMAI. *Sham*-eye.
THEUDAS. *Thoo*-dus.
ZEALOTS. *Zel*-uts.

they departed from . . . the council determined more than ever to proclaim His message. In spite of their pain, these men were *rejoicing*! They were honored to be dishonored for Jesus, and dignified by their indignity on His behalf. [See question #5, page 264.]

42. And daily in the temple, and in every house, they ceased not to teach and preach Jesus Christ.

The apostles made it their *daily* practice to go right back to the *temple* grounds where they had been arrested and to *teach and preach Jesus Christ*—the very "crime" for which they had been arrested and beaten. In addition, they continued to instruct the believers in their homes. Thus, whether in public or in private settings, regardless of the cost, they *ceased not* telling others about Jesus. The example of their unconquerable faith and devotion continues to challenge us today.

THEY COULD NOT BE SILENCED

San Francisco, California, is said to be a city that takes nostalgia seriously. Many are familiar with the old popular song about the "little cable cars" that "climb halfway to the stars." The city spends millions of dollars to keep those quaint remnants of the romantic past in operation.

San Francisco is also famous for its fog—and its foghorns. At one time years ago, more than fifty foghorns located around San Francisco Bay warned ships of dangerous shoals and shores. In November of 1992, the last of the old foghorns was silenced and replaced by an electronic beeper. However, the citizens of San Francisco wouldn't stand for this. Historians denounced the beeper, civic leaders weighed in on the side of history, and radio station KFOG began a campaign to raise the money needed to revive the old

foghorns. After three weeks, the U.S. Coast Guard gave in, and a compromise was reached. If the city would pay for their operation, a couple of the old foghorns would be reactivated.

The Sanhedrin believed that a stern warning followed by a severe beating would silence the apostles. These men had become noisy reminders of an embarrassing, recent past. The Sanhedrin thought that they could get rid of them by dealing with them as they had dealt with Jesus. But the Sanhedrin did not take into account the faith of the apostles. These followers of Jesus knew that He was alive, and they could not be silenced.

Can the same be said of us? —C. R. B.

Conclusion

A. Bold Believers

What was the secret of the incredible boldness of the apostles? Consider the following:

First, the apostles clearly were convinced of the truth of what they were saying and the importance of their message. Their faith in Jesus Christ was the "driving force" behind who they were and what they did. We need to recognize that we are also called to be Christ's ambassadors, just as the apostles were (2 Corinthians 5:20).

Second, the early church prayed for boldness to preach and teach Jesus and used the power given to accomplish that task. We, too, ought to pray for power to do the tasks that God has given us and do them to His glory (Ephesians 3:20, 21).

Third, the apostles were absolutely committed to obeying the Lord regardless of how others might react. They were not surprised by opposition; they expected and accepted it. In fact, they rejoiced in their suffering, considering it an honor to serve Jesus in this manner.

No one ever said that serving Jesus would always be easy or that it would be accepted by others. But we know that as we continue to confess Jesus to others, He will confess us to God (Matthew 10:32, 33). As we honor His name, He will honor ours.

B. Prayer

Our Father, help us to be the ambassadors You have called us to be. Each day, give us opportunities. Each opportunity, give us boldness to respond. Each response, give us wisdom to listen and to speak wisely. And in all we do, may Your love be seen in us. We pray to be like Jesus. In His name, amen.

C. Thought to Remember

Godly boldness is the willingness to take risks in fulfilling our service to God.

Home Daily Bible Readings

Monday, Mar. 19—Ananias and Sapphira Sin and Die (Acts 5:1-11)

Tuesday, Mar. 20—The Power of the Apostles (Acts 5:12-16)

Wednesday, Mar. 21—Life and Faith of Believers (1 Thessalonians 1)

Thursday, Mar. 22—Persecution and Release (Acts 5:17-23)

Friday, Mar. 23—Arrest and Accusation (Acts 5:24-28)

Saturday, Mar. 24—The Answer of the Apostles (Acts 5:29-32)

Sunday, Mar. 25—The Warning of Gamaliel (Acts 5:34-42)

Learning by Doing

This page contains an alternate lesson plan emphasizing learning activities.
Classes desiring such student involvement will find these suggestions helpful.

Learning Goals

After this lesson each student will be able to:

1. Summarize the viewpoints expressed at the apostles' trial before the Sanhedrin and the outcome of the trial.

2. Tell how joyful obedience in the face of opposition can testify to the power of the gospel.

3. Ask God for boldness in confronting a specific situation where a Christian's testimony is needed.

Into the Lesson

Put the words "Boldness is . . ." on a large sheet of poster paper taped to the wall. As your class members enter the room, have each person complete the sentence in his or her own words.

If your classroom does not lend itself to posting something on the walls, or if your students prefer not to write on such a poster, then open the session by asking the class to complete the sentence verbally. Give each person an opportunity to respond with a one-sentence answer before anyone may respond twice.

Make the transition to the Bible study by saying, "Today's lesson looks at a graphic example of boldness. As we read the Scripture text, check to see if the answers we have given describe Peter and John's response during their appearance before the Sanhedrin."

Into the Word

Have a volunteer read Acts 5:27-42 aloud. Then ask your students to suppose that Peter were able to visit or write to your class to help each person be bolder in witnessing for Jesus. Read the text again, one verse at a time, and after each verse ask, "What does this verse suggest that Peter might say to us today?" For example, Acts 5:27 might suggest, "Also be prepared because you never know when you will be called to testify for Jesus."

Or have your class members write a letter such as Peter might have written to encourage Christians to be obedient and bold in sharing their faith in Jesus. Ask half the class to work together to write a letter that Peter might have written the night before his appearance before the Sanhedrin. What might he have anticipated or feared? Have the other half of the class write a letter that Peter might have written the evening after his trial. How would he view his conduct before the Sanhedrin?

Remember how he had failed to stand up for Jesus on the night of Jesus' own trials. What might he now say to encourage us?

Into Life

Have each class member write a song to a familiar melody using the ideas in today's text. Warm up for the writing by working together to list words and ideas the students might want to include. Such a brainstorming might generate this list: *bold, speak up, preach, proclaim, teach, obey, witness, courage, fearless, testify.* If a student were to select the melody of "Stand Up, Stand Up for Jesus," he might then write as follows:

"Speak up! Speak up for Jesus.
Proclaim His name each day.
With boldness tell of Jesus;
It's God we must obey!"

(The directions for this activity are included in the student quarterly, *Adult Bible Class.*)

Then distribute copies of the following True/False quiz. (A copy is included in the *Adult Bible Class.*) Ask each student to complete the quiz as a self-evaluation. (No one will need to reveal his or her results to anyone else in the class. This activity is intended as a personal challenge.)

T F 1. I find it easy to talk to others about my faith in Christ.

T F 2. I often engage others in conversations about Christ.

T F 3. I have personally led a person to become a Christian.

T F 4. I am not ashamed to speak up for Jesus Christ with my family.

T F 5. Everyone at my job knows that I am a Christian.

T F 6. I am always ready to share my faith with others.

T F 7. I often invite people to come to church with me.

T F 8. I am a part of my church's evangelism ministry.

T F 9. I often give people Christian tracts and booklets.

T F 10. I am a bold and confident witness for Jesus Christ.

Close your class session with a prayer. Ask God to help the students evaluate themselves honestly and to yield to His Spirit in those areas where they discern weakness. Pray that each one will be bold in giving witness of Jesus.

Let's Talk It Over

The questions on this page are designed to encourage review of the lesson Scriptures and to promote discussion of the lesson by the class. The answers provided are only discussion starters. Let your class talk it over from there.

1. The Jewish leaders incited the crowd at Jesus' trial to cry out, "His blood be on us, and on our children" (Matthew 27:25). But in the apostles' trial, the leaders objected to having Jesus' blood brought on them. Why is it so hard to accept responsibility for our actions—even if we have promised to do so? What safeguards against making rash promises can you suggest?

It has always been easier to make a promise than to keep it. Sometimes we make conditional promises believing the conditions will not be met. When they are, then we are faced with the consequences of our promise. The one who co-signs a loan for a friend believes the friend will pay the debt and that will be the end of it. But what if the friend does not? Will the cosigner live up to his or her promise? Similarly, the Jewish leaders thought they would never be called into account for Jesus' death. When they were, they could not live up to their promise. We need to give careful thought to everything we say and be sure we make no promises that we are not fully prepared to keep.

2. Peter told the Jewish council that the apostles had to obey the Lord rather than the council. How can we tell when we are in a situation where we need to choose to obey God's will rather than man's laws?

The same Peter who said, "We ought to obey God rather than men" also wrote, "Submit yourselves to every ordinance of man" (1 Peter 2:13). Disobedience to human law can be justified only when there is a clear contradiction between obeying God and submitting to human ordinances.

Some laws may inconvenience us—like zoning laws or building regulations, or tax codes that penalize married couples. Some laws may just seem foolish. But these facts cannot justify violating the law. Only when the law prohibits obedience to God's commands or demands a violation of His commands do we have a right to claim the privilege of "civil disobedience."

3. The council reacted to the apostles' witnessing with murderous rage. What are some more common reactions to the gospel? How can we improve the chances that our witnessing will receive a favorable reaction?

One of the most common reactions to the gospel is apathy. Many people simply do not see how what we are telling them about Jesus can have any effect on their lives. It's like trying to sell a swimming pool to a person who cannot swim!

"Lifestyle evangelism" is the term used to describe witnessing by living the Christian life in front of family members and friends (cf. Matthew 5:16). When our unsaved friends look at us, do they say, "There's something about that person that is different, and that's the way I want to live"? Or do they say, "I don't know what that person has, but I sure don't want it"?

4. Sometimes help comes from unexpected places. Gamaliel—who certainly was no friend of the Christians—actually came to their defense. Why, do you suppose, did he do that? What, if anything, can we learn from this incident?

Gamaliel may well have been acting strictly from political expediency. He may have believed that the apostles represented little if any real threat and did not want to make martyrs of them. At the same time, we should realize that even unsaved persons can be people of integrity. Even though Gamaliel did not agree with the Christians, perhaps he did recognize that they had done nothing worthy of death and refused to be a party to the council's deadly intents.

Another issue is divine sovereignty. God can use anyone to do His will. In Old Testament times, God used the Assyrians and Babylonians as instruments of judgment against His sinning people, and He used Cyrus to bring the captive Hebrews home. Later He used Caesar Augustus to move Mary and Joseph from Nazareth to Bethlehem, where Jesus was to be born.

5. After being threatened and beaten by the Sanhedrin, the apostles thought it a privilege to be "counted worthy to suffer shame for [Jesus'] name." How can we develop such an attitude? How important is it to do so?

More and more Christians are being forced to choose between their faith and the culture. Those who choose faith will find increasingly that they are ridiculed and harassed about their choices. We can get upset about this, try to change things by political means, or just generally complain. Or we can continue to be faithful and testify of Jesus, recognizing that it is a blessing to suffer as Christians (Matthew 5:11, 12; 1 Peter 4:12-16).

Empowered to Serve

DEVOTIONAL READING: Micah 4:1-8.

BACKGROUND SCRIPTURE: Acts 6:1—8:3.

PRINTED TEXT: Acts 6:1-8; 7:55—8:1a.

Acts 6:1-8

1 And in those days, when the number of the disciples was multiplied, there arose a murmuring of the Grecians against the Hebrews, because their widows were neglected in the daily ministration.

2 Then the twelve called the multitude of the disciples unto them, and said, It is not reason that we should leave the word of God, and serve tables.

3 Wherefore, brethren, look ye out among you seven men of honest report, full of the Holy Ghost and wisdom, whom we may appoint over this business.

4 But we will give ourselves continually to prayer, and to the ministry of the word.

5 And the saying pleased the whole multitude: and they chose Stephen, a man full of faith and of the Holy Ghost, and Philip, and Prochorus, and Nicanor, and Timon, and Parmenas, and Nicolas a proselyte of Antioch;

6 Whom they set before the apostles: and when they had prayed, they laid their hands on them.

7 And the word of God increased; and the number of the disciples multiplied in Jerusalem greatly; and a great company of the priests were obedient to the faith.

8 And Stephen, full of faith and power, did great wonders and miracles among the people.

Acts 7:55—8:1a

55 But he, being full of the Holy Ghost, looked up steadfastly into heaven, and saw the glory of God, and Jesus standing on the right hand of God,

56 And said, Behold, I see the heavens opened, and the Son of man standing on the right hand of God.

57 Then they cried out with a loud voice, and stopped their ears, and ran upon him with one accord,

58 And cast him out of the city, and stoned him: and the witnesses laid down their clothes at a young man's feet, whose name was Saul.

59 And they stoned Stephen, calling upon God, and saying, Lord Jesus, receive my spirit.

60 And he kneeled down, and cried with a loud voice, Lord, lay not this sin to their charge. And when he had said this, he fell asleep.

1a And Saul was consenting unto his death.

GOLDEN TEXT: The word of God increased; and the number of the disciples multiplied in Jerusalem greatly; and a great company of the priests were obedient to the faith.
—Acts 6:7.

Lesson Aims

After this lesson students should be able to:

1. Relate how Stephen faithfully served the Lord through helping the needy and through giving his life for Christ.

2. Tell why every act of service, whether great or small, is needed in Christ's kingdom.

3. Identify someone who has faithfully served the Lord for many years, and make specific plans to express appreciation to that person.

Lesson Outline

INTRODUCTION
    A. April Fool?
    B. Lesson Background
 I. SEVEN MEN CHOSEN (Acts 6:1-8)
    A. Sensitive Matter (v. 1)
    B. Proposed Solution (vv. 2-4)
      No Spiritual Robots
    C. Unanimous Approval (vv. 5, 6)
    D. Astonishing Results (vv. 7, 8)
II. ONE MAN MARTYRED (Acts 7:55—8:1a)
    A. Stephen Sees Jesus (vv. 55, 56)
    B. Stephen Is Stoned (vv. 57, 58)
    C. Stephen Dies (vv. 59—8:1a)
      Martyrs
CONCLUSION
    A. "I'm Just a . . ."
    B. Prayer
    C. Thought to Remember

Introduction

A. April Fool?

Grandma was an enthusiastic gardener. She eagerly waited each year for the time when she could get her tools and her hands into the rich soil of her vegetable bed and begin growing good things to eat once again. The first of April was usually about the right time for groundbreaking.

One year Grandma hoped to have some help from younger and stronger hands. Her grandson had taken to muscle building with an eagerness at least as great as Grandma's zest for gardening. His iron pumping was producing visible results that he was not reluctant to display before any willing audience. The backyard garden plot would be a great place for a demonstration.

Things didn't work out quite that way, though. Garden tools just didn't fit hands better suited to iron weights, and arms that were impressive at lifting barbells just couldn't manage a hoe. There was power in those young muscles, but to gardening with Grandma they responded with only an "April Fool!"

Today (April 1) might be a good time to ask what our God-given abilities were designed for and what we are doing with them. Are we playing the fool by putting these abilities on display for self-promotion? Or are we giving the kind of service that is due the Giver? Stephen served—to the ultimate degree!

B. Lesson Background

The first five chapters of Acts expand upon the promise given by Jesus to the eleven apostles just before He ascended into Heaven: "Ye shall receive power, after that the Holy Ghost is come upon you: and ye shall be witnesses unto me both in Jerusalem, and in all Judea, and in Samaria, and unto the uttermost part of the earth" (Acts 1:8). Acts 1–5 is concerned primarily with the spread of the gospel throughout Jerusalem and Judea.

Acts 5:14 notes that, following the sudden and sobering deaths of Ananias and Sapphira and the continued working of miracles by the apostles, "believers were the more added to the Lord, multitudes both of men and women." Not even the threats of the Jewish ruling council could stifle this movement. The apostles, who were beaten on orders from the council, responded by "rejoicing that they were counted worthy to suffer shame" for the name of their Lord. The concluding verse of chapter 5 notes their continued zeal: "And daily in the temple, and in every house, they ceased not to teach and preach Jesus Christ" (v. 42). With such growth, however, came new problems and challenges that the church had to address.

I. Seven Men Chosen
(Acts 6:1-8)

A. Sensitive Matter (v. 1)

1. And in those days, when the number of the disciples was multiplied, there arose a murmuring of the Grecians against the Hebrews, because their widows were neglected in the daily ministration.

Those days describes a time of growth and opportunity for the church that continued in spite of the threats against the apostles recounted in the previous chapter. Before the Day of Pentecost, one hundred and twenty had prayed together (Acts 1:15); then on that day three thousand declared themselves obedient followers of Jesus as Lord and Christ (Acts 2:41). Daily additions soon brought the number of converts to five thousand men (Acts 2:47; 4:4), and to that were added the "multitudes" mentioned in Acts 5:14. Here *the number of the disciples* continued to be *multiplied*.

At this point in the church's growth, all of these believers were Jewish. Most were Jews by birth; they lived in the land promised to Abraham and his descendants, spoke its language (Aramaic), and followed its customs. Others were proselytes (Gentile converts to Judaism). They were Jews, but they were *Grecians* in language and culture. Some of these may have been among the three thousand converted on the Day of Pentecost (note the various lands mentioned in Acts 2:8-11). They may have remained in Jerusalem to become a part of the fellowship of believers in Jesus (Acts 2:42-47). Not having homes or employment in Jerusalem, some of these—and especially the widows—would have been among those who were most dependent on the *daily ministration* provided from the pooled resources of the church.

It would be difficult for any organization to continue for very long in a collection and distribution of material resources without someone's being—or feeling—slighted. "We/they" feelings are hard to avoid where distinct groups of people are involved. Occasionally those who are "outsiders" may complain because they see the more "established" participants as the beneficiaries of special favors. [See question #1, page 272.]

B. Proposed Solution (vv. 2-4)

2. Then the twelve called the multitude of the disciples unto them, and said, It is not reason that we should leave the word of God, and serve tables.

The *twelve* apostles had been chosen, appointed, empowered, and instructed by Jesus to preach, teach, and work miracles in bearing witness to His death and resurrection. For them to begin giving so much time to benevolence management that they neglected their divinely assigned work would be definitely wrong. Caring for the needy was right and good, but it did not have to be administrated by the apostles. [See question #2, page 272.]

A similar problem is faced when ministers of the gospel find themselves busy with matters involving facilities or finances. It is also faced by every Christian in choosing how he or she will spend available time. Choices must be made, not only between the good and the bad, but between the good and the better.

3. Wherefore, brethren, look ye out among you seven men of honest report, full of the Holy Ghost and wisdom, whom we may appoint over this business.

The problem had arisen among the people, so it was only right to let the solution be found *among* them. Apostolic authority would lead in shaping the program, but the people must choose the personnel from among themselves. *Seven men* would be an adequate number to lead in addressing the concern. In order to handle the finances, the men must be known for their transparent honesty. To preserve the sacred purpose of the entire enterprise, they must be Spirit-filled. To steer the right course in personal relationships, they must possess godly *wisdom*.

These seven men are often referred to as "deacons," from the Greek *diakonos*. The basis for this seems to be the use of two other words from the same root as *diakonos* in this passage. The daily "ministration" in verse 1 is from *diakonia*, and the verb for "serve tables" in verse 2 is from *diakoneo*. However, the Bible never explicitly refers to the seven as deacons. While modern deacons are often responsible for the more "material" matters of church life, the two best known of the seven (Stephen and Philip) were especially noted for their speaking and evangelism (Acts 6:9, 10; 8:5, 26-40; 21:8).

4. But we will give ourselves continually to prayer, and to the ministry of the word.

The apostles were not taking a "sabbatical." They would give full-time *ministry*, or service (again the word is *diakonia*), to their primary assignment of providing spiritual leadership through teaching and *prayer*.

NO SPIRITUAL ROBOTS

At one time or another, many busy persons have wished that they could duplicate themselves so they could do all the work that they just don't seem to have time to accomplish. A Georgia preacher, inspired by Disney World's robotic figure of President Lincoln, has tried to do something like this. Just as the Jerusalem church chose seven helpers, this preacher has built seven robots to help him preach the gospel! One of the figures cost a quarter of a million dollars: it is an "apostle Paul" that is able to shake hands, cross its leg, and deliver a thirteen-minute sermon about Jesus' appearance to Paul (Saul at the time) on the road to Damascus.

The apostles found themselves unable to administer the Jerusalem church's benevolence program to widows. The seven men chosen by the church to carry out this ministry were not just "clones" of the apostles; they were men "of honest report, full of the Holy Ghost and wisdom." They were genuine men of God whom the church knew could be entrusted with this important task.

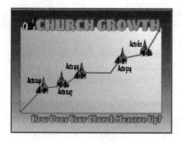

Visual for
lesson 5

Use today's visual to note the rapid growth of the early church. Discuss how the modern church can recapture the same vitality as the early church had.

The world may be amused by robotic figures that can imitate human behavior and even deliver a speech in mechanical fashion. However, if we wish to amaze the world with the power of the gospel as the first-century Christians did, it will require more of us than merely "going through the motions," mechanically giving lip service to Christ, or doing good deeds because it is what we have been "programmed" to do.   —C. R. B.

C. Unanimous Approval (vv. 5, 6)

5. And the saying pleased the whole multitude: and they chose Stephen, a man full of faith and of the Holy Ghost, and Philip, and Prochorus, and Nicanor, and Timon, and Parmenas, and Nicolas a proselyte of Antioch.

We are not told exactly how the choice of the seven men was made. It must have reflected a procedure that was familiar and generally accepted among the believers. All of the seven chosen had Greek names; thus it would appear that the Grecians' complaint was being respected. But we must not attach too much importance to the names, for two of the twelve apostles (Andrew and another Philip) also had Greek names.

Stephen is named first among the seven and is described most fully. That prepares the reader for the record of Stephen's activity that will follow. *Philip*, later referred to as "the evangelist" (Acts 21:8), is named second. The reference to Nicolas as a *proselyte* and as being from *Antioch* foreshadows the prominence of Antioch as a city where the gospel was first preached to Jews and Gentiles alike, and where the disciples were first called Christians (Acts 11:19-26).

6. Whom they set before the apostles: and when they had prayed, they laid their hands on them.

The "multitude" of believers (v. 5) made their choices and presented their candidates for apostolic commissioning (similar to the modern practice of "ordination" of certain leaders). The laying on of the apostles' hands provided the special endowment by which Stephen and Philip were able

to work miracles (Acts 6:8; 8:5-8, 13-20). Perhaps others of the seven also performed miracles, but we are not told of this in the Scriptures.

D. Astonishing Results (vv. 7, 8)

7. And the word of God increased; and the number of the disciples multiplied in Jerusalem greatly; and a great company of the priests were obedient to the faith.

Positive results came almost immediately from the wise and effective handling of the Grecians' complaint. *The word of God increased*: the gospel went forth bearing additional fruit among folk who observed and respected what was done. Once more the word *multiplied* is used to describe the church's phenomenal growth. Most astonishingly, many converts came from the group that had most vigorously opposed the apostles' preaching—the *priests* (Acts 4:1-3; 5:17, 18). [See question #3, page 272.]

8. And Stephen, full of faith and power, did great wonders and miracles among the people.

At this point our attention is directed to *Stephen*, where it remains through the account of his message and martyrdom.

Beyond the measure of the Spirit and of wisdom required of the seven (v. 3) and the degree of faith found in Stephen personally (v. 5), he is here described as *full of faith* (more literally, *grace*) *and power*. He moved swiftly beyond a serving of tables to the working of *wonders and miracles*, thus presenting the message of Christ most effectively *among the people* who had chosen him and to whom he was committed.

Not everyone, however, was favorably impressed with Stephen. Some, apparently of mixed national backgrounds, disputed with him. Failing in that effort to discredit Stephen's ministry, they brought charges of blasphemy against him before the Sanhedrin; and he was brought to trial to answer the charges. In response, Stephen traced the course of Jewish history from its beginning to the current hour. He highlighted the continual rejection by God's people of both His message and His messengers. The crowning sin, said Stephen, lay in the Jewish leaders' rejection and killing of Jesus. That accusation brought an immediate and hostile reaction from the council (Acts 6:9—7:54).

II. One Man Martyred
(Acts 7:55—8:1a)

A. Stephen Sees Jesus (vv. 55, 56)

55. But he, being full of the Holy Ghost, looked up steadfastly into heaven, and saw the glory of God, and Jesus standing on the right hand of God.

Stephen had already demonstrated a loyalty to Christ that was oblivious to the threats and attacks of his accusers. His attention was riveted on a vision infinitely higher than the hate-contorted faces of his accusers. That vision was reflected in his own face, which they had already seen "as it had been the face of an angel" (Acts 6:15).

As Isaiah had seen God's glorious presence when he received his prophetic assignment (Isaiah 6:1-5), so Stephen now *saw* it in the closing hour of his earthly life. But he also saw something more. In the position of highest honor and authority, at the *right hand of God*, he saw *Jesus*. Jesus had said that He would be seen in *glory* seated at the right hand of power (Matthew 26:64; cf. Ephesians 1:20; Colossians 3:1; Hebrews 1:3). What everyone will see at last, Stephen saw at that moment. But Stephen saw yet more; he saw Jesus *standing*—perhaps even rising to His feet as though to welcome His faithful witness home in a magnificent gesture of divine approval. [See question #4, page 272.]

56. And said, Behold, I see the heavens opened, and the Son of man standing on the right hand of God.

As clearly as a man with perfect eyesight sees what is before him on an earthly plane, Stephen saw beyond the wide-flung door of Heaven. He saw, not simply a man called Jesus, but the One who had offended the Jewish leaders by describing Himself with the messianic term *Son of man*. The Sanhedrin had charged Jesus with blasphemy because of His use of this title (Mark 14:61-64). Now Stephen was about to be charged with this same offense because he had dared to refer to Jesus in the same way. Furthermore, he had magnified his offense by saying that he saw in Heaven that very One *standing* at the *right hand* of Almighty God! It was enough to throw the council into a screaming rage!

B. Stephen Is Stoned (vv. 57, 58)

57. Then they cried out with a loud voice, and stopped their ears, and ran upon him with one accord.

The accusers had heard more than enough. This presumptuous miracle worker had to be silenced! To make sure they heard no more, they *stopped their ears* (by either putting their fingers into their ears or their hands over them). Then, with all reasonable communication ended, they *ran* like a pack of wolves *with one accord*. They were united in one mindless purpose—to destroy their victim.

58. And cast him out of the city, and stoned him: and the witnesses laid down their clothes at a young man's feet, whose name was Saul.

Leviticus 24:16 prescribed death by stoning as punishment for blaspheming the name of the Lord; Deuteronomy 17:2-7 directed taking the offender to the city gate for the execution. The *witnesses* whose testimony convicted the offender were to throw the first stones.

In order to give their arms more freedom of movement, those casting stones laid aside their heavy outer garments and put them at the *feet* of *Saul* (later Paul), who may have been an observer for the Sanhedrin at this execution. What a remarkable introduction to the man who would later become the Lord's apostle to the Gentiles!

C. Stephen Dies (vv. 59—8:1a)

59. And they stoned Stephen, calling upon God, and saying, Lord Jesus, receive my spirit.

While the hurtled stones were taking their toll, Stephen was praying loudly enough to be heard and understood over every other sound. His words echoed Jesus' prayer from the cross: "Father, into thy hands I commend my spirit" (Luke 23:46).

60. And he kneeled down, and cried with a loud voice, Lord, lay not this sin to their charge. And when he had said this, he fell asleep.

Did Stephen at this point sink to his knees in weakness or deliberately in prayer? The *loud voice* of his final words, like those of his crucified Lord (Luke 23:46), indicate a continuing force of will and a clear mind. Stephen's words of forgiveness are once again similar to those of the Master: "Father, forgive them; for they know not what they do" (Luke 23:34). [See question #5, page 272.]

The reference to death as a falling *asleep*—as a rest from labor and suffering—was used by Jesus in reference to Jairus's young daughter (Luke

---

How to Say It

ANANIAS. An-uh-*nye*-us.
ANTIOCH. *An*-tee-ock.
ARAMAIC. Air-uh-*may*-ick.
DIAKONEO (Greek). dih-*ah*-ko-*neh*-o (strong accent on *neh*).
DIAKONIA (Greek). dih-*ah*-ko-*nee*-uh (strong accent on *nee*).
DIAKONOS (Greek). dih-*ah*-ko-nawss.
GRECIANS. *Gree*-shunz.
JAIRUS. *Jye*-rus or *Jay*-ih-rus.
JUDAISM. *Joo*-day-iz-um.
LAZARUS. *Laz*-uh-rus.
NICANOR. Nye-*cay*-nor.
NICOLAS. *Nick*-uh-lus.
PARMENAS. *Par*-meh-nas.
PROCHORUS. *Prock*-uh-rus.
PROSELYTE. *prahss*-uh-light.
SAMARIA. Suh-*mare*-ee-uh.
SANHEDRIN. San-*heed*-run or San-huh-drin.
SAPPHIRA. Suh-*fye*-ruh.
TIMON. *Ty*-mon.

8:52, 53) and to Lazarus (John 11:11-14). The figure is nowhere more appropriate than in reference to Stephen's well-earned rest at the end of a turbulent day and at the end of service rendered courageously in the name of Christ Jesus.

MARTYRS

As the Vietnam war spilled over into neighboring countries, Cambodia fell to the Khmer Rouge (Kuh-*mair* Rouge)—the Communists who would later immerse the country in a veritable bloodbath. Minh Tien Voan (Min *Tee*-en *Vo*-an) was a Cambodian staff member of World Vision, a Christian relief organization. As the attack began on Phnom Penh (Peh-*nahm* Pen), the capital of Cambodia, Minh had an opportunity to leave the country by chartered plane. World Vision personnel urged him to do so and thus save his life. He refused with these words: "The people will need us Christians when the country starts to suffer."

A few days later, U.S. government personnel began to evacuate the American embassy in Phnom Penh, in the face of an inevitable Communist takeover of the city. The Americans offered Minh a seat on a helicopter with them. He refused this offer as well. Eventually Minh was arrested and executed for giving Bibles to the peasants.

We who live in a free nation and enjoy safety from persecution for our Christianity may find it hard to relate to stories of people like Minh Tien Voan and Stephen. Seldom, if ever, are we called upon to risk much of anything for our faith. But the life-and-death stories of these and many other Christian martyrs, both ancient and modern, testify to what it means to be committed—*really* committed—to Christ.   —C. R. B.

8:1a. And Saul was consenting unto his death.

Saul's role here may have been more active than is apparent. The Sanhedrin risked being called to account for this illegal act—since only the Romans could authorize capital punishment. But it is difficult to identify specific persons in the midst of mob violence; only those who stand out in some way are easily fingered. Some have suggested that Saul's *consenting* took the form of accepting personal responsibility for the stoning of Stephen by putting himself in a conspicuous position, guarding the cloaks of the actual assailants.

This scene remained etched in Paul's memory. Concerning his own apostleship he wrote, "I am the least of the apostles, that am not meet to be called an apostle, because I persecuted the church of God" (1 Corinthians 15:9). After his conversion, when he had returned to Jerusalem he prayed, "When the blood of thy martyr Stephen was shed, I also was standing by, and consenting unto his death, and kept the raiment of them that slew

him" (Acts 22:17-20). To Timothy, Paul described himself as one "who was before a blasphemer, and a persecutor, and injurious: but [who] obtained mercy" (1 Timothy 1:13). Thus Stephen's willingness to die in the name of Jesus was transformed from an act that Saul supported to one that reminded him of God's wondrous grace.

Conclusion

A. "I'm Just a . . ."

Perhaps it is hard to think of Stephen as one chosen, appointed, and empowered to "serve tables"—the time-consuming task for which the apostles could ill afford to neglect their God-given responsibilities. What a waste of this man's superior ability! But suppose Stephen had refused or neglected the less notable service? How would he have received the subsequent opportunities to serve the Lord through miracles, the brilliant defense of the gospel, and a heroic likeness to his Lord in death?

Jesus once said, "Whoever can be trusted with very little can also be trusted with much" (Luke 16:10, *New International Version*). Remember that in the work of the Lord no one is "just" anything. There are no unworthy opportunities to serve to the glory of God!

B. Prayer

Thank You, our Father, that to Your children You give power to match the assignments that You also give. Help us not to shirk our responsibilities but to find in You the power to accomplish Your tasks. In Christ we pray. Amen.

C. Thought to Remember

Whatever you are doing in the Lord's work, be faithful.

Home Daily Bible Readings

Monday, Mar. 26—Chosen to Serve (Acts 6:1-7)

Tuesday, Mar. 27—Stephen Arrested (Acts 6:8-15)

Wednesday, Mar. 28—Stephen Speaks of Abraham and Isaac (Acts 7:1-8)

Thursday, Mar. 29—Stephen Speaks of Joseph (Acts 7:9-16)

Friday, Mar. 30—Stephen Speaks of Moses (Acts 7:20-35)

Saturday, Mar. 31—Stephen Speaks of God's Blessings (Acts 7:36-50)

Sunday, Apr. 1—Stephen Martyred Before Saul (Acts 7:51—8:1)

Learning by Doing

This page contains an alternate lesson plan emphasizing learning activities.
Classes desiring such student involvement will find these suggestions helpful.

Learning Goals

After participating in this lesson, each student will be able to:

1. Relate how Stephen faithfully served the Lord through helping the needy and through giving his life for Christ.

2. Tell why every act of service, whether great or small, is needed in Christ's kingdom.

3. Identify someone who has faithfully served the Lord for many years, and make specific plans to express appreciation to that person.

Into the Lesson

To introduce the lesson, use one of the following activities.

Help Wanted Ads

Have your class write help wanted ads for positions in Christian service. What qualities would be essential? What qualities would be helpful? What would the compensation package look like?

For example, a help wanted ad from Acts 6:1-4 might read, "Large metropolitan church seeks several men to administer benevolence program for church widows. Applicants must be full of the Holy Spirit and wisdom, responsible, and able to function without close supervision. Grecian heritage would be helpful. Apply in person to the twelve apostles."

Circle Response

On a poster taped to the wall or on a white board write: "Nothing is more spiritual than the way a person handles money." Ask each person to tell why he or she agrees or disagrees with this statement with a one-sentence response. No one may respond twice until each person has had the chance to respond once. This activity will help less vocal members to venture out and participate. It will also help to quiet more vocal members who may unintentionally dominate the class.

Into the Word

A dramatic reading of today's text will help bring the account to life for your class members. Warm up for the dramatic reading by identifying the emotions and attitudes of the voices in each verse. Decide whether each narrative verse should be read by a man or a woman. Then assign members to be narrators, an apostle, and Stephen; and have the cast read Acts 6:1-8; 7:55—8:1a.

To explore the passage, give a copy of the text—with wide margins—to each class member. Have your students read the text and make a mark in the margin beside each verse, using one of the marks defined below:

?   "I have a question about this verse."
*   "I have a comment I'd like to make about this verse."
+   "We need more of this in our church!"
↑   "I am inspired and challenged by what this verse says."

Complete the activity in class yourself; this will provide a good gauge of how long to allow for the activity. Then ask the following questions:

"Who has a verse marked with a question mark?" Field the questions, looking for answers in the text as much as possible.

"Who has a verse marked with an asterisk?" Take the comments and discuss the observations made for as long as you think is appropriate.

"Who has a verse marked with a plus sign?" What items or activities do the students think are needed? Why? Can your class help to make these things happen?

"Who has a verse marked with an *up* arrow?" Discuss what the students find challenging. What will they do about these challenges?

Into Life

Service Project

Widows have always had a special place in the life of the church. And some widows have always been neglected by the church. Probably there are widows in your church and community who feel neglected. Lead your class in planning a project that will minister to the needs of widows in your church. Possibilities include help with transportation, friendly visits in person and by phone, completing chores requiring strength and agility, household repairs, etc.

Appreciation Letter

Lead your class in writing letters of appreciation to people who have demonstrated a Stephen-like dedication to whatever needs to be done. People should exhibit the qualities of Stephen, must have served in more than one capacity, and must have moved on to positions of greater responsibilities. Bring thank-you cards, envelopes, stamps, and pens to class along with a church directory for addresses.

Let's Talk It Over

The questions on this page are designed to encourage review of the lesson Scriptures and to promote discussion of the lesson by the class. The answers provided are only discussion starters. Let your class talk it over from there.

1. The Greek widows felt there was some discrimination in the early church. What should we do to assure that this is not a problem today?

Most church growth experts believe that homogeneous churches grow best—that is, churches in which the membership looks alike. People choose a church not only for the gospel, but for reasons of culture and personal preferences. Thus, say these experts, while the gospel is for everyone, a particular local church may not be. As a result, they will attempt to "market" the church to a limited demographic segment.

Others, however, believe that a church must make every effort to see that its membership matches the demographic mix of the people in its ministry area. To do anything else, they say, is to compromise the gospel for the sake of numbers.

The gospel is, indeed, for everyone. Discuss how your church implements that truth. Do you try to reach people of every racial, ethnic, social, gender, and age distinction? Or do you deliberately aim for a homogeneous congregation? If the latter, what do you do for the sake of the people in other demographic categories?

2. The apostles said, in essence, "This is not our job. Find someone else to take care of it." When is it appropriate for a person to refuse to participate in a worthy ministry, and when would refusal be an act of arrogance? Why?

The apostles did not refuse the ministry of serving the widows because it was "beneath them" or because they just did not want to do it. Instead, they recognized that they had a divine commission. Their foundational role in the church made it imperative that they do what they were called to do, for no one else could do it. When a person has a role that no one else can fill, then he or she must fill it even if it means the person will be unable to participate in other ministries. Every Christian ought to follow this principle.

3. How important do you think the successful handling of the matter of care for the widows was to the church growth reported in verse 7? Why?

We are tempted to think that what happens within the church is separate from our outreach efforts and has no bearing on them. But the unity of the church is a strong testimony to the world, and disharmony speaks volumes as well. What

impressed the watching world about the early Christians was the way they loved each other. The same thing will impress the world today!

4. Stephen saw Jesus standing at the right hand of the Father. Elsewhere the Bible tells us He *sat* at the Father's side (Hebrews 1:3). What significance do you see in the fact that Jesus was standing in Stephen's vision?

The lesson writer suggests Jesus was standing to welcome Stephen into Heaven. That is speculation, but surely it implies that Jesus was taking particular interest in His martyr.

We can be assured that Jesus takes a similar interest in our own situation, especially when we suffer for His sake. We do not have to be facing a murderous mob to get Jesus' attention. When a coworker makes a snide remark about our church attendance or our refusal to participate in gossip, Jesus notices. When a family member accuses us of acting "holier-than-thou" because we put faithfulness to Christ ahead of family, Jesus does not miss it. When a close friend gets angry because we refuse to participate in some inappropriate entertainment, the Lord nods His approval. We can almost hear Him say, "Blessed are you when people insult you, persecute you and falsely say all kinds of evil against you because of me. Rejoice and be glad, because great is your reward in heaven" (Matthew 5:11, 12, *New International Version*).

5. The natural reaction of one who is hurt by another is to seek vengeance—or at least justice. But Stephen prayed for mercy on behalf of his attackers, just as Jesus had done. How can disciples today develop a gracious spirit that seeks mercy even for those who hurt them?

Jesus told us to love even our enemies. Unfortunately, many of us do not know what love is. Love is more than a warm feeling. It is more than simply not hurting another. Love *(agape)* is the practice of active intelligent goodwill toward another without regard for a response. That it is active means it takes action—it takes the initiative. That love is intelligent means it is deliberate—we think about ways we can demonstrate love. Love is seeking the other's best interest, even ahead of our own. When we develop the habit of acting in this manner toward people, then even their hostile reactions can be met with a Christlike love.

Witnessing Beyond Jerusalem

DEVOTIONAL READING: John 4:19-24.

BACKGROUND SCRIPTURE: Acts 8.

PRINTED TEXT: Acts 8:4-8, 26-39.

Acts 8:4-8, 26-39

4 Therefore they that were scattered abroad went every where preaching the word.

5 Then Philip went down to the city of Samaria, and preached Christ unto them.

6 And the people with one accord gave heed unto those things which Philip spake, hearing and seeing the miracles which he did.

7 For unclean spirits, crying with loud voice, came out of many that were possessed with them: and many taken with palsies, and that were lame, were healed.

8 And there was great joy in that city.

. . . .

26 And the angel of the Lord spake unto Philip, saying, Arise, and go toward the south, unto the way that goeth down from Jerusalem unto Gaza, which is desert.

27 And he arose and went: and, behold, a man of Ethiopia, a eunuch of great authority under Candace queen of the Ethiopians, who had the charge of all her treasure, and had come to Jerusalem for to worship,

28 Was returning, and sitting in his chariot read Isaiah the prophet.

29 Then the Spirit said unto Philip, Go near, and join thyself to this chariot.

30 And Philip ran thither to him, and heard him read the prophet Isaiah, and said, Understandest thou what thou readest?

31 And he said, How can I, except some man should guide me? And he desired Philip that he would come up and sit with him.

32 The place of the Scripture which he read was this, He was led as a sheep to the slaughter; and like a lamb dumb before his shearer, so opened he not his mouth:

33 In his humiliation his judgment was taken away: and who shall declare his generation? for his life is taken from the earth.

34 And the eunuch answered Philip, and said, I pray thee, of whom speaketh the prophet this? of himself, or of some other man?

35 Then Philip opened his mouth, and began at the same Scripture, and preached unto him Jesus.

36 And as they went on their way, they came unto a certain water: and the eunuch said, See, here is water; what doth hinder me to be baptized?

37 And Philip said, If thou believest with all thine heart, thou mayest. And he answered and said, I believe that Jesus Christ is the Son of God.

38 And he commanded the chariot to stand still: and they went down both into the water, both Philip and the eunuch; and he baptized him.

39 And when they were come up out of the water, the Spirit of the Lord caught away Philip, that the eunuch saw him no more: and he went on his way rejoicing.

Apr 8

GOLDEN TEXT: They that were scattered abroad went every where preaching the word.—Acts 8:4.

Continuing Jesus' Work
Unit 2: Witnessing in Judea and Samaria
(Lessons 5-8)

Lesson Aims

After this lesson students should be able to:

1. Summarize Philip's evangelistic efforts among the people of Samaria and with the Ethiopian eunuch.

2. Tell how Philip's encounter with the eunuch illustrates important principles of personal evangelism.

3. Plan a specific way to use these principles in his or her witness to someone this week.

Lesson Outline

INTRODUCTION
    A. Stirring Up the Nest
    B. Lesson Background
I. TO SAMARITANS NEARBY (Acts 8:4-8)
    A. Going and Telling (vv. 4, 5)
    B. Confirming the Word (vv. 6, 7)
    C. Enjoying the Results (v. 8)
      Church on Fire
II. TO ONE FROM FAR AWAY (Acts 8:26-39)
    A. Directions From Heaven (vv. 26-29)
      The Distasteful Ones
    B. Questions Raised (vv. 30, 31)
    C. Text Provided (vv. 32-35)
    D. Gospel Accepted (vv. 36-38)
    E. Men Separated (v. 39)
CONCLUSION
    A. Cause for Rejoicing
    B. Prayer
    C. Thought to Remember

Introduction

A. Stirring Up the Nest

Residents of our retirement home sit for hours to watch a dozen tiny birds whose residence is a glass-enclosed aviary. Most fascinating is the emergence of recently hatched babies from their nests to make use of the flying space provided. One wee bird stayed too long in his crowded nest and became so crippled that he remained a "hopper" among those flying above and around him. That is a condition not to be desired, either among God's creatures or God's people.

Moses made this point in his song celebrating God's deliverance of the Israelites from Egypt: "As an eagle stirreth up her nest, fluttereth over

her young, spreadeth abroad her wings, taketh them, beareth them on her wings: so the Lord alone did lead him [Israel], ... He made him ride on the high places of the earth" (Deuteronomy 32:11-13).

Similarly, the persecution endured by the early church in Jerusalem may be seen as a stirring up of the nest in which it came into being. Thus was it persuaded to tumble out and to use and develop its wings in order to embark on the worldwide flight for which it was intended. Today's lesson recounts some of the first brief flights beyond the church's "hatching nest."

B. Lesson Background

While the Jerusalem church began "having favor with all the people" (Acts 2:47), conditions did not remain favorable. The apostles, as the Lord's spokesmen and the leaders of the church, endured persecution (Acts 4:1-3; 5:17-42). Later, opposition was directed against Stephen (one of the seven chosen to help administer the benevolence ministry for widows). Saul of Tarsus, who kept watch over the clothing of those who stoned Stephen to death, quickly rose to leadership in the persecution of the believers in Jerusalem. Acts 8:1-3 tells the story: "At that time there was a great persecution against the church which was at Jerusalem; and they were all scattered abroad throughout the regions of Judea and Samaria, except the apostles."

Thus the believers were dispersed in all directions: southward and westward in Judea and northward to Samaria. Meanwhile, the apostles continued to carry on their special work in Jerusalem.

I. To Samaritans Nearby
(Acts 8:4-8)

A. Going and Telling (vv. 4, 5)

4. Therefore they that were scattered abroad went every where preaching the word.

The early disciples of Jesus took the gospel with them wherever they went. They probably did not announce formal gatherings where they addressed audiences with sermons and lectures. A more likely scenario is excitement generated in personal conversation, heralding the good news that had changed the believers' lives and driven them from their homes. As strangers in a community, they had every reason to say why they were there. The *word* of Christ was the dominant, motivating power in their lives. What else was there to talk about?

What, by the way, should a Christian today talk about when he introduces himself to a stranger? [See question #1, page 280.]

5. Then Philip went down to the city of Samaria, and preached Christ unto them.

The *Philip* mentioned here was not the apostle, since the apostles had remained in Jerusalem. This man was one of the seven who were chosen by the church in Jerusalem and set apart by the apostles to conduct the daily distribution of supplies to the needy (Acts 6:1-6). He was known some years later as "Philip the evangelist" (Acts 21:8). By then he was living in Caesarea and serving as host to Paul and his companions (including Luke, who is part of the "we" mentioned in the record) on their way to Jerusalem.

The *city of Samaria* to which Philip *went* may have been the ancient capital of the northern kingdom of Israel (known as Sebaste in the first century), or it may have been another city in Samaria, such as the one where Jesus talked with the woman at Jacob's well (John 4:4-7).

B. Confirming the Word (vv. 6, 7)

6. And the people with one accord gave heed unto those things which Philip spake, hearing and seeing the miracles which he did.

If Philip's hearers included individuals who had witnessed Jesus' visits to their territory, then a foundation for faith existed already. Added was the evidence provided through Philip's ability to work *miracles*. This power apparently came with the laying on of the apostles' hands when the seven were set apart to their task (Acts 6:5-8; 8:14-19). The word and the works made a convincing combination. [See question #2, page 280.]

7. For unclean spirits, crying with loud voice, came out of many that were possessed with them: and many taken with palsies, and that were lame, were healed.

The scope of Philip's miracle-working ministry resembled that of Jesus. First noted is spiritual affliction—corrected, though not without the departing demons' noisy objections. Mentioned next is *palsies*—most likely a reference to various kinds of paralysis. The last named affliction is clearly physical—lameness. The fact that *many . . . were healed* had a powerful impact.

C. Enjoying the Results (v. 8)

8. And there was great joy in that city.

This outcome seems obvious, but most appropriate. Bodies and spirits had been made whole. Most significant, eternal life had been received by many; for "when they believed Philip preaching the things concerning the kingdom of God, and the name of Jesus Christ, they were baptized, both men and women" (v. 12).

The remainder of our printed text tells how *joy* came to another person to whom Philip brought the word of life in Christ.

CHURCH ON FIRE

In June of 1990, fire ravaged a church building in Burlingame, California, doing a million dollars worth of damage. Eventually, the minister of the congregation admitted to pouring gasoline on the building and lighting it. He said that he wanted to collect the insurance money so that his church could update the fifty-five-year-old structure.

The minister claimed that he didn't mean to burn down the entire building; his plan simply got out of hand. In fact, one of his fellow ministers came to his defense, describing him as "a very dedicated man . . . a real man of God, with a genuine concern." Maybe this just goes to show that having a "genuine concern" for others is not all that is required to be a leader of God's people. A sense of integrity would also help!

Of course, there are many ministers who would like to "set the church on fire"—in a spiritual sense. Those who are most successful at this follow the example of Philip: they proclaim Christ faithfully and watch the gospel bear fruit in the lives of individuals who commit themselves to Christ. In every time and place the transformation that occurs in those who accept Christ proves that God is still creating spectacular changes in human beings through those who are "on fire" for Him. —C. R. B.

II. To One From Far Away (Acts 8:26-39)

Acts 8:9-25 includes the account of two men named Simon and their relationship to Philip's ministry among the Samaritans. One Simon, a skillful illusionist, or magician, became convinced of the gospel through seeing that Philip's miracles were real. This Simon was among those who were baptized. The other Simon (the apostle Peter) came with John from Jerusalem to see what was happening in Samaria and to convey special powers of the Spirit by laying hands on the believers. When Simon the magician tried to

They that were scattered abroad went every where preaching the word. Acts 8:4

Visual for lesson 6

Today's visual suggests a number of modern applications of Acts 8:4. Discuss additional ways you and your class can spread the good news.

buy this ability to give the Spirit to others, Peter responded with a stern rebuke. After further ministry in this location, the two apostles returned to Jerusalem, preaching in other Samaritan villages along the way.

A. Directions From Heaven (vv. 26-29)

26. And the angel of the Lord spake unto Philip, saying, Arise, and go toward the south, unto the way that goeth down from Jerusalem unto Gaza, which is desert.

Why was Philip to make this journey? What was there to justify his leaving the evangelizing of Samaria and taking a long walk alone into the *desert* country of Judea? Such questions must have occurred to him, but he accepted the message of the *angel* as God's directive. He knew that his responsibility was to obey. *Gaza* was the southernmost of five ancient Philistine cities and was located near the Mediterranean coast. [See question #3, page 280.]

27. And he arose and went: and, behold, a man of Ethiopia, a eunuch of great authority under Candace queen of the Ethiopians, who had the charge of all her treasure, and had come to Jerusalem for to worship.

Breathtakingly abrupt, the narrative leaps from Philip's departure—*he arose and went*—to his encounter with *a man of Ethiopia* (modern Sudan), located south of Egypt. This man served as an official responsible for the treasury of *Candace queen of the Ethiopians* (*Candace* was a title of queens in Ethiopia much as *Caesar* was a title of Roman emperors).

In addition, this man was a *eunuch*, as were many attendants in royal courts. (Eunuchs were believed to be less likely to become involved in questionable behavior with any ladies of the court.) He had traveled *to Jerusalem for to worship*, perhaps at one of the major national feasts. Whether he was born a Jew or had become a proselyte (a convert to the Jewish faith), we do not know. But being a eunuch, he would not have been permitted to go inside the courts of the temple at Jerusalem (Deuteronomy 23:1).

28. Was returning, and sitting in his chariot read Isaiah the prophet.

No doubt this journey by *chariot* from Jerusalem to the eunuch's homeland (well over a thousand miles) must have been uncomfortable at times. But we know how he was spending some of the long hours: he was reading his Bible! Specifically he was reading from a scroll of *Isaiah*, perhaps in the Greek translation (the Septuagint), made approximately three centuries earlier in Egypt. Some suggest that the eunuch purchased the Isaiah scroll in Jerusalem during his visit there and was now taking the opportunity to examine it.

29. Then the Spirit said unto Philip, Go near, and join thyself to this chariot.

If God had something in mind for this man in the *chariot*, why did He not convey that message directly by His angel or by His Spirit and leave Philip to continue his work in Samaria?

For whatever reason, that is not the way God works. Each person receives the gospel of Christ from another person. "How shall they believe in him of whom they have not heard? and how shall they hear without a preacher?" (Romans 10:14). The "preacher" may be an apostle such as John, conveying the saving gospel through Scripture (John 20:30, 31). It may be a Christian friend saying through letters what is sometimes spoken. But a human messenger of the gospel has always been God's instrument for the salvation of mankind—even "hand-picked" prospects such as the Ethiopian eunuch and Saul of Tarsus (Acts 9:6).

THE DISTASTEFUL ONES

A long-cherished myth of evolutionary biology involves the viceroy butterfly. It was believed to mimic the coloration of monarch and queen butterflies, which have a taste that birds do not like. In 1862 Walter Bates developed a theory that one species can learn to mimic the sound, appearance, or smell of another species in order to deceive its predators.

One hundred and thirty years later, two Florida biologists decided to test Bates's hypothesis and found that (at least in the case of the three species mentioned above) it was not true! They removed the wings from specimens of the three varieties of butterflies and discovered that

---

How to Say It

ASHDOD. *Ash*-dod.
AZOTUS. Uh-*zo*-tus.
CAESAR. *See*-zer.
CAESAREA. Sess-uh-*ree*-uh.
CANDACE. *Can*-duh-see.
ETHIOPIANS. Ee-thee-*o*-pea-unz.
EUNUCH. *you*-nick.
GAZA. *Gay*-zuh.
ISAIAH. Eye-*zay*-uh.
MEDITERRANEAN. *Med*-uh-tuh-*ray*-nee-un (strong accent on *ray*).
PHILISTINE. Fuh-*liss*-teen or *Fill*-us-teen.
SAMARIA. Suh-*mare*-ee-uh.
SAMARITANS. Suh-*mare*-uh-tunz.
SEBASTE. Seh-*bas*-tee.
SEPTUAGINT. Sep-*too*-ih-jent.
TARSUS. *Tar*-sus.

birds found them *all* to be distasteful. It wasn't the viceroy's protective coloration that caused birds to avoid them after all.

In New Testament times, most Jews found it "distasteful" to have contact with certain classes of people—Gentiles, Samaritans, tax collectors, and eunuchs, for examples. Such groups were numbered among the "outcasts" of first-century society. But then came Philip, preaching the gospel of Christ among the Samaritans and then responding to the call of God to tell an Ethiopian eunuch about Christ—and all of this apparently with no reluctance! His example says that no one is "distasteful" to God; no one is outside the circle of His love.

Have *we* drawn any circles that leave certain "distasteful" people on the outside?   —C. R. B.

B. Questions Raised (vv. 30, 31)

30. And Philip ran thither to him, and heard him read the prophet Isaiah, and said, Understandest thou what thou readest?

The man in the chariot was reading aloud, perhaps to fix his own attention on the text, or possibly to include an otherwise unmentioned driver of the chariot. Philip *heard* enough to know what was being read and to ask a very wise question about it. No one could fully understand the passage being read by the eunuch without recognizing its links to the gospel of Christ. The question was a rather direct one to ask of a complete stranger, but this reader did not mind. [See question #4, page 280.]

31. And he said, How can I, except some man should guide me? And he desired Philip that he would come up and sit with him.

Far from being offended by Philip's question, the eunuch welcomed it as a possible solution to his problem. There was room in the chariot for another passenger, and Philip was warmly invited to *sit* with the treasurer. Neither of these two men, so different in nationality and background, hesitated for a moment to examine God's Word with the other!

C. Text Provided (vv. 32-35)

32, 33. The place of the Scripture which he read was this, He was led as a sheep to the slaughter; and like a lamb dumb before his shearer, so opened he not his mouth: in his humiliation his judgment was taken away: and who shall declare his generation? for his life is taken from the earth.

The source of the eunuch's reading was the best known of Isaiah's songs about God's Suffering Servant. We find it in Isaiah 53:7, 8. It compares God's servant with a *sheep* or a *lamb* in the creature's quiet acceptance of the most violent

treatment, whether in shearing or in slaughter. One is led to think of Jesus' steadfast refusal to answer or complain against the slander and *humiliation* to which He was subjected before and during His crucifixion (1 Peter 2:21-23).

In all of this, as Isaiah prophesied, Jesus' *judgment* (or justice) *was taken away*; that is, He was denied every basic right to a fair trial, either by the Jewish council or by the Roman court. Justice gave way to the clamor for His crucifixion.

The reference to the Servant's *generation* has been interpreted more than one way. If it refers to Jesus' contemporaries, the question *who shall declare his generation?* is asking how one can even speak of a generation so evil as to put Him to death. If it refers to Jesus' descendants, the question could be asking how Jesus can have any at all if His *life is taken from the earth*.

One may wonder why this text in Acts differs in places from the passage as found in Isaiah 53. What we see in Acts is a translation that more closely resembles the Greek text that was commonly used in New Testament times.

34. And the eunuch answered Philip, and said, I pray thee, of whom speaketh the prophet this? of himself, or of some other man?

Obviously Isaiah was describing someone. Was it himself or someone else who fulfilled the role of God's Suffering Servant? The same question remains troublesome to those who deny its obvious answer in Jesus of Nazareth! To them it produces an uneasiness that they often find difficult to cope with.

35. Then Philip opened his mouth, and began at the same Scripture, and preached unto him Jesus.

What an opportunity was presented to the evangelist, and what a text was provided! It was both natural and necessary for Philip to show how the facts of the gospel fulfilled the word picture drawn by Isaiah. From the eunuch's question that followed (verse 36), it is apparent that Philip's preaching *unto him Jesus* included showing how a believer participates in the death and resurrection of Jesus through being baptized— buried and raised according to His command (Matthew 28:18-20; Romans 6:1-4; Colossians 2:11, 12).

D. Gospel Accepted (vv. 36-38)

36. And as they went on their way, they came unto a certain water: and the eunuch said, See, here is water; what doth hinder me to be baptized?

Even the desert country of Judah is not entirely without springs, streams, and pools. Such waters seem to have been rare enough to excite the eunuch when he saw one. Having been taught by

Philip concerning baptism, the eunuch was eager to fulfill this command.

Note that while the teaching about salvation had to come from Philip, the idea of immediate action came from the eunuch. No pressure, prodding, or exhortation was needed here. This man believed and desired to do as he had been taught.

37. And Philip said, If thou believest with all thine heart, thou mayest. And he answered and said, I believe that Jesus Christ is the Son of God.

This verse does not appear in some early manuscripts of Acts, nor in most of the newer translations. It is, however, quoted in some very early Christian writings, and it appears to represent a procedure that was followed in the early church. Baptism was, and is, for believers—believers in *Jesus Christ* as *the Son of God*.

38. And he commanded the chariot to stand still: and they went down both into the water, both Philip and the eunuch; and he baptized him.

The Scripture is amazingly explicit in recording the procedure that followed. Did the inspired historian consider that future generations might question the need for the burial aspect of baptism into Christ? Otherwise why should he be so specific in saying that both the baptizer and the candidate *went down both into the water* to carry out the act (immersion) that is inherent in the word *baptized*? The eunuch was deliberately making an all-out commitment. A limited expression was not, and is not, appropriate. His dripping garment would dry out; his spirit of obedience to the Lord Jesus would not!

E. Men Separated (v. 39)

39. And when they were come up out of the water, the Spirit of the Lord caught away Philip, that the eunuch saw him no more: and he went on his way rejoicing.

Home Daily Bible Readings

Monday, Apr. 2—Philip Preaches in Samaria (Acts 8:4-8)
Tuesday, Apr. 3—Simon the Magician (Acts 8:9-13)
Wednesday, Apr. 4—Peter Confronts Simon the Magician (Acts 8:14-25)
Thursday, Apr. 5—Philip and the Ethiopian Eunuch (Acts 8:26-31)
Friday, Apr. 6—Those Excluded From the Congregation (Deuteronomy 23:1-7)
Saturday, Apr. 7—The Suffering Servant (Isaiah 53)
Sunday, Apr. 8—The Eunuch Is Baptized (Acts 8:32-40)

The Holy *Spirit*, who had brought Philip into contact with the homeward-bound Ethiopian (v. 29), had other work for the evangelist to do in towns along the Mediterranean coast, from Azotus (known as Philistine Ashdod in the Old Testament) and finally to Caesarea (v. 40). There Paul and Luke found him approximately a quarter of a century later (Acts 21:8)—the final time Philip is mentioned in the New Testament.

The newly baptized eunuch apparently continued *on his way* to Gaza, Egypt, and finally home to Ethiopia. While we know nothing certain of what became of him there, we would like to think that (in keeping with the spirit of the book of Acts) he told others of the Christ he had found through the prophecy of Isaiah and the testimony of the man who approached him as he journeyed homeward. With him, as with the Samaritans to whom Philip had taken the gospel, there was "great joy." [See question #5, page 280.]

Conclusion

A. Cause for Rejoicing

"I'll go on my way rejoicing."

A friend of mine said this habitually as he took his departure. The words were those used to describe the Ethiopian eunuch following his obedience to the gospel, but the spirit of joy was my friend's own and it was real. What was he rejoicing about? Almost everything, but mostly things related to Jesus and the life available in Him. If you asked him to be specific, you didn't have time to hear him recite, one by one, all the reasons for his joy.

What, though, were the causes of the eunuch's rejoicing? They are not named, and we can't know them all. Surely these are some: he had been introduced to the Savior prophesied by Isaiah; that Savior had come to die for him and for people throughout the world; God could be worshiped in his homeland of Ethiopia as well as in Jerusalem; and life eternal was his in Jesus Christ. The list of blessings was endless. Why shouldn't he go on his way rejoicing?

Why shouldn't we?

B. Prayer

Thank You, our Father, for faithful followers of Christ who brought His gospel to us where we were. May we be equally as faithful in conveying it to others where they are. For Jesus' sake, amen.

C. Thought to Remember

Our new friend nearby needs to know the best Friend of all. It's a grand privilege to introduce the one to the other!

Learning by Doing

This page contains an alternate lesson plan emphasizing learning activities.
Classes desiring such student involvement will find these suggestions helpful.

Learning Goals

After this lesson each student will be able to:

1. Summarize Philip's evangelistic efforts among the people of Samaria and with the Ethiopian eunuch.

2. Tell how Philip's encounter with the eunuch illustrates important principles of personal evangelism.

3. Plan a specific way to use these principles in his or her witness to someone this week.

Into the Lesson

Say to your class, "In sixty seconds, tell the person sitting next to you about the person who shared the gospel with you the first time it made sense. After sixty seconds, it will be your partner's turn. Remember that you have only sixty seconds, so be brief. Ready, set, go."

Make the transition to the Bible study by saying, "Our Bible lesson today looks at two groups that were influenced by the evangelism of Philip. As we study our text today, maybe we can see some insights that will be helpful in our efforts to present the gospel in a way that 'makes sense' to those with whom we share it."

If this "neighbor nudge" activity doesn't seem right for your class, then guide the class in brainstorming for ethnic and cultural groups that are often neglected in local church evangelism. Tape a large poster to the wall and use a broad-tipped marker to list the groups the students mention.

Make the transition to the Bible study by saying, "Our Bible lesson today looks at two ethnic and cultural groups that were influenced by the evangelism of Philip. As we study the text, let's look for some insights that will be helpful in our efforts to take the gospel to the ends of the earth."

Into the Word

Have a volunteer read Acts 8:4-8, 26-39 aloud. Observe that almost every verse of this text suggests principles of evangelism that are true and valid for all times and for all cultures.

Provide paper and pens and challenge your class members to identify principles of evangelism for every verse that is appropriate. For example, Acts 8:4 shows that all Christians are to announce the Word wherever we go. Acts 8:5 gives us the central focus of our message—we proclaim Christ. Acts 8:8 assures us that joy will fill the place where Christ is preached and acknowledged. Acts 8:26 teaches us to be sensitive to God's leading. Acts 8:27 illustrates immediate obedience and the inclusion of high-profile, influential people in our efforts. Acts 8:28 suggests watching for people who have an interest in the Bible or in spiritual matters. Acts 8:29 shows that God will guide those who are open to His leading. Acts 8:30 illustrates urgency, listening to others, and asking pointed questions to discern understanding. Acts 8:31 cautions to wait for an invitation to move closer. Acts 8:32-35 shows that we should be able to begin at any point in Scripture and share the gospel of Jesus. Acts 8:36 indicates that baptism is important as a part of one's accepting Christ. Acts 8:38 makes it clear that baptism is by immersion. Acts 8:39 tells us to expect joy in the life of the new convert to Christ.

Option

We often use Bible drama with children, but it is also effective with adults. The characters can all read their lines from their Bibles; memorizing lines is not necessary. Understanding the character and projecting the emotions and concerns of the character are important.

Acts 8:4-8 lends itself to drama with a narrator. Prepare a group to dramatize this and note the serious nature of the demonic elements. For Acts 8:26-39, assign parts for a narrator, the angel, the Holy Spirit, Philip, and the Ethiopian.

Into Life

Provide pens and paper for your class to write evangelistic letters to people with whom they would like to share the gospel. Explain that they could introduce the topic like this: "In our Bible class today, we studied the account of Philip talking to a man about Christ, and I thought about how I've been wanting to talk to you about Jesus. The man in the story was interested in religious discussion, just as you are. Our lesson said that Philip told him the good news about Jesus, and I would like to do the same with you."

Invite class members to read their letters aloud. It will encourage the listeners, and the reader will be encouraged by the response of the listeners. Ask for suggestions to improve each presentation.

Close the class period by dividing into prayer partners to pray for the letters and their impact on the recipients. Then encourage the students to mail the letters early this week.

Let's Talk It Over

The questions on this page are designed to encourage review of the lesson Scriptures and to promote discussion of the lesson by the class. The answers provided are only discussion starters. Let your class talk it over from there.

1. It has been said that "the blood of martyrs is the seed of the church." We know this was true in the first-century church, as the persecuted believers "went every where preaching the word." How does that fact influence the way you think about the kinds of opposition to your faith that you face?

It seems to be a principle of both the physical and spiritual realms that when we face resistance, we are likely to become stronger. We need to remember James's words to "count it all joy" when we are persecuted (James 1:2).

Now, what most of us face today can hardly be called "persecution." Still, we do face opposition from time to time. Rather than complain about it and give up in the face of it, we must stand firm for our faith. If we cannot endure a little opposition, how will we stand if outright persecution should someday be our lot?

2. It is apparent that the miraculous signs were a persuasive factor in Philip's ministry and witness among the Samaritans. What are the most persuasive factors in our witness to the lost?

Of course, we must have an intelligent understanding of the gospel that we share (1 Peter 3:15). We cannot effectively persuade non-believers apart from a reasonable articulation of the evidences that support our faith. But for many persons today, this is not enough.

While we may not be able to confirm the truth of our words with the miraculous signs and wonders that Philip used, we all have one powerfully persuasive piece of evidence at our disposal—example. Modeling Christ's love in our relationships is the most persuasive factor in our witness. Albert Schweitzer said, "Example is not the main thing in influencing others. It is the *only* thing."

3. An angel told Philip where to go to find a receptive person with whom to share the gospel. How do we determine when and where to share the gospel today? How do we find people who are receptive to the message?

The parable of the sower reminds us that much of our efforts will be expended sowing seed on resistant ground. Our responsibility is to share the gospel so that "whosoever will may come."

Of course, we want to use good judgment. If we have opportunity to share the gospel in one of two or more locations or situations, then we need to make an effort to determine which one represents the best stewardship of our time and resources. The rest we leave in God's hands, and trust that He by His providence will put us in the right place at the right time to share with those whose hearts are open to the gospel. But with that understanding, let us be careful not to squander such opportunities when they arise.

4. Philip heard the Ethiopian reading a prophecy about Jesus, and this gave him a good idea about how to approach the man with the good news. How can we broach the subject of Jesus with people? What opportunities should we watch for?

Sometimes people are obviously interested in the Bible and what it has to say. We can tell by what they say or by their presence at church events. At other times, however, it may not be so easy to tell—or they may not be interested until we pique their interest. Paul did that in Athens by observing the city's statuary (Acts 17:22ff.). We need to notice what people are interested in, what they talk about, and what goals they pursue. Then we can observe how these are consistent with or in contrast to a Christian worldview. From that, perhaps we can tell why we hold to the latter and what doing so has done for us.

What movies are playing in the local theaters? Can you use their message as an opening for the gospel—either by way of comparison or contrast?

5. The eunuch, Acts tells us, "went on his way rejoicing" after his baptism. Is this joy only for the newly converted, or is it for all believers? How should we see this joy expressed in the life of the church?

Of course, all believers should experience the joy of salvation. Note, however, that joy is not always expressed in unbridled exuberance. Sometimes joy is a quiet peace in spite of life's turmoil. Sometimes it is seen in the satisfaction that being with brothers and sisters in Christ provides. Indeed, sometimes it is seen in expressive displays of emotion, but usually such displays are more properly called "happiness." *Happiness* is an outward expression related to one's circumstances. *Joy* is much deeper; it transcends the present experience and anticipates, by faith, the final victory.

Proclaiming the Risen Lord

DEVOTIONAL READING: John 20:1, 11-18.

BACKGROUND SCRIPTURE: Luke 24:1-12; Acts 9:1-31.

PRINTED TEXT: Luke 24:1-10; Acts 9:19b-22, 26-29a.

Luke 24:1-10

1 Now upon the first day of the week, very early in the morning, they came unto the sepulchre, bringing the spices which they had prepared, and certain others with them.

2 And they found the stone rolled away from the sepulchre.

3 And they entered in, and found not the body of the Lord Jesus.

4 And it came to pass, as they were much perplexed thereabout, behold, two men stood by them in shining garments:

5 And as they were afraid, and bowed down their faces to the earth, they said unto them, Why seek ye the living among the dead?

6 He is not here, but is risen: remember how he spake unto you when he was yet in Galilee,

7 Saying, The Son of man must be delivered into the hands of sinful men, and be crucified, and the third day rise again.

8 And they remembered his words,

9 And returned from the sepulchre, and told all these things unto the eleven, and to all the rest.

10 It was Mary Magdalene, and Joanna, and Mary the mother of James, and other women that were with them, which told these things unto the apostles.

Acts 9:19b-22, 26-29a

19b Then was Saul certain days with the disciples which were at Damascus.

20 And straightway he preached Christ in the synagogues, that he is the Son of God.

21 But all that heard him were amazed, and said; Is not this he that destroyed them which called on this name in Jerusalem, and came hither for that intent, that he might bring them bound unto the chief priests?

22 But Saul increased the more in strength, and confounded the Jews which dwelt at Damascus, proving that this is very Christ.

. . . .

26 And when Saul was come to Jerusalem, he assayed to join himself to the disciples: but they were all afraid of him, and believed not that he was a disciple.

27 But Barnabas took him, and brought him to the apostles, and declared unto them how he had seen the Lord in the way, and that he had spoken to him, and how he had preached boldly at Damascus in the name of Jesus.

28 And he was with them coming in and going out at Jerusalem.

29a And he spake boldly in the name of the Lord Jesus.

GOLDEN TEXT: Why seek ye the living among the dead? He is not here, but is risen.
—Luke 24:5, 6.

Continuing Jesus' Work
Unit 2: Witnessing in Judea and Samaria
(Lessons 5-8)

Lesson Aims

After participating in this lesson, a student should be able to:

1. Describe the appearance of angels to the women at Jesus' tomb and Saul's earliest testimony of the resurrection.

2. Tell how the evidence for Jesus' resurrection is convincing for believers today.

3. Praise God for Jesus' resurrection and for the gospel message it validates.

Lesson Outline

INTRODUCTION
  A. The Darkest Hour
  B. Lesson Background
 I. THE WOMEN SEE AND TELL (Luke 24:1-10)
  A. Amazing Discovery (vv. 1-3)
  B. Wonderful News (vv. 4-8)
  C. Excited Report (vv. 9, 10)
    Not a Hoax
II. SAUL TESTIFIES OF JESUS (Acts 9:19b-22, 26-29a)
  A. In Damascus (vv. 19b-22)
    A Grave Matter
  B. In Jerusalem (vv. 26-29a)
CONCLUSION
  A. Stirring Up the Witnesses
  B. Prayer
  C. Thought to Remember

Introduction

A. The Darkest Hour

"The darkest hour is just before the dawn."

Most of us have heard this saying. Perhaps we have spoken the words in an effort to encourage someone during a difficult time. But if anyone has examined it literally in relation to nights and mornings, we have not seen his report.

There is an all-important area, however, in which this adage is true; and it is an area that touches every person's life in a very significant and powerful way. We refer to Jesus' death and resurrection and to the difference that those events make in how one deals with death whenever he has to confront its harsh reality. At that critical point, resurrection becomes more than just a doctrine; it is the unshakable basis of hope for one who believes and lives in Jesus.

Here is a summary of that message of hope: "That Christ died for our sins according to the Scriptures; and that he was buried, and that he rose again the third day according to the Scriptures: and that he was seen"—by many who knew Him best and grieved most deeply at His dying (1 Corinthians 15:3-8). In Jesus the deepest darkness does give way to brightest dawn—a truth that demands to be reported.

B. Lesson Background

One man, Luke, served as God's recorder for both passages of Scripture before us today. The two passages have this feature in common: each follows an account of death and resurrection, and each leads to the spreading of the news that Jesus is risen.

Luke 23 tells how the Jewish council delivered Jesus to the Roman authorities, who were persuaded to crucify Him. The final two verses of the chapter note that Galilean women who had followed Jesus and supported His ministry (Luke 8:1-3) witnessed His death, then watched as His body was entombed by Joseph of Arimathea (John 19:38-42). Not satisfied with the hundred pounds of myrrh and aloes already used to wrap Jesus' body, the women prepared spices and ointments to show their own respect for Jesus. Then, beginning at sundown on Friday, they rested through the Sabbath, as the law prescribed, before visiting the tomb and hearing the astonishing news that Jesus had risen.

Acts 9 carries us approximately seven years forward into the history of the church and to the life of Saul, a fervent Pharisee and opponent of the gospel. His eagerness to persecute Christians took him to Damascus, where he expected to arrest believers and bring them to Jerusalem for punishment. But Saul himself was "arrested" on the way by Jesus Himself, speaking from Heaven. Saul "surrendered" and asked for orders. Those orders took him on to Damascus for further instructions, given by a disciple named Ananias: "Arise, and be baptized, and wash away thy sins, calling on the name of the Lord" (Acts 22:16).

Saul (writing as the apostle Paul) later referred to his baptism as a death-and-resurrection experience with Christ: "Know ye not, that so many of us as were baptized into Jesus Christ were baptized into his death? Therefore we are buried with him by baptism into death: that like as Christ was raised up from the dead by the glory of the Father, even so we also should walk in newness of life" (Romans 6:3, 4).

What happened in Jerusalem after Jesus' resurrection? We learn this from Luke 24. And what happened in Damascus after Saul's spiritual resurrection in Christ? We learn this from Acts 9.

I. The Women See and Tell
(Luke 24:1-10)

A. Amazing Discovery (vv. 1-3)

1. Now upon the first day of the week, very early in the morning, they came unto the sepulchre, bringing the spices which they had prepared, and certain others with them.

The first day of the week is usually called Sunday; but because of what happened on this day, Christians often refer to it as the Lord's Day. This is most likely the meaning of John's reference to "the Lord's day" in Revelation 1:10.

We have noted Luke's reference to the women from Galilee who witnessed Jesus' death and burial (Luke 23:55, 56). Mentioned earlier as ones who "had been healed of evil spirits and infirmities" (Luke 8:1-4) are Mary Magdalene, Joanna (the wife of Herod's steward), Susanna, and "many others." Two of these, Mary Magdalene and Joanna, are mentioned with the group at the tomb, along with Mary the mother of James and some "other women" (Luke 24:10).

From the other Gospel accounts we learn that one of these women was Salome (Mark 16:1). We also learn that, while Mary Magdalene came to the tomb with other women, at some point she became separated from them. John's account (John 20:1, 2) indicates that when Mary saw that the stone had been rolled away from the tomb, she immediately ran to tell Peter and John that someone had taken the body of Jesus (though she was mistaken). Peter and John then ran to the tomb to investigate (though Luke mentions only Peter's journey in v. 12). Mary Magdalene returned alone to the tomb, where Jesus appeared to her (John 20:11-18). [See question #1, page 288.]

2. And they found the stone rolled away from the sepulchre.

Joseph of Arimathea had completed his burial of Jesus by rolling a great *stone* before the opening of the *sepulchre*. Pilate had ordered the stone sealed and guarded to prevent the removal of Jesus' body (Matthew 27:62-66). This stone had been a subject of concern to the women as they approached the *sepulchre* (Mark 16:3), but they quickly discovered that their anxiety was unnecessary. An angel from Heaven had *rolled away* the stone. Thus were all hindrances removed that would keep anyone from entering and examining the empty burial place (Matthew 28:2-4). As some have noted, the stone was rolled away, not to let Jesus out, but to let witnesses in.

3. And they entered in, and found not the body of the Lord Jesus.

The women *entered in* and looked around. The *body* of Jesus was gone, but its wrappings lay in place, and to one side was the napkin that had been about Jesus' head. This was noted especially by Peter and John when they were summoned to the sepulchre a short while later (John 20:1-8).

B. Wonderful News (vv. 4-8)

4. And it came to pass, as they were much perplexed thereabout, behold, two men stood by them in shining garments.

It is only natural that the women were *much perplexed* by what they saw: the once-secure tomb was opened, and the body they had watched being placed inside was missing—without a trace of forcible removal.

Suddenly *two men stood by them in shining garments.* Both their apparel and their message identified them as angels. One had removed the stone from the doorway of the tomb and proceeded to address the women (Matthew 28:2-7).

5. And as they were afraid, and bowed down their faces to the earth, they said unto them, Why seek ye the living among the dead?

Zechariah (the father of John the Baptist), Mary the mother of Jesus, and the shepherds near Bethlehem all had shown the same natural response to the sudden and glorious appearance of angels (Luke 1:12, 29, 30; 2:9, 10). The women *bowed* to the ground to avoid facing the brilliance before them.

The angels' message was not slow in coming: *Why seek ye the living among the dead?* It sounds like a rebuke, but how else could their news be expressed so briefly, plainly, and powerfully? A tomb is no place to look for a living person.

6. He is not here, but is risen: remember how he spake unto you when he was yet in Galilee.

The angels' statement that Jesus *is not here, but is risen* confirmed the news implied in the angel's question. The announcement should not have come as a surprise, however, to anyone who had followed Jesus' ministry and heard His teaching in these women's home district of *Galilee*. Jesus' own predictions of His suffering, death, and resurrection had been directed mostly

"Why seek ye the living among the dead? He is not here, but is risen."

Luke 24:1, 6

Display today's visual as you discuss Luke 24:4. Discuss: "While we can't all see angels to assure us that Jesus has risen, how can we have confidence in the resurrection?"

Visual for lesson 7

to His apostles (Matthew 16:21; 17:22, 23; Mark 8:31; 9:31; Luke 9:21, 22; 18:31-33), but they were a part of His public teaching available to men and women alike. Now the teaching was authenticated by a dramatic visual aid.

7. Saying, The Son of man must be delivered into the hands of sinful men, and be crucified, and the third day rise again.

Jesus had been clear about the events of His final days. Judas betrayed Jesus *into the hands* of the Jewish leaders, who in turn delivered Him to the Romans with a demand that He be *crucified*. Those events happened as predicted; therefore, why shouldn't His resurrection on the *third day* have been expected? There was really no place for uncertainty or confusion.

Should we be surprised, however, at the disciples' failure to hear and understand Jesus' words? Are we better than they at shaping our actions to what God's Word says, rather than to what we expect or wish it to say?

8. And they remembered his words.

These women needed only to have the truth brought to their attention. Having *remembered* what Jesus said and having experienced the fulfillment of His *words*, they were ready to go and tell others. [See question #2, page 288.]

C. Excited Report (vv. 9, 10)

9. And returned from the sepulchre, and told all these things unto the eleven, and to all the rest.

Apparently the women from Galilee were lodging together in Jerusalem and were in close contact with the apostles. So they returned to share with their fellow disciples the glorious news of Jesus' resurrection. Such news is still important enough to be told with breathless excitement wherever we can find a hearer.

The *eleven* apostles had been the twelve until the defection and self-destruction of Judas. Peter and John were the first of the group to learn of the empty tomb, and they did not at first grasp the entire story (John 20:1-10). They ran to the scene to examine the empty tomb.

10. It was Mary Magdalene, and Joanna, and Mary the mother of James, and other women that were with them, which told these things unto the apostles.

Mary Magdalene and *Joanna* are named among the Galileans whom Jesus had healed of evil spirits and various infirmities (Luke 8:2, 3). *Mary the mother of James* seems to have had a son among the apostles—"James the less" (Mark 15:40). He and his companions, however, did not accept the report. To them, talk of a resurrection seemed as "idle tales" (v. 11). [See question #3, page 288.]

Luke's summary lists the women together, but we have already noted that Mary Magdalene had made her report to Peter and John separately—apparently without having seen the angels (John 20:2). Peter and John, then, must have been separated from the other apostles and were evidently closer to the tomb than they. Mary Magdalene had time to find them and to return to the tomb behind them before the other women made their report. Mark 16:9 tells us that Jesus "appeared first to Mary" outside the tomb (as reported in John 20:11-17). His second appearance was to the other women as they were on the way to tell the apostles about seeing the angels at the tomb (Matthew 28:9). At some point the apostles all came together, except for Thomas, and Jesus appeared to them as well (Luke 24:33-49; John 20:19-24).

NOT A HOAX

Leroy Johnson is an authority on the history of Death Valley National Park. In 1998 a friend told him that he had found a wooden chest containing the possessions of one of the "forty-niners" (the miners who flocked westward during the California "gold rush"). A document in the chest was dated January 2, 1850. At first, Johnson believed it to be authentic.

However, as Johnson and other historians examined the chest and its contents more carefully, they found several discrepancies in its contents. A ceramic bowl bore a distinctive trademark that was not in use until 1914. Two tintype photos in the chest were of a kind not patented until several years after 1850. It became obvious that the chest was a hoax, even though the man who said he found it continued to claim otherwise.

Throughout history skeptics have called the resurrection of Christ a hoax. But the Gospel accounts will not allow such a view to stand. They include the testimony of the women who were first to arrive at the tomb and discover it empty. (Women in that society were already held in disregard; imagine the added scorn that would result from concocting such an outlandish story.) Eventually the men to whom they told the news were able to examine the evidence and believe.

None of these individuals had anything to gain by fabricating a hoax that would have made them look foolish. Today, because of their testimony, we can declare with confidence, "Now is Christ risen from the dead" (1 Corinthians 15:20).

—C. R. B.

II. Saul Testifies of Jesus (Acts 9:19b-22, 26-29a)

Here our focus shifts to a man whose name as well as his life was changed by his proclamation of the risen Christ. When first we meet him in the Scripture, he is known as Saul of Tarsus.

A. In Damascus (vv. 19b-22)

19b. Then was Saul certain days with the disciples which were at Damascus.

This verse follows the account of Saul's baptism into Christ, after which he was given nourishment. For a *certain* number of *days* he remained in *Damascus* in the company of followers of Jesus, who were now his friends, not his foes.

20. And straightway he preached Christ in the synagogues, that he is the Son of God.

Saul had journeyed to the *synagogues* in Damascus with letters authorizing him to seek out and arrest any persons who had defected to the "way" of Christ Jesus (Acts 9:1, 2). Now he entered those synagogues with a very different mission: to proclaim Jesus as the *Christ, the Son of God!*

In Damascus Saul began the pattern that he followed throughout his evangelistic career, even as apostle to the Gentiles. The gospel was the power of God for salvation to every believer, "to the Jew first, and also to the Greek" (Romans 1:16). So in every city the apostle first went to the synagogue, where he would find Jews who possessed a knowledge of the prophetic Scriptures and thus a background for an understanding of the gospel. He would preach in the synagogue as long as he had a receptive hearing and leave only when he was rejected and compelled to do so (Acts 13:45, 46; 17:1-9).

21. But all that heard him were amazed, and said; Is not this he that destroyed them which called on this name in Jerusalem, and came hither for that intent, that he might bring them bound unto the chief priests?

Saul's hearers *were amazed.* His reputation had preceded him to Damascus, especially among those who had the most to fear from his arrival there. Included in that number was Ananias, the disciple whom God persuaded to lead Saul to the new life in Christ (Acts 9:10-18). [See question #4, page 288.]

22. But Saul increased the more in strength, and confounded the Jews which dwelt at Damascus, proving that this is very Christ.

As time passed, Saul became more and more effective in his presentation of the gospel. He thwarted the objections of *the Jews* in *Damascus* by his ready answers to their arguments and assertions. By laying the Old Testament Scriptures alongside the facts of Jesus' life, death, and resurrection, Saul proved that Jesus is *very* (i.e., truly) *Christ,* the promised Messiah.

Verses 23-25 (not included in the printed text) note that "after . . . many days" the Jews made plans to kill Saul, forcing him to leave the city. The "many days" apparently includes the three years mentioned in Galatians 1:15-18, during

---

How to Say It

ANANIAS. An-uh-*nye*-us.
ARABIA. Uh-*ray*-bee-uh.
ARIMATHEA. *Air*-uh-muh-*thee*-uh (strong accent on *thee*).
BARNABAS. *Bar*-nuh-bus.
CAESAREA. Sess-uh-*ree*-uh.
CORNELIUS. Cor-*neel*-yus.
DAMASCUS. Duh-*mass*-cus.
GALILEANS. Gal-uh-*lee*-unz.
MAGDALENE. *Mag*-duh-leen or Mag-duh-*lee*-nee.
PHARISEE. *Fair*-ih-see.
SEPULCHRE. *sep*-ul-kur.
SYNAGOGUES. *sin*-uh-gogs.
TARSUS. *Tar*-sus.
ZECHARIAH. Zek-uh-*rye*-uh.

---

which Saul went to Arabia and then returned to Damascus. The Scripture does not say what he did in Arabia. Perhaps the Lord instructed him during this time, preparing him for the special ministry he would have.

A GRAVE MATTER

The "Y2K bug" generated a lot of hoopla and consternation in the last few years leading up to January 1, 2000. Our tendency to rely on high-tech solutions to even the most mundane of life's problems created some rather interesting dilemmas.

One form of the "bug" that received very little hype was definitely a low-tech matter. Many older people whose spouses had died in the late twentieth century had dual headstones placed on the grave plots where they would eventually be buried with their mates. On each stone, beneath the person's own name, had been engraved the numerals "19" followed by a blank space to be filled in at the time of the person's death. In the late 1990s, it was estimated that a quarter of a million gravestones were inscribed this way. The cost for changing an inscription (so that the blank space was preceded by "20") ran as high as two thousand dollars.

Saul had a different "gravestone" problem. His encounter with the risen Christ was a "grave" matter, for it forced him to acknowledge that Jesus' gravestone had indeed been rolled away. When he finally admitted this, it revolutionized his life. He began proving that Jesus was the Messiah, confounding those who had known him formerly as a persecutor of the church.

Regardless of when we live—whether early in the first millennium as Saul did, or early in the third as we do now—once the risen Christ takes control of our lives, all things become new.

—C. R. B.

B. In Jerusalem (vv. 26-29a)

26. And when Saul was come to Jerusalem, he assayed to join himself to the disciples: but they were all afraid of him, and believed not that he was a disciple.

Rescued from the wrath of the unbelieving Jews, Saul returned to *Jerusalem*, where once more his reputation preceded him. There he *assayed*, or tried, *to join himself to the disciples*. But the Jerusalem faithful were skeptical. Was this an effort to spy on them in an attempt to arrest and punish even more of their number?

27. But Barnabas took him, and brought him to the apostles, and declared unto them how he had seen the Lord in the way, and that he had spoken to him, and how he had preached boldly at Damascus in the name of Jesus.

Saul could not have found a better "sponsor" in his efforts to work with the church at Jerusalem than *Barnabas* provided in bringing him to the apostles. Specifically, Peter and James (the Lord's brother) are mentioned in Galatians 1:18, 19. (That James is called an apostle in this passage most likely reflects his position of leadership in the Jerusalem church.)

Barnabas's willingness to "go out on a limb" for someone whose conversion was being questioned was an appropriate gesture for one known as the "Son of Encouragement" (Acts 4:36, *New International Version*). He also seems to have done his homework by investigating the reports of Saul's conversion. He was able to report confidently that Jesus had appeared and *spoken* to Saul on the way to *Damascus*, and that Saul had risked his life to speak *boldly* for Christ in that city.

Home Daily Bible Readings

Monday, Apr. 9—The Empty Tomb (Luke 24:1-10)

Tuesday, Apr. 10—Jesus Appears to Saul (Acts 9:1-9)

Wednesday, Apr. 11—Ananias, a Reluctant Witness (Acts 9:10-19a)

Thursday, Apr. 12—Saul Preaches and Leaves Damascus (Acts 9:19b-25)

Friday, Apr. 13—Saul in Jerusalem (Acts 9:26-31)

Saturday, Apr. 14—Peter Heals Aeneas and Raises Dorcas (Acts 9:32-43)

Sunday, Apr. 15—Have Faith! God Will Provide (Psalm 63)

Why, we wonder, were the details of Saul's conversion not better known by the apostles before Barnabas told them? Perhaps because in his preaching, Saul talked about Jesus rather than about himself.

28, 29a. And he was with them coming in and going out at Jerusalem. And he spake boldly in the name of the Lord Jesus.

Barnabas's support on behalf of Saul accomplished its purpose. Now Saul was *with* (rather than against) the disciples in *Jerusalem* in all their activities. Saul continued to speak *boldly in the name of the Lord Jesus*—a proclamation in which he seems never to have been as effective in Jerusalem as he was afterward in other places. Apparently the disciples could forgive his acts of persecution more readily than the Jews could forgive his conversion! [See question #5, page 288.]

Conclusion

A. Stirring Up the Witnesses

When Peter stood before those gathered in the house of Cornelius in Caesarea, he spoke plainly of the life and ministry and the death and resurrection of Jesus. He said that God showed the risen Savior openly, "not to all the people, but unto witnesses chosen before of God, even to us, who did eat and drink with him after he rose from the dead. And he commanded us to preach unto the people" (Acts 10:40-42).

Peter was right, but now that we have reviewed the events of the resurrection morning we know the rest of the story: Peter didn't know that Jesus was alive again until some women told him, and at first he didn't believe what he heard! Consider also the case of Saul of Tarsus, who saw and heard Jesus on the Damascus road. An otherwise unknown disciple named Ananias was responsible for giving Saul further instructions once he entered Damascus.

Frontline proclaimers of the gospel still have a constant need for supportive, encouraging, and sometimes direct "nudges" from common folk in the congregation. Whether one's task is done in public or behind the scenes, we are *all* essential to the effective proclamation of the gospel.

B. Prayer

We praise You, our gracious God, for the glorious privilege, not only to know and serve Your risen Son our Lord, but to have a part in making Him known to others. May we do our part joyously and well. In His name, amen.

C. Thought to Remember

Christ the Lord is risen! Spread the news!

Learning by Doing

This page contains an alternate lesson plan emphasizing learning activities.
Classes desiring such student involvement will find these suggestions helpful.

Learning Goals

After this lesson each student will be able to:

1. Describe the appearance of angels to the women at Jesus' tomb and Paul's earliest testimony of the resurrection.

2. Tell how the evidence for Jesus' resurrection is convincing for believers today.

3. Praise God for Jesus' resurrection and for the gospel message it validates.

Into the Lesson

Have your class members sit in groups of four to discuss these two statements: "The resurrection of Jesus Christ is the best-attested event in history," and "The resurrection of Jesus Christ is the most controversial event in history." Do they agree or disagree? Why? What evidence can they cite to support their positions? Allow about five minutes for the discussions.

Make the transition to the Bible study by saying, "The resurrection of Jesus Christ is the foundational doctrine of Christianity. Today's lesson includes a look at the effect of the resurrection of Jesus Christ on the apostle Paul. Be watching in today's study for how the resurrection of Jesus should affect us today."

Into the Word

Have one or two volunteers read the text aloud: Luke 24:1-10; Acts 9:19b-22, 26-29a. Then choose one or both of the following activities to lead your class in a study of the text. Or assign the dramatic monologue to half of the class and the paraphrase to the other half.

Dramatic Monologue

A dramatic monologue tells a story from the perspective of the author but with the dimensions of emotion and excitement added by the reader. Ask the learners to work in groups of two or three to identify the emotion behind the account. Have them give reading instructions for each verse. For example, Luke 24:1 should be read in a subdued and sad voice, with verse two swelling with question and wonder. Acts 9:19 should be read with excitement and awe; verse 20, with boldness.

Paraphrase the Text

Provide paper and pens for each class member to use in writing a paraphrase of today's text. A paraphrase restates the author's ideas in one's own words, including explanations. Luke 24:1 might be paraphrased, "Early Sunday morning, just as it was beginning to dawn, the women arrived at the tomb that Joseph of Arimathea had made available for the burial of the body of Jesus. They had prepared spices to use in the formal burial of Jesus' body."

Into Life

Choose one or more of the following activities to conclude your session.

Hymn Study

Distribute hymnals to the learners and have each one identify his or her favorite resurrection hymn. Then have them find as many allusions, references, or quotations of today's text as they can find in the hymns they chose.

Close the session by singing one stanza and a chorus of each of several favorite hymns.

Personal Testimony

Ask each learner to prepare a two-minute testimony on the topic, "What the resurrection of Jesus means to me." Prepare by asking these questions: How do you know for sure that Jesus rose from the dead? What was your life like before you accepted Christ? What specific changes has the resurrection of Jesus made in your life?

Poetry Writing

Several people in your class probably enjoy poetry, and even people who do not necessarily like poetry will write a simple kind of poetry called a cinquain (*sing*-cane) if you walk them through the steps. Write a cinquain with your whole class by writing the answers to these questions on successive lines on a poster.

• What is a one-word title for this episode?
• What are two words that describe the title?
• What three words describe your feelings about the title?
• What four words express action about the title?
• What is a one-word synonym for the title?

Here is an example based on Luke 24:1-10.

RISEN
ALIVE AGAIN
FILLED WITH JOY
TELLING OTHERS THE NEWS
RESURRECTION

Let's Talk It Over

The questions on this page are designed to encourage review of the lesson Scriptures and to promote discussion of the lesson by the class. The answers provided are only discussion starters. Let your class talk it over from there.

1. From the different Gospel accounts we get different details about the events of the resurrection. How would you reply to someone who challenged the accuracy of the Gospel reports on the basis of these differences?

Skeptics have challenged the veracity of the Gospel records for centuries. One fact that we must always keep in mind is that no contradiction exists unless one account affirms what another denies or denies what another affirms. The fact that different writers record different details simply proves that the accounts are independent testimonies from separate witnesses. Putting them all together gives us a more complete picture than any one account provides.

2. The women who came to the tomb of Jesus must have had a vivid memory of much that Jesus said and did during His ministry. Why do you think they did not remember what He said about His resurrection?

Some things are lost from memory because we just don't consider them worth remembering. This could not have been the case with these women.

Sometimes we forget because of a traumatic experience. To avoid painful memories, the mind seems to block recall of the experience or anything related to it. The horrific events at Calvary could certainly account for such a memory loss. Jesus' predictions of His resurrection included predictions of His crucifixion.

Another reason we forget is that some things do not fit well with our expectations. Though Jesus had predicted His death and resurrection, none of that seemed to fit the disciples' expectations, so they probably had a difficult time remembering what He had said.

Jesus knew how important our memory of this reality would be. Thus, He gave us the Lord's Supper and said, "Do this in remembrance of me."

3. What kind of evidences can we provide for people to whom the claims of the resurrection seem like nonsense or "idle tales"?

We often talk about "doubting Thomas," but the Gospel records are clear that none of the apostles believed in the resurrection until he actually saw Jesus. So how *can* we convince people today?

There are many clear evidences that we can use to help convince the mind of one who doubts,

but one of the best is the reality of Christ's resurrection power in our own lives. We are living evidence that God can bring life out of death. "Therefore, if anyone is in Christ, he is a new creation; the old has gone, the new has come!" (2 Corinthians 5:17, *New International Version*). So in the process of marshaling your arguments and evidences, don't forget that the most convincing evidence is your own new life in Christ.

4. It is not easy to live down one's reputation. Occasionally, a dramatic conversion raises questions about the authenticity of the person's relationship with Christ. How can we deal with this positively in the church?

We must remember that our pre-conversion state is often described in rather graphic terms: we were God's "enemies" (Romans 5:10) and "by nature the children of wrath" (Ephesians 2:3). So the dramatic conversion may be more our perception than God's. From His perspective it is always a dramatic, life-changing experience—nothing short of bringing life out of death.

Perhaps the most important thing we can do is simply to be patient until the fruit of repentance is in evidence. In the meantime, we need to be like Barnabas (Acts 9:26, 27; 11:25, 26) and encourage, nurture, and pray for all our new brothers and sisters, regardless of their pre-Christian life situation.

5. Occasionally new believers will find that friends and family members react negatively, or even with hostility, to their decision to accept Christ. How can we support and encourage such believers so that they are not drawn back into their old pattern of life?

For all their faults, the opponents of the way of life do seem to hang together. It may be this sense of belonging to a group that we most need to replace in the new believer's life. If Satan can get the person to feel lonely or isolated, then he may be able to woo the person back to his kingdom of darkness. The church needs to be a support group, a family. It needs to provide a place "where everybody knows your name"! If the church is large, small groups like the Sunday school or "cell groups" are essential. Ministry teams can also provide this kind of support, and new members ought to be encouraged to get involved in them as soon as possible.

Gentiles Receive the Spirit

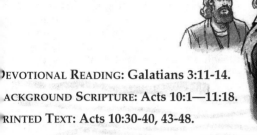

DEVOTIONAL READING: Galatians 3:11-14.

BACKGROUND SCRIPTURE: Acts 10:1—11:18.

PRINTED TEXT: Acts 10:30-40, 43-48.

Acts 10:30-40, 43-48

30 And Cornelius said, Four days ago I was fasting until this hour; and at the ninth hour I prayed in my house, and, behold, a man stood before me in bright clothing,

31 And said, Cornelius, thy prayer is heard, and thine alms are had in remembrance in the sight of God.

32 Send therefore to Joppa, and call hither Simon, whose surname is Peter; he is lodged in the house of one Simon a tanner by the sea side: who, when he cometh, shall speak unto thee.

33 Immediately therefore I sent to thee; and thou hast well done that thou art come. Now therefore are we all here present before God, to hear all things that are commanded thee of God.

34 Then Peter opened his mouth, and said, Of a truth I perceive that God is no respecter of persons:

35 But in every nation he that feareth him, and worketh righteousness, is accepted with him.

36 The word which God sent unto the children of Israel, preaching peace by Jesus Christ: (he is Lord of all:)

37 That word, I say, ye know, which was published throughout all Judea, and began from Galilee, after the baptism which John preached;

38 How God anointed Jesus of Nazareth with the Holy Ghost and with power: who went about doing good, and healing all that were oppressed of the devil; for God was with him.

39 And we are witnesses of all things which he did both in the land of the Jews, and in Jerusalem; whom they slew and hanged on a tree:

40 Him God raised up the third day, and showed him openly.

· · · · · · · · · · · · ·

43 To him give all the prophets witness, that through his name whosoever believeth in him shall receive remission of sins.

44 While Peter yet spake these words, the Holy Ghost fell on all them which heard the word.

45 And they of the circumcision which believed were astonished, as many as came with Peter, because that on the Gentiles also was poured out the gift of the Holy Ghost.

46 For they heard them speak with tongues, and magnify God. Then answered Peter,

47 Can any man forbid water, that these should not be baptized, which have received the Holy Ghost as well as we?

48 And he commanded them to be baptized in the name of the Lord. Then prayed they him to tarry certain days.

Apr 22

GOLDEN TEXT: God is no respecter of persons: but in every nation he that feareth him, and worketh righteousness, is accepted with him.—Acts 10:34, 35.

Continuing Jesus' Work
Unit 2: Witnessing in Judea and Samaria
(Lessons 5-8)

Lesson Aims

After this lesson students should be able to:

1. Recall significant details of the conversion of Cornelius and his household.

2. Tell how this event demonstrates the universal nature of the gospel.

3. Identify a group in their own community that has little or no presence in the church, and make plans to reach people within that group with the gospel.

Lesson Outline

INTRODUCTION
  A. Barriers
  B. Lesson Background
  I. AN AUDIENCE IS PREPARED (Acts 10:30-33)
    A. Angel's Message (vv. 30-32)
    B. Cornelius's Response (v. 33)
  II. AN APOSTLE SPEAKS (Acts 10:34-40, 43)
    A. God Has No Favorites (vv. 34, 35)
      A Fundamental Truth
    B. Jesus Is Savior of All (vv. 36-38)
    C. Others Bear Witness (vv. 39, 40, 43)
  III. THE SPIRIT SHOWS APPROVAL (Acts 10:44-48)
    A. Amazing Interruption (vv. 44-46a)
    B. Apostle's Question (vv. 46b, 47)
      Artistic License
    C. Gentiles' Baptism (v. 48)
CONCLUSION
  A. Who Was Addressed?
  B. Who Is Addressed?
  C. Prayer
  D. Thought to Remember

Introduction

A. Barriers

All too familiar in our time are the walls, both visible and invisible, that separate ethnic groups, nations, and other categories of humanity. No division is more deeply rooted than the Biblically recognized cleavage of humanity between Jew and Gentile—between those of the "commonwealth of Israel" and those considered "strangers from the covenants of promise" (Ephesians 2:12).

Perhaps that division was nowhere more forcefully presented than in the stern warning carved in the wall separating the outer court of the temple in Jerusalem from the inner courts: "No foreigner may enter within the barricade which surrounds the temple and enclosure. Anyone who is caught doing so will have himself to blame for his ensuing death."

B. Lesson Background

The church came into being in Jerusalem during a Jewish feast (Pentecost) through the preaching of the apostles (all Jewish) to Jews from many places. While Jesus had commanded His followers to teach all nations (Matthew 28:18-20) and to go into all the world with the gospel (Mark 16:15, 16), the church was slow to grasp the all-inclusive scope of that commission. It took some dramatic nudging on God's part to convince even the most outspoken apostle that Gentiles, too, were legitimate recipients of divine grace through the gospel.

Cornelius, the first Gentile to hear the gospel, was a centurion in the Roman army. He was stationed in the city of Caesarea, located on the Mediterranean coast about sixty-five miles northwest of Jerusalem. This man worshiped the one true God, practicing the virtues expected of devout Jews, such as prayer, fasting, and generosity to the poor (Acts 10:1, 2, 22, 30). Such was the strength of his example that "all his house" followed the same pattern of living (v. 2).

An angel appeared to Cornelius one day as he was praying during the middle of the afternoon. He directed Cornelius to send for the apostle Peter, who was at Joppa, about thirty miles down the coast. The angel told precisely where the apostle would be found and what his message would be. Immediately Cornelius dispatched three of his trusted servants to Joppa (Acts 10:1-8).

When the travelers reached their destination the next day, Peter was on the rooftop of the house where he was staying, awaiting his noon meal. While there he "fell into a trance" and saw a vision of various creatures being let down before him in what appeared to be a sheet. He then heard a voice command him to slay and eat these animals. Peter refused, claiming that they were "unclean." The voice told Peter that he should not label as unclean what God had cleansed. This vision occurred three times, and Peter was left wondering what it meant (vv. 9-17). [See question #1, page 296.]

At that very moment, the delegation from Caesarea arrived and asked for Peter. He received the men and arranged for them to be lodged overnight. The next day he left with them, accompanied by six fellow Christians from Joppa (Acts 11:12). When the men arrived at Caesarea, they found Cornelius awaiting them, along with many friends and relatives whom he had invited to his home. Cornelius had to be dissuaded from bowing before the apostle, who went on to explain that God had persuaded him to break the Jewish/Gentile barrier by accepting Cornelius's invitation.

Peter then asked, "I ask therefore for what intent ye have sent for me?" (vv. 17-29). Today's printed text begins with Cornelius's answer.

I. An Audience Is Prepared
(Acts 10:30-33)

A. Angel's Message (vv. 30-32)

30. And Cornelius said, Four days ago I was fasting until this hour; and at the ninth hour I prayed in my house, and, behold, a man stood before me in bright clothing.

Cornelius began by recounting what had happened *four days* earlier. The *man . . . in bright clothing* was later identified by Cornelius's messengers to Peter as "a holy angel" (Acts 10:22). He had appeared to Cornelius *at the ninth hour*, or three o'clock in the afternoon.

31. And said, Cornelius, thy prayer is heard, and thine alms are had in remembrance in the sight of God.

Certainly Cornelius was living in a manner that fulfilled God's desire for His people under the Old Covenant: "to do justly, and to love mercy, and to walk humbly with thy God" (Micah 6:8). God honored Cornelius's devotion by making special arrangements for him to hear about Jesus. [See question #2, page 296.]

32. Send therefore to Joppa, and call hither Simon, whose surname is Peter; he is lodged in the house of one Simon a tanner by the sea side: who, when he cometh, shall speak unto thee.

The angel's directions were clear. They included names, a location, and an occupation. It is worth noting that Peter was staying with a *tanner*, whose work would have required handling the skins of dead animals. Since these were unclean according to Jewish law (see Leviticus 11), some see this as an indication that Peter was already starting to rid himself of certain Jewish prejudices even before his vision of the unclean animals.

Here, as in the case of the Ethiopian eunuch (Acts 8:26-39) and Saul of Tarsus (Acts 22:6-16), divine intervention brought the hearer and the messenger together; the human messenger brought the gospel. That was what Peter was coming to *speak*: "words, whereby thou and all thy house shall be saved" (Acts 11:14).

B. Cornelius's Response (v. 33)

33. Immediately therefore I sent to thee; and thou hast well done that thou art come. Now therefore are we all here present before God, to hear all things that are commanded thee of God.

God is no respecter of persons:
but in every nation he that feareth
him, and worketh righteousness,
is accepted with him.
Acts 10:34, 35

Visual for lesson 8

Today's visual is a vivid reminder of the truth that Peter perceived at the home of Cornelius: God does not play favorites!

Could any evangelist find a better prepared audience than the one that welcomed Peter that day? The people had come together on their own initiative with a desire to listen. They recognized a responsibility *before God* to hear His instructions. They were not interested in small talk and human opinion; they wanted their preacher to tell them what God had to say.

II. An Apostle Speaks
(Acts 10:34-40, 43)

A. God Has No Favorites (vv. 34, 35)

34. Then Peter opened his mouth, and said, Of a truth I perceive that God is no respecter of persons.

God had just given Peter a "crash course" on the *truth* that He is *no respecter of persons*. Peter now understood how that lesson applied to the present situation. "I now realize," he said, "how true it is that God does not show favoritism" *(New International Version).* [See question #3, page 296.]

35. But in every nation he that feareth him, and worketh righteousness, is accepted with him.

Old Testament history provides notable examples of God's interest in people of *every nation*—not just those of Israel. One is Ruth the Moabitess, who believed in and served God and is named among the human ancestors of the Lord Jesus (Matthew 1:5).

We are not to assume from this verse that people can become acceptable to God through their works. For one to possess true *righteousness* before God means doing so on His terms, not one's own. That means having the "righteousness . . . which is through the faith of Christ, the righteousness which is of God by faith" (Philippians 3:9). This is what Cornelius lacked.

A FUNDAMENTAL TRUTH

In February of 1942, President Franklin D. Roosevelt signed Executive Order 9066—the decree that caused approximately 120,000 Japanese-Americans to be interned until World War II was over. The order came just two months after the Japanese attack on Pearl Harbor, amidst a widespread hysteria about foreigners, particularly those who looked different from the "average" American. Rumors about "treasonous" Japanese circulated widely. For example, some were claiming that Japanese farmers were planting their tomato crops in arrow-shaped patches that would direct Japanese bombers toward California armament factories!

After the war, it became obvious that certain U.S. officials had knowingly lied to the American people. There was no evidence that any of the Japanese-Americans were siding with Japan. Attorney General Francis Biddle would later say that the internment of the Japanese was "ill-advised, unnecessary, and unnecessarily cruel."

This statement also describes what happens when Christians allow racial and cultural pride and/or paranoia to affect the way they treat others in the church or withhold the gospel from others in society. In our text, Peter stated a fundamental principle of the gospel and then acted on it by telling Cornelius and those gathered with him about Christ.

The gospel is *the* solution to the racial and cultural divisions in the world and in the church. Has this truth found its place in *our* hearts?

—C. R. B.

B. Jesus Is Savior of All (vv. 36-38)

36. The word which God sent unto the children of Israel, preaching peace by Jesus Christ: (he is Lord of all:)

Peter began his message essentially where John begins his Gospel (1:1-3, 14): with Jesus as *the word*—the ultimate expression of God's nature

---

Home Daily Bible Readings

Monday, Apr. 16—Cornelius Sends for Peter (Acts 10:1-8)

Tuesday, Apr. 17—Peter's Vision (Acts 10:9-16)

Wednesday, Apr. 18—The Men at the Gate (Acts 10:17-23a)

Thursday, Apr. 19—Peter Goes to Caesarea (Acts 10:23b-33)

Friday, Apr. 20—Gentiles Hear the Good News (Acts 10:34-43)

Saturday, Apr. 21—Gentiles Receive the Holy Spirit (Acts 10:44-48)

Sunday, Apr. 22—Peter's Report in Jerusalem (Acts 11:1-18)

---

and will, sent to earth as God's message of love. Jesus was born and grew up as one of *the children of Israel*, and His ministry was to them first (Matthew 10:5, 6; Mark 7:27). However, Peter also noted that *he is Lord of all*, including those Gentiles whom he was addressing.

37. That word, I say, ye know, which was published throughout all Judea, and began from Galilee, after the baptism which John preached.

Peter's hearers were not totally "in the dark" concerning Jesus. They did *know* something about Him. As a Roman army officer, Cornelius must have been aware of events that had some impact on the peace and safety of the area under his jurisdiction (even if he were not stationed in Caesarea during Jesus' ministry). Such information would have included the news of multitudes who flocked to the Jordan valley to hear *John* the Baptist and to obey his command of *baptism*. Even greater multitudes were attracted by the teaching and miracles of Jesus in *Galilee*. In Capernaum Jesus had healed the servant of another Roman centurion who humbly requested it (Matthew 8:5-13). Reports of this probably would have been of special interest to Cornelius.

38. How God anointed Jesus of Nazareth with the Holy Ghost and with power: who went about doing good, and healing all that were oppressed of the devil; for God was with him.

Peter called attention to two aspects of Jesus' public ministry: that it was a ministry of *power* provided by the *Holy Ghost* (Luke 4:17-19) and that this power was used for *doing good* to others. Jesus never used His power to His own advantage, but always for the *healing* of others—to make them spiritually and physically whole. This placed Jesus in continual conflict with *the devil*, whom He had come to destroy (Hebrews 2:14, 15; 1 John 3:8). [See question #4, page 296.]

C. Others Bear Witness (vv. 39, 40, 43)

39. And we are witnesses of all things which he did both in the land of the Jews, and in Jerusalem; whom they slew and hanged on a tree.

In contrast to the widely published reports of Jesus' ministry was the more precise and intimate testimony of the apostles, whom the Lord chose to be in His company throughout His ministry from its beginning at John's baptism until His ascension into Heaven (Acts 1:21, 22). This group was the *we* for whom Peter spoke.

The phrase *the land of the Jews* describes Palestine in general and also points to the Jewish leaders as the ones who opposed Jesus and brought about His crucifixion. Their hostility stands in stark contrast to the loving work of God in empowering, approving, and glorifying His one and only Son. The reference to being *hanged on a tree* identified the crucifixion with the curse pronounced in Deuteronomy 21:22, 23 and referred to in Galatians 3:13, where we are told that Jesus was "made a curse for us." There was no limit to the shame and suffering that Jesus bore for us!

40. Him God raised up the third day, and showed him openly.

God's definitive answer to man's hostility toward Jesus was given in Jesus' resurrection on the *third day* following His death. The appearances of Jesus after His resurrection were done *openly*, leaving no doubt in the witnesses' minds that Jesus was indeed alive.

43. To him give all the prophets witness, that through his name whosoever believeth in him shall receive remission of sins.

Cornelius was likely familiar with some of the teachings of the Old Testament *prophets*. Now he was able to see their words in a new light, as he understood their united *witness* to the Christ of whom Peter spoke. *Remission of sins* in the *name* of Jesus was the theme of Jesus' commission to His apostles (Luke 24:47) and of their preaching (Acts 2:38).

III. The Spirit Shows Approval (Acts 10:44-48)

A. Amazing Interruption (vv. 44-46a)

44. While Peter yet spake these words, the Holy Ghost fell on all them which heard the word.

Peter had fulfilled his assignment; now God took over, showing His approval of what was taking place. The sudden coming of the Holy Spirit indicated that these who were hearing the gospel were allowed to do so without regard to their nationality. Acts 11:15 tells how Peter reported the matter later to the church in Jerusalem: "As I began to speak, the Holy Ghost *fell* on them, as on us at the beginning."

Peter's reference to the "beginning" clearly refers to what the apostles experienced on the Day of Pentecost (Acts 2:1-4). However, what happened in Jerusalem and what was happening in Caesarea were not exactly the same. On the former occasion, the Spirit fell on the apostles before they spoke, enabling them to be heard in languages familiar to their widely mixed audience. Here the Spirit came on the listeners and ended the sermon. At Pentecost the Spirit put the stamp of God's power on the speakers and the message; here He put the stamp of God's approval on the hearers and their reception of the message.

45, 46a. And they of the circumcision which believed were astonished, as many as came

How to Say It

CAESAREA. Sess-uh-*ree*-uh.
CAPERNAUM. Cuh-*per*-nay-um.
CORNELIUS. Cor-*neel*-yus.
ETHIOPIAN. Ee-thee-*o*-pea-un.
EUNUCH. *you*-nick.
JOPPA. *Jop*-uh.
MEDITERRANEAN. *Med*-uh-tuh-*ray*-nee-un (strong accent on *ray*).
MOABITESS. *Mo*-ub-ite-ess.
NAZARETH. *Naz*-uh-reth.
TARSUS. *Tar*-sus.

with Peter, because that on the Gentiles also was poured out the gift of the Holy Ghost. For they heard them speak with tongues, and magnify God.

Peter had been wise in taking with him six fellow Christians—all Jewish, of course—when he accompanied Cornelius's messengers to Caesarea. (They could later serve as witnesses to what had happened.) This was an extraordinary experience for these men. They are described as being *of the circumcision*, which highlights their distinction from the Gentiles gathered with them (cf. Ephesians 2:11). And now they saw and heard evidence that these Gentiles were receiving an outpouring of the Holy Spirit similar to what the apostles received on the Day of Pentecost. These Gentiles were speaking in *tongues*, or languages, that they had not learned (just as the apostles had done on Pentecost), and they were obviously expressing praise to God. [See question #5, page 296.]

B. Apostle's Question (vv. 46b, 47)

46b, 47. Then answered Peter, Can any man forbid water, that these should not be baptized, which have received the Holy Ghost as well as we?

Whereas Peter had "doubted" the meaning of the vision that he had seen earlier in Joppa (Acts 10:17), here he grasped immediately the significance of what had happened. A seemingly impregnable barrier was coming down. These Gentiles who had just heard the gospel should be *baptized* as readily as any of the Jews who had expressed a desire to follow Christ.

Some may question whether the sequence of events described here indicates that Cornelius and those Gentiles gathered with him *received the Holy Ghost* prior to their baptism in water (mentioned in the next verse). But this "receiving" experienced by the Gentiles was Peter's way of referring to the baptism of the Spirit that the apostles (*we*) had received at Pentecost. (Note his words in Acts 11:15, 16.) Just as the baptism of the Spirit at Pentecost had preceded the instructions about baptism to Jews, here it preceded the instructions about baptism to Gentiles. It indicated to Peter that the "keys of the kingdom" (Matthew 16:19) were to be used to allow Gentiles—who had been previously excluded—to enter. Thus Peter proceeded to offer to the Gentiles in Caesarea the opportunity to obey the gospel and to be baptized. They would then receive the indwelling of the Spirit promised to every baptized believer, according to Acts 2:38.

ARTISTIC LICENSE

Think for a moment about the works of some famous artists: Salvador Dali's surreal "landscapes," for example; or Pablo Picasso's distorted human faces; or Henry Moore's heavy, rounded interpretations of human or animal figures. "Artistic license" is how we describe the process that is involved in creating all of these designs.

A strange example of this phenomenon can be found on the wall of the Pacific Bell building in Los Angeles. It is a sculptured map of the world, with the continents represented fairly accurately—but that's where reality stops. The position of the continents has been changed so that the eastern tip of Brazil lies just west of Alaska, the tip of South Africa rests above the northern reaches of Norway, and Australia pretty well fills the gap between Panama and Spain. The world as we know it has been strikingly rearranged.

When God poured out His Spirit on the Gentiles in Cornelius's house, He was rearranging the spiritual world as Peter had known it. Peter saw the implications of this and asked, "Can anyone forbid the baptism of these people?" The answer then, as now, is that the gates to God's kingdom are open to all peoples in all places.

God's "artistic license" has given us a completely new way of looking at the world. Isn't it a beautiful piece of work?   —C. R. B.

C. Gentiles' Baptism (v. 48)

48. And he commanded them to be baptized in the name of the Lord. Then prayed they him to tarry certain days.

This matter was important and was not to be delayed. Peter had begun the teaching of these individuals; now he conveyed the command for them *to be baptized.* His work, however, did not end there. *Certain days*—we know not how many—of fellowship and teaching were necessary in order for these new converts to learn the Lord's commands and to embark on an exciting walk with Him.

Conclusion

A. Who Was Addressed?

God had sent His angel, not to present the gospel to Cornelius, but to provide a human preacher of the saving word. But this occasion also provided a vital learning experience for many besides Cornelius. These others needed to learn the lessons that it taught.

Peter needed to learn that Jesus is the Savior of Jew and Gentile alike. Peter received his lesson on a rooftop in Joppa; he saw it illustrated in Caesarea.

Other Jewish Christians stood in great need of the same lesson. A beginning was made with the six believing Jews who had gone with Peter to Caesarea. Later they were present with him in Jerusalem when he explained to the church there exactly what had happened in the house of Cornelius (Acts 11:12-18).

The family and friends whom Cornelius had gathered to hear the gospel learned a priceless lesson—that God is no respecter of persons and that Jesus is a Savior for *every* person. That, however, was a lesson that the church needed to learn as well—and it took time for the lesson to sink in.

B. Who Is Addressed?

A vastly larger audience is affected by the "double-barreled" message of the Scripture before us today. First, the gospel message is for everyone of every ethnic, national, political, economic, social, and religious background and persuasion. Second, the message of salvation is the same for all: that "Christ died for our sins according to the Scriptures; and that he was buried, and that he rose again the third day according to the Scriptures" (1 Corinthians 15:3, 4).

If Christ is the Savior of all, it follows, then, that there is no other Savior for any! And if we who are followers of that Savior do not let others know of Him, who will?

C. Prayer

All glory and praise to You, our Father, for the depth and breadth of Your all-inclusive love. By Your Spirit enlarge our love, we pray, to include those who have not yet been so blessed. Use us as instruments to convey Your mercy. In Jesus' name, amen.

D. Thought to Remember

"As many of you as have been baptized into Christ have put on Christ. There is neither Jew nor Greek, there is neither bond nor free, there is neither male nor female: for ye are all one in Christ Jesus" (Galatians 3:27, 28).

Learning by Doing

This page contains an alternate lesson plan emphasizing learning activities.
Classes desiring such student involvement will find these suggestions helpful.

Learning Goals

After participating in this lesson, students will be able to:

1. Recall significant details of the conversion of Cornelius and his household.

2. Tell how this event demonstrates the universal nature of the gospel.

3. Identify a group in their own community that has little or no presence in the church, and make plans to reach people within that group with the gospel.

Into the Lesson

Begin your class by giving a copy of this agree-disagree survey to each class member. Have each learner mark his or her level of agreement or disagreement, on a scale of 9 to 1, before each statement (9=strongest agreement; 5=completely neutral, no opinion; 1=strongest disagreement).

___ 1. Our church needs to be more diverse in its ethnic and cultural makeup.

___ 2. Our congregation needs to reach out to people with different national origins.

___ 3. People of different ethnic and cultural backgrounds would be comfortable in our church.

___ 4. If converts from our missionaries visited our congregation, they would be warmly received.

___ 5. Appealing to one ethnic (homogeneous) group is a valid church growth principle.

Into the Word

Ask a volunteer to read aloud Acts 10:30-48. Then choose one or both of the following activities to explore the meaning of the text.

Journal or Diary Entry

Provide pens and paper for your class to write journal or diary entries that Peter, Cornelius, a member of Cornelius's household, or one of Peter's Jewish Christian companions might have written during the three days covered in our text. Try to make sure that at least one learner is writing an entry for each character in the text.

Ask the participants to prepare by reading the text with the perspective of the selected person in mind. For example, when Peter saw his vision, he probably did not yet understand its full meaning or implication. After his presentation of the gospel to Cornelius, his understanding was broadened, and he had to change lifelong habits and attitudes.

Allow about ten minutes for writing. Then ask volunteers to read their journal entries aloud.

Dramatic Reading

Assign people in your class to prepare a dramatic reading of today's text. Assign the parts to Cornelius, the angel, Peter, and a narrator.

Read through the text a verse at a time, and discuss the voice, tone, and attitude of the speaker in each verse. For example, consider Cornelius's tone in Acts 10:30 and 31. Was he proud of his piety that prompted the visit of an angel? Probably not, but how does he relate the information in verse 30 and 31 without sounding arrogant or filled with pious pride? Verse 33 would be spoken with rising excitement and anticipation. How will you portray the outbreak of tongues in verses 44-46? This will doubtless prompt a discussion of the nature of tongues. Make sure you have read the commentary section thoroughly or have obtained help from another reliable source.

Once those questions are answered, have the "cast" read through the text in dramatic fashion.

Into Life

Provide each student with a sheet of poster board, some markers, and some mounting tape. Ask the learners to make posters with verses that describe the universal nature of the gospel. Tell them that you will use these posters to decorate your classroom. Encourage your learners to examine the following verses and to select one that appeals to them. Then write the verse in large letters and decorate the poster for display. The verses are Matthew 28:18-20; Mark 16:15, 16; John 3:16; Acts 1:8; or Romans 10:11-13.

In addition, or instead of, the poster project, challenge your class to list the ethnic, cultural, or national groups living within the circle of influence of your congregation who are not being effectively evangelized by your church. Are there any changes in attitude, style, or action that your congregation would have to make in order to reach these groups more effectively? What efforts have been made to reach them in the past? What leaders would need to be contacted to implement an outreach project to these groups? (This activity is included in the student quarterly, *Adult Bible Class*.)

Let's Talk It Over

The questions on this page are designed to encourage review of the lesson Scriptures and to promote discussion of the lesson by the class. The answers provided are only discussion starters. Let your class talk it over from there.

1. Peter's experience was very disturbing to him. He was asked to do something that violated his conscience and threatened his identity. As a Christian, how do you decide how far outside your comfort zone you are willing to go to reach out to someone who is not yet a Christian?

For Peter and others, observance of the law was a mark of identity and evidence of faithfulness. Even though Peter was a Christian, he was still a Jew. Up until this time, submission to the New Covenant had never challenged his continued faithfulness to the Old.

There are some practices we find comfortable and even comforting today as well. Some of these are important matters of faithfulness; on these we must not compromise or change. But others are mere traditions, and on these we need to be flexible. The old slogan is still valid: "In matters of faith, unity; in matters of opinion, liberty; in all things, love."

2. The lesson writer says, "God honored Cornelius's devotion by making special arrangements for him to hear about Jesus." Do you think God always honors devotion in this way? Why or why not?

Since Jesus is the only means of salvation, we may find it comforting to think that God, who knows the heart, will ensure that every person with a responsive heart will get an opportunity to hear the gospel of Christ. Such a practice is certainly within God's prerogative, but the Bible nowhere affirms that He does so.

What the Bible does affirm is our responsibility to "preach the gospel to every creature" (Mark 16:15). We cannot know whether our opportunities to present the gospel have been providentially arranged or not, but our responsibility remains the same. We dare not fail in this task!

3. Does the phrase, "I now realize" (v. 34, *New International Version*), have a familiar ring to you? How often have you been willing to say that with honesty and humility?

It was not easy for Peter to say, "I now realize that I have been wrong about what I believed regarding God's plan for the Gentiles." Nor is it easy for us to say, "I now realize that I didn't have all the facts," or, "I now realize that I was misinformed," or, "I now realize that I was too quick to

pass judgment," or, "I now realize that my understanding of that passage of Scripture was inadequate." If we will honestly and humbly admit our mistakes when we become aware of them, we will have a greater degree of credibility when we voice our opinions and relate facts. Our efforts to edify fellow believers and to evangelize the lost will become more effective as a result.

4. Peter said Jesus "went about doing good." Is our church known for "doing good"? Why or why not? What can we do to be more like Jesus in this area?

Many churches have shied away from doing good because of the degree to which other churches have abandoned the task of evangelism for the "social gospel." It is true that evangelism is our priority, but it is also true that the Bible says much about doing good (cf. Matthew 25:31-46; James 1:27). Often it is an effort at supplying physical needs that opens a door for evangelism.

What projects or ministries can your class suggest? Can you start (or help maintain) a food pantry to supply non-perishable food items to those in need? Can you establish a relationship with a local grocer so that you can issue vouchers that can be redeemed for food items or other essentials? How about a used-clothing exchange?

5. Peter was wise to take six fellow Christians with him to Caesarea. They could later serve as witnesses to what had happened. In what situations should Christian leaders today demonstrate the same kind of wisdom?

Wisdom is always in order, but some situations seem to call for it more than others. One of the biggest problems facing our culture and the church itself is sexual immorality. A Christian leader should take every precaution against the appearance of evil or the opportunity for temptation. Is a Christian man providing transportation for a church event? He would be wise not to take a woman home last. Is he counseling a woman? It is a good idea to have another person (perhaps a secretary) present and to sit in sight of this person. (The church may need to install a window in the door of the room where counseling is done.) The counselee can be seated out of sight, but the counselor should be visible. These ideas may sound old-fashioned, but wisdom never goes out of style.

The Church in Antioch

April 29
Lesson 9

DEVOTIONAL READING: Ephesians 3:7-12.

BACKGROUND SCRIPTURE: Acts 11:19-30; 13:1-3.

PRINTED TEXT: Acts 11:19-30; 13:1-3.

Acts 11:19-30

19 Now they which were scattered abroad upon the persecution that arose about Stephen traveled as far as Phoenicia, and Cyprus, and Antioch, preaching the word to none but unto the Jews only.

20 And some of them were men of Cyprus and Cyrene, which, when they were come to Antioch, spake unto the Grecians, preaching the Lord Jesus.

21 And the hand of the Lord was with them: and a great number believed, and turned unto the Lord.

22 Then tidings of these things came unto the ears of the church which was in Jerusalem: and they sent forth Barnabas, that he should go as far as Antioch.

23 Who, when he came, and had seen the grace of God, was glad, and exhorted them all, that with purpose of heart they would cleave unto the Lord.

24 For he was a good man, and full of the Holy Ghost and of faith: and much people was added unto the Lord.

25 Then departed Barnabas to Tarsus, for to seek Saul:

26 And when he had found him, he brought him unto Antioch. And it came to pass, that a whole year they assembled themselves with the church, and taught much people. And the disciples were called Christians first in Antioch.

27 And in these days came prophets from Jerusalem unto Antioch.

28 And there stood up one of them named Agabus, and signified by the Spirit that there should be great dearth throughout all the world: which came to pass in the days of Claudius Caesar.

29 Then the disciples, every man according to his ability, determined to send relief unto the brethren which dwelt in Judea:

30 Which also they did, and sent it to the elders by the hands of Barnabas and Saul.

Acts 13:1-3

1 Now there were in the church that was at Antioch certain prophets and teachers; as Barnabas, and Simeon that was called Niger, and Lucius of Cyrene, and Manaen, which had been brought up with Herod the tetrarch, and Saul.

2 As they ministered to the Lord, and fasted, the Holy Ghost said, Separate me Barnabas and Saul for the work whereunto I have called them.

3 And when they had fasted and prayed, and laid their hands on them, they sent them away.

**Apr
29**

GOLDEN TEXT: As they ministered to the Lord, and fasted, the Holy Ghost said,
Separate me Barnabas and Saul for the work whereunto
I have called them.—Acts 13:2.

Continuing Jesus' Work
Unit 3: Spreading the Gospel Into All the World
(Lessons 9-13)

Lesson Aims

After participating in this lesson, a student should be able to:

1. Recount how the church at Antioch was strengthened in its growth and how it then sent forth workers to expand the church's outreach.

2. Explain the importance of developing godly leadership in the church.

3. Identify an individual who needs encouragement in the Lord's work, and plan a specific way to become a "Barnabas" to that person.

Lesson Outline

INTRODUCTION
    A. They Crucified Jesus
    B. They Stoned Stephen
    C. They Killed James
    D. Lesson Background
  I. PRODUCING A CHURCH (Acts 11:19-21)
    A. Talking to Brethren (v. 19)
    B. Crossing Barriers (v. 20)
    C. Receiving God's Blessing (v. 21)
 II. RESPONDING TO A NEED (Acts 11:22-24)
    A. Proper Concern (v. 22)
    B. Proper Representative (vv. 23, 24)
III. MATURING (Acts 11:25-30)
    A. Team Teaching (vv. 25, 26)
    B. Prophetic Warning (vv. 27, 28)
    C. Genuine Caring (vv. 29, 30)
     Growing Up
IV. REACHING OUT (Acts 13:1-3)
    A. Expanding Leadership (v. 1)
    B. Extended Concern (vv. 2, 3)
     Thinking "Young"
CONCLUSION
    A. A Great Church's Witness
    B. A Great Church's Leaders
    C. A Great Church's Encouragements
    D. Prayer
    E. Thought to Remember

Introduction

Experts in gardening offer this advice: "If you want to get rid of that undesirable growth in your flower bed, don't try to dig it out. All of the little roots will just reach out in every direction. Let the ground lie fallow for about two years. Each time a sprout comes up, give it a shot of weed killer. After a while it will all die, and you can plant your flowers."

Undesirable objects, when aggressively attacked, often seem to thrive. The desires and intentions of the attacker backfire. Those who initially found the church "undesirable" found it equally resistant to their efforts to stamp it out. Persecution only made it stronger!

A. They Crucified Jesus

"This will bring an end to it," the authorities thought as they watched Jesus die the agonizing death of crucifixion. But their actions were subject to an Authority higher than theirs. The crucifixion was part of God's grand plan "before the foundation of the world" (1 Peter 1:20). It demonstrated His love and His grace, and it was the prelude to the resurrection of Jesus, which destroyed the power of death once for all.

B. They Stoned Stephen

"No one can talk to the powers that be like that. We'll show these followers of Jesus who's really in control." But the ones who hurled the stones that brought about Stephen's death heard only forgiveness and hope from the dying martyr's lips. The results were definitely not what they anticipated: "Therefore they that were scattered abroad went every where preaching the word" (Acts 8:4). The church at Antioch, as we shall see, began as a result of that scattering.

C. They Killed James

Not long after the church at Antioch began, "Herod the king stretched forth his hands to vex certain of the church. And he killed James the brother of John with the sword" (Acts 12:1, 2). Perhaps Herod figured that an assault on the key leadership of the church would silence its voice. That strategy failed just as badly as the others had. The church was briefly vexed, but quickly vitalized. One apostle's death did not stop its witness; it stirred and strengthened it.

D. Lesson Background

In last week's lesson, we watched God certify the Gentiles as candidates for His kingdom by using Peter to extend His invitation to them. The Holy Spirit's stamp of approval (demonstrated in the same manner as Peter had seen it manifested on the Day of Pentecost with the apostles) made it all "official": God wants Gentiles in His family!

In today's lesson we shall see how a church full of Gentiles not only received approval and encouragement (from God and from Barnabas), but also seized the initiative in serving others and in carrying out Jesus' Great Commission.

I. Producing a Church
(Acts 11:19-21)
A. Talking to Brethren (v. 19)

19. Now they which were scattered abroad upon the persecution that arose about Stephen traveled as far as Phoenicia, and Cyprus, and Antioch, preaching the word to none but unto the Jews only.

Earlier we cited Acts 8:4, which notes how *the persecution that arose about Stephen* (following his martyrdom) resulted in the followers of Jesus being *scattered abroad*. Here we see additional "fallout" from that futile effort to silence believers. In trying to quench the fire surrounding Jesus, the religious authorities succeeded only in fanning the flames. Fearing for their lives, the followers of Jesus left their homes and possessions—but they didn't leave their faith.

Three areas of ministry are mentioned in this verse. The first is *Phoenicia*. This area was located northward, beyond Samaria and Galilee, and included the long fertile plain between the Lebanon mountains and the Mediterranean Sea. It also included the cities of Tyre and Sidon. That churches were established in these important cities is evident from Acts 21:3, 4 and 27:3. *Cyprus* was the foremost island of the eastern Mediterranean. It was the home of Barnabas (Acts 4:36).

Most important in today's study is the city of *Antioch*. (This was Antioch of Syria, not the Antioch in Pisidia mentioned in Acts 13:14.) Antioch provided fertile soil for the gospel, for many *Jews* resided here. At this time in history, Antioch was the third largest city in the world (following Rome and Alexandria, Egypt). It was also a corrupt city, badly in need of spiritual and moral revival. But that was about to change.

B. Crossing Barriers (v. 20)

20. And some of them were men of Cyprus and Cyrene, which, when they were come to Antioch, spake unto the Grecians, preaching the Lord Jesus.

Some of these believers had come to Jerusalem from *Cyprus* and from *Cyrene* (located in northern Africa), and there they had embraced the good news. They were anxious to share it with their fellow Jews in *Antioch*, but they had a passion to do more. So they started to tell their neighbors who were *Grecians* about the *Lord Jesus*.

C. Receiving God's Blessing (v. 21)

21. And the hand of the Lord was with them: and a great number believed, and turned unto the Lord.

The enthusiasm of these followers of Jesus caught people's attention, the truth reached hungry hearts, *and a great number believed.* [See question #1, page 304.]

II. Responding to a Need
(Acts 11:22-24)
A. Proper Concern (v. 22)

22. Then tidings of these things came unto the ears of the church which was in Jerusalem: and they sent forth Barnabas, that he should go as far as Antioch.

Many of the leaders in the *Jerusalem* church may have been quite puzzled by the news of events in Antioch. Could God really be blessing this surge among the Gentiles?

We must, however, give these men credit for being open to the possibility that what was happening in Antioch was of God. They searched among themselves for someone to send and decided on the man who had come to be called the "Son of Encouragement" (Acts 4:36, *New International Version*). He was someone known for his fair play; the apostles knew he would make an honest assessment.

When a need for an encourager arises in the church, are people likely to think of you?

How to Say It

AGABUS. *Ag*-uh-bus.
ALEXANDRIA. Al-ex-*an*-dree-uh.
ANTIOCH. *An*-tee-ock.
ANTIPAS. *An*-tih-pus.
BARNABAS. *Bar*-nuh-bus.
CAESAR. *See*-zer.
CLAUDIUS. *Claw*-dee-us.
CYPRUS. *Sye*-prus.
CYRENE. Sye-*ree*-nee.
GRECIANS. *Gree*-shunz.
HEROD. *Hair*-ud.
LUCIUS. *Lew*-shus.
MANAEN. *Man*-uh-en.
MEDITERRANEAN. *Med*-uh-tuh-*ray*-nee-un
    (strong accent on *ray*).
NIGER. *Nye*-jer.
PHOENICIA. Fuh-*nish*-uh.
PISIDIA. Pih-*sid*-ee-uh.
SAMARIA. Suh-*mare*-ee-uh.
SIDON. *Sye*-dun.
SIMEON. *Sim*-ee-un.
SYRIA. *Sear*-ee-uh.
TARSUS. *Tar*-sus.
TETRARCH. *teh*-trark or *tee*-trark.
TYRE. Tire.

B. Proper Representative (vv. 23, 24)

23, 24. Who, when he came, and had seen the grace of God, was glad, and exhorted them all, that with purpose of heart they would cleave unto the Lord. For he was a good man, and full of the Holy Ghost and of faith: and much people was added unto the Lord.

Barnabas is this writer's favorite Christian. What a man! Wouldn't it be great if your friends and loved ones would feel constrained to print verse 24 on your headstone?

It seemed to take no time at all for Barnabas to discern the Holy Spirit's blessing on the Antioch church. True to his reputation, Barnabas *exhorted* (encouraged) *them all* to remain faithful *unto the Lord.*

Barnabas also realized that he did not want to return to Jerusalem. Exciting things were happening in Antioch, and he was not content with merely observing them. He wanted a piece of the action! He also thought of someone else whose abilities made him well suited for ministering in Antioch.

III. Maturing
(Acts 11:25-30)

A. Team Teaching (vv. 25, 26)

25, 26. Then departed Barnabas to Tarsus, for to seek Saul: and when he had found him, he brought him unto Antioch. And it came to pass, that a whole year they assembled themselves with the church, and taught much people. And the disciples were called Christians first in Antioch.

Acts 9:30 notes that *Saul* had been sent away to *Tarsus* (his hometown) when some in Jerusalem had plotted to kill him. That was where Barnabas *found* him. He *brought* Saul *unto*

Home Daily Bible Readings

Monday, Apr. 23—The Church in Syrian Antioch (Acts 11:19-24)
Tuesday, Apr. 24—Barnabas and Saul in Antioch (Acts 11:25-30)
Wednesday, Apr. 25—James Killed and Peter Imprisoned (Acts 12:1-5)
Thursday, Apr. 26—Peter Delivered From Prison (Acts 12:6-19)
Friday, Apr. 27—Barnabas and Saul Commissioned (Acts 12:24—13:3)
Saturday, Apr. 28—Paul, a Prisoner for Christ Jesus (Ephesians 3:1-6)
Sunday, Apr. 29—Paul's Ministry to the Gentiles (Ephesians 3:7-13)

Antioch, recognizing that the church there needed his kind of personality, commitment, and gifts, and that Saul needed a place to serve. The two men worked well together in Antioch; whereas *much people* had been led to the Lord (v. 24), now *much people were taught.* [See question #2, page 304.]

Some believe that the *disciples* were being ridiculed when the locals began to call them *Christians*. Others suggest that it was a grudging kind of admiration: "All those people can talk about is Jesus Christ. Christ this! Christ that! They're *Christ*-ians!"

Still others believe that the name *Christians* was a name given by God to the followers of Jesus. They note that the Greek word translated *called* in this verse is used elsewhere in the New Testament of God's calling, warning, or speaking to someone. Many who hold this view see this name as the fulfillment of a prophecy in Isaiah 62:2: "And the Gentiles shall see thy righteousness, and all kings thy glory: and thou shalt be called by a new name, which the mouth of the Lord shall name." The "new name" of *Christians* would have been particularly appropriate for the believers in Antioch, where the gospel had begun to make significant inroads among Gentiles.

B. Prophetic Warning (vv. 27, 28)

27, 28. And in these days came prophets from Jerusalem unto Antioch. And there stood up one of them named Agabus, and signified by the Spirit that there should be great dearth throughout all the world: which came to pass in the days of Claudius Caesar.

Communication between the church at Jerusalem and the church at Antioch continued through *prophets* who traveled *from Jerusalem unto Antioch*. Here God used a man named *Agabus* to foretell a period of *great dearth*, or *famine, throughout all the world* (that is, the Roman Empire). According to records of that time, famines occurred in various parts of the empire during the reign of Claudius, A.D. 41-54. (This incident also introduces Luke's readers to Agabus, who predicted Paul's arrest in Jerusalem in Acts 21:10-14.)

C. Genuine Caring (vv. 29, 30)

29, 30. Then the disciples, every man according to his ability, determined to send relief unto the brethren which dwelt in Judea: which also they did, and sent it to the elders by the hands of Barnabas and Saul.

This is another demonstration that the assessment Barnabas made concerning the church at Antioch was on target. The grace of God was evident in those people (v. 23), and it manifested itself in their eager response when confronted with the need of fellow believers in *Judea*. They gave *every man according to his ability*—a plan similar to that which Paul recommended to the Corinthians (1 Corinthians 16:1, 2).

The *brethren* in Judea would have suffered particular hardships from any famine. Many had been impoverished because of the persecution of Christians that followed the martyrdom of Stephen (Acts 8:1). Since the gospel had come to Antioch as a consequence of that persecution (Acts 11:19, 20), the believers in that city felt a special responsibility to assist fellow Christians in Jerusalem and the surrounding area.

The church in Antioch sent their gift with *Barnabas and Saul* (perhaps these two led a delegation from the church). No one man's integrity was compromised by having him carry that money alone. Sending the most notable leaders in the church with the offering gave the gesture a special measure of dignity. In addition, the fact that the men who brought the offering had some ties to the Jerusalem church (especially Barnabas) would serve to strengthen the bond between that church and the church in Antioch. [See question #3, page 304.]

GROWING UP

For several years we have been hearing a lot about aging "baby boomers." If we were to believe some of the reports in the media, we would think that this is the first generation ever to be faced with wrinkles, graying hair (or balding scalp), and the onset of that chubbiness around the waist known as "middle-age spread."

One "boomer" has described his generation as "the most populous, schooled, indulged, narcissistic and persistently adolescent generation in American history." Nevertheless, "Father Time" has a way of making his presence known. The last of the boomers are now approaching forty years of age, the clock is ticking, and some are not handling it well!

However, at some point members of every generation have to acknowledge that they are no longer young and must learn to "grow up." This usually means starting to look outward and considering what legacy they will leave behind.

We have no evidence that the church in Antioch was particularly preoccupied with its own welfare. What we *do* find is that this congregation was "growing up." The Christians there took upon themselves the responsibility of sending famine relief to Christians in Judea. No adolescent self-centeredness was present; the church exhibited a sincere concern for others. It is a model that every maturing congregation should follow.   —C. R. B.

IV. Reaching Out
(Acts 13:1-3)
A. Expanding Leadership (v. 1)

1. Now there were in the church that was at Antioch certain prophets and teachers; as Barnabas, and Simeon that was called Niger, and Lucius of Cyrene, and Manaen, which had been brought up with Herod the tetrarch, and Saul.

Apparently *Barnabas* and *Saul* had been able to do some mentoring with the Antioch church, resulting in the assembling of a leadership team. Like most good teams, this one brought several different personalities and backgrounds together. [See question #4, page 304.]

The nickname of *Simeon* suggests that he may have been a dark-complexioned man. Some think that he was the man known as Simon of Cyrene (a man from Africa and probably black), who carried the cross for Jesus (Matthew 27:32). *Lucius*, who is identified as being from *Cyrene*, could very well have been one of the "men of Cyprus and Cyrene" who first began sharing the gospel with the Gentiles in Antioch (Acts 11:20). The Greek text says that *Manaen* was literally a "foster brother" of *Herod* the tetrarch (that is, Herod Antipas), who was the son of Herod the Great; thus, Manaen was *brought up with* Herod. Herod Antipas had John the Baptist killed, and he participated in the trials of Jesus (Matthew 14:1-11; Luke 23:6-12). Obviously Manaen's life took a very different turn!

B. Extended Concern (vv. 2, 3)

2, 3. As they ministered to the Lord, and fasted, the Holy Ghost said, Separate me Barnabas and Saul for the work whereunto I have called them. And when they had fasted and prayed, and laid their hands on them, they sent them away.

Observe that God had brought these men together as leaders; now it was time for two of them to *separate* from the others and begin an important new venture in the Lord's work. It is evident that all of these men had been seeking the Lord's leading for their ministry, not only in Antioch but to the world. Their desire for His leading was clear from their actions: they *fasted* and they *prayed*.

Fasting is still an important spiritual discipline for the church and for individual Christians. Fasting can take place when an individual has a reason to repent and to seek God's forgiveness and renewal. It can be done when one is seeking some specific direction from God. And it can be done when a church is setting men and women aside to a special purpose in the business of Christ's kingdom. That is what was taking place in Antioch: "God, we want Your will to be done here on earth (and all over the earth) as it is in Heaven." [See question #5, page 304.]

THINKING "YOUNG"

A "senior moment" is what happens occasionally to many people in their fifties and older—a friend's name, a familiar word, or even an entire thought just slips from one's mind. It happens to everyone: studies show that most people lose thirty percent of their memory between the ages of twenty and seventy-five.

A memory training specialist at Stanford University has apparently found a way to reverse this trend. She teaches a two-week-long course for seniors (the age group, not the high school or college class) that encourages them to "think young." This involves trying to look at certain objects the way younger people would—for example, analyzing details in paintings and thus, in the words of a psychiatrist at Stanford, "increasing their visual imaging ability." The psychiatrist notes that eighty-five percent of the students increased their memory skills from thirty to fifty percent over a five-year period.

Churches grow older, too, and often forget their reason for existence. Leaders settle into comfortable positions and sometimes stay there by insisting on maintaining the status quo and by never entertaining any new ideas.

How different was the church in Antioch! Its leaders were visionary, energetic, and responsive to the leading of the Spirit of God. They could imagine the whole world wanting to know about Jesus. So they sent out some of their best and brightest on a journey that eventually filled the pagan Roman Empire with the gospel! —C. R. B.

Conclusion

A. A Great Church's Witness

The church at Antioch was a great church because it began through the efforts of Christians who refused to have their faith snuffed out by persecution. They left the things that were less important and carried with them the one thing that was (and is) forever important. And they didn't keep this to themselves. They seemed to be indifferent to financial loss, to the pressure of persecution, and to the anxiety caused by having to "pull up stakes" and relocate their families.

B. A Great Church's Leaders

Antioch was also a great church because its leaders responded to opportunities for service. Barnabas recognized that Saul possessed abilities that the church needed and made a determined

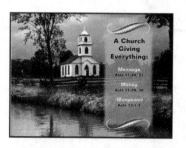

Visual for lesson 9

Use the visual for today's lesson to challenge your students to make your church like the church at Antioch.

effort to find him and add him to the leadership team. Then they multiplied themselves by working with and training "faithful men" who were ready to step up and serve (2 Timothy 2:2). And these men were totally unselfish. While they could have remained together and watched great things unfold in Antioch, they sensed the world's need and heard the world's call—which was really the call of Christ to carry His message to the world. So they commissioned two members of their team and sent them out.

C. A Great Church's Encouragements

In addition, Antioch was a great church because it watched and imitated the style of an encourager (Barnabas). Notice, church leader, the privilege and the sobering reality in this! A congregation, to a significant degree, will take on the personality of its leaders. No church can grow past the spiritual strength, the personal faith, and the passion for Christ that dwells in the hearts of its leaders. When the "mother church" in Jerusalem had a need, the "daughter church" in Antioch rushed to her aid and offered its encouragement. And the disciples sent their best—both in a financial and a personal sense—to fulfill that need.

D. Prayer

Dear God, empower us with the courage that will make us more like these first Christians, who could not keep the good news to themselves and who let it have an impact on every facet of their lives and their church. Thank You for sending Your Holy Spirit to work in Your church. We pray that You will be pleased at seeing that power at work in us, and that our neighbors will know our passion so well that they will call us *Christians.* In Jesus' name, amen.

E. Thought to Remember

Encouragement is a most important key to a growing church.

Learning by Doing

This page contains an alternate lesson plan emphasizing learning activities.
Classes desiring such student involvement will find these suggestions helpful.

Learning Goals

After this lesson each student will be able to:

1. Recount how the church at Antioch was strengthened in its growth and how it then sent forth workers to expand the church's outreach.

2. Explain the importance of developing godly leadership in the church.

3. Identify an individual who needs encouragement in the Lord's work, and plan a specific way to become a "Barnabas" to that person.

Into the Lesson

Begin your class with one or both of the following activities.

Neighbor Nudge

Tell the class, "Turn to the person next to you and tell him or her all you can about the most encouraging person that you know. After thirty seconds your partner will have a chance to describe his or her most encouraging person."

Skit

Ask two of your learners to prepare a skit showing a typical couple looking for a new church home. Each person is adamant that his or her interests and concerns be heard. Issues might include the preacher, the worship style, the time factor, the youth program, the people, etc.

Make the transition to the Bible study by saying, "What is it that people *need* to be looking for in a church? Today we are going to study a great church in the Bible—the church at Antioch. Let's see if we can find what made it a great church."

Into the Word

Ask a volunteer to read aloud Acts 11:19-30; 13:1-3. Then choose one or more of the following Bible study activities.

Introduction of the Speaker

Give each person a sheet of paper and a pen. Then say, "Pretend that you have been asked to introduce Barnabas as the speaker at a special church event. Study today's text along with Acts 4:36, 37; 9:26, 27. Write out your introduction notes."

Group Study

Assign your learners to groups of three or four. Ask them to study today's text and put together a description of a great church. They may want to design a church brochure for the church at Antioch. What qualities of this congregation should be included? What design features would be important to it? Each group should be ready to share the brochure with the rest of the class.

Acrostic

"The disciples were called Christians first in Antioch" (Acts 11:26). Use the word "Christian" as an acrostic to list the qualities that make a person or church "Christian." Write the word "Christian" in large letters vertically down a piece of poster board. Then use each letter to identify a characteristic or quality that defines a person or a church as "Christian." For example, the letter "S" in *Christian* could stand for "**S**peaking About Christ" (Acts 11:19, 20).

Into Life

Use one or both of these activities to close the class session with application.

Encouragement Project

Observe that Joseph was renamed Barnabas ("Son of Encouragement," Acts 4:36, *New International Version*) by the apostles. He was an encourager! Every congregation has people who are in desperate need of encouragement. Design a Barnabas project in which you encourage someone who needs it—and we all do!

How do you encourage someone? A word fitly spoken, a note or small gift at just the right time, a hand on the shoulder or pat on the back, a helping hand in a difficult project, or recognition for what the person has done or is doing. What fits your situation? Make your plan and put it into practice.

Prayer Pyramid

Have your class divide into pairs. Ask each pair to take two minutes to offer prayers of thanks for the *history* of your church. After two minutes, ask each pair to join another pair and pray for two minutes for the *purpose* of your church. After two minutes, ask each group of four to join another group of four and pray for your *church leaders* for two minutes. After two minutes, ask each group of eight to join another group of eight and pray for your church's *missionaries*. Continue the process until everyone is in one big circle praying together for the church.

Let's Talk It Over

The questions on this page are designed to encourage review of the lesson Scriptures and to promote discussion of the lesson by the class. The answers provided are only discussion starters. Let your class talk it over from there.

1. The believers described in Acts 11:19-21 were obviously enthusiastic about sharing their faith in Jesus Christ. How can we stir up more enthusiasm in our congregation for witnessing and evangelism?

Enthusiasm often comes with know-how. Church members may be indifferent toward evangelism because they do not know how to share their faith. Every congregation should find some way to make regular instruction in evangelism available to its members.

Enthusiasm often comes with experience. When a person plays some role in winning another individual to Christ, it brings a joy and excitement like no other. Those who are experienced in evangelism do well when they enlist other members to join them in making evangelistic calls.

2. Barnabas went and found Saul and brought him back to Antioch to help with the work there. How important do you think it is today to find a partner with whom we can share in the Lord's work? Why?

Jesus made it a practice to send His disciples out in pairs on their missions (Mark 6:7; Luke 10:1). In the early church, that practice was continued. Think, for example, of Paul and Barnabas and later Paul and Silas. Such a practice yields many benefits. The two can encourage one another when they encounter difficulties. They can be accountable to one another, praying for one another and administering constructive criticism when necessary. Partners can work out mutually agreeable procedures for completing their work. During a call, for example, one may take the lead in conversation, while the other devotes himself to silent prayer. If the partners are sharing the work of teaching a Bible class, one may handle the basic Biblical teaching while the other concentrates her attention on memorization of Scripture or working with crafts.

3. We could say that the church at Antioch was successful in "growing through giving." What role does stewardship play in the growth of the church today? How can we encourage believers to grow in this area of their faith?

It is possible for members to drop a dollar or two in the offering plate each Sunday and feel no involvement with the church and its ministry. But when they are led to give sacrificially for the cause of Christ, they are more likely to grow in enthusiasm for what the church is doing. This is in line with Jesus' observation that "where your treasure is, there will your heart be also" (Matthew 6:21). Intelligent sacrificial giving is an act of faith. When it is practiced, it stretches and deepens faith. A faith that has come alive through giving may well become eager for further challenges: evangelism, teaching, leadership, missionary work, benevolent work, etc.

4. How desirable would you say it is to draw in people of different personalities and backgrounds to form a leadership team? Why?

Someone has made the statement: "If the two of us think exactly alike, then one of us is unnecessary." That is applicable to a leadership team in the church. If most of the members exist only to rubber-stamp the ideas of their most outspoken colleague, not much will be accomplished. When all contribute out of a vast wealth of faith, education, experience, imagination, and ingenuity, the church's work can be enriched. It is also important to note here that leaders should be eager learners. If they represent different backgrounds, they can learn from one another. And as they learn, they have the potential of growing into increasingly more effective ministers, elders, deacons, women's leaders, youth leaders, etc.

5. What are some ways in which the church at Antioch provides a model for the church that aspires to be a great missionary church today?

The church at Antioch sent out missionaries. We assume that involved financial support, and we know that it included prayer support. Since prayer was an integral part of the calling and commissioning of Barnabas and Saul, we can have no doubt that the church leaders and members surrounded the entire venture with prayer. Today a church must invest a significant portion of its income and a significant emphasis in its prayer life to missions, if it is to be a missionary church. We further note that when Barnabas and Saul returned to Antioch, they were given ample opportunity to report on their missionary labors (Acts 14:26, 27). A missionary church today is one that likewise demonstrates an eagerness to hear about what has happened on the field.

Mission to Gentiles

DEVOTIONAL READING: Psalm 96.

BACKGROUND SCRIPTURE: Acts 13, 14.

PRINTED TEXT: Acts 13:4, 13-15, 42-52.

Acts 13:4, 13-15, 42-52

4 So they, being sent forth by the Holy Ghost, departed unto Seleucia; and from thence they sailed to Cyprus.

. . . .

13 Now when Paul and his company loosed from Paphos, they came to Perga in Pamphylia: and John departing from them returned to Jerusalem.

14 But when they departed from Perga, they came to Antioch in Pisidia, and went into the synagogue on the sabbath day, and sat down.

15 And after the reading of the law and the prophets, the rulers of the synagogue sent unto them, saying, Ye men and brethren, if ye have any word of exhortation for the people, say on.

. . . .

42 And when the Jews were gone out of the synagogue, the Gentiles besought that these words might be preached to them the next sabbath.

43 Now when the congregation was broken up, many of the Jews and religious proselytes followed Paul and Barnabas; who, speaking to them, persuaded them to continue in the grace of God.

44 And the next sabbath day came almost the whole city together to hear the word of God.

45 But when the Jews saw the multitudes, they were filled with envy, and spake against those things which were spoken by Paul, contradicting and blaspheming.

46 Then Paul and Barnabas waxed bold, and said, It was necessary that the word of God should first have been spoken to you: but seeing ye put it from you, and judge yourselves unworthy of everlasting life, lo, we turn to the Gentiles.

47 For so hath the Lord commanded us, saying, I have set thee to be a light of the Gentiles, that thou shouldest be for salvation unto the ends of the earth.

48 And when the Gentiles heard this, they were glad, and glorified the word of the Lord: and as many as were ordained to eternal life believed.

49 And the word of the Lord was published throughout all the region.

50 But the Jews stirred up the devout and honorable women, and the chief men of the city, and raised persecution against Paul and Barnabas, and expelled them out of their coasts.

51 But they shook off the dust of their feet against them, and came unto Iconium.

52 And the disciples were filled with joy, and with the Holy Ghost.

GOLDEN TEXT: I have set thee to be a light of the Gentiles, that thou shouldest be for salvation unto the ends of the earth.—Acts 13:47.

Continuing Jesus' Work
Unit 3: Spreading the Gospel Into All the World
(Lessons 9-13)

Lesson Aims

After this lesson a student should be able to:

1. Summarize Paul's message in Antioch of Pisidia and the people's responses.

2. Compare Paul and Barnabas's methods of evangelism with modern evangelistic practices.

3. Write a letter to a missionary or missionary family, encouraging them in their important work for the Lord.

Lesson Outline

INTRODUCTION
  A. A Team Effort
  B. Lesson Background
  I. THE MISSION BEGINS (Acts 13:4, 13-15)
    A. First Stop—Cyprus (v. 4)
    B. Adjustment Made at Perga (v. 13)
    C. Pattern Set in Antioch (vv. 14, 15)
      Targeting the Audience
 II. THE MISSION EXPANDS (Acts 13:42, 43)
    A. Gentile Seekers (v. 42)
    B. Jewish Seekers (v. 43)
III. THE MISSION MATURES (Acts 13:44-52)
    A. Dealing With Jealousy (vv. 44, 45)
    B. Encouraging the Gentiles (vv. 46-48)
      The "NIMBY" Syndrome
    C. Success and Distress (vv. 49-52)
CONCLUSION
  A. The Protective
  B. The Receptive
  C. Prayer
  D. Thought to Remember

Introduction

A. A Team Effort

A few years ago, a Christian leader, speaking at a workshop, reported a conversation that he had with a new convert. This leader had cared about the other man for quite some time. Patiently he had worked at building a relationship, studying the Bible, speaking to him about Jesus, and answering his questions. Then the man was ready to declare his faith. The leader had the privilege of baptizing him into Christ. A few days later, while they were talking about his new life, the teacher seemed to take great pride in how he had led the man to faith in Christ. The new believer

told his friend, "You know, you're not the only one who led me to Christ. Several other people helped me come to this decision. It was just that you were in the right place at the right time to finish the job."

Paul put it in these terms: "I have planted, Apollos watered; but God gave the increase" (1 Corinthians 3:6). That's one of the beautiful things about the church; it's a *body*. Every Christian is called to use his gifts and his personality for the good of the body's growth. One of us can talk easily. Another can understand the deeper doctrinal issues and thus add insights to our classes. Still another does a wonderful job of demonstrating the mercy of God and the love of Christ through personal kindnesses and eager service. Others are very good at demonstrating and promoting Christian fellowship.

Shortly after the verse cited above, Paul added, "We are laborers together with God" (1 Corinthians 3:9). We are to work *together* in order to present the gospel to those who desperately need good news. Some of us plant, others water, and, in time, the harvest comes. Sometimes it comes in ways that we will never see this side of Heaven. [See question #1, page 312.]

B. Lesson Background

Last week we watched the church in Antioch begin, mature through sound teaching, share its blessings, develop leaders, and commission Barnabas and Saul to go (on Christ's behalf and as their representatives) to places as yet untouched by the gospel. Today's lesson begins where last week's ended. The two men are on their way.

I. The Mission Begins
(Acts 13:4, 13-15)
A. First Stop—Cyprus (v. 4)

4. So they, being sent forth by the Holy Ghost, departed unto Seleucia; and from thence they sailed to Cyprus.

Acts 13:3 (the final verse of last week's printed text) notes that "they" (the prophets and teachers in the Antioch church) sent Barnabas and Saul on their mission. Verse 4 emphasizes that the two men were *sent forth by the Holy Ghost*. Recall from last week's study that, following the leading of the Spirit, the other prophets and teachers in the Antioch church had "laid their hands" on Barnabas and Saul and commissioned them to this special venture. Fasting and prayer also accompanied this pivotal response to the need of the world for the gospel.

Both in his Gospel and in the book of Acts, Luke demonstrates a close attention to details.

This becomes clear as one reads his account of Paul's missionary endeavors. Here he notes that Barnabas and Saul *departed unto Seleucia.* Seleucia was the seaport city of Antioch, located about sixteen miles westward. The town has no other significance than being the place from which the missionary team left.

The team's first stop was the island of *Cyprus.* Why Cyprus? That was the home of Barnabas (Acts 4:36). Since he was known there, it would be a somewhat easier place to get a hearing. In addition, believers from Cyprus had come to Antioch to help start the church there (Acts 11:19, 20). Thus Barnabas and Saul may have been hoping to begin their task in rather friendly surroundings.

B. Adjustment Made at Perga (v. 13)

13. Now when Paul and his company loosed from Paphos, they came to Perga in Pamphylia: and John departing from them returned to Jerusalem.

Our printed text does not include the record of what took place on Cyprus. The team began preaching at Salamis, on the eastern coast of Cyprus. They then moved westward approximately one hundred miles to Paphos, on the other side of the island. There Sergius Paulus, a local official, wanted to hear the word of God from Barnabas and Saul. But Bar-jesus (Elymas), a sorcerer who was an attendant of the official, tried to distract him, "seeking to turn away the deputy from the faith" (v. 8). Saul (who in verse 9 is called Paul for the first time) told the sorcerer that the Lord would strike him with blindness, which immediately happened. Sergius Paulus, who must have witnessed all of this with amazement, "believed, being astonished at the doctrine of the Lord" (v. 12).

The team then traveled northward (over the Mediterranean Sea) to what is now western Turkey. Specifically, *they came to* the province of *Pamphylia,* located along the southern coast, and arrived at *Perga,* the capital of the province. At this point, John Mark, who had been serving Barnabas and Saul as a "minister" (v. 5), or as an apprentice/assistant, *returned* to his home in *Jerusalem.*

Exactly why John Mark left the group has been the subject of much speculation. Some believe that he became homesick or missed his mother—apparently a committed Christian woman who provided accommodations for the church (Acts 12:12). He may have resented how Paul had begun to take on more leadership responsibilities than Barnabas, who was, after all, a relative of John Mark (Colossians 4:10). Others suggest that John Mark feared the more rugged, threatening terrain and inhabitants that awaited the group in the territory of Pamphylia.

Whatever Mark's reason, Paul seems to have considered it unjustified. He refused to include John Mark on a second trip (Acts 15:36-39). In time, however, John Mark's service was valued by Paul and he became a "comfort" to the apostle (Colossians 4:10, 11). [See question #2, page 312.]

C. Pattern Set in Antioch (vv. 14, 15)

14. But when they departed from Perga, they came to Antioch in Pisidia, and went into the synagogue on the sabbath day, and sat down.

From *Perga,* Paul and Barnabas proceeded to *Antioch in Pisidia* (a province to the north), about one hundred ten miles away. This city had a large Jewish population. It was here that Paul and Barnabas established a pattern that they and their co-workers would follow whenever they began to evangelize a city. They *went into the synagogue* first and took part in the *sabbath day* worship. The synagogue was a natural place to present Jesus as the Christ to Jews, whose knowledge of the Scriptures provided a foundation on which Paul and his companions could build.

TARGETING THE AUDIENCE

The *National Enquirer,* the *Weekly World News,* and the *Star* are tabloids found at the checkout lanes in supermarkets just about everywhere. The purchase of one or more is part of the weekly shopping ritual for many people. Even those of us who don't buy the tabloids must admit to occasionally scanning the eye-catching headlines.

A headline that few of us could keep from noticing was seen in one issue of the *Weekly World News.* It read, "Satan Escapes From Hell." Beside the headline was pictured a cloud of oily smoke escaping from an exploding oil well. With

Home Daily Bible Readings

Monday, Apr. 30—Barnabas and Saul Preach in Cyprus (Acts 13:4-12)

Tuesday, May 1—Paul and Barnabas in Pisidian Antioch (Acts 13:13-25)

Wednesday, May 2—Paul Preaches About the Messiah (Acts 13:26-41)

Thursday, May 3—Responses to Paul's Sermon (Acts 13:42-52)

Friday, May 4—Paul and Barnabas in Iconium (Acts 14:1-7)

Saturday, May 5—Paul and Barnabas in Lystra and Derbe (Acts 14:8-20)

Sunday, May 6—Return to Syrian Antioch (Acts 14:21-28)

a bit of imagination, one could see a grotesque face in the cloud.

There is a ready audience for salacious gossip and incredible stories—a subculture easily tapped by the tabloid editors, who know that placing their publications by the supermarket checkout lanes will entice the buyers. That's an important principle of marketing.

Paul and Barnabas knew that certain people could be counted on to be present at a specific place and time: they could be found in the synagogue on the Sabbath day. Here was an audience—a subculture—already prepared to hear the gospel because it was familiar with the Old Testament Scriptures, which Jesus had come to fulfill. It was an open door that Paul and Barnabas used, with encouraging results.

The sensationalism of the tabloids is not a good model for us in sharing the gospel, but the wisdom of the apostles is.   —C. R. B.

15. And after the reading of the law and the prophets, the rulers of the synagogue sent unto them, saying, Ye men and brethren, if ye have any word of exhortation for the people, say on.

In a synagogue service, portions from *the law and the prophets* were read, then someone in the assembly addressed those who had gathered. One of the duties of *the rulers of the synagogue* was to designate someone for this duty. Often visitors, such as Paul and Barnabas, were asked to speak. Paul would have been an especially appropriate choice, given his background of training in the Jewish faith (Acts 22:3).

II. The Mission Expands
(Acts 13:42, 43)

A. Gentile Seekers (v. 42)

42. And when the Jews were gone out of the synagogue, the Gentiles besought that these words might be preached to them the next sabbath.

Our printed text moves to the outcome of Paul's address in the *synagogue*, which began with God's deliverance of Israel from bondage in Egypt and concluded with a proclamation of Jesus as the One through whom "all that believe are justified from all things, from which ye could not be justified by the law of Moses" (Acts 13:39). Most likely those present that day had never heard anything like this before. Yet the message was received favorably, particularly by *Gentiles* who wanted to hear more about it on the *next sabbath*. [See question #3, page 312.]

B. Jewish Seekers (v. 43)

43. Now when the congregation was broken up, many of the Jews and religious proselytes

followed Paul and Barnabas; who, speaking to them, persuaded them to continue in the grace of God.

Some in the *congregation* did not want to wait a week. They were so eager to learn more of what *Paul and Barnabas* were saying about Jesus that they *followed* these two, clinging to their every word. These results were, thus far, just what the missionaries had wanted. They were preaching Jesus as the promised Messiah to their brethren, *the Jews*; and they were also able to introduce Him to the Gentiles by way of the *religious proselytes* (Gentiles who had converted to Judaism).

Obviously these individuals were not far from the kingdom. The good news was drawing them. And Paul and Barnabas were excited to encourage them to keep moving forward, growing in their understanding of *the grace of God*.

III. The Mission Matures
(Acts 13:44-52)

A. Dealing With Jealousy (vv. 44, 45)

44, 45. And the next sabbath day came almost the whole city together to hear the word of God. But when the Jews saw the multitudes, they were filled with envy, and spake against those things which were spoken by Paul, contradicting and blaspheming.

New ideas are fine, unless they begin to supplant established ones. And they are fine as long as they do not engage the interest of significant numbers of people. When, on *the next sabbath day*, *almost the whole city* came to *hear* what Paul and Barnabas had to say, the Jewish leaders could feel their control slipping away. Perhaps it appeared to them that their synagogue was being taken over by these "outsiders."

The issue at hand was not a matter of right and wrong, nor was it a doctrinal disagreement, at least initially. True, these men had said some shocking things—things that seemed radical to some. But it seems that the authorities became concerned only when those teachings began to draw a popular following and to threaten the status quo. So *filled with envy* were they that they mounted a mud-slinging campaign in an attempt to discredit Paul and Barnabas. Unfortunately, the scenario described in these verses proved to be "par for the course" for the missionary team as they moved from city to city.

B. Encouraging the Gentiles (vv. 46-48)

46. Then Paul and Barnabas waxed bold, and said, It was necessary that the word of God should first have been spoken to you: but seeing ye put it from you, and judge yourselves unworthy of everlasting life, lo, we turn to the Gentiles.

Paul and Barnabas refused to ignore those who had for so long been God's chosen people. As Paul would later write to the Roman Christians, "I am not ashamed of the gospel of Christ: for it is the power of God unto salvation to every one that believeth; to the Jew first, and also to the Greek" (Romans 1:16; cf. 2:10). The Jews would get the *first* opportunity to embrace the New Covenant relationship and the *everlasting life* that God was offering through Jesus. But when they rejected it, Paul and Barnabas were prepared to *turn* immediately to the *Gentiles*, who were eager to hear. [See question #4, page 312.]

47. For so hath the Lord commanded us, saying, I have set thee to be a light of the Gentiles, that thou shouldest be for salvation unto the ends of the earth.

That the gospel invitation should go to the Gentiles was in keeping with God's plan as revealed in the Old Testament. Here Isaiah 49:6 is quoted, in which God's servant is *commanded* to be *a light of the Gentiles*. Simeon had alluded to this passage when Joseph and Mary brought Jesus to the temple (Luke 2:32). And while Jesus is the light of the world (John 8:12), He has also appointed His followers to be the light of the world (Matthew 5:14) and to go *unto the ends of the earth*. (Read again Jesus' Great Commission as recorded in Acts 1:8.)

48. And when the Gentiles heard this, they were glad, and glorified the word of the Lord: and as many as were ordained to eternal life believed.

These Jews in Antioch scorned the idea that they were "unworthy" (v. 46) of God's favor. But the *Gentiles* (needless to say) were thrilled. *As many as* were open to the *word* of truth and who were ready to accept God's grace were ready to receive the gift of *eternal life* (Romans 6:23).

The phrase *as many as were ordained to eternal life believed* does not mean that certain individuals were chosen to believe. The verb

translated "ordained" can also mean "placed, positioned, or determined" and appears in the Greek text in a form that can signify an action done by one's self to one's self. It means that those who wanted to place themselves in a position to receive eternal life believed. (Others, such as the Jews described in verse 46, did not want to place themselves in that position.)

THE "NIMBY" SYNDROME

Some time ago, when the world seemed like a kinder and gentler place, the prospect of a new church building going up in a neighborhood was seen as a positive thing. A new church was an indication that "good people" were in the neighborhood and that the social order would be preserved and strengthened.

But times have changed. Today, communities are more likely to resist the construction of a new church building in their midst. People don't want to put up with the noise and traffic it will bring. And if it is the "wrong kind" of church—either architecturally or theologically—people are fearful of the effect it will have on the community. (And we must admit that what is called a "church" today *is* sometimes rather weird—in either architecture or doctrine!) It's another example of what has been labeled the "NIMBY" syndrome—*Not In My Back Yard*: "Don't bother me. Go somewhere else if you want to change things."

While that was the attitude of the Jewish leaders in Antioch, it certainly wasn't what the Gentile community was thinking. They *liked* what they heard about the Christian faith. They *wanted* the church in their "back yard" because the gospel offered them forgiveness and hope.

Does *our* church offer the community a similar message?   —C. R. B.

C. Success and Distress (vv. 49-52)

49. And the word of the Lord was published throughout all the region.

Not only to those here in Antioch but *throughout all the region* the message proclaimed by Paul and Barnabas spread. Most likely this was done through the efforts of new believers, not the missionary team. The gospel moves so much more quickly that way—and that is just as true today as it was on that first missionary journey. [See question #5, page 312.]

50. But the Jews stirred up the devout and honorable women, and the chief men of the city, and raised persecution against Paul and Barnabas, and expelled them out of their coasts.

In Paul's day, as is true in our day, trouble in the church is spread much more successfully through indirect means than by direct. If the

I have set thee to be a light of the Gentiles, that thou shouldest be for salvation unto the ends of the earth.

Acts 13:47

Visual for lesson 10

Use today's visual to illustrate verse 47 of the text. Discuss how Christians today can be a "light" to those who do not know Jesus.

Jewish leaders had stood up and lectured against Paul and Barnabas, it might have had little effect. But they *stirred up* trouble behind the scenes. "Did you know that these men are not dependable people?" Then the one who heard that told another person, "I heard from a reliable source that you can't count on what this Paul says. He's a troublemaker." And a third person, if his emotions have been deeply stirred, will say (with more anger than the first two), "We have to get these people out of here. They're trying to force their beliefs on everyone!" If you ask that third person to explain what he means and where he got his information, he probably can't tell you. But he's sure that it's true.

This verse notes that the Jews in Antioch aimed their disruptive efforts at some of the *devout and honorable women* and the *chief men of the city*. (Some believe that these women were the wives of the chief men.) It was easier for the "city fathers" simply to get rid of the source of the nuisance than to take time to investigate what was happening and see that justice was done. So Paul and Barnabas were told to leave the city. (Here the word *coasts* designates the region surrounding the city.)

51. But they shook off the dust of their feet against them, and came unto Iconium.

When Paul and Barnabas *shook off the dust of their feet*, they were signaling the end of their responsibility toward the unreceptive Jewish authorities. Certainly they must have been frustrated at having to leave the new believers behind so soon. But we can see from the next verse that the seed of the gospel had taken root.

52. And the disciples were filled with joy, and with the Holy Ghost.

These young Christians in Antioch demonstrated exemplary dedication. We might have expected them to become frightened or angry when

their teachers were forced out of town. But they were full of *joy* because of their salvation. And the Holy Spirit was working in their lives and in their church. Later, when Paul and Barnabas came back through Antioch, they could set aside leaders (Acts 14:21-23) and encourage the believers to remain faithful.

Conclusion

A. The Protective

Many times we have heard how difficult it is to move some people from their familiar neighborhoods. Their surroundings may be dangerous or even life-threatening. The living conditions may be primitive. An opportunity for a healthier, more peaceful environment is offered. But "we want to stay home." As someone once put it, "Come weal or come woe, our status is quo."

Was the message that Paul and Barnabas were preaching true? To the Jewish leaders in Antioch, that didn't matter. It was different—that was the real problem.

It is not the Jews who shrank back to protect the comfort of their synagogue who should be our models. They judged themselves unworthy of everlasting life.

B. The Receptive

Our heroes in Antioch should be those who *did* judge themselves worthy of everlasting life. They were filled with joy to hear about the forgiveness of sins and about the One whom God had raised from the dead to provide that forgiveness. They were receptive to an offer from God that would provide the life that they were unable to provide for themselves. This was good news. This was *great* news!

Yes, it would change things. But these people were ready to be changed. What a joy to find and to teach such receptive hearts!

C. Prayer

Our Father, we acknowledge that we are those who are responsible to carry the message of eternal life to others. If we do not, who will? You do not want us to ignore anyone. Give us the energy, insight, compassion, and clarity to share the good news of Jesus and to carry out that task regardless of how our hearers respond. In Jesus' name, amen.

D. Thought to Remember

"The Lord is not slack concerning his promise, as some men count slackness; but is long-suffering to us-ward, not willing that any should perish, but that all should come to repentance" (2 Peter 3:9). God wants us *all*!

How to Say It

ANTIOCH. *An*-tee-ock.
APOLLOS. Uh-*pahl*-us.
BAR-JESUS. Bar-*jee*-zus.
BARNABAS. *Bar*-nuh-bus.
CYPRUS. *Sigh*-prus.
ELYMAS. *El*-ih-mass.
ICONIUM. Eye-*co*-nee-um.
PAMPHYLIA. Pam-*fill*-ee-uh.
PAPHOS. *Pay*-fahss.
PERGA. *Per*-guh.
PISIDIA. Pih-*sid*-ee-uh.
SELEUCIA. Sih-*lew*-shuh.
SERGIUS PAULUS. *Ser*-jih-us *Paul*-us.

Learning by Doing

This page contains an alternate lesson plan emphasizing learning activities.
Classes desiring such student involvement will find these suggestions helpful.

Learning Goals

After participating in this lesson, each student will be able to:

1. Summarize Paul's message in Antioch of Pisidia and the people's responses.

2. Compare Paul and Barnabas's methods of evangelism with modern evangelistic practices.

3. Write a letter to a missionary or missionary family, encouraging them in their important work for the Lord.

Into the Lesson

Many new churches have been planted with well-developed strategies. As a result, these churches have had impressive beginnings and immediate growth. Check with your preacher— he probably knows of such a church. If there is one nearby, you may be able to get someone to come and tell their story. Or you can contact an evangelistic or church-planting ministry in your area and invite someone from the organization to come and address the class.

After this report, divide the class into groups of four or five. Ask each group to develop a strategy for planting a new church. The location has no nucleus of believers to begin the work, so the church is starting from scratch. Give each group a chance to report on its suggested strategy to the rest of the class.

Make the transition to the Bible study by saying, "The beginning of a new church can lay the foundation for years of growth, or it can sow the seeds of self-destruction. We've heard some modern-day plans for a new church planting. Now let's look at one of the first church-planting teams and study its strategy."

Into the Word

Have a volunteer read Acts 13:4, 13-15, 42-52. Then divide your class into four groups to explore this text. Give each group one of the assignments below.

Group 1: Summary

Today's lesson focuses on the portion of Acts 13 that records the ministry of Paul and Barnabas in Antioch of Pisidia. First, summarize the message that Paul and Barnabas preached there, and second, summarize the response of the people. Be ready to report the results of your study with the rest of the class.

Group 2: Concordance Study

Assign this group to find what the rest of the New Testament says about John Mark. Look at each of the passages, and don't forget the Gospel of Mark: Acts 12:12, 25; 13:5; 15:37-39; Colossians 4:10; 2 Timothy 4:11; Philemon 24; and 1 Peter 5:13. Be ready to share the results of your study with the entire class.

Group 3: Map Study

Provide a map of the Mediterranean area for this group to study. Ask the group to trace the travels of Paul and Barnabas through Acts 13. Be sure to distinguish between and locate the two cities with the name of Antioch. Be ready to share the results of your study with the entire class.

Group 4: Principles of Evangelism

The fourth group has the assignment of identifying some principles of evangelism from Acts 13. For example, verse 1 could suggest that well-developed churches should be receptive to the opportunity to share leaders to plant new congregations. Verse 2 implies that fasting and prayer are essential to the planting of new churches. Verse 4 records that Barnabas began his trip by returning to the island of his birth. Jesus said to the former demoniac, "Go home to your family and tell them how much the Lord has done for you, and how he has had mercy on you" (Mark 5:19, *New International Version*). Be ready to share the results of your study with the rest of the class.

Into Life

Provide all of the materials for each of your class members to write a letter of encouragement to a missionary. Your missions committee will be glad to provide you with names and addresses of missionaries supported by your congregation.

Today many missionaries have access to e-mail. This medium has enabled missionaries to publish newsletters and distribute them worldwide immediately. Prayer requests and answers can be communicated instantaneously. You might even arrange for your class to visit an Internet chat room with a missionary for an on-line chat. Be aware of time zone differences.

Conclude the session with a time of prayer for specific missionaries your church supports, new churches in your area, and the evangelistic efforts of your own congregation.

Let's Talk It Over

The questions on this page are designed to encourage review of the lesson Scriptures and to promote discussion of the lesson by the class. The answers provided are only discussion starters. Let your class talk it over from there.

1. Paul described evangelism in terms of one person's planting and another's watering (1 Corinthians 3:6-8). What are some evangelistic tasks members can perform in today's church?

If evangelism is the primary task of the church, then virtually every ministry should be evangelistic in some way. Inviting friends to come along to worship services and special outreach events is one task we all can perform. The person who cleans the building and makes sure the lights are on and the heat (or air conditioning) is set properly is preparing the seedbed for someone else to sow the Word. The person who cares for small children is removing distractions so that the visitor can hear the message and come to faith.

Other members may go beyond this and pass out tracts or other Christian literature to unsaved people, share a brief word of personal testimony and the plan of salvation, or even answer questions or respond to the excuses of the unsaved. But it is clear that the evangelistic enterprise offers some kind of work for everyone.

2. Paul was so put out with John Mark for not completing the first missionary trip that he refused to take him on the next one. The issue even caused Paul and Barnabas to separate (Acts 15:36-41). In time, however, the rift was healed. What do you think is the key to resolving conflicts between Christian brothers?

We do not know who was "at fault" in this disagreement. Perhaps both sides were at fault to some degree. But reconciliation does not depend on determining who is at fault. A commitment to faithfulness to the Lord's work is the key issue. John Mark seems to have demonstrated that he could be faithful, and Paul recognized that. If we are committed to the Lord's work, then we should be able to work with any brother or sister who shares that commitment, even if we disagree from time to time.

3. "The Gentiles besought that these words might be preached to them . . ." (Acts 13:42). That indicates a wonderful openness to the gospel. Who in our culture—in our community— is open to the gospel? How can we tell?

We are often inclined to assume that the unsaved people in our community simply are not interested in the gospel. "They would attend our church's services if they were interested," we may reason. But what if we assumed that people were open to the gospel? How would that affect the way we approach them? They may think of the church as being preoccupied with money or with "telling people how they ought to live." If only they knew that we serve a God who loves us! If only they understood that we teach a way of defeating death and living eternally in peace and joy! Surveys show that people are very interested in "spiritual" things—but they have a distorted view of how to satisfy their interest. Perhaps there are many more "open" people than we realize.

4. Paul and Barnabas broke off their evangelistic efforts toward the Jews to concentrate on teaching the Gentiles. What are some factors that might lead us to curtail our evangelistic efforts toward a particular individual or family?

Can I justify continuing to spend my time trying to convince a stubborn unbeliever, when other more receptive individuals may be awaiting my witness? Am I the only witness available? Perhaps there are others who will prove more convincing for this person than I have been. Another factor to consider is evidence of a hardening. One may find that an individual is growing more resistant toward his efforts, rather than exhibiting signs of emerging faith and penitence. Or one may prayerfully determine that it is time to step out of the picture to let God's Spirit work.

5. The lesson writer notes how quickly the gospel can be spread by new believers. How can we make the best possible use of the evangelistic enthusiasm of new believers?

It is wise to set up a series of home Bible studies with a new believer. These studies can be an evangelistic tool if we encourage him or her to invite family members and friends to participate. Similarly, if the church has a class for new converts and those thinking about becoming Christians, we can urge the new believer to bring in honest inquirers from his circle of acquaintances. We also should instruct the new believer in ways he can share his personal testimony, help him master a brief presentation of the plan of salvation, and make sure there is an adequate supply of tracts and other literature for the new convert and others to use in personal evangelistic efforts.

The Jerusalem Conference

DEVOTIONAL READING: Romans 3:21-26.

BACKGROUND SCRIPTURE: Acts 15:1-35.

PRINTED TEXT: Acts 15:1, 2, 6-15a, 19, 20.

Acts 15:1, 2, 6-15a, 19, 20

1 And certain men which came down from Judea taught the brethren, and said, Except ye be circumcised after the manner of Moses, ye cannot be saved.

2 When therefore Paul and Barnabas had no small dissension and disputation with them, they determined that Paul and Barnabas, and certain other of them, should go up to Jerusalem unto the apostles and elders about this question.

. . . .

6 And the apostles and elders came together for to consider of this matter.

7 And when there had been much disputing, Peter rose up, and said unto them, Men and brethren, ye know how that a good while ago God made choice among us, that the Gentiles by my mouth should hear the word of the gospel, and believe.

8 And God, which knoweth the hearts, bare them witness, giving them the Holy Ghost, even as he did unto us;

9 And put no difference between us and them, purifying their hearts by faith.

10 Now therefore why tempt ye God, to put a yoke upon the neck of the disciples, which neither our fathers nor we were able to bear?

11 But we believe that through the grace of the Lord Jesus Christ we shall be saved, even as they.

12 Then all the multitude kept silence, and gave audience to Barnabas and Paul, declaring what miracles and wonders God had wrought among the Gentiles by them.

13 And after they had held their peace, James answered, saying, Men and brethren, hearken unto me:

14 Simeon hath declared how God at the first did visit the Gentiles, to take out of them a people for his name.

15a And to this agree the words of the prophets.

. . . .

19 Wherefore my sentence is, that we trouble not them, which from among the Gentiles are turned to God:

20 But that we write unto them, that they abstain from pollutions of idols, and from fornication, and from things strangled, and from blood.

May 13

GOLDEN TEXT: We believe that through the grace of the Lord Jesus Christ we shall be saved, even as they.—Acts 15:11.

Lesson Aims

After this lesson students should be able to:

1. Explain the issue that occasioned the Jerusalem Conference, and summarize how the Conference addressed it.

2. Tell how traditions sometimes obscure the simplicity of the gospel of grace.

3. Confess any burdensome "yokes" that they have placed on others, and praise God for the grace freely given in Jesus Christ.

Lesson Outline

INTRODUCTION
   A. Jumping Through Hoops
   B. Lesson Background
 I. CONTROVERSY (Acts 15:1, 2)
   A. The Issue (v. 1)
     A Beautiful World
   B. The Disagreement (v. 2)
 II. CONFIRMATION (Acts 15:6-15a)
   A. Peter's Testimony (vv. 6-11)
   B. James's Counsel (vv. 12-15a)
III. CAUTIONS (Acts 15:19, 20)
   A. For the Jewish Believers (v. 19)
     "Don't Trouble Them"
   B. For the Gentile Believers (v. 20)
CONCLUSION
   A. It's Easy to Bully
   B. It's Easy to Split
   C. It's Harder to Heal, but Right
   D. Prayer
   E. Thought to Remember

Introduction

A. Jumping Through Hoops

About a dozen young adults in medical school at the local university attend church together, and it has been a great encouragement to see their steadfast faith and to listen to them talk about some of their experiences. It's exciting to think about the many years of ministry that they can have as professional healers who know the real Healer.

One day, during a conversation with a third-year student, the preacher at the church asked, "Why are your supervisors so hard on you? Why the long hours, the 'all-nighters'? Is there some

lesson that they're trying to teach you? Do they want to toughen you up, or teach you how to handle sleep deprivation so that you will be better able to handle those early-morning emergencies? There's got to be a reason for it."

"Actually there's not," she said. "The supervisors put us through it only because *their* supervisors and teachers put *them* through it. There's no real reason for it at all. There's nothing about it that is designed to make us better doctors."

In many places, the "rules of the game" dictate that to be legitimate, you must jump through the same hoops that everyone else has had to jump through. It wouldn't be right for you to have the same credentials that I have if you took an easier route to obtain them!

Does that happen in the church? Today's lesson focuses on a time when it did.

B. Lesson Background

In last week's lesson, we considered both the successes and the frustrations that were experienced by Paul and Barnabas and their co-workers during the first missionary journey. Acts 14 (the chapter between last week's lesson and today's printed text) tells what else took place on that journey. In some respects conditions became worse: in Lystra, for example, Paul was stoned and left for dead (Acts 14:19, 20). But there were blessings, too: people kept turning to Christ, and they came in numbers large enough for the team to go back through all of the towns where they had preached and ordain elders in the churches that had been established there (Acts 14:21-23).

The conclusion of chapter 14 records the team's return to its sending congregation in Antioch of Syria. There they reported to that remarkably vibrant young church all that had happened during their endeavor. They also determined to remain in Antioch and work with the church there for a "long time" (vv. 24-28). They were set to enjoy the kind of furlough that the most fortunate missionaries today enjoy—exchanging blessings with the sponsoring congregation and its leaders, and being refreshed and encouraged for the next trip. Then trouble came to town.

I. Controversy
(Acts 15:1, 2)

A. The Issue (v. 1)

1. And certain men which came down from Judea taught the brethren, and said, Except ye be circumcised after the manner of Moses, ye cannot be saved.

These *men* who *came down from Judea* to Antioch and *taught the brethren* had no authority to do so. In the letter that was composed as a result of the meeting in Jerusalem, the leadership in Jerusalem noted that "certain . . . went out from us . . . to whom we gave no such commandment" (Acts 15:24). They may well be the same ones whom Paul described as "false brethren unawares brought in, who came in privily to spy out our liberty which we have in Christ Jesus, that they might bring us into bondage" (Galatians 2:4).

These unauthorized visitors said, *Except ye be circumcised after the manner of Moses, ye cannot be saved*. Of course, there was more involved in this matter than circumcision. As Paul explained, "Every man that is circumcised . . . is a debtor to do the whole law" (Galatians 5:3). In effect, the Gentile Christians in Antioch were being told that, without following the system of Jewish ritual observance, they could not be considered Christians.

A BEAUTIFUL WORLD

Every public library (and many private homes) used to have a globe of the world in them. The various land areas and seas were shown, as well as the political boundaries separating the nations. We don't often see globes anymore, probably because an atlas (or more recently, a computer program) provides much clearer detail and more useful information.

Now, for those who have an interest in globes (and in works of art), there is a particular globe advertised as "the world's finest." It features more than twenty different semi-precious stones, including lapis lazuli oceans and countries represented by amethyst, jade, jasper, tigereye, and other specimens. An effort has even been made to use the stones in the areas of the globe appropriate to their origin. The price of almost eight hundred dollars guarantees that most of your neighbors won't have one; thus, your view of "the world" will be unique among your circle of friends.

The Jewish Christians who came to Antioch and made certain demands of the Gentile Christians had their own unique view of the world, and they did not appreciate the variety that others were trying to bring to it. For them, the church could be only Jewish; the law of Moses was the only "mosaic" they could imagine.

These people did not realize that what God has in mind for His church is a far more beautiful "globe"—one made up of precious stones from every people of the world, not just a few. It's an idea that some Christians still find difficult to accept.   —C. R. B.

B. The Disagreement (v. 2)

2. When therefore Paul and Barnabas had no small dissension and disputation with them, they determined that Paul and Barnabas, and certain other of them, should go up to Jerusalem unto the apostles and elders about this question.

One can easily see how *no small dissension and disputation* arose as a result of this turn of events, especially in light of Paul and Barnabas's recent missionary travels among the Gentiles. They had been preaching and teaching messages such as the one that Paul delivered in Antioch of Pisidia: "Be it known unto you therefore, men and brethren, that through [Jesus] is preached unto you the forgiveness of sins: and by him all that believe are justified from all things, from which ye could not be justified by the law of Moses" (Acts 13:38, 39). To sanction what the other teachers were proposing would have had the effect of negating all that had just been accomplished in places like Antioch.

Since the two groups disagreed so strongly on such a crucial matter (that is, what was necessary for salvation), they agreed to take the *question* to the *apostles* and to those who were *elders* in the well-established church in *Jerusalem*. [See question #1, page 320.]

II. Confirmation
(Acts 15:6-15a)

A. Peter's Testimony (vv. 6-11)

6, 7. And the apostles and elders came together for to consider of this matter. And when there had been much disputing, Peter rose up, and said unto them, Men and brethren, ye know how that a good while ago God made choice among us, that the Gentiles by my mouth should hear the word of the gospel, and believe.

This gathering (often referred to as the Jerusalem Conference, as in our lesson title) seems to have been preceded by a private meeting in which Paul and Barnabas related details of their ministry among the *Gentiles* to the elders and apostles (Acts 15:4; Galatians 2:2). The public discussion began with the proposition expressed by some believers who also were (or had been) Pharisees, insisting that the Gentiles comply with the law of Moses (v. 5). Perhaps these were the same teachers who had taught this doctrine in Antioch, calling forth the need for this conference.

As in Antioch, there was *much disputing* over the issue. Then *Peter rose up* to speak. He was the one whom God had used to expand the church's outreach to include the Gentiles. Peter reminded those present that the fundamental issue they were discussing was something that God had already decided *a good while ago*. God had sent Peter a vision (the same one three times) in order to teach him that God is "no respecter of persons" (Acts 10:34). Peter then went straight from the vision and its explanation to meet some men who had been sent from Cornelius. He correctly put the two events together and went with them to Cornelius's house in Caesarea.

8. And God, which knoweth the hearts, bare them witness, giving them the Holy Ghost, even as he did unto us.

While the apostle was talking about Jesus to those gathered in Cornelius's home, the Holy Spirit fell on those Gentiles in a Pentecost-like manifestation (note Peter's words *even as he did unto us*), thus certifying that God did indeed want these people to receive His salvation (Acts 10:44-47). [See question #2, page 320.]

9. And put no difference between us and them, purifying their hearts by faith.

Peter did not suggest that these Gentiles be circumcised, but baptized, as the expression of their *faith* in Jesus as Lord and Christ (Acts 10:47). This was similar to what had occurred on the Day of Pentecost, when, following the coming of the Holy Spirit on the apostles, Peter had preached to the Jews in Jerusalem and held them responsible for the crucifixion of Jesus, whom "God hath made . . . both Lord and Christ" (Acts 2:36). He then called for his listeners to repent and to be baptized (v. 38).

Thus both Jews and Gentiles had been given the same opportunity to be justified *by faith*. Without circumcision! Without a commitment to keeping the law! There was *no difference* between Jews and Gentiles in how they could be saved.

10. Now therefore why tempt ye God, to put a yoke upon the neck of the disciples, which neither our fathers nor we were able to bear?

The issue was not what Peter had said or done, but what God had decided. He has established a new way—a better way—for individuals to become His children. "Who has ever kept all the law?" Peter's question implied. It is a *yoke* too heavy for anyone to *bear*, and, now that it has been replaced by a better way, it is wrong to force it on anyone. [See question #3, page 320.]

11. But we believe that through the grace of the Lord Jesus Christ we shall be saved, even as they.

Jesus is the way, the truth, and the life (John 14:6). He is the One through whom Jews, who have failed to keep the law of Moses, are *saved*. He is the One through whom Gentiles, who have failed to live up to the "law written in their hearts" (Romans 2:15), are *saved*. The way of law has been rendered obsolete by *the grace of the Lord Jesus Christ*.

B. James's Counsel (vv. 12-15a)

12. Then all the multitude kept silence, and gave audience to Barnabas and Paul, declaring what miracles and wonders God had wrought among the Gentiles by them.

Visual for lesson 11

The visual that corresponds with lesson 11 illustrates Acts 15:11. It is also an important reminder for any believer in Jesus.

Barnabas and Paul followed Peter's testimony with their report of what God had done through them during their missionary travels. They testified of the *miracles and wonders* that *God had wrought among the Gentiles*. It was clear that God had been in this entire undertaking, "confirming the word" and "bearing them witness" through these signs (Mark 16:20; Hebrews 2:3, 4).

13. And after they had held their peace, James answered, saying, Men and brethren, hearken unto me.

The next speaker was *James*, who summarized what had been said thus far and offered a plan for addressing the issue at hand. While there were two apostles known as James, this James was most likely the half-brother of Jesus (Matthew 13:55). James the brother of John had been put to death by this time (Acts 12:1, 2), and James the Less is never mentioned except in lists of the apostles. John notes that during Jesus' earthly ministry His brothers did not "believe in him" (John 7:5) as the Son of God. But the risen Christ appeared to James (1 Corinthians 15:7), and he became a prominent leader in the Jerusalem church. Paul included him among those "who seemed to be pillars" in the church (Galatians 2:9). This James also wrote the epistle of James.

14. Simeon hath declared how God at the first did visit the Gentiles, to take out of them a people for his name.

James used Peter's Hebrew name of *Simeon*, or Simon, perhaps because he was appealing primarily to Jewish Christians. Peter had summarized his experience in the house of Cornelius and its significance. Those *Gentiles* who were willing to accept the gospel were to be welcomed into God's New Covenant *people*. James emphasized this and then cited the authority that his hearers would respect the most. [See question #4, page 320.]

15a. And to this agree the words of the prophets.

Prophets such as Isaiah (Isaiah 11:10; 54:3), Jeremiah (Jeremiah 16:19), and Malachi (Malachi

1:11) looked ahead to a time when Gentiles would be included among those who acknowledged God's name. In his remarks, James proceeded to quote from the prophet Amos (Amos 9:11, 12), emphasizing the Lord's promise to "build again the tabernacle of David" so that Gentiles might seek the Lord (Acts 15:16-18). Thus, what was happening with the Gentiles was not Peter's idea or Barnabas and Paul's doing; it was the fulfillment of God's plan.

III. Cautions
(Acts 15:19, 20)

A. For the Jewish Believers (v. 19)

19. Wherefore my sentence is, that we trouble not them, which from among the Gentiles are turned to God.

James declared his *sentence*, or judgment, regarding this sensitive matter. The Gentile believers had been troubled by the teaching being spread by those who had come from Judea to Antioch. They would have been especially concerned about attempts to make them keep the complicated code of regulations that had been developed by the Pharisees and teachers of the law. None of the Jewish people (not even the leaders) had been able to keep every regulation.

"God is not imposing such rigid standards on these new believers," James asserted. Jews and Gentiles enter the kingdom of God in the same way, and keeping the law is not the way. Trusting Jesus is the way. However, there were some areas of concern that the Gentile believers needed to be aware of, and James proceeded to mention those.

"DON'T TROUBLE THEM"

What do you think is absolutely *essential* to the Christian faith? What might be placed in the category of *opinion*? Church history includes many attempts to move items up the list from opinion to essential, resulting in the creation of new "churches" or denominations.

Even the movements that have claimed to be "non-denominational Christians" have had to struggle with this problem. The "Restoration Movement," which began around the turn of the nineteenth century "to unite Christians in all the sects" (as the founders put it), has divided over many issues. One of the most familiar slogans of this movement is, "In matters of faith, unity; in matters of opinion, liberty; in all things, love." However, like many summations of truth, this one is easy to remember and very difficult to apply!

First-century Jewish Christians were telling Gentiles that they couldn't keep their Gentile culture and still be Christians. In essence, they had to become Jews. But the apostles answered,

"Don't trouble them" with matters that are not essential. That's good advice for us as well. It doesn't quite answer all of our questions, but it does indicate the spirit with which we should approach sensitive issues.

God sent the Savior to smooth the pathway to Heaven, not to place obstacles on it.   —C. R. B.

B. For the Gentile Believers (v. 20)

20. But that we write unto them, that they abstain from pollutions of idols, and from fornication, and from things strangled, and from blood.

In some respects, this list of requirements is what we might expect; in others, it may seem rather surprising. For the Gentile believers to be told to *abstain from* the worship of *idols* (and thus from the spiritual *pollutions* that would come from doing that) makes sense. The second of the Ten Commandments told God's people not to make any graven image (Exodus 20:4). Nothing created must be allowed to substitute for God—nothing in God's natural creation, nor anything created by the hands of those made in God's image.

To state a firm restriction against *fornication* makes good sense as well. God had commanded His people Israel not to commit adultery (Exodus 20:14). Throughout the Scriptures there are strong warnings against any form of sexual immorality.

These two warnings were especially appropriate for Gentile Christians. The pagan worship in cities where the gospel was making inroads often included a mixture of idol worship and illicit sexual activity. Christians must not be idolaters or fornicators. They cannot worship other gods, and they cannot worship their own flesh.

But why ask the Gentiles to abstain *from things strangled, and from blood*? These last two items appear to cover concerns that were important in the Jewish law (Genesis 9:4; Leviticus 17:13, 14;

How to Say It

ANTIOCH. *An*-tee-ock.
BARNABAS. *Bar*-nuh-bus.
CAESAREA. Sess-uh-*ree*-uh.
CORNELIUS. Cor-*neel*-yus.
ISAIAH. Eye-*zay*-uh.
JEREMIAH. Jair-uh-*my*-uh.
LYSTRA. *Liss*-truh.
MALACHI. *Mal*-uh-kye.
PISIDIA. Pih-*sid*-ee-uh.
SIMEON. *Sim*-ee-un.
SYRIA. *Sear*-ee-uh.

Deuteronomy 12:16, 23, 27), but they are never emphasized in any proclamation of the gospel. Why impose them on Gentiles? [See question #5, page 320.]

Some students believe that these commands were added as an aid to Christian fellowship—not as a requirement for salvation. An important part of fellowship, especially in the early church where people with Jewish and non-Jewish backgrounds were coming together, was the readiness to understand and appreciate the sensitivities of others in the church. (It still is important.) The idea of eating the meat of strangled animals or of eating blood would have been highly offensive to Jewish believers. For the Gentile believers to respect these sensitive areas would make fellowship between Jews and Gentiles (particularly sharing meals together) much more harmonious.

Conclusion

A. It's Easy to Bully

The Jewish Christians in Jerusalem had history on their side. They were from God's chosen people. The apostles (the leaders of the church) were Jews. The Gentile Christians were fewer and newer. They had much to learn about their new faith. They simply knew that they had been introduced to something (and Someone) that had changed their lives. If the leaders in Jerusalem had chosen to exercise their full authority, most likely whatever they decreed would have been done by those new (Gentile) Christians.

It's usually easy for the more prominent, more "official" individuals involved in a disagreement to exert their authority, state their demands, and get their way. But it isn't Christlike.

B. It's Easy to Split

The tension between Jewish Christians and Gentile Christians could have increased to the point where the church suffered a major setback. The Gentile believers in Antioch could have reacted in anger to the teachings of the ones who came from Judea. They could have started "their own church," one more sensitive to the Gentile heritage. That's what many Christians do today when there is conflict. One group becomes two—and the credibility of the church in the eyes of the community is strained.

C. It's Harder to Heal, but Right

Better than bullying and better than splitting is healing. That is what the churches of Antioch and Jerusalem did. Contributing to this peaceful resolution, no doubt, was the fact that some effort had already been made to build bridges between the two churches. Upon hearing of the spread of the gospel into Antioch, Jerusalem had sent Barnabas to encourage the new believers (Acts 11:22, 23). Upon hearing of a coming famine, the Antioch church had sent a relief offering to the Christians in Judea. Barnabas was instrumental in this as well (Acts 11:27-30). It is easier for churches (or individual Christians) to find healing in strained relationships when those relationships are built around the love of Jesus.

Healed relationships mean that everyone has to do some giving. When it is the right thing to do, some apologies have to be made—and accepted. Compromises must be worked out in matters that are not of primary importance. Probably no one will get his way entirely; no group will get all it wants.

How do we respond if we are involved in such a situation? Do we "hang in there" and make the sacrifices necessary to maintaining peace? Or do we "throw a fit" and go home angry?

These are the times when it helps to think about what God wants. How does He respond to division within His family? How does He respond to the demonstration of love and encouragement? It should not be hard for us to know when He is smiling and when He is sad.

D. Prayer

Lord, in a difficult world please strengthen Your church that she might be what You wish her to be. Use us all, both leaders and followers, to spread the good news that Jesus Christ has come to save and that He is Lord. Through Him we pray, amen.

E. Thought to Remember

"Behold, how good and how pleasant it is for brethren to dwell together in unity!" (Psalm 133:1).

Home Daily Bible Readings

Monday, May 7—Paul and Barnabas in Jerusalem (Acts 15:1-5)

Tuesday, May 8—Questions and Responses (Acts 15:6-12)

Wednesday, May 9—James Cites Scripture (Acts 15:13-18)

Thursday, May 10—Decision About Gentiles (Acts 15:19-29)

Friday, May 11—Response to the Letter (Acts 15:30-35)

Saturday, May 12—Paul and Barnabas Separate (Acts 15:36-41)

Sunday, May 13—Timothy Joins Paul and Silas (Acts 16:1-5)

Learning by Doing

This page contains an alternate lesson plan emphasizing learning activities. Classes desiring such student involvement will find these suggestions helpful.

Learning Goals

After this lesson students should be able to:

1. Explain the issue that occasioned the Jerusalem Conference, and summarize how the Conference addressed it.

2. Tell how traditions sometimes obscure the simplicity of the gospel of grace.

3. Confess any burdensome "yokes" that they have placed on others, and praise God for the grace freely given in Jesus Christ.

Into the Lesson

Copy the story from the Introduction to the lesson, "Jumping Through Hoops." Ask a class member to read the illustration to introduce the lesson. Then ask your class to cite other examples of rigidly holding to the past long after the reason for doing so has expired. Here is a classic that you can have another person read:

Two sisters were discussing the preparation of ham for a family gathering. One asked the other why they always cut the end off the ham before putting it in the roaster pan. Her sister responded, "I don't know. That's just the way Mom always did it." Not satisfied with that explanation, they decided to call their mother to find the reason. "Mom, why did you always cut the end off the ham before putting it in the roaster pan?"

"Because, it was too long for the roaster pan," their mother replied.

Into the Word

Have your class read today's text—Acts 15:1, 2, 6-15a, 19, 20—as a choral reading. Assign a person or group of people to read the parts of a narrator, the Jewish brethren, Peter, and James.

The narrator will read verse 1 until the Jewish brethren speak. The narrator will read verses 2, 6, and 7 until Peter speaks. The narrator will read verses 12 and 13 until James speaks. (You could have one or two persons compose the report that Barnabas and Paul gave, as summarized in verse 12, and give that report before going on to verse 13.) James finishes the printed text.

Ask the class to form small groups (four to six members in each) and study each verse for insights to use in resolving church problems. For example, verse 1 might suggest that disputes should be expected. We should not be so naive as to assume that there will be no conflicts in church life. Verse 2 infers that if there is a sharp dispute and debate, those involved can appeal to church leaders, even from another congregation, to sort out disagreements. Verse 6 says that the apostles and elders met to consider this question, which implies that the discussion was the primary purpose of the meeting. Have a class member write each group's insights on a poster or on the chalkboard.

Into Life

In Acts 15:11, Peter turns the phrase on the Jews by saying, "But we believe that through the grace of the Lord Jesus Christ we shall be saved, even as they." In other words, "We get to Heaven the same way they do!"

This verse echoes down the corridors of time and still resounds as truth. Encourage your class to memorize this verse together. Read the verse aloud in unison. Each time you read it, emphasize a different word. You may want to stop and discuss the importance of the word emphasized. For example, the word *we* shows that Peter's belief is in stark contrast to the belief of the Jewish brethren who wanted the Gentiles to follow the Jewish law, including the practice of circumcision. The term *grace* stands in contrast to human effort or legalistic requirements of the law.

If time allows, point out that while the issue in Acts 15 is whether a person must be circumcised to be saved, today's churches wrestle with other issues relating to salvation. Give your class copies of the following "Yes-No" quiz. Learners are to tell whether the Bible mentions each action as necessary for a person to be saved. Have your Bible and a concordance ready to answer the lively discussion that will follow!

1. Observe the Lord's Supper
2. Tithe
3. Confess their sins
4. Confess that Jesus is Lord
5. Repent
6. Be baptized
7. Pray the sinner's prayer
8. Go forward in a church service
9. Join your local church

(The directions for this activity are included in the student quarterly, *Adult Bible Class*.)

Close your class time with a period of directed prayer. Include confession for relying too rigidly on tradition as well as praise for God's grace freely given in Christ Jesus.

Let's Talk It Over

The questions on this page are designed to encourage review of the lesson Scriptures and to promote discussion of the lesson by the class. The answers provided are only discussion starters. Let your class talk it over from there.

1. Most churches have their share of "dissension and disputation." When is that a legitimate part of the church's business, and when is it merely disruptive?

Too much dissension and disputation in the church occurs in connection with relatively trivial matters: what color to paint the nursery walls, whether or not to sing every stanza of every worship hymn, how much to pay the custodian, etc. It may be necessary, however, to engage in some dissension and disputation when problems involving doctrinal and moral errors arise. Is a church officer guilty of an extra-marital affair? Is a teacher denying the bodily resurrection of Christ? Are certain members fomenting division by insisting on the necessity of speaking in tongues? Then it may take a bit of dissension and disputation to correct these matters. Certainly it is not wise merely to ignore them.

2. God "knoweth the hearts" of those with whom we share the gospel. How important do you think it is to keep that in mind? Why?

Acceptance of the gospel is always a matter of the heart and leads to a purification of the heart (see verse 9). But we cannot see people's hearts; only God can. We must always remember that God is at work whenever the gospel is shared. Only He can bring salvation. Only He knows, even in advance, which hearts will be softened by the gospel and which ones will be hardened. Our duty is faithfulness—perhaps in planting or in watering, as noted in last week's discussion. But God gives the increase.

3. What kinds of unscriptural "yokes" have you seen some Christians try to put on the necks of others? How can we be sure we are not guilty of the same?

In some churches the subject of dress becomes a "yoke." How people dress for church attendance or even other occasions may become a source of contention. While dress codes in schools, camps, and other gatherings serve a legitimate purpose, these must never become tests of fellowship. Other believers adopt stringent standards regarding recreational practices and urge them on others. Attending movies, playing cards, and playing pool used to be sources of great controversy. Those who participated in such activities were

judged harshly—and may still be in some circles. But while the specific occasions for conflict may vary—and your class may be able to suggest several specifics—the critical issue remains the same: if it is not essential to salvation, a practice or belief must not be allowed to divide brothers and sisters in Christ. Even if we do not care to participate in the same activities—and we are not compelled to do so—we must not suggest that they are any less Christians because they do.

4. James called Peter by his Hebrew name, Simeon. We might see this as a concession to the Jewish Christians to whom he was about to make his appeal. What are some concessions we can make to appeal to people with whom we disagree—concessions that may help us to be heard but in no way compromise our message?

Names were very important to the Jewish people. So while it may seem a mere matter of semantics to us, the use of Peter's Hebrew name may have been significant to these believers. If we can use a pleasant term or avoid a pejorative one in a discussion, we may find we get a better hearing than if our speech is inflammatory. If we can accept a person's narrow view of "right behavior" as an honest attempt at holiness, we may get a better hearing even as we appeal for greater liberty in what the person expects of others. Good manners never compromise sound doctrine.

5. Suppose a new believer said to you, "I thought we lived under grace! Why, then, did the apostles and elders send this letter with *rules* to follow?" How would you respond?

It is no violation of the doctrine of grace to command a believer to avoid idolatry. Jesus Christ is the one Lord (1 Corinthians 8:6), and it is not possible to serve Him faithfully while also serving false gods. If we are to be true to the Christ of the Bible, we must insist on His gospel of grace as the only way to salvation and eternal life. Accepting that gospel has always included accepting Jesus as Lord—which includes a commitment to obeying Him. Jesus Himself said, "If ye love me, keep my commandments" (John 14:15). We are not saved by compliance with rules, like the ones cited in the apostles and elders' letter. But we cannot reject the Lord's rules and still call Him Lord. (See Matthew 7:21-23.)

Responding to Need

DEVOTIONAL READING: Philippians 1:3-11.

BACKGROUND SCRIPTURE: Acts 16:6-40.

PRINTED TEXT: Acts 16:9-15, 25-33.

Acts 16:9-15, 25-33

9 And a vision appeared to Paul in the night; There stood a man of Macedonia, and prayed him, saying, Come over into Macedonia, and help us.

10 And after he had seen the vision, immediately we endeavored to go into Macedonia, assuredly gathering that the Lord had called us for to preach the gospel unto them.

11 Therefore loosing from Troas, we came with a straight course to Samothracia, and the next day to Neapolis;

12 And from thence to Philippi, which is the chief city of that part of Macedonia, and a colony: and we were in that city abiding certain days.

13 And on the sabbath we went out of the city by a river side, where prayer was wont to be made; and we sat down, and spake unto the women which resorted thither.

14 And a certain woman named Lydia, a seller of purple, of the city of Thyatira, which worshipped God, heard us: whose heart the Lord opened, that she attended unto the things which were spoken of Paul.

15 And when she was baptized, and her household, she besought us, saying, If ye have judged me to be faithful to the Lord, come into my house, and abide there. And she constrained us.

·   ·   ·   ·   ·   ·   ·   ·   ·   ·   ·

25 And at midnight Paul and Silas prayed, and sang praises unto God: and the prisoners heard them.

26 And suddenly there was a great earthquake, so that the foundations of the prison were shaken: and immediately all the doors were opened, and every one's bands were loosed.

27 And the keeper of the prison awaking out of his sleep, and seeing the prison doors open, he drew out his sword, and would have killed himself, supposing that the prisoners had been fled.

28 But Paul cried with a loud voice, saying, Do thyself no harm: for we are all here.

29 Then he called for a light, and sprang in, and came trembling, and fell down before Paul and Silas,

30 And brought them out, and said, Sirs, what must I do to be saved?

31 And they said, Believe on the Lord Jesus Christ, and thou shalt be saved, and thy house.

32 And they spake unto him the word of the Lord, and to all that were in his house.

33 And he took them the same hour of the night, and washed their stripes; and was baptized, he and all his, straightway.

May 20

GOLDEN TEXT: Come over into Macedonia, and help us.—Acts 16:9.

Continuing Jesus' Work
Unit 3: Spreading the Gospel Into All the World
(Lessons 9-13)

Lesson Aims

After this lesson a student should be able to:

1. Give the significant details of the conversions of Lydia and the jailer in Philippi.

2. Tell how these incidents demonstrate the importance of presenting the gospel in a manner that is sensitive to people's needs.

3. Pray for courage and sensitivity in presenting Christ to someone this week.

Lesson Outline

INTRODUCTION
  A. Decisions
  B. Lesson Background
 I. SEEING A VISION (Acts 16:9, 10)
  A. A Pleading Man (v. 9)
  B. A Prepared Man (v. 10)
    Responding to a Call of Distress
 II. ANSWERING THE CALL (Acts 16:11-15)
  A. Traveling to Philippi (vv. 11, 12)
  B. Finding a Place of Prayer (v. 13)
  C. Teaching Lydia (vv. 14, 15)
III. HELPING A JAILER (Acts 16:25-33)
  A. Prisoners' Praise (v. 25)
    Praying During a Crisis
  B. Sudden Earthquake (v. 26)
  C. Troubled Jailer (vv. 27-30)
  D. Joyful Household (vv. 31-33)
CONCLUSION
  A. A Changed Family
  B. An Enlarged Family
  C. A Family of New Individuals
  D. Prayer
  E. Thought to Remember

Introduction

A. Decisions

One of the most impressive qualities distinguishing the apostle Paul is his decisiveness. Certainly there were times when he was tentative and even afraid (cf. 1 Corinthians 2:3). But generally speaking, he seems to have been a man who was able to make a decision and move forward aggressively without turning back or regretting what he had done.

Someone may respond, "Well, if God gave me a vision of what He wanted me to do [such as what we see in today's lesson], I'd move forward aggressively too!" And at times we may wish for such guidance. But we must never underestimate the importance of the guidance provided for us in the Scriptures. There God has provided general directions for us (and even some specific directions that can be learned from the teachings and experiences that are recorded).

Most likely all of us have wrestled with how God indicates His will for us in daily situations. Perhaps we have sensed times when God was blocking our plans, as He did when Paul's missionary team intended to go to Asia and Bithynia, but was forbidden by the Spirit (Acts 16:6, 7). At other times, even though we have not seen a vision offering us guidance, we have sensed that a certain course of action is God's will.

Many who claim that they want to know God's will have not spent sufficient time in the Book where it is found! If we determine to be decisive in obeying God's clear will as recorded in Scripture, we will be better prepared for trusting Him on those occasions when His will is not as clear.

B. Lesson Background

Armed with the confirmation of their ministry that had come from the decision of the Jerusalem Conference, Paul and Barnabas prepared to proceed with their task of taking the gospel to the Gentiles. First, they returned to Antioch and conveyed the decisions of the Conference, which brought great encouragement to the church there. Jesus Christ *alone* is the way to salvation; Gentiles are *not* required to bear the additional weight of keeping the regulations and rituals of Judaism. One of the representatives from the Jerusalem church (Silas) enjoyed the fellowship in Antioch so much that he decided to stay for a while. (He probably did not anticipate that he would become Paul's next traveling companion.)

At one point during their stay in Antioch, Paul suggested to Barnabas, "Let's go back and visit the churches that were established on our last trip. We should see how they are doing."

"Great idea!" said Barnabas. "And why don't we take John Mark along with us?"

"Oh, no!" said Paul. "Don't you remember how he deserted us? We don't need someone that unreliable."

Acts 15:39 notes "the contention was so sharp between them" that Paul and Barnabas decided to separate. Barnabas took Mark and headed for Cyprus. Paul then chose Silas as his new partner and went to visit the churches that had been started during the first missionary journey.

From that point Luke's account focuses on the travels of Paul and Silas. In Lystra, Paul and Silas were joined by Timothy, a young man who showed great promise and eventually became an exemplary leader. (That's what happens when more experienced Christians watch carefully for faithful and capable young people and invest time, prayer, example, and instruction in them.)

While Paul desired to visit churches that were already established, he was also eager to break new ground with the gospel. He wanted to go westward into the province of Asia. In some manner, however, the Holy Spirit prohibited him from doing so. He then tried to turn northward. Again the Spirit said no.

Then Paul and his team came to Troas, where he received his "marching orders." Without delay, he responded!

I. Seeing a Vision
(Acts 16:9, 10)
A. A Pleading Man (v. 9)

9. And a vision appeared to Paul in the night; There stood a man of Macedonia, and prayed him, saying, Come over into Macedonia, and help us.

Across the Aegean Sea from Troas was the territory of *Macedonia*. (It is northern Greece today.) As God had earlier guided Peter by means of a vision (Acts 10:9-16), here He revealed to Paul what the next step of his journey should be. [See question #1, page 328.]

B. A Prepared Man (v. 10)

10. And after he had seen the vision, immediately we endeavored to go into Macedonia, assuredly gathering that the Lord had called us for to preach the gospel unto them.

Here is the decisiveness in Paul that was mentioned earlier. *Immediately* plans were made to go into *Macedonia*. Notice also that the travel team is described as *we*. This is the first of the *we* sections in the book of Acts (they are found in 16:10-17; 20:5—21:18; and 27:1—28:16). Here it means that Luke, the author of the book of Acts,

Visual for
lesson 12

Where Is God Calling You?

Today's visual reminds us that not everyone is called to "Macedonia," but God does call each of us to service.

joined Paul and his companions in Troas. (Verse 8 refers to *they* as "passing by Mysia" and coming to Troas.) Now it is *we* until the imprisonment of Paul and Silas in Philippi. [See question #2, page 328.]

RESPONDING TO A CALL OF DISTRESS

A distress call from off the Florida coast was received by the United States Coast Guard. When the rescue team arrived, it found a sixteen-foot boat being dragged in circles by something that had attached itself to the boat's anchor rope. Even the boat's ninety-horsepower engine was useless; it was being pulled steadily out to sea.

The Coast Guard rescue boat attached its winch to the motorboat's anchor rope. Eventually, the rescue team pulled to the surface a giant manta ray that measured eighteen feet in width and was estimated to weigh more than a ton. It could have pulled the boat to the bottom of the ocean had it been able to reach deep water.

The man from Macedonia whom Paul saw in his vision was also issuing a distress call. His cry for help was a plea for someone to bring the gospel message to him and his people. They were feeling the devastating effects of a sinful pagan culture that was pulling them down to certain spiritual and moral destruction.

This crisis call was heard by those who had what was needed to accomplish a rescue: the right message and the right spirit. The gospel had the power to save, and Paul and his team were willing to take it to others. The church has the same message today and the world's need is the same. The question is whether the church has the right spirit—a willingness to go where the message is needed.   —C. R. B.

II. Answering the Call
(Acts 16:11-15)
A. Traveling to Philippi (vv. 11, 12)

11. Therefore loosing from Troas, we came with a straight course to Samothracia, and the next day to Neapolis.

Notice, once again, Luke's careful attention to detail as he charts the course of the missionary team's travels. Apparently nothing significant happened on *Samothracia* (an island in the northeastern Aegean Sea) or in *Neapolis* (the seaport city for Philippi). These were simply stops made in the process of answering the "Macedonian call."

12. And from thence to Philippi, which is the chief city of that part of Macedonia, and a colony: and we were in that city abiding certain days.

Philippi was the first European city where Paul preached. Luke describes it as a *chief city*. This does not mean that Philippi was the capital city; Thessalonica was the capital. But Macedonia was divided into four districts, and Philippi was a leading city in the specific *part* of Macedonia where it was located. Philippi was also considered a Roman *colony*, meaning that it was self-governing and that the citizens were exempt from many of the taxes that were imposed on other portions of the empire.

B. Finding a Place of Prayer (v. 13)

13. And on the sabbath we went out of the city by a river side, where prayer was wont to be made; and we sat down, and spake unto the women which resorted thither.

Earlier we noted that Paul's usual practice upon arrival in a city was to locate the synagogue and begin his evangelistic efforts there. Since Paul did not follow this same procedure in Philippi, most students conclude that there was no synagogue to be found there. Ten Jewish men were required to establish a synagogue, so the absence of a synagogue suggests that there were not many Jews in the city. Thus, *on the sabbath* Paul and his companions searched for a place *where prayer was wont* (or accustomed) *to be made.* Here they found a group of *women*—perhaps Jewish, perhaps Gentile proselytes. No men are mentioned as leading or even participating; perhaps the women were quite eager to have some men present who would join them and teach them.

C. Teaching Lydia (vv. 14, 15)

14. And a certain woman named Lydia, a seller of purple, of the city of Thyatira, which worshipped God, heard us: whose heart the Lord opened, that she attended unto the things which were spoken of Paul.

Out of all the women in the group (we do not know how many were present), one is mentioned by name—*Lydia*. She was a businesswoman from *Thyatira* (a *city* in the Roman province of Asia). Luke describes her as *a seller of purple.* This could mean that she sold cloth that had been dyed purple or that she sold the dye that was used in the process. Perhaps she dealt in both. Since this was a rather expensive procedure and since purple garments were usually in demand, Lydia was probably quite well-to-do.

It is interesting that the church in Thyatira is one of the seven churches addressed by Jesus in the book of Revelation (Revelation 2:18-29). Perhaps Lydia and her co-workers returned there with the gospel message and were instrumental in starting the church.

Luke's record also tells us that Lydia was someone *whose heart the Lord opened.* This should be understood to mean that the Lord used the efforts of Paul and his companions (the message that

they spoke and the sincerity of their lives) to prepare Lydia to believe the gospel and thus to open up a new field of service. Whatever is accomplished by the efforts of faithful Christian workers is considered the Lord's work (Acts 14:27; 15:12) and is done for His glory. [See question #3, page 328.]

Lydia was one of those remarkably attentive, perceptive, and responsive individuals who are willing to hear and examine the gospel message and to accept it without hesitation as the truth. Remember that there have always been faithful women such as she who have played a significant role in the Lord's work.

15. And when she was baptized, and her household, she besought us, saying, If ye have judged me to be faithful to the Lord, come into my house, and abide there. And she constrained us.

Lydia's *household* may have included other women who worked with her in the purple cloth/dye business, family members, or both. They had also come to the riverside to pray and had listened to Paul's message. They, too, accepted it as the truth, and, along with Lydia, they were *baptized.* Thus it is evident that when Paul talked about Jesus as the Son of God and urged those who listened to accept Him as Savior and Lord, he must have talked about Christian baptism as the necessary and appropriate response.

Although a new convert, Lydia seems to have grasped immediately the importance of Christian hospitality. Apparently she either owned or rented (so that she could use it during business trips) a *house* in Philippi (another indication of her wealth). Evidently this was a fairly roomy house, for she and her household had room for living and sleeping; and there was enough additional room for providing temporary quarters for the traveling evangelists. That she *constrained them* means that she insisted that Paul and his companions accept her offer, which they did.

III. Helping a Jailer
(Acts 16:25-33)

A. Prisoners' Praise (v. 25)

25. And at midnight Paul and Silas prayed, and sang praises unto God: and the prisoners heard them.

Not everything in Philippi went as smoothly as did the encounter with Lydia and the other women. Verses 16-24 of Acts 16 tell how the missionary team encountered a young woman who was "possessed with a spirit of divination" and engaged in "soothsaying" (fortune-telling). She identified Paul and his companions as servants of God who were proclaiming the way of salvation. After many days of this, Paul became "grieved" at the woman's behavior. She was speaking the truth; however, the gospel was not being helped by testimony from that kind of source! So Paul cast the spirit out of the woman. Her "handlers," who had been making plenty of money from her ability, became angry. They seized Paul and Silas, brought exaggerated charges against them to the authorities, and had them thrown into prison.

But Paul and Silas were not ordinary prisoners! Instead of cursing their fate, they *prayed* to God. And instead of complaining, they *sang praises*. Nor was this a private time of worship, for the other *prisoners heard them*. [See question #4, page 328.]

PRAYING DURING A CRISIS

One foggy day, Amber Scott was sitting in her car at a railroad crossing, waiting for a train to pass. Suddenly, a truck rear-ended her car, shoving it under a freight car in the middle of the train. The engineer was unaware of what had happened and did not stop.

Scott's car was caught by the train and dragged down the tracks. During the terrifying, seven-minute ride that followed, she called 911 on her cell phone. Her call was broken off, however, because the roar of the train made it impossible for the dispatcher to hear Scott's voice. So she called her mother, but that call was broken off as well.

Scott realized that she had one other resource at her disposal: she prayed. She later said, "I prayed to the Lord all the way down the track." At the end of the ordeal, her car was "totaled"; but she escaped with only minor injuries.

When Paul and Silas were arrested and imprisoned in Philippi, their response was the same as Amber Scott's: they prayed—and they sang hymns as well! As it turned out, they did not escape with "minor injuries," since they had been beaten with "many stripes." Nevertheless, they knew where to turn for strength and help. The result was that God rescued them and that others were influenced by their faith.

The world is watching how we Christians deal with adversity. May our actions be a testimony to our faith.   —C. R. B.

B. Sudden Earthquake (v. 26)

26. And suddenly there was a great earthquake, so that the foundations of the prison were shaken: and immediately all the doors were opened, and every one's bands were loosed.

The other prisoners may have thought their new "guests" a bit strange, but the things that soon began to happen were even stranger! *Suddenly there was a great earthquake*. With the doors of the cells *opened* and the restraining *bands*, or chains, broken, the prisoners could have escaped easily.

C. Troubled Jailer (vv. 27-30)

27. And the keeper of the prison awaking out of his sleep, and seeing the prison doors open, he drew out his sword, and would have killed himself, supposing that the prisoners had been fled.

The *keeper of the prison* had one main job—to "keep" the *prisoners* in custody. If they were to escape, it would mean his life for theirs. Assuming that the prisoners had used the earthquake as their opportunity to flee, this jailer was certain that suicide would be less painful than the sentence that his superiors would carry out on him.

28. But Paul cried with a loud voice, saying, Do thyself no harm: for we are all here.

If the jailer could not see the prisoners, how did *Paul* know what the jailer was about to do? Was it darker in the cell so that the prisoners could see the jailer but he could not see them? Did he give a cry of despair, announcing his lethal intentions? Did God reveal to Paul what the jailer was about to do? We do not know the answers, but we do know that Paul *cried* out from the darkness and assured the jailer that no one had fled.

29, 30. Then he called for a light, and sprang in, and came trembling, and fell down before Paul and Silas, and brought them out, and said, Sirs, what must I do to be saved?

How to Say It

AEGEAN. Ay-*jee*-un.
ANTIOCH. *An*-tee-ock.
BARNABAS. *Bar*-nuh-bus.
BITHYNIA. Bih-*thin*-ee-uh.
CHRYSOSTOM. *Krih*-suss-tum or Krih-*sahss*-tum.
CORINTH. *Cor*-inth.
LYDIA. *Lid*-ee-uh.
LYSTRA. *Liss*-truh.
MACEDONIA. Mass-eh-*doe*-nee-uh.
MYSIA. *Mish*-ee-uh.
NEAPOLIS. Nee-*ap*-o-lis.
PHILIPPI. Fih-*lip*-pie or *Fill*-ih-pie.
PHILIPPIAN. Fih-*lip*-ee-un.
SAMOTHRACIA. Sam-o-*thray*-shuh.
THESSALONICA. Thess-uh-low-*nye*-kuh (strong accent on *nye*).
THYATIRA. *Thy*-uh-*tie*-ruh (strong accent on *tie*).
TROAS. *Tro*-az.

Perhaps the jailer had heard about Paul and Silas or had even heard them speak prior to their arrest. Apparently he knew Paul and Silas were preaching a message of salvation. Now deeply distressed over the crisis confronting him, he turned to Paul and Silas for help: "I have heard you talking about salvation—*what must I do to be saved?*"

D. Joyful Household (vv. 31-33)

31. And they said, Believe on the Lord Jesus Christ, and thou shalt be saved, and thy house.

Paul and Silas gave a short answer that required a longer explanation. The next verse tells us about that.

32. And they spake unto him the word of the Lord, and to all that were in his house.

Paul and Silas continued to teach *the word of the Lord* to both the jailer and *his house* (servants who lived with him or members of his family or both). They explained who the Lord Jesus Christ is and what believing in Him involves.

33. And he took them the same hour of the night, and washed their stripes; and was baptized, he and all his, straightway.

The jailer demonstrated his gratitude for how Paul and Silas had saved his life, both in a physical and in a spiritual sense. He *washed their stripes*, cleaning the wounds that had been caused by the earlier beating. Then *straightway* (without any delay) the believing household was taken to a place where they could be buried and raised with Christ in baptism. John Chrysostom, one of the outstanding preachers of early church history, wrote of the Philippian jailer: "He washed and was washed. He washed them from their stripes, and he himself was washed from his sins." [See question #5, page 328.]

Conclusion

A. A Changed Family

The jailer did not neglect his duty when he took Paul and Silas to his house, where he could care for their wounds. They were still in his custody—just not in the prison. It was the city officials who had neglected their duty (Acts 16:35-40).

We are told that the jailer "rejoiced, believing in God with all his house" (v. 34). Undoubtedly Heaven rejoiced as well (Luke 15:7). Everything in a household changes when those within it are "in Christ"—when He is recognized as the true Head of that home. Those in Philippi who saw the jailer the next day noticed a different man.

B. An Enlarged Family

Lydia was already a God-fearer before she became a Christian. She was also a successful businesswoman. She provided a living for those employees within her "household." She likely had a rather large sphere of influence.

When Lydia became a Christian, she expressed her newfound faith by granting the missionaries the hospitality of her home. She had become part of a new and different kind of household—the "household of faith" (Galatians 6:10).

When we become "in Christ," we join a worldwide fellowship of brothers and sisters. Our family becomes larger.

C. A Family of New Individuals

Whatever happened to the fortune-telling girl in Philippi after the spirit of divination was cast out of her? It requires an assumption for us to say that she became part of the church in Philippi, but some believe that she was. She knew something about Jesus, even when she was telling fortunes. Perhaps she continued to learn of Him after being set free from the control of the evil spirit.

Paul later wrote to the church that would soon be established south of Philippi (in Corinth), "Therefore if any man be in Christ, he is a new creature: old things are passed away; behold, all things are become new" (2 Corinthians 5:17). When we are in Christ, we are part of a family of forgiven individuals who, by God's Spirit, begin living the lives of new people.

D. Prayer

Having considered, Father, how Paul and his companions responded to Your call, we ask that You would reinforce our determination to respond—quickly and decisively—to the needs in our sin-scarred world. In Jesus' name. Amen.

E. Thought to Remember

"And after he had seen the vision, immediately we endeavored to go" (Acts 16:10).

Home Daily Bible Readings

Monday, May 14—Paul's Vision About Macedonia (Acts 16:6-10)

Tuesday, May 15—In Philippi: The Conversion of Lydia (Acts 16:11-15)

Wednesday, May 16—Paul and Silas in Prison (Acts 16:16-24)

Thursday, May 17—Songs at Midnight (Acts 16:25-29)

Friday, May 18—The Message of Salvation (Acts 16:30-34)

Saturday, May 19—An Invitation to Abundant Life (Isaiah 55:1-11)

Sunday, May 20—Public Exoneration (Acts 16:35-40)

Learning by Doing

This page contains an alternate lesson plan emphasizing learning activities.
Classes desiring such student involvement will find these suggestions helpful.

Learning Goals

After participating in this lesson, each student will be able to:

1. Give the significant details of the conversions of Lydia and the jailer in Philippi.

2. Tell how these incidents demonstrate the importance of presenting the gospel in a manner that is sensitive to people's needs.

3. Pray for courage and sensitivity in presenting Christ to someone this week.

Into the Lesson

Open today's class period with one of the following activities.

Sing a Hymn

Sing a hymn that describes the desire of Paul's heart evidenced in today's lesson. A good choice is "I'll Go Where You Want Me to Go." Provide copies for all members or project the words on a screen or wall where everyone can see them. (This hymn is in the public domain. If you choose another, be sure it is also in the public domain or that you have permission from the copyright holder to copy it.) Sing through all stanzas of the hymn. Then discuss the words with your class.

Make the transition to the Bible study by saying, "This hymn describes a commitment to share God's message wherever He wants us to go. Our lesson today finds Paul searching for his next ministry location and following God's leading."

Map Study

Ask a small group to trace the travels of Paul in Acts 16 on a map of the Mediterranean world. Be prepared to share the results with the entire class. Maps are available at most Christian bookstores. The locations mentioned in Acts 16 are listed below, but note that Paul did not visit each of these sites. Use your Bible to note which ones he actually visited and what is said about the locations on the list that Paul did not visit.

Cities: Derbe, Lystra, Iconium, Troas, Neapolis, Philippi, and Thyatira.

Larger Regions: Phrygia, Galatia, Asia, Mysia, Bithynia, Macedonia, and Samothracia.

Into the Word

If your class has both men and women, you may want to divide them into two groups. Ask the women to study Acts 16:9-15 and the men to study Acts 16:16-33. As they study, have them look for information that could be used if they were assigned to introduce Lydia (or the Philippian jailer) as the speaker for a women's (men's) retreat. They should include family, occupation/business, how she (he) became a Christian, and the impact the gospel has made in her (his) life.

Into Life

Paul and his companions went looking for people like Lydia. Lydia was a religious woman who was open, ready, and receptive to the gospel message they had to offer. Have each of the learners select a partner to go with him or her (as Paul did). Brainstorm for a list of people who might be open to listening to the gospel. Then say, "Choose one person whom you and your partner will go to see this week. Develop a plan for how you and your partner will share the gospel with this person. Choose a method from this list that you will use: invite the person to a church event (worship service, Bible study, or other), share your personal testimony, give the person a Christian tract, write a witnessing letter, share a meal with the person, and your better idea!"

In contrast to Lydia, whom Paul went seeking, the jailer in Acts 16 was a person whom God brought into Paul's life. Often we are unprepared to strike up a conversation with such people. Have your class consider each of these statements and check any that might be good to use:

1. "I'll bet it's been a long time since someone invited you to a Bible study. How long has it been?"

2. "I find that our preacher's messages are easy to listen to and have practical application to my life. Would you like to go with me to church next Sunday?"

3. "I'm supposed to talk to someone about the good news of Jesus for a class I'm in at church. Could I talk to you for a few minutes?"

4. "I am really enjoying our Bible study at church. Would you like to go with me next week?"

5. "Did you know that you can know for sure that you are going to Heaven?"

6. "If someone were to ask you, 'What must I do to be saved?' what would you tell them?" (The directions for these activities are included in the student quarterly, *Adult Bible Class*.)

Let's Talk It Over

The questions on this page are designed to encourage review of the lesson Scriptures and to promote discussion of the lesson by the class. The answers provided are only discussion starters. Let your class talk it over from there.

1. We do not expect a vision to direct us to a particular individual, family, or other group with the gospel. What are some ways in which we receive our "Macedonian call"?

One of the most obvious ways is a person's or family's visiting the services of our church. This may be evidence of a spiritual hunger that we should be eager to satisfy. Also, there are times when non-Christian friends and acquaintances will ask us to pray for them. We can promise to do that, and we can also strive to help them know the One to whom we pray. Another Macedonian call may come when someone we know faces a severe crisis. A death in the family, a serious illness, the loss of a job, the break-up of a marriage, and other such crises can soften a person's heart and make it receptive to the gospel. We must be there at such times.

2. The pronoun *we* in verse 10 indicates that Luke, the author of Acts, joined Paul's team. How important is building a team to the success of Christian ministries? How do you know when to enlist help and when to do the job yourself?

The descriptions of the church as a body illustrate the need for teamwork. Just as the mission of the entire church requires the varied gifts and talents of a variety of members, so do the missions of each ministry group. Jesus Himself enlisted twelve special helpers in His own ministry, and we do well to follow His example.

Whenever we find people capable of helping in a ministry is the right time to enlist help. Of course, we do not want to take people away from other ministries for which they are better suited or saddle individuals with too many ministry responsibilities. But every Christian should be involved in some ministry effort. As people come to the Lord, and as we assess their ability to serve in a particular ministry, they ought to be challenged to get involved.

3. The lesson writer says, "Whatever is accomplished by the efforts of faithful Christian workers is considered the Lord's work." What significance does that add to what you do for the Lord?

If what we do for the Lord is actually the Lord working through us (see Philippians 1:6; 2:13), then what an exciting thing it is to serve the Lord! As amazing as the Lord's own ministry

was, full of miracles and awe-inspiring messages, Jesus said His followers would do "greater works than these" (John 14:12). We are the heirs of that promise, as God works in us to do even greater works than Jesus did in His earthly ministry. Since He has died and been resurrected, He now offers eternal life to those who believe in Him (John 3:16). And we are the instruments of that ministry (Romans 10:14; 2 Corinthians 5:18, 20).

4. Many believers—and not a few unbelievers—pray when confronted with a crisis. What does it take to be able to sing praises as Paul and Silas did in the Philippian jail? How quick are you to praise God in the midst of a crisis?

One might say that Paul and Silas had an advantage over us. They were clearly suffering for their faith. They, like the disciples in Jerusalem in the earliest days of the church, were "rejoicing that they were counted worthy to suffer shame for his name" (Acts 5:41). Our crises are not always so clearly an issue of faith. We may not associate our suffering with the name of Jesus.

Still, we ought to give God praise. James said we should "count it all joy" when we have trials, because God will use those experiences to develop patience in us (James 1:2-4). If we face our trials with faith and even joy, then we will also be a witness to others, just as Paul and Silas were to the other prisoners and to the jailer.

5. Both Lydia and the jailer expressed some form of Christian grace immediately upon their conversions. Lydia provided the missionaries a place to stay, and the jailer treated their wounds. How important are such behaviors in the life of a new Christian? Why?

John the Baptist warned his hearers to "bring forth . . . fruits meet for repentance" (Matthew 3:8). While such works are not instrumental in salvation, they are an indication of the genuineness of one's repentance. If one who is in Christ is a "new creature" (2 Corinthians 5:17), then he or she ought to demonstrate a "newness of life" (Romans 6:4). Caring for others within the body is certainly one means of living out the new life a believer has in Christ. Such concern directed at those outside the church can also be a powerful witness to them and may be the instrument God uses to draw them to the cross of Christ as well.

Serving With Humility

DEVOTIONAL READING: 1 Corinthians 15:1-11.

BACKGROUND SCRIPTURE: Acts 20:13-38.

PRINTED TEXT: Acts 20:17-32.

Acts 20:17-32

17 And from Miletus he sent to Ephesus, and called the elders of the church.

18 And when they were come to him, he said unto them, Ye know, from the first day that I came into Asia, after what manner I have been with you at all seasons,

19 Serving the Lord with all humility of mind, and with many tears, and temptations, which befell me by the lying in wait of the Jews:

20 And how I kept back nothing that was profitable unto you, but have showed you, and have taught you publicly, and from house to house,

21 Testifying both to the Jews, and also to the Greeks, repentance toward God, and faith toward our Lord Jesus Christ.

22 And now, behold, I go bound in the spirit unto Jerusalem, not knowing the things that shall befall me there:

23 Save that the Holy Ghost witnesseth in every city, saying that bonds and afflictions abide me.

24 But none of these things move me, neither count I my life dear unto myself, so that I might finish my course with joy, and the ministry, which I have received of the Lord Jesus, to testify the gospel of the grace of God.

25 And now, behold, I know that ye all, among whom I have gone preaching the kingdom of God, shall see my face no more.

26 Wherefore I take you to record this day, that I am pure from the blood of all men.

27 For I have not shunned to declare unto you all the counsel of God.

28 Take heed therefore unto yourselves, and to all the flock, over the which the Holy Ghost hath made you overseers, to feed the church of God, which he hath purchased with his own blood.

29 For I know this, that after my departing shall grievous wolves enter in among you, not sparing the flock.

30 Also of your own selves shall men arise, speaking perverse things, to draw away disciples after them.

31 Therefore watch, and remember, that by the space of three years I ceased not to warn every one night and day with tears.

32 And now, brethren, I commend you to God, and to the word of his grace, which is able to build you up, and to give you an inheritance among all them which are sanctified.

GOLDEN TEXT: None of these things move me, neither count I my life dear unto myself, so that I might finish my course with joy, and the ministry, which I have received of the Lord Jesus, to testify the gospel of the grace of God.—Acts 20:24.

Continuing Jesus' Work
Unit 3: Spreading the Gospel Into All the World
(Lessons 9-13)

Lesson Aims

After this lesson a student should be able to:

1. Summarize Paul's farewell speech and exhortation to the Ephesian elders.

2. Tell what this passage says about the responsibilities of leaders in the local church.

3. Plan a way to express encouragement to a leader in the church and purpose to do so more frequently.

Lesson Outline

INTRODUCTION
  A. Take Heed to Yourselves
  B. Take Heed to the Flock
  C. Lesson Background
I. PAUL'S EXAMPLE (Acts 20:17-27)
  A. Consistent in Lifestyle (vv. 17, 18)
  B. Determined in Service (v. 19)
  C. Faithful in Teaching (vv. 20, 21)
  D. Undaunted by Suffering (vv. 22-24)
  E. Without Regrets (vv. 25-27)
    Leading by Doing
II. PAUL'S EXHORTATION (Acts 20:28-32)
  A. A Charge (v. 28)
  B. A Warning (vv. 29-31)
  C A Trust (v. 32)
    "Win One for the Gipper"
CONCLUSION
  A. Born to Lead
  B. Built to Lead
  C. Prayer
  D. Thought to Remember

Introduction

A. Take Heed to Yourselves

Leadership in the Lord's church is not (and never has been) easy. No one ever said that it would be. Good leaders will not complain when the going gets tough, for they are aware that such times are unavoidable. They keep modeling faith. They keep growing. They keep caring. They determine to lead by loving, not lording; by modeling, not mandating; and by being servants, not sovereigns.

Good leaders do not take a defensive posture that assumes "those people in the pews don't know what they're talking about." Instead, they ask, "How can we serve more effectively and communicate our decisions and dreams more clearly?" They may go on a devotional retreat and pray. They may search the Scriptures together, reminding themselves of the divinely mandated dimensions of their task. They may divide into groups that study issues such as shepherding, peacemaking, and overseeing; then return to the larger group with suggested plans of action.

Such efforts as these can be part of the efforts that leaders make to "take heed" to themselves. Their primary concern should be this: what can we do to be God's men and God's leaders over the flock that He has entrusted to our care?

B. Take Heed to the Flock

Most every congregation has people who are hurting. Some are hurting because of the self-inflicted pain of their sin. Some are hurting through no fault of their own; the sin of others has wrought havoc in their lives. Some hurt and don't know why. Some react to their hurt by trying to inflict pain on someone else.

Both those who are hurt and those who are hurting others need help—divine help and the help of mature Christians. The church's leaders are to be at the forefront of those who want to make a difference in such individuals' lives. Elders are to "take heed" to the flock—the bleating, confused, vulnerable, sometimes stubborn flock—whom God loves and wants to keep in His fold. Their model is the Good Shepherd, who laid down His life for His sheep (John 10:15).

C. Lesson Background

At one point Paul had desired to go into the province of Asia, where Ephesus was located, and preach the gospel. However, the Holy Spirit had forbidden him to do so (Acts 16:6). Shortly afterward, Paul saw a vision of a man from Macedonia pleading with him to come there. Paul's response to that vision was the beginning of his second missionary journey (described in Acts 16:11—18:22). Last week's lesson was taken from Paul's ministry in Philippi, which was his first preaching stop in Macedonia.

Paul did not forget about the needs in Asia. At the conclusion of his second missionary journey he finally arrived there (Acts 18:18-21). There he left Priscilla and Aquila until he himself could return, which he did during his third missionary journey (Acts 19:1). He spent three years there (Acts 20:31), preaching and teaching, establishing a church, and developing capable leadership. Eventually Paul had to leave Ephesus when his evangelistic success threatened the local idol makers and caused a near riot (Acts 19:23-40).

However, Paul had done his work well; a healthy church was firmly in place, and a group of leaders had been set apart to guide it. But Paul's hasty departure meant that some of his work had gone undone. Returning from his third journey, Paul determined to sail past Ephesus in order to reach Jerusalem by the celebration of Pentecost (Acts 20:16). (Perhaps the situation was still too tense in Ephesus, and Paul thought it better not to go back in person.)

Still, Paul was quite concerned about the church in Ephesus. When the ship on which he was traveling stopped at Miletus (about thirty miles south of Ephesus), Paul determined that he would have enough time to send for the elders of the church and meet with them. He reminded these men of what they had been taught before, called their attention to the kind of loving leadership that he had modeled, warned them of threats to their flock, and encouraged them to remain faithful. His words continue to speak powerfully to leaders in Christ's church today.

I. Paul's Example
(Acts 20:17-27)

A. Consistent in Lifestyle (vv. 17, 18)

17. And from Miletus he sent to Ephesus, and called the elders of the church.

As noted above, Paul had chosen to bypass *Ephesus* on his way to Jerusalem. But once the ship reached the harbor at *Miletus*, he realized that he would have time to contact the *elders of the church* in Ephesus and arrange a meeting. (Perhaps the ship had to remain at Miletus a while for repairs or loading.) [See question #1, page 336.]

18. And when they were come to him, he said unto them, Ye know, from the first day that I

Home Daily Bible Readings

Monday, May 21—Paul in Athens (Acts 17:16-34)

Tuesday, May 22—Paul in Corinth (Acts 18:1-11)

Wednesday, May 23—Paul in Ephesus (Acts 19:1-10)

Thursday, May 24—Paul in Macedonia and Greece (Acts 20:1-6)

Friday, May 25—Paul in Troas and Miletus (Acts 20:7-16)

Saturday, May 26—Paul Speaks to the Ephesian Elders (Acts 20:17-24)

Sunday, May 27—Paul's Summary and Farewell (Acts 20:25-38)

came into Asia, after what manner I have been with you at all seasons.

Paul began his remarks to the elders by reminding them of the foundation on which he had built his ministry with them. He had led by an example that began *from the first day* that he arrived in the province of *Asia*. The fact that Paul could say *ye know* indicates that he had nothing to hide from these men. His conduct gave him no reason to be ashamed. Paul's example had remained intact *at all seasons*: during both good times and times of pressure and persecution, his commitment to Christ never wavered. This was the kind of leadership that he had modeled for these elders and that he wanted them to demonstrate. Particularly during the difficult days that lay ahead (vv. 29, 30), they would need to be men of faith, wisdom, and service. [See question #2, page 336.]

B. Determined in Service (v. 19)

19. Serving the Lord with all humility of mind, and with many tears, and temptations, which befell me by the laying in wait of the Jews.

Paul had a strong emotional attachment to the church of Ephesus, as noted by his reference to *many tears* (see also v. 31). No doubt that attachment helped to strengthen his resolve to minister to the Ephesians in spite of the obstacles he faced. We have already noted the opposition that arose from the silversmiths, recorded in Acts 19:23-41. Here we see that there was in Ephesus, as in many other cities, opposition from *the Jews* as well.

C. Faithful in Teaching (vv. 20, 21)

20. And how I kept back nothing that was profitable unto you, but have showed you, and have taught you publicly, and from house to house.

Once again, Paul emphasized the open and aboveboard nature of his ministry: he *kept back nothing*. He shared with the Ephesians everything he knew about Christ and anything that would be *profitable* to their walk with Him and their witness for Him.

Publicly, and from house to house is a good teaching pattern for church leaders in any era. If we are being faithful to Jesus' Great Commission to teach, baptize, and teach (Matthew 28:19, 20), then teaching opportunities—both in public settings and in the privacy of people's homes—will present themselves regularly. An elder should be able to teach in both settings.

21. Testifying both to the Jews, and also to the Greeks, repentance toward God, and faith toward our Lord Jesus Christ.

The pattern of Paul's evangelistic outreach was "to the Jew first, and also to the Greek" (Romans 1:16). Paul and his companions preached to *Jews* first when they entered a city, then shared with *Greeks* (Gentiles) as other doors opened.

Repentance toward God expresses what repentance really means. In true repentance there is sorrow for sin and the confession of one's guilt before God. But what makes it true *repentance* is the turning around *toward God*—the change of direction—in one's life. Before I am a Christian, I take my own advice and go my own way. I am my own boss. When I become a Christian, Jesus is my boss. Whereas I formerly answered to myself and no one else, I now answer to God.

In the same way, *faith* is described as being *toward our Lord Jesus Christ*. Our faith has meaning and substance. As John stated it in the purpose for writing his Gospel: "that ye might believe that Jesus is the Christ, the Son of God; and that believing ye might have life through his name" (John 20:31).

D. Undaunted by Suffering (vv. 22-24)

22. And now, behold, I go bound in the spirit unto Jerusalem, not knowing the things that shall befall me there.

Paul was headed for *Jerusalem, not knowing the things* that he would face. True, there were those present in Jerusalem who were fiercely hostile to the gospel. But Paul wanted to bring the financial assistance that various churches had collected to help the poverty-stricken believers in that city (1 Corinthians 16:1-4; 2 Corinthians 9:1-5, 12-14).

The phrase *bound in the spirit* may be similar to Paul's references to being the Lord's "prisoner" (Ephesians 3:1; 4:1; 2 Timothy 1:8; Philemon 1, 9). The Holy Spirit had already revealed to him that bonds awaited him (see v. 23), so he might well say that he was already bound—already a prisoner—in spirit (or in the *Spirit*, as in some translations). Or we might take the word *bound* to signify Paul's personal compulsion in his own spirit to go to Jerusalem. (We might say he was "bound and determined" to go.) Either way, we see the urgency Paul felt about going on to Jerusalem.

"Finish the Race . . ."

"Complete the task the Lord Jesus has given."

Today's visual illustrates verse 24 of the text and challenges the viewer to take the same attitude as Paul had toward ministry.

Visual for lesson 13

23. Save that the Holy Ghost witnesseth in every city, saying that bonds and afflictions abide me.

Paul was certain that he would experience opposition and even *bonds* in Jerusalem. Later this was confirmed through a prophetic message from Agabus (Acts 21:10, 11). (The word *abide* in this verse means "await.")

24. But none of these things move me, neither count I my life dear unto myself, so that I might finish my course with joy, and the ministry, which I have received of the Lord Jesus, to testify the gospel of the grace of God.

Most important to Paul—more important to him than his personal welfare or safety—was his *ministry*. He had been assigned the introduction of *the gospel of the grace of God* to the Gentiles. Like a marathon runner, Paul wanted to *finish* his *course* in triumph. Such an achievement would give him great *joy*. [See question #3, page 336.]

Did Paul finish the course as he planned? The answer is clear from the final chapter of 2 Timothy: "I have fought a good fight, I have finished my course, I have kept the faith" (2 Timothy 4:7).

E. Without Regrets (vv. 25-27)

25. And now, behold, I know that ye all, among whom I have gone preaching the kingdom of God, shall see my face no more.

Paul's statement that the Ephesian elders would *see* his *face no more* raises a question, in light of the fact that it appears Paul did return to Ephesus at a later time (see 1 Timothy 1:3). Perhaps Paul was simply stating what he believed to be true at this point; in other instances, he made plans that he then had to change for some reason (2 Corinthians 1:15, 16, 23).

26, 27. Wherefore I take you to record this day, that I am pure from the blood of all men. For I have not shunned to declare unto you all the counsel of God.

Those in Ephesus and "all they which dwelt in Asia" had "heard the word of the Lord Jesus" (Acts 19:10). Anyone who rejected the gospel had only himself to blame; his *blood* would be upon his own head. Paul had done his job.

LEADING BY DOING

James Russell Wiggins thinks retirement is a waste of labor and talent. Of people in their sixties who are still sound in mind and body, but who are relaxing in retirement communities, he asks, "How can a society support such idleness?"

Note that Wiggins is not some young fellow worrying about "old folks" getting so many Social Security benefits that the system may bankrupt itself long before *he* gets to retirement age. On the contrary, when Wiggins made those comments, he was ninety-five years old and still editing the *Ellsworth American*, a weekly newspaper in the town of Ellsworth, Maine. It's a job he's been doing since 1922! This gentleman is living up to the advice he gives to others.

The apostle Paul is someone else who lived up to the advice he gave. When the elders of the church at Ephesus came to meet him at Miletus, Paul gave them some advice about how they should conduct themselves as leaders of God's people. But this was not a case of "Do as I say, not as I do." He reminded these men of the character of his own life and leadership. He had given himself in service and faithfully declared "all the counsel of God" to all who would listen.

It was a good example for that time, and it is for ours.   —C. R. B.

II. Paul's Exhortation
(Acts 20:28-32)
A. A Charge (v. 28)

28. Take heed therefore unto yourselves, and to all the flock, over the which the Holy Ghost hath made you overseers, to feed the church of God, which he hath purchased with his own blood.

Here Paul's words provide a description of the purpose of leadership in the Lord's church. Leaders must first *take heed . . . unto* themselves. Paul gave similar counsel to Timothy: "Take heed unto thyself, and unto the doctrine; continue in them: for in doing this thou shalt both save thyself, and them that hear thee" (1 Timothy 4:16). The leader's commitment to his own spiritual development determines how far and how well he will be able to lead others.

Paul also describes the elders of the church as *overseers* of *the flock*. The word for *overseer(s)* is rendered in other places as "bishop(s)" in the *King James Version* (Philippians 1:1; 1 Timothy 3:1; Titus 1:7). In later usage a bishop came to designate an official who had authority over a group of churches. But in the New Testament there was a plurality of bishops over each congregation, not one bishop over several congregations.

The task of oversight involves the duty to *feed the church of God*. The word translated *feed* literally means "to shepherd." Biblical oversight is not expressed primarily through decision-making or exerting authority in a dictatorial manner. Peter tells elders to "feed [i.e., shepherd] the flock of God . . . taking the oversight thereof, not by constraint, but willingly; . . . neither as being lords over God's heritage, but being ensamples to the flock" (1 Peter 5:2, 3). Elders hold each other accountable; they meet the needs of their flock; they give responsible oversight to the direction of the church's ministries; they provide spiritual food by seeing that the Word of God is taught. After all, the church is not the elders'; it is *the church of God*. [See question #4, page 336.]

Paul then gives an additional reason for taking such special care of God's church: it has been *purchased with his own blood*. The Greek phrase can be translated, "the blood of His own," thus referring to the priceless sacrifice that Jesus made to obtain mankind's redemption from sin.

B. A Warning (vv. 29-31)

29. For I know this, that after my departing shall grievous wolves enter in among you, not sparing the flock.

The church is not exempt from attack by the devil and any whom he can use. In fact, he is constantly engaged in such activity! It is his intention to disrupt the church, to raise doubts in the minds of her members, and to put Christians at odds with each other. He will attack from outside the church, but often from the inside.

Paul's reference to *grievous wolves* calls to mind Jesus' warning about wolves "in sheep's clothing" (Matthew 7:15). It may seem hard to imagine that a church could fall prey to the influence of such forces after three years of constant, faithful teaching from an apostle (Acts 20:31). And yet, later portions of the New Testament indicate that this was so. Paul sent 1 Timothy (and probably 2 Timothy) to Ephesus, where Timothy was having to confront those whose doctrine was suspect (1 Timothy 1:3, 4). Some have suggested that the epistle of 1 John was sent to the churches of Asia, which would have included Ephesus. There we read of the influence of false teachers who were questioning whether Jesus came in the flesh (1 John 4:1-3). Finally, Jesus' words to the church in Ephesus (Revelation 2:1-7) indicate that it was being influenced by corrupting and disruptive elements. It is no surprise that Paul counseled these elders to "watch" (v. 31).

30. Also of your own selves shall men arise, speaking perverse things, to draw away disciples after them.

How to Say It

AGABUS. *Ag*-uh-bus.
AQUILA. *Ack*-wih-luh.
EPHESIANS. Ee-*fih*-zhuns.
EPHESUS. *Ef*-uh-sus.
MACEDONIA. Mass-eh-*doe*-nee-uh.
MILETUS. My-*lee*-tus.
PHILIPPI. Fih-*lip*-pie or *Fill*-ih-pie.
PRISCILLA. Prih-*sil*-uh.

Paul warned that the influences described in verse 29 would not come from outside the church; they would originate *of your own selves*. Sadly, it is sometimes true that the church is severely harmed by its *own*—by *men* who are interested in building a following rather than following Jesus. [See question #5, page 336.]

31. Therefore watch, and remember, that by the space of three years I ceased not to warn every one night and day with tears.

The depth of Paul's commitment to the believers in Ephesus is clear from these words. He poured both time (*night and day* for *three years*) and emotional involvement (*tears*) into their spiritual maturity. The "wolves" (v. 29) would have only their own selfish interests at heart.

C. A Trust (v. 32)

32. And now, brethren, I commend you to God, and to the word of his grace, which is able to build you up, and to give you an inheritance among all them which are sanctified.

Although Paul (the Ephesians' teacher, encourager, and model for leadership) was leaving these elders, he was not leaving them alone. He could still *commend* these men *to God, and to the word of his grace*. The apostolic instruction they had received would serve them well as a reliable guide in the face of future threats. Today we have these recorded in the New Testament Scriptures. By following them, we too can lay hold of the *inheritance* promised to all who faithfully serve Jesus.

"WIN ONE FOR THE GIPPER"

Perhaps the most famous plea in all of sports history is, "Win one for the Gipper." George Gipp played football for the University of Notre Dame. He was a "natural"—an outstanding athlete who became famous for leading his team to spectacular comeback victories over superior foes, sometimes playing exceptional football even with serious injuries.

Gipp played his last game during the 1920 season. Injured and sick with a fever, he came into a game against Northwestern for only one play and threw a fifty-five-yard touchdown pass. He died a few weeks later of pneumonia.

Eight years later, Notre Dame was playing a much stronger, undefeated Army team. At halftime neither team had scored. In the Notre Dame locker room, coach Knute Rockne said to his team, "Boys, I want to tell you a story." Then he related Gipp's deathbed conversation with him: "Sometime, Rock, when . . . things are going wrong and the breaks are beating the boys—tell them to go in there with all they've got and win just one for the Gipper." With the team sobbing,

Rockne said, "All right, boys. This is the game. Let's get one for the Gipper." Notre Dame won the game that day, 12-6.

Paul's final words to the elders of the church at Ephesus were words of encouragement. He had set the example. He knew that final victory would be theirs. It can be ours, too, if we are faithful to follow that example and serve Jesus. —C. R. B.

Conclusion

A. Born to Lead

We've all probably heard the term "born leader." There is certainly some measure of truth in that phrase. Some individuals possess a leadership personality that can be seen while they are still children. Their peers just naturally seem to follow them. Such individuals may lead well, or they may lead poorly. But they have an ability to convince and draw followers.

On the other hand, some very fine people never become leaders. They appear to lack that hard-to-define something that gains a following.

B. Built to Lead

It is incorrect, however, that only those born with certain instincts or a certain style of personality can lead. We can study the godly leaders of the Old and New Testaments and learn from the way they led. (We can also study bad examples and learn from them as well!) As we do so, we can seek to use the talents and abilities with which we are blessed to serve the Lord's church and to encourage others. In this way, many Christians "grow" into leadership positions. They are "built," not "born."

Any leader needs to keep in mind these words of Jesus: "For unto whomsoever much is given, of him shall be much required" (Luke 12:48). If you are a leader in the Lord's church, determine above all else to be a follower of Jesus.

C. Prayer

Father in Heaven, more than to be leaders we want to be *followers*—followers of Your Word, of Your Son, and of the path of service to which You point us. If we are presently serving as leaders in Your church, help us to do that with the courage, compassion, and humility that Paul displayed. We ask in the name of the Head of the church, amen.

D. Thought to Remember

Are you an elder, called to shepherd and oversee the flock of God (as the men from Ephesus in today's lesson)? Are you part of the flock? Each of us has the same responsibility: serve the Lord—faithfully, readily, and humbly!

Learning by Doing

This page contains an alternate lesson plan emphasizing learning activities.
Classes desiring such student involvement will find these suggestions helpful.

Learning Goals

After this lesson each student will be able to:

1. Summarize Paul's farewell speech and exhortation to the Ephesian elders.

2. Tell what this passage says about the responsibilities of leaders in the local church.

3. Plan a way to express encouragement to a leader in the church and purpose to do so more frequently.

Into the Lesson

Here is another chance to train and develop a new teacher! Probably there is someone in your class who has the potential of being a teacher. Ask that person to help you by preparing a brief lecture on the background material for today's lesson. Provide a copy of the commentary for this week. The lecture will need to cover in a summary fashion Paul's travels between Acts 16 and today's text in Acts 20. Help your prospective teacher have a successful experience. Offer help with content, especially with visuals. An outline in print or an overhead projection transparency would help any new teacher. Allow from three to five minutes for this part of the lesson. Be sure to follow up with a debriefing session, an evaluation of the lecture, and a thank-you note.

In addition to the activity above, or in place of it if time is short, have the following sentence written on a chalkboard in your room or on a poster prominently displayed: "What does it take to be a good leader?" If possible, arrange the chairs in small clusters of four to six. When the learners arrive, ask them to work in small groups to discuss this question. Have each group select someone to record and summarize the group's discussion and report to the whole class. Allow five to seven minutes for discussion; then ask for reports.

Into the Word

Ask a volunteer to read aloud Acts 20:17-32. Observe that this text and 1 Peter 5:1-4 are two of the most comprehensive descriptions of the office of elder, overseer, and shepherd (the three terms, or verb forms of the terms, are all used to describe the same group of men) in all of the New Testament. Assign a task force to compare these two passages by listing in two columns the teaching of each passage. The chart might begin something like this:

ACTS 20:17-32	1 PETER 5:1-4
All 3 terms used to describe the group	All 3 terms used to describe the group
The terms are all plural	The terms are all plural
Not because of greed	Not because of greed

Allow the task force to work while other groups of learners participate in the following activities. After ten or twelve minutes, call for reports from all groups.

Leadership Study Posters

Make three posters to use in studying Paul's teaching about leadership in Acts 20:17-32. Title the first poster, "COMMITMENT," the second, "CHARACTER," and the third, "CONDUCT." Assign a group and a recorder for each poster and provide a broad-tipped marker. As the group studies each verse, have the learners suggest words or phrases to be listed on each poster. A recorder can be selected to do the writing.

For instance, Paul's example is foundational in Acts 20:18, so the word *example* should go on the CONDUCT poster. *Serving with humility* goes on the CHARACTER poster, from verse 19. *Ready for persecution* is implied from verse 19 and should appear on the COMMITMENT poster. *Teaching publicly and in homes*, from verse 20, belongs on the CONDUCT poster.

Bible Dictionary

Adult Bible teachers have the responsibility not just to teach the Bible but also to teach their class members how to study the Bible for themselves. Borrow Bible dictionaries from your church library or your minister's study. Divide the class into small groups, and have each group research each of the following terms: elders (v. 17), church (v. 17), humility (v. 19), repentance (v. 21), faith (v. 21), grace (v. 24), gospel (v. 24), joy (v. 24), kingdom of God (v. 25), overseers (v. 28), and sanctified (v. 32).

Into Life

Our churches are filled with leaders who have served for years with too little appreciation or encouragement. Probably someone in your class has a great testimony of how an elder in the church has influenced his or her life. Ask such a person to give a short testimony of such a man's service. Encourage all your learners to write notes with similar messages to other leaders in the church.

Let's Talk It Over

The questions on this page are designed to encourage review of the lesson Scriptures and to promote discussion of the lesson by the class. The answers provided are only discussion starters. Let your class talk it over from there.

1. The elders of the church at Ephesus must have sacrificed time and money in order to meet with Paul at Miletus. What, if anything, can we learn from their example?

While Ephesus was not far from Miletus, it must have required a significant amount of time for the elders to make the round trip and to meet with Paul. If any of these men were day laborers, the economic impact of such a trip would have been significant. But they certainly must have regarded the sacrifice as worthwhile in that they gained spiritual insights and encouragement from Paul. Today's leaders—as well as anyone else involved in a ministry for the Lord—must also be willing to invest some time and money in seminars, workshops, reading material, and anything else that can strengthen them in their work.

2. Paul reminded the Ephesian elders of his manner of life while he was among them—his example. How important is one's example? Why?

It is easy to point out that a teacher's example must match his words in order to have credibility. But it is equally important that we all display an example of faithfulness—even those of us who do not consider themselves to be teachers.

Each of us has a certain amount of influence—perhaps on a young person, on a co-worker, or on someone else. And what attracts people, even more than what we say, is our lifestyle. Long after any particular thing we have said is forgotten, someone will remember a kindness shown—or a rude behavior. If we would lead others to Jesus, it will be by a consistent example of showing love.

3. Paul was determined to complete his ministry. What would it mean for you to "complete your ministry"? What prioritizing needs to be in place for you to do that?

For Paul this was a lifetime issue. He pursued his ministry all his life, in whatever circumstances he found himself. Ministry, or serving the Lord, should be a lifetime issue for each of us, as well. However, the specific ministry in which we serve may well change from time to time.

To complete such a ministry requires that we set goals. How will we know whether we have completed a ministry if we do not know what it is we wish to complete? Once goals are set, we can establish priorities and intermediate steps toward

completion. Then, if we want to move into a different area of service, we can do so with the satisfaction of having completed a valuable ministry rather than the frustration of just "growing tired" or "getting burnt out" in a particular position.

4. Paul urged the elders "to feed the church of God." How is that done today?

This question introduces several issues related to teaching the Word of God. One is who should teach. The elders cannot do it all. What role do they take in selecting or approving teachers?

A second issue is what is taught. New, inexperienced Christians need "milk" (1 Corinthians 3:1, 2; 1 Peter 2:2), which symbolizes the basic teachings of the Bible. As believers mature, they need meat or solid food (Hebrews 5:12-14). At this stage they should master deeper New Testament doctrines. And all along they must receive generous helpings of "the bread of life" (John 6:35), being kept in constant contact with the person, miracles, teachings, death, and resurrection of Jesus Christ. What role does the church leadership take in developing or approving graded curriculum?

Another issue concerns making sure that the teaching is received. Is it enough to establish Sunday school classes and small groups if less than half of the congregation takes advantage of these? What should—what can—church leaders do to feed the part of the flock that does not show up at regular "feeding times"?

5. The devil still seeks to undermine the church from within. What precautions can be taken to keep this from happening?

Are "wolves" trying to sneak in among the various flocks of God's people? It is possible that the devil may have his hand-picked agents infiltrating Bible-believing churches and endeavoring to sow as much false teaching in them as possible. But there is probably a greater danger when sincere but poorly taught members allow the devil to use them as his spokesmen. Remember that this happened to Peter (Matthew 16:21-23), and it can surely happen to believers today. Church members must be taught to recognize the devil's devious tactics, his twisting of the truth, and his outright lies. Every Christian ought to give diligence to knowing the truth of the Bible so he or she can easily recognize that which is false.

Summer Quarter, 2001

Division and Decline

Special Features

Lessons

Unit 1: A Kingdom Divided

Unit 2: Prophecies of Judgment

Unit 3: Decline and Fall

About These Lessons

"United we stand; divided we fall." We've all heard those words, and the truth of them seems apparent. Yet we still find ourselves choosing up sides and dividing ourselves one from another. This series of lessons warns against such division. When the nation of Israel became two nations, both were weaker, and both eventually collapsed. Let the church heed the warning.

Jun 3

Jun 10

Jun 17

Jun 24

Jul 1

Jul 8

Jul 15

Jul 22

Jul 29

Aug 5

Aug 12

Aug 19

Aug 26

Quarterly Quiz

The questions on this page may be used in several ways: as a pretest at the beginning of the quarter; as a review at the end of the quarter; or as a review after each lesson. The questions are based on the Scripture text of each lesson (King James Version). ***The answers are on page 340.***

Lesson 1

1. Rehoboam asked for a period of _____ _____ before he responded to the people's request. (two days, three days, or seven days?) *1 Kings 12:5*
2. Rehoboam first consulted the older men who served with his father, _____. *1 Kings 12:6*
3. The younger men counseled Rehoboam to be a servant to the people whom he would rule. T/F *1 Kings 12:10, 11*

Lesson 2

1. To whom did Elijah say that it would not rain except by Elijah's word? *1 Kings 17:1*
2. God told Elijah to hide by the brook called _____. *1 Kings 17:3*
3. Because of God's provision for the widow, her barrel of _____ and her cruse of _____ never ran out. *1 Kings 17:16*

Lesson 3

1. Where did Elijah and the prophets of Baal gather? *1 Kings 18:20*
2. How many prophets of Baal were present? *1 Kings 18:22*
3. How many stones did Elijah use to rebuild the altar of the Lord? *1 Kings 18:31*

Lesson 4

1. King Ahab asked Micaiah about going into battle at a certain city. Which one? *1 Kings 22:15*
2. Which king of Judah was with Ahab on this occasion? *1 Kings 22:18*

Lesson 5

1. Amos condemned the sins of Judah, but he said nothing about Israel's sins. T/F *Amos 2:6*
2. Amos accused the people of Israel of selling the _____ for silver and the _____ for a pair of shoes. *Amos 2:6*

Lesson 6

1. Amos compared the day of the Lord with a man running from a _____, then meeting a _____. *Amos 5:19*
2. Amos said, "Let _____ run down as waters, and _____ as a mighty stream." *Amos 5:24*

Lesson 7

1. What was the name of Hosea's wayward wife? *Hosea 1:3*

2. What were the names of her three children, who illustrated God's dealings with Israel? *Hosea 1:4, 6, 9*

Lesson 8

1. Hosea described the time when God called His "son" Israel out of _____. *Hosea 11:1*
2. Hosea predicted that the _____ would rule God's people because they refused to return to Him. (Egyptian, Assyrian, or Babylonian?) *Hosea 11:5*

Lesson 9

1. Micah told his hearers that the Lord had brought them out of Egypt and "sent before" them three individuals. Who were they? *Micah 6:4*
2. Micah also told of what _____ king of Moab had wanted to do to Israel and how _____ had answered him. *Micah 6:5*
3. What three things did Micah say the Lord requires? *Micah 6:8*

Lesson 10

1. Isaiah saw his vision of the Lord in the year of whose death? *Isaiah 6:1*
2. One of the seraphim approached Isaiah with something in his hand. What was it? *Isaiah 6:6*
3. What question did Isaiah hear the Lord ask? What answer did Isaiah give? *Isaiah 6:8*

Lesson 11

1. During the reign of Ahaz, two kings "went up toward Jerusalem to war against it." Who were they? *Isaiah 7:1*
2. Who said, "I will not ask, neither will I tempt the Lord"? *Isaiah 7:12*
3. Isaiah promised that the virgin's son would be called _____. *Isaiah 7:14*

Lesson 12

1. Isaiah told a story of a _____ planted in a fruitful hill. (garden, tree, or vineyard?) *Isaiah 5:1*
2. Isaiah described those who "rise up early in the morning" to follow _____ _____. *Isaiah 5:11*

Lesson 13

1. In the ninth year of King Hoshea the king of Assyria captured _____. (Damascus, Jerusalem, or Samaria?) *2 Kings 17:6*
2. God sent His servants the _____ to urge His people to turn from evil. *2 Kings 17:13*

Lessons That Must Be Learned

by John W. Wade

MOST OF US LOOK FORWARD to summer as a time of vacations—at the beach, in the mountains, or with family and friends in some other part of the country or the world. As a result we are not very happy with anything that hinders or restricts our anticipated pleasures. We try to avoid any activities that are too "serious." Thus we may wonder why this quarter's lessons address such a somber issue as the division and decline of God's people—the nations of Israel and Judah. The obvious answer is that we need very much to learn about this portion of the past because there are some clear and sobering parallels between that ancient civilization and our own.

Most of your students are aware that our civilization has many problems, the majority of which are of our own making. Many agencies, public and private, are trying to address some of these problems, and their efforts are commendable. These efforts alone, however, cannot offer real solutions. While the reason for this is obvious, many are unwilling to face it. It is simply this: the source of most of our problems lies deeply imbedded in our hearts. Like the prophet Isaiah, we are a people of "unclean lips," dwelling "in the midst of a people of unclean lips" (Isaiah 6:5). Until we recognize this, even our best, most well-intentioned efforts at changing the world will be futile.

"He who does not learn from history," the American philosopher George Santayana once observed, "is condemned to repeat it." This is not to say that history is a series of cycles, each of which repeats itself in every detail. But it does recognize that similar actions and behaviors often lead to similar results. That is the reason that the study of Old Testament history can be of great benefit in every age. In fact, that is the reason these ancient records have been preserved: "Now all these things happened unto them for ensamples: and they are written for our admonition, upon whom the ends of the world are come" (1 Corinthians 10:11).

Unit 1: A Kingdom Divided

Lesson 1 deals with the controversy that led to the tragic division of God's people into two nations—Israel to the north and Judah to the south. The differences that led to this division had been simmering beneath the surface for some time, but the arrogant, self-centered Rehoboam proved to be the catalyst that brought them to an explo-

sive climax. Had a wiser, humbler man come to the throne at the time, the division might have been avoided—or at least delayed, and some of the issues resolved.

Lesson 2 introduces us to the prophet Elijah, whose ministry begins quite suddenly. In many respects Elijah epitomizes the prophetic ministry of the Old Testament, for he was a courageous man who spoke out against evil without concern for his personal safety.

Lesson 3 focuses on Elijah's dramatic confrontation with the prophets of Baal on Mount Carmel. There God's power triumphed decisively, prompting the people to fall on their faces and proclaim that the Lord, not Baal, was the true God. Had the people followed through on this verbal commitment and expressed its truth through their daily living, much heartache would have been avoided.

Micaiah, who is the hero of **lesson 4**, was a contemporary of Elijah and had to deal with the same king, Ahab, whom Elijah confronted. Although his brief encounter with Ahab is the only incident in Micaiah's life that the Bible relates, this episode shows us that Micaiah was a man of courage and character. Ahab had surrounded himself with prophets who were nothing more than yes-men. When Micaiah was encouraged to follow their lead, he refused to do so. To go against the wishes of a powerful king like Ahab was courting death, yet this bold prophet faced such a possibility with calm assurance. In our age of sycophants and flattery, we could use a few Micaiahs.

Unit 2: Prophecies of Judgment

This unit focuses on four prophets who lived in the eighth century B.C. Two of them ministered in Israel and the other two in Judah. Although these men lived more than twenty-seven hundred years ago, their messages seem as contemporary as this morning's newspaper.

In **lesson 5** we learn about Amos, who was a shepherd and fruit farmer when God called him to a prophetic ministry. Although not a "professional" prophet, Amos showed a commitment to God and a courage that empowered him to deliver God's message to the northern kingdom. He spoke out with firmness and clarity against the people's greed, sexual immorality, and idolatry.

Lesson 6 provides further insight into the ministry of Amos. He denounced in no uncertain terms the people's empty, insincere worship—going through rituals without any real desire to know the Lord and serve Him. He also declared that the "day of the Lord" would not be a day of light, as popular opinion supposed, but a terrifying day of judgment.

Lesson 7 introduces us to Hosea, whose marriage became intertwined with his ministry. His wife Gomer's infidelity served as a symbol of Israel's unfaithfulness to God.

Lesson 8 tells how Hosea continued to plead with God's wayward people. He described God's love for them while they were still in Egypt. Even though God had led them out of bondage there, the people turned to false gods. As a result, they would fall to the Assyrians. God's refusal to give up on His people may serve to encourage those who have been tempted to give up on friends or family members who have rejected their efforts to witness of God's love.

Lesson 9 introduces us to Micah, whose ministry was in Judah. Micah denounced the false prophets who had convinced the corrupt leaders that God would protect them. He criticized judges who were guilty of taking bribes and perverting justice, and religious leaders who were carrying out their tasks solely for money. Although they were worshiping according to the appropriate rituals, these acts were clearly an offense to God. Instead of sacrifices, God required His people to "do justly, and to love mercy, and to walk humbly with" God (Micah 6:8).

Unit 3: Decline and Fall

In one of the most dramatic scenes of God's confrontation with a human being, **lesson 10** allows us to witness God's call to Isaiah. Isaiah was overwhelmed by a vision of God "high and lifted up" (Isaiah 6:1). After he was purged of his sins, he answered the call to go and speak God's message to a people who had already hardened their hearts against it. Under such circumstances, we can only marvel that Isaiah was willing to accept God's call.

Lesson 11 includes the prophecy, often cited during the Christmas season, that a virgin would bear a Son and call him Immanuel. This message of hope came in the midst of a national crisis, as Judah found herself threatened by the Assyrians. In the midst of this crisis, King Ahaz refused to call on God for a sign that would give him encouragement and assurance. Such arrogance, however, did not close the matter. Through Isaiah, God gave the wonderful sign of the virgin and her special Son.

Lesson 12 notes how Isaiah used a parable of a vineyard to get Judah's attention. In the parable Israel and Judah are represented by the vineyard.

God expected the "fruit" of justice and righteousness from His people, but instead they brought forth greed and oppression. God had heard the cries of the oppressed and promised to exact justice from those who had made a farce of His laws. The lesson concludes with Isaiah's ringing denunciation of those responsible for such defiance of God's authority, pronouncing a series of woes upon them.

The last lesson of the quarter lowers the curtain on the nation of Israel. God's patience was not unlimited, and when the people continued to worship pagan gods—even sacrificing their children to them—He could no longer stay His hand of judgment. He permitted the Assyrians, noted in the ancient world for their brutality, to capture Samaria, the capital of Israel, and to lead thousands of her citizens into captivity.

As you teach this lesson, try to help your students see parallels between life and religion in ancient Israel and in our own times. For example, while we no longer worship the idols of Baal or Molech, we do have our gods—such as material possessions and money—and these can be just as demanding. To sacrifice a baby to a pagan god would be unthinkable today. Yet, through abortion, we murder babies on a monstrous scale compared with ancient Israel (and call it "pro-choice" to justify it). Encourage your class to search for these parallels.

Learning these lessons from the history of God's people can help us avoid repeating some of their failures—but only if we have the courage to apply these lessons.

Answers to Quarterly Quiz on page 338

Lesson 1—1. three days. 2. Solomon. 3. false. **Lesson 2**—1. Ahab. 2. Cherith. 3. meal, oil. **Lesson 3**—1. Mount Carmel. 2. four hundred fifty. 3. twelve. **Lesson 4**—1. Ramoth-gilead. 2. Jehoshaphat. **Lesson 5**—1. false. 2. righteous, poor. **Lesson 6**—1. lion, bear. 2. judgment, righteousness. **Lesson 7**—1. Gomer. 2. Jezreel, Lo-ruhamah, and Lo-ammi. **Lesson 8**—1. Egypt. 2. Assyrian. **Lesson 9**—1. Moses, Aaron, and Miriam. 2. Balak, Balaam. 3. "to do justly, and to love mercy, and to walk humbly with thy God." **Lesson 10**—1. King Uzziah. 2. a live coal. 3. "Whom shall I send, and who will go for us?" "Here am I; send me." **Lesson 11**—1. Rezin of Syria and Pekah of Israel. 2. Ahaz. 3. Immanuel. **Lesson 12**—1. vineyard. 2. strong drink. **Lesson 13**—1. Samaria. 2. prophets.

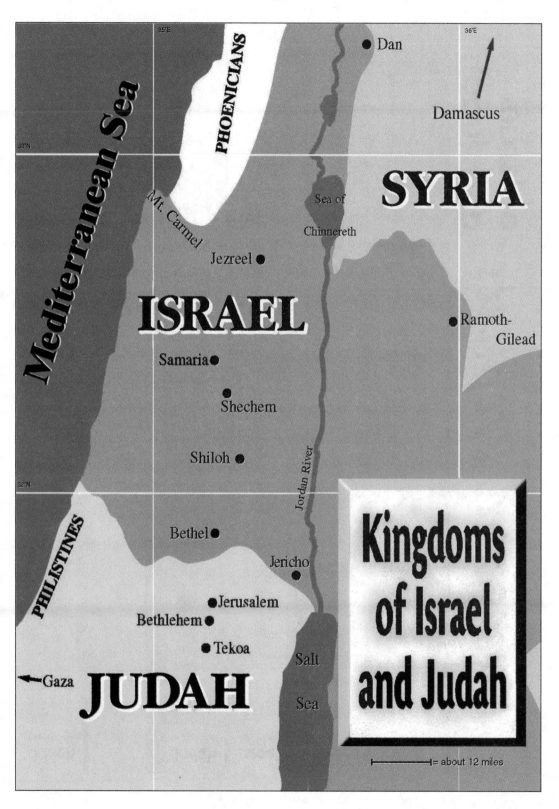

342

Kings and Prophets of Israel and Judah

Headlines and Headliners

A Creative Way to Summarize Biblical Truths

by Ronald G. Davis

THIS QUARTER'S LESSONS form a "Big News" series of studies, focusing on politicians, pundits, prophets, and patrons. Death and destruction, failure and foolishness, fill the pages. Had there been printing presses and journalists, the headlines would have been bold and blaring. Changes occurred so suddenly and drastically that early and late editions would have required major readjustments of the front pages almost daily. Such were the times of "Division and Decline."

When God's prophets tried to catch the attention of God's people with graphic and pithy words, the people proved to be "prophetically illiterate." They could not—or did not choose to—listen and heed. When God's spokesmen unfurled the banners of truth, the people of Israel and Judah used them to shine their idols and polish their accumulated gold. Headlines became deadlines, and in turn, deadlines became death lines. For some, this meant being buried in the graves of their homeland; others suffered the misery of slavery and death in a foreign land.

Capsules and Captions

Perceptive teachers and writers have long recognized the great learning value of capsulized truths—short, memorable statements that summarize the bigger, deeper truths of the lesson. The "Thought to Remember" segment of each lesson in this commentary is an example of that very practice. Indeed, lesson titles themselves serve much the same function (and probably deserve much more attention and notice than most adult teachers give to them!). Having such statements on regular display in the classroom offers real reinforcement and review possibilities. Having learners compose "headlines" based on the printed texts offers opportunities for genuine reflection and reasoning.

Consider how such teacher-created and such learner-generated ideas can be a part of the instructional design in the adult classroom.

The Teacher as "Editor"

In the field of journalism, editors often have the task of determining titles or section headings within a given piece of material. The Sunday school teacher of adults can play the same role in the classroom, giving titles to the parts or to the whole of a particular lesson.

As an introductory exercise, a "front page" of the *Jerusalem Journal* or the *Samaria Sunset* could carry thirteen items, one for each lesson in the quarter. Compare the following "headlines" with the lessons to be studied. Can you match each one with a lesson? Try your skill; then check your responses with the answers below.

- "King Opts for Youth Movement in His Council"
- "Relocation Plans in Full Swing"
- "Meteorological Madman Menaces Monarch"
- "New Song Sweeps Charts"
- "Mountaintop Experience Proves Fatal"
- "Bad News—Good News; Which Do You Want?"
- "Prophet Lies to Tell the Truth"
- "Local Man Called to Be Prophet"
- "Three or Four Is Enough"
- "Redevelopment of Urban Areas Planned"
- "Lions and Bears and Serpents—Oh, My!"
- "Once Loved, Twice Rejected"
- "Holy Man Marries Unholy Woman"

Here is the suggested order of how the lessons are matched with the headlines: lessons 1, 13, 2, 12, 3, 11, 4, 10, 5, 9, 6, 8, 7. Did you decide differently on some? Good! From such differences of opinion and interpretation, a worthy discussion and explanation can often result. This is just the kind of careful thinking every teacher of adults wants to see in the class. (A teacher might want to display a large replica of a "front page" in the classroom and add relevant "headlines" week by week throughout the quarter.)

This same kind of headline display can be used with an individual lesson: create and display a headline for each verse, but do not identify the verse it represents. Then have the learners match each headline with the appropriate verse. Consider this example for lesson 7, "God's Love for Israel," taken from Hosea 1 and 2: 1:2—"Finding a Wife In Israel"; 1:3—"Prophet Weds Suddenly"; 1:4—"Jezreel to Be Reeled In"; 1:5—"When the Bow Breaks"; 1:6—"Daughter Given Merciless Name"; 1:7—"Army Not Good Enough to Defend Judah"; 1:8—"Third Child Not a Charm"; 1:9—"Contract to Be Broken"; 1:10—"Population Projected to Reach Uncountable Numbers"; 1:11—"Two Nations to Be Reunited Under One King"; 2:1—"Stop Thinking in Negatives"; 2:2—"Leader Calls for New Morality"; 2:3—"Naked

Ambition; Unquenchable Thirst"; 2:4—"Children Suffer From Parents' Mistakes."

Displaying or simply reading such headlines in random order and asking the class to match each to a relevant verse can encourage close examination of the text. Again, occasional disagreement can be used to good learning advantage. (Some headlines may fit more than one verse.)

Another idea is to reveal or read all "headlines" in the same order as the verses, asking learners to explain how each capsulizes (or fails to capsulize) the main idea of a specific verse. Class members may well be able to "edit" certain headlines to represent better the truth stated in each. For example, suggesting that the word *Adulterous* be inserted before *Parents'* in the entry for Hosea 2:4 may be an improvement.

A third way the teacher can serve as "editor" is to give the class several "headlines" for a lesson (or a lesson segment or verse) and ask the group to decide which is the best one to represent the truth presented. Consider this example for lesson 2, in which Elijah tells King Ahab about a coming drought, is fed by ravens beside the Brook Cherith, and then travels to Zidon and aids a poverty-stricken widow. Here are three headline choices: "Where's Elijah? Witnesses See Him One Place, Then Another"; "Prophet Curses King, Comforts Pagan Woman"; "From A (Ahab) to Z (Zidon), Elijah Goes." Ask learners to choose which one best summarizes the lesson truth and to be prepared to "defend" their choices.

The Learner as "Reporter"

Although a teacher can encourage thinking through capsulized truths that he has written, even more thinking may take place if the learner himself must create the words. Before a teacher asks the learners to do some "headline writing," he will probably have to demonstrate the activity with one of the ideas suggested above. But once he does, some learners will find themselves doing the activity mentally as they look at different texts and lessons.

One simple way to get started is to work collectively, either as a class or in small groups. Asking for a list of "key words" is a good place to begin. For lesson 1, the list would probably include such words as *Rehoboam, yoke, lighter, counsel, old, young, scorpions,* and others. Once the group has a list, call for someone to incorporate as many as possible in a summary statement. For the words suggested above, one might propose, "Rehoboam Rejects the Old, Takes Counsel of the Young." Someone with a bit more imagination might suggest, "King Readies a Yoke of Scorpions: Watch Out!" One of the learners might develop the list of key words and ideas with the entire group and then ask smaller groups to pen the "headlines." These headlines can be shared with everyone after a few minutes of deliberation.

A second way to have learners devise the "headline" statements would be to give each learner a verse from the printed text and to ask each to compose a headline for the verse's main idea. Several words in the verse should be highlighted, particularly verbs and other key words. Ask the learners to use one or more of the highlighted words or related words in each headline. For lesson 13, one could highlight 2 Kings 17:6 as follows: "In the ninth year of Hoshea the *king* of Assyria *took* Samaria, and *carried* Israel *away* into Assyria, and *placed* them in Halah and in Habor by the river of Gozan, and in the *cities* of the Medes." Verse seven could be marked as, "For so it was, that the *children* of Israel had *sinned* against the Lord their God, which had brought them up out of the land of Egypt, from under the hand of Pharaoh king of Egypt, and had *feared* other *gods*." Imaginative class members will create headlines such as, "Israel Carried Away by King's Placement Plan," and "Faithless Children Forget; Fear False Gods," respectively. Having each adult read the headline that he or she prepared and calling for others to identify the relevant verse will facilitate a careful look at the text and what it says (and implies).

If your class seats itself in a circular pattern, the headlines can be distributed silently, and each learner can write the verse number he or she believes best reflects what is written. As the numbers begin to add up, learners may be checking the text against previous markers' judgments. (Not an ineffective learning activity in itself!)

Of course, if the class is in the habit of participating in a variety of writing activities, all the teacher will need to do is ask members to create "headlines" for units, lessons, or verses. And they can be encouraged by being reminded that there are no right and wrong answers. Headlines can be matter-of-fact, declarative statements, enigmatic phrases, or alliterative axioms. Though brief, they can plant the seed of a "germ idea" that will often result in a full-grown, fruitful plant. That's what every teacher of adults wants and that's what the Lord's kingdom must produce: mature, reproducing disciples.

The church needs a few more headlines touting the good news of good deeds done. The church needs a few more headliners, willing to step forward so that Jesus Christ can be lifted up before others who need to see the gospel in action. Making both the church and Christ more attractive to the world—that's exactly what Bible study is designed to accomplish. That's exactly what the teacher of adults wants to happen.

Rehoboam: An Unwise Decision

June 3
Lesson 1

DEVOTIONAL READING: Matthew 11:27-30.

BACKGROUND SCRIPTURE: 1 Kings 12; 2 Chronicles 10:1—11:12.

PRINTED TEXT: 1 Kings 12:3b-13, 16.

1 Kings 12:3b-13, 16

3b And Jeroboam and all the congregation of Israel came, and spake unto Rehoboam, saying,

4 Thy father made our yoke grievous: now therefore make thou the grievous service of thy father, and his heavy yoke which he put upon us, lighter, and we will serve thee.

5 And he said unto them, Depart yet for three days, then come again to me. And the people departed.

6 And king Rehoboam consulted with the old men, that stood before Solomon his father while he yet lived, and said, How do ye advise that I may answer this people?

7 And they spake unto him, saying, If thou wilt be a servant unto this people this day, and wilt serve them, and answer them, and speak good words to them, then they will be thy servants for ever.

8 But he forsook the counsel of the old men, which they had given him, and consulted with the young men that were grown up with him, and which stood before him:

9 And he said unto them, What counsel give ye that we may answer this people, who have spoken to me, saying, Make the yoke which thy father did put upon us lighter?

10 And the young men that were grown up with him spake unto him, saying, Thus shalt thou speak unto this people that spake unto thee, saying, Thy father made our yoke heavy, but make thou it lighter unto us; thus shalt thou say unto them, My little finger shall be thicker than my father's loins.

11 And now whereas my father did lade you with a heavy yoke, I will add to your yoke: my father hath chastised you with whips, but I will chastise you with scorpions.

12 So Jeroboam and all the people came to Rehoboam the third day, as the king had appointed, saying, Come to me again the third day.

13 And the king answered the people roughly, and forsook the old men's counsel that they gave him.

. . . .

16 So when all Israel saw that the king hearkened not unto them, the people answered the king, saying, What portion have we in David? neither have we inheritance in the son of Jesse: to your tents, O Israel: now see to thine own house, David. So Israel departed unto their tents.

GOLDEN TEXT: If thou wilt be a servant unto this people this day, and wilt serve them, and answer them, and speak good words to them, then they will be thy servants for ever.—1 Kings 12:7.

Division and Decline
Unit 1: A Kingdom Divided
(Lessons 1-4)

Lesson Aims

After participating in this lesson, students should be able to:

1. Describe the circumstances that led to the division of Israel into two kingdoms.

2. Give illustrations (from current events or from their personal experiences) of how following bad advice produced problems.

3. Take steps to deal with a difficult decision or situation they are currently facing by seeking wise and godly counsel.

Lesson Outline

INTRODUCTION
  A. Advice Not "Fit for a King"
  B. Lesson Background
 I. THE PEOPLE'S REQUEST (1 Kings 12:3b-5)
  A. Plea for Mercy (vv. 3b, 4)
  B. Rehoboam's Response (v. 5)
 II. REHOBOAM'S ADVISERS (1 Kings 12:6-11)
  A. Older Men (vv. 6, 7)
    Leadership=Servantship
  B. Younger Men (vv. 8-11)
III. REHOBOAM'S CHOICE (1 Kings 12:12, 13, 16)
  A. Harsh Reply (vv. 12, 13)
  B. Tragic Results (v. 16)
    Generation Gaps
CONCLUSION
  A. Conflict or Compromise?
  B. Speak Softly
  C. Prayer
  D. Thought to Remember

Introduction

A. Advice Not "Fit for a King"

Kings George I, George II, and George III ruled England during the eighteenth century. The first two were weak, ineffective rulers. As a result, the English Parliament became more and more aggressive in governing the country. During this period of parliamentary rule, Britain's empire grew and her trade expanded. Then, in 1760, George III came to the throne. At his coronation his mother advised him, "Be king, George. Be king!"

One of the first steps George III took in his efforts to "be king" was to discharge his able prime minister, William Pitt. Then he began a series of measures that antagonized many leaders both in England and in her colonies. The eventual result was the American Revolution and the colonies' independence—all because George made the foolish mistake of listening to bad advice.

Rehoboam's efforts to "be king" led to similar tragic results—the division of his kingdom. He chose to listen to the brash words of his young advisers rather than heed the advice of his father, King Solomon: "Pride goeth before destruction, and a haughty spirit before a fall" (Proverbs 16:18).

B. Lesson Background

King Solomon began his reign as king of Israel about 971 B.C. Because he realized that he was relatively young and inexperienced when he came to the throne, he humbly asked God for wisdom to rule his people well. God granted Solomon his request, and for some time his kingdom prospered. Solomon embarked on extensive building programs (including the temple in Jerusalem and his own palace) that greatly enhanced the kingdom materially. But as the years passed, Solomon compromised his faith by entering foreign alliances that were "sealed" by his marriages to pagan wives. Many of these women brought their false religions to Israel, corrupting the people with their beliefs and practices.

This sad turn of events brought God's judgment upon Solomon: "The Lord was angry with Solomon, because his heart was turned from the Lord God of Israel, which had appeared unto him twice" (1 Kings 11:9). God then sent the prophet Ahijah to seek out Jeroboam, whom Solomon had made a leader of one of the groups of laborers that Solomon commissioned from the tribes of Israel (1 Kings 5:13, 14; 11:28). Ahijah dramatized his message by taking his outer garment and tearing it into twelve pieces. These twelve pieces symbolized the twelve tribes of Israel. Ten of these pieces the prophet gave to Jeroboam, signifying that he would become the leader of ten of the tribes (1 Kings 11:29-31).

Through some means the king apparently learned of Ahijah's message and sought to kill Jeroboam. Some students suggest that the statement that Jeroboam "lifted up his hand against the king" (1 Kings 11:26) indicates that he tried to initiate some kind of rebellion against Solomon. Whatever the cause of the king's suspicion, Jeroboam fled to Egypt, where he remained until Solomon's death (1 Kings 11:40). When Solomon's son Rehoboam ascended the throne, he journeyed to Shechem for the coronation service, which is the point at which today's printed text begins.

I. The People's Request
(1 Kings 12:3b-5)
A. Plea for Mercy (vv. 3b, 4)

3b. And Jeroboam and all the congregation of Israel came, and spake unto Rehoboam, saying.

The city of Shechem was located about thirty miles north of Jerusalem in a valley between Mount Gerizim and Mount Ebal. It was a city with great historical significance for the nation of Israel. Abraham had built an altar there (Genesis 12:6, 7—where it is called "Sichem"). Later Jacob purchased "a parcel of a field" in that vicinity, where he pitched his tent and erected an altar (Genesis 33:18-20). "Jacob's well," which guides in the Holy Land still show to modern tourists, was also located in this territory (John 4:5, 6). Joshua's farewell address, during which he urged the Israelites to be faithful to God's covenant with them, was delivered at Shechem (Joshua 24:1ff.). With so much history associated with it, one can see why Shechem was selected as the place for the coronation of *Rehoboam* as Israel's king. Of far greater significance, however, is that *he* went to Shechem rather than having the people come to Jerusalem "to make him king" (1 Kings 12:1). This suggests to many students that there was already a certain measure of dissension among the people.

Furthermore, the fact that the Israelites had "sent and called" for *Jeroboam* to return from Egypt (vv. 2, 3) provides additional evidence that trouble was brewing. Although Jeroboam had been in exile, he was apparently so well respected that the people wanted him to serve as their spokesman when they met with Rehoboam. If Rehoboam was aware of his father's suspicions toward Jeroboam (1 Kings 11:40), the latter's return at this particular time surely must have been unsettling to Rehoboam.

4. Thy father made our yoke grievous: now therefore make thou the grievous service of thy father, and his heavy yoke which he put upon us, lighter, and we will serve thee.

Years earlier, when the nation of Israel first wanted a king, Samuel had warned the people that having a king would carry certain negative consequences (1 Samuel 8:10-18). His dire predictions that a king would levy a heavy tax burden upon them and conscript their sons and daughters for his service had come to pass during the reign of Solomon (1 Kings 5:13, 14; 9:15, 22). Now the people wanted relief. They were not asking for the complete abolition of all taxes or other burdens laid upon them by Solomon. All they were asking was that Rehoboam would *make* their *heavy yoke . . . lighter*, and then they would *serve* him.

Certainly this was not an unreasonable request of a new king. Nor did the people complicate the issue by giving an ultimatum. Their statement left open the question of what they would do if Rehoboam denied their request.

B. Rehoboam's Response (v. 5)

5. And he said unto them, Depart yet for three days, then come again to me. And the people departed.

Living in Solomon's palace, Rehoboam may well have been isolated from the people and their hardships. Thus it was reasonable for him to take some time to examine the facts and evaluate the situation before he made a decision. On the other hand, Rehoboam may simply have been stalling for time—like many politicians do today when they are confronted with hard decisions. Regardless of his motives, the people were willing to give him time to consider the matter.

II. Rehoboam's Advisers
(1 Kings 12:6-11)
A. Older Men (vv. 6, 7)

6. And king Rehoboam consulted with the old men, that stood before Solomon his father while he yet lived, and said, How do ye advise that I may answer this people?

The first step Rehoboam took in determining how to *answer this people* was a wise one. He *consulted with the old men* who had counseled *Solomon his father*. They had observed the mistakes that had ruined Solomon's once-promising reign. They saw how his growing extravagance had placed an increasingly heavy burden on the people by demanding that they furnish both the manpower and the taxes necessary to complete and maintain his many projects and enterprises. No doubt, these men had heard some of the complaints that the people had made. [See question #1, page 352.]

7. And they spake unto him, saying, If thou wilt be a servant unto this people this day, and wilt serve them, and answer them, and speak good words to them, then they will be thy servants for ever.

VISUALS FOR THESE LESSONS

The visual pictured in each lesson (e.g., page 349) is a small reproduction of a large, full-color poster included in the *Adult Visuals* packet for the Summer Quarter. The packet is available from your supplier. Order No. 492.

These senior counselors advised Rehoboam to become *a servant unto this people.* [See question #2, page 352.] This was quite different from the usual demeanor of ancient monarchs, who were notorious for their arrogant and haughty behavior. The last thing in the world they would think of becoming was a servant. They desired instead to be served.

These wise old men, however, were declaring a great truth: a ruler who is willing to serve the people will soon have subjects who are willing to serve him. Jesus was a perfect model of this kind of servant leadership (Matthew 20:25-28). And while many pay lip service to it, few leaders in politics, business, or even the church have truly understood this principle.

LEADERSHIP=SERVANTSHIP

Nearly a millennium after Rehoboam's older and wiser advisers counseled the new king to "be a servant," Jesus of Nazareth taught, "If any man desire to be first, the same shall be last of all, and servant of all" (Mark 9:35). Those who are greatest in God's kingdom are those who lead by serving. Jesus is living proof of that truth. He came to serve and to save us, and He never wavered from that purpose. He illustrated servanthood dramatically when He stooped to wash His disciples' feet.

Rehoboam rejected the wisdom of leading by serving. Instead, he looked for advice that would allow him to gratify his pride and exploit his power. His ironhanded tactics irreversibly divided the nation of Israel.

Someone has wisely observed, "You cannot teach what you do not know; you cannot lead where you will not go." All leaders (whether presidents, preachers, or parents) should hang this motto on their walls. Truly effective leadership

Home Daily Bible Readings

Monday, May 28—Jeroboam Versus Rehoboam (1 Kings 12:1-9)
Tuesday, May 29—An Unwise Decision Made (1 Kings 12:10-15)
Wednesday, May 30—The Northern Tribes Secede (1 Kings 12:16-24)
Thursday, May 31—Jeroboam's Golden Calves (1 Kings 12:25-33)
Friday, June 1—Revolt Against Rehoboam (2 Chronicles 10:1-11)
Saturday, June 2—Division of the Kingdom (2 Chronicles 10:12-19)
Sunday, June 3—Judah and Benjamin Fortified (2 Chronicles 11:1-12)

results from humble servantship. Rather than grasping a scepter and wielding a sword, reach for a basin and a towel. That is what Jesus would do.
—R. W. B.

B. Younger Men (vv. 8-11)

8. But he forsook the counsel of the old men, which they had given him, and consulted with the young men that were grown up with him, and which stood before him.

We can only guess at Rehoboam's motives for rejecting *the counsel of the old men.* Perhaps he had turned to them first simply out of courtesy, knowing ahead of time that he would not take their advice. Or he may have resented the fact that their words, in effect, criticized the actions of his father. Perhaps Rehoboam also realized that if he followed their counsel, he would have to do without some of the privileges that Solomon had enjoyed. Rehoboam was like many of us: when someone gives us advice we don't like, we turn to someone else who we think will give advice more to our liking.

In Rehoboam's case, this meant consulting some *young men.* This was a group of his peers—men whom he knew better, for they had *grown up with him.* We usually feel more comfortable among people we have grown up with or have known for a long time. Apparently these younger men had been Rehoboam's companions or servants in the palace, since they had also *stood before him.* They knew how he thought and knew the answers that he wanted to hear.

9. And he said unto them, What counsel give ye that we may answer this people, who have spoken to me, saying, Make the yoke which thy father did put upon us lighter?

In speaking to these younger men, Rehoboam posed his question differently from the way he consulted the older counselors. In speaking to the older men he asked, "How do ye advise that *I* may answer this people?" (v. 6). But to the young men he asked, *What counsel give ye that **we** may answer this people?* Quite obviously Rehoboam identified with, and felt at ease with, the younger men more than the older men.

10. And the young men that were grown up with him spake unto him, saying, Thus shalt thou speak unto this people that spake unto thee, saying, Thy father made our yoke heavy, but make thou it lighter unto us; thus shalt thou say unto them, My little finger shall be thicker than my father's loins.

In sharp contrast to the response of the older counselors, the answer of these *young men* showed utter contempt for the *people.* As companions of Rehoboam, these men had probably lived lives of ease and comfort. Such a lifestyle had left them with little understanding of the plight of the general populace, who were burdened by a heavy tax load. Thus, these men had little or no sympathy for the people's suffering. No doubt, this was one reason Jeroboam was considered a fitting representative for the people (vv. 2, 3): he had worked among them (1 Kings 11:28) and was aware of their grievances. [See question #3, page 352.]

The arrogance of these young advisors to Rehoboam is almost beyond belief. They acknowledged that Solomon had placed a heavy *yoke*, or burden, upon the people, but they urged Rehoboam to increase that burden rather than grant relief. They even told Rehoboam the words he should use: *My little finger shall be thicker than my father's loins* [waist]. The meaning of this proverbial expression was quite clear: Rehoboam's weakest actions would be more severe than his father's strongest actions.

11. And now whereas my father did lade you with a heavy yoke, I will add to your yoke: my father hath chastised you with whips, but I will chastise you with scorpions.

While the reference to *whips* and *scorpions* could have been figurative, on occasion Solomon's overseers may have used actual whips on their workers. Some commentators have suggested that *scorpions* describes an especially painful whip in which pieces of metal or bone were embedded to cause lacerations in the flesh of the victim. [See question #4, page 352.]

III. Rehoboam's Choice
(1 Kings 12:12, 13, 16)

A. Harsh Reply (vv. 12, 13)

12, 13. So Jeroboam and all the people came to Rehoboam the third day, as the king had appointed, saying, Come to me again the third day. And the king answered the people roughly, and forsook the old men's counsel that they gave him.

When the three days that *Rehoboam* had requested had passed, *all the people*, led by *Jeroboam*, again assembled to hear the king's response to their petition. No doubt they had used this time to discuss possible replies he might make. Had he responded favorably to their petition, they probably would have been willing to return home, supportive of Rehoboam. But they also must have considered the possibility that Rehoboam would reject their request.

Sadly, *the king answered the people roughly*, ignoring the wisdom of his father: "A soft answer turneth away wrath: but grievous words stir up anger" (Proverbs 15:1). Even a gentle answer might not have placated the people, but a harsh

Visual for lesson 1

The visuals packet contains a map of the divided kingdom that will be useful today and throughout the quarter.

See page 347 for ordering information.

answer was certain to fan the flames of their dissatisfaction.

B. Tragic Results (v. 16)

16. So when all Israel saw that the king hearkened not unto them, the people answered the king, saying, What portion have we in David? neither have we inheritance in the son of Jesse: to your tents, O Israel: now see to thine own house, David. So Israel departed unto their tents.

Rehoboam's brash rejection of the people's request broke open wounds that actually had been festering for many years. During the time of the judges, tensions manifested themselves on at least three occasions (Judges 8:1-3; 12:1-6; 20:1-48). Later, after King Saul's death, only Judah crowned David as king, while the northern tribes remained loyal to Saul's house, crowning his son Ish-bosheth king (2 Samuel 2:8-10). In addition, following Absalom's revolt and David's return to power, the northern tribes briefly supported a rebel named Sheba (2 Samuel 19:41—20:22). In fact, the words spoken here to Rehoboam are strikingly reminiscent of those that initiated Sheba's revolt against David (2 Samuel 20:1).

To your tents, O Israel. Some students interpret this as a call to arms. It is a reasonable assumption, but not required. It may have been simply a call for the people to leave the meeting with the king and to depart to their homes. Regardless of the immediate intent, however, the eventual result of this response is clear. Negotiations between Rehoboam and the northern tribes were angrily terminated. The northern tribes voiced their allegiance to Jeroboam as king, and Ahijah's prophecy of the kingdom's division came to pass. [See question #5, page 352.]

GENERATION GAPS

"Senior Saints" are sometimes heard to say, "I must have been born several years too late." They mean, of course, that they are not comfortable living in eras dominated by the tastes and

How to Say It

ABSALOM. *Ab*-suh-lum.
AHIJAH. Uh-*high*-juh.
EBAL. *Ee*-bull.
GERIZIM. Guh-*rye*-zim or *Gair*-ih-zeem.
ISH-BOSHETH. Ish-*bo*-sheth.
JEROBOAM. Jair-uh-*bo*-um.
REHOBOAM. Ree-huh-*bo*-um.
SHEBA. *She*-buh.
SHECHEM. *Shek*-em or *Shee*-kem.
SICHEM. *Sigh*-kem.

preferences of a younger generation. On the other hand, the young are restless and rebellious because they too are uncomfortable with what they consider the rigid expectations and "old-fashioned" ways of their elders.

Rehoboam is a prime example of this youthful rebelliousness, except that his issues and agendas held implications much more far-reaching than those normally faced by the younger generation. His choices and decisions affected thousands of people; indeed, the history of a nation was significantly altered by the generation gap between this "upstart" ruler and the "old men" who had served his father, but whose advice he curtly brushed aside.

The conflict that arose when Rehoboam took the throne was never resolved. The kingdom was divided and tribes of God's family became virtual enemies. Fortunately, families usually survive the generation gaps between teens and parents. But will the church overcome whatever generational conflicts threaten the "unity of the Spirit"? God help us if mere opinions and preferences are allowed to divide us! —R. W. B.

Conclusion

A. Conflict or Compromise?

Throughout the centuries, church history has been marred by conflicts of all kinds. Many times the church has found itself in conflict with the forces of the secular world. In these situations the church has had to stand and fight, for to compromise with evil would lead the church to abandon its very reason for being in the world. Jesus warned Christians to anticipate these struggles, and He has promised to be with us when we face them.

However, not all church fights have pitted the church against the world. All too often those who wore the name of Christ have fought against one another. In some situations the faithful have had little choice but to stand and fight. When those within the church seek to subvert the basic doctrines of the church—such as the authority of the Scriptures, the virgin birth of Christ, and the bodily resurrection of Christ—the faithful dare not compromise. We must "earnestly contend for the faith which was once delivered unto the saints" (Jude 3).

Yet candor forces us to acknowledge that not all the controversies within the church deal with crucial matters of faith. We may try to make it appear that we are contending for the faith when in reality we are contending only for our personal opinions. In situations such as this, reasonable compromise is certainly most appropriate. The "bigger picture"—the accomplishment of the mission of the church—must receive top priority.

One of Rehoboam's problems was that he could not distinguish between those policies that were essential to the strength of his kingdom and those that reflected his own personal preferences. He was more concerned about maintaining personal power than seeking the good of the entire kingdom. As a result, what power he did have was irreversibly weakened.

B. Speak Softly

When Solomon came to the throne as a young man, he did so with appropriate humility. He confessed to God that he was "but a little child" not knowing "how to go out or come in." With such an attitude, it is not surprising that he asked for wisdom to rule his people well (1 Kings 3:7-11). Unfortunately, the blessings that God granted Solomon gradually caused him to forget his initial humility and fall victim to pride.

As Rehoboam grew up in the royal household, pampered and surrounded by luxury, he saw few signs of Solomon's humility. Instead, he saw a degree of wealth and power that kept him from developing a compassion for the people that he was called upon to lead. As we have noted, he seemed oblivious to his father's warnings about pride (Proverbs 16:18) and about the importance of a "soft answer" (Proverbs 15:1). What a terrible price the nation paid for Rehoboam's negligence!

C. Prayer

Dear Lord, protect us from stubborn pride. Teach us to learn how to compromise gracefully over issues that are not vital to the Christian faith. Show us how to forgive when we have dealt harshly with others. In the name of the humble Lamb of God we pray. Amen.

D. Thought to Remember

Be discerning about whose advice you follow. Seek counsel from godly people whom you know and trust.

Learning by Doing

This page contains an alternate lesson plan emphasizing learning activities.
Classes desiring such student involvement will find these suggestions helpful.

Learning Goals

After this lesson each student will be able to:

1. Describe the circumstances that led to the division of Israel into two kingdoms.

2. Cite illustrations (from current events or personal experiences) of how bad advice produced problems.

3. Take steps to deal with a difficult decision or situation he or she is currently facing by seeking wise and godly counsel.

Into the Lesson

Prepare poster board visuals for groups of about five people. At the top of each poster board write these headings over three columns: *Adviser, Advice Given, Results of the Advice.* As learners arrive, ask each one to join a group and write a personal or other illustration of good advice or bad advice. These may be political, practical, or personal bits of advice.

Conclude this activity by telling the class that advice is an extremely important part of life. We seek advice on how or where to buy automobiles, how to discipline children, how to be a good spouse, where to buy a house, what schools are best, and more. When we seek advice, we must be certain the adviser is worth hearing, and we must choose whether or not to follow the advice. Today's Scripture shows the importance of looking for good advisers.

Into the Word

Give each person a letter-sized sheet of paper. At the top of the paper should be a major heading, "Making Decisions (1 Kings 12:3b-13, 16)." Over the first column write "Good Moves!" and over the second column write "Bad Moves!" Down the left-hand side of the page, list the following labels: verses 3b and 4, verse 5, verses 6 and 7, verse 8, verses 12 and 13.

Before beginning the Bible study, give a brief lecture on the lesson background from your lesson commentary. Emphasize the circumstances that led to the division of Israel into two kingdoms. You may write the list of principal characters as you lecture about them (Solomon, Ahijah, Jeroboam, Rehoboam). You may also show a map of the divided kingdom of Israel. (Use visual 1 from the *Adult Visuals* pack. See page 349.)

After the mini-lecture, you may choose to have the small groups do the worksheets or have the learners do them individually. Read the Scripture lesson. Ask the groups or individuals to go back and write the good moves or bad moves Rehoboam made in making his decision. The answers for the "Good Moves" column are as follows: *verses 3 and 4: Identify the problem; verse 5: Take time in making important decisions; verses 6 and 7: Consult persons with experience.* Verse 8 can be listed under both columns: *Consult friends.* Verses 12 and 13 will be listed under the "Bad Moves" column: *"Followed bad advice."*

After completing this exercise, ask the following discussion questions: "Why do you think Rehoboam chose to favor the advice of the young men rather than that of the old men?" and "What was the impact of Rehoboam's decision on Israel?"

Make the transition to application by reminding the class that good counsel is extremely important in making good decisions.

Into Life

The application will take place through three brief activities. The first activity is to brainstorm principles in seeking advice. Ask the class to share what they believe are important principles in seeking advice. While they suggest these principles, have a class member write them on a marker board or a chalkboard. Some of the principles were mentioned in the Bible study.

The second activity is to apply these principles to three hypothetical situations. List the following situations on poster board or a transparency and have small groups answer these two questions about one of the situations: "Whom would you seek as advisers in this situation?" and "Why are these advisers appropriate?"

SITUATION 1: A church worship committee is considering making the worship service more contemporary by blending choruses with hymns and adding more instrumentation to the service.

SITUATION 2: A young mother and father have different views on disciplining their child.

SITUATION 3: A single Christian woman has been asked to marry a non-Christian young man who has been coming to church with her.

After completing the above exercise, remind the class that the same principles are appropriate when giving advice as when seeking it. Conclude by having the class read together the closing prayer printed on page 350. (Provide copies or write it on the chalkboard.)

Let's Talk It Over

The questions on this page are designed to encourage review of the lesson Scriptures and to promote discussion of the lesson by the class. The answers provided are only discussion starters. Let your class talk it over from there.

1. Rehoboam consulted some advisers when facing a decision. What are some ways to get good counsel when we are trying to make a crucial decision?

First, admit your weaknesses, biases, and blind spots. Then pray for godly wisdom (James 1:5), both to evaluate the situation on your own and to evaluate the counsel you receive.

The next step is asking qualified advisers for input. Some Christians meet regularly with mature Christians whom they have asked in advance to act as counselors or mentors. Others have partners with whom they meet to provide mutual encouragement and accountability. Either of these situations provides ready access to someone who can serve as an adviser. Alternatively—or in addition to these—it is wise to look for someone who demonstrates godly character and wisdom on a consistent basis. If possible you should try to find someone who has handled positively situations similar to your own.

2. The elders whom Rehoboam consulted suggested that he "be a servant unto this people this day." By hindsight we know their advice was better than the counsel of the young men. How good do you think it is for leaders today? What kind of leaders—political leaders, church leaders, *any* leaders?

Servant leadership has been extolled in churches for years. Certainly that is the model the New Testament gives for church leaders. This text suggests it is workable in political situations as well. Unquestionably, the greatest example of a servant-ruler is Jesus. Almighty God was willing, not only to save us, but to save us by serving us. If we see service as helping people to achieve their potential, then the concept of servant-leadership makes sense in every situation. Rehoboam could have served his people by recognizing God's purposes for Israel and then helping them draw closer to God and keep His commands.

3. The lesson writer notes that the younger counselors may have grown up in ease and comfort, and that this may have contributed to their lack of sensitivity for the people's plight. How can leaders identify with the people whom they lead, especially if they come from different backgrounds from their own?

Background is not nearly as important as relationships. People may come from different backgrounds, but when they work and worship and even play together, differences diminish. Leaders need to spend time with the people for whom they are responsible. Fellowship events and retreats are good additions to the church program to enable the leaders to mix with the congregation in a more informal atmosphere than the Sunday morning worship. Visiting members in their homes or inviting the members into their own homes are also excellent ways to get to know people and to build common ground.

4. The counsel of the younger men was opposite that of the elders, so Rehoboam had to evaluate the advice and make his own decision. How should we evaluate the counsel that we receive?

The most common way is to take the advice we like, the advice that most nearly conforms to our own instincts in the matter. That is what Rehoboam did, and the result was disastrous!

Instead, we should consider whether the advice agrees with Biblical principles, what biases the adviser may have, what assumptions he or she makes, and how trustworthy the person has been in the past. If the advice disagrees with our own inclinations, we should give it extra consideration. Does the counselor have a valid reason for his or her position? Is he or she exposing one of those blind spots that we know we all have? This entire exercise is futile if we are not willing to follow wisdom instead of our own preferences.

5. How should we respond when leaders act unreasonably?

The northern tribes rejected Rehoboam's leadership altogether. On the other hand, David remained loyal even when King Saul tried to kill him. God has commanded that we "be subject unto the higher powers" of civil government (Romans 13:1). At the same time, Peter and the other apostles occasionally defied civil authority (Acts 4:18-20; 5:29). We must keep our allegiance to God and His will primary in our lives. After that we obey civil authorities, church leaders (Hebrews 13:17), and others. When there is a direct conflict, we obey God rather than man. Otherwise, we must submit, no matter how unreasonable or unpopular the leaders may be.

Elijah: A Prophet Appears

DEVOTIONAL READING: Job 36:5-11.

BACKGROUND SCRIPTURE: 1 Kings 17.

PRINTED TEXT: 1 Kings 17:1-16.

1 Kings 17:1-16

1 And Elijah the Tishbite, who was of the inhabitants of Gilead, said unto Ahab, As the LORD God of Israel liveth, before whom I stand, there shall not be dew nor rain these years, but according to my word.

2 And the word of the LORD came unto him, saying,

3 Get thee hence, and turn thee eastward, and hide thyself by the brook Cherith, that is before Jordan.

4 And it shall be, that thou shalt drink of the brook; and I have commanded the ravens to feed thee there.

5 So he went and did according unto the word of the LORD: for he went and dwelt by the brook Cherith, that is before Jordan.

6 And the ravens brought him bread and flesh in the morning, and bread and flesh in the evening; and he drank of the brook.

7 And it came to pass after a while, that the brook dried up, because there had been no rain in the land.

8 And the word of the LORD came unto him, saying,

9 Arise, get thee to Zarephath, which belongeth to Zidon, and dwell there: behold, I have commanded a widow woman there to sustain thee.

10 So he arose and went to Zarephath. And when he came to the gate of the city, behold, the widow woman was there gathering of sticks: and he called to her, and said, Fetch me, I pray thee, a little water in a vessel, that I may drink.

11 And as she was going to fetch it, he called to her, and said, Bring me, I pray thee, a morsel of bread in thine hand.

12 And she said, As the LORD thy God liveth, I have not a cake, but a handful of meal in a barrel, and a little oil in a cruse: and, behold, I am gathering two sticks, that I may go in and dress it for me and my son, that we may eat it, and die.

13 And Elijah said unto her, Fear not; go and do as thou hast said: but make me thereof a little cake first, and bring it unto me, and after make for thee and for thy son.

14 For thus saith the LORD God of Israel, The barrel of meal shall not waste, neither shall the cruse of oil fail, until the day that the LORD sendeth rain upon the earth.

15 And she went and did according to the saying of Elijah: and she, and he, and her house, did eat many days.

16 And the barrel of meal wasted not, neither did the cruse of oil fail, according to the word of the LORD, which he spake by Elijah.

GOLDEN TEXT: The barrel of meal wasted not, neither did the cruse of oil fail,
according to the word of the LORD, which he spake by Elijah.
—1 Kings 17:16.

Division and Decline
Unit 1: A Kingdom Divided
(Lessons 1-4)

Lesson Aims

After this lesson students should be able to:

1. Tell how God provided for Elijah during the three-year famine described in the text.

2. Tell some ways in which God provides for His people today.

3. Suggest a specific way they can demonstrate dependence on the Lord.

Lesson Outline

INTRODUCTION
- A. A Termite and a Prophet
- B. Lesson Background
- I. ELIJAH'S MINISTRY BEGINS (1 Kings 17:1-7)
  - A. Elijah's Courage (v. 1)
  - B. God's Care (vv. 2-7)
    - *Unusual Providence*
- II. GOD DIRECTS ELIJAH (1 Kings 17:8-16)
  - A. Widow in Zarephath (vv. 8, 9)
  - B. Elijah's Request (vv. 10, 11)
  - C. Desperate Condition (v. 12)
  - D. Elijah's Assurance (vv. 13, 14)
  - E. God's Provision (vv. 15, 16)
    - *The Grace of Giving*
- CONCLUSION
  - A. "What Goes Around Comes Around"
  - B. Courage and Patience
  - C. Prayer
  - D. Thought to Remember

Introduction

A. A Termite and a Prophet

According to an old legend, there once lived a wicked giant. The animals of the forest lived in fear of him because he often tortured and killed many of them just for sport. The giant lived in a castle perched high on a cliff overlooking the sea. From this vantage point he could observe anyone who dared approach him.

One day the animals met and began to plot how they might rid themselves of this evil tyrant. The elephant, the largest animal in the forest, volunteered to climb the steep path and attack the giant. But the giant saw him coming, rushed out to meet him, seized him, and threw him into the sea. After watching this, the animals were even more fearful. Finally, however, the lion—

the bravest animal in the forest—agreed to try and fight the giant. But he met the same fate that had befallen the elephant.

As the animals cowered in fear, they heard a tiny voice say, "I have a plan to defeat the giant." Looking around, they discovered a tiny termite emerging from an old log. The other animals scoffed, "If the elephant and the lion could not defeat the giant, what chance do you have?"

"Be patient and wait," replied the little insect as he started toward the castle. Arriving there undetected by the giant, the termite crept inside the castle and began to eat away at one of the massive timbers that held the castle in place. Many months after the termite began his work, the castle suddenly collapsed into the sea, carrying the giant to his doom and securing a victory that the most powerful animals of the forest could not achieve.

This is similar to the situation that faced the northern kingdom of Israel. A wicked king, Ahab, and his wicked wife, Jezebel, were in power. God could have used the mighty armies of Israel's enemies to challenge Ahab. Instead, he chose an obscure prophet, Elijah, who suddenly appeared on the scene to demonstrate to Ahab and to God's people who was really "in power."

B. Lesson Background

Our previous lesson focused on Rehoboam, who became king when his father Solomon died. Rehoboam's arrogant rejection of the people's request for relief from the burdens of an extravagant reign led to a revolt that divided the kingdom.

For approximately the next three hundred and fifty years, the history of God's people comprised the history of two separate kingdoms—the northern kingdom (Israel) and the southern kingdom (Judah). During that time, relations between the two ranged from cooperation in the face of a common enemy to bitter conflict. The Bible notes that, following the division of the kingdom, "there was war between Rehoboam and Jeroboam all their days" (1 Kings 14:30). Tensions continued during the reigns of later kings (1 Kings 15:16).

The northern kingdom never experienced any degree of stability until the reign of Omri, who came to power in approximately 885 B.C. (almost fifty years after the division). Although Omri brought prosperity to the northern kingdom, he "wrought evil in the eyes of the Lord, and did worse than all [kings] that were before him" (1 Kings 16:25). Perhaps his most grievous evil was allowing the influence of his pagan neighbors to the north, who worshiped many false gods, to infiltrate his kingdom. This is indicated by the fact that Omri's son Ahab, who ascended the throne in 874 B.C., married Jezebel, described as "the daughter of Ethbaal king of the Zidonians" (1 Kings 16:31). Most likely this was a marriage designed to seal an alliance between Israel and the Phoenicians to the north. Jezebel, however, was a strong-willed woman, who was also a fervent worshiper of Baal and never missed an opportunity to promote his worship. Thus this marriage, though arranged for political reasons, wrought spiritual disaster in Israel; for it allowed Baal worship to gain a foothold.

It was at this crucial time in the northern kingdom's history, when pagan worship was making serious inroads among God's people, that God called Elijah (in approximately 860 B.C.) to confront a powerful but corrupt couple and to counter their influence on behalf of the true God.

I. Elijah's Ministry Begins
(1 Kings 17:1-7)

A. Elijah's Courage (v. 1)

1. And Elijah the Tishbite, who was of the inhabitants of Gilead, said unto Ahab, As the LORD God of Israel liveth, before whom I stand, there shall not be dew nor rain these years, but according to my word.

The name *Elijah* means "The Lord is God." The Scriptures tell us nothing about Elijah's family; he appears rather suddenly, without any introduction. Even what we learn from this verse is not entirely clear. The expression *of the inhabitants* comes from the word *tishbe,* so many translations have "from Tishbe in Gilead" rather than *of the inhabitants of Gilead.* Gilead was the territory east of the Jordan River, extending from the northern end of the Dead Sea northward to the Yarmuk River, south of the Sea of Galilee. The location of Tishbe is not certain. Some place it north of the Jabbok River in Gilead. Others associate it with a site in the tribal land of Naphtali. If the latter is correct, then Elijah would have been a Tishbite by ancestry even though he was living in the land of Gilead at this time.

Kings and Prophets of Israel and Judah

Visual for lesson 2

This listing of the kings and prophets of Israel and Judah is in the Adult Visuals *packet. It will be useful throughout this quarter.*

Ahab reigned over Israel twenty-two years. During that time he "did evil in the sight of the Lord above all that were before him." He "went and served Baal, and worshipped him," and "reared up an altar for Baal" in Samaria (the capital of the northern kingdom). He "did more to provoke the Lord God of Israel to anger than all the kings of Israel that were before him" (1 Kings 16:29-33). Elijah was called of God to confront Ahab with his sins and to remind him of Israel's real King, to whom Ahab was accountable.

The ministry of Elijah began with a sobering announcement of God's judgment. The prophet's first words authenticated his message: *As the Lord God of Israel liveth, before whom I stand.* The Lord, not Baal, was still in charge of Israel, in spite of Jezebel's aggressive efforts on behalf of Baal. The judgment was that there would *not be dew nor rain these years.* (There are two references to this incident in the New Testament, Luke 4:25 and James 5:17, both indicating that *these years* amounted to three and a half years.) Elijah's words constituted a direct challenge to Baal on behalf of Israel's true God, for Baal was believed by his followers to be the god of fertility—both in human beings and in all of nature. Thus, it was believed, Baal controlled the rain and other factors that were necessary for crops to grow. Such a challenge as Elijah's would leave no doubt as to who was really in charge of the elements. [See question #1, page 360.]

B. God's Care (vv. 2-7)

2, 3. And the word of the LORD came unto him, saying, Get thee hence, and turn thee eastward, and hide thyself by the brook Cherith, that is before Jordan.

Once Elijah had delivered his message, God ordered him to *hide.* During the time of famine, God's messenger and word would be withdrawn from His people. Most likely Elijah's personal safety was also a factor. Since Palestine has a dry season that generally lasts from May to October, some time may have elapsed before it became obvious that Elijah's prophecy was being fulfilled. When that became apparent, Ahab would probably try to kill him. [See question #2, page 360.]

God instructed Elijah to go *eastward* and take refuge *by the brook Cherith.* While there is some disagreement about its location (it is spelled "Kerith" in some modern versions), this was probably a small stream east of the *Jordan* River, emptying into the Jordan or one of its tributaries.

4. And it shall be, that thou shalt drink of the brook; and I have commanded the ravens to feed thee there.

God not only supplied a hiding place for Elijah, but He also provided water and food. The *brook*, which was probably fed by springs, would supply water for a time, and the food would be brought by *ravens*. Obviously such behavior would have been most unusual for ravens, but the God who created them would have no difficulty in commanding them to act in this manner.

UNUSUAL PROVIDENCE

My wife and I never had to miss or postpone any meals while raising three children on a preacher's salary (which can be a real challenge sometimes). But occasionally our provisions came from unlikely sources. No one in our family will ever forget the several meals whose source was a neighbor's pumpkin patch. Cooked pumpkin would have been an ordinary treat; we found batter-dipped, fried pumpkin *blossoms* to be an extraordinary treat! (They taste almost as good as morel mushrooms.)

I never would have guessed that God would supplement our grocery budget with such an unusual entrée. Elijah must have wondered, too, at God's rather bizarre providence. How could ravens possibly supply his food? Later, he must have been at least a little surprised that a penniless widow would be chosen to give him his "room and board."

Truly the Lord provides in unexpected and even miraculous ways. Elijah believed God's promise, despite the unlikely nature of the resources available. Dare we doubt His providence simply because we can't see the possibilities? God nurtures our trust by demonstrating His great, and often mysterious, faithfulness. —R. W. B.

5. So he went and did according unto the word of the LORD: for he went and dwelt by the brook Cherith, that is before Jordan.

We wonder why Ahab did not seize Elijah immediately and either imprison him or kill him. Perhaps he did not believe that the prophet, or his God, could harm him. Most likely Elijah did not tarry long in Ahab's presence to give the king time to act. He seems to have set out at once for the hiding place God had provided for him.

6. And the ravens brought him bread and flesh in the morning, and bread and flesh in the evening; and he drank of the brook.

The *brook* Cherith was isolated enough to provide both security and solitude for Elijah.

7. And it came to pass after a while, that the brook dried up, because there had been no rain in the land.

The *brook* was probably fed by springs, but a prolonged drought would have dried up even these springs. God was signaling to Elijah that it was time for him to begin a new phase in his ministry. [See question #3, page 360.]

II. God Directs Elijah
(1 Kings 17:8-16)
A. Widow in Zarephath (vv. 8, 9)

8, 9. And the word of the LORD came unto him, saying, Arise, get thee to Zarephath, which belongeth to Zidon, and dwell there: behold, I have commanded a widow woman there to sustain thee.

This new phase in Elijah's ministry took him to *Zarephath*. This town was located on the Mediterranean Sea about halfway between the two Phoenician cities of Tyre and Sidon (spelled here as *Zidon*). At this point in history the town was under the control of Sidon.

Sending Elijah to Phoenicia, the very center of Baal worship, and telling him that he would find sustenance from a *widow* (often the poorest of the poor in the ancient world) may seem like another unusual way to provide for him. For now, however, God's hand of judgment (expressed through the famine) remained on the nation of Israel. His blessing was about to be experienced by a non-Israelite. Jesus later used this incident to rebuke those in the Nazareth synagogue for their scornful attitudes and to emphasize God's concern for others outside the scope of the "chosen people" (Luke 4:23-26). [See question #4, page 360.]

B. Elijah's Request (vv. 10, 11)

10. So he arose and went to Zarephath. And when he came to the gate of the city, behold, the widow woman was there gathering of sticks: and he called to her, and said, Fetch me, I pray thee, a little water in a vessel, that I may drink.

In making his way from his hiding place by the brook Cherith, it is likely that Elijah traveled along the east side of the Jordan River as far north as its headwaters at Dan. From there he would have traveled westward to *Zarephath*. By taking such a route, he would have been able to avoid Ahab, who had begun a search all over the kingdom for him (1 Kings 18:8-10).

When Elijah approached *the gate of the city*, he saw a *widow woman* who was *gathering . . . sticks* to build a fire for cooking. At that point he apparently did not know that this was the woman who would feed him. Thirsty from his long travels, he asked for *a little water in a vessel*. To provide a drink of water to strangers was considered a common courtesy in this part of the ancient world. Even though the drought had reached into Phoenicia, the springs there were fed from the peaks of the Lebanon Mountains and thus would still contain water when most other sources had dried up.

Judging from the widow's words to Elijah in verse 12, it is difficult to know whether she was a follower of the true God or was simply acknowledging the Lord as Elijah's God (note her reference to "*thy* God"). Perhaps the woman was a refugee from Israel or had in some other way learned of the true God. We are reminded of Jesus' ministry in this same area, during which a Greek woman came desiring that Jesus cast a devil out of her daughter (Mark 7:25, 26).

11. And as she was going to fetch it, he called to her, and said, Bring me, I pray thee, a morsel of bread in thine hand.

The widow's response to Elijah's request for a drink may have been the clue indicating to him that this was the woman whom God had mentioned earlier. So he added the request that she *bring* him *a morsel of bread*—which would have been more available than any other food.

C. Desperate Condition (v. 12)

12. And she said, As the LORD thy God liveth, I have not a cake, but a handful of meal in a barrel, and a little oil in a cruse: and, behold, I am gathering two sticks, that I may go in and dress it for me and my son, that we may eat it, and die.

The widow was not immediately able to comply with the prophet's request. She did not have a *cake* (loaf) of bread. While this area of Phoenicia did have water available for drinking, it had not been able to escape other consequences of the drought. The widow had just enough *meal* (flour) and *oil* to provide something for her and her son to *eat*. After that they faced starvation. While some students interpret her reply as an excuse for denying food to Elijah, it is possible that the widow was offering an apology for not being able to provide for him more adequately.

D. Elijah's Assurance (vv. 13, 14)

13. And Elijah said unto her, Fear not; go and do as thou hast said: but make me thereof a little cake first, and bring it unto me, and after make for thee and for thy son.

The words *fear not* are found on several occasions in the Scriptures when a person was confronted with an overwhelming or frightening situation. This woman certainly needed such reassurance because she knew that she had barely enough flour and oil to prepare food for herself and her son. Yet this stranger was asking to be fed *first*!

14. For thus saith the LORD God of Israel, The barrel of meal shall not waste, neither shall the cruse of oil fail, until the day that the LORD sendeth rain upon the earth.

Thus saith the Lord God of Israel. By this expression Elijah stated the authority for his reassuring words to the woman. As is so often the case, when God gives He gives bountifully. He would provide the woman with *meal* and *oil* until the drought was over.

E. God's Provision (vv. 15, 16)

15, 16. And she went and did according to the saying of Elijah: and she, and he, and her house, did eat many days. And the barrel of meal wasted not, neither did the cruse of oil fail, according to the word of the LORD, which he spake by Elijah.

Encouraged by the prophet's words, the woman proceeded to do as *Elijah* had asked. And God did indeed miraculously provide for her, her son, and Elijah. The *many days* included not only the time that Elijah stayed with the woman, but the time that passed until the rains returned.

THE GRACE OF GIVING

I can remember when my father's income was less than one-tenth of my present salary. Yet I know that Dad was a faithful tither to the church and gave other offerings besides. My parents believed God's promise to supply all of our needs (Philippians 4:19) when we make His kingdom our priority (Matthew 6:33). And God rewarded their faith by providing for our family.

Sacrificial giving is illustrated and commended repeatedly in Scripture. Jesus praised the widow who gave "all that she had, even all her living" (Mark 12:41-44) to the temple treasury. She was perhaps unwittingly following the example of the widow in our lesson today, who also gave her very last resources to provide for the needs of God's prophet.

Writing to the Corinthian Christians, the apostle Paul illustrated the "grace of giving" by telling of the Macedonian Christians, who gave abundantly despite undergoing "a great trial of affliction" (2 Corinthians 8:1-4). They considered it a

---

Home Daily Bible Readings

Monday, June 4—Omri Reigns Over Israel (1 Kings 16:21-28)
Tuesday, June 5—Ahab Reigns Over Israel (1 Kings 16:29-34)
Wednesday, June 6—Elijah Predicts a Drought in Israel (1 Kings 17:1-7)
Thursday, June 7—The Prayer of Faith (James 5:13-18)
Friday, June 8—The Widow of Zarephath (1 Kings 17:8-16)
Saturday, June 9—Elijah Raises the Widow's Son From Death (1 Kings 17:17-24)
Sunday, June 10—God's Goodness (Job 36:5-11)

privilege to share their meager possessions with needy brothers and sisters. Paul exhorted the Corinthians to "abound in this grace also" (v. 7).

How many of today's Christians understand the "grace of giving"? The Macedonians did because they "*first* gave their own selves to the Lord" (v. 5). So must we.   —R. W. B.

Conclusion

A. "What Goes Around Comes Around"

Most of us have probably heard this saying. And probably we would admit that, while what goes around may not *always* come around, quite often that statement proves true—as the widow in today's lesson learned. She was willing to give the last morsel of food she had to feed a hungry prophet. She had not asked for nor expected any reward for her sacrifice; nevertheless, she was rewarded by receiving enough food to last her and her son through a severe famine.

This principle still holds true today. A church in Georgia earned a reputation for helping other churches in time of need, including a Florida church whose building was struck by a hurricane. Then a disastrous flood seriously damaged the building of the congregation in Georgia. In the weeks that followed there was an outpouring

---

How to Say It

AHAB. *Ay*-hab.
BAAL. *Bay*-ul.
CHERITH. *Key*-rith.
ELIJAH. Ee-*lye*-juh.
ETHBAAL. Eth-*bay*-ul.
GILEAD. *Gil*-ee-ud.
JABBOK. *Jab*-ok.
JEROBOAM. Jair-uh-*bo*-um.
JEZEBEL. *Jez*-uh-bel.
KERITH. *Key*-rith.
MACEDONIANS. Mass-eh-*doe*-nee-uns.
NAPHTALI. *Naf*-tuh-lye.
NAZARETH. *Naz*-uh-reth.
OMRI. *Ahm*-rye.
PHOENICIANS. Fuh-*nish*-uns.
REHOBOAM. Ree-huh-*bo*-um.
SAMARIA. Suh-*mare*-ee-uh.
SIDON. *Sigh*-dun.
TISHBE. *Tish*-be.
TISHBITE. *Tish*-bite.
TYRE. Tire.
YARMUK. *Yar*-mook.
ZAREPHATH. *Zar*-ih-fath.
ZIDON. *Zye*-dun.
ZIDONIANS. Zye-*doe*-nee-uns.

---

of aid from those whom they had helped and from others who learned of their need. Indeed, in this case what went around came around.

Of course, the most vivid illustration of this principle is yet to come. In Matthew 25:31-46 we read of Jesus' description of the final judgment. It tells of what He will say to those who have involved themselves in such acts as giving food to the hungry, drink to the thirsty, and clothing to the naked. Although those who have provided such help have not done so for a reward, Jesus will grant them the greatest reward of all—a glorious welcome into Heaven.

B. Courage and Patience

Elijah was a man of great faith and courage. He needed both to confront a wicked king like Ahab. But once he had pronounced God's judgment through the famine, God wisely took him "out of the picture" for some time. From what the Scriptures indicate, Elijah was a man of action, and he must have chafed while waiting until God was ready to use him again. Left to his own counsel, he might have preferred to remain near the king and his cohorts, caring little that it could mean death. However, raw courage must always be tempered with cautious wisdom. Although Elijah may have accepted God's restraint reluctantly, accept it he did—and survived to carry on a far more important ministry than dying a martyr's death.

In many places in the world today, Christians have to worship and carry out their ministries in secret. For example, in China there are perhaps thousands of "house churches" where Christians meet quietly and without any public announcement. Raw courage might lead some to want to proclaim their faith boldly in the streets, but to do so would certainly mean persecution or even death. Most of these believers have carried on their ministries with appropriate discretion, patiently praying and waiting for that day when they can proclaim their Lord from the housetops.

C. Prayer

Almighty God, we thank You for men like the prophet Elijah—men of faith, prayer, and courage, who were able to confront evildoers in places of power with Your words of judgment. May we pray seeking similar faith and courage—not just for dramatic confrontations but for the little challenges that we face every day. In Jesus' name we pray. Amen.

D. Thought to Remember

Let us learn from the example of Elijah—"a man subject to like passions as we are" but whose "effectual fervent prayer" availed much (James 5:16-18). [See question #5, page 360.]

Learning by Doing

This page contains an alternate lesson plan emphasizing learning activities.
Classes desiring such student involvement will find these suggestions helpful.

Learning Goals

After this lesson each student will be able to:

1. Tell how God provided for Elijah during the three-year famine described in the text.

2. Tell some ways in which God provides for His people today.

3. Suggest a specific way he or she can demonstrate dependence on the Lord.

Into the Lesson

Ask the class members to work in groups of three. Each learner is to tell the others in his or her group about someone whose life demonstrates *trusting God to provide for one's needs.* The learners should know personally the people whom they describe, but they are not to reveal names.

After the groups have finished sharing, tell the class that one of the names used to describe God is *Jehovah-jireh*, which means "God provides" or "God is our provider" (Genesis 22:13, 14). God's care and provision for His people are dramatically illustrated in today's text.

Into the Word

During the week before class, ask a class member to prepare a brief lecture on, or a synopsis of, the lesson background and verse 1 of the text. Give this person a photocopy of the commentary notes on these sections. He or she may want to use a map of the divided kingdom as well.

To open the Bible study, tell the fable of the termite and the giant found on page 354. Be sure to include the concluding thoughts comparing this story with Ahab and Elijah. Then ask the person you have recruited to give a synopsis of the lesson background.

Ask a volunteer to read 1 Kings 17:1-16 aloud. Distribute the following discussion questions to the groups of three that worked together earlier, and ask each group to choose a recorder to write a one-sentence answer to each question.

1. Why do you think Elijah used the phrase, "As the Lord God of Israel liveth"?

2. The text does not tell how Ahab responded to Elijah's message. How do you think he responded?

3. Why do you think God told Elijah to hide?

After the groups or the class discusses these questions, read verses 8 and 9 and give a brief lecture on the background of Zarephath. Then ask the groups to discuss and write one-sentence answers to these two questions:

1. Why do you think Elijah asked the widow to feed him first?

2. Why do you think she complied with his request?

After the groups have completed their study, tell the class that the story of the widow doesn't end here. As the remaining verses of 1 Kings 17 record, her son suddenly became ill and died. But Elijah, through God's power, restored the boy's life.

Into Life

Prepare a visual with three columns under the major heading "Jehovah-jireh" (God Provides). Over column 1 write "Elijah." Over column 2 write "Widow." Over column 3 write "Believers Today." Appoint someone to act as "scribe" to write the class's answers on the visual.

Ask, "What did God provide for Elijah?" Answers may include food, water, safety, and assurance. Then ask what He provided for the widow. Answers may include food, security, her son's life, and a demonstration of His power.

Tell the class, "Now comes the tough question. What does this lesson teach us about God? What do we learn through Elijah about trust in and dependence on God? Will God always provide for our needs? Let's start with the easier question: 'What does God provide for every disciple of His?'" List their answers in column 3. Answers may include salvation, an inheritance, Heaven, hope, peace, a family, etc. The list could be long.

Observe that, even though God is our provider, He does not promise believers that they will *never* experience hardship or even extreme deprivation of basic needs. Ask the class to suggest illustrations of this truth. Summarize by pointing out that trusting God to provide is not always easy. Sometimes it is difficult to see His providence. But Jesus' Sermon on the Mount reminds us of God's care for us. Read Matthew 6:25-34.

To make the lesson personal, ask each class member to identify at least one area of his or her life that needs to demonstrate more patience and trust that God will provide. Ask them to write that at the top of a three-by-five card that you distribute. Then ask each learner to compose a one- or two-sentence prayer committing himself to trusting God in that situation. Each one is to carry the card through this coming week, praying each day the prayer written on it.

Let's Talk It Over

The questions on this page are designed to encourage review of the lesson Scriptures and to promote discussion of the lesson by the class. The answers provided are only discussion starters. Let your class talk it over from there.

1. God could have arranged to demonstrate His power over nature (and thus over the pagan gods) in a much shorter time period if He had chosen to. What benefit do you see in His using such a slow process to teach His people this lesson?

The deeply rooted paganism that dominated the culture of Israel did not rush in by storm. It was accepted gradually over the course of many years. To counteract this, God executed a long-term miracle—one that would remind Ahab and his people every day for three and a half years that Jehovah is the one true God.

Israel was being confronted by God (through Elijah) with orders to do an about-face. In times like these, people very often need time to develop conviction before following through with a major decision in life. A quick decision to follow Christ is not always best. When we encourage our friends to count the cost of Christianity, we are not discouraging them from belief but rather helping them to prepare for a long-term relationship with Christ that will not be shaken.

2. God told Elijah to hide from Ahab. In other places God tells His followers to stand up and not be afraid of their enemies. How do you know when to stand up and confront the evil in society and when to retreat and "hide" for a time?

Elijah did confront Ahab (v. 1). After that, further confrontation would have been meaningless until the truth of Elijah's prediction had become evident. Then Elijah would confront the wicked king, and the people, once again.

When taking a confrontational stand has the potential for good, then we must not shrink back. But if the confrontation will simply polarize the issue or further divide people, silence might be the best course of action.

Seldom is the issue for us a life-and-death matter, as it was for Elijah. Many missionaries have faced such choices when revolution or other violence has threatened their field of labor. Do they stay or do they flee? Both choices have been made honorably.

3. How long Elijah waited by the brook Cherith no one knows, but it seems to have been a period of some weeks, if not several months. What do you suppose he did during this time? What do you do with extended periods of "down time"?

The Bible gives no clue about Elijah's activity during this time, except for the note in James that Elijah was a man of prayer. We would be very surprised if this were not a spiritual retreat for the prophet, spending long times in prayer. Surely he gave thanks for his miraculous provision by the ravens and for the stream as long as it ran. No doubt, he prayed for the nation of Israel and for his countrymen.

In the fast pace of contemporary society, "down time" seems hard to come by. Do we appreciate it when it comes, or do we champ at the bit to get back into the race? Do we take the opportunity to find spiritual renewal? Do we *seek* such times for renewal?

4. The lesson writer notes that Elijah went to "the very center of Baal worship." How can we take the message of the gospel to the very centers of modern idolatry today—the centers of materialism, secularism, false spiritualism, and others?

Sadly enough, we often see just the opposite happening: secularism, materialism, and the like are infiltrating the church. We need to be alert to the subtle lures of these "idols" and teach believers to stand on the truth of God's Word. Then we need to equip the believers to take a stand for truth when challenged by the disciples of these false "gods." The church needs to do more to make its presence known in the community. Perhaps it can do so by sponsoring public events, hosting support groups such as Alcoholics Anonymous, or welcoming Girl Scout or Boy Scout troops into its building. Maybe a well-designed web site on the Internet would help. Try to get specific about ways to get the church's presence and message more publicly known.

5. Read James 5:17. How would you explain to a new believer the point of this verse?

It is not surprising that Christians today tend to feel "smaller" than the Biblical prophets and apostles who interacted directly with God and heard His spoken word. Yet the point of this verse is that God desires our prayers no less than He desired Elijah's—that God takes our prayers just as seriously and responds to them just as readily. It does not matter if a person has been a believer for twenty years or twenty days; God wants us to pray with equal fervor.

Israel: Called to Decide

DEVOTIONAL READING: Joshua 24:14-18.

BACKGROUND SCRIPTURE: 1 Kings 18.

PRINTED TEXT: 1 Kings 18:20, 21, 30-39.

1 Kings 18:20, 21, 30-39

20 So Ahab sent unto all the children of Israel, and gathered the prophets together unto mount Carmel.

21 And Elijah came unto all the people, and said, How long halt ye between two opinions? if the LORD be God, follow him: but if Baal, then follow him. And the people answered him not a word.

. . . .

30 And Elijah said unto all the people, Come near unto me. And all the people came near unto him. And he repaired the altar of the LORD that was broken down.

31 And Elijah took twelve stones, according to the number of the tribes of the sons of Jacob, unto whom the word of the LORD came, saying, Israel shall be thy name:

32 And with the stones he built an altar in the name of the LORD: and he made a trench about the altar, as great as would contain two measures of seed.

33 And he put the wood in order, and cut the bullock in pieces, and laid him on the wood, and said, Fill four barrels with water, and pour it on the burnt sacrifice, and on the wood.

34 And he said, Do it the second time. And they did it the second time. And he said, Do it the third time. And they did it the third time.

35 And the water ran round about the altar; and he filled the trench also with water.

36 And it came to pass at the time of the offering of the evening sacrifice, that Elijah the prophet came near, and said, LORD God of Abraham, Isaac, and of Israel, let it be known this day that thou art God in Israel, and that I am thy servant, and that I have done all these things at thy word.

37 Hear me, O LORD, hear me, that this people may know that thou art the LORD God, and that thou hast turned their heart back again.

38 Then the fire of the LORD fell, and consumed the burnt sacrifice, and the wood, and the stones, and the dust, and licked up the water that was in the trench.

39 And when all the people saw it, they fell on their faces: and they said, The LORD, he is the God; the LORD, he is the God.

GOLDEN TEXT: And Elijah came unto all the people, and said, How long halt ye between two opinions? if the LORD be God, follow him: but if Baal, then follow him. And the people answered him not a word.—1 Kings 18:21.

Division and Decline
Unit 1: A Kingdom Divided
(Lessons 1-4)

Lesson Aims

After this lesson students should be able to:

1. Give the important details of the confrontation on Mount Carmel between Elijah and the prophets of Baal.

2. Describe how people today "halt" between serving God and following "idols."

3. Express an uncompromising faith in the Lord God.

Lesson Outline

INTRODUCTION

   A. Looking for Loopholes

   B. Lesson Background

 I. THE SETTING (1 Kings 18:20, 21)

   A. Ahab's Summons (v. 20)

   B. Elijah's Challenge (v. 21)

     Silence Is Golden?

 II. THE PREPARATION (1 Kings 18:30-35)

   A. The Altar (vv. 30-32)

   B. The Sacrifice (vv. 33-35)

III. THE CLIMAX (1 Kings 18:36-39)

   A. Elijah's Prayer (vv. 36, 37)

   B. God's Answer (v. 38)

     Fire From Heaven

   C. The People's Response (v. 39)

CONCLUSION

   A. Like King, Like People

   B. Halting Between Two Opinions

   C. Prayer

   D. Thought to Remember

Introduction

A. Looking for Loopholes

Pericles, a respected statesman in ancient Athens, was once approached by a group of citizens who wanted a popular decree changed. "Don't you realize," said Pericles, "that we have a long-standing law that forbids the taking down of any tablet upon which a decree is written?"

"Yes, we understand the law," said one of the group, a lawyer noted for his cleverness. "But there is no need to take the tablet down. We need only to turn it around so that it can no longer be read. There is no law against that."

Times haven't changed much since then. In fact, this lawyer's viewpoint is quite prevalent in our society today. Those who hold this viewpoint do not come out openly and attack the moral standards that have served our society so well. Instead, they use legal technicalities (sometimes called "loopholes") to circumvent the obvious intent of laws, thereby violating their real spirit. Compounding this tragedy is the fact that this practice is becoming more prevalent among some of the most influential of leaders and seems to be widely approved by many citizens.

Christians need to stand as fearless Elijah did and ask, "How long halt ye between two opinions? if the Lord be God, follow him." We dare not be content with "loopholes."

B. Lesson Background

The verses between last week's lesson and today's tell how Elijah left Phoenicia and returned to Israel. On his way to see King Ahab he met Obadiah, an official in Ahab's administration, who had been sent to hunt for water and grass for the king's animals. Through Obadiah, Elijah sent word that he wanted to speak with the king.

When the two met, Ahab's immediate response was to blame the prophet for the trouble that had befallen his kingdom: "Art thou he that troubleth Israel?" (1 Kings 18:17). [See question #1, page 368.] Elijah quickly informed the king that *he*, Ahab, was the real troubler of Israel.

Elijah challenged the king to assemble all Israel on Mount Carmel, along with four hundred fifty prophets of Baal and four hundred "prophets of the groves." The "groves" were either trees or wooden posts that were centers of worship of the Canaanite goddess Asherah (who was considered the "lover" of the god Baal). Implied in Elijah's challenge—or perhaps explicitly stated but not recorded for brevity—was that some kind of test would be conducted that would demonstrate which god was superior and which of them (Elijah or Ahab) was really "he that troubleth Israel."

Nothing more is said about the four hundred prophets of Asherah who were invited to Mount Carmel. Since they are described as those who ate at Jezebel's table (v. 19), perhaps she encouraged them not to participate in what she considered a foolish exercise.

I. The Setting
(1 Kings 18:20, 21)

A. Ahab's Summons (v. 20)

20. So Ahab sent unto all the children of Israel, and gathered the prophets together unto mount Carmel.

Mount Carmel is a high ridge that projects out into the Mediterranean Sea, dividing the plain of Esdraelon to the northeast from the coastal plain to the southwest. It was approximately seventeen miles away from Jezreel, where Ahab kept a palace (1 Kings 21:1). Thus Mount Carmel was located where Baal worship was strongest.

We can only guess why Ahab would accept Elijah's challenge. The effects of the drought may have driven him to the point that he was willing to try anything to bring it to an end. Or perhaps he was arrogant enough to believe that the prophets of Baal would somehow overwhelm or embarrass Elijah and thus rid his kingdom of the man whom Ahab considered Israel's "troublemaker."

B. Elijah's Challenge (v. 21)

21. And Elijah came unto all the people, and said, How long halt ye between two opinions? if the LORD be God, follow him: but if Baal, then follow him. And the people answered him not a word.

When Elijah addressed those who had gathered on Mount Carmel, he wasted no time on diplomatic pleasantries but got right to the point: *How long halt ye between two opinions?* Some issues in life are best resolved by reasonable compromise. But on this issue there was no middle ground, no shade of gray. Elijah's plea is reminiscent of Joshua's: "Choose you this day whom ye will serve" (Joshua 24:15).

Elijah's description of the people's behavior, to *halt*, was a fitting one. It describes one who hops or walks with a limp. From that, it sometimes was used to refer figuratively to one who hesitated or wavered. (The *New International Version* has, "How long will you waver between two opinions?") The Hebrew word also meant to leap or dance; in fact, it is used in verse 26 to describe the way the prophets of Baal "*leaped* upon the altar" as they cried out to him. Perhaps the Biblical writer intended a little play on words by using it both of the Israelites' hesitation and of the prophets who led them to believe that they could serve both the Lord and Baal at the same time.

But Elijah would have none of this. The people must choose between either *the Lord or Baal.* Perhaps Elijah reminded his audience that the Lord was the God of their fathers—Abraham, Isaac, Jacob, and Moses. He is a God of mercy, but He is also a jealous and holy God who will tolerate no competition. [See question #2, page 368.]

However, in the minds of the people there appeared to be some advantages to following Baal. He was the god of fertility, and his worshipers often engaged in illicit sexual activity as a religious rite. Furthermore, Baal worship was the religion of Ahab and Jezebel—and it is usually a good idea to be on the side of those in power.

Torn between these two alternatives, *the people answered him not a word*. They knew that if they acknowledged that they had violated the First Commandment ("Thou shalt have no other gods before me"), they would have to repent and change their ways. And they also knew that they could not plead ignorance or mitigating circumstances, which might get them off the hook. On the other hand, they may have hoped that if they remained quiet perhaps Elijah would simply go away, or the false prophets would kill him. And so they said nothing! It was a very different response from the one that followed Joshua's similar appeal (Joshua 24:16-18). Their silence set the stage for the confrontation that followed. [See question #3, page 368.]

SILENCE IS GOLDEN?

Whoever coined the phrase, "Silence is golden," just may have been the grandfather of twins and triplets, all born within a three-month period! I'm guessing that because I myself am such a grandfather. Having spent considerable time helping to care for my five new grandchildren, I have my own definition of peace: when no babies are crying!

As the phrase is normally used, "Silence is golden" means that saying nothing at all is often the best kind of communication. Certain circumstances call for few words—the kind of quiet that actually speaks volumes.

Elijah's challenge to the Israelites to state their religious loyalty was not such a time! Still, they "answered him not a word." They offered no refutation, no defense, no reply. Perhaps they felt the sting of God's reproach. Perhaps they had become so used to the pattern of compromise that they did not know how to respond when asked to take a stand.

Whatever the reason, Israel's weak and sorry condition teaches us an important lesson: sometimes silence is *not* golden; sometimes it's simply "yellow."

—R. W. B.

"If the Lord be God, follow him: but if Baal, then follow him."

Visual for lesson 3

The visual for today's lesson is a dramatic illustration of verse 21. Display it as you begin to discuss that verse.

II. The Preparation
(1 Kings 18:30-35)
A. The Altar (vv. 30-32)

30. And Elijah said unto all the people, Come near unto me. And all the people came near unto him. And he repaired the altar of the LORD that was broken down.

Verses 22-29 provide the details of how the test was to be carried out. The prophets of Baal were to prepare a bullock for sacrifice, laying it on firewood as a burnt offering without lighting it. Then they were to pray that Baal would send fire to consume the sacrifice. From morning until noon they called upon their god, but nothing happened. Elijah began to chide them, claiming that their god must be busy, or on a journey, or asleep. At this, the prophets of Baal cried louder and even cut themselves in their frenzy, yet when evening came "there was neither voice, nor any to answer, nor any that regarded" (v. 29).

When it was more than obvious that nothing was going to happen, Elijah called the people to gather around him. He wanted to make sure that they were in a position to observe his actions carefully so that they could later serve as credible witnesses. First, he *repaired the altar of the Lord that was broken down*. This may have been one of the altars that were destroyed as a result of the promotion of Baal worship during Ahab's reign (1 Kings 16:32; 19:10). It was probably not an elaborate altar, but one made of rough, uncut stones that had been gathered in the area.

31, 32. And Elijah took twelve stones, according to the number of the tribes of the sons of Jacob, unto whom the word of the LORD came, saying, Israel shall be thy name: and with the stones he built an altar in the name of the LORD: and he made a trench about the altar, as great as would contain two measures of seed.

Elijah selected *twelve stones* for the *altar*, representing the twelve *tribes* of *Israel*. Although the tribes were by now divided into two nations, Judah and Israel, the prophet's action conveyed the message that in the eyes of God they were still one nation. [See question #4, page 368.]

Next, Elijah dug a *trench* around the altar. (No doubt this seemed quite odd to the onlookers.) The phrase *two measures* is literally "two seahs." A seah was a unit of measure equal to about a third of a bushel. If this refers to volume, the trench was not very large. Some, however, believe that the term is describing depth, which would make the trench much larger.

B. The Sacrifice (vv. 33-35)

33. And he put the wood in order, and cut the bullock in pieces, and laid him on the wood, **and said, Fill four barrels with water, and pour it on the burnt sacrifice, and on the wood.**

That Elijah *put the wood in order* apparently means he prepared the *sacrifice* as prescribed in Leviticus 1:3-9. This would be another demonstration that the people were still living under God's laws and were expected to observe them.

Then Elijah did something especially unusual. He ordered that *four barrels* of *water* be poured over the sacrifice and *on the wood* used to start the fire. These *barrels* should not be thought of as the large drums that we often associate with barrels today, but as jars similar to those that women balanced on their heads when they carried water.

One may wonder how this much water could have been available during a time of severe drought. Most likely a spring continued to flow somewhere down Mount Carmel—perhaps sustained by an underground source.

34, 35. And he said, Do it the second time. And they did it the second time. And he said, Do it the third time. And they did it the third time. And the water ran round about the altar; and he filled the trench also with water.

Elijah had water poured on the sacrifice a *second* then a *third time*. By now the purpose of the trench was obvious. So much water had been poured on the altar that it ran down and filled the trench. Such actions assured that there would be no basis whatsoever for any charges of fraud or trickery on Elijah's part.

III. The Climax
(1 Kings 18:36-39)
A. Elijah's Prayer (vv. 36, 37)

36. And it came to pass at the time of the offering of the evening sacrifice, that Elijah the prophet came near, and said, LORD God of Abraham, Isaac, and of Israel, let it be known this day that thou art God in Israel, and that I am thy servant, and that I have done all these things at thy word.

The Hebrew text literally reads, "And it came to pass at the offering of the sacrifice." However, since the law required that two sacrifices be offered daily (Exodus 29:38-42), this may well have been the time of the evening sacrifice (about 3:00 P.M.). Once again, Elijah's purpose may have been to remind the people of God's approved practice concerning sacrifice, even though the people of the north no longer worshiped in Jerusalem.

37. Hear me, O LORD, hear me, that this people may know that thou art the LORD God, and that thou hast turned their heart back again.

Elijah addressed his prayer to the *Lord*—that is, Jehovah—using God's unique name that He had revealed to Moses (Exodus 3:13, 14). Elijah was calling the people's attention to the God of the covenant—the covenant that had been made many centuries before with Abraham, Isaac, and Jacob. He was also calling the people back to their responsibilities under that covenant. *Thou hast turned their heart back again.* Elijah was so confident of the people's response that he prayed as if it had already happened.

B. God's Answer (v. 38)

38. Then the fire of the LORD fell, and consumed the burnt sacrifice, and the wood, and the stones, and the dust, and licked up the water that was in the trench.

As soon as Elijah concluded his prayer, God acted—and with authority! *The fire of the Lord fell,* and in an awe-inspiring demonstration of His mighty power everything used to arrange the sacrifice was instantly *consumed.*

Some, wishing to minimize the miraculous element in this event, propose that a bolt of lightning struck the altar and the sacrifice. If so, this would have been a most unusual lightning bolt, for there was no sign of rain at the time. The clouds and rain and any accompanying lightning came later (1 Kings 18:41-45). Even so, a bolt of lightning from a cloudless sky that hit at just the right time and in just the right place would have been just as much a miracle! [See question #5, page 368.]

FIRE FROM HEAVEN

Fire possesses great potential for both productive energy and destructive power. The Chicago fire of 1871 is a classic illustration of the latter. So are the forest fires that annually scorch thousands of acres of land and result in the tragic loss of life and property.

On the productive side, fire heats our homes, generates energy for industry, cooks our food, and powers all sorts of engines. It can be either helpful or harmful, but it is nearly always evidence of power. In the Scriptures, fire is often a symbol of the power of God's Spirit. Perhaps the clearest illustration of this is the "tongues like as of fire" that appeared over each of the apostles on the Day of Pentecost (Acts 2:1-4).

The fire that fell in response to Elijah's prayer was unmistakably a demonstration of the power of Israel's true God, and it fulfilled two important purposes. The sacrifice and altar that Elijah had prepared were consumed (along with everything surrounding them), but the faith of Israel was renewed and empowered.

God's Spirit provides "heat" to warm our hearts with love and conviction and "light" (through the words of the Scriptures) to guide our paths. The world needs to see such fire as evidence that "the Lord, he is the God." Pray for

How to Say It

AHAB. *Ay*-hab.
ASHERAH. Uh-*she*-ruh.
BAAL. *Bay*-ul.
CANAANITE. *Kay*-nun-ite.
CARMEL. *Car*-mel.
ELIJAH. Ee-*lye*-juh.
ESDRAELON. *Es*-druh-*ee*-lon (strong accent on *ee*).
ETHBAAL. Eth-*bay*-ul.
JEZEBEL. *Jez*-uh-bel.
JEZREEL. *Jez*-ree-el or *Jez*-reel.
KISHON. *Kye*-shon.
MEDITERRANEAN. *Med*-uh-tuh-*ray*-nee-un (strong accent on *ray*).
OBADIAH. O-buh-*dye*-uh.
OMRI. *Ahm*-rye.
PERICLES. *Pair*-ih-cleez.
PHOENICIA. Fuh-*nish*-uh.
SEAH. *seh*-ah.
SIDONIANS. Sigh-*doe*-nee-uns.

fires of revival to be poured out on our nation and to the ends of the earth!   —R. W. B.

C. The People's Response (v. 39)

39. And when all the people saw it, they fell on their faces: and they said, The LORD, he is the God; the LORD, he is the God.

The people's response was immediate. They knew very well that they had seen the powerful hand of God dramatically displayed. This was no time for theological discussions about the relative power of Jehovah and Baal. They knew what they had seen, and they acted accordingly: *they fell on their faces!* Western culture may not prescribe this posture, but in that time and culture it was an appropriate posture that showed fear, awe, and reverence.

At the beginning of this test, Elijah had boldly challenged the people to choose between Jehovah and Baal. They now made their choice quite obvious: *The Lord, he is the God.* This manifestation of God's power could not be denied.

The remaining verses of 1 Kings 18 tell of some of the events that followed the incident at Mount Carmel. First, the prophets of Baal were taken down to the brook Kishon (just north of Mount Carmel) and there executed. Then, after informing Ahab that rain was on the way, Elijah went to the top of Mount Carmel and began to pray. After praying, he sent his servant to look toward "the sea" (i.e., the Mediterranean Sea) for signs of rain. When he returned and reported that he saw nothing, Elijah sent him back again.

This was repeated until the seventh time, when the servant returned with the message that he saw a cloud "like a man's hand." Soon the sky grew dark, then "there was a great rain." Ahab, following the prophet's earlier instructions to return to Jezreel, had already started back in his chariot; but Elijah ran ahead of the chariot and arrived at the city first. Clearly it was a day of triumph for the Lord's prophet.

Conclusion

A. Like King, Like People

Rulers, whether they are hereditary monarchs, military dictators, or elected officials, have an obligation before God to provide good government for their people. But just as important, though often overlooked, is their responsibility to provide good models for their people. The reigns of Omri and his son Ahab show the tragic results that follow when rulers do not live up to this second responsibility. These two rulers imported the worship of Baal into the northern kingdom and in the process infected their people with it. Ahab compounded the problem by marrying Jezebel, daughter of Ethbaal of the Sidonians (1 Kings 16:31). She became a vigorous missionary for the cause of Baal, assembling four hundred fifty prophets of Baal and four hundred prophets of Asherah. With such aggressive support for the worship of Baal, it should be no surprise that many of the people became followers of this false religion.

In recent years, we have seen the flouting of God's moral laws by various national leaders. As shocking as some of these activities have been, even more serious is the impact that this type of behavior has had on society in general. That our society is experiencing a serious decline in moral standards, both public and private, is obvious to anyone who takes a serious look at the situation. And, as in Elijah's time, those who take a stand for Biblical teachings on morality are often labeled as "old-fashioned" or "bigoted" by those outside the church and sometimes as "legalists" by fellow believers.

B. Halting Between Two Opinions

Jehovah God is a jealous God: "Thou shalt have no other gods before me" (Exodus 20:3). He is an uncompromising God who is unwilling to accept divided allegiance from His followers. We cannot serve God and mammon (Matthew 6:24). Satan, on the other hand, is quite willing to make whatever concessions are necessary to gain an entrance into people's hearts. He has no objection to people's attending church and even becoming "Christians" so long as he can maintain a foothold in their lives. His soothing message of compromise falls on receptive ears. If we listen to him long enough, we are likely to find ourselves ensnared in his trap.

This was the situation in Israel in Elijah's day. Many of the people probably considered themselves faithful followers of God. They had no real interest in becoming fully committed, dedicated followers of Baal. They wanted to serve Jehovah and at the same time enjoy some of the pleasures that the priests of Baal promised to his followers. Elijah confronted this attitude by hurling at the people a challenge that left no room for compromise: "How long halt ye between two opinions?"

When we fall for Satan's clever call to compromise, we find that the keen edge of moral discernment becomes blunted, and we no longer have the insights or the courage to stand firmly for the right. This is perhaps best illustrated by the people's response to Elijah's challenge: they "answered him not a word." They were drifting aimlessly in a sea of compromise, with no courage and no convictions.

May the words and example of Elijah encourage us to stand firmly on the truth of the Bible—without compromise.

C. Prayer

Dear Lord, we thank You for servants such as Elijah, who stood faithfully in the face of overwhelming odds. Grant us, we pray, the same kind of courage to serve You where You have called us, even when the odds we are up against seem overwhelming. In our Master's name we pray. Amen.

D. Thought to Remember

"Choose you this day whom ye will serve" (Joshua 24:15).

Home Daily Bible Readings

Monday, June 11—Elijah Is Sent to Ahab (1 Kings 18:1-6)

Tuesday, June 12—Elijah Meets and Challenges Ahab (1 Kings 18:7-19)

Wednesday, June 13—Elijah and the Prophets of Baal (1 Kings 18:20-29)

Thursday, June 14—Choose Whom You Will Serve (Joshua 24:14-18)

Friday, June 15—Elijah's Triumph for God (1 Kings 18:30-40)

Saturday, June 16—The Drought Ends (1 Kings 18:41-46)

Sunday, June 17—Elijah Flees, Then Meets God (1 Kings 19:1-18)

Learning by Doing

*This page contains an alternate lesson plan emphasizing learning activities.
Classes desiring such student involvement will find these suggestions helpful.*

Learning Goals

After this lesson each student will be able to:

1. Give the important details of the confrontation on Mount Carmel between Elijah and the prophets of Baal.

2. Describe how people today "halt" between serving God and following "idols."

3. Express an uncompromising faith in the Lord God.

Into the Lesson

Use a large marker to write each of the letters of the word *FAITHFUL* on a different sheet of construction paper in large print. Begin the session by giving one sheet to each of eight class members. Ask them to arrange themselves so they spell a word. When they have formed the word *FAITHFUL*, thank them and ask them to mount their letters on a wall or bulletin board.

Then ask each class member to find a partner and to tell him or her the name of an Old Testament character who modeled faithfulness to God and how the character did so. After a few moments, make the transition to Bible study by telling the class that God has continually reminded His people of His expectation of faithfulness to Him. Today's text provides one example, and it will serve as a reminder for us today.

Into the Word

Read 1 Kings 18:20, 21, 30-39. Then divide the class into groups of four or five. Give each group a piece of poster board, a marker, and a piece of paper with one of the following three tasks. If you have more than three groups, give duplicate tasks to some. If you do not have enough learners to form three groups, then omit some of the tasks or do them as whole-class activities.

Task 1: Pretend you are a reporter covering this miraculous call to faithfulness. List approximately five significant facts about this event that need to be developed in the news article. Write a "quotable quote" from the event that can be used in the article. Write the opening line and a headline for the article.

Task 2: Decide what are crucial characteristics of a faithful follower of God. List those characteristics by building an acrostic around the word *faithful*. Example: using the letter "t" you might cite "truthful" as a characteristic. Other crucial characteristics may also be written on the poster.

Task 3: Select from the text a "key verse" that serves as a motto for this lesson. Print that verse on the poster board. Then identify and list "idols" that tempt people to be unfaithful to God.

After each group has completed the tasks, ask the group or groups with task 1 to report their findings. After the report, give a brief lecture about the temptations Baal brought to the Israelites. See the lesson commentary notes on the Lesson Background, verse 21, and the Conclusion. Then ask the group or groups with task 2 to report their findings. After this report ask the class to name additional characteristics of the faithful life. Write these new suggestions on the poster. After the group or groups with task 3 report, affirm the key verse. Then ask the class to suggest additional "idols" that cause today's believers to waver between faithfulness and unfaithfulness. Add these to the poster as they are given.

Into Life

Make the transition to application by observing that most of us struggle with faithfulness in several areas of our lives. Most of us would like to honor God with greater faithfulness to Him.

Give each person a letter-size sheet of paper with the heading "My Commitment to Faithfulness." Below the heading print these words: "As I read Elijah's call to faithfulness to God, I am thankful that I generally honor Him with these characteristics of faithfulness." . . . Almost midway down the page print, "As I read today's text I confess I feel guilty about not being faithful to God in this area of my life." . . . Near the bottom of the page print, "My plan to honor God by being more faithful to Him includes." . . .

Ask the class members to look at the poster created earlier for task 2. Using this list of characteristics of a faithful life, learners should complete the first part of the worksheet. After they complete this task, ask them to identify areas of their lives where they need to demonstrate more faithfulness to God. Write those areas on the second part of the worksheet. Then give the learners time to complete the strategy exercise near the bottom of the worksheet.

Conclude this lesson by having the class sing together the song "I Surrender All" or "I Give All." (Provide songbooks.) Close the lesson with prayer, asking God to be honored by and to bless the commitments made today by His people.

Let's Talk It Over

The questions on this page are designed to encourage review of the lesson Scriptures and to promote discussion of the lesson by the class. The answers provided are only discussion starters. Let your class talk it over from there.

1. Ahab blamed Elijah for the drought in Israel. How should we respond to people who blame God for the difficulties they face in life?

The popular myth is that if people are basically good and don't do anything really bad, such as killing someone, then God will reward them with health, wealth, and happiness in this life and Heaven in the life to come. Even Christians sometimes buy into a "health and wealth" theology, raising the standards somewhat from the secular world, but still expecting a payoff for good behavior. Unfortunately, the view is not Biblical.

Some have said, "If God were all-good and all-powerful, then there would be nothing bad in the world." Thus, they reason, there is no God—or He is not all-powerful or He is not good! They make their own standards for what God ought to be or do. We need to show them the evidence for the God of the Bible, who is both all-powerful and all-good, but who also allows free will and has done so since the beginning. The exercise of man's free will has introduced sin and pain and death into what was once a perfect creation.

2. Suppose a friend says he thinks it is unfair for God to demand people to live with uncompromising devotion to Him. How would you answer your friend?

God is the Creator of the universe! He owns everything in it and possesses all authority to determine what is right and wrong for humanity. As the clay cannot question the potter or the book its author, so we have little room to make demands. Beyond that, God is holy, the author of goodness. His "jealous" demand for allegiance is based on the requirements of perfect righteousness. Furthermore, God wants to pour out unimaginable grace on His people. His jealousy reflects the fact that He wants only what is best for us.

3. The people hesitated and remained silent after Elijah asked them to declare their loyalty to God or Baal. How does such indecision hurt the body of Christ today?

The familiar adage is true: "All that is required for evil to prosper is for good men [and women] to do nothing." When Christian people hesitate to speak up against evil, then evil is tolerated and accepted. This happens in the church as well as outside it.

In addition, it is the example of those who take a stand that often encourages others to do so. An attitude of hesitation and indecision sets exactly the wrong example for younger believers and fails to prepare the next generation of Christians for bold witnessing to the truth of the resurrection.

4. Elijah used twelve stones to build the altar, one for each of the tribes of Israel. How important are symbols to us today? What symbols are especially important to you?

In all walks of life symbols are important. They serve as reminders of special events and special people. They serve as tokens of love and faithfulness. A golden band worn on the third finger of the left hand speaks of a lifetime commitment to one special person. A loaf and a cup speak of the atoning sacrifice of our Lord. A cross or a portrait of Christ similarly inspire us. Recently many have found the initials "W.W.J.D." to be a motivational symbol.

It is human nature to attach greater significance to objects than their intrinsic worth. It's the reason we keep photo albums, ticket stubs, and other mementos and souvenirs. Let your class members tell of the symbols they find most helpful to their faith and devotion.

5. Wouldn't it be great to call fire from Heaven to vindicate us before the secularists and materialists today who scoff at the idea of serving God! What evidence can we cite for our faith?

The world has scored many great victories in semantics, as seen in the expression *science vs. religion*. Science is seen as an objective study of hard facts. Religion is made to appear completely subjective and repressive of any evidence that would discredit it if given a fair hearing.

In frustration, we may well wish to pull off some great demonstration like Elijah's to show that "religion" is factual and that the God in whom we believe is real. Actually, science itself provides evidence of God, and an honest investigation of facts provides many evidences for our faith. The most important is the evidence for the resurrection. The empty tomb declares the power of the One who could not be held inside it. Jesus' friends could not have stolen His body; Jesus' enemies did not hide the body. Jesus rose again!

Micaiah: Courageous Prophet

DEVOTIONAL READING: **Proverbs 12:13-22.**

BACKGROUND SCRIPTURE: **1 Kings 22:1-40.**

PRINTED TEXT: **1 Kings 22:15-28.**

1 Kings 22:15-28

15 So he came to the king. And the king said unto him, Micaiah, shall we go against Ramoth-gilead to battle, or shall we forbear? And he answered him, Go, and prosper: for the LORD shall deliver it into the hand of the king.

16 And the king said unto him, How many times shall I adjure thee that thou tell me nothing but that which is true in the name of the LORD?

17 And he said, I saw all Israel scattered upon the hills, as sheep that have not a shepherd: and the LORD said, These have no master: let them return every man to his house in peace.

18 And the king of Israel said unto Jehoshaphat, Did I not tell thee that he would prophesy no good concerning me, but evil?

19 And he said, Hear thou therefore the word of the LORD: I saw the LORD sitting on his throne, and all the host of heaven standing by him on his right hand and on his left.

20 And the LORD said, Who shall persuade Ahab, that he may go up and fall at Ramoth-gilead? And one said on this manner, and another said on that manner.

21 And there came forth a spirit, and stood before the LORD, and said, I will persuade him.

22 And the LORD said unto him, Wherewith? And he said, I will go forth, and I will be a lying spirit in the mouth of all his prophets. And he said, Thou shalt persuade him, and prevail also: go forth, and do so.

23 Now therefore, behold, the LORD hath put a lying spirit in the mouth of all these thy prophets, and the LORD hath spoken evil concerning thee.

24 But Zedekiah the son of Chenaanah went near, and smote Micaiah on the cheek, and said, Which way went the Spirit of the LORD from me to speak unto thee?

25 And Micaiah said, Behold, thou shalt see in that day, when thou shalt go into an inner chamber to hide thyself.

26 And the king of Israel said, Take Micaiah, and carry him back unto Amon the governor of the city, and to Joash the king's son;

27 And say, Thus saith the king, Put this fellow in the prison, and feed him with bread of affliction and with water of affliction, until I come in peace.

28 And Micaiah said, If thou return at all in peace, the LORD hath not spoken by me. And he said, Hearken, O people, every one of you.

GOLDEN TEXT: Micaiah said, As the LORD liveth, what the LORD saith unto me, that will I speak.—1 Kings 22:14.

Division and Decline
Unit 1: A Kingdom Divided
(Lessons 1-4)

Lesson Aims

After this lesson students should be able to:

1. Recount the circumstances under which Micaiah courageously refused to compromise God's message.

2. Tell why standing for God's truth is such a challenge in today's world.

3. Express appreciation to someone who, like Micaiah, has paid a price for being true to God's message.

Lesson Outline

INTRODUCTION
    A. An Excellent Spine
    B. Lesson Background
  I. DISASTROUS PREDICTION (1 Kings 22:15-18)
    A. Micaiah's Sarcasm (v. 15)
    B. Ahab's Response (v. 16)
      Under Oath
    C. Micaiah's Message (v. 17)
    D. Ahab's Disgust (v. 18)
 II. DISTRESSING VISION (1 Kings 22:19-23)
    A. The Lord on His Throne (v. 19)
    B. A Lying Spirit (vv. 20-23)
III. DISTURBING ANNOUNCEMENT (1 Kings 22:24-28)
    A. Zedekiah's Anger (v. 24)
    B. Micaiah's Reply (v. 25)
    C. Ahab's Anger (vv. 26, 27)
    D. Micaiah's Promise (v. 28)
      Stretching the Truth
CONCLUSION
    A. The Rest of the Story
    B. A Rare Commodity
    C. Prayer
    D. Thought to Remember

Introduction

A. An Excellent Spine

Charles Spurgeon, the renowned nineteenth-century preacher, was once conducting a Bible study with a group of boys. One boy was asked to read from Daniel 6:3: "Then this Daniel was preferred above the presidents and princes, because an excellent spirit was in him." But the boy misread part of the verse and said, "An excellent spine was in him." We may smile at the boy's mistake; but even if his reading was wrong,

he hit upon an important truth. Daniel *was* great because of his "excellent spine"—his great courage in the face of difficult circumstances.

Some two and a half centuries earlier, Micaiah demonstrated "an excellent spine" under similar conditions. Surrounded by false prophets who spoke words favorable to King Ahab, Micaiah refused to go along with the majority. As a result, he endured the scorn of the king, who had him imprisoned. But Ahab learned, at the cost of his life, that he could not imprison the Lord's truth.

B. Lesson Background

The previous lesson focused on Elijah's confrontation with Ahab and the false prophets of Baal on Mount Carmel. The display of God's mighty power there should have brought Ahab to his knees in contrite repentance; however, his wife Jezebel determined to seek revenge against Elijah. The prophet fled to the wilderness of Judah, where God spoke to him and encouraged him to remain faithful to his prophetic task (1 Kings 19:1-18).

First Kings 20 then records Israel's involvement in two battles with Ben-hadad, king of Syria (also called Aram), during a two-year span. On both occasions Ahab defeated the Syrian forces in fulfillment of a promise given by a prophet of the Lord. After the second battle, Ahab made a treaty with Ben-hadad (against the will of the Lord, as indicated in 1 Kings 20:34-43). Apparently this treaty involved the return of certain cities to Israel that the Syrians had captured. One of these was Ramoth in Gilead (called Ramoth-gilead in today's text). (For the location of Gilead, see the comments on 1 Kings 17:1 in lesson 2, page 355.) Ramoth was located in the eastern part of this territory.

The Syrians, however, had not honored Ahab's treaty. (Syria's possession of Ramoth gave the Syrians easier access to Israelite territory.) After three years had passed (1 Kings 22:1), Ahab decided to attack the Syrians. By this time he was on good terms with Jehoshaphat, the king of Judah. So when Jehoshaphat came to visit Ahab in Samaria, Ahab asked for his assistance in recapturing the city of Ramoth-gilead. Jehoshaphat was willing to ally himself with Ahab in such a venture, but he wanted to be sure that the campaign carried the blessings of the Lord. To reassure him, Ahab brought in four hundred men, apparently a group of court prophets, and asked them whether he should go into battle against the Syrians at Ramoth-gilead. To a man they agreed (1 Kings 22:6). But Jehoshaphat was suspicious of such a unanimous response. "Is there not here a prophet of the Lord besides, that we might inquire of him?" he asked (v. 7).

Ahab admitted that there was such a prophet, Micaiah, but apparently he was in prison. "I hate him," said Ahab, "for he doth not prophesy good concerning me, but evil" (v. 8). But when Jehoshaphat insisted that he wanted to hear Micaiah, Ahab reluctantly sent for him. The officer sent to bring Micaiah informed the prophet about the situation and urged him not to cause trouble, but to bring the same message to the king that the other prophets had brought. Micaiah, unwilling to compromise himself or his God, responded, "What the Lord saith unto me, that will I speak" (v. 14). [See question #1, page 376.]

I. Disastrous Prediction (1 Kings 22:15-18)

A. Micaiah's Sarcasm (v. 15)

15. So he came to the king. And the king said unto him, Micaiah, shall we go against Ramoth-gilead to battle, or shall we forbear? And he answered him, Go, and prosper: for the LORD shall deliver it into the hand of the king.

When Micaiah stood before the two kings, he delivered the same message as that of the other prophets: *Go* to *Ramoth-gilead* and *prosper*. But his words were so dripping with sarcasm that Ahab could not miss their real intent. [See question #2, page 376.]

B. Ahab's Response (v. 16)

16. And the king said unto him, How many times shall I adjure thee that thou tell me nothing but that which is true in the name of the LORD?

Angered by Micaiah's reply, Ahab demanded that the prophet *tell* the truth. But Ahab did not really want to hear the truth. This entire procedure was nothing more than a show for the benefit of Jehoshaphat. What Ahab really wanted Micaiah to say were words that would encourage Judah's king to accompany him in the campaign to take Ramoth-gilead from the Syrians.

UNDER OATH

"Do you swear to tell the truth, the whole truth, and nothing but the truth?" Nearly everyone is familiar with the courtroom question that places witnesses under oath. Unfortunately, what nearly everyone is also familiar with is that not all who take this solemn oath always tell the whole truth. Some commit the crime of perjury by lying on the witness stand.

As a prophet of the Lord, Micaiah was bound to be truthful. He was compelled by his own calling and integrity to say only what God told him. God cannot lie, and neither could Micaiah.

It took great courage for Micaiah to tell King Ahab a truth he did not want to hear. And it takes courage today to speak truth that one knows will not be well received. Jesus is the truth (John 14:6), yet millions reject Him and His teachings. Many do not want to hear our personal testimony of the Savior and Lord we know, but we remain "under oath" to speak all the truth—warnings as well as promises—in love.

Pray that God will make you a bold witness for Him.   —R. W. B.

C. Micaiah's Message (v. 17)

17. And he said, I saw all Israel scattered upon the hills, as sheep that have not a shepherd: and the LORD said, These have no master: let them return every man to his house in peace.

Micaiah proceeded to relate two visions that revealed the true word of the Lord to Ahab. First, he described the nation of *Israel* as *sheep* who were *scattered* because there was no longer a *shepherd* to lead them.

D. Ahab's Disgust (v. 18)

18. And the king of Israel said unto Jehoshaphat, Did I not tell thee that he would prophesy no good concerning me, but evil?

Ahab did not need an interpreter to help him understand the meaning of Micaiah's vision. He quickly realized that the prophet was predicting Ahab's removal from office. The reason the people were pictured as having no "master," or leader, was because Ahab would no longer be present to lead them.

But instead of heeding Micaiah's warning, Ahab used it to prove his earlier charge (v. 8) that the prophet carried a grudge against him and was out to get him. This is a time-honored method of avoiding having to face painful truth: blame the messenger and either ignore him, discredit him, or even arrange to dispose of him.

Home Daily Bible Readings

Monday, June 18—Israel and Judah Become Allies (1 Kings 22:1-5)
Tuesday, June 19—The Lying Prophets of Ahab (1 Kings 22:6-12)
Wednesday, June 20—Bad Advice for Jehoshaphat (2 Chronicles 18:4-11)
Thursday, June 21—Micaiah Predicts Failure (1 Kings 22:13-28)
Friday, June 22—Micaiah's True Answer (2 Chronicles 18:12-27)
Saturday, June 23—Defeat and Death of Ahab (1 Kings 22:29-40)
Sunday, June 24—Jehoshaphat, Jehoram, and Ahaziah's Reigns (1 Kings 22:41-53)

II. Distressing Vision
(1 Kings 22:19-23)

A. The Lord on His Throne (v. 19)

19. And he said, Hear thou therefore the word of the LORD: I saw the LORD sitting on his throne, and all the host of heaven standing by him on his right hand and on his left.

Micaiah was not easily intimidated. Even though he realized that he could be endangering his life if he said anything more, he refused to remain silent. He told of another vision in which he *saw the Lord* in a position similar to that of an ancient ruler: *sitting on his throne*. And, just as a ruler was often surrounded by his advisers, the Lord was surrounded by *all the host of heaven*. The word *host* often refers to armies; *heavenly host* or *host of heaven* refers both to celestial bodies and to spiritual beings such as angels who worship God (Nehemiah 9:6). From the succeeding verses we know that the host in Micaiah's vision also included evil spirits—perhaps in the same way that Satan presented himself before the Lord in Job 1:6; 2:1. [See question #3, page 376.]

B. A Lying Spirit (vv. 20-23)

20. And the LORD said, Who shall persuade Ahab, that he may go up and fall at Ramoth-gilead? And one said on this manner, and another said on that manner.

Micaiah's vision continued with a description of how the Lord asked the members of the host of Heaven *who* would *persuade Ahab* to go to his downfall *at Ramoth-gilead*. Again, this was similar

---

How to Say It

AHAB. *Ay*-hab.
AHAZIAH. Ay-huh-*zye*-uh.
AMON. *Ay*-mun.
ARAM. *Air*-um.
BAAL. *Bay*-ul.
BEN-HADAD. Ben-*hay*-dad.
CARMEL. *Car*-mel.
CHENAANAH. Kih-*nay*-uh-nah.
ELIJAH. Ee-*lye*-juh.
JEHORAM. Jeh-*ho*-rum.
JEHOSHAPHAT. Jeh-*hosh*-uh-fat.
JEZEBEL. *Jez*-uh-bel.
JOASH. *Jo*-ash.
MICAIAH. My-*kay*-uh.
RAMOTH-GILEAD. *Ray*-muth-*gil*-ee-ud (strong accent on *gil*).
SAMARIA. Suh-*mare*-ee-uh.
SYRIA. *Sear*-ee-uh.
ZEDEKIAH. Zed-uh-*kye*-uh.

---

to the way in which an earthly ruler would ask his advisers for help in solving a specific problem.

21-23. And there came forth a spirit, and stood before the LORD, and said, I will persuade him. And the LORD said unto him, Wherewith? And he said, I will go forth, and I will be a lying spirit in the mouth of all his prophets. And he said, Thou shalt persuade him, and prevail also: go forth, and do so. Now therefore, behold, the LORD hath put a lying spirit in the mouth of all these thy prophets, and the LORD hath spoken evil concerning thee.

These verses (and the entire scene described in Micaiah's vision) have created no little controversy among Bible students. We are told clearly in Scripture that God cannot lie (Titus 1:2). Yet in this passage He appears to be encouraging, if not causing, lying. Two ways to understand Micaiah's vision have been suggested.

Some believe that the vision is not to be taken literally, as a description of actual events occurring in Heaven. They point out that God does not need the "advice" of the host of Heaven; He possesses all wisdom and knowledge. They also claim that the false prophets surrounding Ahab did not need an evil spirit to make them say what they did. They were guided primarily by their own selfish interests. In this view the *lying spirit* was a personification of the attitude that governed the false prophets, and the vision was a symbolic way of saying that God allowed the prophets to speak falsely and lure Ahab to his death. A second view takes the vision more literally. It holds that the lying spirit was a demon, or perhaps the devil himself. (Some suggest that one of God's spirits, or angels, could have assumed the role of a lying spirit in order to carry out God's judgment against Ahab.)

Whether we take this scene literally or figuratively, we must keep in mind that God's actions did not violate Ahab's freedom of choice in this matter. God allowed the lying spirit to work among him and the false prophets; but these men, by their own defiance of God and His truth, had opened their lives to such an influence. Ahab, because of his unparalleled wickedness (1 Kings 21:25, 26), had placed himself under God's judgment. He had rejected the path of life and chosen the path of death (Deuteronomy 30:19).

III. Disturbing Announcement
(1 Kings 22:24-28)

A. Zedekiah's Anger (v. 24)

24. But Zedekiah the son of Chenaanah went near, and smote Micaiah on the cheek, and said, Which way went the Spirit of the LORD from me to speak unto thee?

Zedekiah was mentioned earlier in 1 Kings 22 as one of the prophets who predicted victory for Ahab and even used a visual aid to reinforce his "prophecy" (v. 11). He seems to have been the spokesman for the court prophets. He was so incensed by Micaiah's words that he slapped him *on the cheek.*

Zedekiah then asked Micaiah, *Which way went the Spirit of the Lord from me to speak unto thee?* The meaning of *Spirit* here is different from its meaning in verses 21-23. Zedekiah was asserting that he, not Micaiah, had the Spirit of prophecy sent by God. His sarcastic question asked, "How did the Spirit leave me and go to you?"

B. Micaiah's Reply (v. 25)

25. And Micaiah said, Behold, thou shalt see in that day, when thou shalt go into an inner chamber to hide thyself.

Micaiah's reply stated an important truth: the real test of any prophecy is whether or not it is fulfilled in the way it was stated (Deuteronomy 18:21, 22). Micaiah was quite willing to have his and the court prophets' conflicting prophecies tested in this manner. Would Ahab go into battle and meet disaster as Micaiah had predicted? Or would he go into battle and triumph as the court prophets had predicted? The answer would come, declared Micaiah, when Zedekiah would have to go into hiding from those who were angry that his advice had led to Ahab's death. At that point he would no longer be able to maintain the pretense that he really spoke for God. The fact that he had lied would be undeniable. [See question #4, page 376.]

C. Ahab's Anger (vv. 26, 27)

26. And the king of Israel said, Take Micaiah, and carry him back unto Amon the governor of the city, and to Joash the king's son.

Ahab was furious with Micaiah and his message. The king's immediate concern was that it might upset Jehoshaphat so much that he would return to Judah and not accompany him on his campaign against Syria. Thus he ordered *Amon the governor* [perhaps we would use the term "mayor"] *of the city* of Samaria to put Micaiah *back* in prison (implying that he had been there previously). *Joash* may have been Amon's assistant or involved in some other way in administering the prison. He is called *the king's son,* which some commentators think may be a title for an important official rather than a description of Joash's relationship to Ahab.

27. And say, Thus saith the king, Put this fellow in the prison, and feed him with bread of affliction and with water of affliction, until I come in peace.

Visual for lesson 4

Today's visual draws from Micaiah's warning in verse 28 to challenge believers today to hearken to the Word of God.

Ahab not only sent Micaiah to *prison* but placed him on a very restricted diet—*bread* and *water*—as further punishment. The reference to *affliction* may mean that Micaiah was to be given only enough food and water to keep him alive, but not enough to satisfy his hunger.

The words *until I come in peace* had an ominous ring to them. Ahab meant that when he returned from battle, he would administer a more severe punishment to Micaiah, perhaps even death. But these words were ominous only for Ahab. He was being presumptuous to assume that he would return in peace, as the next verse indicates.

D. Micaiah's Promise (v. 28)

28. And Micaiah said, If thou return at all in peace, the LORD hath not spoken by me. And he said, Hearken, O people, every one of you.

Micaiah refused to be intimidated by Ahab or the court prophets. Instead of going back quietly to his cell, he made one further pronouncement. If Ahab did *return at all*, it would be clear evidence that Micaiah had not spoken the truth. Micaiah was willing to submit his prophecy to the test suggested in Deuteronomy 18:21, 22. By these words he signed his own death warrant, in effect, for if Ahab did return, he almost certainly would execute the prophet.

Hearken, O people, every one of you. Micaiah's final words before being taken to prison were not limited to those around him. He wanted as many as possible to be aware of what had just transpired, so that all of them could later recognize who really spoke for God. [See question #5, page 376.]

STRETCHING THE TRUTH

A wife chided her husband: "I don't mind your little half-truths, but you keep telling me the wrong half!" Some individuals justify themselves when they tell less than the whole truth by rationalizing: "It was just a little white lie."

Sometimes truth is stretched so far that it snaps back with destructive force.

Micaiah resisted any temptation to tell a lie that would have favored King Ahab and secured his own freedom from imprisonment. Micaiah recognized that he was accountable to a far greater King than Ahab. That King had issued a command against "bearing false witness." That King hates a "lying tongue" (Proverbs 6:17), and He warns that unrepentant liars shall join other unforgiven sinners one day in the "lake which burneth with fire and brimstone" (Revelation 21:8). The concept of "little" or "white" lies reflects man's thinking, not God's.

Don't try to stretch the truth; "stretch" your life so that it conforms to the truth.   —R. W. B.

Conclusion

A. The Rest of the Story

Our lesson text ends with Micaiah's prediction of disaster for Ahab if he went into battle against the Syrians. The concluding verses of 1 Kings 22 tell us how his prophecy turned out.

Ahab chose to disregard Micaiah's warning and was able to persuade Jehoshaphat to accompany him on the campaign to retake Ramoth-gilead. However, to provide some additional "insurance" that Micaiah's prediction would not come true, Ahab persuaded Jehoshaphat to wear his clothing into battle.

Predictably, the results were nearly disastrous for the king of Judah. The king of Syria had ordered his troops to concentrate on capturing or killing Ahab. Seeing someone dressed in the garb of Ahab, they attacked Jehoshaphat's chariot and might have seized him had he not cried out.

In the meantime, at another place on the battlefield, Ahab apparently felt quite secure in his disguise. Suddenly an enemy archer shot an arrow at random. It found a chink in the king's armor and he bled to death in his chariot. Without a leader the hosts of Israel left the battlefield and scattered to their homes, fulfilling Micaiah's prophetic vision (v. 17). Ahab's body was carried back to Samaria and buried. Later his chariot was washed out, and the dogs licked up his blood, fulfilling a prophecy of Elijah (1 Kings 21:19).

The Scriptures are silent about what happened to Micaiah. With Ahab dead, he may have been released from prison. On the other hand, Jezebel remained the real power behind Ahab's two sons and successors, Ahaziah and Jehoram. She may have had the prophet executed.

B. A Rare Commodity

Some months ago I was speaking to a friend who is a businessman in a different part of the state where I live. When I inquired about how his business was doing, he informed me that he had sold it. When I asked him what kind of a sales contract he had entered into to complete the transaction, he replied, "We didn't sign a contract. We just shook hands on the deal."

"But," I protested, "you can't do business on a handshake."

"You can still do it that way down where I live," came his reply.

This conversation caused me to stop and think a bit about the business climate where I and most people live. In our society integrity has become an increasingly rare commodity. We feel its absence in every area of our lives. As a result, we have become cynical about our relationships in all kinds of circumstances.

Modern advertising usually tells some truth about the product it attempts to sell, but it doesn't tell us all the truth. When we see a good deal advertised, we have learned to ask, "What about the fine print?" Experience has taught us that the fine print often nullifies what the headlines advertise.

Politicians have built their careers on promising what they cannot (or do not intend to) deliver. Lawyers can cleverly twist words in such a way that their clients can avoid the legal consequences of their deeds. Students habitually cheat, claiming that "everybody does it." Even religious leaders sometimes betray their sacred calling, leading astray many in their flocks through either a theology or a lifestyle that rejects Biblical standards.

Must we as Christians be reduced to a cynicism that accepts this decline of values that is so prevalent in what many call a "post-Christian" culture? Or can we resist? The examples of Elijah and Micaiah, about whom we have studied in the past three lessons, show us that we do not have to surrender to the values of our culture. Their lives demonstrated a commitment to God that left no room for compromise. And they demonstrated that commitment by their integrity—a rare commodity in our times, but one that the world must see if our witness is to communicate clearly on Christ's behalf.

C. Prayer

O God, You have called us out of this world to become Your holy servants. Now send us back into the world to serve the needs of those all about us who have lost their way and need the light that only You can offer. In Jesus' name we pray. Amen.

D. Thought to Remember

One person and God make a majority.

Learning by Doing

This page contains an alternate lesson plan emphasizing learning activities.
Classes desiring such student involvement will find these suggestions helpful.

Learning Goals

After participating in this lesson, each student should be able to:

1. Recount the circumstances under which Micaiah courageously refused to compromise God's message.

2. Tell why standing for God's truth is such a challenge in today's world.

3. Express appreciation to someone who, like Micaiah, has paid a price for being true to God's message.

Into the Lesson

Tell the class that there are times when it is tough to speak God's truth. For example, the listener might be hostile or antagonistic to Christianity or be too close of a friend. Ask the class members to share what they think would be a tough situation for them to speak a truth from God. They may do this in small groups or share with the whole class. As they report these situations, list them on a marker board or chalkboard.

Make the transition to Bible study by telling the class that we are going to be encouraged by someone who successfully shared God's truth in a threatening situation. This little-known character probably had a degree of fear because he was facing a powerful authority. His courageous truthfulness did get him in trouble, but he faithfully delivered God's message. His adventure teaches us a lesson about courage, truthfulness, integrity, and priorities. The man's name is Micaiah. (Write *Micaiah* on the board.) Like Elijah, he was a prophet during the reign of King Ahab.

Into the Word

Read 1 Kings 22:15-28 and deliver a brief lecture on the lesson background. Then ask the learners to form groups of five or six people. Each group will work together to write the dialogue of the main characters in contemporary English and then act out the incident, using their paraphrased dialogues for scripts.

To prepare for this activity, make large name tags for each main character: King Ahab, Micaiah, Jehoshaphat (even though he doesn't speak), and Zedekiah. (Write each name on a letter size piece of paper and use a string to hang it from the appropriate actor's neck.) Preparations for the activity should also include a piece of paper for each class member, listing the verses and speaker down the left side. The group will write their paraphrase down the right side. The left-side column should list v. 15, King Ahab to Micaiah, Micaiah to King Ahab; v. 16, King Ahab to Micaiah; v. 17, Micaiah's vision/prophecy; v. 18, King Ahab to Jehoshaphat; vv. 19-23, Micaiah's vision/prophecy; vv. 24, 25, Zedekiah to Micaiah, Micaiah to Zedekiah; vv. 26, 27, King Ahab (to court prophets?); v. 28, Micaiah to King Ahab (and to the people).

Give each group a photocopy of the lesson commentary notes on verses 21-24 with the words *lying spirit* and *Zedekiah* highlighted. This material will help groups interpret and paraphrase the dialogue. Be ready also to visit each group and clarify sections of the story as needed.

After the groups have finished, ask them to assign readers and read the paraphrase to their own groups. Then ask one of the groups to perform its dialogue for the entire class. Give the readers the name tags to help class members remember the characters.

After the reading (and applause!), give a brief lecture. Use this time to fill in details and to clarify the story as needed.

Into Life

Use the following discussion questions to guide the class in applying this Scripture to life.

1. Focus on the prophet Micaiah for a moment. What do you learn about godly living from this event in his life? (List the answers given on the chalkboard.)

2. Micaiah took a courageous stand for truth in a hostile environment. Today's Western world is also becoming increasingly hostile to Christianity. What lessons do you learn for today's Christian living in today's world?

3. Who are some persons you have known who have taken a courageous stand for Christ's truth? They may have even paid a price for that stand!

Remind the class that, to have this kind of courageous testimony, we must do two things: we must know God's Word, and we must make a determination to be faithful to the truth *before* a confrontation challenges us. Give the learners three-by-five cards and ask each to write a personal vow to God that addresses both issues above. Some may wish to tape these commitments to the inside covers of their Bibles.

Let's Talk It Over

The questions on this page are designed to encourage review of the lesson Scriptures and to promote discussion of the lesson by the class. The answers provided are only discussion starters. Let your class talk it over from there.

1. Micaiah said, "What the Lord saith . . . that will I speak." Why do believers today sometimes shy away from talking about certain matters with nonbelievers, even when God's Word speaks clearly about such issues? How can we develop the boldness to speak up?

Some fear the social stigma of being called fundamentalists, right-wing fanatics, or bigots. Unfortunately, there are many times when we do not speak up for what the Bible says because we do not know what it says!

We need to be sure we are spending time in the Word, letting it fill our lives and allowing it to guide our behavior and decision making. Then we need to work on showing love to others, including those with whom we disagree. When we demonstrate our love for others by doing tangible acts of goodness, we will have some credibility in our claim to love the sinner even while hating the sin.

2. Micaiah's first message was apparently so sarcastic in tone that the king knew the words were not to be taken at face value. How appropriate is the use of sarcasm today? Under what conditions is it proper? When is it improper? Why?

The word *sarcasm* comes from two Greek words: *sarx,* meaning flesh, and *kazein,* to cut or tear. Literally, then, it suggests a cutting or tearing of the flesh. Sometimes sarcasm seems to do just that, as a sarcastic jab cuts a person down or tears at his self-esteem. But Micaiah directed his comments at the issue; his was not a personal attack. Such a use is sometimes helpful, portraying the weakness of the position in a way that a simple declaration seems unable to accomplish.

Another caution: sometimes irony and sarcasm are not recognized as such—especially when they appear in print and have no facial expressions or tone of voice to interpret them. In such cases they are worse than worthless, seeming to support exactly the opposite position the writer intended!

3. Micaiah was a true prophet. When he said, "Hear . . . the word of the Lord," he spoke with divine authority. How should we respond when a person claims to have a message from God?

"From God" is a phrase we dare not take lightly. Regardless of how pure one's motivation is, when he prefaces his own opinion with these words, he is taking the Lord's name in vain and assuming authority that is not his. The phrase itself does not make a person more trustworthy; false teachers and church leaders with selfish agenda have often used such a phrase (Titus 1:10-14).

On the other hand, since we have the Word of God, we are able to convey a message "from God." In other words, where the Bible speaks, we too can speak with authority. But when the Bible is silent, we need to admit that we have only our own opinion to offer.

4. When someone challenges the truthfulness or accuracy of what we have said, the natural response is to make a defense. Micaiah was willing to say, "Wait and see." When should we take a "wait and see" attitude, and when should we defend our position?

Too often we argue about issues that simply cannot be resolved by debate. One deacon remembers the discussion in a meeting one way and another recalls it differently. Neither will convince the other, but a look at the minutes could settle the matter. When such a disagreement arises, we should decide to wait and see what an authoritative source can tell us instead of defending our position to the point of alienating our brothers and sisters.

At other times, however, the source of truth may be right at hand—such as when the issue is one of Biblical truth. In such cases we need to get the Bible and look to it for the answer. Then we should defend that truth against any who would seek to discredit or diminish it.

5. "Hearken, O people, every one of you." Thus Micaiah warned those who heard him to pay attention to what God had said. The language sounds archaic, but the message is needed just as much today. How can we urge contemporary people to pay attention to what God says?

Our example is as instructive as anything. We must live in such a way as to declare our unquestioning faith in God's Word. Then we need to seek fresh ways to communicate it, using all the tools of the modern age to assist us. Sometimes the world rejects our message because we "package" it in outdated terminology and methods. We should feel free to change the way we deliver the message as long as the message itself—the Word of God—remains unchanged!

Judgment on Judah and Israel

DEVOTIONAL READING: **Hebrews 10:26-31.**

BACKGROUND SCRIPTURE: **Amos 1, 2.**

PRINTED TEXT: **Amos 1:1, 2; 2:4-10.**

Amos 1:1, 2

1 The words of Amos, who was among the herdmen of Tekoa, which he saw concerning Israel in the days of Uzziah king of Judah, and in the days of Jeroboam the son of Joash king of Israel, two years before the earthquake.

2 And he said, The LORD will roar from Zion, and utter his voice from Jerusalem; and the habitations of the shepherds shall mourn, and the top of Carmel shall wither.

Amos 2:4-10

4 Thus saith the LORD; For three transgressions of Judah, and for four, I will not turn away the punishment thereof; because they have despised the law of the LORD, and have not kept his commandments, and their lies caused them to err, after the which their fathers have walked:

5 But I will send a fire upon Judah, and it shall devour the palaces of Jerusalem.

6 Thus saith the LORD; For three transgressions of Israel, and for four, I will not turn away the punishment thereof; because they sold the righteous for silver, and the poor for a pair of shoes;

7 That pant after the dust of the earth on the head of the poor, and turn aside the way of the meek: and a man and his father will go in unto the same maid, to profane my holy name:

8 And they lay themselves down upon clothes laid to pledge by every altar, and they drink the wine of the condemned in the house of their god.

9 Yet destroyed I the Amorite before them, whose height was like the height of the cedars, and he was strong as the oaks; yet I destroyed his fruit from above, and his roots from beneath.

10 Also I brought you up from the land of Egypt, and led you forty years through the wilderness, to possess the land of the Amorite.

GOLDEN TEXT: Thus saith the LORD; For three transgressions of Judah, and for four, I will not turn away the punishment thereof; because they have despised the law of the LORD, and have not kept his commandments.—Amos 2:4.

Division and Decline
Unit 2: Prophecies of Judgment
(Lessons 5-9)

Lesson Aims

After this lesson each of your students should be able to:

1. Summarize Amos's message of judgment against Judah and Israel in today's text.

2. Illustrate how the sins that Amos cited are prevalent in our society.

3. Develop a message of warning of God's judgment on contemporary sin.

Lesson Outline

INTRODUCTION
    A. Without Official Approval
    B. Lesson Background
I. AMOS THE PROPHET (Amos 1:1, 2)
    A. The Man (v. 1)
    B. The Message (v. 2)
    "Here Comes the Judge"
II. JUDGMENT AGAINST JUDAH (Amos 2:4, 5)
    A. The Reason (v. 4)
    B. The Result (v. 5)
    Intolerable Tolerance
III. JUDGMENT AGAINST ISRAEL (Amos 2:6-8)
    A. Greed (vv. 6, 7a)
    B. Immorality (v. 7b)
    C. Blasphemy (v. 8)
IV. LESSONS FROM THE PAST (Amos 2:9, 10)
    A. Judgment Against the Amorites (v. 9)
    B. Deliverance in the Exodus (v. 10)
CONCLUSION
    A. Being Judgmental
    B. Prayer
    C. Thought to Remember

Introduction

A. Without Official Approval

"I was no prophet, neither was I a prophet's son," confessed Amos (Amos 7:14), frankly admitting that he was not a card-carrying member of the prophets' "union" and thus lacked any official status in recognized clerical circles.

But Amos was neither the first nor the last to proclaim God's message outside "official" channels. Consider Micaiah, who proclaimed God's message without hesitation in spite of how it contradicted Ahab's court prophets. Consider John the Baptist, whose rustic lifestyle seemed eccentric to some but whose powerful preaching prepared the way for the Messiah. Consider Jesus, of whom the religious leaders of His day asked, "How did this man get such learning without having studied?" (John 7:15, *New International Version*). Finally, consider Jesus' apostles. Although recognized as "unlearned and ignorant men," their boldness on behalf of Jesus caused the Jewish leaders to marvel (Acts 4:13).

God can use anyone to declare His good news. In some cases His most effective witnesses are those who have "non-professional" status.

B. Lesson Background

During the approximate century that passed since the events covered in last week's lesson, a number of significant changes occurred in Israel (the northern kingdom). The dynasty of Omri, which included Omri, Ahab, and his two sons, Ahaziah and Jehoram, had been replaced by the dynasty that began with the reign of Jehu. Under this dynasty, Israel enjoyed substantial prosperity, which reached its peak during the long reign of Jeroboam II, who ruled from 785 to 745 B.C. The prophetic ministry of Amos occurred near the middle of Jeroboam's reign, at about 760 B.C.

Perhaps the most important reason for Israel's prosperity during this time was the weakness of its neighbors, particularly the Syrians to the north and the Assyrians to the east. Both of these peoples had caused problems for Israel during the previous century. During this power vacuum, Jeroboam II expanded his territory, regaining some of the land that had been lost by his predecessors. The result was a growing prosperity that reminded some of the "glory days" under David and Solomon. However, despite the nation's impressive outward appearance, its spiritual condition was deteriorating rapidly. This was the problem that Amos had come to address.

I. Amos the Prophet
(Amos 1:1, 2)

A. The Man (v. 1)

1. The words of Amos, who was among the herdmen of Tekoa, which he saw concerning Israel in the days of Uzziah king of Judah, and in the days of Jeroboam the son of Joash king of Israel, two years before the earthquake.

Amos was the earliest of that grand quartet of eighth-century prophets that included Hosea, Micah, and Isaiah. They brought God's message to all of God's people: Amos and Hosea preached in *Israel*, while Micah and Isaiah brought God's message to Judah.

All that we know about Amos is what we learn from his writing. Here we are told that he *was among the herdmen of Tekoa.* He later describes himself as one who "followed the flock" (Amos 7:15). He also mentions that he was "a gatherer of sycamore fruit" (7:14). His hometown of *Tekoa* was located on a ridge about six or seven miles south of Bethlehem.

As noted earlier, Amos had no official credentials qualifying him to serve as a prophet. When he was challenged by Amaziah, the high priest at Bethel, he frankly acknowledged that he was not a prophet in the generally accepted sense, nor was he "a prophet's son" (Amos 7:14). This probably means that Amos was not one of the "sons of the prophets" (2 Kings 4:38; 6:1), who apparently comprised a kind of "training school." His authority came directly from God: "The Lord took me as I followed the flock, and the Lord said unto me, Go, prophesy unto my people Israel" (Amos 7:15). [See question #1, page 384.]

Amos carried out his ministry during the reigns of *Uzziah* in *Judah* and of *Jeroboam* II in Israel. The prophet adds a specific chronological reference to date his ministry—*two years before the earthquake.* This earthquake is also referred to in Zechariah 14:5. Archaeological excavations at Hazor, a city in Israel eight or ten miles north of the Sea of Galilee, have provided evidence of an earthquake that occurred sometime around 760 B.C.

B. The Message (v. 2)

2. And he said, The LORD will roar from Zion, and utter his voice from Jerusalem; and the habitations of the shepherds shall mourn, and the top of Carmel shall wither.

Amos journeyed from his home in Tekoa to Bethel, a distance of about twenty-five miles. Bethel was one of two places (Dan was the other) where Jeroboam I had set up golden calves in order to keep his subjects in the northern kingdom from going to the temple in Jerusalem to worship (1 Kings 12:25-29). Bethel had become the more prominent of the two locations and was known as "the king's chapel" (Amos 7:13).

The Lord is depicted as a roaring lion, terrifying in His judgment. Such language reflects the world of the shepherd, with which Amos was quite familiar. The lion was one of the animals from which a shepherd had to protect his flock (1 Samuel 17:34, 35). While the Lord wanted to be the protecting Shepherd of Israel (Psalm 23), here He is portrayed as coming to harm Israel as He exercises judgment upon them for their sins. [See question #2, page 384.]

Zion was a common designation for *Jerusalem.* Here was located the temple, the earthly symbol of God's presence with His people. Amos reminded his audience that it was from here that God would pronounce judgment, not from Dan or Bethel, where the rulers of Israel had set up rival sanctuaries.

The habitations of the shepherds shall mourn. God's judgment would include a drought that would make it difficult for shepherds to find places to feed their sheep. So severe would be the effects of this drought that even *the top of Carmel shall wither.* Recall the extended drought that God sent during the time of Elijah and Ahab. Even when this drought was at its worst, Elijah was able to get water on Mount Carmel to pour on top of his sacrifice (1 Kings 18:33-35). Thus, for this location to wither signified a severe drought indeed.

"HERE COMES THE JUDGE"

The late Sammy Davis, Jr., is remembered, not only for his musical talent, but also for his work as a comedian. One of his most memorable routines was called "Here Comes the Judge." Davis wore a judge's robe and sat behind a huge bench as if in a courtroom. Many found the unorthodox "judgments" that his character handed down to be entertaining. Harry Anderson, star of the television series *Night Court,* got laughs as well with his caricature of a judge who dressed and behaved in a non-conformist style. There is often genuine humor in characterizations that are non-stereotypical.

Amos was no "stereotypical" or "cookie cutter" clone of the prophets of his time and place. He really did not have the credentials considered necessary to qualify him for such a job. He *was* authorized, however, by the Supreme Judge of all the earth. It was God's indictment that he boldly brought against Israel and Judah. He needed no other validation, degree, or license.

God often appoints unlikely candidates to deliver His messages and render His judgments. Consider the "motley crew" of twelve whom He used to begin the church. Consider *us,* whom He has commissioned to preach "repentance and

The Lord will roar from Zion, and utter his voice from Jerusalem ... and the top of Carmel shall wither.
Amos 1:2

Visual for lesson 5

The visual for today's lesson dramatically illustrates God's warning in verse 2. Display this poster as you begin your Bible study.

remission of sins" to the nations (Luke 24:47). His commandment alone qualifies us to be "prophets" and "judges" to our time and to our world.   —R. W. B.

II. Judgment Against Judah
(Amos 2:4, 5)

A. The Reason (v. 4)

4. Thus saith the LORD; For three transgressions of Judah, and for four, I will not turn away the punishment thereof; because they have despised the law of the LORD, and have not kept his commandments, and their lies caused them to err, after the which their fathers have walked.

In the intervening verses of chapters 1 and 2, Amos had pronounced God's judgment upon many of Israel's neighbors—Syria (1:3-5), Philistia (1:6-8), Phoenicia (1:9, 10), Edom (1:11, 12), Ammon (1:13-15), and Moab (2:1-3). He then turned his attention to *Judah*. By including Judah in his condemnations, Amos indicated to his audience that he was not just a preacher from Judah who was expressing a personal prejudice against Israel.

As Amos preached against Israel's enemies, his audience may have voiced hearty approval, as these peoples had often been a "thorn in the side" of God's people. Many in Israel would have been just as enthusiastic of Amos's condemnation of Judah, for the enmity between Israel and Judah was long-standing. A few, however, might have been keen enough to realize where Amos's line of reasoning was leading—straight toward Israel.

With the phrase *for three transgressions of Judah, and for four*, Amos was not specifically enumerating only three or four sins. This appears to be a rhetorical device that the prophet used to introduce each of the Lord's condemnations. It was a way of saying that the sins of a nation had accumulated to the point where God could no longer withhold His judgment. In condemning the other nations, Amos mentioned specific sins of which they were guilty. He followed the same pattern in denouncing Judah's sins. The people had *despised the law of the Lord*, thus violating His covenant with them.

Furthermore, they had been involved in *lies*, which had *caused them to err*. The Hebrew word rendered *lies* may refer to the false gods that the people had chosen to worship instead of the true God. In doing so, they were only duplicating the sins *their fathers* before them had committed. [See question #3, page 384.]

B. The Result (v. 5)

5. But I will send a fire upon Judah, and it shall devour the palaces of Jerusalem.

In Amos's indictment of *Judah*, *Jerusalem* was specifically singled out for punishment. This was the center of Judah, both religiously and politically, and its leaders bore a great deal of the responsibility for the sins of the people. For that reason, Jerusalem would be subjected to a *fire*, probably as a result of invading armies. The fulfillment of Amos's words occurred when the army of Nebuchadnezzar, king of Babylon, destroyed the city, including the temple, in 586 B.C.

INTOLERABLE TOLERANCE

Twenty-first century society is bending over backward to grant the moral freedom of choice to every soul, no matter how a person's choices may offend God, endanger lives, and/or contaminate the culture. It is called "tolerance." Calling sin "sin" is viewed as judgmental and unsophisticated. Standing for God's absolutes is ridiculed as "primitive" or at least "ultra-conservative." All manner of perversions, obscenity, exploitation, and godlessness is tolerated in the name of "freedom" and "choice."

The moral uncertainty of our times is not so very different from that of Amos's day. His neighbors, too, were tolerating all kinds of sinful

---

How to Say It

AHAB. *Ay*-hab.
AHAZIAH. Ay-huh-*zye*-uh.
AMAZIAH. Am-uh-*zye*-uh.
AMMON. *Am*-mun.
AMORITES. *Am*-uh-rites.
ASSYRIANS. Uh-*sear*-ee-unz.
BABYLON. *Bab*-uh-lun.
CARMEL. *Car*-mel.
EDOM. *Ee*-dum.
ELIJAH. Ee-*lye*-juh.
HAZOR. *Hay*-zor.
HOSEA. Ho-*zay*-uh.
JEHORAM. Jeh-*ho*-rum.
JEHU. *Jay*-hew.
JEROBOAM. Jair-uh-*bo*-um.
JOASH. *Jo*-ash.
MICAIAH. My-*kay*-uh.
MOAB. *Mo*-ab.
NEBUCHADNEZZAR. *Neb*-yuh-kud-*nez*-er (strong accent on *nez*).
OMRI. *Ahm*-rye.
PHILISTIA. Fuh-*liss*-tee-uh.
PHOENICIA. Fuh-*nish*-uh.
SYRIA. *Sear*-ee-uh.
TEKOA. Tih-*ko*-uh.
UZZIAH. Uh-*zye*-uh.

and ungodly behavior. They needed to be told of impending punishment for their transgressions. God warned them that He would deliver them into the hands of their enemies because they were so disobedient and unrepentant.

So-called "tolerance" eventually becomes intolerable to God. True, He is patient with us, for He wants no one to perish (2 Peter 3:9). But justice ultimately will prevail. Sin will earn its wages (Romans 6:23). Unforgiven unbelievers will suffer "the second death" (Revelation 21:8).

Who, like Amos, will warn them of what is coming? Who will call them to repentance?

—R. W. B.

III. Judgment Against Israel
(Amos 2:6-8)
A. Greed (vv. 6, 7a)

6. Thus saith the LORD; For three transgressions of Israel, and for four, I will not turn away the punishment thereof; because they sold the righteous for silver, and the poor for a pair of shoes.

Some students believe that the first sin for which Israel was indicted was that of bribing judges so that they would return false verdicts against the *righteous*. However, the rest of the sentence, which seems to be a repetition of the first part, appears to be directed at the sin of selling *poor* people into slavery. A man who fell into debt and could not pay his way out would be sold as a slave. Even his wife and children might be enslaved in this manner. The people had so trivialized human life that they would sell a person *for a pair of shoes*.

7a. That pant after the dust of the earth on the head of the poor, and turn aside the way of the meek.

Amos used biting sarcasm as he cited the people's avarice. They were so greedy that they even wanted the *dust* that the *poor* had on their heads. This may be a way of saying that their greed for land had become so intense that they wanted even this meager amount of dust. Perhaps it refers to how the poor sprinkled dust in their hair as a sign of mourning over their impoverished state. The rich wanted to deny them even this small token of their despair.

B. Immorality (v. 7b)

7b. And a man and his father will go in unto the same maid, to profane my holy name.

This may refer to *a man and his father* who both used a female slave for their sexual pleasures, or to both men consorting with the *same* prostitute. Some students take the view that such a woman was a sacred prostitute, and in visiting

her these two men were engaging in pagan worship as well as in breaking the law that forbade sexual promiscuity. God's law demanded sexual purity, and those who violated that law were guilty of profaning His *holy name*. How tragic that a father would set such a disgusting example for his son!

C. Blasphemy (v. 8)

8. And they lay themselves down upon clothes laid to pledge by every altar, and they drink the wine of the condemned in the house of their god.

The *clothes laid to pledge* describes the heavy outer garments that the poor wore during the day and used as a cover at night. When these were held as security for a debt, they were to be returned by nightfall so that the debtor would not have to sleep without protection from the cold (Exodus 22:26; Deuteronomy 24:12, 13). But instead of observing the law, the creditors were keeping the garments and using them as their own in the temple. Given what Amos said in verse 7b, it may be that their lying down *by every altar* involved the kind of sacred prostitution encouraged by pagan worship.

They drink the wine of the condemned. This may refer to wine that was given in pledge for a debt or paid as a fine. Apparently people were consuming this wine during drunken gatherings that took place *in the house of their god*. The worship of some of the pagan gods included such occasions of drunken revelry. [See question #4, page 384.]

IV. Lessons From the Past
(Amos 2:9, 10)
A. Judgment Against the Amorites (v. 9)

9. Yet destroyed I the Amorite before them, whose height was like the height of the cedars, and he was strong as the oaks; yet I destroyed his fruit from above, and his roots from beneath.

God's use of the personal pronoun *I* here emphasizes His faithfulness to His people as contrasted with the people's unfaithfulness to Him. Here *Amorite* seems to be a general term for the people who inhabited Canaan when the Israelites entered the promised land (Genesis 15:16). The words Amos used to describe them (*like the height of the cedars* and *strong as the oaks*) call to mind the Israelites' description of their size (Numbers 13:33). But God had given the Israelites victory over these foes—a victory so complete that it is described as including both the *fruit* and the *roots* of these mighty *oaks*.

The message here is a two-edged sword. On the one hand it is a fearsome reminder of what can happen when God judges a people. Just as

He removed the Amorite (Canaanites) from the land, He can remove Israel from the land when their sin becomes similar to that of their predecessors. The other side is a message of comfort. God can take care of His people, as surely as He cared for them in giving them the land in the first place.

B. Deliverance in the Exodus (v. 10)

10. Also I brought you up from the land of Egypt, and led you forty years through the wilderness, to possess the land of the Amorite.

During the exodus from *Egypt*, God demonstrated His power in various ways. The *forty years* of wandering were the result of the Israelites' disobedience. Still, God had guided them and provided them food and water as they traveled. Their clothes did not wear out during their wandering (Deuteronomy 8:4).

Although Amos preached a message that strongly condemned the sins of God's people, he also offered them the opportunity to repent and return to God. By referring to significant events in Israel's history, the prophet reminded the people of how much God had loved and cared for them. How could they be so callous toward a God who had done so much for them? [See question #5, page 384.]

Conclusion

A. Being Judgmental

When one takes a stand for the truth, he is likely to be accused of being "judgmental" or a "hypocrite." In our tolerant, anything-goes society, to be so branded marks one as a pariah and even an outcast in some groups. Of course, it never seems to occur to the person making the charges that in so doing he is being judgmental.

Home Daily Bible Readings

Monday, June 25—Prophecy Against Syria (Amos 1:1-5)

Tuesday, June 26—Judgment on Damascus (Jeremiah 49:23-27)

Wednesday, June 27—Prophecy Against Gaza and Tyre (Amos 1:6-10)

Thursday, June 28—Prophecy Against Edom and Ammon (Amos 1:11-15)

Friday, June 29—Prophecy Against Moab and Judah (Amos 2:1-5)

Saturday, June 30—Prophecy Against Israel (Amos 2:6—3:2)

Sunday, July 1—Penalties for Disobedience (Leviticus 26:14-22)

Those who accuse others of being judgmental often quote Jesus' words: "Judge not, that ye be not judged" (Matthew 7:1). What such people fail to understand is that Jesus was condemning biased, misguided judgments. Only a few sentences later He urges His listeners to make all kinds of judgments: to choose the strait gate rather than the broad way, to beware of false prophets, and to judge a tree by its fruit (vv. 13-20).

There is certainly nothing wrong with making judgments. In fact, it is impossible to exist without making judgments. And many of the judgments we make are about trivial matters—which tie goes best with this suit or which restaurant we shall patronize today. Other judgments are far more important, although they may not involve moral decisions—such as which college I will attend or which job offer I shall accept.

Still other judgments are profoundly moral and have life-changing implications. The most important judgment we will ever make in this life is the answer we give to the question, "What think ye of Christ?" (Matthew 22:42).

By contemporary standards Amos would have been branded "judgmental." In fact, he went out of his way to be judgmental, leaving his home in Judah and traveling to the neighboring kingdom of Israel to make his judgmental pronouncements. It is quite obvious that Amos did not receive a very friendly welcome in Bethel, especially from those whom he was criticizing. The priest at Bethel, Amaziah, accused him of conspiring against the king, Jeroboam II.

The next time you are called judgmental for standing for the truth, avoiding sinful actions, or criticizing someone who is engaging in immoral activities, count it a compliment. You are in good company—Amos, John the Baptist, the apostle Paul, and Jesus Christ, among others. Just be sure of one thing, however: make certain that you are standing firm for the right, not just for your opinion of what is right. Amos received a special revelation from God for his ministry. We cannot expect that kind of revelation, but we do have God's revelation in the Bible. On it we can and must stand firm.

B. Prayer

We thank You, Father, for men like Amos who boldly proclaimed the truth in a society that did not want to hear the truth. Grant us the same courage to speak forthrightly to our own society. In Jesus' name we pray. Amen.

C. Thought to Remember

The same God who gave a ministry to Amos, a humble shepherd, has a ministry for each of us—regardless of our occupation.

Learning by Doing

This page contains an alternate lesson plan emphasizing learning activities.
Classes desiring such student involvement will find these suggestions helpful.

Learning Goals

After this lesson each student will be able to:

1. Summarize Amos's message of judgment against Judah and Israel in today's text.

2. Illustrate how the sins that Amos cited are prevalent in our society.

3. Develop a message of warning of God's judgment on contemporary sin.

Into the Lesson

Prepare a handout with a large "Behavior Meter" on it. (See below.) Give the handout to groups of five or six people and ask each group to indicate a place on the meter that the members believe best characterizes our nation's society. Then ask where they would put the meter mark for the society of the 1950s. Where do they think the mark will go twenty years from now?

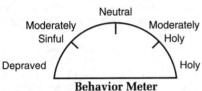

Behavior Meter

Say, "We are going to study a prophet who became a 'behavior meter' for Israel. He listed their sins and pronounced God's judgment to come."

Into the Word

Prepare a brief lecture to introduce the setting for today's study. Prepare a poster or an overhead projector transparency with the following outline: Prosperity and Poverty, The Prophetic Quartet, Amos's Occupation, Amos's Credentials, The Timing and Target of the Prophecy. The notes in the lesson commentary on the Lesson Background and verses 1 and 2 (pages 378, 379) will give the information needed for this presentation.

Next, give each learner a highlighting marker and a photocopy of Amos 2:4-10. Explain the words "for three transgressions . . . and for four . . ." in verses 4 and 6 (see page 380). Then ask each person to highlight words or phrases in the text that give word pictures or images of sin or of God's punishment.

When they have finished, display a visual on which you have already listed the word pictures or images of sin. *(They "despised the law of the Lord," had "not kept his commandments," "walked after lies," v. 4; "sold the righteous for silver, and*

the poor for a pair of shoes," v. 6; they would "pant after the dust . . . on the head of the poor" and "turn aside the way of the meek," a "man and his father [went] in unto the same maid," v. 7; they would "lay themselves down upon clothes laid to pledge by every altar, and . . . drink the wine of the condemned in [an idol's temple]," v. 8.) Use your lesson commentary to explain the more confusing images.

Second, review the list of sins and ask the class members to write a contemporary name for, or an illustration of, each sin. *(For example, selling the righteous for silver might be the equivalent of taking advantage of one's employees to make a bigger profit at their expense.)* Write these names or illustrations beside (or under) the sins listed, using a different color marker.

Third, ask the class to identify which of these sins the prophet would also charge against our nation. Place an asterisk (*) beside these.

Into Life

Tell the students that "we have identified the sins and punishments of the Israelites in Amos's list, and we have also identified some of the sins of our culture. Let's imagine that you are the prophet to carry God's message of warning to our nation. What would you say?" Give the original groups of five or six people another handout, as described below, on which they can write a judgment and warning to our nation. They will use Amos's prophecy as a pattern. Use terminology similar to verses 4-8 ("for three transgressions . . . and for four," etc.), but with modern locations and modern sins taken from your earlier list).

After the groups complete this exercise, ask them to read their pronouncements to the rest of the class. If you have a large class with many groups, two groups can simply exchange papers and read each other's pronouncements.

Then ask the class to share ideas about what we can do about these sins present in our society. Ask a volunteer to write abbreviations of answers on a chalkboard. After the list is completed, share in a prayer time for our nation. Choose five class members, and ask each to word a prayer for one of the following: forgiveness for our nation's sinfulness, guidance for our national, state, and local political leaders, guidance for the education of our children, strength for our churches, and a faithful testimony for each class member.

Let's Talk It Over

The questions on this page are designed to encourage review of the lesson Scriptures and to promote discussion of the lesson by the class. The answers provided are only discussion starters. Let your class talk it over from there.

1. Amos acknowledged that he was not an official "prophet" (7:14). God often chooses people from unlikely backgrounds for special tasks. What are some of the characteristics that mark spokespersons for God?

In one sense the Lord has commissioned all of those who have received Jesus as Savior to tell of His mercies and bring others into a saving relationship (see Matthew 28:18-20). Some, however, have received special giftedness to communicate this message in callings identified in Ephesians 4:11-13. Students may note qualities like ability to communicate, good knowledge of God's Word, and good interpersonal skills. Notice in Ephesians 5, however, the importance of living as children of light. Do not let the importance of one's personal relationship with the Lord go unmentioned.

2. Amos pictured the Lord as a lion about to plunder the flock of Israel. That image was contrary to the popular image of the Lord as a shepherd and must have been startling to Amos's hearers. What images do people today have of God? How might we appropriately challenge those images to call people to repentance?

The shepherd metaphor was an appropriate one, as seen in Psalm 23. It pictured only one aspect of God's nature, however. God was a shepherd to those who would follow His commands, but to the rebellious He became a lion of judgment. Too often the people of our day picture God in ways wholly separate from the God of the Bible. They make up their own images of God and expect Him to be what they imagine. To some He is an impersonal "force"; to others He is a beneficent grandfather. The church must challenge such false notions with Biblical descriptions of God, who is holy and just as well as loving. Only when God is seen for who He is can men and women receive the blessings He wants to give them.

3. Amos cited specific sins of which his people were guilty: despising God's law, breaking His commandments, lying, and continuing in their fathers' sins. If God sent a prophet to denounce the sins of our nation, what specific sins would he condemn? What can we do to turn people away from such sins?

Any number of specific sins might be mentioned in this discussion, but surely the careless disregard for life and morality must be at the top of the list. When personal convenience is treasured over the lives of innocent babies, God's heart must break. When solemn vows of fidelity are trashed in favor of what seems to be the promise of a more comfortable life, God must shake His head in disgust. The church must be careful to uphold the standards of the Bible in the example of its members. Then it must demonstrate both the importance of adherence to those standards and the grace that is available through Jesus when people do not follow them.

4. Amos chastised the Israelites for greed and sexual promiscuity. The same sins had plagued the nation before and would continue to grieve God at later dates in history. These two sins are devastating to God's people. How do they gain access and even acceptance among God's elect?

In Amos's day resistance to sexual impurity was weakened by the practices of pagan religions. In that context orgies were not only accepted but were used to please their false gods. In our day, the "worship" of beauty and continued exposure to sexual infidelity through the media dull our senses. When the practice becomes tolerated even among those who have been entrusted with leadership, the condemned practices are soon regarded as normal rather than damaging.

Greed also slips in almost unnoticed when folk are told again and again that they deserve better. Soon it is treated almost as a sign of God's blessing. We need to beware that we are not lured into accepting the unacceptable (see Colossians 2:8).

5. With the example of the Amorites, God was calling His people to look back at history to discover what would happen to the disobedient. What lessons from history could we cite to show that God's judgment will eventually be rendered on His unfaithful people?

That is precisely the point of this lesson. The judgment on Israel of which Amos warned is only one of several. God judged Adam and Eve in Eden. He judged the Egyptians for enslaving His people. He judged and delivered His people repeatedly through the period of the judges. The Assyrian and Babylonian captivities were also acts of severe judgment. How many more examples do we need to see that God takes sin seriously?

Empty Offerings

DEVOTIONAL READING: Malachi 1:6-14.

BACKGROUND SCRIPTURE: Amos 3–5.

PRINTED TEXT: Amos 4:2-5; 5:18-24.

Amos 4:2-5

2 The Lord GOD hath sworn by his holiness, that, lo, the days shall come upon you, that he will take you away with hooks, and your posterity with fishhooks.

3 And ye shall go out at the breaches, every cow at that which is before her; and ye shall cast them into the palace, saith the LORD.

4 Come to Bethel, and transgress; at Gilgal multiply transgression; and bring your sacrifices every morning, and your tithes after three years:

5 And offer a sacrifice of thanksgiving with leaven, and proclaim and publish the free offerings: for this liketh you, O ye children of Israel, saith the Lord GOD.

Amos 5:18-24

18 Woe unto you that desire the day of the LORD! to what end is it for you? the day of the LORD is darkness, and not light.

19 As if a man did flee from a lion, and a bear met him; or went into the house, and leaned his hand on the wall, and a serpent bit him.

20 Shall not the day of the LORD be darkness, and not light? even very dark, and no brightness in it?

21 I hate, I despise your feast days, and I will not smell in your solemn assemblies.

22 Though ye offer me burnt offerings and your meat offerings, I will not accept them; neither will I regard the peace offerings of your fat beasts.

23 Take thou away from me the noise of thy songs; for I will not hear the melody of thy viols.

24 But let judgment run down as waters, and righteousness as a mighty stream.

GOLDEN TEXT: Let judgment run down as waters, and righteousness as a mighty stream.
—Amos 5:24.

Division and Decline
Unit 2: Prophecies of Judgment
(Lessons 5-9)

Lesson Aims

After participating in this lesson, your students should be able to:

1. Recite key points of Amos's condemnation of Israel's misuse of wealth and its empty rituals of worship.

2. Explain the connection between true worship and a godly life, and tell why that link must never be broken.

3. Take steps to make times of corporate worship more realistic and less ritualistic.

Lesson Outline

INTRODUCTION
  A. A Heart Full of Whales
  B. Lesson Background
 I. GOD'S CONDEMNATION OF ISRAEL (Amos 4:2-5)
  A. Arrogance in Prosperity (vv. 2, 3)
    Obligations of Affluence
  B. Emptiness in Worship (vv. 4, 5)
 II. THE DAY OF THE LORD (Amos 5:18-20)
  A. No Light (v. 18)
  B. No Escape (v. 19)
  C. Only Darkness (v. 20)
III. INDICTMENT OF FALSE WORSHIP (Amos 5:21-24)
  A. Feast Days and Assemblies (v. 21)
  B. Offerings (v. 22)
  C. Music (v. 23)
  D. God's Desire (v. 24)
    Seven-day Religion
CONCLUSION
  A. Justice and Righteousness
  B. Prayer
  C. Thought to Remember

Introduction

A. A Heart Full of Whales

A whaling vessel was in port being prepared for a long voyage in search of whales. On Sunday the captain of the ship attended worship services in the little village chapel. He seemed quite attentive throughout the sermon, but later, when the minister spoke to him, it was obvious that the sermon had made no impression on him. "How is it," asked the minister, "that you could seem so attentive during a sermon and yet apparently never hear a word I said?"

"The fact is," replied the captain, "all the time you were preaching I was thinking about where I would be most likely to find whales. There was no room in my heart for anything but whales."

Probably not many today attend worship services with their hearts full of whales. But, as in Amos's day, some fill them with thoughts of making profits and pursuing pleasures.

B. Lesson Background

In the previous lesson we were introduced to the prophet Amos and his ministry to Israel, the northern kingdom. You may want to review with your class the historical setting of Amos's ministry provided in the Lesson Background to that study. During this period Israel was free from foreign threats and as a result was enjoying general prosperity. [See question #1, page 392.]

Many blame poverty for the many social ills we face, and it is true that poverty provides a variety of temptations. But prosperity carries with it its own temptations. While people sometimes blame God for their difficulties and fail to thank Him for the blessings they have, those who are doing well are tempted to credit their prosperity to their own intelligence and hard work, neglecting to thank God for their blessings. Sometimes they are inclined to look scornfully at the poor, blaming their plight on their own laziness or ignorance.

Greed also impairs one's worship. When material comforts control a person's life, that one is not likely to engage in meaningful worship. Affluent Israelites may have attended worship services regularly and given generously, but they did so with wrong motives. Jesus called His disciples' attention to the same problem when He commended a widow and her two mites in contrast to the much larger donations given by the rich (Mark 12:41-44; Luke 21:1-4). Empty ritual can never substitute for the kind of relationship with God that gives worshipers a genuine concern for others.

As we study this lesson today, we should be able to see many parallels between conditions in ancient Israel and conditions in our own country today, approximately twenty-seven hundred years later. In doing so, we should also keep in mind that less than forty years after Amos prophesied, God's punishment came upon Israel in the form of Assyrian armies who crushed the nation and carried thousands away into captivity.

In the first verse of Amos 4, the prophet directed his words to the "kine of Bashan." Bashan was the fertile plateau east of the Jordan River, stretching to the north from the Yarmuk River south of the Sea of Galilee to Mount Hermon. In the ancient world it was famous for the exceptional cattle that were nourished on its lush pastures. Here "kine [that is, cows] of Bashan" is used as a metaphor to describe the rich women of Samaria who oppressed the poor to maintain their luxuriant lifestyle.

I. God's Condemnation of Israel (Amos 4:2-5)

A. Arrogance in Prosperity (vv. 2, 3)

2, 3. The Lord GOD hath sworn by his holiness, that, lo, the days shall come upon you, that he will take you away with hooks, and your posterity with fishhooks. And ye shall go out at the breaches, every cow at that which is before her; and ye shall cast them into the palace, saith the LORD.

The plight of the poor and oppressed in Israel had not gone unnoticed. God had withheld His judgment for a time, but His *holiness* now arose to demand punishment. Amos described the impending disaster that God had in store for Samaria: the people would be led away like fish on *hooks*. Some of the reliefs (pictures engraved on stone) and inscriptions left behind by the Assyrians portray this treatment of captive peoples. Usually they were led away with a rope fastened to a hook that pierced the nose or lower lip. (Note the description, in 2 Kings 19:28, of how God promised to treat the Assyrians.)

Amos also spoke of the people's *posterity*, or children, as being taken away *with fishhooks*. Again, Assyrian records (both written records and pictures) include portrayals of children being led into captivity. One of the most terrible aspects of sin is that innocent children sometimes have to suffer the consequences of their parents' sins.

And ye shall go out at the breaches. The destruction of the walls of Samaria would leave gaping holes through which the captives could be led out. Note again the reference to *every cow,* reminiscent of the "kine of Bashan" in verse 1.

It is difficult to know what the phrase *ye shall cast them into the palace* means. The Hebrew text here is not very clear. Another suggested reading is, "You will be cast out toward Harmon." If this is correct, then Amos's words may refer to Mount Hermon or to some other area where the people's captors would take them.

OBLIGATIONS OF AFFLUENCE

Being a Christian in the Western world today poses both special privileges and special responsibilities. We enjoy freedom of worship, and we usually don't have to fear imprisonment or torture for expressing our faith. But there is a certain peril in privilege, particularly where material wealth is concerned. Our stewardship responsibilities are greater because we are stewards over

more possessions. Jesus said, "From everyone who has been given much, much will be demanded; and from the one who has been entrusted with much, much more will be asked" (Luke 12:48, *New International Version*).

There is always the temptation to credit ourselves instead of God's blessing for our abundance. If we yield to this temptation, we will be less likely to make appropriate preparations for Jesus' return. We will also have far less influence for Christ in this world than we could have.

Israel, too, was prosperous; its people had come to trust in their wealth and what it brought them rather than in God. But the inescapable judgment of God, declared Amos, was sentencing them to defeat and exile. Can we learn from Israel's experience? Will we avoid the same sins?

Sadly, history can and does repeat itself. Pray that our nation will forsake its wicked ways and turn to God, who will hear from Heaven and heal our land (2 Chronicles 7:14). —R. W. B.

B. Emptiness in Worship (vv. 4, 5)

4. Come to Bethel, and transgress; at Gilgal multiply transgression; and bring your sacrifices every morning, and your tithes after three years.

Jeroboam I had established a center of worship at *Bethel* to keep the people of the northern kingdom from going to the temple in Jerusalem to worship (1 Kings 12:25-30). Amos boldly stepped forward and challenged this unauthorized practice. He condemned the false worship at Bethel by sarcastically urging the people to continue in it: *Come to Bethel, and transgress.* They were transgressing, both through their worship at an unapproved site and by their attempts to worship God while living in defiance of His authority in their daily conduct.

Gilgal was the site where the Israelites camped after crossing the Jordan River, just prior to beginning their conquest of Canaan (Joshua 4:19). Apparently it, like Bethel, had become a center of worship (Hosea 4:15; 12:11; Amos 5:5).

The fact that the people brought *sacrifices every morning* indicates that they had erected altars at Bethel and Gilgal. Thus they were careful to observe certain commands set forth in the law (morning and evening sacrifices are commanded in Exodus 29:38-42). Yet in Bethel these sacrifices were being offered to the golden calf set up there by Jeroboam, not to the true God.

The phrase *your tithes after three years* calls to mind the teaching of the law of Moses about tithing. The law commanded that every three years the Israelites were to bring the tithes of that year's produce and store it away in order to provide for the needs of Levites, strangers, orphans, and widows (Deuteronomy 14:28, 29; 26:12). Students disagree as to whether this "third-year tithe" was the same as, or in addition to, the annual tithe (Deuteronomy 14:22). The Hebrew term may also be rendered "every three days." If this translation is accepted, then Amos would have been using sarcasm once again to highlight the people's spiritual condition. Even if they offered tithes every three days, it would be meaningless in view of their failure to obey God's law in their daily living.

5. And offer a sacrifice of thanksgiving with leaven, and proclaim and publish the free offerings: for this liketh you, O ye children of Israel, saith the Lord GOD.

Continuing his sarcastic tone, Amos urged the people to *offer a sacrifice of thanksgiving with leaven.* Including leaven in any offering involving fire was forbidden (Leviticus 2:11). By doing so the people were once more substituting their will for the expressed will of God in His law.

Amos also told his audience to *proclaim and publish the free offerings: for this liketh you. Free offerings* means "freewill offerings." *This liketh you* means that the people liked to receive public acclaim for such offerings. Instead of coming humbly with their gifts, they were coming boastfully because this brought them the praise of others. Consider how Jesus described the phony worshipers of His day: "When thou prayest, thou shalt not be as the hypocrites are: for they love to pray standing in the synagogues and in the corners of the streets, that they may be seen of men" (Matthew 6:5). [See question #2, page 392.]

II. The Day of the Lord
(Amos 5:18-20)
A. No Light (v. 18)

18. Woe unto you that desire the day of the LORD! to what end is it for you? the day of the LORD is darkness, and not light.

The day of judgment on God's enemies is often referred to in Scripture as *the day of the Lord.* (Additional references include Isaiah 13:6, 9; Joel 1:15; 2:1, 2, 11, 31; 1 Thessalonians 5:2; 2 Peter 3:10.) Those to whom Amos preached believed that such a day was coming—they even longed for it. The problem was that they did not see this as a day of judgment against them. Amos made it clear, as we have seen in the previous part of our printed text, that a time of judgment was coming upon the people of Israel for their sins. Clearly God was not pleased with them. But their prosperity had blinded them to spiritual realities. With times so good (so they thought), how could the day of the Lord possibly be a day of *darkness, and not light?*

Are we in any way like these ancient Israelites? Do we live our lives as if this world is all that matters? Is our measure of contentment with life based on how well we are doing materially? Every day that passes brings us one day closer to the time that we will be called to stand before the judgment seat of Christ (Romans 14:10). What are we doing to prepare ourselves for that day? [See question #3, page 392.]

B. No Escape (v. 19)

19. As if a man did flee from a lion, and a bear met him; or went into the house, and leaned his hand on the wall, and a serpent bit him.

To explain what the day of the Lord would be like for unprepared people, Amos used illustrations that were familiar to his audience. The *lion* has been extinct in Palestine for centuries, but in ancient times it frequented the thickets along rivers. Both Samson (Judges 14:5, 6) and David (1 Samuel 17:34, 35) had successful encounters with lions. The *bear* refers to the Syrian brown bear, now also extinct in Palestine.

Imagine the humor in the word picture painted by Amos. A man is running for his life to escape from a lion. He reaches a point where he figures he can finally relax, only to see a bear coming! He flees from the bear and eventually comes to his *house,* thinking that surely he will be safe there. Feeling at ease, he leans his *hand on the wall*—and a snake bites him! (This probably refers to an opening in a wall, perhaps a window, where a snake could hide.) The point of Amos's illustration is obvious: when the day of the Lord arrives, there will be no way to escape the wrath of God.

C. Only Darkness (v. 20)

20. Shall not the day of the LORD be darkness, and not light? even very dark, and no brightness in it?

Darkness is often associated with God's judgment or with that which is evil or undesirable. Jesus speaks of those who in the day of judgment will be cast out into "outer darkness" (Matthew

8:12; 25:30). Whether that day will be one of *light* or of darkness is up to us and is determined by our relationship with Jesus.

III. Indictment of False Worship (Amos 5:21-24)

A. Feast Days and Assemblies (v. 21)

21. I hate, I despise your feast days, and I will not smell in your solemn assemblies.

Although the people were keeping the prescribed *feast days*, God rejected their worship because there was such a glaring contradiction between their profession of faith and their daily living. The *smell* of the burnt offerings presented in their *solemn assemblies* was unacceptable to Him. When God gave instructions in the law of Moses concerning sacrifices, He had described the "sweet savor" that would rise from them (Leviticus 1:9, 13, 17). But God had also warned that if His people rebelled against Him, dire consequences would follow: "I will make your cities waste, and bring your sanctuaries unto desolation, and I will not smell the savor of your sweet odors" (Leviticus 26:31). Amos was announcing that Israel had deteriorated to such a sorry state. [See question #4, page 392.]

B. Offerings (v. 22)

22. Though ye offer me burnt offerings and your meat offerings, I will not accept them; neither will I regard the peace offerings of your fat beasts.

In the previous verse Amos had condemned the people's "solemn assemblies," which had reached the point of being nothing more than empty rituals and a perversion of true worship. Now he turned his attention specifically to the various offerings that the people brought.

The *burnt offerings* are the most commonly mentioned offerings in the Old Testament. Only male animals (without blemish) were used for this offering, and the entire animal was burned

Today's visual features a dramatic photograph of Yellowstone Falls to illustrate the message of Amos 5:24. Post it as you begin to discuss that verse.

Visual for lesson 6

on the altar. Leviticus 1 includes the regulations concerning the burnt offering. The term *meat offerings* is more accurately rendered "grain offerings," for these were made of "fine flour." These were the only bloodless offerings required by the law of Moses. Regulations for them are found in Leviticus 2. *Peace offerings* could be made with either male or female animals. A portion of the animal was eaten by the priests and the rest by the worshiper. These are further described in Leviticus 3.

C. Music (v. 23)

23. Take thou away from me the noise of thy songs; for I will not hear the melody of thy viols.

David and other psalmists wrote many *songs* that had become incorporated into Israel's worship. The building of Solomon's temple had stimulated the development of music, both vocal and instrumental, as a part of public worship. Apparently this emphasis on music had been continued in the places of worship established in the northern kingdom. (The term *viols* describes an instrument similar to a harp.)

God's objections were not to the music itself, but to the attitudes of the worshipers. Perhaps their emotions were soothed by the pleasant sounds. But unless they came before God with humble hearts, what they did was merely for personal pleasure. It was not true worship.

D. God's Desire (v. 24)

24. But let judgment run down as waters, and righteousness as a mighty stream.

Here *judgment* means justice. Amos wanted both *justice* and *righteousness* to govern the people's relationship with their fellow Israelites. Of course, both of these qualities can never become a reality without a proper relationship with God. The Ten Commandments are instructive here: the first four deal with man's relationship with God while the other six cover man's relationship with others. Neither part of the Commandments is complete without the other.

Using a vivid word picture once again, Amos pleaded with the people to allow justice and righteousness to flood the land like a *mighty stream*. He pictured the change as something that would be ongoing—not like a desert wadi (where water ran after a sudden rain only to dry up later), but like a perennial stream that issued life-giving water throughout the year. [See question #5, page 392.]

SEVEN-DAY RELIGION

Times really don't change much. Hundreds of years after Amos delivered God's warnings to the Israelites concerning their neglect of justice and righteousness, Jesus had to teach the worshipers of His day the same lessons. "Woe unto you, scribes and Pharisees, hypocrites! for ye pay tithe of mint and anise and cummin, and have omitted the weightier matters of the law, judgment, mercy, and faith: these ought ye to have done, and not to leave the other undone" (Matthew 23:23). Same sin—same condemnation!

True religion is walked as well as talked. Sabbath-keepers in ancient Israel were failing to live by their professed faith. Today Sunday superficiality is the practice of many Christians who give just one day a week to God. They see their time categorized as either "spiritual" or "secular." Worship is fine in its time and place, but "business is business."

Many churches have recognized the importance of using the church facilities seven days a week. Even more essential is the living out of Christian principles and gospel truth seven days a week. God will be pleased, and the world will be given a clearer view of what Christianity really is.

—R. W. B.

Conclusion

A. Justice and Righteousness

For much of the previous century, conservative, Bible-believing Christians (often referred to as evangelicals) were not leaders in working for social justice. There were historical reasons for this. Early in the century, theological liberals, having abandoned many of the beliefs essential to the Christian faith, turned their energies to working for social justice in the world. The focus on these efforts led to the term "social gospel," which became associated with liberal theology. Evangelicals, wanting nothing to do with liberalism in any form, abandoned these concerns for social justice, giving their energies instead to evangelism and missions.

It would be unfair, however, to accuse evangelicals of abandoning all concern for the needy and helpless. They have built orphanages and homes for the elderly. They have supported missions in the inner cities, ministering to drug addicts, alcoholics, prostitutes, and the homeless. They have given generously to international parachurch organizations that minister to human needs around the world.

If Amos were to return to the twenty-first century, how would he view our society now? Evangelicals generally hold that the best route to social reform is to convert people to Jesus Christ. If people are genuinely committed to Jesus and His teachings, they will be concerned for individuals such as the sick, the homeless, the orphans, the widows, and the hungry. Certainly Amos would give his approval to this.

At the same time, many of the evils of our society are deeply imbedded in our social structures and our laws. Those of us who live in democratic societies, where as citizens we have an opportunity to shape our laws, must recognize the special responsibility that is ours to work for justice in our society. As Christian citizens, we need to keep ourselves well informed about public issues and express our beliefs through the ballot box and through whatever involvement in public life that we believe is God's desire for us. This will be no easy task, for in a chaotic society like ours there are often no simple answers to complicated problems. In some instances we may have to accept compromises, settling for something that may be an improvement but falls short of achieving the best.

Amos was an advocate of both justice and righteousness. Let us work for both of these important goals—for righteousness, in bringing people into a right relationship with God through Jesus Christ, and for justice, in bringing a Christian perspective to the issues of our day that are crying for solid answers.

B. Prayer

Father, we are often disturbed by the suffering and injustice that we see all about us. Sometimes it seems overwhelming. Keep us from comfortably accepting our world as it is. Give us the strength and wisdom to do whatever we can wherever we are to bring about the justice and righteousness that Amos spoke about. Through the Prince of peace we pray. Amen.

C. Thought to Remember

Empty, hollow worship will neither please God nor have an impact on the world for Him.

Home Daily Bible Readings

Monday, July 2—A Prophet's Privilege and Responsibility (Amos 3:3-8)

Tuesday, July 3—The Doom of Samaria (Amos 3:9—4:5)

Wednesday, July 4—Israel Rejects Correction (Amos 4:6-13)

Thursday, July 5—A Call to Repentance (Amos 5:1-15)

Friday, July 6—The Day of the Lord (Amos 5:16-20)

Saturday, July 7—God Despises Worship Without Righteousness (Amos 5:21-27)

Sunday, July 8—Corruption of the Priesthood (Malachi 1:6-14)

Learning by Doing

This page contains an alternate lesson plan emphasizing learning activities.
Classes desiring such student involvement will find these suggestions helpful.

Learning Goals

After this lesson each student will be able to:

1. Recite key points of Amos's condemnation of Israel's misuse of wealth and its empty rituals of worship.

2. Explain the connection between true worship and a godly life, and tell why that link must never be broken.

3. Take steps to make times of corporate worship more realistic and less ritualistic.

Into the Lesson

Observe that children will sometimes call other children names when they are angry. Sometimes they use the names of animals. Ask the class what a child might imply when calling someone a chicken. A pig. A dog. A cow.

Then tell the class that you know of an *adult* who called a number of prominent women "cows." And he was a preacher! Ask, "Why do you think a preacher would call women 'cows'? What do you think he was implying?"

Let the class suggest answers, but do not comment on the answers one way or the other. After some discussion, say, "Actually, this preacher was making a point about the worship these women and others in Israel practiced. We will see what he meant in today's adventure with Amos."

Into the Word

Prepare a visual to help your learners understand the lesson background. The visual should have the heading "Empty Offerings." Under this should be listed four major points for your brief presentation: Israel's Prosperity, Diluted Worship, Cows of Bashan, Coming Captivity. Use the Lesson Background and commentary notes (see pages 386, 387) to prepare and deliver a brief lecture on these four points. Then tell the class that the focus of Amos's address is the approach of God's judgment against the people's empty, ritualistic worship.

Read Amos 2:2-5 and ask, "Why does Amos tell his listeners to go to Bethel and Gilgal to sin? What is he implying?" Then explain these phrases: "Bring your sacrifices every morning . . . your tithes after three years . . . a sacrifice of thanksgiving," and "free offerings."

Ask a volunteer to read Amos 5:18-24. Then form small groups to discuss the following sets of questions based on this text. (You should have these questions printed on a handout or a large visual to which the groups can refer.)

1. The Israelites longed for the "day of the Lord." What do you think they expected to happen on the day of the Lord? Why would Amos pronounce "woe" to these expectant Israelites?

2. Why would God hate their religious feasts and not accept their offerings and music?

3. Why the pronouncement in verse 24? What did God expect of the Israelites?

After a few minutes, ask each of three volunteers to report on one of the questions and tell what his or her group concluded.

Into Life

Ask the groups to continue to work together. Each group is to discuss only one of the following tasks. If you have more than three groups, have some of the groups discuss the same task.

Task 1: Innocent children sometimes suffer the consequences of their parents' sins (Amos 4:2, 3). Cite contemporary illustrations of this principle and write recommendations for parents.

Task 2: Amos emphasizes social responsibility. Read Matthew 25:31-46. Then list some of the characteristics of a person who fulfills God's will in this area. Also list implications this passage suggests for the contemporary church.

Task 3: Worship is influenced by our values and behavior. Considering what had happened to the worship of the Israelites, offer suggestions of how to keep Christian worship expressions genuine and not merely ritualistic.

After the groups finish, introduce Group 1 by telling the class there are often helpful subtopics packed into the big picture of Scripture. One of those is in today's text, and it has to do with sin's consequences on our children. Ask a representative from Group 1 to share the group's findings.

Introduce Group 2 by telling the class that this group addressed one of the major issues of Amos's message—social justice and responsibility. Ask a representative to share Group 2's conclusions.

Introduce Group 3 by reminding the class that the worship of the Israelites was not acceptable because of their hearts and behavior. Allow a representative from Group 3 to offer suggestions on how to keep worship fresh, personal, and genuine. After the report, remind the class that God seeks worshipers whose lives reflect worship of Him, not simply people who go to worship.

Let's Talk It Over

The questions on this page are designed to encourage review of the lesson
Scriptures and to promote discussion of the lesson by the class. The answers
provided are only discussion starters. Let your class talk it over from there.

1. During Amos's day, Israel was enjoying a period of prosperity. For them, wealth was like a poison. But it is not just Israelites who succumb to the deceit of becoming self-sufficient. How can having too much affect our relationship with God?

Affluence brings a false sense of security. Citizens in Israel probably attributed their prosperity to their own intelligence and hard work. Enjoying the benefits of wealth made the people crave even more, even if acquiring additional wealth forced them to compromise or even give up their devotion to God. Feeling self-sufficient, they began to lose their sense of need for God. Israel's prosperity was making them soft. Proud people who live in the world's richest nations need to take heed.

2. Amos 4:4, 5 describes Israel's empty and ritualistic worship. Some would accuse today's church of practicing empty worship as well. How do we distinguish real worship from empty worship?

The practice of worship has become almost a science today. In many churches the worship service is carefully choreographed and rehearsed so that it becomes a performance, a production worthy of Broadway.

John 4:23 and 24 remind us that real worship is done in spirit and in truth. Real worship involves a heart that is close to God's (Matthew 15:8) and a humble spirit (Psalm 95:6).

It is good to prepare for worship, and worship leaders often need to practice. But the intent must always be to give glory to God, not to put on a show that honors the performers. As always, the attitude is the most critical element.

3. First John 5:13 assures us that we can "know" that we have eternal life. While it is important that we have that confidence, is it possible to become overconfident regarding judgment—even as the people in Israel did? What should be our attitude regarding "the day of the Lord"?

With almost any single text, we might extract a truth and still not understand its full meaning. First John 5:13 does give us assurance in the Christian life, but to understand the verse we need to keep in mind all of what the Bible says

about our relationship with the Lord. Saving faith is not a single event, like buying a ticket. It is a relationship. A man who ignores his wife or takes her for granted will jeopardize his marriage. The same is true of our relationship with God. The just shall live—continually—by faith.

This lesson was the one that Amos was trying to bring home to the nation of Israel. Just because they were God's chosen didn't mean that they could become arrogant and self-directed in their lifestyle. God wanted a faithful nation. Without that relationship they would be disowned.

4. The language of verse 21 is strikingly harsh. What do you think would cause God to "hate" or "despise" our worship assemblies or practices today? What should be our response?

The same thing that led to the rejection of Israel's worship will make our worship unacceptable to God—hypocrisy. If we think we can make a great show of piety and devotion to God by singing hymns (or contemporary choruses) without giving God our hearts, then we are as misguided as the people of Israel! If we think we can ignore the needs of the people around us and then come before the Lord in worship, we have not comprehended what it means to love God. "If a man say, I love God, and hateth his brother, he is a liar: for he that loveth not his brother whom he hath seen, how can he love God whom he hath not seen?" (1 John 4:20). We can worship "in spirit and in truth" (John 4:24) only when our worship is a natural expression of the love and devotion that we demonstrate every day—not just one day a week.

5. What can we do, as individuals or as a church, to "let judgment run down as waters, and righteousness as a mighty stream"?

Talk about specific needs in your own community that need to be addressed. Is there a homeless shelter that you could help to equip or staff? Is there a family who lost its home to a fire or other disaster? Are there single mothers who could use some help with their children but cannot afford child care? Are there issues coming up on the ballot this fall that demand a united front from believers to secure justice for some segment of the community? Of course, in all these matters, do not overlook the power of prayer!

God's Love for Israel

DEVOTIONAL READING: Psalm 100.

BACKGROUND SCRIPTURE: Hosea 1, 2.

PRINTED TEXT: Hosea 1:2—2:4.

Hosea 1:2-11

2 The beginning of the word of the LORD by Hosea. And the LORD said to Hosea, Go, take unto thee a wife of whoredoms and children of whoredoms: for the land hath committed great whoredom, departing from the LORD.

3 So he went and took Gomer the daughter of Diblaim; which conceived, and bare him a son.

4 And the LORD said unto him, Call his name Jezreel; for yet a little while, and I will avenge the blood of Jezreel upon the house of Jehu, and will cause to cease the kingdom of the house of Israel.

5 And it shall come to pass at that day, that I will break the bow of Israel in the valley of Jezreel.

6 And she conceived again, and bare a daughter. And God said unto him, Call her name Lo-ruhamah: for I will no more have mercy upon the house of Israel; but I will utterly take them away.

7 But I will have mercy upon the house of Judah, and will save them by the LORD their God, and will not save them by bow, nor by sword, nor by battle, by horses, nor by horsemen.

8 Now when she had weaned Lo-ruhamah, she conceived, and bare a son.

9 Then said God, Call his name Lo-ammi: for ye are not my people, and I will not be your God.

10 Yet the number of the children of Israel shall be as the sand of the sea, which cannot be measured nor numbered; and it shall come to pass, that in the place where it was said unto them, Ye are not my people, there it shall be said unto them, Ye are the sons of the living God.

11 Then shall the children of Judah and the children of Israel be gathered together, and appoint themselves one head, and they shall come up out of the land: for great shall be the day of Jezreel.

Hosea 2:1-4

1 Say ye unto your brethren, Ammi; and to your sisters, Ruhamah.

2 Plead with your mother, plead; for she is not my wife, neither am I her husband: let her therefore put away her whoredoms out of her sight, and her adulteries from between her breasts;

3 Lest I strip her naked, and set her as in the day that she was born, and make her as a wilderness, and set her like a dry land, and slay her with thirst.

4 And I will not have mercy upon her children; for they be the children of whoredoms.

GOLDEN TEXT: I will have mercy upon the house of Judah, and will save them by the LORD their God.—Hosea 1:7.

Lesson Aims

After this lesson students should be able to:

1. Tell how Hosea's marriage to an unfaithful wife illustrates God's love for His people, even when they are unfaithful.

2. Suggest how Christians may be tempted toward spiritual infidelity even as Israel was.

3. Offer a prayer of repentance for past infidelities to the Lord.

Lesson Outline

INTRODUCTION
  A. Blasted Into Usefulness
  B. Lesson Background
 I. AN UNUSUAL MARRIAGE (Hosea 1:2-9)
  A. Choice of a Wife (vv. 2, 3a)
  B. Birth of a Son (vv. 3b-5)
  C. Birth of a Daughter (vv. 6, 7)
    God's "Last Nerve"
  D. Birth of a Second Son (vv. 8, 9)
II. PROMISE OF BETTER TIMES (Hosea 1:10—2:1)
  A. God's People Multiplied (v. 10)
  B. God's People United (1:11; 2:1)
    Iron Hands/Velvet Gloves
III. HEARTBREAK OF SIN (Hosea 2:2-4)
  A. Marriage Vows Broken (v. 2)
  B. Infidelity Punished (vv. 3, 4)
CONCLUSION
  A. A Double Tragedy
  B. Prayer
  C. Thought to Remember

Introduction

A. Blasted Into Usefulness

Several years ago my family and I stood on the bank of the Saint Lawrence River and watched great ocean freighters lock through the Saint Lawrence Seaway. Across the river we could see Canada and the city of Montreal, but we did not see a single ship on the river. At this point the river, while it was quite wide, was too swift and shallow for navigation.

"Why," asked one of our children, "can the big ships go through here but not on the river?"

"Blasting," was my reply. "Blasting a channel through solid rock by using tons of dynamite. It was a long, hard job, but it was the only way the river could be made navigable. It had to be blasted into usefulness."

Hosea may have been a thoughtful, sensitive person even before God called him to be a prophet. Yet for him to be effective in carrying out his ministry, it was necessary for God to deepen his sensitivity. Thus God used Hosea's personal tragedy of a broken marriage, painful though it was, as a means of making him a more compassionate and insightful prophet. In effect, Hosea was blasted into usefulness.

B. Lesson Background

Like Amos, Hosea's ministry was to Israel (the northern kingdom); but unlike Amos, who was from Judah (the southern kingdom), Hosea was most likely from Israel. Like Amos, Hosea prophesied during the reign of Jeroboam II, who ruled Israel from 793 to 753 B.C. (Hosea 1:1; Amos 1:1). Unlike Amos, Hosea is described as prophesying during the reigns of four kings of Judah—Uzziah, Jotham, Ahaz, and Hezekiah (Hosea 1:1). This means that Hosea's ministry probably lasted into the final quarter of the eighth century B.C. If so, he may well have witnessed the fall of the northern kingdom to Assyria in 722 B.C. (which Amos may not have). Since the only king of Judah that Amos mentions is Uzziah (Amos 1:1), Hosea was probably a younger contemporary of Amos. He was also a contemporary of the prophets Isaiah and Micah.

I. An Unusual Marriage
(Hosea 1:2-9)

A. Choice of a Wife (vv. 2, 3a)

2. The beginning of the word of the LORD by Hosea. And the LORD said to Hosea, Go, take unto thee a wife of whoredoms and children of whoredoms: for the land hath committed great whoredom, departing from the LORD.

It was noted during the studies from Amos (lesson 5, page 378) that Israel experienced great prosperity during the reign of Jeroboam II. Spiritually and morally, however, the nation was undergoing a serious decline. To speak *the word of the Lord* during such times required someone specially prepared for the heartbreak of scorn and rejection. God was about to guide Hosea through such a period of preparation.

Go, take unto thee a wife of whoredoms. Such a command seems shocking, even inconceivable, to us. As a result, some students take this incident as a vision or an allegory rather than the record of actual events. However, no mention is made of a dream or vision; and the fact that the woman's name (Gomer) has no allegorical significance seems to rule out this approach.

Although Gomer was described as *a wife of whoredoms*, this does not necessarily mean that she was an immoral woman when Hosea married her. It may be a description of what she became through the influence of the sexually promiscuous society in which she lived. While faithful to Hosea at the beginning of their marriage, eventually Gomer yielded to the temptations surrounding her and turned to a life of immorality. The phrase *wife of whoredoms* thus warned Hosea of the heartache that lay ahead for him. [See question #1, page 400.]

For the land hath committed great whoredom, departing from the Lord. The reason given for Hosea's marriage fits well with the understanding of Hosea and Gomer's relationship described in the previous paragraph. Just as Israel began as God's faithful people, then departed from His way, so did Gomer begin as a faithful wife to her husband Hosea, only to "depart" from him to pursue other lovers.

The reference to *children of whoredoms* seems to indicate that the children born following Hosea and Gomer's marriage would follow the sordid lifestyle of their mother, not the righteous lifestyle of their father. This would have been as painful for Hosea to see as was the adulterous activity of his wife.

3a. So he went and took Gomer the daughter of Diblaim.

Even though Hosea may have had serious reservations about God's command, he obeyed without voicing these—an indication that God had selected the right man for this very unusual and demanding task. [See question #2, page 400.]

B. Birth of a Son (vv. 3b-5)

3b, 4. Which conceived, and bare him a son. And the LORD said unto him, Call his name Jezreel; for yet a little while, and I will avenge the blood of Jezreel upon the house of Jehu, and will cause to cease the kingdom of the house of Israel.

The text makes it clear (by saying *bare him a son*) that this first child was the child of Hosea and not the child of an illicit relationship. God chose the *name* for the son, *Jezreel*, which means "God sows" or "scatters." This was also the name of a city located south and west of the Sea of Galilee, overlooking the valley of Jezreel. Approximately a hundred years earlier Jezreel had been the scene of Jehu's massacre of Jezebel and the house of Ahab (2 Kings 9:30-37; 10:1-7, 11). Following these actions, Jehu had attempted to bring about a religious reform by carrying out a bloody purge of the followers of Baal (2 Kings 10:18-28). God rewarded Jehu's efforts by declaring that four generations of his descendants would reign on the throne of Israel, though God was not pleased with the excessive amount of *blood* shed nor with Jehu's failure to keep His law faithfully (10:30, 31). As a result, a punishment similar to the one that had befallen Ahab's house awaited *the house of Jehu*.

In 753 B.C. Jeroboam died. He was succeeded by his son Zechariah, who was assassinated within six months, thus ending the rule of the fourth generation (2 Kings 15:8-12). Only some thirty years remained until the destruction of *the kingdom of the house of Israel* in 722 B.C.

5. And it shall come to pass at that day, that I will break the bow of Israel in the valley of Jezreel.

I will break the bow of Israel. The *bow* represented Israel's might. Following the death of Jeroboam II, Israel never again regained her military strength. Certain portions of the land such as the *valley of Jezreel* (to the north of the city of Jezreel) fell prey to the Assyrians in 733 B.C., several years before Israel itself fell.

C. Birth of a Daughter (vv. 6, 7)

6. And she conceived again, and bare a daughter. And God said unto him, Call her name Lo-ruhamah: for I will no more have mercy upon the house of Israel; but I will utterly take them away.

Hosea's second child was a daughter, who also was given an unusual name—*Lo-ruhamah*, which means "not pitied" or "no mercy." Commentators have noted that this child was not said to have been born "to him" (Hosea), unlike Jezreel (v. 3). This may indicate that this second child was born through an illicit relationship, thus marking the beginning of Gomer's adultery.

The message behind the name Lo-ruhamah was closely tied to that of Jezreel, for both signified God's judgment upon *the house of Israel*. Israel's repeated rejection of God and His covenant had exhausted His patience. *No more* would they be shown *mercy*.

Visual for lesson 7

Display visual 7 at the beginning of your class time today. It pictures the three children of Hosea's wife and their very significant names.

GOD'S "LAST NERVE"

Sometimes a parent who is running out of patience with his or her young children is heard to say, "You kids are getting on my last nerve!" Unless the children's behavior improves, some form of punishment usually will follow—especially after Dad's or Mom's last nerve has "snapped." Even the most kind and loving parents occasionally exhaust every last shred of patience; then justice is administered swiftly, and often painfully, upon strong-willed children who disregard clear instructions and ample warnings.

Israel had become a childish nation. She had been privileged to experience God's love and care in many unique ways. His covenant commandments were unmistakably clear. Yet the "chosen nation" repeatedly rebelled and disobeyed, in spite of God's warnings about such behavior. Finally the people got on "God's last nerve." The message came through Hosea: "No more mercy!"

The parallels to our contemporary moral and spiritual bankruptcy are sobering, to say the least. Will our nation be wise enough to learn from the lessons of history? Such wisdom begins with fearing the Lord. Our Father's patience does have limits.   —R. W. B.

7. But I will have mercy upon the house of Judah, and will save them by the LORD their God, and will not save them by bow, nor by sword, nor by battle, by horses, nor by horsemen.

Although *Judah* had followed Israel into idolatry and apostasy, she had not fallen so far that her situation was beyond God's *mercy*. Nearly twenty years after the destruction of the northern kingdom, Judah, like Israel, felt the wrath of Assyria at its very doorstep. But then *the Lord their God*, without using any of the usual weapons of war, destroyed the entire Assyrian army and spared His people and His city (2 Kings 19:32-37). [See question #3, page 400.]

D. Birth of a Second Son (vv. 8, 9)

8, 9. Now when she had weaned Lo-ruhamah, she conceived, and bare a son. Then said God, Call his name Lo-ammi: for ye are not my people, and I will not be your God.

Since mothers in the ancient Near East nursed their children up to three years, this amount of time probably had lapsed between the birth of the daughter and the birth of the second *son*. Again, note that this child is not described as born to Hosea.

Call his name Lo-ammi. This son's name meant *not my people.* God's explanation for this name amounted to a reversal of His earlier promise that Israel would be His people and that He would be their God (Leviticus 26:12). However, as the following verses indicate, this was not God's final word on the matter. Just as His promise could be reversed, so could His judgment.

II. Promise of Better Times (Hosea 1:10—2:1)

A. God's People Multiplied (v. 10)

10. Yet the number of the children of Israel shall be as the sand of the sea, which cannot be measured nor numbered; and it shall come to pass, that in the place where it was said unto them, Ye are not my people, there it shall be said unto them, Ye are the sons of the living God.

Verses 10 and 11 mark a sharp break with the previous verses, which had been filled with gloom and impending judgment. Hosea's inspired vision saw beyond the destruction of his people to a day when they would *be as the sand of the sea, which cannot be measured nor numbered.* Though once rejected and shown no mercy (v. 6), they would again be called *the sons of the living God.* This may refer to the time when some of the descendants of those taken captive in 722 B.C., along with some of the refugees from Judah, were able to return from their captivity in 538 B.C. and make the promised land their home.

Note, however, Paul's quotation of this passage in Romans 9:26. Here the apostle sees Hosea's promise as embracing not just the physical descendants of Abraham, but his spiritual seed as well—Christians, who by faith are considered children of Abraham (Galatians 3:6-9). This makes the reference to the sand of the sea significant, for it is reminiscent of the promise God made to Abraham concerning his descendants (Genesis 22:15-18).

B. God's People United (1:11; 2:1)

11. Then shall the children of Judah and the children of Israel be gathered together, and appoint themselves one head, and they shall come up out of the land: for great shall be the day of Jezreel.

Hosea also described the day when *Judah* and *Israel*, divided for some two hundred years at the time of his ministry, would once more be *gathered together* under *one head* and would *come up out of the land.* Some suggest that his words were fulfilled when Cyrus the Great conquered the Babylonian Empire and issued a decree allowing the Jewish captives who chose to do so to leave the land of their captivity and return to their homeland (Ezra 1:1-4).

But the return from captivity in Babylon is but a shadow of the full implications of this passage. Like the previous verse, it should be viewed as a messianic prophecy looking forward to the coming of Christ. Only then will the unity described in this verse come to pass, as individuals from both Judah and Israel (along with Gentile believers) are brought together in the church under *one head*, Jesus Christ, to make up the "Israel of God" (Galatians 6:16).

The verse concludes with the promise that *great shall be the day of Jezreel.* Earlier Jezreel was described as a place associated with Israel's punishment (Hosea 1:4, 5). Now, however, the situation is reversed, and Jezreel becomes a place of blessing. The name Jezreel ("God scatters" or "sows") takes on a positive meaning in this verse, as God "scatters" the people, not in judgment as before, but in a sowing that will result in abundant growth. [See question #4, page 400.]

IRON HANDS/VELVET GLOVES

Parenting may be the most difficult job in the world. One of its biggest challenges involves administering discipline. Even permissive parents realize sooner or later that children need to be punished in some manner. The hard part is balancing justice with mercy.

Our Father in Heaven is a master of loving discipline. In fact, "whom the Lord loveth he chasteneth" (Hebrews 12:6); and it really does "hurt Him more" when He punishes His children. Israel had to be chastened severely, yet even with Hosea's prophecy of imminent punishment came the additional promise of God's merciful plan to bring His people together—a plan that came to pass under the saving lordship of Jesus Christ.

Our God is indeed an awesome God—perfectly just, yet full of compassion. His love is often tough, but His "iron hands" are clothed with "velvet gloves." His mercy is everlasting.

—R. W. B.

2:1. Say ye unto your brethren, Ammi; and to your sisters, Ruhamah.

Having just promised better times for God's people, Hosea was told to remove the *Lo* that had prefixed the names of his children. *Lo* is the Hebrew word for "not"; thus the names reflected the brighter future ahead. (*Ammi* means "my people"; *Ruhamah* means "receiving mercy.") Those who are part of God's people under the New Covenant will recognize each other as *brethren* and as *sisters* on the basis of the mercy of God that all have experienced.

Later in this chapter Hosea reiterates these promises by using the names of the three children (vv. 22, 23). Peter used similar language

when he described what God has done for all those who were formerly excluded from the people of God but who, through Jesus, are now included (1 Peter 2:10).

III. Heartbreak of Sin
(Hosea 2:2-4)

A. Marriage Vows Broken (v. 2)

2. Plead with your mother, plead; for she is not my wife, neither am I her husband: let her therefore put away her whoredoms out of her sight, and her adulteries from between her breasts.

In spite of Hosea's words concerning the glorious future that lay ahead for God's people, the prophet had to confront the painful reality of the present situation involving his wayward wife. Hosea's children were asked to *plead with* their *mother* (Gomer), for by this time she had left Hosea to live a life of immorality. Perhaps Hosea himself had tried and failed to win her back. Failing in this effort, he had declared the marriage covenant broken: *she is not my wife, neither am I her husband.*

Hosea's children were to beg their mother to *put away her whoredoms . . . and her adulteries.* This may refer, not just to the activities of prostitution, but to the seductive adornment by which Gomer attracted her partners. It was not enough for her simply to leave a life of adultery; she had to leave behind whatever might tempt her to return to that lifestyle.

B. Infidelity Punished (vv. 3, 4)

3. Lest I strip her naked, and set her as in the day that she was born, and make her as a wilderness, and set her like a dry land, and slay her with thirst.

Home Daily Bible Readings

Monday, July 9—The Prophet Hosea's Marriage (Hosea 1:1-5)

Tuesday, July 10—The Births of Loruhamah and Lo-ammi (Hosea 1:6-9)

Wednesday, July 11—Blessing Followed by Chastisement (Hosea 1:10—2:7)

Thursday, July 12—Israel's Humiliation and Punishment (Hosea 2:8-13)

Friday, July 13—The Lord's Hope for His People (Hosea 2:14-18)

Saturday, July 14—Unfaithful Israel to Be Restored (Hosea 2:19-23)

Sunday, July 15—Invitation to Praise (Psalm 100)

A husband was responsible to provide clothes and other needs for his wife (Exodus 21:10). Hosea, the betrayed husband, was prepared to take away all the gifts of clothing and other adornments that he had showered upon his wife. In the same way, God (the betrayed "husband" of Israel) would *strip* Israel of all the blessings He had provided for her in such abundance.

The phrase *in the day that she was born* probably refers to the time when Israel was enslaved in Egypt and was called to be God's "holy nation" (Exodus 19:6). At that time she was as naked and helpless as a newborn baby.

Hosea then used another word picture to depict Israel's desolate condition resulting from her punishment—a *wilderness* and a *dry land*. This comparison reminded the Israelites of the nation's forty years of wandering in the wilderness after the exodus. Unless Israel repented of her wicked ways and returned to the Lord, she would revert to a condition similar to the desperation of those days. At that time God had provided water in the desert, but this time He would *slay her with thirst.*

4. And I will not have mercy upon her children; for they be the children of whoredoms.

One of the great tragedies of sin is its impact upon the children of those who become caught in its deadly snare. The children of Gomer would become known as *children of whoredoms*—participants in the same shameful acts as their mother. They would experience the judgment of God upon the northern kingdom, which was just a few years away. [See question #5, page 400.]

Conclusion

A. A Double Tragedy

Hosea had to cope with a double tragedy—the infidelity of his wife and the moral collapse of his nation. When did Hosea first realize that Gomer was unfaithful to him? Did some of her actions arouse suspicions that he ignored at first, refusing to believe that his beloved had betrayed him? Or did the realization come suddenly, on the day she left home to pursue openly her adulterous activities? Although we are spared the sordid details of Hosea's broken marriage, we are aware of enough broken homes and marriages to understand the situation.

When did Hosea first realize that Israel was guilty of spiritual infidelity in her relations with the Lord? Perhaps he realized, long before his prophetic ministry began, the moral decadence into which Israel had fallen. He may have spoken out occasionally against many of the actions that he knew were wrong. Yet he was not ready to speak with authority until God called him to his unique ministry.

Suppose Hosea were to return today. He would not need the eyes of a divinely inspired prophet to see that our nation is trapped in the quicksand of depravity. If we continue on this course, our judgment will be as certain as that of ancient Israel.

Hosea certainly did not enjoy being a prophet of gloom and doom, yet that was the message he had to deliver to Israel. In the same way, most of us do not enjoy being the bearers of bad tidings. Yet if we are to fulfill our responsibilities as Christian parents and leaders, we must speak out and do so in no uncertain terms. We must call out for integrity and justice in high places, marketplaces, and remote places.

B. Prayer

O holy God, we pray that You will give us the strength and the understanding to speak to our times. Hold back Your judgment upon us—a judgment that we clearly deserve—and grant Your mercy that we may yet repent and turn to You. In Your Son's name we pray. Amen.

C. Thought to Remember

Both an unfaithful person and an unfaithful nation will eventually experience the wrath of God.

How to Say It

AHAB. *Ay*-hab.
AHAZ. *Ay*-haz.
AMMI. *Am*-my.
ASSYRIAN. Uh-*sear*-ee-un.
BAAL. *Bay*-ul.
BABYLONIAN. Bab-uh-*low*-nee-un.
CYRUS. *Sigh*-russ.
DIBLAIM. Dib-*lay*-im.
GOMER. *Go*-mer.
HEZEKIAH. Hez-ih-*kye*-uh.
HOSEA. Ho-*zay*-uh.
ISAIAH. Eye-*zay*-uh.
JEHU. *Jay*-hew.
JEROBOAM. Jair-uh-*bo*-um.
JEZEBEL. *Jez*-uh-bel.
JEZREEL. *Jez*-ree-el or *Jez*-reel.
JOTHAM. *Jo*-thum.
LO-AMMI. Lo-*am*-my.
LO-RUHAMAH. *Lo*-roo-*hah*-muh (strong accent on *hah*).
MICAH. *My*-kuh.
RUHAMAH. Roo-*hah*-muh.
UZZIAH. Uh-*zye*-uh.
ZECHARIAH. Zek-uh-*rye*-uh.

Learning by Doing

This page contains an alternate lesson plan emphasizing learning activities.
Classes desiring such student involvement will find these suggestions helpful.

Learning Goals

After this lesson each student will be able to:

1. Tell how Hosea's marriage to an unfaithful wife illustrates God's love for His people, even when they are unfaithful.

2. Suggest how Christians may be tempted toward spiritual infidelity even as Israel was.

3. Offer a prayer of repentance for past infidelities to the Lord.

Into the Lesson

If a class member is currently dealing with infidelity in his or her marriage, make adjustments to the lesson plan as needed to be sensitive.

Select two women and three men from among the early arrivals to the classroom to prepare a drama giving a synopsis of Hosea's marriage (Hosea 1:2-8; 3:1-3). They should not use a narrator but dramatize the story in first person. Give them signs to wear. These signs should have the names of Hosea, Gomer, Jezreel, Lo-ruhamah, and Lo-ammi on them. Send the group to a hallway, a corner, or another room to make preparations.

While the drama group is making preparations, write the word *Infidelity* on the chalkboard or marker board. Discuss these questions:

1. What are some of the causes or reasons for marital unfaithfulness?

2. What is some of the "fallout" or damage that comes from marital infidelity?

3. Why is reconciliation often very difficult in cases of marital infidelity?

Into the Word

Begin your Bible study with an explanation of Hosea's background and God's command to him about marriage. Note that Hosea's wife bore three children; then form at least three study teams to give reports on the meaning and significance of the names of these children. Give each team a photocopy of a portion of the lesson commentary as follows, and ask the group to report the significance of its assigned name to the rest of the class: *Team 1:* Jezreel, 1:3b-5; *Team 2:* Lo-ruhamah, 1:6, 7; *Team 3:* Lo-ammi, 1:8, 9. After they have finished their work but before they report, ask the drama team to make its presentation. Then ask representatives from the study teams to report on the significance of the children's names.

After these presentations, have a volunteer read aloud Hosea 1:2—2:4. Then deliver a short lecture emphasizing the following points: Israel's unfaithfulness or adultery; the imagery in Hosea's marriage; Israel's fall (see the commentary on 1:5, 6, 8, 9); Judah's hope (see the commentary on 1:7); Israel's hope (see the commentary on 1:10, 11); God's plea (see the commentary on 2:1-4). Help the class members follow the lecture by putting these points on strips of poster board. As you mention each point, tape or fasten the appropriate piece of poster board to the wall.

Into Life

Remind the class that spiritual infidelity is the real theme of this drama in Hosea's life. Draw the class's attention back to the questions discussed in the lesson Introduction. Ask the same questions but with an emphasis on unfaithfulness to God.

1. What are some of the causes or reasons for unfaithfulness to God?

2. What is the fallout or damage caused from unfaithfulness to Him?

3. Why is reconciliation often difficult? For whom is it most difficult—us or God? Why?

Then tell the groups, "Your task is to warn today's believers about how Christians are tempted to be spiritually unfaithful. How can you do that?" Ask each group to choose one of the following means to communicate the warning and to write or prepare the prophetic message. A group may write a radio announcement, write an e-mail notice to churches, write a description of a video game, or prepare a poster. If time does not permit this activity, simply ask these discussion questions: "What are some of the ways Satan tempts contemporary Christians to be spiritually unfaithful? What do you think are some of his favorite and most effective tools?"

Ask, "What can our Sunday school class do to encourage Christians to remain faithful?" List the answers on poster board.

Then ask the class to let this lesson become very personal. All of us have been unfaithful to our Heavenly Father at times. Otherwise we wouldn't need a Savior. Give each class member a three-by-five card. As they reflect on their sins, they are to write a prayer of repentance. The prayer should start with these words: "I am sorry, Lord, because. . . ." They should also write their gratitude for God's grace. Begin this part of the prayer with "I thank You, Lord, for. . . ."

Let's Talk It Over

The questions on this page are designed to encourage review of the lesson Scriptures and to promote discussion of the lesson by the class. The answers provided are only discussion starters. Let your class talk it over from there.

1. Gomer was certainly a spiritual mismatch for one of God's prophets. More importantly, she represented the spiritual misfits of the day. What social practices of today are "out of step" with God's call and damaging to spiritual health?

This discussion could include many social "ills" (e.g., sexual promiscuity, drinking, smoking, greed, dancing, or even immodesty). To answer this question, it is important that we honestly examine those practices that are expressly forbidden by Scripture. Such behavior must not be condoned. We must also be careful, however, not to use the Scriptures to try to prove a point when there is no definitive statement made. In these matters we can point to potential harm, but we must realize that for some this may not be an issue at all. In these gray areas 1 Corinthians 10:23 becomes very beneficial: "All things are lawful for me, but all things are not expedient: all things are lawful for me, but all things edify not."

2. The lesson writer observes that Hosea obeyed the Lord in spite of any reservations he may have had about God's command. What have you done in spite of personal reservations simply because you believed it was the right thing to do? How has God blessed you for that?

Too often the opposite situation is played out: a believer knows what God's Word says but acts contrary to it because "I just know God would not want me to be unhappy!" Such excuses have been used to justify unwarranted divorces and any number of other sins. But perhaps you have class members who can tell of the time they began to tithe even though they weren't sure how to make ends meet—and how the Lord has blessed them. Maybe a public figure can tell of taking a stand on an issue even when others called it "political suicide." Perhaps a wife can tell how she forgave an unfaithful husband when her friends said, "Dump him." Observe that obeying God is always the right thing to do, even when we do not know what the outcome of our actions will be!

3. God said He would judge Israel, but Judah would be spared. Their deliverance would come, not by their own strength, but "by the Lord their God." What lessons, if any, do you think that has for us today?

For one thing, it illustrates salvation. Ephesians 2:8-10 tells us we are saved by God's grace, not by any works that we might do. Judah was likewise saved by God's grace. Still, King Hezekiah's faithful leadership and, especially, his prayers for the city of Jerusalem (see 2 Kings 19:15-20), were instrumental in God's provision of His grace. As we confront the moral problems of our own culture, we need to follow Hezekiah's example. We need to pray and work for the right, trusting that God will "do exceeding abundantly above all that we ask or think" (Ephesians 3:20).

4. God cited several blessings that would come when those who were formerly not His people could be called "the sons of the living God." Paul cites this passage in Romans 9:26, and Peter alludes to it in 1 Peter 2:10. What blessings have you experienced since becoming a part of the people of God? What blessings do you imagine we would see if a large majority of our nation turned to the Lord?

Every believer should be able to cite specific benefits of being a Christian. These are not likely to be material or financial blessings, although there may be some of those. Restored relationships, peace of mind in spite of financial reverses, and hope for the future are more likely responses.

If the nation as a whole turned to Christ, imagine the results! Crime would drop dramatically. Sharing, in the same manner as the early church practiced, would provide for the needs of the poor. Cooperation would replace distrust between "management" and "labor" so that businesses could become more profitable and the profits fairly shared by all. Politicians would seek office in order to serve, not simply to have more power and wealth.

5. In Hosea 2:3, 4 the prophet metaphorically described the results of Gomer's unfaithfulness. What are some of the results that can be expected when God's people turn their backs on Him?

In the short run there may be no distinguishable difference at all! God is patient, waiting for sinners to return to that which is right. Justice does not always come immediately, but it will come. God will judge according to righteousness and truth. Those who turn their backs on God may have peace for a season, but not for eternity.

God's Compassion for Israel

DEVOTIONAL READING: Psalm 103:8-14.

BACKGROUND SCRIPTURE: Hosea 11.

PRINTED TEXT: Hosea 11:1-9.

Jul 22

Hosea 11:1-9

1 When Israel was a child, then I loved him, and called my son out of Egypt.

2 As they called them, so they went from them: they sacrificed unto Baalim, and burned incense to graven images.

3 I taught Ephraim also to go, taking them by their arms; but they knew not that I healed them.

4 I drew them with cords of a man, with bands of love: and I was to them as they that take off the yoke on their jaws, and I laid meat unto them.

5 He shall not return into the land of Egypt, but the Assyrian shall be his king, because they refused to return.

6 And the sword shall abide on his cities, and shall consume his branches, and devour them, because of their own counsels.

7 And my people are bent to backsliding from me: though they called them to the Most High, none at all would exalt him.

8 How shall I give thee up, Ephraim? how shall I deliver thee, Israel? how shall I make thee as Admah? how shall I set thee as Zeboim? mine heart is turned within me, my repentings are kindled together.

9 I will not execute the fierceness of mine anger, I will not return to destroy Ephraim: for I am God, and not man; the Holy One in the midst of thee: and I will not enter into the city.

GOLDEN TEXT: I drew them with cords of a man, with bands of love: and I was to them as they that take off the yoke on their jaws, and I laid meat unto them.—Hosea 11:4.

Division and Decline
Unit 2: Prophecies of Judgment
(Lessons 5-9)

Lesson Aims

After participating in this lesson, students should be able to:

1. Summarize Hosea's message of God's compassion for His people.

2. Tell how God's words and actions toward Israel modeled those of a loving parent.

3. Give thanks for the stubborn, steadfast love of our heavenly Father.

Lesson Outline

INTRODUCTION
  A. Whose Hand Is on the Wheel?
  B. Lesson Background
I. HISTORY OF GOD'S LOVE (Hosea 11:1-4)
  A. Love Extended (v. 1)
  B. Love Rejected (v. 2)
  C. Love Like a Parent's (vv. 3, 4)
II. HEARTBREAK OF GOD'S LOVE (Hosea 11:5-9)
  A. Israel's Punishment (vv. 5, 6)
    Not Slow, But Patient
  B. Israel's Backsliding (v. 7)
  C. God's Stubborn Love (vv. 8, 9)
CONCLUSION
  A. A Backsliding Nation
  B. "This Is Going to Hurt Me"
  C. Prayer
  D. Thought to Remember

Introduction

A. Whose Hand Is on the Wheel?

Years ago, when I was about six or seven, I went for a ride with my father in the family car. After a while Dad said to me, "Would you like to drive, Son?" Of course, like any boy my age, I wanted to drive; so I climbed onto Dad's lap and grabbed the steering wheel. Under my guidance the car veered first to the right and then to the left, but somehow it managed to stay on the street and even to stop at a corner.

During my drive I saw a friend standing on the sidewalk beside the street. I shouted, "Look at me—I'm driving!" Later, he questioned whether I was really driving. "Sure I was," I answered. "Didn't you see me holding the steering wheel?"

In reality, of course, it was my father's strong arms that handled the steering wheel. It was his steady feet that controlled the brake, the clutch, and the accelerator. I was like the Israelites in Hosea's day, who thought that all the blessings they had received had come through their own efforts. They had forgotten, to their shame, that God was the One who had provided all those blessings.

B. Lesson Background

In last week's study we noted that Hosea was called to his prophetic ministry at a time when Israel was experiencing great prosperity. We also saw how God used the tragedy of Hosea's broken marriage to illustrate His love for Israel. In spite of Gomer's infidelity, Hosea later attempted to rescue her from the slavery that her prostitution had brought upon her (Hosea 3:1-3). This painful series of events helped Hosea gain a deeper understanding of God's love for Israel—a nation that had committed spiritual prostitution by spurning God's love and pursuing the gods of her pagan neighbors.

While Hosea reminded God's people of His love for them, he also had to warn them of coming judgment, which would be executed through the conquering armies of Assyria. Yet those warnings were also indicators of God's love, for He was encouraging the people to repent and return to Him so that they could be spared that judgment.

I. History of God's Love
(Hosea 11:1-4)

A. Love Extended (v. 1)

1. When Israel was a child, then I loved him, and called my son out of Egypt.

Old Testament history includes frequent references to Israel's bondage in Egypt and to the glorious deliverance that God accomplished through the exodus. These references were a way of reminding the people of God's mercy toward them and of their responsibility to obey Him (1 Samuel 12:6-8; Nehemiah 9:6-9; Psalm 78:12-55; Jeremiah 7:21-26; Daniel 9:15). Often they describe the exodus in terms of the mighty power that God demonstrated. Here Hosea uses it as an illustration of how much God *loved* His people. [See question #1, page 408.]

Israel was a child. This seems to call attention to the fact that the Egyptian bondage occurred at a time when Israel was just beginning to develop as a nation. Hosea may also have desired to picture God's people being as helpless as children, totally unable to free themselves from their slavery. Like little children, they could not defend themselves. But when they "cried . . . by reason of the bondage," God "heard their groaning" (Exodus

2:23, 24) and came to their rescue. Just as a new-born child needs extra care, so did the nation of Israel in her infancy.

I . . . called my son out of Egypt. God instructed Moses to say to Pharaoh, "Israel is my son, even my firstborn: and I say unto thee, Let my son go, that he may serve me" (Exodus 4:22, 23). Matthew says this prophecy was fulfilled again when Joseph and Mary took the child Jesus to Egypt and remained there until after after the death of Herod (Matthew 2:13-15).

B. Love Rejected (v. 2)

2. As they called them, so they went from them: they sacrificed unto Baalim, and burned incense to graven images.

Whereas Israel's departure from God was illustrated earlier by a wayward wife, here it is illustrated by a wayward son. *As they called them, so they went from them.* The first *they* and the second *them* in this passage refer to God's spokesmen, the prophets. The first *them* and the second *they* refer to the people at large. Many times God had appealed to His people through the prophets. Yet they rejected those messengers just as callously as they had forgotten their deliverance from Egypt. "Yet many years didst thou forbear them, and testifiedst against them by thy Spirit in thy prophets: yet would they not give ear" (Nehemiah 9:30).

Having forgotten God, *they sacrificed unto Baalim.* While the Israelites were in Egypt, they may have been tempted to serve some of the Egyptian gods; but once they entered Canaan, they were enticed by the Canaanite deities—here described as the Baalim. Baal was considered the head of the Canaanite gods and was worshiped as the source of fertility and productivity. Baal was worshiped differently and given different attributes in different locales, thus the use of the plural *Baalim* or *Baals*, as in most newer translations.

Because Palestine received minimal rainfall, its pagan inhabitants considered it important to appease a fertility god like Baal to insure good crops and families with many children. The fertility rites in which worshipers of Baal participated often involved immoral activity with sacred prostitutes. Some of this also involved burning *incense to graven images.* This was a clear violation of the Second Commandment (Exodus 20:4).

C. Love Like a Parent's (vv. 3, 4)

3. I taught Ephraim also to go, taking them by their arms; but they knew not that I healed them.

Ephraim and Manasseh were sons of Joseph. Ephraim had received a special blessing from his grandfather, Jacob (Genesis 48:5-22), and the tribe of Ephraim came to occupy a position of prominence when the Israelites reached the promised land. When the kingdom became divided, Jeroboam, who was from the tribe of Ephraim (1 Kings 11:26), became king of the northern kingdom (Israel). Perhaps for that reason Ephraim appears to have been acknowledged as the leading tribe of the north. The designation *Ephraim* is often applied to the entire northern kingdom, as in this verse and throughout Hosea.

I taught Ephraim also to go. Hosea depicts a parent teaching a child to walk. Parents tend to be very protective during the early stages of their children's development. They watch their young ones carefully as they pull themselves up and take a few hesitating steps while hanging on to the crib railing or a chair. From time to time the parents offer them a hand and help them take a few awkward steps. Finally, when they take those steps without any help or support, the parents express their approval and support with enthusiasm. What a wonderful picture of the care and patience of our loving God! [See question #2, page 408.]

They knew not that I healed them. Here another aspect of God's love is shown. Today, even with all of our miracle drugs, little children sometimes become desperately ill. During those anxious times the parents keep a constant watch over their little ones, trying to soothe their pain and provide whatever comfort they can. Every other concern becomes secondary to that of nursing the children back to health. Once more, this is a beautiful description of our Father's compassion for us.

Here, however, Hosea notes how God's people responded to His concern. Usually when children fall and cut or bruise themselves, they know they can turn to their parents for help, for experience

---

How to Say It

ADMAH. *Ad*-muh.
ASSYRIAN. Uh-*sear*-ee-un.
BAAL. *Bay*-ul.
BAALIM. Bay-uh-*leem*.
CANAANITE. *Kay*-nun-ite.
EPHRAIM. *Ee*-fray-im.
GOMER. *Go*-mer.
GOMORRAH. Guh-*more*-uh.
HOSEA. Ho-*zay*-uh.
JEHU. *Jay*-hew.
JEROBOAM. Jair-uh-*bo*-um.
MANASSEH. Muh-*nass*-uh.
SAMARIA. Suh-*mare*-ee-uh.
SHALMANESER. Shal-mun-*ee*-zer.
SIDDIM. *Sid*-im.
SODOM. *Sod*-um.
ZEBOIM. Zeh-*bo*-im.

"I drew them with cords of a man, with bands of love."

Visual for
lesson 8

The visual for today's lesson pictures a tender scene of a father walking with his child. Display it at the beginning of your session.

has taught them to do so. But the Israelites seemed completely oblivious to all that God had done for them and treated His kindness toward them with contempt.

4. I drew them with cords of a man, with bands of love: and I was to them as they that take off the yoke on their jaws, and I laid meat unto them.

Hosea used yet another word picture to illustrate how much God loved His people. He compared God's dealings with Israel with those of a farmer with one of his animals. The portrayal of those who *take off the yoke on their jaws* may describe how a farmer removed the heavy wooden yoke from around the face of an animal (such as an ox) so that the animal could eat more easily. It may also picture what took place at the end of a day when the animal's work was done. Thus had God dealt gently with His people. He had not forced affection from them, but *drew them with cords of a man, with bands of love.*

And I laid meat unto them. Mealtime (or the end of a day) brought, not only relief from the burden of the yoke, but also food. (*Meat* in the King James Version is usually a general reference to any kind of food.) [See question #3, page 408.]

II. Heartbreak of God's Love
(Hosea 11:5-9)

A. Israel's Punishment (vv. 5, 6)

5. He shall not return into the land of Egypt, but the Assyrian shall be his king, because they refused to return.

Hosea turned rather abruptly from speaking of God's love to declaring God's judgment. *He shall not return into the land of Egypt.* Previously Hosea had said that the people would return to Egypt (Hosea 8:13; 9:3). Apparently he had been speaking figuratively, using the Israelites' experience in Egypt to represent the nation's future bondage to Assyria. Some students believe that the expression *He shall not return into the land of Egypt* is a

reference to Israel's attempts to ally itself with Egypt in order to gain assistance in its struggle against Assyria. These attempts were part of the reason that the Assyrians eventually invaded Israel and destroyed Samaria (2 Kings 17:3-6). If that understanding is correct, then Hosea was predicting that those attempts would fail.

But the Assyrian shall be his king. Approximately a century earlier the Assyrian ruler Shalmaneser III had traveled westward and forced Jehu, king of Israel, to pay him tribute. But then Assyrian power waned. By the time Jeroboam II was king, Israel found itself free of the threat of Assyrian interference and enjoyed a period of significant prosperity. That prosperity would come to a bitter end when the revitalized Assyrians returned westward with a renewed military might that was virtually impossible to withstand.

The reason for this tragic turn of events was really quite simple: *because they refused to return.* The people's continual rejection of God and His covenant, in spite of frequent warnings, could result only in their receiving His punishment.

NOT SLOW, BUT PATIENT

Parents who threaten misbehaving children with repeated ultimatums, yet never follow through with punishment, are training their offspring to ignore all disciplinary warnings. They are creating individuals who will learn how to disregard authority and flaunt disobedience, and whose actions will come to have far more serious consequences for society. Such methods are unhealthy and destructive, and they certainly do the children no favors.

God's warnings to Israel were not empty threats. He always means what He says and says what He means. And though God takes no delight in the punishment of His beloved children (Ezekiel 33:11), He does chasten all whom He loves (Hebrews 12:6).

That God's punishment is not always immediate has sometimes been misunderstood as indifference on His part. Backsliders in Hosea's day allowed themselves to be lulled into complacency. They were lured into sinful unfaithfulness by what seemed to them an absence of retribution for their transgressions. Like the scoffers described by Peter (2 Peter 3:3, 4), they thought, "Nothing has changed; we see no reason to worry or to repent." Skeptics of our day also doubt that they will ever have to pay the "wages of sin."

But make no mistake—"payday" will come! The unrepentant and the unforgiven "shall be punished with everlasting destruction from the presence of the Lord" (2 Thessalonians 1:9). Remember, however, that this is not how God wants to treat us. He "is long-suffering . . . not willing that any should perish, but that all should come to repentance" (2 Peter 3:9).   —R. W. B.

6. And the sword shall abide on his cities, and shall consume his branches, and devour them, because of their own counsels.

The sword shall abide on his cities. The Israelites may have believed that they would be safe inside Samaria and their other fortified *cities*; but no walls would be able to protect them from the devastation of the coming Assyrian onslaught. Eventually Samaria fell, following a three-year siege (2 Kings 17:5). Assyrian records from this time note that approximately thirty thousand Israelites were carried into captivity.

The term *branches* is rendered "bars of their gates" in recent versions. It may reflect part of the process involved in conducting the siege of a city—using battering rams to create a breach in the city's defenses.

Once more the reason for this turn of events is stated: *because of their own counsels.* This calamity was coming upon the people because the leaders who were responsible for the spiritual welfare of the people had chosen to follow false gods rather than return to Jehovah (Hosea 4:4-12).

B. Israel's Backsliding (v. 7)

7. And my people are bent to backsliding from me: though they called them to the Most High, none at all would exalt him.

The phrase *bent to backsliding from me* pictures someone who is stubbornly moving away from God. Hosea indicates that the backsliding of the Israelites was not an uncommon or infrequent action, but that the people had become *bent to*, or strongly inclined to, this behavior. (The *New International Version* reads, "My people are determined to turn from me.") Even though Israel had turned away from God again and again, God continued to love them. These words convey some of the heartache experienced by God as He pondered how His own people could treat Him with such scorn.

The use of the word *backsliding* in several Old Testament passages has led to its being used by Christians to describe one who has fallen away from the faith. Old-time revivalists often aimed their messages at the backsliders in the church or in the community. However, one rarely hears the word being used in Christian circles today. (Perhaps it is considered too judgmental or harsh.)

The statement *though they called them to the Most High, none at all would exalt him* is similar to verse 2, and is best understood as a reference to the ministry of God's prophets. *Though they* [the prophets of God] *called them* [the people of Israel] to return to God, virtually *none* of them *would exalt him.* The nation was rapidly becoming ripe for divine judgment. [See question #4, page 408.]

C. God's Stubborn Love (vv. 8, 9)

8. How shall I give thee up, Ephraim? how shall I deliver thee, Israel? how shall I make thee as Admah? how shall I set thee as Zeboim? mine heart is turned within me, my repentings are kindled together.

Yet again God expressed His never-dying love for His people, in spite of their ongoing rebellion against Him. If God administered the judgment they deserved, they would be utterly destroyed, as were *Admah* and *Zeboim.* These two cities were located in the Valley of Siddim at the southern end of the Dead Sea (Genesis 10:19; 14:2; Deuteronomy 29:23). Because of their sinfulness, they were destroyed along with Sodom and Gomorrah in the time of Lot. If the Israelites remembered their history, they realized that these cities had been destroyed without leaving a trace. It should have served as a grim reminder of the punishment that lay in store for them, unless they repented of their rebellion.

That God's *heart is turned within* Him suggests that He has a heavy heart because His righteousness requires Him to punish His people. It is not unlike the feeling a loving parent experiences when he realizes that a child must be punished for a particular action and that there is no alternative.

The word for *repentings* used here is not the usual Hebrew word for "repent." We should not understand this to mean that God repents in the same way that human beings are required to repent. The word describes God's feelings or emotions toward His people and how difficult it is for Him to punish them. Even though justice required that the Israelites be punished, such action brought sorrow to God. [See question #5, page 408.]

9. I will not execute the fierceness of mine anger, I will not return to destroy Ephraim: for I am God, and not man; the Holy One in the midst of thee: and I will not enter into the city.

Because of His compassion, God would not utterly *destroy Ephraim.* God's mercy would prevail over His justice. God is *not man,* who, in a similar situation of being betrayed, might completely unleash his anger upon his offender. Though betrayed by His people, God would not give up on them. He declared, *I will not enter the city*—for the purpose of bringing complete destruction.

In the verses that follow, Hosea allows a gleam of hope to penetrate the desolation in Israel's immediate future. The people would indeed suffer under the heavy hand of Assyrian oppression and be carried into captivity; yet the time would come when the Lord would "place them in their houses" (Hosea 11:10, 11).

Conclusion

A. A Backsliding Nation

God used His miracle-working power to free the Hebrew people from bondage in Egypt. He guided them through the wilderness—an experience that should have lasted only a few months but, because of their unbelief (Hebrews 3:16-19), was extended to forty years. He further blessed His people by leading them into the promised land, where they were able to live in houses that they had not built and to enjoy fruit from vines they had not planted. Yet, even as they were enjoying these blessings, they were enticed by pagan gods and repeatedly turned away from the Lord Jehovah.

God did not allow this backsliding to go unpunished. He allowed neighboring peoples to oppress His people. However, before each occurrence of discipline, God sent first the judges and then the prophets to call His people back to Him. Hosea was one of the last of these messengers to warn the northern kingdom. The failure of the north to heed his warning led to its destruction within a few years after Hosea conveyed the word of the Lord.

And yet, through all of these failures, there was always a remnant—a handful of the faithful—who gave heed to God's message and did repent. God used this faithful remnant to keep alive the hope of a Messiah who would offer salvation, not only to Israel but to the entire world.

Our nation, like ancient Israel, has become a backsliding nation, forgetting all the blessings

God has poured out upon us. By almost every standard that can be applied, our nation has abandoned the values that made us great. Crime, drugs, broken homes, illegitimate births, and abortions give evidence of our decline.

Our nation has no shortage of messengers to call us from our backsliding. From church pulpits and over radio and television come constant appeals to hear and obey the message that can save us. But many have closed their ears, preferring instead to worship at the shrines of our modern Baals—success, affluence, and pleasure.

Is there any hope for our nation, or have we already gone beyond the point of no return? We could very well allow ourselves to become paralyzed by pessimism. It is vital, as we study ancient messengers of God such as Hosea, that we take hope in the fact that God is exceedingly patient in dealing with wayward people. Hosea also shows how God can use a faithful remnant to accomplish His purposes. May we commit ourselves to being a part of that remnant.

B. "This Is Going to Hurt Me"

When we were youngsters and got into trouble that warranted serious punishment, our parents sometimes prefaced their actions with the words: "This is going to hurt me more than it will you." We didn't believe it at the time, and only later, when we had become parents, did we begin to understand what our parents were talking about.

In today's lesson Hosea describes God's "parenting" of His child Israel. He also tells us that, although God had to administer punishment to Israel, He took no pleasure in it. It was going to hurt Him more than it did the Israelites.

We often think of God as being high and exalted and quite different from us—and, of course, He is! But He is also a loving Father who feels pain when we turn away from Him and who never ceases to love us and long for our return. If our nation is to return to God, it will happen only when a faithful remnant begins to demonstrate through their lives an eagerness to love others and a fervent desire to serve sacrificially so that the Lord's kingdom may grow.

C. Prayer

O God, we pray that we will humbly receive from this ancient prophet the message You have for us. Like Hosea, may we surrender our lives to You so that we can share that message with others. Thank You for Your steadfast love. In our Lord's name we pray. Amen.

D. Thought to Remember

"Whom the Lord loveth he chasteneth" (Hebrews 12:6).

Home Daily Bible Readings

Monday, July 16—A Call to Repentance (Hosea 6:1-6)

Tuesday, July 17—God's Love for Israel (Hosea 11:1-7)

Wednesday, July 18—God's Great Compassion (Hosea 11:8—12:1)

Thursday, July 19—Thanksgiving for God's Mercies (Psalm 103:8-14)

Friday, July 20—The Long History of Rebellion (Hosea 12:2-14)

Saturday, July 21—Judgment on Israel (Hosea 13:4-16)

Sunday, July 22—A Plea for Repentance (Hosea 14)

Learning by Doing

This page contains an alternate lesson plan emphasizing learning activities.
Classes desiring such student involvement will find these suggestions helpful.

Learning Goals

After this lesson, each student will be able to:

1. Summarize Hosea's message of God's compassion for His people.

2. Tell how God's words and actions toward Israel modeled those of a loving parent.

3. Give thanks for the stubborn, steadfast love of our heavenly Father.

Into the Lesson

Before class, prepare enough slips of paper to tape one to the bottom of every chair in the classroom. Use three colors of paper, one color for each of the following questions. On one-third of the papers write, "When I think of a good parent, _____'s name comes to mind because. . . ." On another third write, "One thing I want from or for my child is _____ because. . . ." On the remaining third write, "I think the most difficult aspect of parenting young children is _____ because. . . ."

Ask each person to reach under his or her seat, remove the slip of paper taped there, and write a response to the statement. Give the students two or three minutes to do this. Then have the learners form groups of three to six people, making sure that at least one person with each of the three questions is included in each group. Allow the group members to share their answers and viewpoints with each other. Then ask a few volunteers to share their responses with the whole class.

Make the transition to Bible study by noting that God uses several different images to describe His relationship with His people. And one of those images is that of a parent. This imagery, which fills our text, is still appropriate today.

Into the Word

From last week's lesson, review the story of Hosea's broken marriage and Gomer's infidelity. Explain that this marriage illustrates Israel's infidelity and God's love, which will be important in this lesson as well. Also explain the name "Ephraim" in verse 3. Tell the class that today's text gives the heart of God's message to Israel and packs warnings and encouragements to our nation and churches today.

Put the following outline on a large visual.

1. Two Imageries (rebellious children and stubborn calf) (vv. 1-4)

2. Judgment and Punishment (vv. 5, 6)

3. Backsliding Israel (v. 7)

4. God's Stubborn Love (vv. 8, 9)

Ask each group (from the earlier grouping) to write a paraphrase of a portion of the text, using imagery and words easily understood in our culture. Each group should be assigned one of the sections of the outline. A recorder is to write the group's paraphrase on poster board.

After the group reports on verses 1-4, explain "Baalim" and emphasize the unfaithful history and continual rebellion of Israel. (See page 403.) After the group shares its paraphrase of verses 5 and 6, use your lesson commentary to tell of Assyria's impact on Israel. After the group reports on verse 7, explain the concept of "backsliding." After the last group offers its paraphrase of verses 8 and 9, explain "repentings" and emphasize God's continuing love.

Into Life

Ask the class to continue to work in their groups as we apply the lesson to life. Ask the groups to jot down notes about what they think God would say to our nation through the prophet about the following:

1. The prophet's word about our roots and formative years.

2. The prophet's evidences of our backsliding or unfaithfulness.

3. The prophet's word about God's heartache concerning our nation's unfaithfulness.

4. The prophet's encouraging word to the faithful followers in our nation.

After they complete this task, ask representatives of the groups to share their findings about the issues above.

Ask the learners to suggest specific issues that we should pray about with respect to (1) our nation, (2) our church, and (3) our personal lives. List the suggestions under three headings on the chalkboard. In addition, provide pens and paper and ask each learner to write down all the suggestions that are offered.

When you have three good lists, ask the groups to pray together. Assign one of the lists to each group, and ask each group member to pray concerning one or two of the issues on the group's list. At the end of the class session, encourage the learners to take their lists home and to pray about these matters on a daily basis.

Let's Talk It Over

The questions on this page are designed to encourage review of the lesson Scriptures and to promote discussion of the lesson by the class. The answers provided are only discussion starters. Let your class talk it over from there.

1. Hosea called on the people to remember their roots and their relationship to God as children. What would remind us of how God has changed us and how we need to depend on Him?

Each of us has a personal pilgrimage that led us to a place where we knew that we needed God. Sometimes we can find encouragement in knowing the stories of others. By examining our roots, much as Hosea did, we can be renewed in our commitment to the God who saved us. Take some time to share these stories.

2. In Hosea 11:3 is a beautiful illustration of God's guiding Ephraim as a parent teaches a child how to walk. What help do we need from God as we learn to walk in His ways?

Dependency usually has a negative connotation. To become dependent on alcohol, drugs, or even an addictive behavior is certainly far from where God wants us to be. But there is a dependency that is absolutely necessary. Solomon wrote, "Lean not unto thine own understanding" (Proverbs 3:5). There are times when God is the only source of strength on which we can depend. Of course, a loving parent wants his or her child to learn to stand on his own. While we always need to depend on God, we also need to learn to take a stand. Include in your discussion some ideas on where to draw the line between leaning on God and standing "on our own"—in a healthy, "dependent" kind of way!

3. The picture of God dealing with Israel as a kind farmer cares for his animals is very similar to the familiar shepherd metaphor (Psalm 23; John 10). What other word pictures can you think of to describe God's care for His people? What makes these images significant to you?

The husband-wife image, noted last week, is reinforced in the New Testament, where the church is called the "bride of Christ." This is especially significant in light of the "marriage supper" imagery in Revelation 19:9. Married couples will especially appreciate this imagery. Perhaps a medical worker will find the image of Jesus as the "Great Physician" especially meaningful. Your learners may also suggest some original images. For example, a blue-collar worker may picture God as a fair and honest employer who works alongside His employees.

4. God's love was not always tender love. Sometimes, as illustrated in Hosea 11:5-7, it had to become tough. What is tough love and how do you perceive that it might be expressed today as God deals with us?

Parents seem to have a "built-in" protective side. To see their children get hurt is more painful to them than enduring the hurt themselves. Remember when your parents said, "This is going to hurt me more than it hurts you"? As children, we probably did not understand what they meant; their punishment really smarted, and we couldn't see how it had hurt them. But now we know what our parents were saying. They were telling us that they were grieved that we had made a wrong decision and were going to have to suffer for it. They were saying that they would rather have us obey than to have to bear these consequences. But if they carried out the punishment, they were also saying that they loved us enough to do something that would deter us from making the same mistake again. The writer of Hebrews (12:5-10) reminds us that "whom the Lord loveth he chasteneth" (v. 6). He disciplines us so "that we might be partakers of his holiness" (v. 10).

5. To be both tender and tough as we handle our children causes us inner turmoil. See how it affected God (verses 8, 9). What happens to church leaders when they are called upon to discipline a disobedient child of God? (It may be possible to think of specific examples.)

Perhaps there is no better pattern for leaders than the advice given in 1 and 2 Timothy. To serve as a leader, Paul wrote, Timothy would have to hold fast to sound words (2 Timothy 1:13), to recognize those sinful practices that would lead others away from God (2 Timothy 3), to study the word of truth (2 Timothy 2:15), and to fight the good fight (1 Timothy 6:12). We should know, however, that this type of confrontation will be met with resistance. Thus, Paul told Timothy to "endure" (2 Timothy 2:3). In contrast to how most people confront, however, Timothy was told to be gentle, apt to teach, and patient (2 Timothy 2:24). God's messengers will understand a little more about God's nature and suffering if they will try to practice this pattern of discipline. Lift your leaders up in prayer and with words of encouragement. Theirs is a difficult task.

What God Requires

DEVOTIONAL READING: Proverbs 21:2, 3.

BACKGROUND SCRIPTURE: Micah 3; 6:1-8.

PRINTED TEXT: Micah 3:5-12; 6:3-8.

Micah 3:5-12

5 Thus saith the LORD concerning the prophets that make my people err, that bite with their teeth, and cry, Peace; and he that putteth not into their mouths, they even prepare war against him:

6 Therefore night shall be unto you, that ye shall not have a vision; and it shall be dark unto you, that ye shall not divine; and the sun shall go down over the prophets, and the day shall be dark over them.

7 Then shall the seers be ashamed, and the diviners confounded: yea, they shall all cover their lips; for there is no answer of God.

8 But truly I am full of power by the Spirit of the LORD, and of judgment, and of might, to declare unto Jacob his transgression, and to Israel his sin.

9 Hear this, I pray you, ye heads of the house of Jacob, and princes of the house of Israel, that abhor judgment, and pervert all equity.

10 They build up Zion with blood, and Jerusalem with iniquity.

11 The heads thereof judge for reward, and the priests thereof teach for hire, and the prophets thereof divine for money: yet will they lean upon the LORD, and say, Is not the LORD among us? none evil can come upon us.

12 Therefore shall Zion for your sake be plowed as a field, and Jerusalem shall become heaps, and the mountain of the house as the high places of the forest.

Micah 6:3-8

3 O my people, what have I done unto thee? and wherein have I wearied thee? testify against me.

4 For I brought thee up out of the land of Egypt, and redeemed thee out of the house of servants; and I sent before thee Moses, Aaron, and Miriam.

5 O my people, remember now what Balak king of Moab consulted, and what Balaam the son of Beor answered him from Shittim unto Gilgal; that ye may know the righteousness of the LORD.

6 Wherewith shall I come before the LORD, and bow myself before the high God? shall I come before him with burnt offerings, with calves of a year old?

7 Will the LORD be pleased with thousands of rams, or with ten thousands of rivers of oil? shall I give my firstborn for my transgression, the fruit of my body for the sin of my soul?

8 He hath showed thee, O man, what is good; and what doth the LORD require of thee, but to do justly, and to love mercy, and to walk humbly with thy God?

Jul 29

GOLDEN TEXT: He hath showed thee, O man, what is good; and what doth the LORD require of thee, but to do justly, and to love mercy, and to walk humbly with thy God?—Micah 6:8.

Division and Decline
Unit 2: Prophecies of Judgment
(Lessons 5-9)

Lesson Aims

After this lesson your students will be able to:

1. Tell how Micah contrasted the message of false prophets with the true requirements of following the Lord.

2. Explain how people today try to please God in ways other than those prescribed by Him.

3. Memorize Micah 6:8, and make it the governing principle of their conduct each day this week.

Lesson Outline

Introduction

A. Canine Theology

A story is told about a medieval monastery located in a high Alpine pass. This monastery served as a refuge and rescue station for travelers caught in snowstorms in the mountains. The monks had worked many years training their renowned Saint Bernard dogs to aid them in their rescue work.

On one occasion an important church official was visiting the monastery. During his visit a terrible blizzard swept across the mountains, and, as usual, the monks sent out their rescue dogs to search for travelers. Soon the dogs returned with two half-frozen men. When they were revived, it was discovered that they were considered heretics and that they had been caught in the storm as they fled the wrath of the church authorities.

The visiting church official was furious because these men had been rescued. "Why didn't the dogs leave them out there to suffer the fate they deserved?" he stormed.

Finally one of the monks spoke up. "It takes many months to train a dog to do rescue work. We find it impossible to teach them the finer points of theology. All they seem able to learn is mercy."

In a world where religious strife has left many people confused about Christianity, we might be better off if differences could be settled by a "canine theology" that taught mercy before it addressed the finer points of theology.

B. Lesson Background

The Scriptures tell us little about the prophet Micah. What we do know about him is found in the first verse of the book of Micah. He was from Moresheth, a small town located about twenty-five or thirty miles southwest of Jerusalem. He prophesied during the reigns of three kings of Judah: Jotham, Ahaz, and Hezekiah, dating him from around 740 B.C. to as late as 690 B.C. This would have made Micah a contemporary of Hosea and Isaiah.

Like Isaiah, Micah's ministry was primarily to Judah, the southern kingdom. As Micah began his ministry, both Judah and Israel were still enjoying the prosperity that they had experienced through much of the first half of the eighth century B.C. But these good times would not last much longer. In 745 B.C. Tiglath-pileser III came to power in Assyria. Under his aggressive leadership, Assyria experienced a resurgence of power, while, at the same time, Israel was becoming increasingly unstable. In 725 B.C. the Assyrians began a siege of Samaria that lasted three years and ended in 722 with the fall of the city and the captivity of thousands of Israel's citizens.

By the end of the eighth century, Jerusalem was also feeling the threat of the Assyrians. But God intervened miraculously on behalf of His people, and the city was spared (2 Kings 19:35).

Although Micah grew up in a rural area, he was quite aware of the problems that were plaguing the land—self-serving leaders, greedy priests, counterfeit prophets, and a populace unconcerned about the injustices that were occurring regularly. He was given the thankless task of warning the people of God's wrath if they did not repent and return to God. But Micah was also given the opportunity to look beyond the dismal state of affairs around him to a time when God would one day bless His people in a marvelous way: "He will turn again, he will have compassion upon us" (Micah 7:19).

I. False Prophets
(Micah 3:5-7)

A. Their Deceptive Message (v. 5)

5. Thus saith the LORD concerning the prophets that make my people err, that bite with their teeth, and cry, Peace; and he that putteth not into their mouths, they even prepare war against him.

Micah had already brought sharp words of rebuke against the political leaders of God's people—the "heads of Jacob" and the "princes of the house of Israel" (Micah 3:1). He would return to them later; now he turned his attention to the religious leaders—in particular, *the prophets that make my people err*. The prophets were responsible for monitoring the moral condition of the nation and for holding the political leaders accountable when their actions violated the standards set by Israel's real Leader.

Micah went on to accuse the false prophets of prophesying merely for the sake of financial gain. This seems to be the meaning of the phrase *bite with their teeth*. As long as the false prophets were well taken care of, they eagerly spoke words of *peace*, saying exactly what their supporters wanted them to say (even while the Assyrian army was preparing to attack the northern kingdom). If certain individuals refused to provide anything for them and would not support them (*putteth not into their mouths*), these phony prophets determined to *prepare war against them*. [See question #1, page 416.]

B. Their Eventual Destiny (vv. 6, 7)

6. Therefore night shall be unto you, that ye shall not have a vision; and it shall be dark unto you, that ye shall not divine; and the sun shall go down over the prophets, and the day shall be dark over them.

These self-proclaimed prophets were really frauds, but they were clever enough to fool many of the people. Micah refused to be intimidated by them: he predicted that the end of their clever schemes was at hand. When the Assyrians eventually entered the northern kingdom and ravaged the land, the false prophets' declaration of peace would be proven empty. No longer would they claim to *have a vision*, and no more would they *divine*. This word refers to the methods of some false prophets, who obtained their messages from the observation of events in nature, such as the flight of birds or the appearance of the entrails of an animal killed in order to discern the will of the gods. Such practices were strictly forbidden by God (Deuteronomy 18:9-14).

7. Then shall the seers be ashamed, and the diviners confounded: yea, they shall all cover their lips; for there is no answer of God.

The word *seers* describes individuals who received their messages through dreams or visions from God. In some such manner, Micah "saw" the word of the Lord (Micah 1:1). Those who claimed to have seen such visions but had not (cf. Jeremiah 23:16) would *be ashamed*.

Diviners, as noted under the previous verse, received their messages by means that God had declared to be unacceptable. Such deceivers would be *confounded*, meaning embarrassed or disgraced. They would *all cover their lips* and speak no more, for it would be clear to everyone that God had not spoken through them.

II. Micah, a True Prophet
(Micah 3:8-12)

A. Declaring His Authority (v. 8)

8. But truly I am full of power by the Spirit of the LORD, and of judgment, and of might, to declare unto Jacob his transgression, and to Israel his sin.

Once Micah had swept aside the claims of the false prophets, he was free to present his own credentials. His prophecies did not originate in his imagination, nor were they spoken to make money. Instead, he was *full of power by the Spirit of the Lord*.

No doubt the false prophets made similar claims concerning their authority. Recall lesson 4, in which Micaiah, a true prophet of God, was arrogantly challenged by Zedekiah, who asserted that he had just as much of the Spirit of the Lord as Micaiah claimed to have (1 Kings 22:24). Eventually, said Micaiah, the test of which prophet spoke the truth would come when the future clearly proved whose message was true and whose was false (1 Kings 22:25-28). And so it would be in Micah's case. Part of what he predicted (the destruction of Samaria, for example) would come to pass within the lifetime of some of his listeners. Then they would be able to separate the true prophets from the false ones. [See question #2, page 416.]

B. Condemning Leaders (vv. 9-11)

9. Hear this, I pray you, ye heads of the house of Jacob, and princes of the house of Israel, that abhor judgment, and pervert all equity.

Having established his credibility as a true spokesman of God, Micah then directed his attention once more to the *heads of the house of*

Jacob and the *princes of the house of Israel*. As indicated by verses 10-12, his focus seems to be especially on Jerusalem, also known as Zion.

The corruption of high officials in government has been occurring as long as there have been governments. Whatever the tactics and whatever the era of history, the results are the same: the principles of *judgment* (justice) and *equity* (fairness) are perverted.

10. They build up Zion with blood, and Jerusalem with iniquity.

They build up Zion with blood. Micah's indictment may have been literally true. The resources to build palaces and other imposing buildings in Jerusalem may, in some cases, have been gained through violence. It is more likely, however, that Micah was using forceful figurative language to make his point. The rich and powerful had used shady business deals and clever legal strategies to exploit the poor and powerless and achieve their desired ends. They did not care who was hurt in the process.

11. The heads thereof judge for reward, and the priests thereof teach for hire, and the prophets thereof divine for money: yet will they lean upon the LORD, and say, Is not the LORD among us? none evil can come upon us.

Here Micah targeted his indictment to include those leaders (*heads*) who *judge for reward*, *the priests*, and *the prophets*. Corrupt judges were bad enough, but when priests and prophets—God's representatives and spokesmen—joined in and participated in the same selfish practices, the impact on the nation was especially devastating. Worse yet, these leaders insisted that *the Lord* was *among* them, giving His blessing to their actions. They believed themselves to be immune from judgment or punishment, which is the sense in which the word *evil* is used here.

When God's spokesmen become as shameful and corrupt as the people around them, their message is sapped of any power or influence. And they are only fooling themselves if they think that the Lord will ignore such behavior. [See question #3, page 416.]

"NO NEW SIN UNDER THE SUN"

The ancient Persians, recognizing the seriousness of judicial corruption, devised an effective deterrent. When a judge was convicted of being influenced by bribes, he was executed. Then the hide was flayed from his body, tanned, and used to upholster the next judge's chair. Sitting on such a seat of judgment reminded successors of the stiff punishment for courtroom dishonesty!

Bribery of public officials seems to be a practice common to every society regardless of time and place. Micah noted that in Judah "the heads

---

How to Say It

AHAZ. *Ay*-haz.
ASSYRIA. Uh-*sear*-ee-uh.
BALAAM. *Bay*-lum.
BALAK. *Bay*-lack.
BEOR. *Be*-or.
GILGAL. *Gil*-gal.
HEZEKIAH. Hez-ih-*kye*-uh.
HOSEA. Ho-*zay*-uh.
ISAIAH. Eye-*zay*-uh.
JEREMIAH. Jair-uh-*my*-uh.
JERICHO. *Jair*-ih-ko.
JOTHAM. *Jo*-thum.
MICAH. *My*-kuh.
MICAIAH. My-*kay*-uh.
MOAB. *Mo*-ab.
MORESHETH. *Mo*-resh-eth.
SAMARIA. Suh-*mare*-ee-uh.
SHITTIM. Shih-*teem*.
TIGLATH-PILESER. *Tig*-lath-pih-*lee*-zer (strong accent on *lee*).
ZEDEKIAH. Zed-uh-*kye*-uh.

---

thereof judge for reward" (Micah 3:11). Today we often read or hear of similar actions by which elected officials betray the trust that people have placed in them. Such incidents remind us that sin remains essentially the same because the human heart remains the same—"deceitful above all things, and desperately wicked" (Jeremiah 17:9).

All too often our world wants to address the ills of society by lowering the standards of what is right and wrong. But God's standards don't need any "tinkering." We need to adjust our lives to His standards! —R. W. B.

C. Predicting Judgment (v. 12)

12. Therefore shall Zion for your sake be plowed as a field, and Jerusalem shall become heaps, and the mountain of the house as the high places of the forest.

This verse gives us a clue about the timing of Micah's prophecy because it is cited in Jeremiah 26:18, 19. There we learn that Hezekiah was king of Judah when Micah spoke these words. That means that Samaria probably had fallen to the Assyrians by this time.

How could the people of Judah ignore the implications of this tragedy for them? Did they think that they could escape a similar punishment without making some drastic changes? The passage in Jeremiah also gives us the good news that they did not ignore Micah's prophecy, but turned to God in repentance. Hezekiah himself led in that repentance, but it apparently did not last. The remainder of our printed text comes from a later portion of Micah, and the prophet once again is pleading with the people to repent.

III. God's Challenge
(Micah 6:3-5)

A. His Question (v. 3)

3. O my people, what have I done unto thee? and wherein have I wearied thee? testify against me.

Micah 6 begins with God's statement that He has a "controversy" with His people (v. 2). The setting is similar to a courtroom scene in which witnesses are called to testify. God calls the mountains and the "foundations of the earth" to speak. Having been in existence since long before Israel became a nation, they have observed Israel's behavior throughout history. They can testify as to whether God's "controversy" was justified.

However, the tone of the words in verse 3 is not that of a condemning Judge. This is a loving Father agonizing over His children gone astray. Judah had received blessing after blessing from God, and yet the people had turned from Him. In light of this, how could they answer God's question? How could they *testify against* Him? Parents who have attempted to reason with wayward children can understand the anguish in God's heart as He addresses His people.

B. His Reminders (vv. 4, 5)

4. For I brought thee up out of the land of Egypt, and redeemed thee out of the house of servants; and I sent before thee Moses, Aaron, and Miriam.

God had not given His people any reason to be "wearied" (v. 3) of His treatment of them. Their history was filled with evidence of His love for them. The clearest piece of evidence was the act that had made Israel a nation: God's deliverance of them from bondage in *the land of Egypt*. There was no way that Israel could have escaped from that misery without God's miraculous intervention or apart from those individuals, *Moses, Aaron, and Miriam*, whom He had sent to provide leadership. Each contributed significantly to Israel's beginnings as a nation: Moses was the lawgiver, Aaron was the nation's first high priest, and Miriam was a prophetess (Exodus 15:20, 21).

5. O my people, remember now what Balak king of Moab consulted, and what Balaam the son of Beor answered him from Shittim unto Gilgal; that ye may know the righteousness of the Lord.

The incident involving *Balak king of Moab* and *Balaam* is found in Numbers 22–24. *Shittim* was located in Moab, north of the Dead Sea and east of Jericho. It was one of the last campsites of the Israelites as they prepared to enter the promised land (Joshua 3:1). *Gilgal* was situated between the Jordan River and Jericho and was the people's first place of encampment after they crossed the Jordan River (Joshua 4:19).

As the Israelites proceeded toward the promised land, they conquered the peoples in some of the territories who had stood in their way and refused to let them pass through (Numbers 21:21-35). Balak, realizing the danger that the Israelites posed to his people, hired the prophet Balaam to pronounce a curse upon Israel. But God permitted Balaam to speak only words of blessing on Israel. This was another example of how God had protected and cared for His people.

All of these acts had been done to teach Israel to *know the righteousness of the Lord*. God could not be blamed for the people's sorry condition; He had demonstrated His love for them on numerous occasions.

IV. God's Requirements
(Micah 6:6-8)

A. Suggested Answers (vv. 6, 7)

6, 7. Wherewith shall I come before the LORD, and bow myself before the high God? shall I come before him with burnt offerings, with calves of a year old? Will the LORD be pleased with thousands of rams, or with ten thousands of rivers of oil? shall I give my firstborn for my transgression, the fruit of my body for the sin of my soul?

Here Micah seems to put himself in the position of the people as they respond to the charges that God has brought against them. What must they do to please the Lord? What does He want?

Home Daily Bible Readings

Monday, July 23—Wicked Rulers and Prophets (Micah 3)

Tuesday, July 24—Peace and Security Through Obedience (Micah 4:1-5)

Wednesday, July 25—Restoration Promised After Exile (Micah 4:6—5:1)

Thursday, July 26—The Ruler From Bethlehem (Micah 5:2-6)

Friday, July 27—Future Role of the Remnant (Micah 5:7-15)

Saturday, July 28—God Challenges Israel (Micah 6:1-5)

Sunday, July 29—What God Requires (Micah 6:6-16)

A series of possible answers follows. *Burnt offerings* were commanded in the law of Moses (Leviticus 1). Animals of *a year old* (including *calves*) were often required for sacrifices (Leviticus 9:2, 3; 12:6; 14:10, 11).

On the other hand, perhaps God was interested more in quantity of sacrifices than quality: *will the Lord be pleased with thousands of rams, or with ten thousands of rivers of oil?* (Oil frequently accompanied certain offerings, such as those described in Leviticus 2.)

Finally the prophet proposed a radical act: *shall I give my firstborn for my transgression?* Certainly God never commanded His people to do anything like this! But would He be pleased with someone's desire to give Him something as precious as the firstborn of his children? [See question #4, page 416.]

B. The Right Answer (v. 8)

8. He hath showed thee, O man, what is good; and what doth the LORD require of thee, but to do justly, and to love mercy, and to walk humbly with thy God?

Micah did not mean to imply that the people of Judah should not offer the sacrifices that God had commanded in the law. His point was that all of these sacrifices were meaningless unless they led to a lifestyle that pleased God and followed after what He considered important: seeking justice, loving *mercy*, and walking *humbly* before God. None of this had been kept secret from the people; as Micah said, *He hath showed thee . . . what is good*. But the people chose to ignore these concerns. It has always been easier to follow prescribed rituals than to live out one's faith in everyday settings. [See question #5, page 416.]

KEEPING THE MAIN THING THE MAIN THING

Most of us can recall various neighborhood clubs that we belonged to as children. Usually these clubs were established on rainy or otherwise boring days when we would find ourselves sitting in someone's basement or tree house with nothing to do. Someone would say, "I know! Let's start a club!" Immediate interest would be aroused and, before long, officers were elected, secret handshakes and/or passwords were decided on, and initiation rites were created. Sometimes dues and dress codes were stipulated. The longer it rained, the more organized we became. And the more organized, regulated, and regimented we became, the less likely was the club to exist longer than a week or so. We became so bogged down with details that we forgot our central purpose—to have some fun!

The people of Judah in Micah's day had become obsessed with rites, rituals, and ceremonies, thus forgetting God's primary agenda for them. They were substituting formal sacrifices and programmed "pomp and circumstance" for a humble walk with God and a heartfelt compassion for others. The main things of their religion had ceased to be the main things.

God "hath showed [us] what is good." Are we paying attention? —R. W. B.

Conclusion

A. Some Things Never Change

God's basic requirements for those who would serve Him have not changed. The question raised in Micah 6:8 is one to which Christians today must give serious consideration.

None of what Micah states as important before God requires involvement in elaborate rituals or colorful ceremonies. Even the most simple worship service can produce the changes in us that God requires. All too often (perhaps even unconsciously) we substitute activity and "busyness" for the kind of worship that God really wants.

As the twenty-first century unfolds, we hope for a better century than the twentieth, which was so filled with injustice and so lacking in mercy and humility before God. But in the process of looking forward, we must also look backward to the eighth century B.C. and heed the words of Micah. If we put his challenge into practice, we can help to eliminate some of the violence and bitterness that have plagued our society in recent years.

B. Prayer

God of mercy and justice, teach us how to be humble before You and obedient to You. May our lives so resonate with these virtues that the world will see and become followers of Jesus as we are. In His name we pray. Amen.

C. Thought to Remember

God's priorities must become our priorities.

What does the Lord require of me?

To do justly;

to love mercy;

to walk humbly

with Him.

—from Micah 6:8

Visual for lesson 9

Today's visual, an attractive representation of Micah 6:8, is one you may want to frame and display at any time in your church building, not just to illustrate this lesson.

Learning by Doing

This page contains an alternate lesson plan emphasizing learning activities.
Classes desiring such student involvement will find these suggestions helpful.

Learning Goals

After participating in this lesson, your students will be able to:

1. Tell how Micah contrasted the message of false prophets with the true requirements of following the Lord.

2. Explain how people today try to please God in ways other than those prescribed by Him.

3. Memorize Micah 6:8, and make it the governing principle of their conduct each day this week.

Into the Lesson

Ask the class to suggest some qualities of a good teacher or preacher. Write their ideas on the chalkboard. Remind the class that no teacher or preacher will fit all of these ideals. However, some qualities must be present in any leader. Ask the class to select from your list one or two qualities that must be present in *every* teacher. Place a check mark (✔) beside the answers given. Then put a circle around the qualities that emphasize faithfulness to God's Word. Tell the class, "Teachers and preachers must speak for God; they must be faithful to God's Word and His will. However, there have always been religious leaders who were not. The contrast between the two kinds is seen in today's lesson."

Into the Word

Early in the week, ask a class member to read the incident of Balak and Balaam in Numbers 22–24. Ask this person to prepare a brief summary of the incident to relate to the class.

Begin the Bible study with a brief lecture about Micah and his prophecies. Use the Lesson Background in the lesson commentary. Conclude this lecture by telling the class that, earlier in the book, Micah had condemned the political leaders of Judah. Now he turns his attention to the religious leaders—the prophets and priests.

Ask the class to work in teams of two or three. The teams' first task is to read Micah 3:5-12 and paraphrase each verse by reducing it to one word, one phrase, or one brief sentence. Give this example from verse 9: "Listen up, you religious extortionists!" After the groups have finished, ask a couple of teams to read their paraphrases.

Note that these self-acclaimed prophets were frauds! Use the commentary on verses 6 and 7 to describe these leaders. Point out that Micah, by contrast, came to speak God's truth (v. 8). He indicts these false leaders, saying that they are going to fail and be exposed.

Before studying Micah 6:3-8, tell the class this passage reads like a trial scene. Ask the learners to look at verses 1 and 2. On a visual, write (as you mention these positions and persons), "Accused: Israel; Plaintiff: The Lord; Jury: The hills, mountains, and earth." Ask the teams to read Micah 6:3-8 and discuss the following questions, which you will have copied on a handout that you will distribute at this time.

1. What is the charge implied against Israel?

2. Why did the Lord cite the Israelites' slavery in Egypt in His argument?

3. Why did God ask the questions that are in verses 6 and 7? Was God condemning sacrifices and offerings? What was He implying?

4. What is the bottom line of what God expects of His people?

After the groups have finished their discussion, ask for volunteers to give answers to questions 1 and 2. Then ask the person you recruited earlier in the week to relate his summary of Balak and Balaam's incident. Ask the class, "Why would God include this incident in His argument?" *(The incident is a reminder to be faithful to God's Word and will.)* Continue by asking volunteers to give their answers to questions 3 and 4.

Into Life

Discuss the following questions.

1. What does this text imply about contemporary religious leaders—our ministers, teachers, Bible study leaders, youth coaches, and others?

2. The people hearing Micah's message may have been enthusiastic about offerings and sacrifices, but they missed the point of godly living. What are some of the actions believers today may do as a substitute for godly living? What illustrations would Micah use if he were citing religious practices that we substitute for godly living?

3. Look at Micah 6:8. What does it mean to "do (act) justly" in 2001? What does it mean for Christians today to "love mercy"? How can we "walk humbly with [our] God"?

Distribute three-by-five cards, and ask each learner to draw a scroll on his or her card and to write the words of Micah 6:8 in the scroll. Ask the students to carry these scrolls this week, memorize the words, and make this verse a governing principle for godly conduct in their daily lives.

Let's Talk It Over

The questions on this page are designed to encourage review of the lesson Scriptures and to promote discussion of the lesson by the class. The answers provided are only discussion starters. Let your class talk it over from there.

1. The so-called prophets in Micah's day told the people what they *wanted* to hear rather than what they *needed*. Why would they neglect their office so flagrantly? To what degree is this a danger among church leaders today?

The prophets in Micah's day may have liked the financial gifts that they were receiving for their services. Perhaps it was just more "politically correct" to avoid the tough issues. Any observant student of character knows that everyone prefers being liked to being disliked. Therefore, it is not surprising that the prophets told the people what they wanted to hear—or that the same thing happens today. Thus some church growth "experts" are likely to advocate similar advice today: "Give the people what they want." While that may be okay in terms of methods, we dare not allow it to affect the message.

However, not all the blame rests on these leaders. Paul warned Timothy that some people will look for such teachers, ones who will tell them just what their "itching ears" want to hear (2 Timothy 4:3). May we not be guilty of encouraging our leaders to walk this misguided path!

2. In contrast to the false prophets, Micah boldly proclaimed himself as "full of power by the Spirit of the Lord." How can one tell a "real" spiritual leader from a false or misguided one?

We live in a time when a lot of effort is made to make the successful leader *look* right. Outward appearances, however, have nothing to do with godly leadership. God looks on the heart. How do we check out a leader's heart condition? James 3:13-18 provides a litmus test for those who are claiming wisdom and understanding from God. The real man of God must live a good life, act with humility, and avoid envy and selfish ambition. He must not boast. He must be peace-loving, considerate, submissive, full of good fruit, impartial, and sincere. The person who seeks after such a leader in the church should feel fairly confident that here is the source for sound spiritual advice.

3. Micah condemned the prophets who were "in it for the money." Does that mean we ought not to pay Christian ministers? What is the difference between wanting to be fairly compensated in ministry and being "in it for the money"?

Churches who are served by ministers who are more concerned with pleasing God than in getting paid are blessed, indeed. Sometimes, in fact, they may inadvertently take advantage of such ministers, who will not make pay an issue. Naturally, a minister wants to be compensated to a degree that he can care for his family, provide a home comparable to those of the rest of the church members, and put away something for his later years. But the genuine minister will not often mention compensation. And if you check with the financial secretary, you'll probably discover the minister is one of the church's best givers, too!

4. Micah called on the people to consider what they should do to come back to the Lord. While some of the measures seem rather extreme, they were nonetheless futile! How "extreme" should we become to make sure that we are maintaining a close relationship to God? What will make our efforts more successful than those of the Israelites?

As extreme as these sacrificial offerings may seem, the Israelites must have considered them easier to give to God than what He really wanted.

God wants a contrite heart. We are proud. God wants a humble spirit. We are striving to be self-sufficient. God wants us to give generously. We tend to hoard. God wants us to live peaceably. We hold on to our grudges and try to get others to share in our hatred. When we start on the inside and then take action based on a renewed heart, the actions we take will be pleasing to God—however "extreme" they may appear.

5. Micah makes a distinction between knowing what we are to do and actually doing it. In our personal walk with God, what are those areas where it is tougher to walk the walk rather than just to talk the talk?

Satan will attack each of us where that one is most vulnerable. Thus, the toughest area for one will not be the toughest for another. Still, there are probably several others who share our vulnerability to certain types of temptation. Discussing one's weaknesses with a trusted brother or sister who will pray for that one and offer accountability may be helpful. As James said, "Confess your faults one to another, and pray one for another" (James 5:16).

Isaiah's Call

DEVOTIONAL READING: Acts 26:12-20.

BACKGROUND SCRIPTURE: Isaiah 6.

PRINTED TEXT: Isaiah 6.

Isaiah 6

1 In the year that king Uzziah died I saw also the Lord sitting upon a throne, high and lifted up, and his train filled the temple.

2 Above it stood the seraphim: each one had six wings; with twain he covered his face, and with twain he covered his feet, and with twain he did fly.

3 And one cried unto another, and said, Holy, holy, holy, is the LORD of hosts: the whole earth is full of his glory.

4 And the posts of the door moved at the voice of him that cried, and the house was filled with smoke.

5 Then said I, Woe is me! for I am undone; because I am a man of unclean lips, and I dwell in the midst of a people of unclean lips: for mine eyes have seen the King, the LORD of hosts.

6 Then flew one of the seraphim unto me, having a live coal in his hand, which he had taken with the tongs from off the altar:

7 And he laid it upon my mouth, and said, Lo, this hath touched thy lips; and thine iniquity is taken away, and thy sin purged.

8 Also I heard the voice of the Lord, saying, Whom shall I send, and who will go for us? Then said I, Here am I; send me.

9 And he said, Go, and tell this people, Hear ye indeed, but understand not; and see ye indeed, but perceive not.

10 Make the heart of this people fat, and make their ears heavy, and shut their eyes; lest they see with their eyes, and hear with their ears, and understand with their heart, and convert, and be healed.

11 Then said I, Lord, how long? And he answered, Until the cities be wasted without inhabitant, and the houses without man, and the land be utterly desolate,

12 And the LORD have removed men far away, and there be a great forsaking in the midst of the land.

13 But yet in it shall be a tenth, and it shall return, and shall be eaten: as a teil tree, and as an oak, whose substance is in them, when they cast their leaves: so the holy seed shall be the substance thereof.

Aug
5

GOLDEN TEXT: Also I heard the voice of the Lord, saying, Whom shall I send, and who will go for us? Then said I, Here am I; send me.—Isaiah 6:8.

Division and Decline
Unit 3: Decline and Fall
(Lessons 10-13)

Lesson Aims

After this lesson a student should be able to:
1. Retell the story of Isaiah's vision and call, including his unreserved response.
2. Describe both the privilege and the frustrations of serving the Lord.
3. State the ministry to which he or she believes God is calling, and answer, "Here am I; send me."

Lesson Outline

INTRODUCTION
    A. When the King Calls
    B. Lesson Background
I. ISAIAH'S TEMPLE VISION (Isaiah 6:1-4)
    A. The Lord Seated (v. 1)
    B. Seraphim Standing (v. 2)
    C. Praise Spoken (vv. 3, 4)
II. ISAIAH'S CALL TO SERVICE (Isaiah 6:5-8)
    A. His Unworthiness (v. 5)
    B. His Cleansing (vv. 6, 7)
    C. His Response (v. 8)
        Heed the Call
III. ISAIAH'S MISSION (Isaiah 6:9-13)
    A. Difficult Task (v. 9)
        Go and Tell
    B. Discouraging Response (v. 10)
    C. Duration of the Mission (vv. 11, 12)
    D. Declaration of Hope (v. 13)
CONCLUSION
    A. Cleansed and Called
    B. Mission Impossible
    C. Prayer
    D. Thought to Remember

Introduction

A. When the King Calls

When World War I broke out, railroad stations in London were overwhelmed by individuals trying to reach their destinations before travel restrictions were imposed. Amid the confusion, one man, whose clothes, face, and hands were covered with soot and oil, pushed his way to the head of the line, purchased a ticket, and boarded the train. As soon as he sat down, he fell asleep.

When other passengers got on the train and saw the man, they woke him up and complained about his behavior and appearance. He replied,

"I am a reservist, and my unit has been called up for duty. I am a stoker on a coal-burning ship—a very dirty job. I had put in twenty hours at my job with no break when I received my call. I didn't take time to clean up, because when the king calls, a loyal subject doesn't say, 'Wait until I'm ready!' He responds immediately!"

Isaiah could have made excuses when the Lord asked, "Whom shall I send, and who will go for us?" When the King of kings called, Isaiah responded without delay: "Here am I; send me."

B. Lesson Background

The prophet Isaiah was a contemporary of Micah, whose message we studied in last week's lesson. His lengthy ministry was carried out in Judah during the reigns of four kings—Uzziah, Jotham, Ahaz, and Hezekiah (Isaiah 1:1), meaning that it probably covered well over fifty years (approximately 745 B.C. to 690 B.C.). When Isaiah was first called to the prophetic ministry, Judah, along with Israel, was continuing to experience prosperous times, mainly because Assyria remained in a period of decline. However, as noted in the Lesson Background of last week's lesson, this changed drastically during the second half of the eighth century B.C. Before Isaiah's ministry was concluded, the prophet would see his homeland ravaged by the Assyrians.

According to Isaiah 1:1, Isaiah's father was named Amoz (not to be confused with the prophet Amos). Isaiah was married and had two sons (Isaiah 7:3; 8:1-4). Unlike most other prophets, Isaiah seems to have had easy access to the royal court and was able to speak with kings such as Ahaz and Hezekiah (Isaiah 7:3; 38:1). A later Jewish tradition says that Isaiah was sawn in two during the reign of the wicked king Manasseh. (This may be the incident to which the writer of Hebrews refers in Hebrews 11:37.)

Isaiah is often hailed as the greatest of the writing prophets. His literary style is elevated, and he was given an especially keen sense of God's activity in history, anticipating a day when many nations and peoples would come to the Lord. Because of Isaiah's numerous messianic prophecies, his book has been called the "fifth Gospel."

I. Isaiah's Temple Vision (Isaiah 6:1-4)

A. The Lord Seated (v. 1)

1. In the year that king Uzziah died I saw also the Lord sitting upon a throne, high and lifted up, and his train filled the temple.

Uzziah, who is also called Azariah in the Scriptures (2 Kings 15:1; 2 Chronicles 26:1), had a lengthy reign as *king* of Judah, from 792 B.C.

until *the year* he *died*, which was 740 B.C. During the early part of his reign, he apparently served as a co-regent (or co-ruler) with his father, Amaziah. On the whole Uzziah was a good king, and Judah enjoyed prosperity under his rule. Near the end of his reign, however, he arrogantly tried to usurp the authority of the priests. As a result, he was stricken with leprosy and had to live in a separate house while his son Jotham served as a co-regent until Uzziah's death (2 Chronicles 26:16-23).

Some commentators believe that Isaiah 6 records Isaiah's initial call to the prophetic ministry, and it certainly reads as if it could be just that. However, the fact that this call is not recorded until the sixth chapter rather than in the first suggests to many that Isaiah was already active as a prophet before this event. If so, then his ministry must have taken on a new and more specific direction at this time. Perhaps this experience came after King Uzziah's death to remind Isaiah that *the Lord* was Judah's real King and was still in control. [See question #1, page 424.]

I saw . . . the Lord. How can this be, when John 1:18 tells us that "no man hath seen God at any time"? We should understand Isaiah's experience as a vision rather than a direct encounter with God. It is likely that Isaiah regularly attended the temple; perhaps this vision occurred during one of these occasions.

In his vision Isaiah saw the Lord *sitting upon a throne*, signifying His power and authority. Like an earthly king He wore a robe or *train*, which was so vast that it *filled the temple*, giving further evidence of His majesty.

B. Seraphim Standing (v. 2)

2. Above it stood the seraphim: each one had six wings; with twain he covered his face, and with twain he covered his feet, and with twain he did fly.

The word *seraphim* transliterates a Hebrew plural form (the singular is *seraph*). This is the only place in the Bible where these beings are mentioned. (While there are similarities between the seraphim and the "beasts" described in Revelation 4:6-8, the latter are never called *seraphim*.) Apparently they had human form except that *each one had six wings*. Two (the meaning of *twain*) of these wings were used to cover the *face* (perhaps to protect the seraphim from beholding the glory of God) and two to cover the *feet*. The third pair of wings was used so that the seraphim could *fly*.

The primary function of the seraphim appears to have been to praise God and to serve as His messengers. The term *seraphim* comes from a Hebrew word meaning "to burn"; thus the seraphim were the "burning ones." Some see that as suggestive of their role as purifying agents, as in verses 6 and 7.

C. Praise Spoken (vv. 3, 4)

3. And one cried unto another, and said, Holy, holy, holy, is the LORD of hosts: the whole earth is full of his glory.

Holy, holy, holy: the repetition was likely for emphasis. Some think that speaking these words *one . . . unto another* represents an antiphonal choir, singing in response to one another.

While we usually associate the word *holy* with words like *righteous, pure,* and *good*, the basic meaning of the term is "set apart." God's nature sets Him so far apart from sinful humans, or even from the angels, that these divine qualities have become the basis for our understanding of what it is to be holy.

4. And the posts of the door moved at the voice of him that cried, and the house was filled with smoke.

The energy generated by the praise of the seraphim caused the temple (a solidly built structure) to shake. The filling of *the house* (i.e., the temple) *with smoke* is an indication of the glory of God's presence (Exodus 19:18; 20:18).

II. Isaiah's Call to Service (Isaiah 6:5-8)

A. His Unworthiness (v. 5)

5. Then said I, Woe is me! for I am undone; because I am a man of unclean lips, and I dwell in the midst of a people of unclean lips: for mine eyes have seen the King, the LORD of hosts.

Isaiah's distress, reflected in his cry *Woe is me*, reflects a sense of reverence and overwhelming awe in the presence of Almighty God (something that many today, even among Christians, have lost). Isaiah knew that he was in no way worthy to be experiencing what he was experiencing.

I am undone, confessed Isaiah. He acknowledged his complete helplessness in the presence of a holy God. His *unclean lips* had uttered words that were offensive to God. Furthermore, Isaiah realized that he was not alone in his predicament; he lived among *a people of unclean lips*. Isaiah did not say this in an effort to excuse his condition; he was simply aware that his surroundings were corrupt and that he could not escape their impact. We need to be aware of how we are affected by our culture and how we often (unknowingly) have substituted the world's values for God's standards in our thoughts, words, actions, and priorities. [See question #2, page 424.]

B. His Cleansing (vv. 6, 7)

6. 7. Then flew one of the seraphim unto me, having a live coal in his hand, which he had taken with the tongs from off the altar: and he laid it upon my mouth, and said, Lo, this hath

touched thy lips; and thine iniquity is taken away, and thy sin purged.

Isaiah came to the alarming realization of who he was before a holy God—a sinner, condemned and unclean. He offered no excuse or defense for his actions.

But Isaiah's situation was not hopeless. God knew his need and responded to it by allowing one of the *seraphim* to take a *live coal* from the *altar*—most likely the golden altar in the Holy Place, from which coals of fire were taken into the Most Holy Place on the Day of Atonement (Leviticus 16:12). The seraph then touched Isaiah's lips with the coal. The contact of his lips with fire symbolized a cleansing that purged Isaiah from his sin. (Thus the significance of obtaining one of the coals normally used on the Day of Atonement is clear.)

The presence of fire indicates that Isaiah's cleansing was thorough, but it also suggests that it was painful. Few experiences are more soul-wrenching than having to confess our sins and accept the responsibility for them and for the punishment that often follows.

C. His Response (v. 8)

8. Also I heard the voice of the Lord, saying, Whom shall I send, and who will go for us? Then said I, Here am I; send me.

I heard the voice of the Lord. Up to this point, God had not spoken. There had been no need; His very presence had communicated everything Isaiah needed to know. When God did speak, He asked a question: *Whom shall I send, and who will go for us?* His words do not seem to have been directed specifically to Isaiah. It was almost as if Isaiah were overhearing a conversation in the courts of Heaven. But in Isaiah's mind there was no doubt that the questions were aimed at him. [See question #3, page 424.]

Note the change in pronouns from singular (*I*) to plural (*us*). While this may indicate that God was including the seraphim in His question, some believe that this reflects the presence of the three Persons of the Godhead, much as Genesis 1:26 does ("Let *us* make man in *our* image").

Apparently Isaiah's response was immediate: *Here am I; send me.* He did not ask for time to think the matter over or to count the cost. He volunteered without a moment's hesitation, not even knowing what a *yes* answer might entail.

In Isaiah's case the call to God's service was not specific. It rarely is. When one becomes a member of his nation's armed forces, he usually has no idea where he will eventually serve. In the same way, the moment one becomes a Christian he enlists in the struggle with Satan and becomes a soldier in God's army. But he may have little or no idea where he will eventually be used in that struggle or the price he will have to pay.

HEED THE CALL

Moses received his unique assignment to lead the Israelites out of bondage in Egypt during a unique encounter with a burning bush. The apostle Paul received his "wake-up call" in the form of a blinding light on the road to Damascus. Most of us do not experience such a dramatic summons into the Lord's service. I remember how my father was called into the ministry by the quiet discipling efforts of faithful church elders. It was not a spectacular type of "call," but it certainly made an impact on his life.

No universal pattern of circumstances characterizes God's call to Christian service. It comes in a variety of ways. However, Isaiah's call teaches us certain particulars that prepare us to receive God's call, no matter the circumstances in which that call may come. Isaiah was *humble* before the Lord; he was *remorseful* and *penitent* in acknowledging his sin; and he responded as a *willing* servant to God's plea for workers.

In one way or another, God calls each of His children to work in His kingdom. To what task is He calling you? Are you listening for His "still small voice" with humility, penitence, and willingness? You, too, can hear and heed His call.

—R. W. B.

III. Isaiah's Mission (Isaiah 6:9-13)

A. Difficult Task (v. 9)

9. And he said, Go, and tell this people, Hear ye indeed, but understand not; and see ye indeed, but perceive not.

Isaiah's task consisted of a pair of actions—he was to *go and tell*. The message he was to deliver was also stated in pairs: *Hear . . . but understand not; and see . . . but perceive not.* The Hebrew text suggests the meaning, "Keep on hearing, yet

Visual for lesson 10

The visual for today's lesson makes a missionary application. Discuss what your church is doing to support efforts to "go" with the gospel.

How to Say It

AHAZ. *Ay*-haz.
AMAZIAH. Am-uh-*zye*-uh.
AMOZ. *Ay*-mahz.
ASSYRIA. Uh-*sear*-ee-uh.
AZARIAH. Az-uh-*rye*-uh.
BABYLON. *Bab*-uh-lun.
DAMASCUS. Duh-*mass*-kus.
HEZEKIAH. Hez-ih-*kye*-uh.
JOTHAM. *Jo*-thum.
MANASSEH. Muh-*nass*-uh.
MESSIANIC. mess-ee-*an*-ick.
MICAH. *My*-kuh.
SERAPH. *sair*-uff.
SERAPHIM. *sair*-uh-fim.
TEIL. tile.
TEREBINTH. *ter*-uh-binth.
UZZIAH. Uh-*zye*-uh.

never understanding; and keep on seeing, yet never perceiving."

While Isaiah had readily volunteered to do God's bidding, God said his efforts were, for the most part, destined to fail. In spite of all his pleading, *this people* would refuse to pay attention. This does not mean that every individual in the nation would close his ears and eyes to Isaiah's call to repentance. But the nation as a whole was determined to go its own way. Its rejection of God's prophet would confirm the judgment that God had already reserved for His people.

GO AND TELL

It was "Show and Tell" day at my elementary school—a fact that I had failed to remind my mother of until it was time to leave the house! At the last minute, Mom shoved our family bread plate into my hand and sent me off to school. The plate did possess unusual color and texture, but neither my mother nor I had any idea how unique and valuable it was. My teacher, however, recognized it as a fine specimen of centuries-old *Majolica* (Muh-*jah*-lick-uh) ware "worth who-knows-what." Needless to say, I returned home that day with not just a bread plate, but a priceless antique—wrapped, padded, and tied securely. I still own and cherish that plate.

Isaiah's commission to "go and tell" was a typical charge to prophets. He was to be a messenger for God; his message was priceless because it contained divine truth. But it was, for the most part, negative news—not nearly as well received as my plate story and certainly not as happily heard as the good news shared by gospel ambassadors of reconciliation.

The going and telling of Christians in response to Christ's commission is definitely a more joyful job than Isaiah's. Though we must warn sinners of God's wrath and justice, the primary thrust of our message is God's love and mercy. Both warnings and promises are designed to bring people to repentance and salvation. So let us "go, show, and tell," never forgetting the priceless worth of the gospel. —R. W. B.

B. Discouraging Response (v. 10)

10. Make the heart of this people fat, and make their ears heavy, and shut their eyes; lest they see with their eyes, and hear with their ears, and understand with their heart, and convert, and be healed.

Prosperity tends to make people oblivious to prophets such as Isaiah. So when Isaiah challenged the prosperous people of Judah to return to God, they would instead take the easy way of continuing on the same path. Their hearts would grow *fat*, their *eyes* would not *see*, and their *ears* would not *hear*. Thus there was no repentance, no conversion, and no healing. Both Jesus and Paul used this text to describe the adverse reaction of some to their messages (Matthew 13:14, 15; Acts 28:25-27). [See question #4, page 424.]

C. Duration of the Mission (vv. 11, 12)

11, 12. Then said I, Lord, how long? And he answered, Until the cities be wasted without inhabitant, and the houses without man, and the land be utterly desolate, and the LORD have removed men far away, and there be a great forsaking in the midst of the land.

Realizing the hopelessness of the ministry to which he had been called, Isaiah cried out in anguish, *Lord, how long?* "Is there no end to this message of judgment?" he seemed to be asking. To be called to a difficult task is challenging enough; to be called to a task that holds no hope of success can overwhelm an individual with discouragement.

God gave Isaiah an answer to his question, but it was hardly reassuring. Yes, there would be a conclusion to his seemingly hopeless task, but not before disaster had ravaged the land. The *cities* of Judah would be *wasted without inhabitant*, and the *houses* would become empty—*without man* to occupy them. The *land* would be left *utterly desolate*.

Why would such desolation occur? Because *the Lord* would remove *men far away*, leaving the land forsaken. At the very moment Isaiah's call was taking place, changes were occurring on the international scene that, within twenty years, would bring the Assyrian hordes upon Israel (the northern kingdom) and carry her people away.

About twenty years after that, this dreaded foe was camped outside Jerusalem threatening to do there what it had done to Samaria. Jerusalem was spared then (Isaiah 37:36, 37), but that was not the end of her troubles. Within a hundred years, another foreign power, Babylon, would descend upon Judah and carry still more captives far away.

D. Declaration of Hope (v. 13)

13. But yet in it shall be a tenth, and it shall return, and shall be eaten: as a teil tree, and as an oak, whose substance is in them, when they cast their leaves: so the holy seed shall be the substance thereof.

Even the *tenth*—the portion of those who remained in the land—would *be eaten*, meaning that they would suffer additional ravaging attacks from their enemies. However, like a strong, resilient tree, this remnant would survive in spite of being subjected to such treatment. The *teil tree* (called *terebinth* in most modern translations) was common in the lower elevations of Israel and Judah. Its great size and long life resembled those of the *oak*. These trees (each symbolic of Judah) would be cut down by Judah's enemies, but their *substance* (meaning their stumps) would provide the *holy seed* that would keep alive a remnant of God's people so that His covenant with Abraham would still be fulfilled through the coming of the Messiah. A similar promise is found in Isaiah 11:1. [See question #5, page 424.]

Conclusion

A. Cleansed and Called

Isaiah's stirring account of his vision of the Lord reminds us that, in one way or another, God calls every Christian to a ministry. But it also points out that, if we are to be effective in that ministry, we must first of all be cleansed, laying aside "every weight, and the sin which doth so easily beset us" (Hebrews 12:1). Just as the cleansing was an agonizing experience for Isaiah, so it is likely to be for us. And yet, the "finished product" will be, in Paul's words, "a vessel . . . meet for the master's use, and prepared unto every good work" (2 Timothy 2:21).

B. Mission Impossible

Several years ago "Mission Impossible" was a popular television program. Each week a team of agents—the "Impossible Missions Force"—was assigned an extremely dangerous task considered to be "impossible." By clever strategies, incredible devices, and great courage they were always able to accomplish their "impossible" mission.

The title of this television program could well summarize the challenge that confronted Isaiah. He was sent to the people of Judah, who had turned away from God, with a message of repentance. But his mission appeared impossible; the people had already closed their minds and their ears to that message. As discouraging as this task may have been for Isaiah, he did not fail, for he was faithful to his duty. Let us remind ourselves that God counts faithfulness as more important than success.

A few of us may be called to some distant and difficult mission field; however, most of us will be called to closer and less dramatic mission fields. Some might consider teaching a junior boys' class an "impossible" mission, yet certain individuals have succeeded in spite of the difficulties. Others would consider ministering to those suffering from drug and alcohol addiction as another task to be filed in the "impossible" category. Yet some have carried out this ministry faithfully in spite of numerous disappointments and setbacks. Others have found their "impossible" mission in bringing hope and comfort to the terminally ill through hospice care.

Is God calling you to a seemingly impossible mission? If so, accept it as Isaiah did. And never forget that God specializes in the impossible.

C. Prayer

Almighty God, as we look around us at our world, we see many "impossible" tasks that need to be done for Your kingdom. Cleanse us from any influences that would hinder our service to You, and give us the courage to undertake these opportunities. In Jesus' name we pray. Amen.

D. Thought to Remember

"Here am I; send me."

Home Daily Bible Readings

Monday, July 30—The Wickedness of Judah (Isaiah 1:1-9)

Tuesday, July 31—Isaiah's Transforming Vision (Isaiah 6:1-8)

Wednesday, Aug. 1—Daniel's Vision of God's Glory (Daniel 10:1-11)

Thursday, Aug. 2—John's Vision of Christ (Revelation 1:9-18)

Friday, Aug. 3—Isaiah's Commission (Isaiah 6:9-13)

Saturday, Aug. 4—A Prayer of Trust (Psalm 25:1-10)

Sunday, Aug. 5—Paul's Vision on the Road to Damascus (Acts 26:12-20)

Learning by Doing

This page contains an alternate lesson plan emphasizing learning activities. Classes desiring such student involvement will find these suggestions helpful.

Learning Goals

After this lesson a student should be able to:

1. Retell the story of Isaiah's vision and call, including his unreserved response.

2. Describe both the privilege and the frustrations of serving the Lord.

3. State the ministry to which he or she believes God is calling, and answer, "Here am I; send me."

Into the Lesson

Remind the class of the old TV series *Mission Impossible*, which was about government agents assigned to tasks or missions that had been deemed "impossible" for other agencies to complete. Ask, "If God were to call you to an 'impossible mission,' which of these assignments might that be?" Then read the following list:

• Teach a junior high boys' class.

• Make teaching calls to prospective Christians.

• Supervise a church building remodeling project.

• Lead music in a worship service.

• Lead a midweek Bible study group.

Ask the class members to call out the mission that would be the most difficult for them to fulfill. Ask a few persons why they think the jobs they mentioned would be "impossible missions."

Then ask, "How would you feel if the Lord asked you to do something that was bound to fail? That's exactly what God asked one of His prophets to do. But Isaiah's willing response becomes a model of humble and unquestioning service for believers today."

Into the Word

Begin the Bible study with a short lecture on the setting by using the lesson commentary notes on the Lesson Background and verse 1. Then divide the class into three groups. Give each group one of the following assignments.

Group 1: Heavenly Worship. Read Isaiah 6:1-4 and Revelation 4:6b-8. List the similarities in these two glimpses of Heavenly worship. Tell what attitudes and lessons you find implied for today's worship services in these visions.

Group 2: Moment in God's Presence. Read Isaiah 6:1-8. Tell what the phrases "a man of unclean lips" and "a people of unclean lips" imply about our attitudes and relationship with God. Explain the significance of the live coal being laid on Isaiah's mouth. What might the pain of this experience imply about confession of sin?

Group 3: Call to Service. (Give this group a photocopy of the lesson commentary for verses 8-13.) Read Isaiah 6:8-13 and the lesson commentary notes on this passage. Be ready to explain Isaiah's "impossible mission": What was his task? How would Judah respond? Why did God bother to send Isaiah? What would be in Judah's future? Review this text by allowing the group members to report their findings.

Into Life

Distribute a "Personal Assessment Sheet," as follows. As a heading for the left column, write, "My Experience With the Lord." Then list the following multiple-choice assessments:

__ 1. The "angel" who placed the "live coal" on the lips of my life was

    A. a stranger

    B. a parent

    C. a church leader

    D. a friend

    E. I'm still waiting for my "angel."

__ 2. If I've had one worship experience where I've had a taste of Heavenly worship, it was

    A. at a church camp.

    B. in a personal devotional time.

    C. at my home church.

    D. in a nature setting.

    E. Other _____

Column two should have the heading "My Experience in Service." Under it write:

1. List the areas of service in which you are presently involved through your church.

2. Suppose God called you to one of the following ministries. Check (✔) the ones that would surprise you.

__ Evangelistic teaching

__ Leading public worship

__ Teaching children/youth

__ Teaching adults

__ Being a foreign missionary

__ Sharing Christ at work

__ Leading a Bible study

__ Preparing to be a minister

__ Providing meals for the homeless

__ Showing hospitality

__ Other _____

Ask each learner to circle the task or ministry he or she feels "called" to do, even though it may be frightening. Close with prayer, asking people to tell the Lord they will be open to His leading.

Let's Talk It Over

The questions on this page are designed to encourage review of the lesson Scriptures and to promote discussion of the lesson by the class. The answers provided are only discussion starters. Let your class talk it over from there.

1. Some people think that Isaiah's grief over King Uzziah's death played a significant part in the timing of this vision. What kind of events cause us to search for God? Do "crisis" oriented encounters with God have a longer lasting impact on us than encounters we have planned, such as regular worship services, revival meetings, retreats, or camps? Why or why not?

Many things can bring an individual to a meaningful encounter with God: the Word, a sermon, a crisis, or the birth of a child, to name a few. For some reason, Christians have come to give unusual credence to "extraordinary" encounters with God, such as the conversion of a drug dealer or other flagrantly immoral person. This has had the unfortunate result of causing some Christians to consider themselves less important to God or to the church because their "testimony" is not dramatic enough. We need to learn that all types of encounters with God can be faith-building and can result in more fruitfulness in God's kingdom. We simply have to be open to Him.

2. How much do we need to come face to face with our sin and sinfulness before we can have a worship experience? Before we can hear or respond to God's call? What is likely to be the result if we skip dealing with our sinfulness and try to move directly to commitment and service?

Help your students appreciate (1) that their sins, great or small, deserve the death penalty in the court of eternal justice and (2) that only the grace of God through Christ provides the necessary pardon for their sins. Individuals who recognize the magnitude and consequences of their sin tend to be more thankful for God's unmerited gift of grace. They appreciate more fully Christ's sacrifice on their behalf. They tend to be more faithful in the most trying circumstances. Jesus said the one who has been forgiven much is the one who loves much (Luke 7:47). The more we appreciate how great is our need for forgiveness, the more we will exhibit our love for Christ.

3. Out of the millions of people who lived during Old and New Testament times, only several dozen people received a special "call" from God. All others received a general call. In what ways today does God "call" people to serve Him? What response does God want from each person?

Many Christians wait so long for a "special call" from God that they become useless to the kingdom. The principle of each Christian's being "gifted" by the Spirit for the purpose of building up the body of Christ is a sufficient "call" for all Christians to get busy in kingdom work. (See Romans 12.) Note also the story entitled "Heed the Call" on page 420 to guide your discussion.

4. Isaiah was told that, in spite of his preaching, Judah's spiritual condition would not improve. What do you think kept Isaiah motivated? What helps you to remain motivated to persevere in God's work when it seems not to be appreciated or fruitful?

Cynical Christians tend to think or say of some groups of people, "Nothing will help *them!*" Their critical focus may be on a specific group of people or on the larger category of all non-Christians. Their pessimism blocks any proactive response toward others. They are resigned to withdraw and focus on piety, making sure they remain faithful. These "negative" or "stagnant" Christians present two types of problems: (1) they discourage other Christians who are working hard to be faithful and fruitful, and (2) they give non-Christians a false measuring stick by which they conclude they are just as moral as most Christians. Remember that God has called us to be faithful to do what we can—not what we can't. We can't *make* another person believe, but we can offer the opportunity. Let's do what we can!

5. The Lord told Isaiah that the nation of Judah would have a spiritual "comeback" after its destruction and captivity. Should we as Christians pray for hard times for our nation so there might be a better possibility for spiritual revival? Why or why not?

Prosperity can be as habit forming as a drug. Thus, Satan can cripple Christians in any nation by helping to maintain prosperity. The new false gods become materialism, consumerism, and comfort. The downfall of Christians often comes through complacency. Still, Isaiah's prayer was not for hard times, but for revival. Perhaps we ought to pray for revival, seek to be good stewards of whatever resources God has put at our disposal, and then leave to God the decision of whether the discipline of hard times is necessary.

Isaiah's Challenge to Rely on God

DEVOTIONAL READING: Psalm 33:1-12.

BACKGROUND SCRIPTURE: Isaiah 7; 2 Kings 16; 2 Chronicles 28.

PRINTED TEXT: Isaiah 7:1-6, 10-17.

Isaiah 7:1-6, 10-17

1 And it came to pass in the days of Ahaz the son of Jotham, the son of Uzziah, king of Judah, that Rezin the king of Syria, and Pekah the son of Remaliah, king of Israel, went up toward Jerusalem to war against it, but could not prevail against it.

2 And it was told the house of David, saying, Syria is confederate with Ephraim. And his heart was moved, and the heart of his people, as the trees of the wood are moved with the wind.

3 Then said the LORD unto Isaiah, Go forth now to meet Ahaz, thou, and Shear-jashub thy son, at the end of the conduit of the upper pool, in the highway of the fuller's field;

4 And say unto him, Take heed, and be quiet; fear not, neither be faint-hearted for the two tails of these smoking firebrands, for the fierce anger of Rezin with Syria, and of the son of Remaliah.

5 Because Syria, Ephraim, and the son of Remaliah, have taken evil counsel against thee, saying,

6 Let us go up against Judah, and vex it, and let us make a breach therein for us, and set a king in the midst of it, even the son of Tabeal.

· · · · · · · · · · · · ·

10 Moreover the LORD spake again unto Ahaz, saying,

11 Ask thee a sign of the LORD thy God; ask it either in the depth, or in the height above.

12 But Ahaz said, I will not ask, neither will I tempt the LORD.

13 And he said, Hear ye now, O house of David; Is it a small thing for you to weary men, but will ye weary my God also?

14 Therefore the Lord himself shall give you a sign; Behold, a virgin shall conceive, and bear a son, and shall call his name Immanuel.

15 Butter and honey shall he eat, that he may know to refuse the evil, and choose the good.

16 For before the child shall know to refuse the evil, and choose the good, the land that thou abhorrest shall be forsaken of both her kings.

17 The LORD shall bring upon thee, and upon thy people, and upon thy father's house, days that have not come, from the day that Ephraim departed from Judah; even the king of Assyria.

Aug 12

GOLDEN TEXT: Therefore the Lord himself shall give you a sign; Behold, a virgin shall conceive, and bear a son, and shall call his name Immanuel.—Isaiah 7:14.

Division and Decline
Unit 3: Decline and Fall
(Lessons 10-13)

Lesson Aims

After participating in this lesson, each student will be able to:

1. Summarize the message that Isaiah gave Ahaz and how the message demonstrated God's control to King Ahaz and the people of Judah.

2. Cite reasons that people today need reassurance of God's control.

3. Share the message of "Immanuel" with someone facing particularly difficult circumstances.

Lesson Outline

INTRODUCTION
   A. God Is the Pilot
   B. Lesson Background
I. ISAIAH REASSURES AHAZ (Isaiah 7:1-6)
   A. A Nation Troubled (vv. 1, 2)
   B. A Prophet Sent (v. 3)
   C. A King Encouraged (vv. 4-6)
     Whom Do You Trust?
II. GOD SPEAKS TO AHAZ (Isaiah 7:10-13)
   A. God's Request (vv. 10, 11)
   B. Ahaz's Refusal (v. 12)
     To Sign or Not to Sign?
   C. God's Rebuke (v. 13)
III. AHAZ RECEIVES A SIGN (Isaiah 7:14-17)
   A. A Virgin's Special Son (v. 14)
   B. A Nation's Dismal Future (vv. 15-17)
CONCLUSION
   A. Immanuel
   B. Prayer
   C. Thought to Remember

Introduction

A. God Is the Pilot

The story is told of a mother and her three children who were taking a long flight together aboard a commercial airliner. About an hour into the flight, the plane unexpectedly ran into some turbulence, which caused it to drop suddenly and shake violently. The passengers became alarmed and some began to scream and cry out. But one of the three children, a six-year-old boy, remained calm throughout the whole episode.

Later one of the attendants stopped and complimented the lad for his remarkable courage when everyone else seemed to panic. "Oh, I didn't have any reason to be afraid," responded the boy. "My daddy is the pilot!"

King Ahaz and the people of Judah, learning that Israel and Syria were conspiring against them, became so frightened that their hearts were shaking like the "trees of the wood . . . moved with the wind" (Isaiah 7:2). The Lord sent Isaiah to Ahaz to give the troubled king the assurance that Judah had nothing to fear from this threat. After all, God—the "pilot" of the universe—was still handling the controls.

B. Lesson Background

In last week's lesson we studied Isaiah's special call to the prophetic ministry in the year that King Uzziah died (Isaiah 6:1). Jotham, who had served as a co-regent with his father, then became king. Although he did not carry out certain needed religious reforms, the Bible includes these words of approval: "he did that which was right in the sight of the Lord" (2 Kings 15:34).

Jotham was succeeded by his son, Ahaz, who did not follow the good examples set by his father and grandfather. Ahaz "did *not* that which was right in the sight of the Lord" (2 Kings 16:2). This created a particularly difficult situation for Judah, in light of the changing international scene at that time. Assyria, under the aggressive leadership of Tiglath-pileser III, had begun making inroads into Israel (the northern kingdom) and Syria. These two nations, which had been at war with each other during the days of the prophet Elijah (see the Lesson Background of lesson 4) had formed a coalition to thwart the Assyrian menace. They were trying to pressure Judah into joining their coalition—a situation that produced the crisis described in the opening verses of our printed text.

I. Isaiah Reassures Ahaz (Isaiah 7:1-6)

A. A Nation Troubled (vv. 1, 2)

1, 2. And it came to pass in the days of Ahaz the son of Jotham, the son of Uzziah, king of Judah, that Rezin the king of Syria, and Pekah the son of Remaliah, king of Israel, went up toward Jerusalem to war against it, but could not prevail against it. And it was told the house of David, saying, Syria is confederate with Ephraim. And his heart was moved, and the heart of his people, as the trees of the wood are moved with the wind.

Rezin the king of Syria and *Pekah . . . king of Israel* were the leaders who had formed a coalition to resist the threat of Assyria. They wanted Judah to join this alliance. When Ahaz refused, both Israel and Syria sent forces to Judah in an attempt to coerce Ahaz's compliance with their demand.

The Biblical record in 2 Chronicles 28:1-8 notes that Judah was soundly defeated during these invasions. Pekah, the king of Israel, "slew in Judah a hundred and twenty thousand in one day, which were all valiant men" (v. 6). The record in Chronicles is clear that all of this took place because Ahaz and Judah "had forsaken the Lord God of their fathers" (v. 6). Among other detestable sins, Ahaz had offered his children to be sacrificed in the fire to pagan gods (v. 3).

It may have been after these attacks that the incident recorded in Isaiah 7 occurred, when Israel and Syria *went up toward Jerusalem to war against it*. In spite of the significant casualties Israel and Syria had inflicted earlier upon Judah, they *could not prevail against* Jerusalem's formidable defenses. However, Judah had been so weakened by its losses that Ahaz and his people had good reason to fear still another assault. Verse 6 of our text indicates that the purpose of such an attack would be to remove Ahaz from the throne, most likely in order to replace him with a king who would be more cooperative with the proposed alliance against Assyria.

The phrase *house of David* could refer to either the royal court of Ahaz or to the entire nation of Judah. It seems that the nation was gripped with a sense of panic upon receiving word of the approaching armies: the king's *heart was moved, and the heart of his people, as the trees of the wood are moved with the wind*. Apparently they had lost all hope. [See question #1, page 432.]

B. A Prophet Sent (v. 3)

3. Then said the LORD unto Isaiah, Go forth now to meet Ahaz, thou, and Shear-jashub thy son, at the end of the conduit of the upper pool, in the highway of the fuller's field.

At this point, Ahaz desperately needed reassurance, and *the Lord*, knowing that need, spoke to *Isaiah* and sent him to *meet* with the troubled king. God also ordered Isaiah to take his *son, Shear-jashub*, with him. The son's unusual name served as an object lesson, for it meant "a remnant will return"—a message similar to that which Isaiah had received during his call from the Lord (Isaiah 6:13). [See question #2, page 432.]

The meeting between Ahaz and Isaiah occurred *at the end of the conduit of the upper pool, in the highway of the fuller's field*. (The verb *full*, from which we get *fuller*, means to wash clothes.) The exact location of this site is unknown. Perhaps the king was conducting a tour of the city's water sources in anticipation of another siege.

C. A King Encouraged (vv. 4-6)

4. And say unto him, Take heed, and be quiet; fear not, neither be faint-hearted for the two tails of these smoking firebrands, for the fierce anger of Rezin with Syria, and of the son of Remaliah.

Fear not—how often we read these words in Scripture at the beginning of a message of hope and encouragement! The phrase *these smoking firebrands* describes *Rezin*, king of *Syria*, and *the son of Remaliah*, who was Pekah, king of Israel. (Pekah was a usurper, an army officer who had murdered the previous king in order to seize the throne. Many scholars believe it is contempt for his behavior that causes him to be referred to, not by his name, but merely as *the son of Remaliah*.) Like torches, these kings' *fierce anger* against Ahaz (for not joining their coalition) would blaze for a short time and then burn out.

5, 6. Because Syria, Ephraim, and the son of Remaliah, have taken evil counsel against thee, saying, Let us go up against Judah, and vex it, and let us make a breach therein for us, and set a king in the midst of it, even the son of Tabeal.

Ephraim was the most prominent tribe of the northern kingdom; sometimes its name was used to refer to the entire kingdom. The two kings who were allied against Ahaz had failed in their earlier attempts to capture Jerusalem, but they were determined to try yet again to *make a breach therein*. If they were successful, they intended to place someone described as the *son of Tabeal* on the throne. We know nothing about this person, though he was probably someone who was sympathetic to the proposed alliance against Assyria.

WHOM DO YOU TRUST?

During World War I, the United States and Russia were enemies. During World War II, the same two countries were allies, for at that point they were facing a common enemy in Germany. Sometimes conflict creates alliances between unlikely powers. Siblings who constantly quarrel and bicker will usually join forces against "outsiders" who threaten either or both of them.

A common enemy (Assyria) made "strange bedfellows" out of Israel and her former enemy, Syria. Those two allied themselves against Judah, which in turn established an alliance with Assyria (2 Kings 16:7), of which the prophet Isaiah strongly disapproved. Far better would have been the outcome if all of God's chosen people in both the northern and southern kingdoms had presented a united front that trusted not in chariots, swords, and spears, but in Jehovah God.

Although the opposition to Christians today seems especially intimidating at times, we need to trust in and depend on God's strength as we fight our battle "against spiritual wickedness in high places" (Ephesians 6:12). All the resources that we need to achieve victory have been provided, but we must determine to use them.   —R. W. B.

II. God Speaks to Ahaz
(Isaiah 7:10-13)

A. God's Request (vv. 10, 11)

10, 11. Moreover the LORD spake again unto Ahaz, saying, Ask thee a sign of the LORD thy God; ask it either in the depth, or in the height above.

In the intervening verses, not included in the printed text (7-9), Isaiah gave Ahaz further encouragement that the campaign directed against him would not stand. There was also, however, a warning issued to Ahaz, whose faith had been less than exemplary to this point: "If ye will not believe, surely ye shall not be established" (v. 9).

The Lord spake again unto Ahaz. Perhaps some time passed until this next occasion when God spoke to the king through Isaiah. It appears that Ahaz had been unwilling to accept Isaiah's previous message of hope, and so the prophet was sent to him again. This time Isaiah encouraged the spiritually unsteady king to *ask* for some kind of *sign* that would convince him of the truth of the prophet's message.

Certainly there are times when asking for a sign is wrong. During Jesus' ministry the Pharisees asked for signs, not to confirm their faith but to find a way to curtail Jesus' popularity with the people (Matthew 12:38-40). Zechariah was made mute for asking, "Whereby [How] shall I know this?" regarding God's promise (Luke 1:18-20). However, when Gideon asked for a sign, God complied (Judges 6:36-40). God knows the heart of the person. He knows whether the request for a sign comes from a true desire to know His will or is an act of doubt and disbelief.

The case before us is different from the above examples because the initiative for the sign came from God. God told Ahaz to ask for a sign, and He gave him a wide range of items for which he could ask: *either in the depth, or in the height above* (probably meaning "anything on earth or in the sky"). While this language suggests a miraculous sign, a sign could involve some natural event that occurred in such a way as to convey a message. In effect, God presented Ahaz with a blank check. [See question #3, page 432.]

B. Ahaz's Refusal (v. 12)

12. But Ahaz said, I will not ask, neither will I tempt the LORD.

In rejecting God's offer to *ask* for a sign, Ahaz seems to appear very pious and reverent toward God: "I will not *tempt the Lord.*" Deuteronomy 6:16 states, "Ye shall not tempt the Lord your God, as ye tempted him in Massah" (referring to the incident found in Exodus 17:1-7). But since God was giving this opportunity to Ahaz, the king's response was actually a blatant defiance of God's authority and a declaration that he himself (without God's help) would determine what he and his nation would do.

It appears that Ahaz had already made up his mind to ask Assyria for help against his enemies, which he proceeded to do (or, perhaps, had already done), according to 2 Kings 16:7-9. Ahaz refused to acknowledge Judah's real King. He trusted the Assyrians (that is, man's power) more than he trusted God. It was a decision he would live to regret (v. 17).

TO SIGN OR NOT TO SIGN?

In recent years great interest has arisen among the general public in angels, miracles, and the "spirit world." The print, film, and video media have responded to and heightened that interest through articles, books, movies, and television shows on these themes. People are reporting miracles of healing and even of "resurrection" (when a person who has been pronounced clinically dead returns to life). Alleged angel and spirit "sightings" seem to be frequent. Human nature strongly desires to believe in the supernatural. That desire can be satisfied by fantasy, superstition, coincidence—or by real evidence.

Ahaz was given the opportunity to name the sign by which the divine nature of Isaiah's message would be validated. However, receiving such a sign would have required the king's personal repentance and obedience. Thus, when offered this unique opportunity, the king declined the invitation. He preferred to continue in sin for another season and to trust in the military might of a godless neighbor (Assyria).

Home Daily Bible Readings

Monday, Aug. 6—Isaiah Reassures King Ahaz (Isaiah 7:1-9)

Tuesday, Aug. 7—The Great Sign (Isaiah 7:10-17)

Wednesday, Aug. 8—Ahaz Reigns Over Judah (2 Kings 16:1-8)

Thursday, Aug. 9—The Assyrians Take Damascus (2 Kings 16:9-20)

Friday, Aug. 10—Ahaz's Apostasy Leads to Defeat (2 Chronicles 28:1-8)

Saturday, Aug. 11—Intervention of Obed (2 Chronicles 28:9-15)

Sunday, Aug. 12—Invasion of Judah and Ahaz's Death (2 Chronicles 28:16-27)

Demanding signs from God can reflect an attitude of doubt rather than faith. But ignoring the evidence of the signs that *God Himself* freely offers reflects intentional and stubborn disbelief. Sinful cynics must take a "leap of doubt" when they refuse to consider the compelling amount of evidence that brings true seekers to the certainty that "God . . . is, and that he is a rewarder of them that diligently seek him" (Hebrews 11:6).

God has given us numerous signs of His great faithfulness that we dare not reject or ignore. As the hymn says, "Morning by morning new mercies I see; All I have needed Thy hand hath provided."

—R. W. B.

The familiar scene on the visual for today's lesson reminds us that Isaiah looked beyond his own political and geographical situation to the birth of the King of kings and Lord of lords!

Visual for lesson 11

C. God's Rebuke (v. 13)

13. And he said, Hear ye now, O house of David; Is it a small thing for you to weary men, but will ye weary my God also?

O house of David. The message concerning the Israelite/Syrian coalition had been sent to the house of David (v. 2), so now the Lord's response given through Isaiah was addressed to it as well. Isaiah had grown tired of Ahaz's arrogance and obstinacy, but even more significant, God had grown *weary* of it as well.

While Isaiah had spoken to Ahaz of *thy God* in verse 11, in this verse he referred to *my God*. The prophet subtly indicated that Ahaz, through his stubborn disbelief, had severed ties with God and His purposes. [See question #4, page 432.]

III. Ahaz Receives a Sign (Isaiah 7:14-17)

A. A Virgin's Special Son (v. 14)

14. Therefore the Lord himself shall give you a sign; Behold, a virgin shall conceive, and bear a son, and shall call his name Immanuel.

Even though Ahaz had refused to ask for a *sign, the Lord* offered to *give* one anyway. The sign is directed to *you,* which is plural in the Hebrew. Thus this sign was not only for Ahaz but for the whole "house of David" (v. 13), or the nation of Judah.

The sign was this: *A virgin shall conceive, and bear a son, and shall call his name Immanuel.* Christians understand this to be one of the most significant of the messianic prophecies (cited in Matthew 1:22, 23). While there has been frequent discussion over the years about the Hebrew word that is translated *virgin,* it is clear from a study of the Hebrew word used by Isaiah in this verse that *virgin* is the best translation of the term. The word is used nine times in the Old Testament, five times in the plural and four times in the singular. In every case the word clearly describes an unmarried woman, though in one instance (Proverbs 30:19) it describes an immoral one. However, for Isaiah's sign to have the significance attached to it, an immoral woman having a child would hardly be appropriate. Also worth noting is the fact that this word has a definite article before it in the Hebrew text ("*the* virgin"). This would call attention to the fact that a special virgin was being described. The Septuagint (the Greek translation of the Old Testament) used a word that clearly means *virgin.*

Some believe that the virgin mentioned by Isaiah was a woman who was a virgin at the time of the prophecy, but who was married (perhaps to Isaiah) at the time the promised child was conceived. Many of these students suggest that the child mentioned in Isaiah 8:1-4 is the same one as prophesied here. As attractive as that kind of consistency may be, the structure of the Hebrew in this verse clearly indicates that the virgin would be a virgin at the time of the conception. Moreover, the birth of a child to a woman who was unmarried at the time of the prophecy and who later married would hardly provide the kind of exceptional "sign" that the Lord had challenged Ahaz to request in verse 11.

Isaiah then proceeded to call attention to the special *son* whom the virgin would bear. The child's uniqueness is clear from the name he is to receive: *Immanuel,* meaning "God with us." Our finite minds find it difficult to comprehend how an infinite God could, through His Son, take on a human form and live among us as a human being. Yet that is exactly what the incarnation means: "the Word was God" and "the Word was made flesh, and dwelt among us" (John 1:1, 14). [See question #5, page 432.]

B. A Nation's Dismal Future (vv. 15-17)

15, 16. Butter and honey shall he eat, that he may know to refuse the evil, and choose the good. For before the child shall know to refuse the evil, and choose the good, the land that thou abhorrest shall be forsaken of both her kings.

Isaiah then used the infancy of the promised child to indicate the time that Judah would be in danger from the current threat of Israel and Syria. He stated that the child's diet would consist of *butter* (a word more accurately rendered "curds") *and honey*. These foods reflect a humble diet, consistent with that of a family of limited financial resources, as Jesus' earthly family was. It is also consistent with the difficult times to come upon Judah because of Ahaz's reliance on Assyria (vv. 20-22). This is what the child would *eat, that he may know to refuse the evil, and choose the good*, that is, "until he knows to reject the evil and choose the good."

How long does it take a child to learn right from wrong? At a very early age (within just a few years) this process is taking place. This meant that the coalition formed against Judah would be short-lived. In fact, within three years after the invasion by Israel and Syria, the Assyrians captured Damascus (capital of Syria) and forced Pekah, king of Israel, from his throne. Thus both Israel and Syria, which had caused Ahaz and Judah so much anxiety, were *forsaken of both her kings*.

17. The LORD shall bring upon thee, and upon thy people, and upon thy father's house, days that have not come, from the day that Ephraim departed from Judah; even the king of Assyria.

Isaiah then informed Ahaz that his land would suffer as it had not suffered in nearly two hundred years—since *the day that Ephraim departed from Judah*. This phrase refers to the time (in 931 B.C.) when the nation of God's people was divided into Ephraim (or Israel, the northern kingdom) and Judah (the southern kingdom). During the reigns of Jeroboam I (the first king of the north) and Rehoboam (the first king of the south) there was continual war (1 Kings 14:30). Isaiah foretold a similar period of chaos that *the king of Assyria* would bring about in Judah.

As noted earlier, Ahaz placed more trust in the king of Assyria (Tiglath-pileser III) than he did in the God of Judah. He appealed to Tiglath-pileser for help against Israel and Syria (2 Kings 16:7-9). While Ahaz may have considered this a solution to his present crisis, in the long run he caused Judah far more problems than he solved. Many of these problems would be left to his son Hezekiah to address (2 Kings 18:13—19:37).

Conclusion

A. Immanuel

Although God used Isaiah as His spokesman and as a special channel to convey His message, the prophet could not have understood fully all the implications of his predictions of God's future acts. He knew, of course, that *Immanuel* meant "God with us." Did he also recognize that he was describing the most significant event in history? Could he have dared to expect the coming of God's own Son into the world?

Of course, we today know how Isaiah's words were fulfilled. We have read Matthew, and he explains it (1:22, 23). May we never allow our familiarity with this passage to diminish our sense of wonder at the glorious thought of Immanuel! It is unfortunate that we usually limit our teaching about the incarnation to the few weeks during the Christmas season. Every day we need to remind ourselves that God's Son did come into the world and that we can receive forgiveness of our sins because He was willing to die for us.

B. Prayer

Almighty God, help us to learn to trust You for help and guidance instead of relying on our own fallible judgments. May we look to Immanuel— God with us—as our source of strength and wisdom. In His name we pray. Amen.

C. Thought to Remember

Immanuel—God with us. What a wonderful thought!

How to Say It

AHAZ. *Ay*-haz.
ASSYRIA. Uh-*sear*-ee-uh.
DAMASCUS. Duh-*mass*-kus.
ELIJAH. Ee-*lye*-juh.
EPHRAIM. *Ee*-fray-im.
GIDEON. *Gid*-ee-un.
HEZEKIAH. Hez-ih-*kye*-uh.
IMMANUEL. Ih-*man*-you-el.
ISAIAH. Eye-*zay*-uh.
JEROBOAM. Jair-uh-*bo*-um.
JOTHAM. *Jo*-thum.
MASSAH. *Mass*-uh.
MESSIANIC. mess-ee-*an*-ick.
PEKAH. *Peek*-uh.
PHARISEES. *Fair*-ih-sees.
REHOBOAM. Ree-huh-*bo*-um.
REMALIAH. Rem-uh-*lye*-uh.
REZIN. *Ree*-zin.
SEPTUAGINT. Sep-*too*-ih-jent.
SHEAR-JASHUB. She-are-*jah*-shub (strong accent on *jah*).
SYRIA. *Sear*-ee-uh.
TABEAL. *Tay*-be-ul.
TIGLATH-PILESER. *Tig*-lath-pih-*lee*-zer (strong accent on *lee*).
UZZIAH. Uh-*zye*-uh.
ZECHARIAH. Zek-uh-*rye*-uh.

Learning by Doing

This page contains an alternate lesson plan emphasizing learning activities.
Classes desiring such student involvement will find these suggestions helpful.

Learning Goals

After this lesson each student will be able to:

1. Summarize the message that Isaiah gave Ahaz and how the message demonstrated God's control to King Ahaz and the people of Judah.

2. Cite reasons that people today need reassurance of God's control.

3. Share the message of "Immanuel" with someone facing particularly difficult circumstances.

Into the Lesson

Have the chairs arranged in circles of four or five, or positioned around tables, as students arrive. At each circle (or table) have a sheet of poster board, a marker, and several hymn and chorus books. Ask students to find lines in songs that indicate God is in control or that we should trust Him as the pilot of our lives. They are to write the name of the song and the specific line(s) reflecting this concept. Examples you might give are "Jesus, Savior, Pilot Me," "This Is My Father's World," or "I Will Call Upon the Lord." Post these lists on a wall as groups report.

Make the transition to Bible study by telling the class that trusting God brings peace to life. Many of our hymns and choruses reflect His providential care. However, trusting Him is easier said than done. Our study in Isaiah reminds us that God sees the big picture and is faithful to His people, even when they are in difficult circumstances.

Into the Word

Use the information in the Lesson Background and the notes on verses 1 and 2 to set the stage for the events of today's lesson. Use a map of the northern and southern kingdoms to show how Jerusalem was under attack. Tell the class that God sent Isaiah to bring hope and good advice to the troubled King Ahaz and the people of Judah.

Since this passage has the potential to be quite confusing, keep the class members together for this study. Read the printed text. Then use the following discussion questions as you work in bits of information from the lesson commentary.

1. God told Isaiah to take his son to meet Ahaz (v. 3). The son's unusual name, Shear-jashub, means "a remnant will return." Why do you think God asked for him to be present?

2. God called the enemies "smoking firebrands" (vv. 4-6). What do you think He meant by this description of the kings of Syria and Israel?

3. Isaiah, in previous chapters, had already told of Judah's doom (vv. 4-6). Why would God now send a message of assurance? (Note: this is a good place to identify Ephraim and Tabeal. Also, use the brief summary of verses 7-9, on page 428, to stress God's encouragement and offer of hope.)

4. Why do you suppose Isaiah told Ahaz to ask for a sign from the Lord, and why did Ahaz refuse (vv. 10-12)? (Explain God's response in verse 13.)

5. Why would a prophecy about Jesus' birth be an appropriate and adequate sign (vv. 14-16)?

6. What was to be the result of Ahaz's faithless choice to call for the Assyrians to deliver Judah (v. 17)? Use the commentary notes to point out that the prophecies about suffering and captivity would come true. They are colorfully emphasized in verses 18-25. However, the prophecies about the remnant also teach us that God was with Judah, guiding the nation in difficult times.

Into Life

God used His prophecy about Immanuel to demonstrate to Ahaz His never-ending care for His people and that He remained in control. Even though they were to face severe hardship and judgment, God demonstrated His mercy. People still need that assurance.

Use the following "case study" to help your students talk about why people need to know that God is in control in life's difficult circumstances and that the coming of Immanuel gives hope.

Albert is a thirty-six-year-old family man. He has two children: Kara is thirteen years old and Chad is ten. Albert's wife, Abby, has just been told she has developed a disease that will cause severe physical disabilities within the next few years. (1) What do Albert and Abby need to remember about God's character and how He works in the lives of His people? (2) What can they tell their children about the Lord through this experience? (3) Why are Christians able to respond differently to trying circumstances from the way unbelievers respond?

Have the groups formed earlier in the session assume Albert's role and write new words to the song "Precious Lord, Take My Hand" or "I Give All." They may use only the first line of the original song. All other words must be new. Allow groups to sing or to read their songs to the rest of the class.

Let's Talk It Over

The questions on this page are designed to encourage review of the lesson Scriptures and to promote discussion of the lesson by the class. The answers provided are only discussion starters. Let your class talk it over from there.

1. Ahaz had put his faith in a political solution, an alliance with Assyria, rather than in God. What can the church do to help Christians increase their trust in God rather than in political solutions? What can we do as Christians to encourage national leaders to seek a godly course first?

Some Christians get so focused on one or two moral issues that they begin to act as if the world can be saved only if everyone agrees with their convictions. Outsiders conclude they would have to become zealots on those issues if they were to "join the church." It is true that Christians need to speak up about moral issues. It is also true that Christians need to remember the spiritual lessons from the experiences of Old Testament nations. The rise and fall of nations were a part of God's plan and method of bringing about a kingdom that would never fall to moral decay or to any enemy.

2. Isaiah took his son with him as an object lesson. What benefits do you think came to Shear-jashub by being present? In what ways would the church be stronger if more Christians took their children or grandchildren along to observe or share in spiritual endeavors?

Turning opportunities for spiritual service into family projects gives children a type of value-laden spiritual education that can be found nowhere else. Children working together on a project in their youth programs is excellent, but the example of dedicated parents can never be duplicated by a youth program. Parents need to be positive in their approach. "We *get* to do this" is much better than "We *have* to do this." And "I'm glad we can work on this together" is superior to "Everybody at church is lazy; we'll have to do it since no one else will."

3. Many people have longed for a "sign" from God. What do you think they are wishing for as a result of a sign? What signs has God already provided for us? How would another sign make a difference?

Jesus had to deal constantly with people looking for a sign. It seems they wanted everything so clear and easy that they would not have to "walk by faith." Many claim that receiving a sign will increase their faith. A sign in the midst of a very

difficult situation may accomplish that. But receiving many signs would lead to a dependence on signs and make faith weak. Learning to "walk by faith" even when God seems to be silent is a worthy goal for all of us. The Christian who develops a deep appreciation of the many "signs" throughout Bible history knows that God has already supplied the faith sustaining information sufficient for each day of the Christian's life.

4. It would be easy to imagine that Isaiah might have grown impatient or angry over the way Ahaz responded to God. How can we handle a similar temptation when someone repeatedly resists our efforts to lead him to Christ?

When our efforts are not working as we had expected, we can have one of two inadequate reactions: flight or fight. Impatience and frustration can result either in our giving up and withdrawing or in our becoming judgmental and launching unfair verbal attacks. God would direct us to focus our efforts on pleasing Him. We are to do the sowing and watering. It is His responsibility for the "increase" (1 Corinthians 3:6). Like Noah, whom God honored (Hebrews 11) for his faithfulness in preaching for 120 years in spite of a lack of converts, we need to do our spiritual work well and do it "as unto the Lord." Another way of looking at this issue is for each to ask, "What would have happened if people gave up on me one day before I decided to become a Christian?"

5. How would you explain the importance of "Immanuel" to a fellow believer? To a nonbeliever? How would you use this concept to comfort a Christian going through difficulty?

"Wow! God *WITH* us!" How blessed can we be? The idea of a distant, uninvolved, and unfeeling God does not readily gain anyone's allegiance; but a God who is present with us brings inspiration and comfort. God is with us on a daily basis just as Jesus was present in the flesh as He walked with His disciples. Every Christian can have assurance that God understands what we go through on a daily basis because He (Jesus) has "been there and done that!" (Compare Hebrews 4:14-16.) Learning to apply this truth and reminding other believers of it is a great source of confidence and comfort in all seasons and circumstances.

Pronouncement of Doom

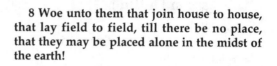

DEVOTIONAL READING: Mark 12:1-9.

BACKGROUND SCRIPTURE: Isaiah 5.

PRINTED TEXT: Isaiah 5:1-8, 11, 18-23.

Isaiah 5:1-8, 11, 18-23

1 Now will I sing to my well-beloved a song of my beloved touching his vineyard. My well-beloved hath a vineyard in a very fruitful hill:

2 And he fenced it, and gathered out the stones thereof, and planted it with the choicest vine, and built a tower in the midst of it, and also made a winepress therein: and he looked that it should bring forth grapes, and it brought forth wild grapes.

3 And now, O inhabitants of Jerusalem, and men of Judah, judge, I pray you, betwixt me and my vineyard.

4 What could have been done more to my vineyard, that I have not done in it? Wherefore, when I looked that it should bring forth grapes, brought it forth wild grapes?

5 And now go to; I will tell you what I will do to my vineyard: I will take away the hedge thereof, and it shall be eaten up; and break down the wall thereof, and it shall be trodden down:

6 And I will lay it waste: it shall not be pruned, nor digged; but there shall come up briers and thorns: I will also command the clouds that they rain no rain upon it.

7 For the vineyard of the LORD of hosts is the house of Israel, and the men of Judah his pleasant plant: and he looked for judgment, but behold oppression; for righteousness, but behold a cry.

8 Woe unto them that join house to house, that lay field to field, till there be no place, that they may be placed alone in the midst of the earth!

. . . .

11 Woe unto them that rise up early in the morning, that they may follow strong drink; that continue until night, till wine inflame them!

. . . .

18 Woe unto them that draw iniquity with cords of vanity, and sin as it were with a cart rope:

19 That say, Let him make speed, and hasten his work, that we may see it: and let the counsel of the Holy One of Israel draw nigh and come, that we may know it!

20 Woe unto them that call evil good, and good evil; that put darkness for light, and light for darkness; that put bitter for sweet, and sweet for bitter!

21 Woe unto them that are wise in their own eyes, and prudent in their own sight!

22 Woe unto them that are mighty to drink wine, and men of strength to mingle strong drink:

23 Which justify the wicked for reward, and take away the righteousness of the righteous from him!

GOLDEN TEXT: Woe unto them that call evil good, and good evil; that put darkness for light, and light for darkness; that put bitter for sweet, and sweet for bitter!—Isaiah 5:20.

Division and Decline
Unit 3: Decline and Fall
(Lessons 10-13)

Lesson Aims

After this lesson each of the students should be able to:

1. Retell Isaiah's parable of the vineyard, and list the sins prevalent in Judah that prompted it.

2. Compare the list of sins with conditions in his or her own community.

3. Suggest a specific action that he or she can take to resist one of the sins cited by Isaiah.

Lesson Outline

INTRODUCTION
   A. "What Have You Done Lately?"
   B. Lesson Background
 I. PARABLE OF THE VINEYARD (Isaiah 5:1-7)
   A. Location (v. 1)
   B. Preparation (v. 2a)
   C. Disappointment (v. 2b)
   D. Questions (vv. 3, 4)
   E. Judgment (vv. 5, 6)
   F. Explanation (v. 7)
     Sour Grapes
II. APPLICATION (Isaiah 5:8, 11, 18-23)
   A. Woe to the Covetous (v. 8)
   B. Woe to the Carousers (v. 11)
   C. Woe to the Scoffers (vv. 18, 19)
   D. Woe to the Perverted (v. 20)
   E. Woe to the Arrogant (v. 21)
   F. Woe to the Drunkards (vv. 22, 23)
     Six Deadly Sins
CONCLUSION
   A. Blessings and Responsibilities
   B. Prayer
   C. Thought to Remember

Introduction

A. "What Have You Done Lately?"

Alben Barkley, vice-president of the United States under President Harry Truman, once told of an incident that occurred when he was a senator from Kentucky. He learned that one of his staunch supporters had backed an opponent in a recent election. Later the senator confronted the man and began to remind him of all the favors he had done for him in the past.

"When you were out of work, didn't I get you a government job?" asked Senator Barkley.

"Yes, you did," the man replied.

"And when your uncle was in jail, didn't I persuade the judge to release him without bail?"

"That's right."

"And didn't I recommend your son for an appointment to the Naval Academy?"

"You sure did."

"Well then," asked the senator, "why did you work on behalf of my opponent after all I had done for you?"

"But, Senator," complained the man, "what have you done for me lately?"

This man's lack of gratitude is regrettable, but it is not as shocking as the ingratitude of the people of Judah in Isaiah's day. God had blessed them in countless ways, yet repeatedly they had turned away from Him to worship pagan gods and engage in immoral living. It was part of Isaiah's responsibility as God's prophet to deliver the message that God's patience with Israel had reached an end. His judgment was close at hand.

B. Lesson Background

"It was the best of times, it was the worst of times." This well-known opening statement from Charles Dickens's *A Tale of Two Cities* appropriately describes the situation in Judah when Isaiah began his ministry. We have noted in previous studies that Isaiah began his ministry during the reign of King Uzziah of Judah and continued it through the reigns of Jotham, Ahaz, and Hezekiah (Isaiah 1:1). Uzziah's reign was a prosperous one, and that prosperity continued into the times of Jotham and even Ahaz—"the best of times." But it was also "the worst of times" because the nation was experiencing serious spiritual and moral decline. Isaiah faced a difficult ministry, to say the least! (Recall the Lord's words to him, found in Isaiah 6:9-13.) The challenges he faced were not greatly different from those that Christian leaders today confront, as economic prosperity causes many to feel apathetic about spiritual matters.

All told, Isaiah's labors covered a period of more than fifty years. It has already been noted that Isaiah seems to have had frequent access to the royal court, for he was able to speak with kings such as Ahaz and Hezekiah (Isaiah 7:3; 38:1). Some students believe he probably served as a kind of counselor to the kings of Judah.

Today's lesson text is taken from Isaiah 5. This chapter does not seem to be directly connected with either the chapters that immediately precede it or those that follow. As a result, there is no consensus among Bible students about where to place this chapter chronologically in Isaiah's ministry, although there is general agreement that it came early in his career.

I. Parable of the Vineyard (Isaiah 5:1-7)

A. Location (v. 1)

1. Now will I sing to my well-beloved a song of my beloved touching his vineyard. My well-beloved hath a vineyard in a very fruitful hill.

Isaiah began with the words, *Now will I sing.* Perhaps Isaiah actually sang his message as a kind of ballad. Some have suggested that this may have been "performed" at the Feast of Tabernacles, which was held in the fall in Jerusalem (mentioned in verse 3) and which celebrated the harvest gathered from the vineyards (Deuteronomy 16:13). Many people would have been in the city for such a joyous occasion, and by singing his message, Isaiah might have attracted a larger audience than he would have otherwise.

The song is actually a parable, a story that makes a strong point. Isaiah's use of a parable here reminds us of how the prophet Nathan used a parable to expose David's sin with Bathsheba (2 Samuel 12:1-7). [See question #1, page 440.]

B. Preparation (v. 2a)

2a. And he fenced it, and gathered out the stones thereof, and planted it with the choicest vine, and built a tower in the midst of it, and also made a winepress therein.

The word *fenced* is better rendered as "dug," meaning that the owner of the vineyard cleared the soil of *stones* so that he could plant his vineyard. This was a common practice in Palestine, where there was little topsoil and many stones. The plot thus prepared was *planted* with *the choicest vine*, and a *tower* was built *in the midst of it.* This was a watchtower, which would allow the owner of the vineyard to guard it against thieves and marauding animals. Finally, a *winepress* was built. This was usually a basin, cut out of the limestone, where the grapes were squeezed by trampling. Below this basin was a second basin into which the juice flowed.

C. Disappointment (v. 2b)

2b. And he looked that it should bring forth grapes, and it brought forth wild grapes.

Everything had been done to insure a bountiful harvest of *grapes*, and the owner of the vineyard had good reason to expect such a crop. But to his disappointment, the vines *brought forth wild grapes.* These grapes were small, sour, and seedy—completely useless.

D. Questions (vv. 3, 4)

3, 4. And now, O inhabitants of Jerusalem, and men of Judah, judge, I pray you, betwixt me and my vineyard. What could have been done
more to my vineyard, that I have not done in it? Wherefore, when I looked that it should bring forth grapes, brought it forth wild grapes?**

As Isaiah began to apply this parable to his audience, he assumed the role of the "well-beloved." He shifted from speaking in the third person (he) to using the first person (*I*). He asked two pointed questions: *What could have been done more to my vineyard?* Why, after all the time and effort I had invested, did it yield only *wild grapes*?

E. Judgment (vv. 5, 6)

5. And now go to; I will tell you what I will do to my vineyard: I will take away the hedge thereof, and it shall be eaten up; and break down the wall thereof, and it shall be trodden down.

Normally a vineyard was protected by a hedge of thick, thorny shrubs or cactuses. (Even today one may see garden plots or houses in Palestine protected in this manner.) Because the vineyard had become such a source of disappointment, the owner determined that he would remove its protection: *I will take away the hedge thereof, . . . and break down the wall.* The wild animals would thus be free to enter the vineyard and "lay it waste," as the next verse describes.

6. And I will lay it waste: it shall not be pruned, nor digged; but there shall come up briers and thorns: I will also command the clouds that they rain no rain upon it.

To *lay* the vineyard *waste* did not require the owner's constant attention. Neglect would accomplish his purpose in a very short time. Every gardener knows that a vineyard or any other plot of ground where the plants are not pruned or cultivated will soon become an eyesore.

Notice that up to a point, Isaiah's reaction to the disappointing vineyard was no different from what anyone else's would have been. But when he stated, *I will also command the clouds that they rain no rain upon it*, the prophet seems to have been preparing his audience for the application of this parable to God's dealings with His people. Only He has authority over the clouds.

F. Explanation (v. 7)

7. For the vineyard of the LORD of hosts is the house of Israel, and the men of Judah his pleasant plant: and he looked for judgment, but behold oppression; for righteousness, but behold a cry.

Now came the explanation of Isaiah's parable: *The vineyard of the Lord of hosts is the house of Israel, and the men of Judah his pleasant plant.* Thus this indictment was directed at all of God's people, both the northern kingdom and the southern kingdom. The Lord was the one who had "planted" His people in a "very fruitful" (v. 1) land. The Lord was the one who had done all He could to provide for and protect His vineyard. For centuries He had blessed His people with deliverance and protection from the enemy nations around them.

God did this for His people so that they would be His "holy nation" (Exodus 19:6) and would produce the kind of "fruit" appropriate for such a people. However, like the owner of the vineyard in the parable, God was sadly disappointed in what He saw. He *looked for judgment* (justice), but instead He found *oppression*. The rulers and the rich were using all kinds of clever schemes to exploit people and keep them under their control. Instead of *righteousness*, there was a *cry*, most likely the anguished outcries of the oppressed.

Because of such a poor "harvest," God determined to do to His vineyard what the owner in the parable did to his. He would remove the "hedge" of protection from His people, abandoning them to their enemies. [See question #2, page 440.]

SOUR GRAPES

In contemporary vernacular, "sour grapes" is a term used to describe disparaging remarks from someone who is jealous of someone else's success. Examples of sour grapes include a contest loser's criticism that the prize was not worth winning anyhow, a small church's put-down of a larger church's methods, and a rejected applicant's contempt for the company who hired someone else for the desired position.

Such jealousy, however, is not among the sins condemned by Isaiah in his description of wayward Judah. The prophet's poetic parable decried the ingratitude of the Israelites and their tragic betrayal of God's trust. God was the owner of the vineyard (the people of Israel and Judah). He prepared and provided everything necessary (and more) for the productivity and security of His people. He had every reason to expect a bountiful harvest of delicious grapes (obedient, faithful lives). But instead, all God reaped from Judah was wild, sour, seedy fruit—a sorry crop worth nothing. No wonder God allowed the "vineyard" to be destroyed.

What more could God have done for Israel? What more can He do for us? He supplies every need, both physical and spiritual. He has made us, saved us, and prepared an eternal home for us. Jesus tells us to "bear much fruit; so shall ye be my disciples" (John 15:8). Are we producing much fruit—or only sour grapes?   —R. W. B.

II. Application
(Isaiah 5:8, 11, 18-23)

After pronouncing God's sentence upon Judah, Isaiah then introduced specific charges against the people. Six statements of indictment were spoken, each of them beginning with the ominous word *Woe*.

A. Woe to the Covetous (v. 8)

8. Woe unto them that join house to house, that lay field to field, till there be no place, that they may be placed alone in the midst of the earth!

Woe is a strong word, signifying much more than a gentle slap on the wrist. It carries the weight of God's righteous indignation. [See question #3, page 440.]

Greed is the sin condemned in this verse—a sin that was also cited by Amos and Micah (Amos 8:4; Micah 2:2). Amos had prophesied a few years before Isaiah; Micah's ministry was contemporary with Isaiah's. (See the chart on page 342.) The rich joined *house to house* by buying up all the property they could until their houses touched one another. Apparently they were doing this at the expense of the poor, creating a kind of monopoly for themselves. Perhaps those who did this rented out other houses as a source of income.

The rich would *lay field to field* by acquiring land adjoining their own. Small farmers who had fallen into debt often had to sell their land to pay off their debts. In the process they were reduced to poverty. The Mosaic law required that in the Year of Jubilee all land was to be returned to the original owners or their heirs (Leviticus 25:8-17), but the rich often had clever schemes to circumvent this law. As a result they were able to live *alone* amid their vast holdings.

B. Woe to the Carousers (v. 11)

11. Woe unto them that rise up early in the morning, that they may follow strong drink; that continue until night, till wine inflame them!

How to Say It

AHAZ. *Ay*-haz.
BATHSHEBA. Bath-*she*-buh.
CORINTH. *Cor*-inth.
HEZEKIAH. Hez-ih-*kye*-uh.
ISAIAH. Eye-*zay*-uh.
JOTHAM. *Jo*-thum.
MICAH. *My*-kuh.
SOPHISTS. *Sah*-fists.
UZZIAH. Uh-*zye*-uh.

Those who *rise up early in the morning* are usually ambitious, hard-working persons who are to be commended for their dedication and diligence. But Isaiah's second woe is reserved for those who show the same kind of enthusiasm for *strong drink*. They are so addicted to alcohol that they get an early start in pursuing their habit. They *continue* drinking *until night*. Obviously, only the rich could engage in this kind of behavior, for a common laborer who tried this would soon become impoverished and unable to provide himself with basic necessities—or with more wine!

C. Woe to the Scoffers (vv. 18, 19)

18. Woe unto them that draw iniquity with cords of vanity, and sin as it were with a cart rope.

The third *woe* was directed toward the arrogant scoffers. The figure that Isaiah uses here (men rather than oxen straining to pull a heavy *cart*) is a striking one. Commentators express different views as to its meaning. Perhaps the best explanation is that these men were having to bear the weight of their sin (and its consequences). Solomon expresses this thought well in the Proverbs: "His own iniquities shall take the wicked himself, and he shall be holden with the cords of his sins" (Proverbs 5:22).

19. That say, Let him make speed, and hasten his work, that we may see it: and let the counsel of the Holy One of Israel draw nigh and come, that we may know it!

Those who reject God's message (and His messengers) often display a defiance toward Him. (Often this is really an attempt to cover their insecurity.) In this case, the defiant ones were telling Isaiah, "You claim that God is working in history. But we don't see any evidence of it. Show us—give us a sign—and then we will believe."

These scoffers sound like some of Jesus' enemies who challenged Him to show them a sign (Matthew 12:38). These men were not seeking after truth; they were interested only in making Jesus look bad. They had closed their minds to any possibility of believing. Even when Jesus was on the cross, they challenged Him, "If he be the King of Israel, let him now come down from the cross, and we will believe him" (Matthew 27:42). But even such a dramatic miracle as that would not have changed their stubborn minds. Peter notes that "scoffers" continue to question whether Jesus will return (2 Peter 3:3, 4).

D. Woe to the Perverted (v. 20)

20. Woe unto them that call evil good, and good evil; that put darkness for light, and light for darkness; that put bitter for sweet, and sweet for bitter!

The Sophists, a school of philosophers in ancient Greece, earned a reputation for being able to "make the worse appear the better part." However, it is obvious that some in Isaiah's day had preceded the Greeks in mastering this skill. Even now there seems to be no shortage of those proficient in this art! [See question #4, page 440.] Certain lawyers have brought disrepute upon their profession by cleverly defining terms in such a way that their clients can avoid the consequences of their evil deeds. Advocates of abortion prefer to define the issue as one of "choice." They call an unborn baby a "fetus," not a human being. Those who want to justify homosexuality speak of an "alternate lifestyle," as if that would make such behavior more acceptable to God.

Many today are tempted to fall into the same trap in one way or another. They don't want to believe that a "loving" God could consign anyone to Hell. Some church members lose their evangelistic zeal by embracing the belief that "one religion is as good as another." Isaiah did not hesitate to pronounce a woe upon those who practice such verbal and moral sleight of hand.

E. Woe to the Arrogant (v. 21)

21. Woe unto them that are wise in their own eyes, and prudent in their own sight!

The apostle Paul said there were some in the church at Corinth who were "measuring themselves by themselves, and comparing themselves among themselves," and as a result were not *wise* (2 Corinthians 10:12). Many today reject God's standards of right and wrong and substitute their own. Since these are almost always easier to meet than God's standards, such individuals begin to feel proud and self-righteous when they are able to live up to their revised standards.

F. Woe to the Drunkards (vv. 22, 23)

22, 23. Woe unto them that are mighty to drink wine, and men of strength to mingle strong drink: which justify the wicked for

Visual for lesson 12

The humorous illustration of a person misreading the chart during an eye exam reminds us we all need to examine how we "spell" good and evil.

reward, and take away the righteousness of the righteous from him!

The sixth of Isaiah's "woes" might seem like a repetition of his second (v. 11), but there is a difference. In the second "woe" Isaiah condemns those who have completely succumbed to the power of *strong drink*. They rise up early in the morning to drink, they drink all day, and they are still drinking at night. In this verse the *woe* seems directed at some kind of public officials who engage in what we might call "binge drinking." They like to demonstrate how *mighty* they are and how much *strength* they possess by how much liquor they can hold. Perhaps they think of themselves (or others think of them) as "heroes." But their drinking smooths the path toward corruption. Their senses and their moral values are dulled so that they *justify the wicked for reward* and deny justice to the *righteous*.

When we note the heartaches caused by the abuse of alcohol today, we are reminded once more of just how contemporary the words of Isaiah are, even though they were uttered some twenty-seven centuries ago.

Six Deadly Sins

The "seven deadly sins" named during the Middle Ages were pride, avarice, gluttony, lust, sloth, envy, and anger. God's list in His condemnation of Judah was not quite the same, though surely the Israelites were guilty of all these sins as well. Isaiah spoke of only six "woes" in our text, but anyone can see that these were "deadly" to the perpetrators: covetousness, carousing, scoffing, perversion of the truth, arrogance, and injustice (sparked by drunkenness).

The latter verses of Isaiah 5 tell of the punishment that would come to these unrepentant sinners. Their destruction and defeat are described in terms of fire, decay, beatings, earthquakes, noise, and darkness. God's judgment will be no Sunday school picnic!

Regardless of the number or the seriousness of your sins, they are punishable by the same "wages"—death (Romans 6:23). Jesus has paid that penalty for you, but you must appropriate His gift of redemption by trusting and obedient faith (John 1:12; Acts 2:38).

"How shall we escape, if we neglect so great salvation?" (Hebrews 2:3). *Woe to us!* —R. W. B.

Conclusion

A. Blessings and Responsibilities

When Isaiah began his ministry in ancient Judah, his nation was enjoying a prosperity similar to that experienced when David was king. These blessings had come from the hand of God, who had been watching over His people from the time of Abraham. But the nation had forgotten that God was the source of their blessings, and because of that, they were using His blessings in the wrong way. Many had become greedy, and this greed had lured them into bribery and other corrupt practices. In a land where there was plenty for everyone to be well fed and properly clothed and housed, the rich were becoming richer at the expense of the poor. Isaiah eloquently pointed out that with all blessings come responsibilities, and the greater the blessings, the greater the responsibilities.

If we cannot see the obvious parallels between our society and the one to which Isaiah preached and appealed in the name of the Lord, then we are either morally blind or willfully ignorant. It should be clear that we who live under the New Covenant instituted by Jesus Christ have received greater blessings than the people of Isaiah's time, and as a result we have far greater responsibilities. Are we living up to them? [See question #5, page 440.]

Remember Jesus' words: "Unto whomsoever much is given, of him shall be much required" (Luke 12:48).

B. Prayer

O God, from whom all blessings flow, may we never forget that You are the source of all our blessings. Grant us the wisdom and the courage to accept the responsibilities that accompany these blessings. Help us to be fruitful in Your service. In Jesus' name, amen.

C. Thought to Remember

Responsibilities should not be seen as burdens to be borne, but as opportunities to help others and to bring glory to God.

Home Daily Bible Readings

Monday, Aug. 13—The Song of the Vineyard (Isaiah 5:1-7)

Tuesday, Aug. 14—Woe Unto Extortioners and Carousers (Isaiah 5:8-17)

Wednesday, Aug. 15—Woe Unto Scoffers (Isaiah 5:18-23)

Thursday, Aug. 16—Foreign Invasion Predicted (Isaiah 5:24-30)

Friday, Aug. 17—The Anger of the Almighty (Isaiah 9:11—10:4)

Saturday, Aug. 18—Assyria Also Judged (Isaiah 10:5-12)

Sunday, Aug. 19—Wicked Tenants of the Vineyard (Mark 12:1-9)

Learning by Doing

*This page contains an alternate lesson plan emphasizing learning activities.
Classes desiring such student involvement will find these suggestions helpful.*

Learning Goals

After this lesson each student will be able to:

1. Retell Isaiah's parable of the vineyard, and list the sins prevalent in Judah that prompted it.

2. Compare the list of sins with conditions in his or her own community.

3. Suggest a specific action that he or she can take to resist one of the sins cited by Isaiah.

Into the Lesson

Write the words *Love Songs* on the chalkboard or on a large poster. As students arrive, have romantic music playing on a CD or cassette player. Ask students to name their favorite love songs and to tell the songs' themes. Examples of themes are declarations of love, disappointment or heartache, separation, and the like. If your class is small, you may hear each person's favorite. Larger classes could have trios or small groups identify their favorites with each other.

Tell the students that today we will read a sad love song. The song is packed with emotion— deep love, tender care, a disappointed lover, anger, and desertion. It is a parable about God's relationship with unfaithful Israel and Judah. It is a powerful parable that teaches us about God's expectations for believers today.

Into the Word

Use the Lesson Background in the commentary pages to set the scene for this study. Be sure to note that this chapter is in poetic form.

During the week before this lesson, ask a person who reads or memorizes Scripture well to be prepared to recite or read Isaiah 5:1-8, 11, 18-23 for the class. This early request will give the person time to become familiar with the flow of the words in this passage of Scripture. Before the reading or recitation, ask the class to close their eyes and enjoy hearing this unusual love song. They will study it closely in a few moments.

After the reading, tell the class that the poetry is written in two verses or thoughts. The first is the song of the vineyard, and the second is the condemnation of sins. First, review the imagery of Israel and Judah hidden in the song of the vineyard (vv. 1-7). Write the following words on the chalkboard as you talk about their significance: *the vineyard, fruitful hill, the fence, the tower, the winepress, wild grapes, removing the hedge and wall, lay it waste, no rain.*

To study the second part of the poetry, tell the class that Isaiah applies the parable by specifically mentioning six charges or sins. Each charge is introduced with the strong word *woe.* Ask the class to define *woe. (Strong word of rebuke, signifying God's righteous indignation.)* Then ask them to locate the six "woes" in the text and to identify the sin condemned in each. Have a class member write these six sins on the chalkboard as they are identified. They may include greed (v. 8), alcohol addiction (v. 11), arrogant scoffing of God (vv. 18, 19), false advice or rationalization of their sins (v. 20), spiritual arrogance (v. 21), and drunkenness that leads to a perversion of justice (vv. 22, 23).

Into Life

Tell the class that Isaiah's words are very contemporary. Ask students to work in teams of two or three persons each to write notes about how each of the six sins are evidenced in today's society. Give each group a piece of poster board with the heading "Applying Isaiah to Life Today." Over the left column write, "Woe to. . . ." Over the right column write, "Contemporary Acts or Evidences of Sin." The teams are to identify and list the sins against which Isaiah invoked the divine "woe" down the left column. In the right column, they are to cite ways these sins are evidenced in life today. Since the discussion could become lengthy, encourage groups to work quickly. They should also spend more time on the sins more prevalent in our culture. Ask volunteers to tell a few of their answers to the whole class.

Remind the class that even though God was speaking to a nation, His heart was breaking because individuals had been unfaithful to His love. He responds similarly when individuals sin today. To make the lesson personal, ask each person to think of some sins or areas of temptation that trouble him or her personally. Give each person a three-by-five card and say, "I'd like each of you to write a prayer on this card. Thank God for His love and patience, confess to God the problem area you have identified, and ask God's guidance in overcoming this temptation." Assure the learners that no one will be required to reveal the information on the card to anyone but God. Encourage them to use these in the coming week to seek God's provision for their spiritual needs. Then close with prayer.

Let's Talk It Over

The questions on this page are designed to encourage review of the lesson Scriptures and to promote discussion of the lesson by the class. The answers provided are only discussion starters. Let your class talk it over from there.

1. The lesson writer compares Isaiah's approach with that of Nathan in 2 Samuel 12. Of course, we are familiar with Jesus' use of parables, too. How might we use parables today to make a spiritual point?

Jesus spoke in parables because they were effective ways of communicating. The story lines grabbed the audience's attention. The puzzle made people think. The analogy and the major point could easily be remembered.

Stories, or parables, have always been effective means of communicating. However, the experts tell us that the next generation will be even more attuned to stories and less to exposition. We may want to work at making storytelling one of our chief weapons in the battle for truth.

2. Suggest different analogies (besides a vineyard) that might be used in a parable to describe our nation's present moral condition and the danger of God's judgment.

There are many different ways of describing the danger a nation or congregation faces if it fails to be faithful to God Almighty. The task of framing a unique and workable analogy also forces the students to think about the terrible implications of the judgment of God. Often the image of "fire and brimstone" is used to warn against God's judgment. Isaiah's parable does not use the fire and brimstone scenario, but it makes the point of destruction just as plainly.

Creating an effective way to communicate God's lifesaving truth is very commendable. But first we must take care that we heed the message ourselves!

3. What are some "woes" God might pronounce on our nation or on an average congregation? How can these woes be effectively communicated to people today?

Use Isaiah's style in today's text to develop this list. The focus can be either on issues that pervade all of society or those of local importance. General issues include an acceptance of naturalism to the exclusion of God's activity in the world (e.g., evolution, secular humanism), a denial of the sanctity of life (seen in abortion, euthanasia, etc.), and the loss of moral absolutes. Local issues might concern efforts to open a strip club in the community, a gambling issue on an upcoming

ballot, or any other issue that is of special concern where you live.

4. List the ways that people today give sin other names so that they "call evil good." How do such labels become accepted, and what harm does that acceptance do? How can we ensure that we are not "brainwashed" by the ungodly changes around us?

Definitions of good and evil can change either slowly or rapidly. Someone makes up a new name for a practice long regarded as evil. A few people say the new name sounds better in mixed company. Another group likes the nonjudgmental nature of the term. Others argue the new phrase is more "politically correct." Soon most people are using the new term. Within months the new term has become ingrained into the nation's vocabulary. Today, adultery has become an "affair" or indiscretion. Homosexuality is "an alternate lifestyle." An unborn baby is just "fetal tissue."

The obvious consequence is that the concepts of sin and guilt are soon destroyed. Without these our need for a Savior is not readily apparent. The task of evangelism is made more difficult because sinners feel no need for the gospel.

5. Christians have proposed many ways to combat the moral drift of our culture. What are some pros and cons of relying on any of the following: (a) focusing only on evangelistic outreach, (b) developing programs that help Christians grow in holiness, (c) starting organizations like MADD (Mothers Against Drunk Driving) to attack moral evils, or (d) developing government programs like DARE (a drug use prevention program) to attack moral evils?

A well-known investment firm advertises that it gains and keeps new customers by focusing on one investor at a time. The church's best strategy would be to work consistently and tirelessly with *individuals* to evangelize the lost, to disciple the believers, and to be change agents in our culture. In the process, the church will be cooperating with God in using each person's gift to the glory of God.

The kingdom is crippled when we fight over which method is the one method for successful church work. The kingdom is also crippled when approaches are championed verbally but never put into action.

Israel Taken Into Captivity

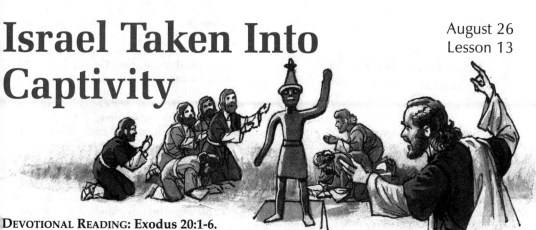

DEVOTIONAL READING: Exodus 20:1-6.

BACKGROUND SCRIPTURE: 2 Kings 17:1-23.

PRINTED TEXT: 2 Kings 17:6-18.

2 Kings 17:6-18

6 In the ninth year of Hoshea the king of Assyria took Samaria, and carried Israel away into Assyria, and placed them in Halah and in Habor by the river of Gozan, and in the cities of the Medes.

7 For so it was, that the children of Israel had sinned against the LORD their God, which had brought them up out of the land of Egypt, from under the hand of Pharaoh king of Egypt, and had feared other gods,

8 And walked in the statutes of the heathen, whom the LORD cast out from before the children of Israel, and of the kings of Israel, which they had made.

9 And the children of Israel did secretly those things that were not right against the LORD their God, and they built them high places in all their cities, from the tower of the watchmen to the fenced city.

10 And they set them up images and groves in every high hill, and under every green tree:

11 And there they burnt incense in all the high places, as did the heathen whom the LORD carried away before them; and wrought wicked things to provoke the LORD to anger:

12 For they served idols, whereof the LORD had said unto them, Ye shall not do this thing.

13 Yet the LORD testified against Israel, and against Judah, by all the prophets, and by all the seers, saying, Turn ye from your evil ways, and keep my commandments and my statutes, according to all the law which I commanded your fathers, and which I sent to you by my servants the prophets.

14 Notwithstanding, they would not hear, but hardened their necks, like to the neck of their fathers, that did not believe in the LORD their God.

15 And they rejected his statutes, and his covenant that he made with their fathers, and his testimonies which he testified against them; and they followed vanity, and became vain, and went after the heathen that were round about them, concerning whom the LORD had charged them, that they should not do like them.

16 And they left all the commandments of the LORD their God, and made them molten images, even two calves, and made a grove, and worshipped all the host of heaven, and served Baal.

17 And they caused their sons and their daughters to pass through the fire, and used divination and enchantments, and sold themselves to do evil in the sight of the LORD, to provoke him to anger.

18 Therefore the LORD was very angry with Israel, and removed them out of his sight: there was none left but the tribe of Judah only.

GOLDEN TEXT: Therefore the LORD was very angry with Israel, and removed them out of his sight: there was none left but the tribe of Judah only.—2 Kings 17:18.

Division and Decline
Unit 3: Decline and Fall
(Lessons 10-13)

Lesson Aims

After participating in this lesson, students should be able to:

1. Tell what today's text says about why the northern kingdom fell to the Assyrians.

2. Tell why God's judgment must be a crucial part of the church's message today.

3. Suggest some credible ways to express God's judgment against sin.

Lesson Outline

INTRODUCTION
  A. When Foundations Erode
  B. Lesson Background
I. ISRAEL'S FALL (2 Kings 17:6)
  A. Samaria Destroyed (v. 6a)
  B. Captives Taken (v. 6b)
II. A HISTORY OF SIN (2 Kings 17:7-12)
  A. Fearing Other Gods (v. 7)
  B. Living as the Pagans (v. 8)
    Etched in Stone
  C. Building Idols (vv. 9-12)
III. A HISTORY OF WARNINGS (2 Kings 17:13-18)
  A. Prophets Sent (v. 13)
  B. Warnings Rejected (vv. 14-17)
  C. Judgment Carried Out (v. 18)
    Barricades on the Road to Hell
CONCLUSION
  A. The Mills of God
  B. Prayer
  C. Thought to Remember

Introduction

A. When Foundations Erode

Several months ago as my family and I were traveling on an interstate highway, the traffic slowed and almost stopped. Up ahead we could see that construction work was in progress. As we approached the construction area, our two lanes were narrowed down to one lane. Soon we came to a bridge, and there the problem became obvious. The fill on the bridge approach had eroded away and the pavement had collapsed. When I later asked about what happened, I was told that at the base of the fill was a spring that had not been properly capped and drained away. As a result, the spring continued to flow, slowly

washing away the fill and allowing the pavement to collapse.

The fall of Israel (the northern kingdom) occurred in a similar manner. Its spiritual and moral weaknesses gradually eroded away its strength. Although the collapse of the nation took place in 722 B.C., the seeds of judgment had been sown over many generations. Only the final destruction came suddenly. Is there a lesson in this for us? And are we willing to heed it?

B. Lesson Background

Today's lesson concludes this quarter's studies, entitled "Division and Decline." We saw *division* in the first lesson, where we studied Rehoboam. It was his decision to listen to foolish counsel that resulted in the division of the kingdom of Israel. Other lessons during the quarter highlighted the *decline* that occurred in both Israel and Judah as the people and their leaders yielded more and more to sin. In today's lesson we see the tragic, but inevitable, result of this pattern: the judgment of Almighty God.

A visitor to Israel and Judah in 750 B.C. would have found both nations prospering and enjoying peace with their neighbors. At the time, both nations were being ruled by strong kings—Jeroboam II in Israel and Uzziah in Judah. In part, the good times had come because Assyria, the primary power to the northeast, was in a period of decline. But the apparent good times were not to last much longer. The external prosperity of Israel in particular masked serious spiritual and moral problems. These problems, however, could not be masked from God, nor from His prophets, who warned of imminent judgment.

In 745 B.C. Tiglath-pileser III came to power in Assyria. He gave immediate attention to reviving its prominence on the world stage. He soon turned his attention westward to Syria and Israel. These two nations had been bitter enemies at one time, but, fearing Assyria's might, they formed a coalition against Tiglath-pileser and tried to force Judah to join them. But none of Israel's efforts, no matter how valiant, could save her from the might of Assyria—for Assyria was God's instrument of judgment against His people.

I. Israel's Fall
(2 Kings 17:6)

A. Samaria Destroyed (v. 6a)

6a. In the ninth year of Hoshea the king of Assyria took Samaria.

The death of Jeroboam II brought a period of turmoil to Israel. Five men occupied her throne in less than twenty years. Sometime around 738 B.C. the Assyrians, under Tiglath-pileser III, seized portions of the land and took captives to Assyria (2 Kings 15:29). The king, Pekah, was later assassinated as the result of a conspiracy led by Hoshea, who then replaced him on the throne. (In Assyrian records Tiglath-pileser III claims responsibility for placing Hoshea on the throne. He may have backed Hoshea in order to gain a more cooperative king to be his vassal.)

However, after about six years, Hoshea rebelled against Assyria (2 Kings 17:4). As a result Shalmaneser V, who had replaced Tiglath-pileser III as king of Assyria, marched against Israel. In 725 B.C. the Assyrians laid siege to Samaria, the capital of Israel. Samaria had been strongly fortified and was able to withstand the siege for three years, finally falling in 722 B.C.

B. Captives Taken (v. 6b)

6b. And carried Israel away into Assyria, and placed them in Halah and in Habor by the river of Gozan, and in the cities of the Medes.

According to the records of Sargon II (who succeeded Shalmaneser V), the Assyrians deported 27,290 people from Samaria. Deportation served two purposes: it provided slaves for the Assyrians, and, by deporting the nation's leaders, it decreased the likelihood of another revolt. As an additional defense against further insurrection, the Assyrians settled in Israel conquered people from other parts of their empire.

The exact location of *Halah* is unknown, but some scholars place it north and east of Nineveh, Assyria's capital. Concerning *Habor*, the text literally reads, "Habor the river of Gozan." Habor was a river that emptied into the Euphrates River; Gozan was a city situated on the Habor. The *Medes* occupied an area east of the Tigris River in what is modern Iran.

II. A History of Sin
(2 Kings 17:7-12)

A. Fearing Other Gods (v. 7)

7. For so it was, that the children of Israel had sinned against the LORD their God, which had brought them up out of the land of Egypt, from under the hand of Pharaoh king of Egypt, and had feared other gods.

The first six verses of this chapter give an explanation of some of the international maneuvering for power that took place during the nine years of Hoshea's reign. These verses seem to place the blame for Israel's fall on Hoshea's flawed political schemes. The verse before us, however, makes it clear that Hoshea was not the only one responsible for the punishment that God administered to the nation. *The children of Israel had sinned*; the people, along with the

Use the same map as you used for lesson 1 to set the scene for today's lesson.

Visual for lessons 1, 13

king, were guilty. They *had feared other gods* in spite of the many centuries during which the true God had blessed them and watched over them. They had forgotten all that He had done for them, including the event that had made them a nation: when He *brought them up out of the land of Egypt.* [See question #1, page 448.]

This verse should not be taken to imply that everyone in Israel had turned away from the Lord. Just as in Elijah's day, there were certainly many who had remained faithful to God (1 Kings 19:18). One of the great tragedies of sin is that in a time of national disaster, the faithful and innocent often have to suffer along with the wicked.

B. Living as the Pagans (v. 8)

8. And walked in the statutes of the heathen, whom the LORD cast out from before the children of Israel, and of the kings of Israel, which they had made.

Every person, whether he acknowledges it or not, orders his life according to some kind of a moral code. Even though that code may not be chiseled in stone or printed in law books, it is still the guide that orders that person's life. It may be rigid and unbending, or it may be very flexible, changing with every new situation. Through Moses, God had given His people the Ten Commandments, written in stone, and along with them other laws covering many aspects of their daily living and their worship of God.

Many people try to combine religious codes with their own personal codes of conduct, resulting in interesting, and often contradictory, systems of right and wrong. This was the situation in ancient Israel. Most of the citizens of Israel probably would have insisted that they were faithful to the laws of Moses. At the same time, they *walked in the statutes of the heathen.*

We don't use the word *heathen* much anymore. It refers to a person or a people who do not acknowledge the true God, but worship false gods. We are more likely to use the word *pagan* for such peoples. When the Israelites entered the land of Canaan, the pagan inhabitants there practiced such sinful acts as cult prostitution and child sacrifice. God ordered the Israelites to *cast out* these sinful people (Deuteronomy 7:1-5), but this command was never completely carried out. Later, godless *kings of Israel* such as Jeroboam I and Ahab (spurred on by his wife Jezebel) invented pagan gods or imported them from foreign lands and encouraged the people to walk in statutes *made* by men, not ordained by God (1 Kings 12:25-33; 16:30-33; 21:25, 26).

ETCHED IN STONE

"It's not etched in stone," we sometimes hear a person say. Such a statement usually means, "Hey, I'm flexible! I'm willing to consider another idea. I'm not locked into this suggestion or rule or date or whatever." If something isn't "etched in stone," it is subject to change.

Israel had treated God's law as if its statutes could be altered, modified, or even erased. But they had intentionally forgotten that the divine Commandments that formed the basis of the law *were* etched in stone—literally! The tablets that Moses brought down from Sinai were inscribed indelibly, and they are part of God's words that "shall not pass away" (Matthew 24:35).

Many people today live by a "revised version" of the Bible. Moral relativity, situation ethics, and the very popular "How could it be wrong when it feels so right?" all play fast and loose with God's truth. But when a command or prohibition is "in the Book," no alterations are allowed. "If any man shall take away from the words of the book of this prophecy, God shall take away his part out of the book of life" (Revelation 22:19).

It's etched in stone!   —R. W. B.

C. Building Idols (vv. 9-12)

9. And the children of Israel did secretly those things that were not right against the LORD their God, and they built them high places in all their cities, from the tower of the watchmen to the fenced city.

This verse and those that follow mention specific ways in which the people did *those things that were not right against the Lord their God.*

The sins of the people included practices done *secretly* and others that were carried out publicly, at the various *high places.* Earlier in Israel's history, some of these places were used in worshiping the Lord (1 Samuel 9:11-14; 1 Kings 3:2). But by the time described in our text, the high places were devoted mainly to pagan worship.

The phrase *from the tower of the watchmen to the fenced city* means "throughout the whole land," from the most isolated vineyard (where a

tower was built in order to watch for thieves or animals) to the most well-defended city. The corruption of the people was a national disgrace.

10. And they set them up images and groves in every high hill, and under every green tree.

The word *images* means "sacred stones" or "obelisks." These were monuments that were set up as objects of worship. The making of images was strictly forbidden by the Second Commandment (Exodus 20:4). [See question #2, page 448.]

The term *groves* describes trunks of trees or posts set up as places of worship for the Canaanite goddess Asherah. Asherah was a pagan fertility goddess, whose "worship" often included illicit sex acts performed in order to induce her to grant fertility to both humans and crops.

11, 12. And there they burnt incense in all the high places, as did the heathen whom the LORD carried away before them; and wrought wicked things to provoke the LORD to anger: for they served idols, whereof the LORD had said unto them, Ye shall not do this thing.

Incense was recognized as a symbol of prayer (Psalm 141:2). In this case, the incense was a symbol of prayers offered to pagan gods, not to

---

How to Say It

AHAB. *Ay*-hab.
ASHERAH. Uh-*she*-ruh.
ASSYRIA. Uh-*sear*-ee-uh.
BAAL. *Bay*-ul.
CANAANITE. *Kay*-nuh-nite.
ELIJAH. Ee-*lye*-juh.
EUPHRATES. You-*fray*-teez.
GOZAN. *Go*-zan.
HABOR. *Hay*-bor.
HALAH. *Hay*-luh.
HOSHEA. Ho-*shay*-uh.
JEROBOAM. Jair-uh-*bo*-um.
JEZEBEL. *Jez*-uh-bel.
MEDES. Meeds.
MOLECH. *Mo*-lek.
NINEVEH. *Nin*-uh-vuh.
PEKAH. *Peek*-uh.
PHARAOH. *Fair*-o or *Fay*-ro.
REHOBOAM. Ree-huh-*bo*-um.
SAMARIA. Suh-*mare*-ee-uh.
SARGON. *Sar*-gon.
SHALMANESER. Shal-mun-*ee*-zer.
SINAI. *Sigh*-nigh or *Sigh*-nay-eye.
SYRIA. *Sear*-ee-uh.
TIGLATH-PILESER. *Tig*-lath-pih-*lee*-zer (strong
         accent on *lee*).
TIGRIS. *Tie*-griss.
UZZIAH. Uh-*zye*-uh.

the Lord. The phrase *whom the Lord carried away* hinted at the punishment the Israelites were to suffer. God had given His people clear warning of this when He first issued His law. If the Israelites failed to obey the Lord, they would be treated as those whom the Lord had cast out of the land (Leviticus 18:26-28).

III. A History of Warnings (2 Kings 17:13-18)

A. Prophets Sent (v. 13)

13. Yet the LORD testified against Israel, and against Judah, by all the prophets, and by all the seers, saying, Turn ye from your evil ways, and keep my commandments and my statutes, according to all the law which I commanded your fathers, and which I sent to you by my servants the prophets.

God gave the Israelites His *law* in order to show them how to live as His people. But that was not all He did. He raised up judges to deliver them from their oppressors in the promised land. He permitted them to have kings, though He recognized that such a request was really not in the people's best interests. In addition the Lord sent *prophets* and *seers* who warned the people to *turn* from their *evil ways*. While the term *prophets* describes the office these messengers held, *seers* calls attention to the means by which they often received their messages from God— through dreams and visions.

B. Warnings Rejected (vv. 14-17)

14. Notwithstanding, they would not hear, but hardened their necks, like to the neck of their fathers, that did not believe in the LORD their God.

In spite of God's efforts to turn His wayward people back from their sinful ways, the words of His messengers fell on deaf ears. They *hardened their necks* like stubborn animals that refuse to obey the person who holds the reins. [See question #3, page 448.]

15. And they rejected his statutes, and his covenant that he made with their fathers, and his testimonies which he testified against them; and they followed vanity, and became vain, and went after the heathen that were round about them, concerning whom the LORD had charged them, that they should not do like them.

They rejected his statutes and the *covenant* that God had *made with their fathers* at Mount Sinai. Instead of God's law becoming a testimony to the people's faithfulness toward Him, it *testified against them*. Instead of building their faith on the many clear evidences of God's guidance, they preferred following *vanity*—the emptiness of the false

gods that were really no gods at all. The *New International Version* reads, "They followed worthless idols and themselves became worthless."

16. And they left all the commandments of the LORD their God, and made them molten images, even two calves, and made a grove, and worshipped all the host of heaven, and served Baal.

The term *molten images* describes idols made by melting precious metal and pouring it into a mold. Specifically noted were the *two* golden *calves* that Jeroboam I had set up at Dan and at Bethel after the kingdom had divided in 931 B.C. (1 Kings 12:25-29). As noted under verse 10, the word *grove* describes a place of worship for the pagan goddess Asherah. Asherah was a consort of *Baal*, whose worship was encouraged by Ahab and Jezebel (1 Kings 16:31, 32).

17. And they caused their sons and their daughters to pass through the fire, and used divination and enchantments, and sold themselves to do evil in the sight of the LORD, to provoke him to anger.

To *pass through the fire* refers to sacrificing infants by fire to the pagan god Molech. The Israelites substituted the God of love with the god of brutality. Is it any wonder that God was provoked to *anger*? Will God be any less angry with our society, which has sacrificed countless numbers of unborn babies a year through abortion?

Divination is the practice of attempting to learn the future through means forbidden by God. Sometimes this was accomplished through trances or dreams. In other cases the entrails of sacrificed animals were "interpreted," or lots were cast, to provide such information. God condemned such practices (Deuteronomy 18:9-14). [See question #4, page 448.]

The word *enchantments* describes the efforts of magicians to invoke the aid of evil spirits to influence human affairs. These activities were also condemned by God. When people turn away from serving God, they often turn to strange and bizarre practices. We see many in our time who have departed from God and His revealed truth to embrace the so-called "New Age" philosophy or some other deceptive cult—or even the occult.

C. Judgment Carried Out (v. 18)

18. Therefore the LORD was very angry with Israel, and removed them out of his sight: there was none left but the tribe of Judah only.

Secular historians might attribute Israel's decline and fall solely to political or military factors. But the divinely inspired historian saw something else. He saw the hand of God's judgment using pagan powers to execute His judgment. *The Lord was very angry with Israel*—and with good reason. For centuries He had watched over Israel, guiding her, protecting her, and sending prophets to warn her when she departed from God's ways. Time and again she had rejected these warnings. And so God *removed them out of his sight*, and only the tribe of Judah survived. But Judah did not learn from Israel's experience, and it also felt God's anger about a hundred twenty years later. The enemy was different (Babylon), but the reason Judah fell was the same reason Israel did—disobedience. [See question #5, page 448.]

BARRICADES ON THE ROAD TO HELL

Some partying teens were speeding down a rural road one night, oblivious to warnings that a bridge was out not far ahead. They flew past a huge yellow and black sign that announced: ROAD CLOSED, 1/2 MILE. Without noticing, they sped past another sign with blinking lights attached: BRIDGE OUT, ROAD CLOSED, 1/4 MILE. In seconds they saw the barricade blocking the edge of a gaping chasm where the bridge used to stand. Startled out of his drunken stupor, the driver slammed on his brakes; but the car crashed through the barrier and plunged into the dark abyss. There were no survivors.

Israel had been warned—repeatedly—of the consequences of its rebellious behavior. God spoke His message of certain judgment through His many prophets. But Israel ignored each barricade that God erected on the slippery slope to destruction. The nation did not survive.

Millions around us are speeding down the road to spiritual death and eternal condemnation. God has provided the barricades of conscience, conviction, and Christ to halt their race toward Hell. Most ignore the warnings, oblivious to the truth. They continue to rebel and resist and reject God's salvation. Among such there will be no survivors. —R. W. B.

Home Daily Bible Readings

Monday, Aug. 20—Assyria Defeats King Hoshea (2 Kings 17:1-6)

Tuesday, Aug. 21—Israel Sinned and Disobeyed God (2 Kings 17:7-13)

Wednesday, Aug. 22—Reasons for Israel's Captivity (2 Kings 17:14-18)

Thursday, Aug. 23—Summary of Israel's Iniquity (2 Kings 17:19-23)

Friday, Aug. 24—Assyria Resettles Samaria (2 Kings 17:24-28)

Saturday, Aug. 25—Pagan Worship Prevails in Samaria (2 Kings 17:29-41)

Sunday, Aug. 26—The One True God (Exodus 20:1-6)

Conclusion

A. The Mills of God

Many are acquainted with the saying, "Though the mills of God grind slowly, yet they grind exceeding small." This one brief statement is a fitting summary of the history of Israel.

From the time that God led His people out of Egypt and into the promised land, He blessed them in many ways. Yet on numerous occasions the people turned from Him and followed other gods. At times they may have fallen into sin unwittingly, simply aping the activities of their neighbors without thinking about the consequences. At other times their sins were a flagrant defiance of God's laws. But whether the people acted unwittingly or arrogantly, God's mills continued to grind toward a day of reckoning.

There were instances in which God gave His people glimpses of what lay ahead for them if they did not repent. During the time of the judges, He allowed them to be threatened and harassed by many of their neighbors. Such treatment usually brought them to their senses (if only briefly), and then the sorry cycle began again. This scenario was repeated, particularly during the time of the divided kingdom, and in spite of the fact that God repeatedly sent prophets to warn His people of the inevitable outcome if they continued in sin. Finally, as recorded in today's lesson, the divine Miller carried out His judgment on the northern kingdom. The promised "grinding" had come to pass.

There ought to be a sobering lesson in this for us today. Our nation has been greatly blessed, materially and spiritually, yet how have we used these blessings? All too often we have squandered them on selfish and sinful pursuits. Do we think that we are any better than ancient Israel or that we can devise a way to avoid judgment?

Listen carefully! Can you hear, above the din of our busy and noisy lives, the steady and ominous grinding of God's righteous mills?

B. Prayer

Righteous God, help us to recognize that as a nation and as individuals we have often fallen far short of the attitudes and behavior that You require of us. Help us to repent while there is still time and to turn to You in humility. In Jesus' name, amen.

C. Thought to Remember

Once to ev'ry man and nation
  Comes the moment to decide,
In the strife of truth with falsehood,
  For the good or evil side.
      —James R. Lowell

Learning by Doing

This page contains an alternate lesson plan emphasizing learning activities.
Classes desiring such student involvement will find these suggestions helpful.

Learning Goals

After this lesson each student will be able to:

1. Tell what today's text says about why the northern kingdom fell to the Assyrians.

2. Tell why God's judgment must be a crucial part of the church's message today.

3. Suggest some credible ways to express God's judgment against sin.

Into the Lesson

Write *Warning!* in large letters at the top of your chalkboard or marker board. Ask, "What warning from your parents did you ignore that got you into some trouble?" Allow each learner to relate an experience to two or three other persons. You may also wish to ask a couple of people to tell the entire class about their experiences.

Tell the class that a foolish disregard of a parent's warning often brings trouble. Even so, when we disobeyed, our parents did not remove us from the family or disown us. There are times when parents, however, do go through the heart-wrenching experience of separating themselves from their children. Ask, "What kind of extreme circumstances might cause a parent to disown his child?" After the class suggests a few answers, emphasize how difficult this action would be for the parent. Observe that, in today's Bible study, we will see what happened when God finally reached a similar point with His people Israel. Along the way we will discover key lessons about living faithfully for the Lord.

Into the Word

Use the commentary notes in the Lesson Background and under verse 6 to establish the setting for today's lesson.

Prepare handouts as follows. Reproduce today's printed text at the top of the page and list these discussion questions below. (Do not include the italicized answers; they are for your convenience.)

1. What was the strategy behind resettling people from captive lands? *(Resettled people were less likely to revolt because they would not be defending their homeland.)*

2. What does verse 7 imply about how widespread idolatry had become? *(Surely not everyone turned away from God, but the vast majority had. Idolatry was very common in the land.)*

3. Why do you think the Israelites were so tempted to follow the practices of the pagans?

(The presence of pagan peoples and their practices were a source of temptation. Their behavior, while sinful, appealed to the base lusts of the Israelites.)

4. Explain the saying "hardened their necks" in verse 14. *(Stubborn resistance to efforts to turn them away from their wrong behavior.)*

5. What do you think the text means when it says the Israelites caused their children to "pass through the fire"? *(Child sacrifice.)*

Distribute the handouts and highlighter pens to the learners in groups of two to four people. (These activities could also be done by the whole class together.) First, ask the groups to read the text and highlight each sin mentioned. Ask them to write in the margins of their handouts a definition, interpretation, or modern application of each sin. Then ask the groups to discuss the questions that are printed on their sheets.

After a few minutes, allow a few volunteers to summarize their answers. You may need to use your lesson commentary to answer questions they may raise about the text. Explain the "images" and "groves" that are mentioned in verse 10 and the sinful practices mentioned in verse 17.

Into Life

Discuss what this lesson implies about teaching God's will and judgment to today's world. Ask the learners to suggest some ways to accomplish that task. Then say, "Every person, whether he acknowledges it or not, orders his life according to some moral code. We are going to allow you to begin defining your moral code and developing a life mission statement."

Prepare and distribute another handout entitled "Living by a Moral Code." List the following questions under the heading, "Defining My Personal Codes": (1) What do I value most in life? (2) What am I passionate about? (3) What are three things that make me angry? (4) What are three things that bring me joy? (5) Where do I spend most of my money? (6) Where or for what tasks do I volunteer? (7) What are my life's most significant accomplishments? (8) How do I want to be remembered after death?

List these questions under the heading, "Summing It Up": (1) Why do I believe I exist? (2) What do I believe is God's purpose for my life? (3) What corrections do I need to make in my code, practices, and goals if I am to bring honor to God?

Let's Talk It Over

The questions on this page are designed to encourage review of the lesson Scriptures and to promote discussion of the lesson by the class. The answers provided are only discussion starters. Let your class talk it over from there.

1. Who is responsible for the moral decline in a nation: the leaders or the citizens? Why? What ought the church to do to fulfill its responsibility regarding moral decline? How?

Unless citizens live under a tyrant who kills all dissenters, both the leaders *and* their followers are responsible for the moral condition of their nation. Christians should pray for opportunities to witness both to the average citizen and the highest officials. Then they should be quick to take those opportunities when they come. A letter to the editor, a voice at the PTA meeting, a vote for a moral candidate, or a reasoned explanation of one's position to a neighbor could be part of the solution. But if one is not alert to it, the chance to make such a contribution might pass away unused.

2. Who or what are the idols in our nation? What sacrifices are being offered to these idols? Which has the most negative influence on the average person: the practices of Christian neighbors or non-Christian neighbors? Why?

The chief god of this age seems to be pleasure. Without embarrassment many people frequent places once thought shameful: topless beaches, campus drinking parties, brothels, etc. Other practices are more subtle but just as dangerous, such as building massive debt to indulge selfish desires or getting ahead at work no matter who gets hurt. People sacrifice time, money, morals, and other people. Ultimately, they sacrifice and sell their souls. Peer pressure is probably the best predictor of the vulnerability of the average Christian. When fellow Christians get caught up in a worldly focus, the negative impact can influence other Christians into straying spiritually.

3. Though Israel followed in the sins of "their fathers," younger generations often tend to act differently from the previous ones. What would it take for the current younger generation to "rebel" by drawing closer to God rather than going farther away from God? What can the church do today to influence the younger generation in this "radical" direction?

In a prosperous time, people have the extra time and money to indulge in new pursuits. It is easy for the younger generation to be attracted to the sensational. Our youth programs must constantly challenge the youth to stand out from and become leaders for their peers. Emphasis on discipleship groups, short-term mission trips, youth conferences, and caring for the needy tend to capture the imagination of youth. They see a way by which they can stand out from the crowd and do something meaningful with their lives. In order for the church to be successful in youth ministry, there must also be a sufficient number of adults in every congregation who will give themselves to making these experiences possible.

4. How harmless or destructive are the culturally accepted "divination" practices like horoscopes and psychic hotlines? Why do you hold this view?

Many argue that these activities are harmless entertainment with no negative spiritual impact. But anything that leads people to place their trust in something other than God creates a spiritual trap for many individuals. Add to that the significant evidence that there may be demonic powers at work in some of these practices, and the wise believer will have serious reservations about participation in them. Many citizens are blind to a cultural slide that desensitizes individuals to evil. (Compare Genesis 6:5.) Without some dissenting voice, our society will begin to include many of the occult worship practices that are strongly condemned in the Old Testament.

5. Many Christians see the spiritual danger facing people or nations, yet they remain silent. After "judgment" falls upon the evildoers, these Christians are quick to say, "They should have known better." What can the local church do to help Christians become proactive in a missionary effort to replace an attitude of passivity or smugness?

God has always been missions oriented. His missionaries included Moses, the prophets, His own Son, and the New Testament church. Any congregation that is not searching for ways to send its own people to the lost has not captured God's vision for His church. A church is wise to give financially to missions. But every church will be even wiser by participating in local efforts to reach people, by sending its own as mission workers (short-term or long-term), by praying for the effectiveness of missionaries, and by keeping a missions emphasis before the congregation.